SOCIAL WORK LAW

SOCIAL WORK LAW

Alison Brammer

School of Law, Keele University

Fourth Edition

PEARSON

Harlow, England • London • New York • Boston • San Francisco • Toronto • Sydney
Auckland • Singapore • Hong Kong • Tokyo • Seoul • Taipei • New Delhi
Cape Town • São Paulo • Mexico City • Madrid • Amsterdam • Munich • Paris • Milan

Pearson Education Limited
Edinburgh Gate
Harlow CM20 2JE
United Kingdom
Tel: +44 (0)1279 623623
Web: www.pearson.com/uk

First published 2003 (print)
Second edition 2007 (print)
Third edition 2010 (print), 2011 (electronic)
Fourth edition published 2015 (print and electronic)

ISBN: 978-1-4082-9405-5 (print)
      978-1-4082-9406-2 (PDF)
      978-1-292-00347-4 (eText)

British Library Cataloguing-in-Publication Data
A catalogue record for the print edition is available from the British Library

Library of Congress Cataloging-in-Publication Data
A catalog record for the print edition is available from the Library of Congress

10 9 8 7 6 5 4 3 2
19 18 17 16

Cover: © Tungphoto/Shutterstock
Print edition typeset in 9.5/12 ITC Giovanni Book by 73
Print edition printed and bound in Slovakia by Neografia

NOTE THAT ANY PAGE CROSS REFERENCES REFER TO THE PRINT EDITION

Brief contents

Contents

Part 2 Children and families 163

7 Supporting children and families 165

8 Children and family breakdown 198

Part 3   Vulnerable adults   395

14   Adult social care   397

15   Mental health   426

Foreword

In the five years since the publication of the last edition of this invaluable book, social workers have had to face enormous changes in the many different and complex legal environments in which they practise their professional skills – a complexity exemplified by the astonishingly long list of statutes which appears in Chapter 1. If the largest and most profound changes have been in family law and the law of community care, there are few chapters which have not required the skilful updating for which we must all be indebted to the author.

In recent years too many social workers have come to feel undervalued, disempowered and deskilled. In part at least this was an unhappy consequence of the way in which care proceedings had come to be dealt with by the courts. Proper implementation of the family justice reforms, already well under way, will, I very much hope, re-position social workers as trusted professionals playing the central role in care proceedings which they should, and must. Social workers are experts. We must recognise them and treat them as such.

Expertise in social work practice, however, is not enough. Given the legal context in which they practise, social workers, as Sir Andrew McFarlane commented in his Foreword to the last edition, need to have a sound knowledge of the legal framework and the law that governs their work. He observed that this book succeeds in providing social workers with the law they need to know in a digestible form. That applies as much to this very welcome new edition, which I commend, both to the experienced and to the less experienced, as an expert guide through the legal thickets.

The Rt. Hon. Sir James Munby
President of the Family Division and of the Court of Protection
Royal Courts of Justice
6 January 2015

Preface

Aims

The aims of this book are to:

- Improve knowledge of law and its application to social work practice.
- Clarify legal terminology, conventions and practice and introduce basic legal skills.
- Identify the statutory responsibilities of social workers.
- Establish links between law and social work values.
- Demonstrate how law can promote good practice and empower service users whilst acknowledging the converse.
- Provide a comprehensive account of 'service user law'.
- Engage with professional and contextual issues surrounding law and social work.

The law covered in this text is specifically that which applies in England and Wales. The law applicable in Scotland and Northern Ireland is not included other than on occasion by way of comparison. Social work practice in statutory Social Services Departments forms the main focus of discussion although it is recognised that an increasing number of people in the social work profession are employed in the private and voluntary sector and where possible relevant issues relating to those areas are addressed.

Terminology

It is important to add a note on terminology at this stage. Language in law and social work practice is always changing – though not necessarily at the same pace. At times a choice had to be made between various terms and styles and a brief explanation for those choices follows.

Throughout the text the term 'service user' is employed rather than 'client'. In practice this term is now more commonly accepted as the appropriate term. The reasoning behind this preference is that reference to 'service user' is less discriminatory as it implies a more active and equal position with the social worker and emphasises that social work practice and the law deals significantly with provision of services and support and is not confined to issues of protection and control. It is recognised that in some particular circumstances the term may not seem appropriate to all or some of the players. For example, in child protection where a parent emphatically denies the existence of 'significant harm' yet action is taken to remove the child, that parent may not perceive herself as a service user or a client and may relate more closely to terms such as victim or adversary.

He is used throughout the text rather than s/he or they, which can appear clumsy, though more acceptable in terms of anti-discriminatory practice. The main reason for use of he is that legislation is framed in these terms, though application of the Statutory Interpretation Act 1978 means that he should be taken to refer to she also. This usage is adopted therefore for reasons of clarity and consistency.

The glossary includes explanation of a range of terms used throughout the book. Some are technical legal terms which are unavoidable and in rare cases may still be expressed in Latin. Other terms are more recent in origin and an explanation is provided of their meaning in the context of social work law. Terms included in the glossary are highlighted in red bold the first time they appear in the text. Abbreviations used are highlighted in black bold in the text at first mention.

Approach

A few thoughts about learning the law will further explain the approach of this text.

Learning social work law is most effective as part of an approach which conforms to what Biggs (1994)[1] describes as 'the qualitative outlook'. Under this premise, students learn in a cumulative fashion through interpretation of new materials with existing knowledge and understanding. The task for teachers of social work law is thus to encourage understanding, not simply to transmit vast amounts of content which can be reproduced in a test situation without any real understanding of the subject matter or its interrelationship with other areas (the quantative outlook). The qualitative approach involves use of activities to help understanding. Elements typically present in this approach include: a positive motivational context; a high degree of learner activity, both task-related and reflective; interaction with others, at peer level and hierarchically; a well-structured knowledge base, that provides depth and breadth for conceptual development and enrichment (Biggs, 1994).

To learn a new subject it is necessary to be aware of expectations, motivation and attitudes. It is possible that some social work students feel that the study of law is imposed on them if they wish to pursue a career in social work, rather than it being a genuine choice. A few students may still consider that law has no relevance to social work and therefore have little commitment to its study. Others may grasp the aspects of law that might be interpreted as oppressive or discriminatory and see their role as fighting against law rather than embracing it as a tool to improve practice.

For some students, reluctance to study law is founded in a preconception that law is dry and boring. A response to such concerns is to encourage students to take some ownership of the study of law by incorporating it fully into their professional development as a social work practitioner. Guiding this approach, is Rogers' (1969)[2] view that significant learning takes place when the subject matter is perceived as having relevance to your own purpose.

To learn law it is necessary to spend some time on basic skills of legal research, 'the ability to find, use and apply legal source material; the ability to read cases and statutes and apply them to new or complex situations' (Kenny, 1994, p. 47).[3] The introduction of these skills should be set against a context of an understanding of the respective roles of social workers and solicitors. In practice social workers should have access to legal advice for complex cases. The aims of studying law as a social worker should not include a desire to turn into quasi-lawyers, but having an appropriate knowledge of law and awareness of how to access the law that supports professional practice.

Before embarking on the study of law as part of a social work course, it is apposite to develop an awareness of the sensitive nature of some areas of study. It is important to acknowledge the possible existence of personal and professional experience of certain issues, e.g. domestic violence, and the need to foster a 'safe' working environment.

One way to achieve this is through the development of 'ground rules' which can if necessary be revisited throughout a course of study. Ground rules might include issues such as: respect for each other's beliefs and opinions, confidentiality within the group, sharing resources, appropriate use of language, time out if appropriate, and full participation. From my experience of following this approach with groups of mature students I would support the view of Egan (1974),[4] that, 'an adult way of learning is best established when a group agrees to and respects and values each other, and that this is best achieved through a contract that establishes ground rules' (in Rowland, 2000, p. 65).

The approach taken in this text is to provide the opportunity to learn law in a way which is relevant to social work practice and develops critical analysis. Chapters therefore include learning objectives, discussion points, signals to evaluate law, including deficiencies in current law and commentary on proposals for reform, case analysis and exercises in the form of case study discussion, as a facet of problem-based learning (Savin-Baden, 2000).[5] A limitation of case studies is that it is not usually possible to provide the amount of detail that would be available in a real situation. This can be a positive feature, however, in that it can encourage questioning and provide for a greater range of options to be considered e.g. a reference in a case study to a 'child in need' as defined by the Children Act 1989, s. 17 might prompt thought or discussion about gate-keeping, prioritisation of services, concepts of need versus protection, ethnocentric interpretations of need, medical versus social need – all issues hidden behind a seemingly straightforward legal term. The companion website will include answers to case studies and exercises.

Keeping ahead of the game – further reading and website addresses

Professionals working in all of the areas covered in this book need to be alert to changes in policy, legislation and case law, all of which impact on practice. Reading a textbook on social work law, however comprehensive, is unlikely to equip the social practitioner fully for the diverse situations which will be encountered. In part this is an inevitable result of the speed of changes and developments in law.

Some sections of this text have had to consider both existing law and future, as yet unimplemented, legislation or proposals for reform. In addition, the potential for challenge of existing law via the Human Rights Act 1998 should not be overlooked and its impact is considered throughout. The approach adopted therefore is to encourage and enable the reader to consider the study of law as a career-long aspect of professional development, and to achieve this to develop the skills necessary to access up-to-date materials and indications of future direction. Three principal features of the book support this aim.

Further reading

Space dictates that certain important publications, such as government policy and consultation documents, can only be referred to in brief. References are provided in further reading to encourage the reader to access the original documents and to expand and develop on the knowledge gained in the text. Certain key documents e.g. 'Working Together to Safeguard Children', will become an essential part of the social work 'toolkit'. The text aims to encourage a critical and reflective approach to the role of law. Published research and academic articles included in further reading support this notion and the requirement for research-based practice. This is a generic text but it is recognised that on qualification most social workers will choose an area of specialism and may wish to research that area in greater depth.

Website addresses

In addition to the more traditional library-based sources of information, there is a wealth of information which can be accessed via the internet. Website addresses are included at the end of each chapter. Sites are included through which significant documents such as government publications can be accessed. In addition, for each topic there are websites listed reflecting the particular issues, e.g. charitable or research-based organisations, which can provide further insight into an area.

Outline of content

The remainder of this text is divided into three parts: the legal context of social work practice; children and families; and vulnerable adults. Criminal justice issues are dealt with in Chapter 13 regarding juvenile offenders and Chapter 18 for adults. Two additional chapters at the end of the text cover asylum law and welfare. Both areas are relevant to each of the three parts of the text but have been positioned at the close of vulnerable adults as it is arguable that asylum seekers and people who are homeless have a vulnerability. There have been significant changes within social work law since publication of the third edition and these are reflected in the updated fourth edition.

Whilst I hope the views in this chapter are persuasive and coherent, ultimately they are expressed by a lawyer. Accordingly, a summary of feedback follows from two exercises carried out with Social Work students.

Why study law?

- relevant to ALL areas of practice
- avoid litigation
- social workers operate within tight guidelines which are dictated by law
- know powers within law and limitations
- understand nature of state's role in protection
- understand clients/service-users' rights and lack of rights – enables empowerment
- advocacy
- defines boundaries of how citizens should behave
- law protects client group and social workers
- social workers need a good working knowledge of the legal system, e.g. access to services
- to fulfil obligations to service users/clients
- to challenge unfair discrimination
- to influence and shape legal systems

- to guard against personal litigation
- social workers work in partnership with other professionals and agencies which are dominated by the legal framework – to know professional boundaries
- because it's interesting!

What are the barriers to use and understanding of the law?

- rigidity
- jargon, language and terminology
- format
- continuous change in some areas, lack of change in others
- contradictory content
- not accessible
- inconsiderate to victim
- subject to interpretation
- discriminatory
- elitist
- tradition, e.g. dress etc. in court setting
- time – adjournments etc.
- too generic
- lack of time and resources to learn
- politics influences changes in law.

The author has endeavoured to explain the law as at 1 June 2014 and some possible developments thereafter are included.

Notes

1. J. Biggs (1994) 'Student learning research and theory: where do we currently stand?', in J. Gibbs (ed.) *Improving Student Learning*. Oxford: The Oxford Centre for Staff Development.
2. C. Rogers (1969) *Freedom To Learn*. Merrill.
3. P. Kenny (1994) *Studying Law*. London: Butterworths.
4. Egan, cited in S. Rowland (2000) *The Enquiring University Teacher*. The Society for Research into Higher Education/Open University Press, p. 65.
5. M. Savin-Baden (2000) *Problem-based Learning in Higher Education, Untold Stories*. Oxford: Oxford University Press.

Author's acknowledgements

As ever I am a grateful to all at Pearson for their efficiency, guidance and tolerance. I'd also like to thank Kelvin Johnstone for his revision of the education chapter and his support and insight into teaching social work law.

DEDICATION

For Rosa

Publisher's acknowledgements

We are grateful to the following for permission to reproduce copyright material:

Figures

Figure 2.1 from *Children Act 1989*, HMSO Chapter 41, contains public sector information licensed under the Open Government Licence (OGL) v3.0. http://www.nationalarchives. gov.uk/doc/open-government-licence; Figure 7.1 from The Framework for Assessment of Children in Need and their Families. DCSF. © Crown copyright material is reproduced with the permission of the Controller of HMSO and Queen's Printer for Scotland, contains public sector information licensed under the Open Government Licence (OGL) v3.0. http:// www.nationalarchives.gov.uk/doc/open-government-licence; Figure 9.3 from Public Law Outline: 2014 update, https://www.justice.gov.uk/downloads/protecting-the-vulnerable/ care-proceeding-reform/plo-flowchart.pdf, Ministry of Justice, contains public sector information licensed under the Open Government Licence (OGL) v3.0. http://www. nationalarchives.gov.uk/doc/open-government-licence; Figure 18.1 from West Mercia Police Authority, reproduced with permission.

Tables

Tables 17.1 and 17.2 adapted from *The Law and Social Work: Contemporary Issues for Practice*, Palgrave (Cull, L.-A. and Roche, J., Eds 2001), reproduced with permission of Palgrave Macmillan.

Text

Text on page 6 from Domains with the Professional Capabilities Framework, http://www. tcsw.org.uk/pcf.aspx, The College of Social Work, accessed 21st March 2014. Correct at time of going to press. The PCF is subject to regular updating; Box on page 114 from *The Human Rights Act – Changing Lives*, 2nd ed., The British Institute of Human Rights (Matthews, L., Sceats, S., Hosali, S. and Candler, J. 2008), reproduced with permission from BIHR; Text on pages 166 and 232 from *Working Together to Safeguard Children: Statutory Guidance on Inter-agency Working to Safeguard and Promote the Welfare of Children*, HM Government (2013), contains public sector information licensed under the Open Government Licence (OGL) v3.0. http://www.nationalarchives.gov.uk/doc/open-government-licence; Boxes on pages 230 and 242 from *X Council v. B (Emergency Protection Orders)* [2004] EWHC 2015 (Fam), contains public sector information licensed under the Open Government Licence (OGL) v3.0. http://www.nationalarchives.gov.uk/doc/open-government-licence; Box on page 398 from Care Bill becomes Care Act 2014, https://www.gov.uk/government/speeches/ care-bill-becomes-care-act-2014, contains public sector information licensed under the

Open Government Licence (OGL) v3.0. http://www.nationalarchives.gov.uk/doc/open-government-licence; Box on page 427 from *Code of Practice to the Mental Health Act 1983 (as amended by the Mental Health Act 2007)*, Department of Health (2007), contains public sector information licensed under the Open Government Licence (OGL) v3.0. http://www.nationalarchives.gov.uk/doc/open-government-licence; Box on page 464 from Care home boss locked disabled patients in his car for THREE hours whilst he visited bookies, *Daily Mail*, 14/12/2007, Mail Online; Box on page 573 from *R (AS)* v. *London Borough of Croydon* [2011] EWHC 2091 (Admin), contains public sector information licensed under the Open Government Licence (OGL) v3.0. http://www.nationalarchives.gov.uk/doc/open-government-licence.

Table of cases

Table of legislation

Table of Statutory Instruments

List of abbreviations

AA	Adoption Act 1976
ABC	Acceptable behaviour contract
ABCPA	Anti-social Behaviour, Crime and Policing Act 2014
AC	Approved clinician
ACA	Adoption and Children Act 2002
ACPC	Area Child Protection Committee
AEA	Action on Elder Abuse
AIA	Asylum and Immigration Act 2004
AMHP	Approved Mental Health Professionals
ASBA	Anti-social Behaviour Act 2003
ASBO	Anti-social Behaviour Order
ASW	Approved Social Worker
BAILII	British and Irish Legal Information Institute
BASW	British Association of Social Workers
CA 1989	Children Act 1989
CA 2004	Children Act 2004
CAF	Common Assessment Framework
CAFA	Children and Families Act 2014
CAFCASS	Children and Family Court Advisory and Support Service
CAMHS	Child and Adolescent Mental Health Service
CAO	Child assessment order
CCRC	Criminal Cases Review Commission
CDA	Crime and Disorder Act 1998
CDCA	Carers and Disabled Children Act 2000
CDS	Criminal Defence Service
C(EO)A	Carers (Equal Opportunities) Act 2004
CHAI	Commission for Healthcare Audit and Inspection
CJA	Criminal Justice Act 2003
C(LC)A	Children (Leaving Care) Act 2000
CMH	Case Management Hearing
CPS	Crown Prosecution Service
CQC	Care Quality Commission
CRE	Commission for Racial Equality
C(RS)A	Carers (Recognition and Services) Act 1995
CSA	Care Standards Act 2000
CSCI	Commission for Social Care Inspection
CSDPA	Chronically Sick and Disabled Persons Act 1970

CTO	Community treatment order
CYPA	Children and Young Persons Act 2008
DASS	Director of Adult Social Services
DCSF	Department for Children, Schools and Families
DDA	Disability Discrimination Act 1995
DfE	Department for Education
DfES	Department for Education and Skills
DoH	Department of Health
DOLS	Deprivation of Liberty Safeguards
DPA	Data Protection Act 1998
DPP	Director of Public Prosecutions
DP(SCR)A	Disabled Persons (Services, Consultation and Representation Act) 1986
DRC	Disability Rights Commission
DTO	Detention and Training Order
DVCVA	Domestic Violence, Crime and Victims Act 2004
DVPO	Domestic Violence Protection Order
DWP	Department for Work and Pensions
EA 1996	Education Act 1996
EA 2002	Education Act 2002
EA 2005	Education Act 2005
EA 2011	Education Act 2011
ECHR	European Convention on Human Rights
ECtHR	European Court of Human Rights
ECT	Electroconvulsive therapy
EHC	Education Health and Care Plan
EIA	Education and Inspections Act 2006
EOC	Equal Opportunities Commission
EPA	Enduring power of attorney
EPO	Emergency protection order
ERA	Employment Rights Act 1996
EWO	Education Welfare Officer
FfA	Fostering for Adoption
FLA	Family Law Act 1996
FMA	Forced Marriage Act
FSM	Free school meals
GR	Gender reassignment
GSCC	General Social Care Council
HA	Housing Act 1996
HCPC	Health and Care Professions Council
HMCS	Her Majesty's Courts Service
HRA	Human Rights Act 1998
HSCA	Health and Social Care Act 2008
HSPHA	Health Service and Public Health Act 1968
IAA	Immigration and Asylum Act 1999
ICS	Integrated Children's System
IEP	Individual education plan
IMCA	Independent Medical Capacity Advocate
IMHA	Independent mental health advocate
IRH	Issues Resolution Hearing
IRO	Independent Reviewing Officer

ISSP	Intensive supervision and surveillance programme
LA	Local authority
LAA	Legal Aid Agency
LAC	Local authority circular
LAC	Looked after children
LASPO	Legal Aid, Sentencing and Punishment of Offenders Act 2012
LASSA	Local Authority Social Services Act 1970
LEA	Local education authority
LGO	Local government ombudsman
LPA	Lasting power of attorney
LSCB	Local Safeguarding Children Boards
MCA 1973	Matrimonial Causes Act 1973
MCA 2005	Mental Capacity Act 2005
MHA 1983	Mental Health Act 1983
MHA 2007	Mental Health Act 2007
MHRT	Mental Health Review Tribunal
MIAM	Mediation Information and Assessment Hearing
MJ	Ministry of Justice
NAA	National Assistance Act 1948
NASS	National Asylum Support Service
NHSA 1977	National Health Service Act 1977
NHSA 2006	National Health Service Act 2006
NHSCCA	National Health Service and Community Care Act 1990
NIAA	Nationality, Immigration and Asylum Act 2002
NR	Nearest relative
NSF	National Service Framework
OASYS	Offender Assessment System
ODPM	Office of the Deputy Prime Minister
PACE	Police and Criminal Evidence Act 1984
PCA	Protection of Children Act 1999
PCCA	Protection of Children Act index
PCC(S)A	Powers of Criminal Courts (Sentencing) Act 2000
PCF	Professional Capabilities Framework
PLO	Public Law Outline
POCA	Protection of Children Act list of adults considered unsuitable to work with children
POVA	Protection of Vulnerable Adults
PSHE	Personal, social, health and economic education
RC	Responsible clinician
RRA	Race Relations Act 1976
RR(A)A	Race Relations (Amendment) Act 2000
SAB	Safeguarding Adults Boards
SAO	School attendance order
SAR	Subject Access Request
SCIE	Social Care Institute for Excellence
SCT	Supervised community treatment
SDA	Sex Discrimination Act 1975
SEN	Special educational needs
SENCO	Special Educational Needs Coordinator
SENDA	Special Educational Needs and Disability Act 2001

SI	Statutory Instrument
SOA	Sexual Offences Act 2003
SRE	Sex and relationships education
SSFA	School Standards and Framework Act 1998
SSI	Social Services Inspectorate
UKBA	United Kingdom Border Agency
UNCRC	UN Convention on the Rights of the Child
YISP	Youth inclusion and support panel
YJB	Youth Justice Board
YJCEA	Youth Justice and Criminal Evidence Act 1999
YOP	Youth Offender Panel
YOT	Youth offending team
YRO	Youth rehabilitation order

Law Reports

AC	Appeal cases
All ER	All England Law Reports
BHRC	Butterworths Human Rights Cases
BMLR	Butterworths Medico-Legal Reports
CCLR	Community Care Law Reports
Ch	Chancery Division
COP	Court of Protection Law Reports
Cr App R	Criminal Appeal Reports
ECHR	European Court of Human Rights
EHRR	European Human Rights Reports
EWCA	England and Wales Court of Appeal
EWHC	High Court of Justice for England and Wales
Fam	Family Division
FCR	Family Court Reporter
FLR	Family Law Reports
IRLR	Industrial Relations Law Reports
QB	Queen's Bench Division
UKHL	UK House of Lords
WLR	Weekly Law Reports

Journals

BJSW	British Journal of Social Work
CC	Community Care
CFLQ	Child and Family Law Quarterly
Crim LR	Criminal Law Review
DCLD	Discrimination Case Law Digest
Fam Law	Family Law
JCL	Journal of Child Law
JSWFL	Journal of Social Welfare and Family Law
LAG	Legal Action Group Bulletin
LS	Legal Studies
MLR	Modern Law Review
NLJ	New Law Journal
SJ	Solicitors Journal

Part 1

Legal context of social work practice

Chapters:

Chapter 1

Introduction to law and social work practice

Learning objectives

To develop an understanding of the following:

- The legal framework for social work.
- The framework for qualification as a social worker.
- Regulation of social work.
- Incorporating an anti-oppressive and anti-discriminatory practice perspective into the study of law.
- The relationship between law and social work practice.
- The skills and knowledge required to work effectively with the law.
- An appreciation of the limitations of law.
- Values which influence social work practice and their link to the law.

Introduction

In this introductory chapter the relationship between law and social work practice and reasons for the study of law are examined. The discussion begins with consideration of why law has become more prominent in social work education and practice, supported by reference to the framework for social work education. Relevant sections of the Local Authority and Social Services Act 1970 are outlined as the major legal framework that establishes Social Services Departments, with relevant additions from the Children Act 2004. A summary of key legislation relevant to social work practice demonstrates further the dominance of law. The chapter continues with explanation of some of the key legal concepts for social work practice: confidentiality; accountability; rights, duties and powers; and the introduction of key values – partnership, choice, empowerment, anti-discriminatory and anti-oppressive practice – and the extent to which these values are supported by the law.

Relationship between law and practice

The relationship between law and social work practice and the place of law as an element in taught social work programmes continues to be the subject of ongoing debate. Polarised views have developed. Both positions on the relationship between law and social work practice are encapsulated in the following quote:

> Deciding when to invoke the law is not a simple matter. Both Blom-Cooper's (1998) view that the law is the beginning and the finish of any action, and Stevenson's belief that an ethical duty of care is the mainspring of social work action, distort by over-simplification the reality of practice. Competence in practice, requires both an acknowledgement of the relevance and applicability of the law and also assessment skills inspired by social work values, theoretical knowledge and practice wisdom.[1]

Law clearly plays an important role in social work practice today. Substantial legislation has been passed in recent years which has a profound effect on social work practice, notably the Children Acts of 1989 and 2004, the Crime and Disorder Act 1998, the Adoption and Children Act 2002, the Mental Capacity Act 2005 and the Care Act 2014. The understanding of law underpins and provides duties and powers for social work, and understanding the statutory and legal requirements is essential for effective and fair social work practice. Nevertheless, research has found that social workers were uneasy about acting as statutory agents.[2] Furthermore, Jones *et al.* found that social workers became stressed when their work brought them into the sphere of law, believing they were considered as having limited credence and status in that field.[3] Recent evidence in a **SCIE** review suggests continuing unease: '… social work students and practitioners experience contact with the law and legal system as stressful'.[4]

Clearly it is not sufficient for instruction concerning pieces of legislation relevant to social work practice, such as the Children Act 1989, to be delivered without reference to contemporary social work practice and the incorporation of social work values relating to oppression, service users' rights and discrimination. Good social work practice is of much greater complexity than simply executing prescribed duties under legislation. Questions of interpretation and application of legislation are not confined to lawyers. The law attempts to balance apparently conflicting principles and practices which must be applied by social workers and key legal judgments have dealt with the relationship between the law and social work practice. For example, in *R v. Gloucestershire County Council, ex parte Barry* [1997] 2 All ER 1, a rather confused picture emerged over the extent to which social workers, in exercising a duty to assess disabled people for support services, can take a local authority's resources into account. Another decision made it clear that where legal remedies are available they must be applied proportionately, as in where a supervision order was made, as a proportionate response to the circumstances of the case rather than the care order applied for: *Re O (A Child) (Supervision Order: Future Harm)* [2001] EWCA Civ 16. Inappropriate use of legal powers is potentially dangerous and has proved damaging to the social work profession in the past.

Preston-Shoot *et al.* (1998) argue that the role of law now has a 'centrality, pre-eminence ... within social work practice'.[5] Even so, it is also true that neither child abuse nor delinquency or other social problems that social workers encounter can simply be legislated away. The effective teaching and learning of social work law must acknowledge the relevance and application of law but that needs to be set against a context of social work values and practice skills. Taking this approach, it is argued that a new academic discipline has emerged, that of 'social work law'.[6]

In the mid 1980s there was significant media interest in social work, with particular emphasis on social workers' apparent lack of knowledge of law and legal procedures arising from a number of significant child abuse inquiry reports. Following these tragedies, research emerged which critically confirmed a deficiency within practitioners to identify and observe legal duties and positively to use available legal powers.[7] Rules and Requirements for the DipSW were published in 1995 (replaced by the new framework – see below) and stated that: 'Students must be required to demonstrate through formal written assessment their understanding and application of the legislation relating to social work in the country in which they train' (para. 3.4.2). CCETSW[8] produced Rules and Requirements relating to legal knowledge (set out as background information at note 9).[9] It is clear then that there has been an expectation for some time that, to be legally competent, a social worker must be able to apply relevant law to factual situations and not simply regurgitate its provisions in the abstract. Knowing which action a social worker might take in response to an emergency, or how a social worker might present materials to a court, requires understanding of the relationship between law and social work practice. Legal knowledge needs to be integrated with other social work knowledge and skills for effective practice. An advice note from the College of Social Work notes in relation to social workers' roles and functions:

> They have a lead role in safeguarding people who may be socially excluded, at risk of abuse or neglect, or who become vulnerable for other reasons. They balance support and protection/safeguarding roles carefully and in keeping with the specific needs and circumstances of the person or family, taking protective action as needed and within the context of legal roles and frameworks.[10]

Understanding and application of law in social work practice is now addressed within the degree framework for social work qualification. Further changes to the qualification framework may follow two significant publications, 'Making the education of social workers consistently effective' by Sir Martin Narey in 2013[11] and 'Re-visioning social work education: an independent review'. by Croisdale-Appleby in 2014.[12]

The qualifying framework

The current social work qualification, a degree in social work, was introduced in September 2003 as an aspect of the Department of Health's (**DoH**) objectives to raise the profile and status of the profession. It replaced the Diploma in Social Work (DipSW). Masters level qualifications in social work are also available at many academic institutions. The degree incorporates an emphasis on practical application of skills and knowledge, including legally-based skills and knowledge. To support this, students spend a minimum of 200 days in practice and, where possible, the expertise of service users and carers is actively involved in shaping and delivering degree programmes.

The precise formulation of the requirement to study law as part of the social work quali-fication changed in 2012 with the introduction of the Professional Capabilities Framework (**PCF**) developed by the Social Work Reform Board and Standards of Proficiency set by the Health and Care Professionals Council. The PCF replaces the TOPSS National Occupational Standards for Social Work in relation to any students admitted to qualifying programmes since 2013.[13]

The Quality Assurance Agency Subject Benchmark Statement (2008) still applies. It will be necessary to become familiar with these requirements in their entirety during the quali-fication process and to be continually aware of the requirements as they inform practice. Here, the focus is on how these requirements impact on social work and the law, and on identifying those requirements of most obvious application.

Standards of Proficiency

The Standards of Proficiency are threshold standards which social workers in England must meet at the end of their training in order to register and enter practice. Key elements of the Standards of Proficiency include the requirement to: be able to practise within the legal and ethical boundaries of their profession (2), understanding current legislation applicable to the work of their profession; be able to practice in a non-discriminatory manner (6); be able to maintain confidentiality (7); be able to maintain records appropriately (10); understand the key concepts of the knowledge base relevant to their profession (13), including under-standing the development and application of relevant law and social policy.

Professional Capabilities Framework

The PCF describes capabilities of social workers at all stages of their career. It has nine do-mains applicable to all roles and settings, effective throughout an individual's social work career. Knowledge, understanding and application of law feature significantly throughout the domains. For example, the 'Values and Ethics' domain (2) requires social workers to be knowl-edgeable about the value base of their profession, its ethical standards and relevant law.

The domains are reproduced below, specific references to the need to study law are high-lighted.

> **1 PROFESSIONALISM – Identify and behave as a professional social worker, committed to professional development**
>
> Social workers are members of an internationally recognised profession, a title protected in UK law. Social workers demonstrate professional commitment by taking responsibility for their conduct, practice and learning, with support through supervision. As representatives of the social work profession they safeguard its reputation and are accountable to the profes-sional regulator.

2 VALUES AND ETHICS – Apply social work ethical principles and values to guide professional practice

Social workers have an obligation to conduct themselves ethically and to engage in ethical decision-making, including through partnership with people who use their services. Social workers are knowledgeable about the value base of their profession, its ethical standards and relevant law.

3 DIVERSITY – Recognise diversity and apply anti-discriminatory and anti-oppressive principles in practice

Social workers understand that diversity characterises and shapes human experience and is critical to the formation of identity. Diversity is multi-dimensional and includes race, disability, class, economic status, age, sexuality, gender and transgender, faith and belief. Social workers appreciate that, as a consequence of difference, a person's life experience may include oppression, marginalisation and alienation as well as privilege, power and acclaim, and are able to challenge appropriately.

4 RIGHTS, JUSTICE AND ECONOMIC WELLBEING – Advance human rights and promote social justice and economic wellbeing

Social workers recognise the fundamental principles of human rights and equality, and that these are protected in national and international law, conventions and policies. They ensure these principles underpin their practice. Social workers understand the importance of using and contributing to case law and applying these rights in their own practice. They understand the effects of oppression, discrimination and poverty.

5 KNOWLEDGE – Apply knowledge of social sciences, law and social work practice theory

Social workers understand psychological, social, cultural, spiritual and physical influences on people; human development throughout the life span and the legal framework for practice. They apply this knowledge in their work with individuals, families and communities. They know and use theories and methods of social work practice.

6 CRITICAL REFLECTION AND ANALYSIS – Apply critical reflection and analysis to inform and provide a rationale for professional decision-making

Social workers are knowledgeable about and apply the principles of critical thinking and reasoned discernment. They identify, distinguish, evaluate and integrate multiple sources of knowledge and evidence. These include practice evidence, their own practice experience, service user and carer experience together with research-based, organisational, policy and legal knowledge. They use critical thinking augmented by creativity and curiosity.

7 INTERVENTION AND SKILLS – Use judgement and authority to intervene with individuals, families and communities to promote independence, provide support and prevent harm, neglect and abuse

Social workers engage with individuals, families, groups and communities, working alongside people to assess and intervene. They enable effective relationships and are effective communicators, using appropriate skills. Using their professional judgement, they employ a range of interventions: promoting independence, providing support and protection, taking preventative action and ensuring safety whilst balancing rights and risks. They understand and take account of differentials in power, and are able to use authority appropriately. They evaluate their own practice and the outcomes for those they work with.

8 CONTEXTS AND ORGANISATIONS – Engage with, inform, and adapt to changing contexts that shape practice. Operate effectively within own organisational frameworks and contribute to the development of services and organisations. Operate effectively within multi-agency and inter-professional settings

Social workers are informed about and pro-actively responsive to the challenges and opportunities that come with changing social contexts and constructs. They fulfil this responsibility in accordance with their professional values and ethics, both as individual professionals and as members of the organisation in which they work. They collaborate, inform and are informed by their work with others, inter-professionally and with communities.

9 PROFESSIONAL LEADERSHIP – Take responsibility for the professional learning and development of others through supervision, mentoring, assessing, research, teaching, leadership and management

The social work profession evolves through the contribution of its members in activities such as practice research, supervision, assessment of practice, teaching and management. An individual's contribution will gain influence when undertaken as part of a learning, practice-focused organisation. Learning may be facilitated with a wide range of people including social work colleagues, service users and carers, volunteers, foster carers and other professionals.

Source: The College of Social Work. Accessed 21st March 2014. Correct at time of going to press. The PCF is subject to regular updating

QAA benchmarks

Students will be expected to demonstrate knowledge before award of a degree, which is to include:

The significance of legislative and legal frameworks and service delivery statements (including the nature of legal authority, the application of legislation in practice, statutory accountability and tensions between statute, policy and practice). The current range and appropriateness of statutory, voluntary and private agencies providing community-based, day-care, residential and other services and the organizational systems inherent within these. The significance of interrelationships with other social services, especially education, housing, health, income maintenance and criminal justice.

The complex relationships between justice, care and control in social welfare and the practical and ethical implications of these, including roles as statutory agents and in up-holding the law in respect of discrimination.

In summary, the study of law as part of a social work programme can be broken down into three component parts:

1. As a structure within which social workers must practise, in many cases giving evidence in court or providing reports for court. Awareness of court procedures and the roles of

others within the justice system may help to ease the anxiety and unease which often accompanies this area of practice and make contact with legal advisers and others in the legal process more effective. Working knowledge of the court system will also enable a social worker to advise and provide support to a service user facing court proceedings.

2. Law as the instrument which gives social workers licence to practise through legal powers, duties and limitations, e.g. the duty to investigate suspicion of abuse, the power to provide support services. An understanding of how law develops and the various sources of law, policy and procedure, and accountability.

3. The need to have an understanding of legal issues which service users may face even though there may not be a direct social work responsibility involved in the issue, e.g. legal remedies for domestic violence.

Regulation of social work

Under the Care Standards Act 2000 (**CSA**), responsibility for training and regulation of social workers was vested in the General Social Care Council (**GSCC**). The Health and Social Care Act 2012 abolishes the General Social Care Council. The Health and Care Professions Council (**HCPC**) now has responsibility for regulation of social work (alongside 15 other health and care professions) and holds the professional register.

The functions of the HCPC in relation to social work are:

- Keeping the register of social care workers.
- Determining standards of education and training required as a condition of registration.
- Giving advice about standards of conduct and performance. (S2ZB, Schedule 3 to the Health Act 1999, inserted by the Health and Social Care Act 2012)

Fitness to practice is assessed by the HCPC now, in place of the GSCC. It is possible for a person to be removed from the register, and there is a right of **appeal** against removal to the First Tier Tribunal (Care Standards). This process and its relation to the Protection of Children Act list (see further in Chapter 9) was considered by the Care Standards Tribunal in *Arthurworrey* v. *Secretary of State for Education and Skills* [2004] EWCST 268 (PC). The applicant, Lisa Arthurworrey, was employed as a social worker by Haringey Council and was allocated the case of Victoria Climbié in 1999. She subsequently gave evidence at the public inquiry into Victoria's death. Following an internal review panel Part 8 inquiry at Haringey, she was suspended from duty and the Council referred her to the Protection of Children Act list. She successfully appealed against inclusion on the list and her name was removed from the list. The tribunal had to consider whether, under the Protection of Children Act 1999, she was guilty of misconduct that harmed a child or placed a child at risk of harm, and unsuitable to work with children (s. 4(3) **PCA** 1999). Such cases would now fall within the Safeguarding Vulnerable Groups Act 2006. Misconduct can include omissions. The 11 particulars of misconduct presented to the tribunal included: failure to conduct a proper interview with Ms Kouao (Victoria's aunt); failure to complete all the tasks required of her and identified at a strategy meeting; and failure to make contact or to take adequate steps to make contact with Victoria.

The tribunal considered the definition of misconduct and noted the need to consider the context in which the individual was working, including levels of support and supervision. In considering whether her actions amounted to misconduct, the tribunal considered five factors which were relevant to all of the allegations: experience, training, the complexity of the case, the question of supervision, and the office environment.

The tribunal found no misconduct and, whilst as a result it did not have to decide on suitability to work with children, it commented that Ms Arthurworrey was a suitable person to work with children, describing her as a 'straightforward and caring individual who has fully acknowledged the mistakes she made in connection with this case'.

As to the use of **POCA** (the Protection of Children Act list of adults considered unsuitable to work with children), the tribunal made it clear that to list an individual for 'professional mistakes should be an unusual occurrence, to be used only in the most clear cut cases'. It suggested that the procedure to remove an individual from the register is the preferable route in cases of mistakes and poor professional practice. The concluding comments of the tribunal were: 'The message that we wish to make beyond the particular case that we have been considering is that Government must ensure that social workers are better trained, better resourced, and better supervised. In this way, it is hoped that the tragedy of Victoria will not be repeated.'

Since the introduction of the register, social workers have appeared before the GSCC (subsequently HCPC) conduct committee. The social worker may be removed from the register or a suspension order or admonishment (caution) may be made. Conduct has included forming inappropriate relationships with clients; being abusive to colleagues; and failure to follow child protection procedures, thereby placing a young person at risk.

For example, the conduct committee of the GSCC ruled that social worker Iftikhar Choudri had exploited the vulnerability of two women, who had 'serious enduring mental health problems'. Choudri had a consensual sexual relationship with Ms X after their professional relationship ended. As well as sharing intimate details of his personal life with Ms X, Choudri also made inappropriate comments to her and another service user, Ms Y. The committee ruled that Choudri should not be able to practise as a social worker because he failed to understand and work within appropriate professional boundaries and abused the power given to him by his professional position.[14]

The standard of proof in conduct hearings is the civil standard, balance of probabilities, even where the matter of concern is of a criminal nature, e.g. an allegation that a social worker stole from a client.

A different scenario arose in *Skervin* v. GSCC [2007] EWCST 1076. Here the GSCC refused an application for registration from S, who held a DipSW, on the ground that he was not of good character, having failed to disclose incidents of poor performance (dismissal for poor time keeping) to a subsequent employer and in his application for registration.

Protection of title

It is an offence for a person to use the title 'social worker' or imply that he is a qualified social worker if he is not registered with the Health and Care Professionals Council.

Legal framework of social work

The statutory context of social work is provided by the Local Authority Social Services Act 1970 (**LASSA**) (as amended) and a summary of the main provisions is a useful reference point.

Section 1 establishes the authorities which have social services functions as county councils, metropolitan and London boroughs and unitary authorities, but not district councils.

Sections 2–5 of the LASSA are repealed by the Children Act 2004 to give effect to the organisational changes introduced following recommendations in the Climbié report.

Personnel requirements specified by the LASSA are amended by the Children Act 2004. The duty to appoint a Director of Social Services is removed and replaced by a requirement to appoint a Director of Children's Services for each children's services authority, and a Director of Adult Social Services (**DASS**). The Director of Children's Services is appointed for the purpose of prescribed functions including those exercisable by the LEA: social services that relate to children; children leaving local authority care; the children's services authority for cooperation, safeguarding and promoting the welfare of children and information databases; and any health services for children that are transferred to the local authority. Within councils there will also be a lead member (councillor) appointed for each area, children's services and adults' services. In some areas children's and adults' services have merged back into a new single department to be led by a single director.

Adequacy of staffing levels is a matter for debate in the current climate of under-resourced local authorities, increasing responsibilities of social services and heavy caseloads carried by individual social workers. It would not be surprising to see this issue raised via judicial review proceedings or as an aspect of a human rights challenge. Whilst 'adequacy' is a difficult term to define, extreme staff shortages, excessive caseloads and unallocated cases would be difficult to defend. *R* v. *Hereford and Worcester County Council, ex parte Chandler* (1992) (unreported) was a case where leave for judicial review was granted, one of the grounds being that C had not received the one-to-one service he required because the authority had inadequate staff in **breach** of its s. 6 duty. The case was settled before hearing by providing the service and compensation.[15] This issue has been formally recognised by Lord Laming in 'The Protection of Children in England: A Progress Report' (2009), prepared following the 'baby P' case, in which he recommends that the Social Work Task Force should: 'develop national guidelines setting out maximum case-loads of children in need and child protection cases, supported by a weighting mechanism to reflect the complexity of cases, that will help plan the workloads of children's social workers'.

Section 7 of the LASSA 1970 contains a number of important provisions. It provides for the Secretary of State to produce directions for the exercise of social services functions (discussed further in Chapter 2); establishes complaints procedures (discussed further in Chapter 4); contains the power for the Secretary of State to require an inquiry into social services functions (discussed in Chapter 9); and provides for the default powers of the Secretary of State (see Chapter 4). The LASSA 1970 also contains a list in Sch. 1 (updated regularly) of the permitted actions or functions of social services authorities.

Summary of key legislation impacting on social work practice and defining service user groups

General

Equal Pay Act 1970

Local Authority Social Services Act 1970

Local Government Act 1972

Interpretation Act 1978

Housing Act 1996

Data Protection Act 1998

Human Rights Act 1998

Access to Justice Act 1999

Immigration and Asylum Act 1999

Public Interest Disclosure Act 1999

Freedom of Information Act 2000

Local Government Act 2000

Nationality, Immigration and Asylum Act 2002

Homelessness Act 2002

Housing Act 2004

Civil Partnership Act 2004

Gender Recognition Act 2004

Domestic Violence, Crime and Victims Act 2004

Equality Act 2006

Safeguarding Vulnerable Groups Act 2006

Health and Social Care Act 2008

Equality Act 2010

Legal Aid, Sentencing and Punishment of Offenders Act 2012

Welfare Reform Act 2012

Protection of Freedoms Act 2012

Health and Social Care Act 2012

Domestic Violence, Crime and Victims (Amendment) Act 2012

Marriage (Same Sex Couples) Act 2013

Legislation relating to children and young persons

Children and Young Persons Acts 1963 and 1969

Family Law Reform Act 1969

Child Abduction Act 1984

Children Act 1989

Human Fertilisation and Embryology Act 1990

Child Support Act 1991

Education Act 1996

Family Law Act 1996

Protection of Children Act 1999

Children (Leaving Care) Act 2000

Special Educational Needs and Disability Act 2001

Adoption and Children Act 2002

Children Act 2004

Children and Adoption Act 2006

Childcare Act 2006

Children and Young Persons Act 2008

Academies Act 2010

Child Poverty Act 2010

Children, Schools and Families Act 2010

Children and Families Act 2014

Legislation relating to adults' services

Mental Health Act 1983

Care Standards Act 2000

Mental Capacity Act 2005

Mental Health Act 2007

Care Act 2014

Criminal justice legislation

Bail Act 1976

Police and Criminal Evidence Act 1984

Public Order Act 1986

Criminal Justice Act 1991

Probation Service Act 1993

Criminal Justice and Public Order Act 1994

Sex Offenders Act 1997

Protection from Harassment Act 1997

Crime and Disorder Act 1998

Youth Justice and Criminal Evidence Act 1999

Criminal Justice and Court Services Act 2000

Powers of Criminal Courts (Sentencing) Act 2000

Sexual Offences Act 2003

Anti-social Behaviour Act 2003

Criminal Justice and Immigration Act 2008

Policing and Crime Act 2009

Crime and Security Act 2010

Anti-social Behaviour, Crime and Policing Act 2014

The above summary does not include *all* legislation which a social worker may encounter in everyday practice. It is, however, a selection of some of the more important pieces of legislation that directly impact on social work practice. There are also areas of overlap as some pieces of legislation could apply, for example, to children and adults, e.g. the Mental Capacity Act 2005, though it tends to be associated more with adult service users. The amount of legislation relevant to adults has reduced drastically as the Care Act 2014 repeals and replaces several pieces of legislation, e.g the National Health Service and Community Care Act 1990. The Local Authority Social Services Act 1970, Sch. 1 contains a comprehensive list of enactments conferring functions assigned to social services committees.

Limitations of law

Whilst accepting that law shapes social work practice and provides social workers with powers and duties, it is also necessary to appreciate the limitations of the law.

- Law will not always provide clear direction – rather it sets boundaries for practice, and there is often a huge discretion on ways to practise within those limits (this may also be seen as an advantage).

- Particular provisions are often open to interpretation and may appear unclear. Sometimes it is necessary to 'wait and see' until case law clarification is produced, e.g. case law on meaning of 'significant harm'.

- Discrete laws may appear to be in conflict with each other.

- Law may not keep pace with practice developments, e.g. greater openness in adoption was not anticipated in the Adoption Act (**AA** 1976) 1976, but the need to consider contact was incorporated into the Adoption and Children Act 2002.

- Legal language may not be updated to reflect terms adopted in practice.

- There are gaps in the law. An example of this is the lack of powers to intervene in adult protection.

- Law may not help a social worker decide when to act; that may be a matter of risk assessment.

- Law may appear to be discriminatory itself, e.g. restriction on voting rights for detained patients under the Mental Health Act 1983, or may be applied in a discriminatory fashion, e.g. police discretion to stop and search exercised disproportionately to include high numbers of young black men.[16]

- Law is reactive rather than proactive – with the exception perhaps of the Human Rights Act 1998, English law tends to react to situations that have occurred, by punishing or providing a remedy, rather than setting out codes of behaviour.

- The law can seem to be a bureaucratic machine, concerned more with processing forms accurately and following procedures than dealing with the central issue in a case. This approach is partly due to the need to follow principles of natural justice and for justice to be seen to be done.

Key legal concepts

Confidentiality

An important source for social workers faced with ethical dilemmas is the 'Code of Ethics for Social Work' adopted by the British Association of Social Workers.[17] In the principles of practice, the code provides the following guidance on maintaining confidentiality:

> Social workers should respect the principles of confidentiality that apply to their relationships and ensure that confidential information is only divulged with the consent of the person using social work services or the informant. Exceptions to this may only be justified on the basis of a greater ethical requirement such as evidence of serious risk or the preservation of life. Social workers need to explain the nature of that confidentiality to people with whom they work and any circumstances where confidentiality must be waived should

be made explicit. Social workers should identify dilemmas about confidentiality and seek support to address these issues.

Source: BASW Code of Ethics 2012

As a starting point in any discussion on confidentiality the social worker can draw guidance from the above statement. It is clear that a presumption of confidentiality of information surrounds much of the work of a social worker but also that there are exceptions which will displace the presumption. Without any principle of confidentiality the extent to which individuals would be prepared to share sensitive and private information would be limited, frustrating the objectives of many areas of social work. An absolute guarantee of confidentiality should never be given to a service user, however, as there are circumstances where the law and good practice require information to be shared. A further qualification is necessary here in that, where it becomes apparent that information of a confidential nature needs to be shared, this should be carried out with sensitivity and limited to the minimum number of people/ agencies necessary. In many situations, if information needs to be shared, the first step will be to ask for permission from the service user or other person who provided the information. As any duty of confidentiality is owed to that person, then once consent is obtained, assuming the individual has the capacity to consent, there should be no concerns about breach of confidentiality provided the information is disclosed in an appropriate way. For example, permission to disclose information to another professional would not justify disclosure to the press. The legal basis which supports confidentiality and is relied upon to justify non disclosure is 'public interest immunity'. For example, in an early case, *D* v. *NSPCC* [1978] AC 171, the House of Lords ruled that the identity of someone who had alleged a child had suffered abuse could not be revealed to the child's parents. The information was immune from **disclosure**.

It may not be possible to maintain confidentiality in the following circumstances.

Statutory duty

Under a limited number of pieces of legislation there is a statutory duty to disclose information. Currently, relevant statutes are the Prevention of Terrorism Act 2005, the Public Health Acts, the Road Traffic Acts, the Misuse of Drugs Act 1971 and the Police and Criminal Evidence Act 1984 (**PACE**). The relevant legislation applies to very specific circumstances and it would be appropriate to obtain legal advice before disclosing on this basis.

Crime and Disorder Act 1998

This legislation is dealt with separately because it contains a section which gives permission for disclosure but does not contain a duty to disclose. Section 115 provides that:

s. 115

(1) Any person who, apart from this subsection, would not have power to disclose information—

   (a) to a relevant authority; or

   (b) to a person acting on behalf of such an authority,

shall have power to do so in any case where the disclosure is necessary or expedient for the purposes of any provision of this Act.

(**CDA** 1998)

Relevant authority includes the police, health authorities, probation and other local authorities.

Interest of the subject

Professionals will often have to share information about an individual in the best interests of that person. This is at the heart of multi-disciplinary work and is supported by a number of official documents. For example, 'Working Together' (2013)[18] states, in the section on sharing information (para 24):

> Fears about sharing information cannot be allowed to stand in the way of the need to promote the welfare and protect the safety of children. To ensure effective safeguarding arrangements: all organisations should have arrangements in place which set out clearly the processes and the principles for sharing information between each other, with other professionals and with the LSCB; and no professional should assume that someone else will pass on information which they think may be critical to keeping a child safe. If a professional has concerns about a child's welfare and believes they are suffering or likely to suffer harm, then they should share the information with local authority children's social care.

(See also *Re G (A Minor)* [1996] 2 All ER 65.) The emphasis must be on sharing relevant information with appropriate professionals who are likely to work with or have an interest in, for example, the protection of a child. The same principle can be applied to the conduct of a child protection conference. 'Working Together' acknowledges that the consequences of failing to share information properly can be grave, 'Serious Case Reviews (SCRs) have shown how poor information sharing has contributed to the deaths or serious injuries of children' (para 23).

Cross-government guidance, 'Information Sharing: Guidance for Practitioners and Managers', has been published (2008) and aims to provide some clarification of this difficult area. The guidance is applicable to child and adult social work and includes: principles of information sharing; core guidance on sharing information including a checklist and flowchart; good practice illustrations; and further guidance on legal issues.

Public interest

There may be occasions where the public interest outweighs the subject's interest in maintaining confidentiality, especially where there is a real threat of harm to others. It is a balancing exercise. In *W v. Egdell* [1989] 1 All ER 1089, a psychiatric report was disclosed to the Home Secretary on the basis that the public interest in the appropriate authorities being made aware of the 'dangerousness' of a patient outweighed the duty of confidence to the patient.

Court order

The need for justice in every case that reaches court provides the public interest to justify disclosure of confidential material in court proceedings. There is a duty to provide all relevant information to the court (whether or not it supports the social worker's argument). Rules of disclosure also mean that most relevant information, including statements, will be exchanged by the parties prior to the hearing. Information which becomes part of the court proceedings in this way cannot be disclosed to anyone beyond the parties to the case without the court's permission. For example, in child protection proceedings the court may authorise disclosure of material which is necessary to enable an expert to conduct an assessment of the child; or for use in criminal proceedings if prosecution of an alleged perpetrator is being considered. The court will order disclosure in other circumstances, for example to a professional body, if it is in the public interest to protect the public from a member of the profession upon a question as to suitability or misconduct.

Further specific guidance on confidentiality in relation to Social Services Departments is contained in circular LAC (88) 17, which should be read in the light of developing case law.

(The provisions of the Data Protection Act 1998 and the Freedom of Information Act 2000 are discussed in detail in Chapter 4.)

Accountability

Accountability in social work practice is an increasingly significant yet complex area. A social worker may be accountable on a number of levels. At the very least, accountability lies to the Social Services Authority in its role as employer and also as holder of the social services functions that are delegated to social workers acting as agents of the authority. Correspondingly, the local authority is liable for the actions of its employees. Only when acting as an Approved Social Worker does a social worker acquire individual **liability** for action. In addition, a social worker must be accountable to the service user, in that it is possible to explain and justify why particular decisions are made. This accountability may be tested via the Local Authority Complaints System if a service user is dissatisfied, by complaint to the local government ombudsman and ultimately by invoking judicial review procedures or action against a public authority under the Human Rights Act 1998. Other formal processes, including the functions of registration and inspection, support the notion of accountability, and in specified areas there is a duty to consult with service users. In cases involving statutory responsibilities towards children, accountability is to the child who is the subject of the case. There are circumstances where the social worker effectively works as an officer of the court and is accountable to the court, e.g. when directed to prepare and present a report or to comply with an undertaking or to follow the court's directions as to supervision of contact. Beyond those clear instances, accountability may also lie to team managers, section heads, practice teachers, the university or other institution during prequalification placements.[19]

(The issue of local authority liability in tort is discussed in the context of challenging decisions in Chapter 4.)

Inspection and regulation

Performance of public services, including social services, is increasingly being monitored through inspection and audit systems as a means of ensuring greater accountability. The role of the HCPC in relation to social work as a profession has been discussed above. The Care Standards Act 2000 also set up a new regulation and inspection body, known as the Care Standards Commission. After the first year of operation its role was taken over by the Commission for Social Care Inspection. At the same time, a second independent inspectorate with a remit covering health services was established, known as the Commission for Healthcare Audit and Inspection (**CHAI**). In both cases the Government objective was to strengthen accountability of those responsible for the commissioning and delivery of health and social services. The Care Quality Commission (**CQC**) took over the functions of CSCI and CHAI, together with the functions of the Mental Health Act Commission as a single inspection body in 2009. Ofsted continues to have responsibility for registration and inspection of children's services.

Duties and powers

Most social work areas of responsibility defined by legislation may be categorised as either duties or powers.

Duties

Where a **duty** is imposed by law, social services are obliged to carry it out; it is a mandatory obligation to carry out a particular function. There is no discretion or allowance for shortfall of resources. Breach of a duty could found an action for judicial review. An example is the duty to carry out an assessment of an adult's needs for care and support under s. 9 of the Care Act 2014. The section reads:

> ### s. 9
>
> **(1)** Where it appears to a local authority that an adult may have needs for care and support, the authority must assess—
> **(a)** whether the adult does have needs for care and support, and
> **(b)** if the adult does, what those needs are.
>
> (Care Act 2014)

The important word is *must*, which suggests an imperative. As a general rule, where 'shall' appears, a duty is imposed.

Powers

Where a **power** is provided, there is an element of discretion. Power provides the authority to act in a particular way but there is scope to decide how to act. An example is the power in para. 16 of Sch. 2 to the Children Act 1989 in respect of children looked after by a local authority.

> ### Sch. 2
>
> **(2)** The authority may—
> **(a)** make payments to—
> **(i)** a parent of the child; ...
> in respect of travelling, subsistence or other expenses incurred by that person in visiting the child;
>
> **(CA 1989)**

The important word is *may*. The authority may act in a particular way; they have a discretion but are not under an obligation. Guidance may be issued, which assists the interpretation of powers.

In some provisions what appears to be a duty is in effect softened by use of terms such as 'as far as is reasonably practicable', introducing some leeway into the obligation. The word 'responsibility' is sometimes used loosely to refer to duties and powers and in so doing suggests a rather fuzzy position. If there is a duty or power contained in legislation, it is preferable to talk in those terms and to be clear about the distinction between the two and the consequences. The circumstances where it would be appropriate to refer to responsibilities are in respect of a professional's ethical code, or in relation to agency policies which cover matters other than those set out in legislation.

Rights

The term 'rights' is open to wide interpretation, ranging from moral rights in the widest sense, through civil, political and cultural rights to a rather more restrictive interpretation of rights as something that an individual is legally entitled to. Unlike other countries which have a formal written constitution, often based on a Bill of Rights, UK law tends not to be expressed in positive rights. Rather it takes a more negative and reactive stance so that it is fair to assume that a person has the right to act in a particular way unless the law expressly prohibits it. This position may change over the years: it has been suggested that the introduction of the Human Rights Act 1998 will result in a rights-based culture and accessible avenues in which challenges can be brought if rights are infringed.

In social work, rights which have already been clearly incorporated into law include:

- The right to an assessment for care and the right of a carer for an assessment of their needs to provide care under the Care Act 2014.
- The right not to be discriminated against in specified circumstances, e.g. provision of goods and services on specified grounds known as protected characteristics, including race, sex and disability.
- The right of a child (if of sufficient understanding to make an informed decision) to refuse a medical or psychiatric examination under the Children Act 1989.
- The right of access to information held about you under the Data Protection Act 1998.

(Chapters 7 and 16 include discussion of children's rights and the rights of vulnerable adults, particularly in cases where capacity is limited.)

Values

It is crucial to recognise that the law does not exist in a vacuum. Each day social workers make numerous difficult decisions relating to the lives of service users. Law is one of many factors that will be balanced in arriving at an appropriate decision reflecting good social work practice. A value system is an essential prerequisite for making such decisions. It is also appropriate for use of law to be informed by a framework of values. Values may influence which route to follow if there are a range of legal options available, e.g. the choice between removing a child or an adult from home if child abuse is suspected, or even whether it is appropriate to have recourse to law at all, recognising that the law itself has deficiencies.

It may be argued that some social work values directly conflict with the objectives of available law. For example, it is difficult to reconcile the values of anti-discriminatory and anti-oppressive practice with some of the terminology utilised in the Mental Health Act 1983 and its tendency to define and categorise individuals by reference to one characteristic, their medical diagnosis of mental health. Conversely, there will be cases where the law can be used directly to support values. For example, it may be empowering for an individual who has been abused to have direct recourse to the Family Law Act 1996 and to obtain an **injunction** removing the abuser from the household. It may also be argued that certain values that are often closely associated with social work are actually enshrined within legislation. For example, Art. 14 of the European Convention on Human Rights, the right not to be discriminated against, supports the social work value encapsulated in the Code of Ethics, i.e. recognising 'the value and dignity of every human being irrespective of origin, race, status, sex, sexual orientation, age, disability, belief or contribution to society'.[20]

Social care legislation is increasingly including statutory principles as explicit statements of the values underpinning the legislation. The Mental Capacity Act code of practice explains that the principles are:

> the values that underpin the legal requirements in the Act. The Act is intended to be enabling and supportive of people who lack capacity, not restricting or controlling of their lives. It aims to protect people who lack capacity to make particular decisions, but also to maximize their ability to make decisions, or to participate in decision-making as far as they are able to do so.[21]

The effect of personal values should also be acknowledged. It is important constantly to question individual values and consider the effect they have on practice. The position taken on a particular issue will probably be arrived at by the application of a combination of personal values, social work values and legal values, as demonstrated by, for example, the issue of whether a mature person with Alzheimer's disease should be able to live independently, be cared for by family members or move to residential accommodation. Factors which influence the position taken will include: personal views on whether you would be willing and able to care for a parent in such circumstances or would want to be cared for by your children; the values of empowerment, autonomy and choice; and the extent to which a person whose capacity is reduced should enjoy the same rights of autonomy, in the context of risk factors associated with living alone. The legal position includes a duty to provide community care support, and a duty to provide residential accommodation, direct payments, issues of substitute decision-making and management of financial affairs.

This example illustrates the complexity of everyday situations social workers will face. An approach based exclusively on either social work values or legal values provides an incomplete picture.

Partnership

Partnership may operate at a number of levels.[22] On at least two levels it is integral to good social work practice.

Service users

Partnership with service users may include working to involve them fully in decision-making processes, whether by provision of appropriate literature and information, advocacy services, etc., or active involvement in, for example, conferences and reviews. The concept of partnership is integral to the philosophy and practice of the Children Act

1989. Yet there is no specific mention of partnership within the Act itself. It features in the Guidance which supports the Act, e.g. Volumes 2 and 3 of the *Children Act 1989 Guidance and Regulations (2010)*,[23] and may be read in to certain provisions, notably, under s. 17, the duty to promote the upbringing of children in need by their families so far as that is consistent with promoting welfare. Whether a true, meaningful partnership can exist between a professional social worker and a service user has been questioned in view of the obvious power imbalance. It may be an objective which is easier to realise in a case where Social Services are providing support to a child in need than in a contested child protection scenario. In the latter case, where the views of the social worker and the parents may be in direct conflict, it is still important that the social worker applies elements of a partnership approach, particularly by keeping lines of communication open, sharing and explaining information and any decisions that have been taken and not adopting an inflexible or adversarial stance. Aldgate (2001) suggests further that some of the key features of partnership with parents are:

- A shared commitment to negotiation and actions concerning how best to safeguard and promote children's welfare.
- A mutual respect for the other's point of view.
- Recognising the unequal nature of power between parents and professionals.
- Recognising that parents have their own needs which should be addressed.
- Good communication skills on the part of professionals.
- The establishment of trust between all parties.
- Integrity and accountability on the part of both parents and professionals.
- Shared decision-making.
- A joint recognition of constraints on the services offered.
- A recognition that partnership is not an end in itself.[24]

Professionals

Another application of partnership may be evident in working relations between different professional groups in an inter-disciplinary framework. The need to work together gained explicit recognition in guidance such as 'Working Together to Safeguard Children' (2013) and 'No Secrets' (2000) and the consequences of failure to work together and share information is well documented in a number of Child Abuse Inquiry Reports.[25] The Youth Offending Teams (**YOTs**) established under the Crime and Disorder Act 1998[26] present a formal template for multi-disciplinary work to prevent youth crime. The Children Act 2004 develops partnership between professionals further. A statutory duty to cooperate with a view to improving children's wellbeing is imposed on children's services authorities and their relevant partners (s. 10). Relevant partners include district councils, police, probation boards, youth offending teams and health authorities. (See further discussion in Chapter 7.)

Choice

Promoting choice has been recognised as an important value for some time, particularly in the context of adults whose decision-making capacity may be limited.[27] The British Association of Social Workers' (**BASW**) Code of Ethics identifies the importance of promoting the interests of service users and advises: 'Social workers should support people to reach informed decisions about their lives and promote their autonomy and independence, provided this does not conflict with their safety or with the rights of others.'

The reality of choice, however, is firmly located in a resources debate. Against a context of community care policy which purports to enable people to live independently in their own homes for as long as possible, across the country individuals whose care needs reach a level that costs more to meet in the community than by residential care may feel they have little real choice. Equally, if local authorities cannot recruit sufficient foster carers or prospective adoptive parents then a young person in a care home may struggle to see how he or she can make a positive choice about his or her home.

Empowerment

Social workers may be able to provide support to an individual and empower that person to take action for him- or herself to improve circumstances. Working in a very paternalistic manner might be seen as restricting opportunities for empowerment. Promoting empowerment is closely linked to anti-oppressive and anti-discriminatory practice and to recognition of rights.[28]

Anti-discriminatory, anti-oppressive practice

The legal context to anti-discriminatory and anti-oppressive practice can be found in core anti-discrimination legislation and various references in other pieces of legislation (see Chapter 6). Good practice in social work has, however, developed beyond these legal minimum standards for anti-discrimination. Anti-discriminatory, anti-oppressive practice is integral to social work. Again, the BASW Code provides direction:

> Social workers should promote and contribute to the development of positive policies, procedures and practices which are anti-oppressive and empowering. They should respect people's beliefs, values, culture, goals, needs, preferences, relationships and affiliations. Social workers should recognise their own prejudices to ensure they do not discriminate against any person or group. They should ensure that services are offered and delivered in a culturally appropriate manner.

This is an area where the role of law has been questioned, in particular because, although the aim of early anti-discriminatory legislation was to alter entrenched attitudes and promote change, is it possible for the law, with its focus on dealing with individual problems, and which itself has been charged with discriminatory practice, to be an instrument of social change? A simple evaluation of the effectiveness of the legislation would suggest that, whilst the legislation and the work of the Equality and Human Rights Commission has broken down some barriers, much systematic discrimination still continues. It is important, however, for social workers to have a basic understanding of anti-discrimination legislation, as there may be circumstances where clients encounter discrimination and may seek their social worker's advice.

In addition, social workers have a legal obligation to comply with the law, and social work actions themselves may be covered by anti-discriminatory legislation. (The scope of existing anti-discrimination legislation is covered in detail in Chapter 6.) At this stage, it is important to be aware of the following central provision of the Equality Act 2010, which supports the need to promote anti-discriminatory and anti-oppressive practice.

> ## s. 149
>
> **(1)** A public authority must, in the exercise of its functions have due regard to the need to—
>
>   **(a)** eliminate discrimination, harassment, victimisation and any other conduct that is prohibited by this Act;
>
>   **(b)** advance equality of opportunity between persons who share a relevant protected characteristic and persons who do not share it;
>
>   **(c)** foster good relations between persons who share a relevant protected characteristic and persons who do not share it.
>
> (Equality Act 2010)

This public sector equality duty applies to all of the nine protected characteristics of the Equality Act. The previous law only included a race and disability equality duty.

Further support may be drawn from the Human Rights Act 1998. Section 6 of the 1998 Act imposes a duty on public authorities to act in compliance with the articles of the European Convention, including Art. 14, which reads:

> ## Art. 14
>
> The enjoyment of the rights and freedoms in this Convention shall be secured without discrimination on any ground such as sex, race, colour, religion, political or other opinion, national or social origin, association with a national minority, property, birth or other status.
>
> **(ECHR)**

This article clearly envisages discrimination on a wider range of grounds than covered by our existing legislation. Although it is currently limited to discrimination in the enjoyment of rights set out under the Convention, the introduction of a free-standing discrimination article is possible in the future.

Other specific provisions in legislation direct anti-discriminatory practice. For example, s. 22(5) of the Children Act 1989 requires that, in making placement decisions, due consideration be given to a child's religious persuasion, racial origin, and cultural and linguistic background.

The structures and provisions of the English legal system can themselves be viewed as disempowering and discriminatory. It is thus essential to deal proactively with issues of equal opportunities. All legislation employs the male pronoun, though under the Interpretation Act 1978 'he' is intended to include 'she'. Unless directly quoting from legislation, it is important to avoid talking in a way which might be construed as sexist and explain the above reasoning if it is necessary for the sake of accuracy. Other 'discriminatory' language has featured in legislation such as the National Assistance Act 1948 which referred to the 'deaf and dumb'.

It is important in acknowledging the limitations of law to recognise that law will not always provide the answers: e.g. in discrimination issues, practice developments have progressed more rapidly than law. Such an approach encourages critical awareness and may reassure those who feel that legal solutions are being imposed on their practice at the expense of other interventions more traditionally associated with social work, which are therapeutically based.

Formal guidance on values and principles

There are examples of value frameworks, sometimes expressed as principles in both legislation and policy guidance. 'No Secrets: Guidance on developing and implementing multi-agency policies and procedures to protect vulnerable adults from abuse',[29] includes a statement that agencies should adhere to the following guiding principles:

1. actively work together within an inter-agency framework;
2. actively promote the empowerment and wellbeing of vulnerable adults;
3. act in a way which supports the rights of the individual to lead an independent life based on self-determination and personal choice;
4. recognise people who are unable to make their own decisions;
5. recognise that the right to self-determination can involve risk and ensure that such risk is recognised and understood by all concerned and minimised wherever possible;
6. ensure the safety of vulnerable adults.

A second example can be found in the Mental Capacity Act 2005, which includes in s. 1 general principles to be followed in relation to individual capacity. The inclusion of principles in a piece of legislation is significant and the principles referred to support good practice.

---

s. 1

The principles

(1) The following principles apply for the purposes of this Act.

(2) A person must be assumed to have capacity unless it is established that he lacks capacity.

(3) A person is not to be treated as unable to make a decision unless all practicable steps to help him to do so have been taken without success.

(4) A person is not to be treated as unable to make a decision merely because he makes an unwise decision.

(5) An act done, or decision made, under this Act for or on behalf of a person who lacks capacity must be done, or made, in his best interests.

(6) Before the act is done, or the decision is made, regard must be had to whether the purpose for which it is needed can be as effectively achieved in a way that is less restrictive of the person's rights and freedom of action.

(**MCA** 2005)

A framework for decision-making

The application of a framework for decision-making provides a logical format in which to balance social work and legal values in order to reach a decision. This approach has been advocated by Braye and Preston-Shoot (1997), and the following simplified version (adapted from the above) can be adopted and applied to the majority of decisions a social worker will face. Given the approach of the media to social work crisis, which focuses on scapegoating, it is essential that processes of decision-making are clear. Further imperatives for openness and transparency in decision-making are provided by the Data Protection Act 1998 and the Human Rights Act 1998. Thus, 'a decision-making framework is both a safety device and a moral imperative'.[30] The framework suggested here is divided into stages of background work and taking action, but it is acknowledged that in practice there may not be a clear dividing line between the two.

Background

- Identify the problem requiring social work intervention, source of referral, background information, previous involvement in the case. How is information to be recorded?
- Obtain further information if necessary, making use of inter-agency contacts.
- Identify the level of risk in the situation – there may be different levels of risk to different people.
- Consider the purpose of intervention – in the long and short term – what do you want to achieve and why?
- Are there competing interests among the individuals concerned (e.g. different assertions of 'rights', safety of professionals may be an issue)?
- Does the legal framework mandate or permit types of action, duties or powers?
- Is it appropriate to seek legal advice at this stage, relevant, e.g., to collection of evidence, immediate protection?

Taking action

- Is an emergency response required, possibly requiring police involvement?
- Is there a level of agreement or is it necessary to invoke formal powers (not mutually exclusive concepts)?
- What guidance exists as to how a decision to intervene is reached – e.g. is a formal meeting such as a planning meeting or case conference required? Who holds the decision-making power in the authority (team manager, director)? Has adequate supervision been present?
- Have consultation responsibilities been complied with?
- Is everybody involved who needs to be – within the agency and in partnership with other agencies, e.g. health, education?
- What mechanisms will achieve the desired outcomes? Is it necessary to go to court; are resources available?
- What review requirements exist after action has been taken?

Chapter summary

- Law provides for the structure of Social Services Departments and the mandate to practise.
- Law sets parameters within which discretion may be exercised in reaching decisions.
- Law does not exist in a vacuum as a discrete entity but should be incorporated into social work practice.

- A value framework should inform use of law and selected values – partnership, empowerment, anti-oppressive and anti-discriminatory practice find some support in the law but may also be interpreted as contradictory in places.

- The concept of accountability is complex and may lie to various bodies, including your employer and the courts.

- The confidentiality of information and records may be protected by public interest immunity. Confidentiality of information and records cannot be guaranteed, however, and it may be necessary to disclose information where it is in the interest of a child, in the public interest, ordered by a court, or as part of multi-disciplinary work.

- A framework for decision-making, incorporating analysis of legal options and values can support good practice and guard against defensive practice.

Websites

Health and Care Professions Council: this body replaced the General Social Care Council and has responsibility for regulation of the social care workforce, including social workers:
www.hcpc-uk.org.uk

British Association of Social Workers: including the Code of Ethics:
www.basw.co.uk

Directgov – the entry point for Government information and services online, this website has an alphabetical listing of central Government departments, agencies and bodies, topics and policies (a really useful bookmark):
www.gov.uk

Further reading

A number of articles and texts explore the relationship between law, social work practice, ethics and decision-making.

Braye, S. and Preston-Shoot, M. (1994) 'Partners in community care? Rethinking the relationship between the law and social work practice' 2 *Journal of Social Welfare and Family Law* pp. 163–84.

Braye, S. and Preston-Shoot, M. (1999) 'Accountability, administrative law and social work practice: redressing or reinforcing the power imbalance?' 21(3) *Journal of Social Welfare and Family Law* pp. 235–56.

Braye, S. and Preston-Shoot, M. (2001) 'Social Work Practice and Accountability' in Cull, L.-A. and Roche, J. *The Law and Social Work.* Basingstoke: Palgrave.

Braye, S. and Preston-Shoot, M. (2006) 'The role of law in welfare reform: critical perspectives on the relationship between law and social work practice' 15(1) *International Journal of Social Welfare* pp. 19–26.

Dickens, J. (2012) *Social Work, Law and Ethics.* London: Routledge.

McLaughlin, K. (2010) 'The social worker versus the General Social Care Council: an analysis of care standards tribunal hearings decisions' 40(1) *British Journal of Social Work.* p. 311. (An interesting examination of the way the tribunal has dealt with social work misconduct cases.)

Preston-Shoot, M. (2000) 'What if? Using the law to uphold practice values and standards' 12(4) *Practice* p. 49.

Preston-Shoot, M., Roberts, G. and Vernon, S. (2001) 'Values in social work law: strained relations or sustaining relationships?' 23(1) *Journal of Social Welfare and Family Law* pp. 1–22.

Preston-Shoot, M. (2014) *Making Good Decisions.* Basingstoke: Palgrave Macmillan.

The following publications address issues of good practice in social work and question future direction of social work education:

Croisdale-Appleby, D. (2014) *Re-visioning Social Work Education: An Independent Review.* London: Department of Health.

GSCC (2008) *Raising Standards: Social Work Conduct in England 2003-08.* London: GSCC.

GSCC (2011) *Professional Boundaries – Guidance for Social Workers.* London: GSCC.

Narey, Sir Martin (2013) *Making the Education of Social Workers Consistently Effective.* London: Department for Education.

Notes

[1] S. Braye and M. Preston-Shoot (1990) 'On teaching and applying the law in social work: it is not that simple' 20(4) *British Journal of Social Work* pp. 333–53, p. 343.

[2] C. Ball, R. Harris, G. Roberts and S. Vernon (1988) 'The Law Report: Teaching and Assessment of Law in Social Work Education', CCETSW.

[3] F. Jones, B. Fletcher and K. Ibbetson (1991) 'Stressors and strains amongst social workers: demands, supports, constraints and psychological health' 21(5) *British Journal of Social Work* pp. 443–69.

[4] S. Braye and M. Preston-Shoot (2005) *Teaching, Learning and Assessment of Law in Social Work Education.* London: Social Care Institute for Excellence.

[5] M. Preston-Shoot, G. Roberts and S. Vernon (1998) 'Social work law: from interaction to integration' 20(1) *Journal of Social Welfare and Family Law* pp. 65–80.

[6] Ibid., p. 65.

[7] DHSS (1991) 'Working Together: Guidelines for Inter-agency Co-operation for the Protection of Children'. London: HMSO.

[8] CCETSW ceased to exist from 2002 upon implementation of the Care Standards Act 2000, which introduced the General Social Care Council (s. 54).

[9] C. Ball, M. Preston-Shoot, G. Roberts and S. Vernon (1995) *Law for Social Workers in England and Wales,* CCETSW: 'Students need to understand:

  i. that the law gives social workers their mandate to practise:
    (a) as employees of the statutory bodies (when, for example, employed as a local authority social worker); or officers of the court (when employed, for example, as a probation officer),
    (b) by defining the various groups of people in respect of whom social workers have duties and powers,
    (c) by defining a social worker's legal functions in relation to each client group;
  ii. that legally accountable powers, when appropriately used, can promote and encourage good social-work practice: e.g. by emphasising the importance of prevention and rehabilitation; by setting out the conditions upon which compulsory intervention is permissible; by ensuring that compulsory intervention with a person's rights takes place in accordance with proper legal safeguards, such as due process of law and adherence to principles of natural justice;
  iii. that the exercise of legal powers may be oppressive or discriminatory if not used in ways that avoid discrimination and respect clients' rights; and that social and legal

institutions and processes, such as the court system, to which social work practice must often relate, are frequently identified as discriminatory and racist in operation and practice.

Students need to know:

i. the substantive law which is relevant to social work practice, and its nature and sources;

ii. the relationship between local authority and probation policy and the law;

iii. the structures and processes of the relevant court and tribunal systems.'

[10] The College of Social Work (2014) 'Roles and Functions of Social Workers in England' Advice Note, (para 3D).

[11] Sir Martin Narey (2013) 'Making the Education of Social Workers Consistently Effective'. Department for Education.

[12] Croisdale-Appleby, D. (2014) 'Revisioning Social Work Education: An Independent Review'. Department of Health.

[13] TCSW (2012) *Professional Capabilities Framework*. London: The College of Social Work.

[14] *Community Care*, 11 December 2007.

[15] Cited in L. Clements (1996) *Community Care and the Law*. London: Legal Action Group Books.

[16] W. Macpherson (1999) *The Stephen Lawrence Inquiry: Report of an Inquiry by Sir William Macpherson of Cluny et al.*. London: The Stationery Office.

[17] The Code referred to may be accessed via the BASW website at www.basw.co.uk.

[18] Department for Education (2013) *Working Together to Safeguard Children*. London: The Stationery Office.

[19] For a full discussion, see S. Braye and M. Preston-Shoot (2001) 'Social Work Practice and Accountability' in L.-A. Cull and J. Roche (eds) *The Law and Social Work: Contemporary Issues for Practice*. Basingstoke: Palgrave.

[20] BASW (1996) 'The Code of Ethics for Social Work', point 6.

[21] Department for Constitutional Affairs (2007) Mental Capacity Act 2005: Code of Practice, p. 19.

[22] See discussion in relation to the use of written agreements in S. Braye and M. Preston-Shoot (1992) 'Honourable intentions: partnership and written agreements in welfare legislation' 21(6) *Journal of Social Welfare and Family Law* pp. 511–28.

[23] Department of Health (2010).

[24] J. Aldgate (2001) 'Safeguarding and Promoting the Welfare of Children in Need Living with their Families' in L.-A. Cull and J. Roche (eds) *The Law and Social Work: Contemporary Issues for Practice*. Basingstoke: Palgrave.

[25] See Department of Health (1991) *Child Abuse: A Study of Inquiry Reports*. London: HMSO; and P. Reder, S. Duncan and M. Gray (1993) *Beyond Blame: Child Abuse Tragedies Revisited*. London: Routledge.

[26] Section 39.

[27] Department of Health/SSI (1989) *Homes Are for Living In*. London: HMSO.

[28] See S. Braye and M. Preston-Shoot (1995) *Empowering Practice in Social Care*. Buckingham: Open University Press.

[29] Department of Health (2000).

[30] S. Braye and M. Preston-Shoot (1997) *Practising Social Work Law*. Basingstoke: Macmillan.

Chapter 2

Sources of law

Learning objectives

To develop an understanding of the following:

- The language, terminology and conventions of law and to become fluent in the use of appropriate legal terminology.
- The substantive content and sources of law that give social workers powers and duties.
- The status of legislation, case law, policy and guidance.
- The process of making legislation.
- The application of case law and the doctrine of precedent.
- Legal research skills and to begin to develop a critical approach to law.
- The process of law reform and in particular the role of the Law Commission.
- The influence of European and International law and Conventions.

Talking Point

The following quotes are drawn from the Law Commission Scoping Report on Adult Social Care (2008):

> Adult social care is in urgent need of reform. It remains a complex and confusing patchwork of conflicting statutes enacted over a period of 60 years. The law is also based on outdated and often discriminatory concepts and gives rise to human rights concerns. A number of significant costs are incurred as a direct result of the complexity of this area of law. Finally, there are concerns about how the law negotiates the tension between local and central planning and decision making. In short it is in need of reform.

> The legislative framework for adult residential care, community care, adult protection and support for carers is inadequate, often incomprehensible and outdated. It remains a confusing patchwork of conflicting statutes enacted over a period of 60 years. There is no single, modern statute to which service providers and service users can look to understand whether (and, if so, what kind of) services can or should be provided.

> The overall aim of the project is to provide a clearer and more cohesive framework for adult social care. This would help to ensure that service users, carers, social care staff, health professionals and lawyers are clear about rights to services and which services are available. It will also aim to modernise the law to ensure that it is no longer based on outdated principles.

Source: **Law Commission**

The law is dynamic and ever changing. Developments and changes in the law can be traced to a variety of sources. Parliament makes new legislation which the courts then develop and clarify through case law. The prompts for reform may be particular social problems or the search for a clearer legal framework, as identified by the Law Commission (whose role is discussed in more detail below) in their recent work on adult social care law. The substance of many of their recommendations in their work on adult social care law can now be found in the Care Act 2014.

Introduction

What appears clear ... is that social work students and practitioners experience contact with the law and legal system as stressful. They are concerned about their lack of familiarity with legal settings, languages and procedures, and about the frequency with which the legal rules change. They express uncertainty about how the law interfaces with social work values and organizational procedures. Furthermore, legal accountability, which might benefit service users, can be unsettling for social work practitioners. They conceptualise the law as intimidating, conflictual, and more likely to be obstructive than empowering.

(Braye and Preston-Shoot, 2005)[1]

Given the above statement, it is essential at an early stage to gain an understanding of law and to develop confidence and enthusiasm in using law. The first step is knowing what law is and where it comes from. That is the focus of this chapter. Sources of law, including case law and legislation, are written and cited in accordance with recognised conventions that can make them appear unduly complicated to a lay person.[2] It is worth spending some time unravelling these conventions so as to become comfortable with direct sources.

Law which is relevant for social work practice is contained in a variety of forms. Much of it is fairly recent and can be linked to Government initiatives, such as the 'Every Child Matters' programme, efforts to tackle social exclusion and efforts to reduce delay in family law proceedings. The process of introducing new law which impacts on social work practice shows no sign of slowing down. For effective practice, it is essential to have an understanding of existing law and also to be aware of likely areas of reform. There will be occasions when it is necessary for a social worker to refer directly to a source of law and understanding law is clearly specified as a requirement within the Professional Capabilities Framework. (See Chapter 1.) Domain 2 requires that, 'Social workers are knowledgeable about the value base of their profession, its ethical standards and relevant law' and in relation to 'Knowledge' in domain 5: 'Social workers understand . . . the legal framework for practice.' In order to meet these requirements and become competent and effective practitioners it is important, at an early stage in a career in social work, to gain familiarity with direct sources of law.

This chapter explains the range of sources of law and the relative importance or status of different types of law, in relation to social work practice. Legislation, as the primary source of law, is considered first, including an explanation of the development of new legislation. This is followed by consideration of rules, regulations, directions, guidance or policy and codes of practice, which supplement primary legislation. The law of the United Kingdom is contained not only in statutes, but also in the form of case law, which collectively is known as the **common law**. The extent to which a legal decision has an influence on subsequent cases through the operation of precedent is considered, and an exercise is offered to provide insight into the way that decisions of the courts are reported.

One of the exciting aspects of the study of social work law is the speed at which it changes and develops. Keeping track of those developments is also one of its most challenging demands. New laws may be driven from a number of directions, some overtly political in nature. A significant amount of law, however, has been introduced following the work of the Law Commission, an independent body, whose role is considered in some detail below. Perhaps the greatest influence on the future development of law in this country is likely to be the Human Rights Act 1998 (which is the subject of Chapter 5). This chapter concludes with reference to the influence of other European and international law conventions.

As a preliminary issue, which has a bearing on all the subsequent sections, the chapter commences with a discussion of the language of law.

Language of law

The use of complicated, sometimes almost unintelligible, legal language has often been cited (by students and others) as a real barrier to understanding law. There are a number of possible responses to this complaint and comments to be made about legal language.

First, to agree! Most lawyers could cite at least one legal provision which they have read and reread and still not understood, or which they consider they could have drafted in a more satisfactory manner. An example of a provision which seeks to introduce a fairly straightforward point, but does so in a convoluted way, is the 'no order' principle of the Children Act 1989. This states:

> ### s. 1
>
> **(5)** Where a court is considering whether or not to make one or more orders with respect to a child, it shall not make the order or any of the orders unless it considers that doing so would be better for the child than making no order at all.
>
> (CA 1989)

In other words, any order made by a court should result in a positive benefit for the child! In practical terms, to use the example of care proceedings, it will be for the local authority to convince the court that, through making the order, the application of the terms of the care plan will be positively better for the child than making no order at all. Secondly, legal language is used to ensure precision and thoroughness in legislation. Certain terms are employed because they have a precise legal meaning; for example, **negligence** and recklessness. It may sometimes be helpful to turn to a law dictionary for help in deciphering difficult terminology. The glossary included in this book explains legal terms which a social worker is likely to encounter.

Thirdly, all professions develop their own special language or jargon and lawyers are no exception. Neither are social workers. An occasion comes to mind when a magistrate asked a social worker, when giving evidence, to talk about brothers and sisters rather than siblings! Increased inter-agency working may lead to development of more shared language in the longer term. Fourthly, legislation does not change at a comparable pace to practice developments. There are numerous examples of use of language in legislation (and case law) which it would be considered unacceptable to use in practice. This is most obvious where legislation made many decades ago is still in common usage. One example is the National Assistance Act 1948, s. 29, which refers to:

> ### s. 29
>
> … welfare of persons who are blind, deaf, dumb or otherwise handicapped, or are suffering from mental disorder of any description, or who are substantially and permanently handicapped by illness, injury, or congenital deformity or such other disabilities as may be prescribed.
>
> (**NAA** 1948)

Aside from any concerns about labelling individuals, it is clear that many of the terms used in this section would now be considered inappropriate or even offensive. Although different views are held, reference to an individual being hearing impaired or without speech is suggested as preferable to referring to an individual as deaf or dumb. It has also become accepted practice now to refer to disability rather than handicap.

Fifthly, in an attempt to leave categories open and broad for interpretation in practice, the law can appear vague and imprecise. In the checklist to the welfare principle of the Children

Act 1989, s. 1(3)(d) refers to the child's 'age, sex, background and any characteristics of his which the court considers relevant'. Later in the Act, at s. 22(5)(c) local authorities are required, when making decisions, to give due consideration to a child's religious persuasion, racial origin and cultural and linguistic background. It is likely that in the welfare checklist 'any characteristics of his' is intended to include religious persuasion, racial origin and cultural and linguistic background; however, it is unfortunate that in the first section of the Act such reference is implicit rather than explicit.

Sixthly, there is a clear movement to introduce greater use of simpler, far clearer language into the legal system. There is a much greater emphasis now on preparing legislation for users, in recognition that legislation that cannot be understood by people whose interests it serves is likely only to bring the law into disrepute. In addition, all Bills and new legislation are now accompanied by detailed explanatory notes. Both the legislation and the explanatory notes are available from the Parliament website.[3] One of the central aims of the reforms[4] of civil justice in the 1990s was to simplify the process of litigation and encourage the use of clearer and simpler language. Many terms commonly used by lawyers might be described as 'legalese' and could be substituted by plain language without affecting their meaning: e.g. 'people' instead of 'persons'; 'under' instead of 'pursuant to'; and 'end' instead of 'expiration'.[5]

There may be cases where legal language conflicts with the principles and practice of anti-discriminatory and anti-oppressive values. In those circumstances it is appropriate to use the preferred terms adopted in practice, unless quoting directly from the particular legal provision.

Legislation

Legislation applicable in England and Wales is introduced by Parliament and the process involves scrutiny and amendment by both the House of Commons and House of Lords. Up to the stage where Royal Assent is given, draft legislation is referred to as a Bill. During the parliamentary process, the content of the legislation may be altered significantly, as a result of debate and amendments; for example, the Children Act 1989 almost doubled in size. Since the introduction of the Government of Wales Act 2006, the National Assembly for Wales has the power to make legislation, specifically applicable to Wales, on a range of devolved matters. As an example, see the Social Services and Well-Being (Wales) Act 2014.

Most new legislation is introduced by the Government, and is preceded by a **white paper** that outlines the proposals and background to the need for reform. A white paper is a command paper presented to Government (usually by a Government minister) as a statement of Government policy. Elements of new laws may be traced back to election manifestos or reflect particular events or circumstances prevailing in society, e.g. greater fear of crime. There may have been a detailed consultation period prior to this, in some cases coordinated by the Law Commission, or other bodies such as the Department of Health or Home Office. As part of the consultation process, a **green paper** may have been published which puts forward proposals for consultation. A notable example is the 'Every Child Matters' green paper published in September 2003, which preceded the Children Act 2004. Most Government proposals for legislation in the forthcoming year of office are announced in the Queen's Speech (prepared by the Cabinet) at the State Opening of Parliament in November each year.

Legislation may also commence as a Private Member's Bill; however, it is now fairly unusual for a Private Member's Bill to become law, because parliamentary time is short and is mainly taken up with Government matters. A well-known example of a Private Member's

Bill is the Abortion Act 1967, which was introduced by David Steel MP. In some cases a Bill may start life as a Private Member's Bill then, as the issue gains the Government's support, a Government Bill on the subject is introduced. Such was the case with the Disability Discrimination Act 1995 (now consolidated into the Equality Act 2010) and the Civil Partnership Act 2004, though in each case some pressure groups were disappointed by what they felt was ultimately a watered-down version of their proposals.

Process of new legislation

The process can be understood as a series of steps beginning with the first reading.

First reading

A Bill can be introduced for first reading in either the House of Commons or the House of Lords. In practice it is more common for Bills to be introduced in the House of Commons, particularly where there are financial implications. There is no debate about the Bill at first reading, the clerk simply reads the title of the Bill and it is then formally printed ready for debate at subsequent stages.

Second reading

Debate on the main principles of the Bill starts at this stage. A vote can be taken on the Bill as a whole at the end of second reading.

Committee stage

Following second reading, all Bills move to a standing committee for further consideration.[6] There are between 16 and 50 members on a committee, which includes a cross-section of political party representation with a majority of members from the Government. The committee can hear evidence from experts, and works through the Bill clause by clause, making amendments, which are drafted by parliamentary counsel, where necessary.

Report stage

The outcome of the committee stage is reported to the House. Further debate takes place and more changes can be made at report stage. Often this will include attempts to restore provisions lost or amended in committee stage, or to remove committee additions.

Third reading

At third reading, debate becomes more focused and is confined to the contents of the Bill. At the earlier second reading the debate will usually have been more wide ranging, involving a review of the Bill in the context of the subject to which it relates. The Bill then moves to the House of Lords.

House of Lords

In the House of Lords a similar process takes place. First reading starts the process, followed by second reading, committee stage, report stage and third reading, following which a motion is put forward. The Bill returns to the House of Commons with the Lords' amendments to it, which must then be considered by the Commons. Amendments may be made to the Bill through the whole process, even at a very late stage, as was seen in the instance of the Adoption and Children Act 2002. A much called-for but controversial late amendment in the House of Commons extended eligibility to adopt to couples, not limited to married couples. It is essential for the two Houses finally to reach agreement on the changes made by each other if the Bill is to succeed, though in limited circumstances it is possible for the Government to use its House of Commons majority to overrule House of Lords opposition.

Royal Assent

The short titles of Bills which have received **Royal Assent** are read out in each House. Obtaining Royal Assent, the signature of the Queen, converts the Bill into an Act of Parliament. It is possible to track the progress of a Bill through Parliament by reference to **Hansard**, the daily official report of each House.[7] To illustrate the timescale legislative passage may involve, the Mental Capacity Act 2005 developed as shown in Table 2.1.

To complete the picture it is worth remembering that the Law Commission started their consultation process around mental capacity in 1989, and the Government white paper 'Making Decisions' was published in 1999.

Commencement

Legislation is not automatically implemented on receipt of the Royal Assent. Often the Act will be brought into force at a later date by a commencement order,[8] or there may be a commencement section at the end of the statute, which specifies the date. Implementation may be delayed for a number of reasons. A delay of two years took place before the Human Rights Act 1998 came into force on 2 October 2000. One reason for this delay was the need for a major training programme to be conducted at all levels of the judiciary. Longer delays may occur: e.g. parts of the Family Law Reform Act 1986 were not implemented until 2001.[9]

Acts may come into force in sections over a period of time and some parts of legislation are never implemented. The Lord Chancellor announced in 2001 that the part of the Family Law Act 1996 relating to reform of divorce laws would not be implemented, following pilot programmes throughout the country, which trialled mediation and compulsory meetings

Table 2.1 Legislative passage of the Mental Capacity Act 2005

House	Stage	Date
Commons	First Reading	17 June 2004
Commons	Second Reading	11 October 2004
Commons	Committee – 12 sittings	19 October – 4 November 2004
Commons	Report	14 December 2004
Commons	Third Reading	14 December 2004
Lords	First Reading	15 December 2004
Lords	Second Reading	10 January 2005
Lords	Committee – 5 sittings	25 January – 8 February 2005
Lords	Report (day 1)	15 March 2005
Lords	Report (day 2)	17 March 2005
Lords	Third Reading	24 March 2005
Commons	Consideration of Lords Amendments	5 April 2005
Commons	Royal Assent	7 April 2005

for divorcing couples, and suggested this part of the Act would be unworkable. These un-commenced provisions have now been repealed by the Children and Families Act 2014.

Amendment

Legislation may continue to be amended after it receives Royal Assent and has been implemented. Amendments are introduced by new legislation in related areas. This provides an opportunity to fine-tune the earlier legislation, update it and ensure consistency without having to repeal the Act and replace it in full. The Children Act 1989 has been amended on a number of occasions, for example, by the Adoption and Children Act 2002 and most recently by the Children and Families Act 2014 (**CAFA**). Amongst other things, the definition of 'harm' as part of the threshold criteria for care proceedings was amended by the **ACA** to include 'impairment suffered from seeing or hearing the ill-treatment of another' (further detail in Part 2). This reflects growing understanding of the impact of domestic violence on children. The disadvantage of this process of amendment is that it becomes more difficult to keep track of the terms of the original Act as amended. Major amendments to sections can be identified by their use of capital letters, e.g. s.14A of the Children Act 1989 establishes the special guardianship order as introduced by the Adoption and Children Act 2002.

Presentation of legislation

Legislation is presented in a standardised format, see Figure 2.1. The title of the Act and its year are printed on the front page, with a Chapter number. This indicates the stage in the parliamentary sitting when the Act is passed, i.e. the Children Act was the 41st Act passed during that parliamentary year. It is followed by 'Arrangement of Sections', a contents list, then a description of the objects of the Act (the preamble), which, in relation to the Children Act 1989, is:

> An Act to reform the law relating to children; to provide for local authority services for children in need and others; to amend the law with respect to children's homes, community homes, voluntary homes and voluntary organisations; to make provision with respect to fostering, childminding and day care for young children and adoption; and for connected purposes.

The language used to refer to parts of a Bill changes after it receives Royal Assent. A Bill is divided into clauses, subclauses and paragraphs. An Act of Parliament, or statute, contains headed sections, subsections and paragraphs which may be organised into parts (e.g. Children Act 1989, Part II – Orders with respect to children in family proceedings; Part III – Local Authority support for children and families). The provisions in an Act are cited according to convention. Section 17(1)(a) of the Children Act 1989, refers to section 17, subsection (1), paragraph (a), of the Children Act 1989 (loosely referred to as the duty to children in need). If not familiar with this section, it would be useful for the reader to take the opportunity to find that section in the Act and see exactly what it says. Schedules at the end of an Act carry the same force of law as the main body of the Act, but often include more detailed or supplemental matters, such as procedural requirements or formalities, transitional arrangements, repeal of earlier legislation and minor amendments.

In practice, to find out if a statute is implemented in part or in full, Butterworth's *Is it in Force?*[10] should provide the answer. Figure 2.2 illustrates the parliamentary process of introducing legislation.

Children Act 1989

CHAPTER 41

LONDON
HER MAJESTY'S STATIONERY OFFICE
£13·40 net

Figure 2.1 Front cover of Children Act 1989
Source: HMSO, Crown Copyright

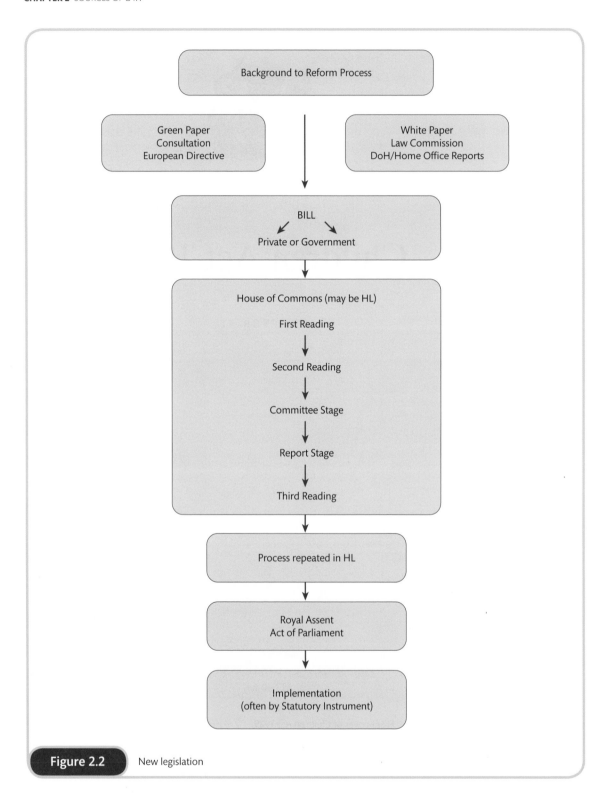

Background to Reform Process

Green Paper
Consultation
European Directive

White Paper
Law Commission
DoH/Home Office Reports

BILL
Private or Government

House of Commons (may be HL)

First Reading

Second Reading

Committee Stage

Report Stage

Third Reading

Process repeated in HL

Royal Assent
Act of Parliament

Implementation
(often by Statutory Instrument)

Figure 2.2   New legislation

Delegated legislation

Delegated legislation, sometimes referred to as secondary legislation, has the same force of law as Acts of Parliament or primary legislation, but is not made by Parliament in the process described above. Examples of delegated legislation are the Children (Leaving Care) (England) Regulations 2001 (SI 2000/2874) and the Court of Protection Rules 2007 (SI 2007/1744).

Most delegated legislation is made by ministers by **statutory instrument (SI)** and is in the form of regulations, orders, rules and byelaws. The preamble to a statutory instrument usually makes clear the authority for its issue, e.g. 'In exercise of the powers conferred by section X of the Y Act, the Secretary of State for (Z department) makes the following regulations...'. A vast body of law is produced this way and often serves to provide the detail to an associated Act of Parliament. The lack of parliamentary scrutiny means that delegated legislation can be introduced fairly quickly. Regulations often deal primarily with process and procedures, e.g. the Children Act 1989 (Representations Procedure) (England) Regulations 2006 (SI 2006/1738). Local authorities may also make secondary legislation in the form of byelaws, and can thus respond to particular issues in their area. This power to make a byelaw will have its source in an Act such as the Public Health Act 1936.

Since devolution, the National Assembly for Wales can also make delegated legislation and guidance where the power to do so is provided by Act of Parliament. This provides the opportunity to more closely reflect priorities set by the Assembly, but it will often share similarities with equivalent provision in England. As an example, it would be useful to compare the guidance prepared in England and Wales on establishing adult protection procedures, 'No Secrets' (England)[11] and 'In Safe Hands' (Wales).[12]

The range of different types of official advice and guidance documents can be confusing, particularly in relation to the question of legal responsibility to comply with their contents. As a general rule, it must be considered professional good practice to comply with any level of official advice. In some cases, however, a difficulty can arise where advice is ambiguous or where each local authority has some scope to interpret advice differently and may actually implement it through a local authority policy. The question must then be asked, to what extent can regional variations be justified as in the public interest?

An outline of the different types of advice documents and their status follows. If there is a doubt over the level of responsibility created by documents, this is an area where (if only to avoid judicial review) it would be prudent to obtain legal opinion. Recognising that legal advice may not always be readily available, a starting point is to refer to Sch. 1 to the Local Authority Social Services Act 1970 (LASSA 1970). This Schedule lists the permitted functions of Social Services Departments.

Regulations

As stated above, regulations carry the force of law. Usually regulations provide the detail, which supplements a duty or power contained in primary legislation. For example, the Local Authority Social Services Complaints (England) Regulations 2006.[13]

Guidance documents

There are a variety of types of guidance documents which, as the term suggests, provide guidance on putting legislation into practice. Guidance relating to social services matters is frequently contained in a circular, issued by the Department of Health. Local authority circulars are automatically issued to every local authority that will be affected by their contents. Circulars can be obtained direct from the Department of Health (or from its website).[14] Circulars are also issued by other departments, such as the Home Office. Within the general term 'guidance', documents are issued of differing status, commonly referred to as formal policy guidance and general practice guidance. Local authorities are under a stronger obligation to follow the former.

Formal policy guidance

It is often clear that guidance is in fact formal policy guidance because it will be identified as issued under the Local Authority Social Services Act 1970, s. 7(1), which states that local authorities shall 'act under the general guidance of the Secretary of State'. Examples of this type of policy guidance include 'Working Together to Safeguard Children' (Department for Education, 2013) and Adoption: Statutory Guidance (Department for Education, 2013). Guidance may be issued by more than one department. The status of this type of guidance was explained by Mr Justice Sedley in the case of *R* v. *Islington London Borough Council, ex parte Rixon* [1997] ELR 66:

> If this statutory guidance is to be departed from it must be with good reason, articulated in the course of some identifiable decision-making process ... In the absence of any such considered decision, the deviation from statutory guidance is in my judgment a breach of law.

From this statement, the consequences of not following this type of guidance are clear.

General practice guidance

Guidance that is not issued under LASSA 1970, s. 7(1) can be regarded as general guidance and of a lower legal status. Again, this type of guidance may be issued as a local authority circular or it may be written as a letter and referred to as a local authority social services letter or it may be a more substantial document such as 'Safeguarding Disabled Children – Practice Guidance (2009).[15] It can be described as advice from the Department of Health rather than as a directive. Practice guidance can be quite detailed and give particular examples of ways in which a local authority or other public body might demonstrate good practice in implementing its responsibilities. For example, 'Achieving Best Evidence in Criminal Proceedings: Guidance on interviewing victims and witnesses and guidance on using special measures' (2011) is practice guidance issued by the Ministry of Justice with the Department of Health, Department for Education and Welsh Assembly Government. Whilst this type of guidance does not carry s. 7 status, it would nevertheless be unwise for a local authority to ignore it. A decision of a local authority which did not have regard to relevant practice advice would clearly be judicially reviewable as one that did not take into account all relevant factors.

Directions

In addition to the duty to exercise functions under guidance, LASSA 1970, s. 7 also refers to the duty to act in accordance with directions.

(1) Without prejudice to section 7 of this Act, every local authority shall exercise their social services functions in accordance with such directions as may be given to them under this section by the Secretary of State.

(2) Directions under this section –

(a) shall be given in writing; and

(b) may be given to a particular authority, or to authorities of a particular class, or to authorities generally.

(LASSA 1970)

Directions have the force of law and must always be complied with (LASSA 1970), e.g. the Complaints Procedure Directions 1990.

Codes of practice

In some pieces of legislation the relevant minister is authorised to make a code of practice. A code of practice, though made further to an Act of Parliament, has a slightly different status to delegated legislation, and does not of itself carry the force of law. Nevertheless, it is clear in many cases that breach of a code will have serious implications. Perhaps the best example of this is in relation to police powers. Codes of practice have been made by the Home Secretary under the Police and Criminal Evidence Act 1984 (PACE). Code C deals with the detention, treatment and questioning of people in the police station. If there is a breach of the code, evidence obtained by the breach may be excluded. (See also Chapter 12.)

Codes of practice carry the advantage that they can be updated regularly, to reflect changes in practice and changes in society, even if the primary legislation does not change. For example, Code C to PACE 1984 was most recently updated in 2013. A code of practice supports the Mental Capacity Act 2005 and the Act imposes a duty to have regard to the code on a variety of people, including independent mental capacity advocates. This gives an indication of the significance of this particular code.

The common law: case law and precedent

The common law comprises decisions of the courts on matters brought before them, known collectively as case law and 'weighted' according to the doctrine of precedent.

Precedent

The doctrine of **precedent** can be explained as the principle that decisions of cases made at the higher level of the court hierarchy are binding on other (lower) courts contemplating a decision (illustrated in Figure 2.3). The highest UK court is the Supreme Court (formerly the House of Lords) and its decisions are binding on inferior courts. Application of the doctrine of precedent promotes certainty and consistency and has been described as a 'convenient

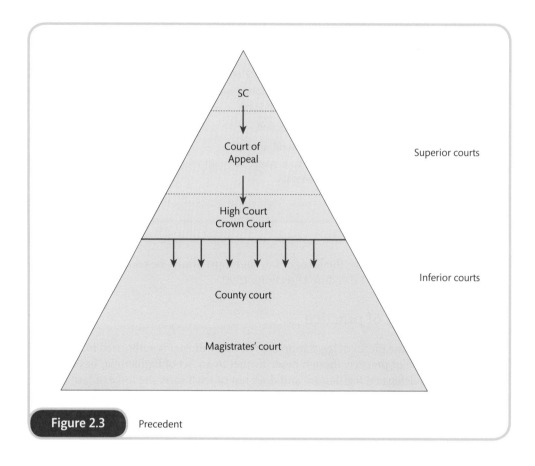

Figure 2.3   Precedent

time saving device',[16] which avoids 're-inventing the wheel' each time an issue requiring a decision comes before a court. It provides an opportunity for the courts to develop, interpret and expand the law, adding detail that it would be impracticable to include in legislation. Disadvantages of precedent are that it can seem unnecessarily restrictive and inflexible and that a 'poor' decision can stand for a long time. The courts are also limited to determination of the issues that people choose to litigate. Huge areas of ambiguous law may remain on the statute book awaiting clarification until an aggrieved individual decides to bring the issue to the attention of the court. Precedent as a term can be used to describe the process outlined, of inferior courts following the decisions of superior courts. It can also be used to describe a particular case, e.g. the *Gloucestershire* decision is a precedent on the issue of resources and assessments[17] (*R* v. *Gloucestershire County Council, ex parte Barry* [1997] 2 All ER 1).

What exactly is binding?

Decisions reached by the higher courts are often incredibly complex and include a range of arguments, which may at times appear to contradict and conflict, either between different judgments or even within one judgment. Not all of the detail included in a judgment is binding on subsequent decisions; only the part of the judgment that is referred to as the ***ratio decidendi***. This roughly translates as the reason for the decision or the central core of reasoning. In some cases it is not always readily apparent and the search for the *ratio decidendi* can become the subject of further legal argument and debate in subsequent cases. Much of the detail of the judgment is classified as **obiter dicta**, or statements made in passing, which are not crucial to the case but may be considered persuasive in subsequent decisions.

The key question in many cases will turn on whether a particular line of precedent has to be followed. In order to avoid a precedent that is unfavourable to the outcome sought, it is necessary to be able to distinguish the case from the case which set the precedent. Cases may be distinguished in a number of ways. It may be possible to distinguish on the facts: i.e. there is a material difference in the facts between the current case and the precedent, which justifies a different decision. Cases may be distinguished on the issues, or on the basis that there is an unclear *ratio* in the case, which it is argued forms the precedent. It may also be argued that the precedent need not be followed because, when that case was heard, key cases that would have influenced the outcome were either omitted or misinterpreted.

Accessing and understanding case law

Case law decisions are published in law reports. Law reports can actually be traced back around 700 years. In fact it is unlikely that, as a social worker, you would need to look at a case from before the 1950s, given the structure and formation of Social Services Departments and the legislation affecting social work responsibilities. It is most likely that access will be to new cases, which may have an effect on existing practices. Law reports contain the full text of a legal judgment and further details about the case.

In 1865 'The Law Reports' were introduced as a series divided according to the court which heard a particular case. The divisions that can be found today are Appeal Cases (**AC**) for cases in the Court of Appeal and Supreme Court, Chancery Division (**Ch**), Queen's Bench (**QB**), and Family Division (**Fam**), for cases heard in each of the respective divisions of the High Court. There are also two 'general' series, which include major cases covering a wide range of issues, known as the All England Law Reports (**All ER**) and the Weekly Law Reports (**WLR**). In addition to these sources, useful reference can be made to the Family Law Reports (**FLR**), the Family Court Reporter (**FCR**) and the Community Care Law Reports (**CCLR**), two specialist series that concentrate on a particular area of law, as their names suggest. With the increasing influence of human rights law sometimes it may also be necessary to find a decision of the European Court of Human Rights. These decisions are contained in the European Human Rights Reports (**EHRR**).

Ombudsmens' decisions are highly relevant to social work practice and, although not binding in the same way as case law from the courts, they may be persuasive. These decisions can be accessed from the local government ombudsman website[18] and a selection have also been reported in the Community Care Law Reports.

Where a short summary of a case is required, it is useful to look in *The Times* newspaper, which provides up-to-date reports of cases decided sometimes as recently as the previous day. A further option is to look at case note sections in certain journals, which have the advantage of incorporating some commentary on the implications of a decision as well as a summary of the facts and judgment. Journals including the *New Law Journal* (**NLJ**), *LAG Bulletin* (**LAG**), *Solicitors Journal* (**SJ**) and *Family Law* (**Fam Law**) have case law sections. Major cases will also be reported more widely and may be subject to media scrutiny on television and in the broadsheet and tabloid press.

Case names are written according to convention and follow a logical pattern. For example, in the case *X (Minors)* v. *Bedfordshire County Council* [1995] 3 All ER 353, an action is brought by 'X' (the letter is used to anonymise the party and '(Minors)' tells us it is a case concerning children), 'v.' means against, followed by the name of the other party, Bedfordshire County Council. The date in square brackets refers to the year in which the case is reported, '3' refers to the volume of the law report for that year, 'All ER' is an abbreviation for the series of law report, here the All England Law Reports, and 353 is the page. Sometimes the title of the case will also include a reference to the level of court where it was heard, e.g. HL refers to the House of Lords. (There is an exercise at the end of this chapter designed to develop understanding of case law.)

Neutral citation

It is now possible to access many case reports on the internet. In recognition of this, a citation system particular to reports available on the web has been developed, known as 'neutral citation', because it is not linked to any particular law report. The citation begins with the year then follows with UKSC (previously UKHL); EWCA Civ or Crim; or EWHC Admin, Fam or COP, and refers respectively to a decision made by the House of Lords or in England and Wales made by the Court of Appeal Civil or Criminal Division or the High Court Administrative or Family Court or Court of Protection. The number following gives the case position for that court, i.e. whether it was the first or thirty-first case heard by the court in that year.

For example: *Re J (Care proceedings: Possible Perpetrators)* [2013] UKSC 9

- [2013] – this case was heard in 2013.
- UKSC – a decision of the Supreme Court.
- 9 – the ninth case heard by the Supreme Court in that year.
- (*Care Proceedings: Possible Perpetrators*) – the substantial issues for the court to consider.

Judge-made law

The volume of law being introduced in the form of primary and delegated legislation has increased dramatically in recent years. It might be suggested that, as a result, the significance of the common law has correspondingly reduced. In fact, as case law often deals with ambiguity and matters of interpretation in legislation, it remains a key element of English law. This highlights an issue which is discussed in detail by Griffith (1991),[19] namely the extent to which the judiciary have a creative function in developing the common law and interpreting statutes. Whilst their suitability for this task continues to be questioned, it seems commonly accepted that judges do create law, and are not confined simply to applying parliamentary legislation. What limits are there on this creative process? Rules of statutory interpretation have developed over the years to assist the judiciary where a statute is unclear, where it does not specifically provide for the situation before the court, or where a complex case appears to relate to apparently conflicting provisions. The judiciary can sometimes be quite creative in making and adapting the common law in the absence of statute. This was clearly illustrated in the development of case law on High Court declarations, prior to the introduction of a statutory framework by the Mental Capacity Act 2005, and the continued use of declarations within the 'inherent jurisdiction' in relation to adults with mental capacity but nonetheless vulnerable (discussed further in Chapter 16).

Practice Directions

As well as giving judgments in decided cases, the courts also issue Practice Directions from time to time. These directions are intended to give guidance on how to conduct particular cases. As an example, in February 2000, the Lord Chief Justice of England and Wales gave a Practice Direction entitled *Trial of Children and Young Persons in the Crown Court*. Its objective was to ensure that the trial process 'should not expose the young defendant to avoidable intimidation, humiliation or distress'. It included the following directions (amongst others):

- The trial should, if practicable, be held in a courtroom in which all participants are on the same or almost the same level.
- The trial should be conducted according to a timetable which takes full account of a young defendant's inability to concentrate for long periods. Frequent and regular breaks will often be appropriate.

Judicial review

A significant body of case law has developed through the process of judicial review, an aspect of administrative law, which is of great importance for public authorities and has produced cases including the *Gloucestershire* decision referred to above. In a judicial review case the central issue is a review of the way a particular decision was taken. It should not normally be seen as an appeal against an unfavourable decision, nor an opportunity for the court to substitute a different decision. Applications for judicial review are brought in the administrative court office of the High Court Queen's Bench Division, which is staffed by nominated, experienced judges. A judicial review may be brought against any body that performs a public function. Local authorities are clearly within that category, as are police authorities, Government ministers, inferior courts and tribunals, and disciplinary bodies such as the General Medical Council.

Judicial review is available to anyone who has a sufficient interest in the matter in question. This is wider than the victim test under the Human Rights Act 1998 (explained further in Chapter 5). The category is intended to exclude vexatious litigants. The grounds for judicial review have developed through a series of cases and include illegality, procedural impropriety and irrationality. A public body acts illegally when it goes beyond its jurisdiction or powers or is said to be **ultra vires**. This can include a failure to follow a specified procedure, or taking into account irrelevant matters when reaching a decision. The grounds for judicial review also extend to cases where a breach of the rules of **natural justice** is argued, such as not being informed of the case against you, or not having the opportunity to present your case: e.g. *R* v. *Harrow London Borough Council, ex parte D* [1990] 3 All ER 12 related to a mother's complaint that she did not know the allegations against her which were discussed at a case conference.

The orders that can be made in a judicial review case include: mandatory orders formerly called **mandamus**, requiring a public authority to carry out its duty; quashing orders, previously known as *certiorari*, which quash a decision; and prohibitory orders, restraining a public body from acting in a particular way. The court can make a declaration on a question of law or rights, or an injunction which regulates behaviour. It is possible for an award of damages to be made in conjunction with any of the above orders. As a preliminary, it is necessary to obtain leave to proceed with an application for judicial review. Normally it will be necessary for the individual to have exhausted any other appropriate remedies before bringing the claim for judicial review. For example, this might include initial reference to the local authority's complaints process and complaint to the **local government ombudsman**.

Law reform

The impetus for law reform may be provided by a variety of sources. Overwhelming public pressure on an issue will be difficult for Government to ignore and may prompt new legislation or speed the process of reform. In many cases new legislation is borne out of a process of research and consultation, which may be led by a particular Government department or an independent body, and influenced by lobbying by interested groups. The work of probably the most significant independent body, the Law Commission, is discussed below. The Children Act 1989 provides a useful illustration as it developed through a combination of the above. Reports recommending reform of areas of child law had been produced by both the Department of Health and the Law Commission. Simultaneously, events in Cleveland heightened public awareness of child abuse and proved a catalyst to the subsequent, and relatively quickly introduced, Act.

The Law Commission

The Law Commission is an independent body comprising five commissioners and various support staff. It was established by Parliament in 1965 to review the law of England and Wales and make proposals for reform when appropriate. The reform process includes stages of research, which may involve comparative analysis with other systems of law, and consultation with interested bodies, lawyers, the general public, academics and experts. Proposals are often accompanied by draft Bills. The Law Commission is responsible for systematic development and reform of law and works on a number of different projects at any given time, usually directed by the Lord Chancellor or the Government in terms of the specific area. The Commission publishes an annual report, which provides details of ongoing work, consultation papers and any resulting legislation. Currently the Commission is conducting a consultation on data sharing between Public Bodies and is working on producing recommendations to reform the law on offences against the person (amongst other projects).

In addition to reform, the Commission also consider **consolidation**, **codification** and **revision** of statutes. Consolidation involves drawing together fragmented legislation on a particular area into one statute. Fragmentation most often occurs where legislation has been repeatedly amended. Revision of statutes ensures that obsolete provisions are repealed. (When the Children Act 1989 was introduced, eight pieces of legislation relating to children were repealed in their entirety and others limited.) A major ongoing project is the codification of the criminal law. The Commission published a Draft Criminal Code in 1989 and from that a number of draft Bills have been produced, which collectively will form a criminal code when enacted. The significance of this objective should not be underestimated. This chapter has shown that English law is contained in two distinct sources, statute and case law. In contrast, most other countries with a more modern constitution have a single code for an area of law. To develop English law similarly should lead to a clearer and more accessible system, which can be understood by lawyers and lay people.

Unfortunately, not all of the Law Commission's recommendations are adopted by Parliament and translated into legislation. In fact, only about two-thirds of their proposals for law reform have become legislation. This is so even in areas where antiquated, inappropriate legislation exists and there is widespread support for reform. It can also take many years for recommendations that are adopted to become law. An obvious example is the Law Commission's work on mental capacity and public powers of protection for vulnerable adults. The Law Commission worked on this area from 1991 to 1995, publishing four consultation documents, a final report and a draft Bill. This was followed by a consultation paper, 'Who Decides?' (1997) and 'Making Decisions' (1999), which contained Government proposals. In the final document the Lord Chancellor gave a commitment to introduce legislation 'when Parliamentary time allows'. That time proved to be in 2005 when the Mental Capacity Act received Royal Assent. The final legislation contains many, but not all, of the Law Commission recommendations. The Care Act 2014 contains some elements of the Law Commission recommendations in relation to public powers of protection for vulnerable adults.

Chapter summary

- There is a vast range of law and official guidance relevant to social work practice and it is located in a number of different sources, including: primary and secondary legislation; policy and practice guidance; directions; codes of practice and case law.

- New legislation is created by Parliament. Starting as a Bill, proposed legislation goes through a process of scrutiny in the House of Commons and the House of Lords until it receives Royal Assent and becomes an Act of Parliament. Most new legislation actually comes into force some time after it receives Royal Assent, by a separate commencement order.

- In addition to primary legislation, social workers should be aware of the range of rules, regulations and guidance frequently issued to supplement the Act, which may be regularly updated. These documents vary in status and, although they may not have the full force of law, failure to comply with the guidance they contain may have severe consequences for an authority.

- The other major source of law in the United Kingdom is case law decided by judges, also known as the common law.

- The significance of a particular case depends in part on the doctrine of precedent, through which decisions of superior courts form precedents which the inferior courts are bound to follow when faced with similar cases.

- Case law can be found in a range of law reports, and is reported in a standardised way which provides a summary of the facts of the case, the judgments of judges who hear the case, the date and the level of court.

- Law is regularly updated, consolidated and reformed and the Law Commission is an important independent body whose task it is to review and offer proposals for reform of the law.

Exercises

The best way to understand case law and legislation is to read some.

Choose one of the cases listed below, all of which are significant cases in social work law (and will be referred to in this text):

R v. Gloucestershire County Council, ex parte Barry [1997] 2 All ER 1

Gillick v. West Norfolk and Wisbech Area Health Authority and Another [1986] AC 112

Re X (Emergency Protection Orders) [2006] EWHC 510

DL v A Local Authority & Others [2012] EWCA Civ 253

1. Locate the case in a law library.

2. Read the case fully, including all the judgments.

3. Identify the following from your case:

   (a) names of parties;

   (b) court/venue;

   (c) name(s) of judge(s);

   (d) date and length of hearing;

   (e) full reference case reported under – which law report;

   (f) headnote;

   (g) catchwords;

   (h) decision;

   (i) judgment;

   (j) cases referred to in judgment;

   (k) points of law;

   (l) legal representatives.

4. Search on the internet for an electronic version of the case and note the neutral citation.

5. Identify the implications of the decision for social work practice.

Access the Adoption and Children Act 2002 and research the following points:

- What is the short title of the Act?
- How many Chapters and how many Schedules does the Act contain?
- Who is eligible to adopt?
- Which part of the Act contains amendments to the Children Act 1989 and how many are there?
- When can local authority foster parents apply to adopt a child they have fostered?
- How long does a child have to live with adopters before an application for adoption can be made?
- How is suitability of adopters to be assessed?
- How many adoption registers are there and what do they cover?
- What are the grounds for dispensing with parental consent to adoption?
- Is the Act fully in force?
- Did any provision come into force earlier than the bulk of the Act – if so, which?

You will also need to have sight of the Children Act 1989 to answer the final two points.

- Identify three differences between the special guardianship order introduced by this legislation and the residence order established under the Children Act 1989.
- Compare and contrast the welfare test and checklist under the ACA 2002 and the Children Act 1989. Are there any significant differences?

For each of the following – identify its source and status, e.g. the Children Act 1989 is primary legislation produced by Parliament.

- The Children Act 1989.
- The definition of murder.

- Code C Detention Treatment and Questioning 2004.
- 'In Safe Hands' (2000).
- *Mabon* v. *Mabon and others* [2005] EWCA Civ 634.
- President's Direction: HIV Testing of Children [2003] 1 FLR 1299.
- The Special Guardianship Regulations 2005.
- *Achieving Best Evidence in Criminal Proceedings: Guidance on interviewing victims and witnesses and guidance on using special measures* (2011).

Websites

The Law Commission website, which includes details of law reform programmes:
http://lawcommission.justice.gov.uk

For legislation and explanatory notes to new legislation:
www.legislation.gov.uk

The official website for Parliament provides information about Parliament, gives access to *Hansard* (the report of parliamentary debates) and judgments of the House of Lords, and tracks progress of Bills before Parliament:
www.parliament.uk

The Home Office site provides information on the progress of law reform in the criminal law arena:
www.gov.uk/government/organisations/home-office

Case law reports are available from a number of websites, some of which are subscription only (e.g. Westlaw). BAILII is generally accessible and provides access to British and Irish legal information including cases and legislation. There is a useful keyword search facility and it is possible to view cases from each of the different courts (and tribunals) and in 'most recent order':
www.bailii.org

Further reading

Encyclopaedia of Social Services and Child Care Law. London: Sweet & Maxwell. (A looseleaf encyclopaedia which is updated regularly and contains legislation, regulations and rules, relevant circulars alongside explanatory text.)

Golding, J. (ed) (2005) *Is it in Force? 2005. A Guide to Commencement of Statutes Passed Since 1st January, 1980 (incorporating statutes not yet in force)*. London: LexisNexis. (Use this text to check whether an Act or any of its provisions have been implemented – usually available for reference in any law library.)

Holland, J. and Webb, J. (2006) *Learning Legal Rules* (6th edn). Oxford: Oxford University Press.

Thomas, P.A. and Knowles, J. (2001) *How to Use a Law Library: An Introduction to Legal Skills* (4th edn). London: Sweet & Maxwell. (An accessible, detailed guide to finding and understanding legal materials.)

Notes

1 S. Braye and M. Preston-Shoot (2005) *Teaching, Learning and Assessment of Law in Social Work Education.* London: Social Care Institute for Excellence.

2 See D. French (1996) *How to Cite Legal Authorities.* London: Blackstone Press.

3 www.parliament.uk.

4 The 'Woolf Reforms'; so called after Lord Woolf CJ, who led the reform of civil procedure.

5 For further information and examples, visit the Plain Language Commission website at www.clearest.co.uk.

6 Occasionally an MP may move for the Bill to go to a special standing committee or a committee of the whole House.

7 Available online at www.hansard-westminster.co.uk.

8 E.g. Criminal Justice and Court Services Act 2000 (Commencement No. 4) Order 2001 (S1 2001/919).

9 By SI 2001/777.

10 J. Gold (ed.) (2005) *Is it in Force? 2005.* London: LexisNexis. A guide to the commencement of statutes passed since 1 January 1980 (incorporating statutes not yet in force).

11 Department of Health (2000) 'No Secrets: Guidance on developing and implementing multi-agency policies and procedures to protect vulnerable adults from abuse'. London: Department of Health.

12 National Assembly for Wales (2000) *In Safe Hands: Implementing Adult Protection Procedures in Wales.* Cardiff: National Assembly for Wales.

13 S1 2006/1681.

14 www.gov.uk/dh.

15 Department for Education.

16 T. Ingman (2000) *The English Legal Process* (8th edn). London: Blackstone Press.

17 For a full discussion of precedent, see T. Ingman (2000) *The English Legal Process* (8th edn). London: Blackstone Press.

18 www.lgo.org.uk.

19 J. A. G. Griffith (1991) *The Politics of the Judiciary* (4th edn). London: Fontana.

Chapter 3

Courts and law officers

Learning objectives

To develop an understanding of the following:

- The organisation and operation of the legal system.
- The background knowledge required to work effectively in legal settings.
- The distinction between civil and criminal law.
- The distinction between public and private law.
- The structure and process of courts and tribunals.
- The roles of various legal personnel and professionals working in the legal system.
- Access to law and representation issues.

> ## Talking Point
>
> At a press conference held to 'mark and celebrate the family justice reforms' implemented in April 2014, the President of the Family Division, Sir James Munby, outlined the importance of the new Family Court:
>
> **The Family Court deals with ALL family cases with the exception of two classes of case reserved for the Family Division: (a) cases under the inherent jurisdiction of the High Court; and (b) international cases. The judiciary of the Family Court includes all levels of judge: High Court Judges, Circuit Judges and Recorders, district judges and magistrates. Wherever possible, all the judges of the Family Court sit under the same roof. England and Wales continue to be divided into geographical areas judicially led and managed by the Designated Family Judge. Within that area, all the locations at which hearings take place are managed and operated as a single Family Court. There is, for the entire local Family Court, a 'single point of entry' for the issue of proceedings and a centralised and unified administration. There is a centralised 'gate-keeping and allocation team', allocating cases at the outset for hearing before an appropriate judge at an appropriate place. There is centralised listing.**
>
> **What does this mean for the children and families we serve? It is the essential underpinning for the new system. Together with fundamental changes in practice and procedure, it will go a long way to eradicating the scourge of delay and giving us a modern, efficient, just and speedy family justice system.**
>
> The court system of England and Wales has developed over centuries and may be regarded as complex and confusing, full of tradition, strange conventions and costumes. The development outlined above, a new Family Court, together with recent changes to the Tribunals system demonstrates ongoing development and some commitment to simplifying the judicial system for the benefit of its users.

Introduction

The English legal system often appears complex to a lay person and this is especially so when it is portrayed inaccurately by the media. This chapter aims to provide sufficient information for an individual who has chosen a social work career, which has close links with law, to overcome this concern.

The chapter offers explanation of the structure of the English legal system, the courts, the role of key personnel in court and the ways in which support can be provided for an individual to have effective access to the law. To bring this information to life, court observation is strongly encouraged and a guide for observation is included at the end of the chapter.

Courts and the English legal system

The hierarchy of the court structure is inextricably bound up with the doctrine of precedent (explained in the previous chapter). It may be helpful to visualise the structure as a staircase climbing from the magistrates up to the Supreme Court. Alternatively, a pyramid shape, again with the Supreme Court as the pinnacle and the magistrates' court at ground level, captures both the hierarchy of the system and also roughly reflects the relative workload at each level. To a certain extent, courts can be distinguished according to whether they deal with civil or criminal cases (though there are overlaps).

Distinguishing between civil and criminal law

There are a number of ways in which the distinction between civil and criminal law can be drawn.

Parties

In a criminal case the dispute is between the state and an individual or 'body'. The parties are referred to as the prosecution and the defence or the accused. The substance of the case is an allegation of behaviour which falls within the definition of a criminal offence (in statute or common law, e.g. theft or murder). It will be a matter over which society as a whole is taken to have an interest in expressing at least its disapproval and ultimately, if proved, may consider it necessary to sentence the perpetrator of the offence.

In a civil case the dispute is between individuals, referred to as the claimant or applicant (previously the term 'plaintiff' was used) and the defendant, or in divorce cases, the petitioner and the respondent.

In criminal or civil cases an 'individual' as described above may, in fact, be something other than a single person, as the term would suggest. It could include a company or corporation, a charity, health authority or local authority.

Civil disputes may be further classified as **private** or **public** matters. In a public matter a body may act on behalf of the state in a civil case. An obvious example of this is where a local authority issues care proceedings in respect of a child in its area. This is a civil matter, but could also be described as an aspect of public rather than private law because it involves a public body exercising a public function. A civil matter, which is private as opposed to public, would include a divorce between two individuals, or could be a **contract** dispute between an individual and a company or public body, the nature of the dispute in these matters, e.g. contract, being the defining issue. It is notable that the Children Act 1989 covers aspects of both the public and private law relating to children.

Remedies

The outcome or **remedy** in a case will differ according to whether it is a civil or criminal matter. In a criminal case the object is to determine the question of guilt and then to make an appropriate disposal. According to different perspectives, this penalty may be framed in terms of punishment, rehabilitation or retribution and includes imprisonment, community orders, fines and compensation orders.

In civil cases an order will be made giving judgment to either party (crudely speaking, the winner). This can include an element of paying the other side's costs. The order that can be made will depend on the type of case and may include injunctions, which order a person to carry out a particular action or order them to refrain from particular action, e.g. a non-molestation order. The most frequent order in civil cases is for compensation or damages to be paid by one party to the other to compensate for loss or damage and special rules and conventions are used to arrive at the level of damages. It will be noted that there is another overlap here, in that a compensation order can also be made in criminal cases. (This order is discussed in more detail in Chapter 18). Also, breach of a civil order may be a criminal offence, e.g. the anti-social behaviour order (discussed in Chapter 13).

Standard of proof

In a civil case the **standard of proof** is known as **balance of probabilities**. This means that the point to be proven has to be more probable than not. In percentage terms this might be understood as a 49:51 per cent balance, i.e. the scales only just have to tip. In a criminal case the standard of proof is higher and is known as **beyond reasonable doubt**. Again, to conceptualise this in percentage terms, it might equate to approximately 97 per cent, a high level but still allowing for a slight degree of doubt. The statue of the Scales of Justice outside the Old Bailey in London serves to remind us of this analogy.

The same circumstances may lead to criminal and civil cases and illustrate the application of the different standards of proof; for example, harm caused to a child may constitute a criminal offence and may give rise to care proceedings. In the criminal case the evidence focuses on whether the court is satisfied 'beyond reasonable doubt' that the defendant caused the harm and should be convicted. In care proceedings the court must be satisfied on a balance of probabilities that the threshold of 'significant harm' is reached and that the child should be made subject of a care order; it is less concerned with precisely attributing blame for injuries caused. A statement from *Re U (A Child) (Serious Injury: Standard of Proof)* [2004] **EWCA** Civ 567 reminds us that 'it by no means follows that an acquittal on a criminal charge or a successful appeal would lead to the absolution of the parent or carer in family or civil proceedings'.

The criminal law has been amended following a number of cases where injuries to children have been caused and care proceedings have been taken but it has not been possible to convict the perpetrator due to evidential difficulties and the higher standard of proof. See, for example, the case of *Re O and N (Children) (Non-accidental Injury: Burden of Proof); Re B (Children)* [2003] **UKHL** 18 (discussed fully in Chapter 9). The relevant criminal law is contained in the Domestic Violence, Crime and Victims Act 2004 (**DVCVA** 2004, amended by DVCV(A)A 2012). Section 5 includes the offence of 'causing or allowing the death or serious injury' of a child or vulnerable adult. The offence applies where a child (or vulnerable adult) dies or suffers serious injury as a result of an unlawful act of a person of the same household, who either caused the death or serious injury or, aware of the risk, failed to protect the child. In such a case more than one adult can be charged with the offence and it is not necessary to establish precisely who caused the death or serious injury and who failed to protect. (The new offence is discussed in more detail in Chapters 9 and 17.)

The standard of proof should not be confused with the **burden of proof**. The burden of proof rests on the party asserting a particular point – 'he who alleges must prove'. In criminal cases it is for the prosecution to prove guilt to a standard beyond reasonable doubt rather than for the defence to prove innocence.

Very occasionally the burden of proof in a criminal case may switch to the defence. For instance, in attempts by the defence to show good cause why the defendant was carrying what was alleged to be an offensive weapon, the burden would be on the defence to prove this and the standard of proof would then be the civil one of balance of probabilities. In a civil case the burden may switch between the parties, particularly if there are counterclaims.

Each of the criteria can be seen to have a number of qualifications or exceptions. Very little in the law is absolutely clear-cut, though there is often an expectation from the public that precision is the very essence of the law. This may also explain why lawyers rarely give advice in terms of absolute 'yes' or 'no' answers; rather, the tendency is to talk along the lines of likelihood and alternative pathways. To draw an accurate distinction between criminal and civil matters or confidently to categorise a case as civil or criminal it is necessary to look

Table 3.1 Distinguishing features of civil and criminal cases

	CIVIL	**CRIMINAL**
Parties	Claimant/applicant and defendant Petitioner and respondent	State/prosecution versus defendant/accused
Remedies	Compensation Injunctions (Costs)	Sentence 'punishment' deterrence/retribution
Standard of proof	Balance of probabilities	Beyond reasonable doubt

Courts	Magistrates
	County Crown
	Tribunals
	Family
	High Court Queen's Bench
	Chancery
	Court of Protection
	       Court of Appeal
	(Civil Division) (Criminal Division)
	    Supreme Court
	European Court of Justice	

NB: Courts listed on central line have both civil and criminal jurisdiction

at the features of the case in entirety. Table 3.1 summarises the differences between a civil and criminal case and identifies the courts with civil and criminal jurisdiction.

Courts exercising civil jurisdiction

Civil cases may be heard in the Supreme Court, the Court of Appeal (Civil Division), the High Court Chancery, Family and the Queen's Bench Division, known as the superior courts. The inferior courts dealing with civil cases are the county court, which has a jurisdiction over the majority of civil cases, including personal injury cases, and the magistrates' court, which, although dealing mainly with criminal matters, hears some civil claims. The new Family Court combines expertise of judges sitting at magistrates, county and high court level. Formerly, the jurisdiction for family cases was spread between the magistrates' **family proceedings court**, the county court, including care centres and the Family Division of the High Court. The majority of civil disputes fall into three categories: personal injury action seeking compensation following an injury; actions for breach of contract; and debt. Some civil cases also involve circumstances where the permission of the courts is required before a particular action can be taken, e.g. a Court of Protection declaration authorising sterilisation of a woman with a learning disability, or approval to remove a child from the jurisdiction. Tribunals also exercise civil jurisdiction.

Outline of a civil case

For every potential civil litigant there are a number of risks to be evaluated. These risks range from the most obvious one of losing the case, through to the effects of delays in the proceedings and the cost of the proceedings. Litigation is unpredictable and can be a very stressful and demanding experience. There will usually be a period of negotiation and exchange of correspondence before a civil action formally begins. If, through this informal process, it is not possible to settle the dispute, court proceedings may be commenced. The detail of the civil system is contained in the Civil Procedure Rules 1998.

Imagine a scenario where a person, John, when visiting his mother in a residential home, is injured by slipping on a pool of water left after a member of staff had been mopping the floor. Despite an initial letter from John to the manager of the home and a further letter from a solicitor to the head office of the company which runs this and a series of other homes, the home has not acknowledged liability or offered any compensation, and John now feels he has no alternative other than to commence proceedings. The process would begin with John filling out a claim form and paying a fee to the court office, which stamps the claim form with the court's official seal. At this stage proceedings are formally issued. Next, within four months, John must serve the claim form, with a response pack, to the home. **Service** is the technical term for delivery of a legal document (usually by first class post). On receipt of the claim form, the home should return an acknowledgement of service and also indicate whether it intends to admit, defend or counterclaim in response to John's claim form. Next, statements of case are produced by both parties, the factual contention of the party bringing the case (John) and (from the care home company) a response to allegations made by John and particular defences that are available. In this example the home might deny that there was water on the floor or argue that, even if there was, it was adequately signposted with an appropriate warning. The court will make an early assessment of the likely complexity of the claim and allocate the claim to one of three case management tracks:

1. *Small claims track:* limited to claims involving less than £10,000 or £1,000 in a personal injury case. It is intended to be both inexpensive and quick.

2. *Fast track:* appropriate for cases which are considered more important and have a value above the small claims limit. In fast track cases it would be usual for the matter to be capable of hearing at a one-day trial with a maximum of two experts for each party. In some fast track cases oral evidence may be excluded.

3. *Multi-track:* all other cases will be allocated to multi-track. These are the cases which typically involve significant amounts of money and are more complex.

A judge will then give some directions for the steps that the parties need to take to progress the claim to final hearing. These directions might include producing photographs. Each party will inspect the other's documents, a process known as **disclosure**, and exchange other types of evidence, including reports of experts and witness statements. Through disclosing these documents in advance some cases will be settled without the need for a full hearing. It should also enable the parties to consider the strength of their claim in the context of all the evidence and should mean that there are no significant surprises at the trial. Cases will be listed for trial as soon as is possible and procedures emphasise the need to reduce any unnecessary delays.

If the case reaches trial, witnesses will be called to give oral evidence, relating to the facts in contention, and other evidence including documents will be considered by the judge. At the conclusion of the trial, judgment will be given in favour of one of the parties. In the example, if the home was found to have been negligent in allowing the pool of water, which caused the injury to John, to be on that floor, it is likely to have to pay John the costs incurred in bringing his claim, including legal advice and representation in court. As part of the judgment an award of damages may also be awarded to John to compensate for his loss, including pain and suffering, loss of earnings, loss of amenity, costs of medical treatment, etc. The risk of having a judgment awarded against you is the real incentive to settle a case!

Courts exercising criminal jurisdiction

Courts that deal with criminal cases are: the magistrates' court, which has both an adult and a youth crime jurisdiction; the Crown Court; the Queen's Bench Division of the High Court; the Criminal Division of the Court of Appeal; and the House of Lords. The starting point in a consideration of a criminal case is the classification of the crime. There are three groups of offences recognised by the criminal law:

1. *Summary offences:* the less serious criminal offences, including numerous motoring and traffic offences, drunkenness offences, threatening behaviour, taking and driving away (TWOC) and are tried by magistrates.

2. *Indictable offences:* the most serious offences, which are tried 'on **indictment**' in the Crown Court, including murder, rape, arson and robbery.

3. *Either way offences:* as the name suggests, may be tried in the magistrates' court or the Crown Court depending on the seriousness of the offence and the preference of the defendant. Either way offences include criminal acts where there is a possible range of seriousness, such as theft, which may be charged in a petty shoplifting case or a major theft of property worth millions of pounds.[1]

Offences may also be classified according to the type of harm done. This is often reflected in the legislation which establishes particular offences, e.g. the Theft Act 1968 or the Sexual Offences Act 2003. Crimes may be committed: against property, e.g. burglary; physical integrity of the person, e.g. rape or assaults; or general public rights of citizenship, e.g. public order offences.

Brief outline of the criminal process

The first stage in the criminal process is arrest. An individual may be arrested on a warrant issued by a magistrate, or, more commonly, by a police officer. On arrest, the suspect must be given a caution, and told what he is being arrested for. Following arrest, a decision will be taken on whether the individual is to be charged with an offence. Following charge the issue of remand must be considered. There is a presumption in favour of bail, which should be refused only in specified circumstances, such as there being substantial grounds to believe that the accused person would abscond, commit a further offence, interfere with witnesses, or otherwise obstruct the course of justice.[2] Conditions may be attached to bail addressing a particular risk, e.g. regular reporting to the police station to ensure attendance at court.

Following charge (a decision that the CPS are increasingly involved with), full control of progress of the case is taken by the Crown Prosecution Service (**CPS**). The CPS will review the evidence that the police have gathered and independently make the decision whether to prosecute, based on likelihood of success and whether prosecution is considered to be in the public interest.

The next stage will depend on the nature of the offence. Summary offences, which are the less serious type of offences where the defendant is not entitled to trial by jury, start and finish in the magistrates' court. Following a guilty plea, which for some cases may be entered by post, the magistrates will proceed to sentence. The prosecution will present an outline of the case and introduce the defendant's **antecedents** after which the defence may present offender mitigation. For not guilty pleas a trial will be scheduled before a bench of three magistrates or a district judge. (A more detailed explanation of sentencing procedure can be found in Chapter 18.)

Either way offences can be dealt with in the magistrates' court or in the Crown Court before a judge and jury. The defendant has the right to elect for Crown Court trial and the magistrates' court may commit the case to Crown Court if they deem it to be sufficiently serious. If the case remains in the magistrates' court and the defendant pleads guilty, the case will proceed to sentence or the magistrates may commit to the Crown Court for sentence if they feel that their powers of sentence are insufficient. Following a not guilty plea the case will be scheduled for trial. Where a defendant is charged with an offence which is triable only on indictment the court will consider bail and any legal matters and send him to Crown Court for trial.

The standard procedure for a trial following a not guilty plea is:

- The prosecution opening speech – usually includes a summary of the evidence which the prosecution intends to call.

- The prosecution will then introduce its evidence, including witnesses, who must take the oath or affirm before giving their evidence. The prosecution asks questions of the witness, known as **examination-in-chief**. The witness must then face questions from the defence, known as a **cross-examination**, the objective of which is to discredit and disprove the truth of the witness's evidence. Following cross-examination the prosecution may **re-examine**, or ask further questions, but that is limited to any new issues which have arisen out of cross-examination, rather than going over and trying to reinforce the evidence already given.

- At the close of the prosecution case, i.e. when the prosecution has provided all the evidence on which it intends to rely, the defence has the opportunity to submit a plea that there is **no case to answer**. If this is accepted the defendant is acquitted.

- Assuming that submission is not successful, the case then proceeds with defence evidence, including, in many cases, the evidence of the accused.

- When all the evidence has been produced, a closing speech is made by the defence.

- In the Crown Court, the judge will sum up for the benefit of a jury. In summing up, the judge deals with points of law and summarises the evidence.

- The foreman of the jury will deliver its verdict, and either the accused will be acquitted, if found not guilty, or, if found guilty, the case moves to sentence. Only if the jury are unable to reach a unanimous decision, will the judge accept a majority verdict.[3] The Chair of the Bench in the magistrates' court delivers the verdict and pronounces sentence.

For cases where there is a possibility of a prison sentence, a pre-sentence report is provided to the court (discussed in Chapter 18). The final stage in the process before sentence is announced is the plea in mitigation, presented by the defence. The range of sentences that may be ordered depends on the offence for which the defendant is convicted. Sentencing options range from absolute discharge, through to fines, **community orders** (replacement for probation and community service), compensation orders, suspended sentence of imprisonment and imprisonment for any period up to life sentence. (These sentencing options are discussed in Chapter 18.)

For a young person charged with a criminal offence, the basic procedure is very similar to that outlined above but the case will usually proceed in the youth court. A range of different sentencing or disposal options is available to the court (and these are dealt with in detail in Chapter 13).

The court structure

The courts are now managed by the Her Majesty's Courts and Tribunal Service, an executive agency of the Ministry of Justice, in place of direct responsibility to the Lord Chancellor.[4]

Magistrates' court

The magistrates' court is the inferior criminal court, dealing with between 95 and 96 per cent of all criminal cases and a significant civil jurisdiction. It is one of the oldest courts and, despite a number of changes over the years, it has retained the basic principle that lay members of the community form this tier of the judiciary. Magistrates' courts are administered by the Courts Service. The main criminal jurisdiction of the magistrates' court comprises trial of summary offences. Appeals lie from the magistrates' court to the Crown Court against sentence and conviction, and to the Queen's Bench Division of the High Court on a point of law or application for judicial review.

Youth court

The youth court is a specialist branch of the magistrates' court (Criminal Justice Act 1991), which deals with defendants aged between 10 and 17. The court will consist of three magistrates (at least one male and one female) who are drawn from the youth court panel, and the procedure is intended to be less formal than in the adult court. Parents are also expected to attend court where the young person is under 16. Observation and reporting by the press is limited. Terminology also differs, with 'finding of guilt' and 'order made upon finding of guilt' used in preference to conviction and sentence. A limited category of criminal proceedings against juveniles are dealt with in the adult magistrates' court or Crown Court, including very serious offences and cases where a juvenile is charged jointly with an adult.

Magistrates' court civil jurisdiction

In addition, the magistrates' court has a significant civil jurisdiction. Prior to the introduction of the new Family Court the magistrates family proceedings court dealt with cases brought under the Children Act 1989 and also the Family Law Act 1996. Due to the special nature of these cases, magistrates sitting in the family proceedings court were required to be members of the family panel and receive special training. Magistrates with specialist training will sit in the new Family Court.

Other aspects of the civil jurisdiction of magistrates' courts include dealing with recovery of council tax, and functions which might be described as administrative.

County courts

There are 217 county courts in England and Wales, exercising a civil jurisdiction. The county court is classified as an inferior court and has tended to deal with less serious civil matters (small claims track and the fast track), work being divided between it and the High Court. Cases in the county courts are heard by circuit judges and district judges (formerly registrars), and are usually listed in the county court for the district where the defendant lives. The county court also includes the small claims court. Partly as a result of the small claims jurisdiction of the county court, it is not unusual for individuals to be unrepresented in the county court. The county court office will offer a certain amount of assistance to a litigant in person and can be a useful source of information, providing a variety of leaflets, etc.

County court jurisdiction is wide and includes: actions for contract or **tort**; trusts and probate; housing matters; cases under the Consumer Credit Act 1974; divorce; discrimination claims in cases not related to employment, e.g. provision of goods and services. Appeals lie to the Court of Appeal (Civil Division). Though it is a civil court, a judge in the county court may commit a person to prison for contempt of court.

For family law matters county courts were designated as family hearing centres, or care centres and adoption centres and cases were heard by specially nominated judges. Those judges will now hear cases in the new Family Court.

Crown Court

The Crown Court is a superior court and deals with indictable criminal offences and those either way offences referred by the magistrates' court. There are 77 branches of the Crown Court in England and Wales, including the Old Bailey in London. Each court centre may actually contain several court rooms. Where the defendant pleads not guilty, a jury will normally sit with the judge. In those cases it is for the jury to determine whether or not the defendant is guilty, and the judge's role is to deal with matters of law, provide a summing up to the jury and pronounce sentence. The Criminal Justice Act 2003 permits cases to be tried by judge alone where there is a real risk of jury tampering, and in certain complex fraud cases. The Crown Court also hears appeals against sentence and conviction by magistrates. In appeal cases a jury is not involved, but the judge will sit with up to four lay magistrates. Circuit judges and recorders hear cases in the Crown Court. Appeals (about 8,000 per year) from the Crown Court lie to the Court of Appeal, Criminal Division, then to the Supreme Court. The Criminal Justice Act 1988 introduced a power for the prosecution to appeal against an over-lenient sentence imposed by the Crown Court as, e.g., in *Attorney-General's Reference (No. 24 of 2001)*; **sub nom** R v. *David Graham Jenkins* (2001) CA C9500543. In that case a sentence of six months' imprisonment for an offence of gross indecency with a 4-year-old child (the defendant's stepdaughter) was unduly lenient and was substituted with a total sentence of 18 months' imprisonment.

The jury

A jury in the Crown Court will have been chosen at random from people in the community aged between 18 and 70 and on the register of electors. The object is to produce a jury that represents the community at large. Some individuals are not eligible to sit on a jury. Included in this category are: the police; lawyers and judges; probation officers and children's guardians; people with a mental illness; members of the clergy; and people with criminal convictions. If called to jury service, it may be possible to be excused if you have already provided jury service in the last two years or if you are aged over 65, an MP, a member of the armed services or a member of the medical profession. In addition, the court has a general discretion and can excuse a person from jury service for a good reason, e.g. exceptional work commitments, caring responsibilities, but probably not holidays. There are limited powers for the prosecution and the defence to object to particular individuals sitting on the jury. In addition, a juror should not take part in a case where he or she has a personal interest or is closely connected to a party or a witness.

The High Court

The High Court deals with civil and criminal cases, including cases which originate in the High Court and appeals from lower courts. Its jurisdiction is so wide that it has been described as a 'hotchpotch'.[5] There are three divisions of the High Court: Family Division, Chancery Division and Queen's Bench Division. Judges in the High Court are referred to as Mr/Mrs Justice Smith, or Smith J.

The Family Division

The Family Division dealt with matrimonial issues, any issues relating to children (and their property), adoption, and exercises the inherent jurisdiction and wardship. The High Court tended to deal with the more complex child care cases, perhaps involving a number of different applications, difficult evidence or cases with an international element. High Court judges will continue to deal with such cases in the new Family Court. In addition, two types of cases will continue to be reserved to the High Court Family Division: the exercise of the inherent jurisdiction in relation to children (wardship) and vulnerable adults; and international cases under the Hague Convention or Brussels IIR.

Prior to the introduction of the Mental Capacity Act 2005, the jurisdiction of the Family Division included the use of declaratory relief. This is an order which the court makes to declare that a particular course of action or treatment would not be considered unlawful and so could not therefore form the basis of a civil action in tort (e.g. a doctor who performs a sterilisation after a declaration has been made authorising the operation could not be sued for battery). Declaratory relief has been used in a range of cases where a person has not been able to give consent to particular medical treatment because of mental incapacity. The basis of the order is the common law doctrine of necessity, guided by application of the best interests of the incapacitated person. A well-known case is *Airedale National Health Service Trust v. Bland* [1993] 1 All ER 821, where a declaration was made stating that it would not be unlawful to withhold medical treatment, nutrition and hydration from a patient in a persistent vegetative state. The jurisdiction extended with courts being prepared to make declarations that deal with wider welfare issues as well as medical issues. This presents an important exercise of the law-making role of the judiciary. Cases relating to lack of capacity of an individual to make a decision are now dealt with under the Mental Capacity Act 2005 in the Court of Protection. Declaratory relief cases may continue to be relevant where an adult has capacity in the sense of the Mental Capacity Act 2005 but is nevertheless considered vulnerable. An example of such a case is *DL v. A Local Authority & Others* [2012] EWCA Civ 253 (discussed in Chapter 17).

The Chancery Division

The Chancery Division deals with a range of specialised work, including bankruptcy, mortgages, land charges, probate (including challenges to wills and administration of estates), revenue law, patents and company law.

Queen's Bench Division

The Queen's Bench Division is the largest division of the High Court and has the widest ranging jurisdiction. Most of the work of this division comprises civil issues which are considered too complex for the county court to deal with or involve larger amounts of money than the county court limit for compensation, for example serious injuries arising out of traffic accidents. The Queen's Bench Division plays an important role in relation to civil liberties. It is the court that can issue the writ of **habeas corpus**, which authorises the release of a detained person.

The majority of judicial review cases commence in the Queen's Bench Division. Judicial review is the process whereby administrative decisions taken by a range of bodies, importantly, including local authorities, can be challenged. An example of a judicial review decision of particular significance for Social Services Departments was the *Gloucestershire* case,[6] which was followed by a series of other cases dealing with the extent to which a local authority's resources can be taken into account in carrying out assessments of individual needs for services. Judicial review plays an important role in ensuring that local authorities and other public bodies do not exceed their powers (*ultra vires*). The basis for intervention by the court is often referred to as *Wednesbury* reasonableness after the case of *Associated Provincial Picture Houses Ltd* v. *Wednesbury Corporation* [1948] 1 KB 223. In essence, a decision may be subject to review if it is so unreasonable that no reasonable authority would have made it. In addition, the authority must have considered all relevant factors and disregarded irrelevant factors.

The Queen's Bench Division also hears appeals on a point of law, from the magistrates' courts and Crown Court.

Court of Protection

The Queen's Bench Division of the High Court used to include a Court of Protection. Under the Mental Capacity Act 2005 a new Court of Protection was established at High Court level. Its jurisdiction flows from the Act and is essentially to make decisions in relation to the property and affairs and healthcare and personal welfare of adults (and children in a few cases) who lack capacity, in their best interests. The court also has the power to make declarations about whether someone has the capacity to make a particular decision. (Further detail on the court's powers are included in Chapter 16.)

Family Court

The Crime and Courts Act 2013 contains provisions to establish a unified Family Court. This single court replaces the jurisdiction of the family proceedings court, the family jurisdiction of the county court (care centres and family hearing centres) and the family work of the High Court. Introduction of the new court flows from the recommendations of the Family Justice Review (2011) chaired by Sir David Norgrove.

It has been argued that having three different courts dealing with family law matters was confusing, and transferring cases between the levels was a cause of delay. With the new Family Court, judges at all levels will be able to sit in the same building. Family Law applications will all be submitted to the Designated Family Hearing Centre and it should be easier to ensure that a judge at the right level is appointed to the case from the beginning. All applications will be considered by a Legal Adviser (Clerk) and/or a District Judge (referred to as gatekeepers) who will allocate the case for hearing by the appropriate level of judge within the Family Court. Actual hearings may take place at the main Designated Family Hearing Centre for the area or at one or more satellite Hearing Centres.

Court of Appeal

The Court of Appeal is housed with the High Court in the Royal Courts of Justice in the Strand, London. The courts have their own Citizens' Advice Bureau to help litigants in person. Usually, three senior judges will sit together to hear cases in the Court of Appeal: they can include the Lord Chancellor, Master of the Rolls, Lord Chief Justice, President of the Family Division, Lords of Appeal in Ordinary and Lords Justices of Appeal, and any High Court judge. Whilst one might expect this court to be very formal, in fact hearings in the Court of Appeal are quite different from hearings in the High Court or Crown Court: it is unusual for witnesses to give evidence; the hearing consists of legal argument from barristers, often including Queen's Counsel; the judges themselves are often interactive and will question counsel about specific points and ask to hear argument relating to particular aspects of the case. Judges are referred to as Lord Justice of Appeal, or Smith LJ. The Court of Appeal hears significantly more cases than the Supreme Court.

Civil Division

The civil arm of the Court of Appeal hears appeals on a variety of civil matters from the High Court, county court and tribunals.

Criminal Division

The Criminal Division of the Court of Appeal hears appeals against sentence from the Crown Court (the majority of its work); appeals against conviction; cases may be referred by the Attorney-General to deal with a point of law or where a sentence imposed is considered unduly lenient. The Criminal Cases Review Commission can refer cases to the Court of Appeal.

The Supreme Court

The Appeal functions of the House of Lords have transferred to the Supreme Court. The objective is to enhance independence of the Law Lords by further separating the functions of the judiciary and Parliament. The Court hears civil appeals from the Court of Appeal, with leave (permission) from the Court of Appeal, or if the Supreme Court had itself given leave. For a criminal case to reach the House of Lords the ground of appeal had to be a point of law.

It is not uncommon for different views to be taken by the judges; reading case reports can give real insight into the complexities of judicial decision-making and the difficulty of arriving at a consensus over some of the issues that are litigated. In some circumstances a majority judgment is given. This could lead to a rather perverse outcome in some cases. For example, in *Gillick*,[7] both the Court of Appeal and the House of Lords delivered majority judgments. The judges in the Court of Appeal and the House of Lords were of a similar level of expertise. In the final analysis, adding together the judges in the Court of Appeal and the House of Lords, it must have been somewhat dissatisfactory for Mrs Gillick to find that, although the final judgment of the House of Lords was against her, and is taken to have established the mature minor principle, in fact more judges supported her view than not! Perhaps this sort of outcome is one of the reasons why it is argued that it is unnecessary to have two senior appeal courts. Judges in the Supreme Court are Lords of Appeal in Ordinary (Law Lords) and referred to as, e.g., 'Lord Smith of Greenshire'.[8]

European Court of Justice

The European Court of Justice, which sits in Luxembourg, is the supreme authority for matters affecting the European Union. Its judgments are binding on all UK courts including the Supreme Court. European Community law is drawn from European Community treaties and legislation adopted by the Council of the European Union, usually in the form of regulations and directives. As Britain is a member of the European Union, UK law automatically includes European regulations. Each member state has some discretion with directives, which are binding but include some flexibility for the member state as to the manner in which the obligations are translated into national legislation. As an example, the European

Equal Treatment Directive 2000 required all member states to introduce anti-discrimination legislation dealing with ageism (among other things) by 2006.[9] In response, the Government introduced the Employment Equality (Age) Regulations 2006 to prohibit age discrimination in employment (now addressed by the Equality Act 2010).

European Court of Human Rights

The European Court of Human Rights sits in Strasbourg and is the supreme authority on the European Convention on Human Rights (ECHR) 1950. The United Kingdom 'incorporated' the ECHR into domestic law via the Human Rights Act 1998 (discussed in Chapter 5) but UK citizens retain a final right of appeal to the European Court of Human Rights.

Coroners' court

> The role of Her Majesty's coroner and the coroner's inquest is under unprecedented scrutiny in the aftermath of the Shipman case, the inquiry into the Bristol heart babies and the Alder Hey Hospital organs scandal. Each has thrown the work of coroners into sharp focus. Yet little is known about what they do and their wide-ranging powers.[10]

In the light of the above quote, it is not surprising that a programme of reform of coroners' courts has taken place. The system is now governed by the Coroners and Justice Act 2009. The aim is for a system which delivers more effective, transparent and responsive justice and coroner services for victims, witnesses, bereaved families and the wider public. The Act creates a new Office of Chief Coroner as head of the coroner system and regional coroners.

The coroner conducts investigations and as part of the investigation determines in each case whether there will be an inquest, to which witnesses will be called to give evidence. The coroner has an inquisitorial role and a wide discretion to decide what witnesses will be called and the type of evidence and questioning. Witnesses may give evidence by live link or behind screens. The duty to investigate a death applies where there are reasons to suspect the deceased died a violent or unnatural death, the cause of death is unknown or the deceased died in custody or state detention (including immigration detention centres, secure mental hospitals, deprivation of liberty orders). Inquests will be held in public and should normally be completed within 6 months of notification of the death. In specified circumstances, including, for example, where the death resulted from an act or omission of a police officer, an inquest must be held with a jury. Rather than a verdict, the coroner must record a conclusion as to how, when and where the deceased came by his death. This conclusion must not be framed so as to suggest civil or criminal liability of a person. Common conclusions include death by natural causes, accident, misadventure and suicide, but there is no specific list.

Tribunals

The court structure outlined so far has been supplemented by a system of around 80 tribunals commonly associated with the rise of the welfare state and exercising administrative and judicial functions. Some of the more important tribunals in social work terms included: the Care Standards Tribunal; Employment Tribunal; Mental Health Review Tribunal; Asylum and Immigration Tribunal; Criminal Injuries Compensation Appeals Panel; and Social Security Tribunal.

The tribunal system was originally intended to provide a quicker and more informal mechanism for dealing with certain specific areas of law than the traditional court system. Tribunal jurisdiction depends on the area of law. For example, the Care Standards Tribunal heard cases relating to regulation of residential homes for adults and children.

A major disadvantage of the tribunal system has been that even before the legal aid reforms, generally legal representation under the Community Legal Service has not been available to assist individuals to bring their case. This effectively deters some individuals from bringing a claim and may disadvantage others who find themselves arguing against experienced lawyers. Despite the lack of financial support, in many areas, because of the issues at stake, it has become commonplace for lawyers to be involved. This may be one reason why tribunals have become increasingly legalistic in their format. Rules of procedure for each tribunal are usually prescribed alongside the principal legislation affecting matters to be heard by the tribunal. Tribunals must give reasons for their decisions[11] and if they make a decision which is mistaken in its application of law a claim for judicial review or appeal to the High Court will lie.

The Tribunals, Courts and Enforcement Act 2007 established a new statutory framework. Two tribunals exist: the First Tier Tribunal and the Upper Tribunal. The First Tier tribunal comprises 'chambers' into which particular aspects of the tribunal jurisdiction are grouped. For example, the 'Social Entitlement Chamber' includes asylum support; criminal injuries compensation; and social security and child support. A second chamber, the 'Health, Education and Social Care Chamber' includes care standards; special educational needs and disability; and mental health reviews. The Upper Tribunal will be mainly for appeals from the first tier tribunal. The easiest way to access tribunal reports is via **BAILII**.[12]

Public and private hearings

As a general principle, court proceedings should normally be held in public, in open court. In a number of circumstances, however, the public and the press will be excluded and a case will be heard privately, or *in camera*. Cases heard *in camera* may still take place in a court room, or, commonly, the case may be heard in chambers (smaller rooms in court buildings). In these circumstances the only people present will be the parties to the dispute and their legal advisers. The majority of cases relating to children are heard *in camera*.

Article 6 of the European Convention on Human Rights is relevant to the public or private nature of hearings. The Article states that:

> ### Art. 6
>
> Everyone is entitled to a fair and public hearing.
>
> (ECHR)

It is unlikely that the effect of this Article will be to require that all cases which have been heard *in camera*, e.g. relating to domestic violence injunctions, will need to be heard in public in future. It is arguable that, if that were the case, Art. 8, respect for private and family life, might be violated. The more likely effect of Art. 6 will be for cases to continue to be heard in private, but for the judgment or decision to be given in public. The European Court of Human Rights ruled on this point in *B* v. *United Kingdom, P* v. *United Kingdom* (2002)

34 EHRR 19. The court found that denial of a hearing and pronouncement of judgment in public in child custody proceedings did not violate the right to a fair trial. The proceedings were described as prime examples of cases where the exclusion of the press and public might be justified in order to protect the privacy of the child. Witnesses should be able to express themselves candidly on highly personal issues without fear of public curiosity or comment. Pronouncing judgment in public would frustrate those aims.

Taking the courts into the twenty-first century

The Courts Service is taking seriously the need to speed up justice and improve communications. Information technology developments which have been piloted include: use of e-mail to notify agencies such as the police and prisons of the outcome of cases; electronic screens outside courts giving details of the progress of cases; electronic presentation of evidence such as photographs, maps and witness statements, and video links to prisons. All Crown Courts now have video link facilities.

Social work involvement in the courts

There is the potential for social workers to be involved professionally with cases at all levels of the court structure. Involvement may be as applicant to the court, or witness, or in giving support to a service user. Table 3.2 outlines the main areas of social work involvement.

Table 3.2 Areas of social work involvement at each level in the court structure

Magistrates' court Civil	Civil proceedings	ASBOs, Curfew Orders, provision of reports
Magistrates' court Criminal court	Youth	Crime and Disorder Act cases Provision of reports
	Adult	Reports to court (Probation Officer's role)
County court	Displacement of nearest relative – Mental Health Act 1983 Discrimination cases	
Family Court	Emergency Protection, Child Assessment Orders, Care and Supervision Orders, Adoption and Placement Orders, Special Guardianship Child Arrangements Orders, Section 37 Investigation Children Act 1989, Exclusion Order – Family Law Act 1996	
Crown Court	Provision of reports in adult criminal cases for juveniles charged with adults	
High Court Family Division	Wardship, Declaratory relief	
Queen's Bench	Judicial review	
Court of Protection	Mental Capacity Act 2005 cases	
Court of Appeal	Appeals on point of law	
Supreme Court	Appeals on point of law	

At each level the social work involvement may vary between applicant, report writer, witness, litigation friend, or may be general support to service user.

Rules of evidence

It should not be necessary for social workers to have an in-depth understanding of the rules of evidence – a complex area of law. A broad understanding of some principles of evidence, however, is an aid to understanding court procedures and will help ensure that information is recorded in a way that enables its use in court. It will also be helpful if a social worker has to give direct evidence or prepare statements for the court. Chapter 4 deals with techniques of giving evidence, sometimes referred to as 'courtcraft', and provides a summary of the main rules of evidence.

Law officers

The legal profession in England and Wales is divided into two main branches: **solicitors** and **barristers**. This contrasts with many other countries where there is simply one type of lawyer or advocate. Justification for continuation of the division is a constant source of debate. Traditionally, the solicitor's role has been to deal with legal work unrelated to court proceedings, such as conveyancing and preparation of cases for court, whereas barristers have presented cases. Increasingly, the divide between these roles is becoming blurred, with solicitors' rights of audience to present cases extended to a wider range of courts.

Solicitors

There are 128,000 practising solicitors in England and Wales, of whom about 75 per cent work in private practice; the remainder are employed in companies or by local or central Government and the Crown Prosecution Service. Once a male-dominated profession, women now represent just over 47 per cent of the profession and 12.6 per cent of the profession are from minority ethnic groups. Greater balance can be expected in the future, as new admissions comprise greater proportions of women and individuals with known ethnicity. Rules of conduct are set down by the professional body for solicitors, the Law Society. An independent body, the Solicitors Regulation Authority, deals with complaints made where the solicitor has broken the rules of professional conduct. The outcomes of complaints are published in the *Law Society's Gazette* and include examples ranging from unbefitting conduct to misuse of client funds. If dissatisfied with the outcome of complaints, the Legal Services Ombudsman may become involved.

Solicitors can offer advice on all areas of law and can represent a client's interests in litigation, including advocacy, and draw up legal documents such as wills and trusts. There is a growing trend towards solicitors developing large firms and associated practices with international offices, as law becomes more complex and solicitors choose to work in specialised areas of law. The analogy of the solicitor to the medical general practitioner still holds true, however, particularly in smaller firms where solicitors will deal with wide-ranging areas of law. Solicitors' dealings with their clients are protected by privilege and generally remain confidential unless the client gives authority to disclose. So, even if a client confesses to his solicitor that he has committed a murder, the solicitor cannot tell anyone.

Since 1994, solicitors with significant experience of advocacy have been able to obtain rights of audience to appear in the higher courts, including the Crown Court and High Court.[13] Solicitor-advocates will still be distinguishable from barristers, as they do not wear wigs and must address the judge from further back in the court. Solicitors may be paid directly by the client, via the Community Legal Service, or through the contingency fee scheme (no win no fee arrangements)[14] and may undertake a certain amount of ***pro bono*** (free) work.

Local authorities have a wide range of legal responsibilities, in social services matters and other areas, and usually employ solicitors to conduct this work. It is important for social workers to know which solicitors in the local authority legal section deal with legal issues arising from social services responsibilities and to build good working relations with them.

Barristers

Barristers, also known as **counsel**, are the smaller of the two branches of the legal profession in England and Wales; there were around 15,500 practising barristers in 2012. Of those barristers, about 65 per cent are male and just over 10 per cent are from an ethnic minority. Senior, more experienced barristers may be appointed Queen's Counsel (QC) and in complex cases a QC and junior barrister will conduct the case. Barristers are regulated by the Bar Council. The majority of barristers are self-employed and operate from offices known as 'chambers', which are managed by a barrister's clerk, effectively the barristers' agent. Chambers tend to be situated near major courts. Barristers are usually instructed or briefed by solicitors, but it has become possible for them to accept instructions direct from lay clients. Barristers have rights of audience in the higher courts and their training focuses on advocacy and evidence. Barristers may also be consulted by solicitors where specialist legal advice, in the form of an opinion, is required. As with solicitors, barristers may take on some cases without charging a fee. Complaints against barristers are dealt with by the Complaints Commission of the Bar Council.

Crown Prosecution Service

The Crown Prosecution Service (CPS), headed by the Director of Public Prosecutions (**DPP**), was set up in 1986. From that date the dual role of the police as investigator and prosecutor was separated,[15] with the Crown Prosecution Service taking on responsibility for all prosecutions. The CPS employs solicitors and barristers and works independently of the police, taking the decision whether to bring a prosecution in a particular case, based on the evidence accumulated by the police. Crown Prosecutors determine whether a person is to be charged in all indictable only, either way or summary offences, where the custody officer is satisfied that in all the circumstances of the case there is at least a reasonable suspicion against the person of having committed an offence (in accordance with Art. 5 of the European Convention on Human Rights) and that at that stage it is in the public interest to proceed. There are some exceptions which the police may continue to charge, including most road traffic offences, absconding and some public order offences.

Guidance is provided by a Code for Crown Prosecutors. A key element of the code is the two-part test for prosecution:

1. examination of the evidence;
2. whether prosecution is in the public interest.

Factors in favour of prosecution include whether the offence was motivated by any form of discrimination or the victim is particularly vulnerable. The most recent edition of the code (7th edn, 2013) recognises that the CPS is a public authority within the meaning of the **HRA** 1998, and must therefore comply with the terms of the European Convention on Human Rights. There are also specific policies which support and underpin the code, e.g. the policy for prosecuting cases of domestic violence.

Criminal Defence Service

The Criminal Defence Service (**CDS**) is modelled on a form similar to the Crown Prosecution Service.[16] A defendant will apply to the court for a right to representation where he wishes to be represented at public expense, and must satisfy the interests of justice test before the request can be granted. The order is known as a Representation Order and the defendant's acting solicitor must have in place a contract (a franchise) with the Legal Services Commission.

Magistrates/Justices of the Peace (JPs)

It is difficult not to have preconceived ideas and stereotypes about different professions, and the law is no exception. Being a highly popular choice for media attention, whether in the tabloids, broadsheet press or on television as the subject of documentaries or, increasingly, in popular entertainment, there are many influences on how we see members of the legal profession. Sadly, the impressions given are not always too close to reality, either in terms of procedural accuracy, or glamour and style! This was illustrated most clearly in a role play exercise carried out with students some years ago. Each member of the group was assigned a part in a courtroom scenario and given guidance on the role to be taken and evidence they could give, but otherwise was free to develop the character as they wished. Three students played the bench of magistrates and came dressed in 'suitable attire'. This consisted of a lounge suit and old school tie for the male magistrate. One female magistrate wore a twinset and pearls and glasses dangling from a long gold chain were perched at the end of her nose. The second female magistrate wore a huge hat covered in artificial flowers and fruit!

It would be difficult to design a better prompt for a discussion on the principles of the magistracy offering justice by one's peers. The example above might suggest that there is a stereotypical view of a magistrate as a judgmental member of the middle class with little in common with many of the individuals who appear in the magistrates' court. Research carried out by Parker *et al.* on magistrates' sentencing practices and ideology in the late 1980s appears to support that view and found a level of mistrust of social workers.[17] The magistracy has received criticism at a number of levels, including inconsistency in sentencing, prejudice and resistance to change.

It is useful to consider some statistics which give an indication of the current makeup of the magistracy. There were 23,244 magistrates in England and Wales in 2013. There are slightly more women than men. The current percentage of magistrates from ethnic minority groups is 8.3 per cent, and recruitment drives aim to increase this further.

All magistrates are appointed by the Lord Chancellor, following recommendation by a local advisory committee. Membership of advisory committees, once a fairly closely guarded secret, is now a public matter. New magistrates may have put themselves forward to the committee, possibly in response to advertising campaigns of the advisory committee, or may be recommended by others, including existing magistrates. Prospective magistrates are interviewed by the advisory committee, which has the task of ensuring that the composition of the bench broadly reflects the community it serves. It is difficult precisely to identify the qualities required in a magistrate but, broadly speaking, magistrates should be of good character, have a good local knowledge and understanding of the local community, be able to work as a member of the team, be able to reach reasoned decisions and on appointment be aged between 18 and 65 years. The following will not be appointed to the magistracy: anyone not of good character and personal standing; an undischarged bankrupt; a serving member of the police or armed forces; a person from an occupation which might conflict with the role of a magistrate; or a close relative of an existing magistrate on the same bench. Magistrates must retire at 70.

In response to criticism that magistrates were untrained and unprepared for the task, the level of training provided has increased in order that magistrates should deliver more consistent and reasoned decisions whilst still retaining the qualities of the laity. Magistrates receive training before they sit in courts, and continue to receive training throughout their service. The training provided places considerable emphasis on the need for consistency in decision-making against the context of current developments. Magistrates' court sentencing guidelines are issued to all magistrates and provide a structure which aims to guide magistrates' decisions on establishing the seriousness of each individual case and the most appropriate disposal (see example in Chapter 18). Training topics include basic rules of court procedure, the implications of the Human Rights Act 1998, sentencing powers and options, and communication skills. Specialist training is provided for work in the family or youth court and for magistrates who will sit as chair in court. Magistrates are unpaid volunteers, but may receive expense allowances. This remains a barrier to the objective of widening recruitment of the magistracy because the issue remains as to who can afford to be a magistrate, and this is likely to distort the representativeness of the bench.

Apart from lay magistrates, there are 142 district judges (magistrates' courts) who are paid professional lawyers. Until recently, they were referred to as stipendiary magistrates. Unlike lay magistrates, they can sit alone and are found mainly in London and in large cities where there is a high volume of work.[18]

Justices' clerk

An important figure in the magistrates' court is the justices' clerk. The clerk has overall responsibility for administration, organisation and finance, but is best known for his or her role in court of giving advice to the magistrates on law and procedure and having overall control of the conduct of the proceedings. The clerk usually reads out the charge and takes the plea in criminal cases, identifies the parties in civil cases and administers the oath. The particular style and demeanour of the clerk can have an enormous impact on the tone of the proceedings, including the level of formality, sympathy towards applications for adjournments, etc. The first question from many advocates arriving at court will be which clerk they have. A justices' clerk will normally be a barrister or solicitor qualified for at least five years. The responsibilities of the justices' clerk have gradually increased beyond keeping a record of the proceedings, and there are a range of decisions which the clerk will take independently of the magistrates, including: allocation of cases to higher courts; appointment of children's guardians; fixing dates of directions and main hearing; serving reports; issuing a **witness summons** and warrant for arrest; extending bail periods; requesting a pre-sentence report or welfare report, etc. In contrast, the role of the clerk in higher courts is mainly administrative because the judiciary are legally qualified.

Judges

Judges are appointed by the Lord Chancellor and are drawn mainly from barristers and, more recently, solicitors. Judges are appointed to a particular level in the court system ranging from 12 Lords of Appeal in Ordinary, who sit in the Supreme Court, through to 35 Lord Justices of Appeal, 108 High Court judges, 654 circuit judges, 1,196 recorders, 446 district judges and 784 deputy district judges. Given that most judges are appointed from the Bar, it is not surprising that there are few women and a small percentage of judges are from an ethnic minority. This inevitably raises questions as to diversity and impact on decision-making.

Attorney-General

The **Attorney-General** is a member of the Cabinet and hence the post is a political appointment. He answers questions in Parliament, advises and represents the Crown (or Government) in any proceedings in our domestic courts of the High Court or above, or in disputes before the European Court of Human Rights. The Attorney-General has to give consent before certain prosecutions can be brought, e.g. incitement to racial hatred under the Public Order Act 1986. The Solicitor General is deputy to the Attorney-General.

Director of Public Prosecutions

The Director of Public Prosecutions (DPP) is head of the Crown Prosecution Service. The duties of the DPP are laid out in the Prosecution of Offences Act 1985. The DPP can represent the Crown when appeals are brought in the Court of Appeal or Supreme Court.

Official Solicitor

The post of Official Solicitor carries a wide remit, including representation of wards of court, conducting litigation for children and for people with a disability, acting as 'friend of the court' (**amicus curiae**) to assist the court, and responsibility for bail and *habeas corpus*. The work of the Official Solicitor relating to children has now been amalgamated into the Children and Family Court Advisory and Support Service (**CAFCASS**), and operates as a non-departmental public body subject to National Standards.[19] In relation to work with children, the Official Solicitor is referred to as CAFCASS Legal Services and Special Casework. The Official Solicitor has a continuing role to play in cases involving adults who lack mental capacity.

Children's guardian

The **children's guardian** is usually a qualified social worker, and the children and family reporter will often have trained as a probation officer. (These roles are dealt with in more detail in Chapter 4.)

Probation service

The probation and the prison services form the National Offender Management Service. Duties of probation include after-care of offenders released from custody, and provision of social inquiry reports to assist courts to determine the most suitable method of disposal. (The role of the probation service is covered in more detail in Chapter 18.)

Lord Chancellor and the Ministry of Justice

The Lord Chancellor, who also holds the title Secretary of State for Justice, heads the Ministry of Justice. The Lord Chancellor no longer sits as a judge. The ministry has responsibility for the National Offender Management Service, prisons and the courts and works with other government agencies.

Access to law and representation issues

It is a reality that in some situations the only advice available to a service user is that of the social worker. For this reason alone, a basic knowledge of the range of law likely to be encountered by a service user is desirable. Even when legal advice has been obtained, a social worker may still have a role in 'interpreting' and explaining that advice. This section considers various avenues for obtaining advice on legal issues and representation if necessary, focusing on the Community Legal Service. It is also worth noting that lawyers are not the only source of legal advice. Social workers working in different specialities can be a useful resource to each other: e.g. education social workers, social workers in hospital settings and approved mental health practitioners can all provide information relating to legal aspects of their area of work.

Trade unions have obvious expertise in employment law and usually provide advice to members in connection with employment matters, and sometimes representation. Examples of areas of likely expertise include unfair dismissal, discrimination at work and whistleblowing.

Voluntary agencies can often provide specialist help to social workers and clients within their area of expertise. Many have legal advisers and helplines and publish useful factsheets, e.g. Action on Elder Abuse, Disabled Parents Network, Counsel and Care, VOICE and the Children's Legal Centre. Support may also be specifically focused to the needs of professionals, e.g. the Association of Child Abuse Lawyers (ACAL) provides practical support for lawyers and other professionals working for adults and children who have been abused.

For many individuals, and for particular types of cases, effective access to the legal system and presentation of a case will be possible only if legal representation is available. The provision of free legal aid and assistance was established after the Second World War and a comprehensive scheme was provided by the Legal Aid Act 1988. It provided for assistance via the green form scheme, civil legal aid, criminal legal aid, assistance by way of representation (ABWOR) and the duty solicitor scheme.[20] That system was reformed into the Community Legal Service run by the Legal Services Commission.

Legal Aid reforms have been introduced by the Legal Aid, Sentencing and Punishment of Offenders Act 2012 (LASPO). The Act, which has been subject to a high level of criticism, restricts availability of Legal Aid to a more limited range of legal issues and will inevitably lead to an increase in the number of **litigants in person** (sometimes also referred to as self-represented litigants). On the face of it the reduction in Legal Aid may achieve the government's objective of financial savings but cases involving litigants in person often take more time, a more pro-active role for the judge and significantly contribute to delays in the legal system. If the issue of concerns is within the areas where Legal Aid is available, a means test determines whether the individual is eligible. There is a calculator tool, 'Can you get legal aid?' on the government website, www.gov.uk.

The Legal Services Commission has been abolished and replaced by the Legal Aid Agency, an executive agency of the Ministry of Justice. The Legal Aid Agency provides civil and criminal legal aid and advice and includes the Public Defender Service. The **LAA** runs a helpline for advice on: debt; housing; family law; welfare benefits; discrimination; and education. Organisations including private practice solicitors, law centres and Citizens Advice Bureaux can provide Legal Aid services if they have a contract with the LAA.

The types of civil Legal Aid include:

- *Legal Help* – advice and assistance on legal entitlement and options.
- *Help at Court* – an adviser is able to speak on your behalf at court without formally acting in the whole proceedings.

- *Family Mediation* – help to reach agreement following relationship breakdown to resolve problems involving children, money and the family home.
- *Family Help* – assistance and representation in family.
- *Legal Representation* – representation at court by a solicitor or barrister.
- *Controlled Legal Representation* – representation at mental health tribunal proceedings or before the First Tier Tribunal in asylum or immigration cases.

Legal Aid is available for:

- debt relating to mortgage possession of the home and involuntary bankruptcy;
- civil legal services provided in relation to breach of the Equality Act 2010;
- Special Educational Needs matters;
- public family law regarding protection of children;
- private family where there is evidence of domestic violence or child abuse;
- child abduction matters;
- representation for child parties in private family cases;
- legal advice in support of mediation;
- domestic violence injunction cases;
- forced marriage protection order cases;
- housing matters including possession and eviction from the home;
- homelessness assistance for people who are homeless or threatened with homelessness;
- injunctions under the Protection from Harassment Act 1997 in the context of housing and ASBO matters in the county court;
- injunctions for gang-related violence;
- mediation to resolve family law disputes;
- applications for asylum;
- inquests into the death of a family member;
- civil claims relating to allegations of abuse and assault;
- Mental Health, Community Care, Actions Against Public Authorities and Public Law will remain in scope with minor amendments.

Legal aid will *not* be available for the following areas:

- asylum support (except where accommodation is claimed);
- consumer and general contract;
- Criminal Injuries Compensation Authority cases;
- debt, except where there is an immediate risk to the home;
- employment cases;
- education cases, except for cases of Special Educational Needs;
- housing matters, except those where the home is at immediate risk (excluding those who are 'squatting'), homelessness assistance, housing disrepair cases that pose a serious risk to life or health and anti-social behaviour cases in the county court;
- immigration cases (non-detention);
- legal advice in relation to a change of name;

- court actions concerning personal data;

- legal advice on will-making for: those over 70, disabled people, the parent of a disabled person, and the parent of a minor who is living with the client but not with the other parent and the client wishes to appoint a guardian for the minor in a will;

- private family law (other than cases where criteria are met regarding domestic violence or child abuse);

- tort and other general claims; and

- welfare benefits, except for advice and assistance for welfare benefits appeals in the Upper Tribunal, and advice, assistance and representation for welfare benefits appeals in the higher courts.

Chapter summary

- In order to understand the court structure in England and Wales it is useful to be able to distinguish between a civil and a criminal case. That distinction is reflected in the way the parties to a case are referred to, the outcome or remedies, and the standard of proof.

- The standard of proof in a civil case is 'balance of probabilities' and in a criminal case it is 'beyond reasonable doubt'.

- The courts exercising civil jurisdiction are the Supreme Court, the Court of Appeal (Civil Division), the High Court, county court and magistrates' court and the Family Court.

- The courts exercising criminal jurisdiction are the Supreme Court, the Court of Appeal (Criminal Division), Queen's Bench Division of the High Court, Crown Court and magistrates' court. The magistrates' court divides into an adult court and a youth court. The level at which a case is tried depends partly on classification of the offence as a summary, either way or indictable offence.

- The courts are organised in a hierarchy, with the Supreme Court as the most senior court and the magistrates' court as the most inferior court. This hierarchy is inextricably bound to the doctrine of precedent.

- A growing body of law is dealt with by tribunals, which are intended to deal with specific areas, e.g. employment law, in a less formal environment.

- In addition to the domestic courts, the European Court of Justice is the most senior court in matters affecting European Community law. The European Court of Human Rights hears cases related to the European Convention on Human Rights.

- The legal profession divides into solicitors and barristers (counsel). Solicitors have tended to deal with preparation of cases whilst barristers appear in court, but that division of work is becoming increasingly blurred. The Crown Prosecution Service is responsible for prosecution of criminal offences and there is a Criminal Defence Service.

- A case will be decided either by magistrates, lay members of the public, in the magistrates' court or by judges in the higher courts. Other significant personnel in the legal system include the Attorney-General, Director of Public Prosecutions, Official Solicitor and Lord Chancellor.

- The Legal Aid Agency has responsibility for provision of legal support. The Legal Aid, Sentencing and Punishment of Offenders Act 2012 restricts the availability of Legal Aid to specified areas of law.

Exercises

Which court?

Identify the court where the following matters are likely to be heard (there may be more than one option in each scenario) and where appropriate advice might be sought in relation to the issues at stake:

- An application for possession of a council house due to rent arrears.
- A claim of unfair dismissal after Jack was 'forced' to resign following racial harassment and name calling on the factory floor and consistent refusals in response to requests for over-time which his contemporaries all enjoyed.
- An uncontested adoption of James, an 18-month-old boy with Down's syndrome.
- A criminal charge of burglary against brothers, Phil (16) and Greg (20).
- An application for an injunction to remove Peter from the home he shares with his girlfriend, Julie, who came to Social Services asking for help after he pushed her down the stairs during an argument.
- A claim for compensation for a broken leg and whiplash caused in a car accident.
- A claim for breach of contract, arising from cancellation of a marquee and catering for 100 people, when Robert and Rachel called off their wedding the night before it was due to take place.
- An application for care proceedings in respect of six children, of three different fathers, two of whom are cared for by maternal grandparents. The father of one child is threatening to take him out of the country to live with his parents in Greece.
- A challenge to the refusal by a pub landlord to serve a group of five adults with learning dis-abilities, the reason given that one of the group was a wheelchair user and it would not be possible to get him out quickly if there was a fire.

Court observation guide

Through observation, students should be able to identify aspects of the roles of personnel in court, the procedure and legal issues. Aim to spend at least a couple of hours in court.

The following questions – some factual matters and others asking for your impression of the proceedings – should help you to get more from your visit. The exercise will be most valuable if you visit a variety of courts and draw comparisons between them.

- What type of court are you in? Is it superior or inferior or is it a tribunal?
- Does the court deal with civil or criminal matters or a combination of these?
- Who is adjudicating – if a judge, what level, and, if magistrates, how many are sitting?
- What are the roles of the clerk and the usher?
- How many parties are represented in court and how many lawyers represent each party, e.g. solicitors only, solicitors and barristers, junior barristers and Queen's Counsel?
- Does the court deal with a number of separate cases or is the case before it scheduled for a long hearing?
- Are there representatives of the press, probation, social services, etc. in court?

- Are there many members of the public watching the proceedings?
- Who is in charge?
- How formal are the proceedings?
- How do the advocates refer to each other?
- How is the judge/magistrate addressed?
- What is the 'dress code' in court?
- What conclusions can you draw from 'body language' in court?
- Are there any 'expert'/'professional' witnesses?
- What types of evidence are adduced, e.g. oral testimony, documents, reports, weapons, plans, photographs?
- Who keeps a record of the proceedings and how?
- Is the courtroom in a modern or traditional court? Sketch the layout.
- Comment on the 'facilities' at the court – are there places to wait comfortably, a tea room, somewhere for children?
- Did the cases raise any issues in relation to social work values?

Websites

The website of the Ministry of Justice:
www.justice.gov.uk

The Courts and Tribunal Service – an executive agency of the Ministry of Justice, for information on courts, procedures and forms:
www.justice.gov.uk/about/hmcts

The Law Society, the professional body for solicitors:
www.lawsociety.org.uk

The Bar Council, the professional body for barristers:
www.barcouncil.org.uk

The Crown Prosecution Service website provides information about the service responsible for prosecuting criminal cases investigated by the police and provides access to the code of practice:
www.cps.gov.uk

The Children and Family Court Advisory Service (CAFCASS):
www.cafcass.gov.uk

The Lay Magistrates Association:
www.magistrates-association.org.uk

The website of the Legal Aid Agency:
www.justice.gov.uk/legal-aid

A useful starting point if you are seeking legal help and advice:
www.clsdirect.org.uk

Citizens' Advice Bureau:
www.citizensadvice.org.uk

The public information site of the Citizens' Advice Bureau:
www.adviceguide.org.uk

Advice UK, a directory of advice-giving agencies:
www.adviceuk.org.uk

The Law Centres Federation will supply details of your nearest law centre:
ww.lawcentres.org.uk

Further reading

Textbooks providing a clear overview of the legal system include:

Boylan-Kemp, J. (2014) *English Legal System – The Fundamentals.* London: Sweet & Maxwell.

Cownie, F., Bradney, A. and Burton, M. (2013) *English Legal System in Context.* Oxford: Oxford University Press.

Genn, H. (2006) *Tribunals for Diverse Users.* London: Department for Constitutional Affairs. (Interesting research into three tribunals: the Appeals Service, Criminal Injuries Compensation Appeals Panel and the Special Educational Needs and Disability Tribunal which found that '... with rare exceptions tribunals treated users from all ethnic backgrounds with courtesy and respect'. The report also highlights the need for the judiciary to have the skills to enable unrepresented parties to present their cases.)

Partington, M. (2013) *Introduction to the English Legal System.* Oxford: Oxford University Press.

Critical examination of the senior judiciary and magistracy is provided by:

Doughty, J. and Murch, M. (2012) 'Judicial independence and the restructuring of family courts and their support services' 24(3) *Child and Family Law Quarterly,* p. 333.

Family Justice Review Panel (2011) *Family Justice Review.* London: Ministry of Justice, Department for Education and Welsh Government.

Griffith, J. A. G. (1991) *The Politics of the Judiciary* (4th edn). London: Fontana.

Parker, H., Sumner, M. and Jarvis, G. (1989) *Unmasking the Magistrates.* Milton Keynes: Open University Press.

Reforms to legal aid are discussed in:

Miles, J., Balmer, N. and Smith, M. (2012) 'When exceptional is the rule: mental health, family problems and the reform of legal aid in England and Wales' 24(3) *Child and Family Law Quarterly,* p. 320.

The increasing number of self represented litigants may find the following guide useful:

Bar Council (2012) *A Guide to Representing Yourself in Court*; available from www.barcouncil.org.uk.

Notes

[1] Either way offences are listed in Sch. 1 to the Magistrates' Courts Act 1980.
[2] Bail Act 1976.
[3] Juries Act 1974, s. 17.
[4] The court service website includes useful information about the way courts operate: see www.courtservice.gov.uk/info_home.htm.

[5] M. Berlins and C. Dyer (1990) *The Law Machine*. London: Penguin.

[6] *R* v. *Gloucestershire County Council, ex parte Barry* [1997] 2 All ER 1 (discussed further in Chapter 9).

[7] *Gillick* v. *West Norfolk and Wisbech Area Health Authority* [1986] AC 112.

[8] The membership (names of judges) is included at the front of the All England Law Reports.

[9] Eurolink Age, 2001.

[10] R. Rhodes-Kemp (2001) 'Is it time for an inquest into the coroner's role?' *The Times* 13 February 2001.

[11] Tribunals and Inquiries Act 1971, s. 12.

[12] The British and Irish Legal Information Institute: www.bailii.org.

[13] Now covered by the Legal Services Act 2007.

[14] Conditional Fee Agreements Order 1998 (SI 1998/1860).

[15] Guidance to Police Officers and Crown Prosecutors issued by the Director of Public Prosecutions under s. 37A of the Police and Criminal Evidence Act 1984.

[16] It came into being in 2001 when, in matters concerning representation in criminal proceedings, the Access to Justice Act 1999 replaced the Legal Aid Act 1988.

[17] H. Parker, M. Sumner and G. Jarvis (1989) *Unmasking the Magistrates*. Milton Keynes: Open University Press.

[18] The Magistrates Association is a good source of information about the magistracy: www.magistrates-association.org.uk.

[19] Consequential amendments have been made to the Adoption Rules, Family Proceedings Rules, Family Proceedings Courts Rules and Magistrates' Courts (Adoption) Rules. For more information, visit the CAFCASS website at www.cafcass.gov.uk/index.htm.

[20] See M. Cousins (1994) 'The politics of legal aid: a solution in search of a problem' 13 *Civil Justice Quarterly* p. 111.

Chapter 4

Social workers' role in law

Learning objectives

To develop an understanding of the following:

- The various roles of a social worker when working with the law.
- The skills employed as a witness.
- The relationship between lawyers and social workers.
- Basic rules of evidence.
- Advocacy.
- The various ways social work decisions may be challenged.
- The concept of whistleblowing and application of the Public Interest Disclosure Act 1998.
- Statutory regulation of record keeping, confidentiality and access to information, the Data Protection Act 1998 and the Freedom of Information Act 2000.

> ### Talking Point
>
> A number of social workers and other professionals struggle with the adversarial nature of court proceedings. Appearing in court can be an intimidating experience for social workers and other professionals, and managing this alongside a continuing relationship with a family is challenging. It is therefore important that all staff are adequately trained before going to court. This should be part of both specialist child protection training and continuing professional development.
>
> The above statement is taken from the report of Lord Laming published in 2009 following the case of Baby P ('The Protection of Children in England: A Progress Report', para. 8.6). More recently, the Family Justice Review (2012) stated, 'Social workers should be taught about relevant legal process and procedure and in particular what the court expects them to present and how to present it' (para. 52).
>
> Increasingly, across all areas of practice, social workers will be called upon to appear in court. Whilst this can be a stressful experience, it can also result in positive outcomes. The need for training is recognised by Laming and it is also important to stress the importance of the relationship between lawyers and social workers working together in legal settings. This chapter considers those areas where this interface is most important, in relation to the specific roles that a social worker may adopt, recognition that social work decisions may be challenged and the skills required to work effectively within the legal system.

Introduction

Previous chapters have described essential features of the English legal system. In this chapter the focus moves to two key areas: consideration of the various roles of the social worker in the legal system and ways in which social work practice can be challenged. Roles include acting as the applicant in proceedings, as McKenzie friend, witness, report writer, member of CAFCASS, appropriate adult and advocate. The chapter continues with an introduction to the concept of 'courtcraft', focusing on the role of the social worker in court, and rules of evidence.

Increasingly, social work practice is being challenged by service users and the legal options for challenge are outlined, followed by consideration of 'whistleblowing' as a mechanism for highlighting and challenging undesirable practices in relation to social work services.

Appropriate record keeping is an essential aspect of the social worker's role and, it may be argued, an increasing burden to the practitioner. Guidance on record keeping and the legal framework for access to records concludes the chapter.

Social work roles in the legal system

Applicant

As representative of the local authority, a social worker may be in the role of applicant in court in a range of proceedings. Usually a solicitor or barrister will conduct the case and the social worker then becomes the key witness in the application. Examples of such cases include: Emergency Protection Orders; Child Assessment Orders; Care and Supervision Orders (and their variation or revocation); application to displace the nearest relative under the Mental Health Act 1983; placement orders in adoption cases; applications for Court of Protection orders in relation to vulnerable adults who lack capacity. (See further discussion of the term 'vulnerable adult' in Chapters 14 and 17.) For many types of proceedings, a report from the social worker will be required by the court. Some principles of report writing are discussed later. The actual application process usually involves completion of standard forms for the court, and these are generally dealt with by the local authority solicitor.

McKenzie friend

The case of *McKenzie v. McKenzie* [1970] 3 All ER 1034 established the principle that where a person is not legally represented (and is therefore known as a litigant in person, or self represented person), he can nevertheless bring someone along to help in court. This person is known as a McKenzie friend. The majority of courts will permit a McKenzie friend to give advice to the individual in court as long as they conduct themselves reasonably. The McKenzie friend cannot directly address the court, as he does not by this status have rights of audience. The involvement of a McKenzie friend has been particularly useful in tribunals, where Legal Aid is not usually available, and it is a role that a social worker may take on. There has been a significant growth in the numbers of litigants in person following recent restrictions on Legal Aid availability. The role of the McKenzie friend is consequently even more important and can offer real assistance to the court.

It is also important to be aware that a service user may be supported by a McKenzie friend who is not a social worker. The role of the McKenzie friend in family proceedings was the subject of *Re O (Children); Re W-R (A Child); Re W (Children)* [2005] EWCA Civ 759. In the first two of the three appeals heard together, litigants in person (individuals who appear in court without legal representation) had been denied the assistance of a McKenzie friend in contact and residence proceedings. In the third, a McKenzie friend had been permitted but severe restrictions were placed on the documentation he was allowed to see. The Court of Appeal allowed the appeals. It noted that Art. 6 ECHR was engaged in any application by a litigant in person for assistance of a McKenzie friend and that there was a presumption in favour of allowing this and ensuring a fair hearing. There was no reason why the McKenzie friend should not have access to court papers, provided they were used solely for the purpose of assisting the litigant in person with his case. This is a particularly important decision given the reduction in public funding for representation.[1]

The court may refuse an application for a particular person to act as a McKenzie friend, as in *Re H* [2012] EWCA Civ 1797, a family law dispute where the McKenzie friend proposed by the father had been intimidating to the mother. Guidance on the role of McKenzie friends is contained in 'Practice Guidance: McKenzie Friends (Civil and Family Courts)' [2010] 2 FLR 962. As a consequence of the increase in litigants in person following legal aid cuts there has been a growth in 'professional' McKenzie friends who offer a service to litigants for a fee.

Witness

The role of the social worker as a witness is considered fully at the end of this chapter. At this stage it is important to note that the witness owes a duty to the court to tell the truth, even if in exceptional circumstances this may mean expressing a personal view which conflicts with the agency stance.

Report writer

In the majority of cases where a social worker is involved in court proceedings he will provide a report for the court. The type of report varies between civil and criminal cases and cases involving young people. In some cases the content is prescribed by regulations or national standards, e.g. pre-sentence reports, permanence reports in adoption cases. In other cases reports provided to court will vary in style according to the author, though certain conventions may be followed.

Reports may be requested by the court exercising a general discretion or by a specific power such as under s. 7 of the Children Act 1989:

---

s. 7

(1) A Court considering any question with respect to a child under this Act may –

    (a) ask an officer of the service; or

    (b) ask a local authority to arrange for –

        (i) an officer of the authority; or

        (ii) such other person (other than a probation officer) as the authority considers appropriate, to report to the Court on such matters relating to the welfare of that child as are required to be dealt with in the report.

...

(5) It shall be the duty of the authority or an officer of the service[2] to comply with any request for a report under this section.

(CA 1989)

It is clear from the wording of the section and reference to 'that' child that the court can ask specific questions pertinent to the particular circumstances of the child concerned, e.g. relating to levels of contact with an estranged parent.

The probation service has a major role in providing reports to the criminal courts. These reports provide information to the court and an element of assessment to assist with sentencing. National standards[3] dictate the content and structure of such reports. When a report is being prepared, the nature and purpose of the inquiry should be made clear to the subject of the report, and their consent should be obtained. Reports will normally be shared with the subject.

Children's guardian

Guardians tend to be experienced social workers. Guardians are part of the Children and Family Court Advisory and Support Services (CAFCASS) formed in 2001. The former term **'guardian *ad litem*'** has been replaced by 'children's guardian' since the creation of CAFCASS.

The role of the guardian *ad litem* was created to provide an independent voice for the child in cases concerning the child's welfare, following the Maria Colwell Report.[4] The role of the guardian was considerably extended by the Children Act 1989 – s. 41 identifies specified proceedings in which a guardian must be appointed by the court. The principal role of the guardian is to prepare a report for the court, following their inquiries, and to safeguard and protect the interests of the child. The guardian will usually conduct interviews with professionals who have had dealings with the case, the parents and other significant adults, as well as the child. The guardian must ascertain the views of the child, but is not bound to follow those views in the final recommendation. If the court does not follow the final recommendation of the guardian, it is required to give reasons for not doing so (*Devon County Council* v. *C* [1985] FLR 1159). Where the views of the child conflict with those of the guardian and the child is of sufficient maturity, the child may be separately represented by their own solicitor. The child needs to have sufficient understanding to participate in the proceedings, giving instructions as the case develops, and the courts have shown some reluctance to permit children to participate directly in adversarial litigation without the protection of a guardian (*Re N (Contact: Minor Seeking Leave to Defend and Removal of Guardian)* [2003] FLR 652). The guardian is usually involved in public law proceedings but increasingly also has a role in some private law proceedings.[5]

In order to carry out the role, guardians are authorised by the Children Act 1989, s. 42 to examine and take copies of all relevant material relating to the child held by the local authority. Increasingly, the guardian is asked to comment on the local authority's care plan for the child, as well as the order that is recommended to the court. Amendments introduced by the Adoption and Children Act 2002 have made it possible to extend the role of the guardian beyond the final care order in some cases. An Independent Reviewing Officer will monitor the care plan and may refer the case to CAFCASS if appropriate, and the guardian may then take the case back to court. This reform can be traced back to *Re S (Children: Care Plan); Re W (Children: Care Plan)* [2002] UKHL 10. (The role of the Independent Reviewing Officer is considered further in Chapter 10.)

CAFCASS has a major role in providing reports to court. It is an amalgamation of the old Court Welfare Service, guardian *ad litem* panels and the children's division of the Official Solicitor's office. This body is independent of the local authority and responsible to the Ministry of Justice. The functions of CAFCASS are set out in s. 12 of the Criminal Justice and Courts Services Act 2000. To:

- Safeguard and promote the welfare of the child.
- Give advice to the court about any application made to it in such proceedings.
- Make provision for children to be represented in such proceedings.
- Provide information, advice and support for children and their families.

(Aspects of the role of CAFCASS are discussed further in Chapters 7 and 9.)

General principles of report writing

In most circumstances, there are some general principles that can be followed in preparing a report for court. These include the following:

- Basic information should be included on the front page, including the name of the court and the case number; the name and date of birth of the subject; the type of application; and the author's name and professional address.
- Clarity and concision of language will always help the reader.
- Avoid dense pages of text and use bullet points (though sparingly – the other risk is to overdo the abruptness).
- Remember who the report is for – and make appropriate adjustments to style and vocabulary.

- Consider the structure and length of the report – there may be guidance to follow.
- Include a chronology of events.
- A genogram may be useful if there is a complex family make-up.
- Avoid jargon (ask a non-interested person to check this out and you may be surprised by how much jargon slips in!).
- Be non-discriminatory in the language used.
- Distinguish between facts and opinion.
- Avoid unnecessary repetition within the report of material available to the court in other documents.
- Remember that it is the business of the court to make findings of fact.
- Conclusions should flow logically from the body of the report.
- Where more than one option is available to the court, set out and discuss each in turn, and make a realistic recommendation.
- Objectivity is all; avoid over-personalising your report, although it is inevitable that you will be drawing upon your experience.[6]
- Increasingly, there are strict timetables for filing of evidence, including reports. Failure to adhere to timetables invites criticism; if unavoidable, it is important to seek court approval.

(Reports in care proceedings are dealt with in more detail in Chapter 9.)

Appropriate adult

Under the Police and Criminal Evidence Act 1984 (PACE) and associated codes of practice, a social worker may be required to act as an appropriate adult in connection with certain vulnerable adults and juveniles who are detained in police custody. For a juvenile, three categories of people may act as appropriate adult: the parent or guardian (or care authority for a child who is looked after); a social worker; or any other responsible adult who is not a police officer or employed by the police. In this capacity, social workers have a positive role to play in safeguarding the rights and civil liberties of the person who is detained.[7] First preference is for the parent, although it is arguable that there are advantages for the police in using a social worker as an appropriate adult in place of a parent or guardian. Social workers are certainly more likely to have an understanding of the process; there is a professional relationship between the agencies and a social worker is less likely to be emotionally involved.

Code C on the detention, treatment and questioning of suspects (updated 2013) outlines the role of the appropriate adult. The role includes more than simple observation, and encompasses advising the person being questioned, observing whether or not the interview is being conducted properly and fairly, and facilitating communication with the person being interviewed. In order to carry out this role, the social worker needs to have some understanding of police powers and procedures at the police station, including the role of the custody officer. The appropriate adult may also exercise certain rights of the individual being detained, including the right to legal advice. In most cases, therefore, both an appropriate adult and a solicitor should be present during questioning of a juvenile or a vulnerable adult. (The role of the appropriate adult in PACE interviews is considered in more detail in Chapters 13 and 18.)

Advocacy

At times it is appropriate or necessary for a child (or adult) to have the support of an advocate to speak on their behalf. The 'advocate' in this context is a skilled person, distinct from the legal advocate in court. Under existing law there is limited statutory recognition of the role and characteristics of advocacy, though the value of advocacy services is recognised in a number of official documents, e.g. Department for Education (**DfE** 2010) 'The Children Act 1989 Guidance and Regulations', vol. 3 'Planning Transition to Adulthood for Care Leavers'. In the absence of a cohesive statutory framework and allocated resources, advocacy schemes have developed piecemeal and are provided throughout the country by a number of major charities such as the Children's Society, VOICE and National Youth Advocacy Service. Providing support for children and young persons or vulnerable adults to make representations and complaints to social services about aspects of service provision is an important role for advocates. In such circumstances the role of the advocate has been described as follows:

> The role of the advocate is to ascertain the wishes and feelings of children and young people and ensure their voice is heard in all decision-making forums, both in and out of court. It also means being proactive in ensuring that children and young people receive their fair share of the resources that they may need in order to fulfil their full potential as adults and citizens of the future.[8]

The Adoption and Children Act 2002 introduced a statutory requirement to make advocacy services available for children and young people who are or wish to make a complaint. The Act amends the Children Act 1989 by introducing a new s. 26A and accompanying regulations and guidance provide further detail.[9] (See further discussion in Chapter 10.)

A further role for advocacy is envisaged by the Mental Capacity Act 2005. This legislation introduces the Independent Mental Capacity Advocate (**IMCA**), whose role is to represent and support people who are faced with a serious decision about medical treatment or accommodation; lack capacity to make the decision for themselves; and do not have any family or friends. (This role is explored further in Chapter 16.) The Independent Mental Health Advocate (**IMHA**) fulfils a similar role in mental health practice.

Working in court

Courtcraft skills

The English legal system is largely based on the adversarial model (as opposed to the inquisitorial model adopted in some other countries).[10] Under this model, evidence is tested and the court will decide on the merits of the application before it, but cannot guarantee to ascertain the 'truth'. There are some differences in approach between civil and criminal cases. Although evidence in care cases must be rigorously tested, family cases follow the paramountcy principle and are increasingly described as non-adversarial. The Court of Appeal explained in *Oxfordshire County Council* v. *M* [1994] 2 All ER 269:

> the game of adversarial litigation has no point when one is trying to deal with fragile and vulnerable people like small children. Every other consideration must come second to the need to reach the right conclusion if possible.

Increasingly, it is recognised that the outcome of a case will depend not only on the relative merits of a case, and the skills of the advocates, but also on the 'performance' of witnesses. The study and development of appropriate skills in court is known as 'courtcraft' and the following section outlines some of the steps that can be taken to prepare to give evidence for the first time, or to improve performance as a witness. Training and practice in this area is vital. Even relatively small-scale role-play exercises can help to ease some of the anxiety that is experienced by most people (including solicitors) before entering court.

Use of the word 'performance' is deliberate. One of the best ways to understand the court experience and to demystify it is to think of it as a theatre, where everyone takes a part: some know their lines better than others, some wear costumes, there are props, the proceedings run according to ritual, with intervals, and the outcome may ultimately prove to be a mystery!

The key to a good court experience is preparation. This starts long before a court hearing is anticipated. In the majority of cases, evidence will be required relating to circumstances some time before the actual hearing. It is vital, therefore, that accurate records are kept from the first referral, and are sufficiently detailed. Records should be dated and recording should take place contemporaneously with events, or as soon as possible afterwards. Relevant information about resources should also be recorded, e.g. the availability of foster carers. Always distinguish between fact and opinion. Records should also include details of notifications to other agencies, their involvement, and any information that has been shared. It is possible that some of the detail that is kept on file may not be presented to the court, because of rules of evidence. These rules vary according to the type of case, in particular depending upon whether it is a civil or criminal matter. An outline of some of the key rules of evidence is provided at the end of this chapter; however, this is an area where guidance should normally be provided by the solicitor representing the local authority.

If the file may be taken into court, it is important to be familiar with the contents so as not to become flustered when searching for a key document. Rules on disclosure of evidence, however, should mean that there are very few surprises during court hearings, and new documentary evidence will not normally be produced at such a late stage. Thorough preparation includes having knowledge, not just of personal evidence and report, if one is to be submitted to the court, but also of any other reports that the court will receive, particularly if there are areas of inconsistency.

Part of the preparation stage should include having a pre-court conference with the lawyer presenting the case, to make sure that there have been no sudden last-minute changes to the case. This may be the local authority solicitor but may also include a 'conference with counsel' if a barrister is presenting the case. The professional relationship between the lawyer presenting the case and the social worker who instructs the lawyer should be seen as another aspect of multi-disciplinary working together where communication is essential. It is vital to remember that, while a social worker is likely to have in-depth knowledge of the case, the solicitor will normally know only what he has been told by the social worker and can present the case only on that basis. Studies of the social worker/lawyer relationship have found that unclear boundaries between the two roles can be a major source of tension and the simplified delineation of roles, i.e. the lawyer advising and the social worker instructing, are difficult to maintain in practice. Dickens (2004) concluded that improved communication and understanding of respective roles is essential here as for all inter-professional relationships.

Preparation also involves being aware of the various legal options available to the court. This is particularly important now that courts have a wide range of disposal options in youth justice cases, and are not limited to granting or refusing the order applied for in family proceedings but can draw on a range of powers. An integral part of the evidence is being able to show that all relevant alternatives have been considered and that the case has been considered on an individual basis rather than within a rigid policy framework.

Moving on from pre-court preparation to the actual hearing, there are further steps that can be taken to reduce stress. These include basic points like checking up on transport arrangements, getting to court in plenty of time, finding which court the case will be heard in if the court building has more than one room, and if possible having a look inside the court and becoming familiar with the layout. The court usher will usually be helpful if approached. Before entering the courtroom, any mobile phones or pagers should be switched off. Dress may be a contentious issue, although it may be argued that it should not be necessary to compromise individual dress sense because you are in a court of law. The counter-argument is that appearance of witnesses is likely to influence the court, at least at a subconscious level, and nothing should detract from the focus of the case, i.e. your clients, the child, or the accused. Once professionals become regular court attenders, it is easy to forget that, for the individual concerned, the issue at stake may be life-changing, and it is important to show some respect for that situation. Dress should therefore be sufficiently formal to demonstrate respect for the occasion without being uncomfortable.

Once the proceedings begin, the social worker's role may be to instruct the solicitor throughout the case or it may be to appear as one of several witnesses.

Giving evidence

When a witness enters the court and is directed to the witness box, he is required to take the oath or **affirmation**, before giving oral evidence to the court. A Christian will hold the New Testament (a Jew will hold the Old Testament) and say: 'I swear by Almighty God that the evidence I shall give shall be the truth, the whole truth and nothing but the truth.' Members of other religions and sects take an oath in a manner and with such ceremony as they declare to be binding: for instance, a Hindu will hold the Gita and state, 'I swear by the Gita that the evidence …' etc.; a Moslem or follower of Islam will swear on the Koran and state, 'I swear by Allah …', etc.

Anyone who does not wish to swear an oath can affirm by saying: 'I do solemnly, sincerely and truly declare and affirm that the evidence I shall give, shall be the truth, the whole truth and nothing but the truth.' Where youths are concerned, the procedure follows that for adults except that the oath reads: 'I promise before … to tell the truth', etc. Where a child under the age of 14 gives evidence, he does so unsworn.

Taking the oath provides a useful opportunity to test voice level, take a few deep breaths and start to focus the mind. It also presents the opportunity to find a position where eye contact with the judge or magistrates is possible. Although the majority of questions will come from the solicitors or barristers, answers should be addressed to the bench or judge. Magistrates should normally be referred to as 'your worship(s)' and judges as 'your honour'. Evidence normally begins with introductions and this is an opportunity to establish expertise as a prerequisite to giving opinion evidence. The case of *F* v. *Suffolk County Council* [1981] 2 FLR 208 stated that the courts will presume that a qualified social worker is an expert for general issues of child care.

The process of giving evidence is divided into three parts. First, the solicitor representing your case conducts examination-in-chief. In many civil proceedings, where a witness statement has been submitted, the witness will simply be asked to confirm the contents of their statement, or may go straight to cross-examination. Where examination-in-chief does take place, evidence should normally be presented as a logical narrative and is the opportunity to present your arguments persuasively. Remember that in examination-in-chief the solicitor cannot ask leading questions. A leading question is one that suggests the answer. For example, 'Did you draw the conclusion that this child had been sexually abused?' would be a leading question, whereas, 'Did you draw a conclusion about this child?', followed by 'What was that conclusion?' would not. Examination-in-chief will usually follow the format and content of the witness statement. Figure 4.1 illustrates how a statement of a social worker in a child care case might be presented.

Case No. ....

In The .... Family Court
Application under Children Act 1989, Section ....
RE [*Name and date of birth of child*]
BETWEEN
.... Applicant
and
.... Respondent
STATEMENT OF EVIDENCE OF
I, ... of [professional address]
WILL SAY:

1. I am a social worker employed by the [*authority*]. I have been the social worker for [*child*] since ...... I hold the [*qualifications and outline of experience*]. I make this statement from facts within my own knowledge and also from interviews with .... and from social work records which are true to the best of my knowledge and belief.
2. [*Description of family whom the case concerns.*]
3. [*Brief outline of presenting problems, which resulted in application being made*].
4. [*History and previous involvement (if any) of family with social services or other professional services*].
5. [*Detailed account of involvement and current evidence. All relevant factual detail and important interviews. Dates and recommendations of any case conferences. If reference is made to matters told to the witness by another person, this should be clear; as should the person's name and professional capacity and circumstances in which the conversation took place*].
6. [*Professional opinions formed resulting from the facts.*]
7. [*Application of the welfare checklist of the Children Act 1989, s.1(3), providing conclusions on each point*].
8. [*Immediate and future plans for the child, including any further investigations*].

I would therefore respectfully recommend that this Honourable Court order that .....
....
I, ..., make this statement believing the contents to be true and I understand that it may be placed before the court.

Signed.........

Social Worker
Dated

Figure 4.1   Sample social worker witness statement in childcare case

In civil cases the current rules encourage advance disclosure of evidence. A strict timetable for filing evidence will be created by the court following the 'Public Law Outline' (2014). (The Public Law Outline is considered in detail in Chapter 9.)

Next comes the (often dreaded) cross-examination. At this stage the most important advice is to keep calm. The objective of the opposing advocate is to discredit and challenge evidence and elicit evidence favourable to the opposition. It is necessary to remain assertive and convincing to counter this attack. This includes being aware of body language as well as oral answers and remembering to address answers to the bench. Taking a moment to turn away from the advocate and towards the bench can provide a vital few seconds of thinking time. The advocate may ask leading questions in cross-examination, but if inappropriate questions are directed to the witness, or the advocate makes statements which the witness is not invited to challenge or comment on, it is really the role of the solicitor to object, rather than the witness. It is acceptable to request that a question be repeated or clarified if it was not heard or understood.

Thirdly, in some cases the witness may be re-examined by his own solicitor on any new points that have arisen in cross-examination. This is the final opportunity to argue the case. Finally, the magistrates or judge may also ask some questions, after which the witness is released.

The following comments from a Registered Homes Tribunal decision give an indication of the qualities to aim for as a witness. It was stated that the registration and inspection officers 'gave their evidence in clear, cogent and convincing terms without any hint of embellishment or animosity towards the **Appellants**'.[11]

Understanding some basic principles of the English legal system and the types of language which will be used (as outlined in these early chapters) can soon make the court experience seem like an extension of everyday practice. The following list outlines three steps to becoming a good witness, in terms of preparation, familiarity and role.

Preparation: know the case

Accurate recording of all events.

Good working relationship with the solicitor.

Provide sufficient copies of all relevant documents.

Basic understanding of rules of evidence.

Knowledge of the range of relevant legal options.

Familiarity: know the court

Locate venue.

Acquaint self with layout of court or tribunal.

Knowledge of procedure of court or tribunal.

Knowledge of the various roles of court personnel.

Role: know yourself

Establish expertise, qualifications and experience.

Consider appropriate behaviour of a witness.

Aim for honest, clear and accurate presentation.

Dress appropriately.

Speak slowly, allowing sufficient time for the clerk to take notes.

Address answers to the bench, not the advocate.

Be aware of the effect of body language.

Avoid any personalised comments.

Keep calm.

> **Reflect**
>
> The performance or characteristic of a witness may be described in many ways – some negative, e.g. aggressive, others positive, e.g. assertive. How can you ensure that the experience is positive and effective?

Rules of evidence

Lawyers will advise upon technical aspects of evidence. A basic understanding is an aid to the preparation of evidence and comprehending the procedures in court. There are three main types of evidence: testimony, to which most of the rules below apply; documents, including **statements of truth** (formerly called **affidavits**); and real evidence, which is produced to the court as exhibits, e.g. objects, photographs, and can include a witness's demeanour.

Admissibility

Evidence must be admissible for it to be heard by the court. Admissibility turns on relevance and is a matter of law, for the magistrates or judge – not the jury – to decide. Broadly speaking, the relevance of an issue will be dictated by the relevant statute or body of case law. For example, the Children Act 1989, s. 31 outlines the criteria upon which evidence can be given in an application for care proceedings. The evidence will be relevant if it logically helps to prove or disprove a **fact in issue**, e.g. evidence to prove or disprove whether the cause of a bruise was non-accidental. The proof may be direct or circumstantial.

Hearsay

There is a general presumption against the admissibility of hearsay evidence in criminal cases. The object of this hearsay rule is to ensure that the court hears the best, most direct evidence available. Hearsay can be explained as: 'Evidence of a fact given to the court in some way other than through the oral testimony of a witness who has first-hand knowledge of that fact, and given as evidence of the truth of that fact.'

Evidence which is given simply to prove that something was said, rather than to prove the truth of the statement, is accepted as an exception to the hearsay rule. This is important, as a social worker may frequently want to report to the court statements made by a service user or child without claiming that the statement is necessarily true. There are other significant exceptions to the rule against hearsay, which have been introduced by statute, e.g. under the Children (Admissibility of Hearsay Evidence) Order 1991.[12] Hearsay evidence is now generally admissible in civil cases. Even where hearsay evidence is admissible, corroboration is likely to be required, and the witness is likely to be cross-examined as to the source and reliability of the hearsay evidence, with a view to undermining the evidence. There has also been some relaxation of the rule against hearsay in criminal proceedings under the Criminal Justice Act 2003.

A case concerning admissibility of hearsay evidence serves to remind us of the significance of the distinction between civil and criminal matters: *Clingham* v. *Kensington and Chelsea Royal London Borough Council* [2001] EWHC Admin 1. The application, in civil proceedings, was for an anti-social behaviour order under s. 1 of the Crime and Disorder Act 1998. The evidence in question consisted of evidence of police officers that would refer to information received from other officers and allegations of anti-social behaviour from members of the public who were too frightened to give evidence or could not be identified. The High Court ruled that the evidence was hearsay but in a civil case it was admissible, though the court would consider what weight to attach to it depending on the full circumstances of the case. The defendants' argument that proceedings for an anti-social behaviour order were akin to criminal proceedings, and therefore criminal rules of evidence should be followed, did not succeed. Nor did the argument that, as some of the evidence was hearsay without the possibility of cross-examination, the trial was not fair as required by Art. 6(1) of the ECHR.

Opinion

Traditionally, as the courts seek facts, there is a preference against opinion evidence. In some cases, however, opinion evidence can be crucial to the outcome and is effectively required by statute, e.g. evidence as to whether a child is 'likely to suffer significant harm' (Children Act 1989, s. 31). In order for opinion evidence to be accepted by the court, it is necessary for the witness to be an expert in the fields about which the opinion is proffered. As a preliminary, therefore, it is necessary to establish the expertise of the witness.

Expert opinion evidence should contain information that goes beyond a level of general understanding which might be expected of a lay person. Expert evidence may need to be defended on the basis of relevant experience and research, and cross-examination on opinion should be anticipated. A social worker will frequently be in the position of an expert witness. Reference to relevant research and theory to support the stance taken in a case is therefore important and care should be taken not to express opinions beyond what can reasonably be supported. As an example, in the following paragraph from *LBL* v. *RYJ, VJ* [2010] EWHC 2665 (COP), a case concerning assessment of capacity of a young woman, Judge Macur describes the social worker who gave evidence:

> I regard that Mr Sinclair is entitled to be recognised as an expert witness in this case. He has been so 'recognized' in these cases as such for over eight years. He has worked as a social worker since 1978 (as 'forensic social work manager' between 1988 and 1998 in a secure unit) and has a good knowledge of the provisions of the Mental Capacity Act. He has practical experience of working with personality disordered patients and clients and is well informed on national resources and developments. He has organised several national conferences on The Management of Personality Disorder as well as teaching and publishing of several articles in this subject. He is regularly instructed to work on behalf of the Official Solicitor and practises as an independent social worker. He has acted in cases concerning children where 'adolescent issues' are the subject of investigation.

(The role of social work and other experts in child care cases is considered in Chapter 9.)

Corroboration

Corroborating evidence is that which backs up evidence already provided. There used to be rules that required a judge to give the jury a 'corroboration warning' in respect of certain classes of witnesses, including complainants in sexual cases, but this has now been abolished.[13] A judge may still give a warning to the jury about accepting a particular piece of evidence, e.g. in *R* v. *Spencer* [1987] AC 128, a case involving the prosecution of members of staff in Rampton Special Hospital for alleged abuse of patients. The jury was warned of the danger of convicting on the unsupported evidence of special hospital patients who, in the words of the court, were of bad character, mentally unstable and may have a common grudge against staff.

The judge has a more general discretion to give a warning in any case where it appears the witness has 'a purpose of his own' to serve. Also, in criminal cases the Criminal Justice and Public Order Act 1994 allows the jury to draw an adverse inference from the accused's failure to answer questions in the police station or failure to give evidence. (This is sometimes incorrectly referred to as abolition of the right to silence.)

Competence

Competence depends on a witness being able to understand the duty to tell the truth and also the extra obligation and sanction involved in the oath or affirmation. Witnesses are generally both **competent** and **compellable**, meaning that they must give evidence, though it may be necessary to secure attendance by a witness summons. Under s. 80 of the Police and Criminal Evidence Act 1984, the spouse of the accused is now competent and compellable to give evidence in respect of an assault or sexual offence committed against her or a child. This provision was introduced due to concerns that women who had suffered domestic violence were frequently reluctant to give evidence against their assailant.

Evidence of children and vulnerable adults

In civil and criminal cases, children (under the age of 14) give evidence unsworn. There are special provisions for children and vulnerable adults to give evidence behind screens or using video link. Videotapes of evidence can be provided for the court. A social worker will often be in the position of supporting children and vulnerable adults who give evidence – and their families – and should be prepared for a range of possible outcomes, including withdrawal of a case by the CPS. (Relevant provisions of the Youth Justice and Criminal Evidence Act 1999 are discussed in more detail in Chapters 13 and 18.)

Relationship with lawyers

The importance of establishing good working relationships with a range of other professionals is now well established. The Children Act 2004, 'Working Together to Safeguard Children' (2013), 'No Secrets: Guidance on developing and implementing multi-agency policies and procedures to protect vulnerable adults from abuse' (2000), and the Crime and Disorder Act 1998 formally recognise this principle. Although sometimes on the periphery of this network, it is important for social workers to establish good working relations with lawyers for the cases that ultimately reach court, but also for the provision of legal advice on a regular basis. Early contact between social workers and solicitors can lead to better final outcomes in the legal process.

In order to build good working relations it is important to be clear about the parameters of the respective roles as solicitor and social worker. In essence, social workers decide whether to become involved in a case and then instruct a solicitor; the solicitor then gives advice and represents the authority in court. A good working relationship will be more flexible than this strict demarcation suggests and will operate along the lines of partnership and cooperation. Sometimes, the solicitor will instruct a barrister for the court hearing. The solicitor will then liaise with the barrister and retain responsibility for day-to-day management of the case and provision of information and materials to the barrister.

What are the barriers that may prevent a good working relationship? A practical barrier comes in the form of contractual arrangements in some authorities, which mean that social workers have less direct access to lawyers, and may have to obtain permission from managers to seek legal advice that the department will subsequently be charged for. Beyond that, some preconceptions held by both professions may militate against effective partnership. Solicitors may be perceived as entrenched in the adversarial tradition and focused on winning cases at all costs, an approach that might not be appropriate in, e.g., child care cases. On the other hand, social workers might be perceived as idealistic and unrealistic about what lawyers can actually achieve within the limits of the law – a quick fix is not always possible. Such preconceptions may actually be rooted in a tension between the values of solicitors and social workers, and concern that some actions of social workers are subject to legal scrutiny. The way forward can include joint training initiatives, formation of multi-disciplinary interest groups, dissemination of information, e.g. legal fact sheets providing summaries of case law developments. In terms of managing individual cases, it is useful to spend time at the initial point of contact demarcating tasks and respective responsibilities.

Social work and the law share certain features because of the professional nature of both jobs. The Royal Commission on Legal Services identified five characteristics of a profession: it has a governing body; it has a specialised field of knowledge acquired by training and experience; admission to the profession is dependent on a period of training, and competence is tested; there is an element of self-regulation; there is a professional ethic.

Lawyers and social workers actually share many skills. Building on common ground can make the task of working together less daunting. Awareness of role boundaries also lays the foundations for establishing constructive ways for solicitors and social workers to work together.[14]

> ### Reflect
>
> Think about the respective roles of lawyer and social worker. Can you identify shared skills, within the different roles?

Challenging social work practice

Invariably there will be situations where aspects of social work decisions (not confined to decisions relating to court processes) will be challenged. As the social worker is normally employed as an agent of the Social Services Authority, whether or not the decision has been taken with the support of legal advice, a decision will be viewed as a decision of the agency. Whilst it is convenient to talk in terms of a decision, what is in fact being challenged may be a course of conduct over a particular case. It is not generally possible for any person to complain in the abstract about the actions of a Social Services Authority; they must normally be personally affected and/or have a personal interest in the case. That stance is certainly supported by the victim test under the Human Rights Act 1998. Other limitations are considered under each avenue for challenge.

Seven potential avenues for challenging social work decisions exist:

- local authority's complaints procedure;
- complaints to the local government ombudsman;
- default power of the Secretary of State;
- judicial review;
- local authority monitoring officer;
- action for damages;
- complaints under the Human Rights Act 1998.

Local authority's complaints procedure

Complaints procedures in relation to both adult services and childcare cases had their foundation in the Local Authority Social Services Act 1970, s. 7B, with specific directions covering the detail of the complaints procedure.[15]

The principal features of the procedures are that: to make a complaint or representation a person must be a qualifying individual; the complaints procedure has an independent element; and there are three stages to the process – the informal stage, the formal stage and the review stage.[16]

Informal stage

A person is a qualifying individual if social services have a power or a duty to provide a service to him/her, and the need for that service is known by the department. The person may already be in receipt of services. When a representation is received from a qualifying individual, the department should first attempt to resolve it informally, acting swiftly in response to representations that may simply be oral at this stage. This informal stage must not be used to dissuade an individual from making a formal complaint. The person can ask to go direct to the formal stage, omitting the informal stage.

Formal stage

If the complaint is not resolved at the informal stage, the Social Services Department must give the complainant an explanation of the formal and review stages of the complaints procedure and invite him/her to make written representations. It is good practice also to offer assistance and guidance on the use of the procedure, and appropriate accessible materials should be available, e.g. leaflets written for people whose first language is not English. All written representations received by the department must be registered. The local authority should consider the complaint and reply within 28 days if possible. If it is not possible to reply within 28 days, an explanation for the delay should be given. After consideration of the complaint the complainant should be notified in writing of the decision.

Review stage

If not satisfied with the decision at the formal stage, the complainant can request a review by a panel. This request should be made within 28 days of notification of the outcome of the formal stage. The panel should then meet within 28 days of receipt of the request to hear the complaint. The panel consists of three people, and at least one must be an independent person, neither a member nor an employee of the authority. The complainant is entitled to make written and oral submissions to the panel and may be accompanied by a person who is able to speak on their behalf, e.g. an advocate or friend rather than formal legal representation. The meeting should be conducted as an informal hearing. The panel can make a recommendation to the local authority, which should be recorded in writing within 24 hours of the hearing. Due to the involvement of an independent person, the panel are not able to make decisions which are binding on the local authority; nevertheless, the local authority must have regard to the panel's recommendations and should depart from them only if there are very good reasons for doing so. The independence of panels and their compliance with Art. 6(1) ECHR was questioned in *R (Beeson)* v. *Dorset CC* [2002] EWCA Civ 1812. The court held that the procedure does not breach Art. 6 because of the availability of recourse to judicial review and, taken together, the panel with the addition of judicial review provides the necessary fairness.

From the time limits outlined, it is clear that from first making the complaint, the process will take a minimum of three months, assuming there is no informal stage. Practice suggests that in fact considerably longer delays are commonplace. There is also the risk that, even if the outcome of the review panel is in the complainant's favour, the local authority is not bound to follow it. Not surprisingly, some complainants may wish to take their complaint a stage further and may explore the additional options below.

The **local government ombudsman** (**LGO**) effectively provides a second tier body to consider any complaints which are unresolved. A person making a complaint must be notified of their right to complain to the LGO.

The Children's Commissioners for Wales and for England may also have a role in examining some cases and monitoring arrangements for complaints. (The Commissioners' roles are discussed in more detail as part of the discussion on children's rights in Chapter 7.)

Local government ombudsman

Also known as the Commissioner for Local Administration, the local government ombudsman can investigate a complaint against a local authority where there has been maladministration, which causes an injustice to the complainant.[17] There are three local government ombudsmen in England dealing with complaints from different parts of the country. Maladministration for these purposes includes: unreasonable delay; bias; disregard of procedures; and incompetence. The complaint should normally have arisen no more than 12 months before the LGO is contacted. In practice, because the ombudsman will normally expect a complaint to have been considered first by the complaints procedure outlined above, this time may be exceeded. The remit of the local government ombudsman has been extended with the introduction of new powers to investigate complaints relating to providers of self funded care. The effect of this development is to introduce consistency between adults who purchase their own care, with an individual budget, direct payments or their own money, with adults whose care has been directly arranged and funded by the local authority, who have had access to this independent complaints service for many years.

A significant number of investigations by the LGO have concerned delays in processing assessments for services. *Investigation into Complaint No. 97/A/2959 against Hackney London Borough Council* (1998) CCLR 66 provides a useful illustration. The case concerned two brothers aged 41 and 39, both with learning difficulties. They had been attending a day centre for about ten years. In 1995, Hackney transferred management of the centre to a charity as part of reorganisation of services for people with learning difficulties and reorganisation of the community care division. The transfer took place on the understanding that Hackney and the charity would reassess the needs of all users of the centre within six months. Despite reminders from the charity and Edward and Robert's parents, Mr and Mrs Foster, the assessment did not commence until 1997. Mrs Foster lodged a complaint, which was upheld in January 1997 by the Social Services Complaints Review Panel concluding that Hackney had been negligent and recommending that the reassessment be carried out within three months. The Director of Social Services wrote explaining that the cause of the delay was lack of resources. By November 1998 Hackney had still not completed risk assessments or a care plan for Edward or Robert.

The local government ombudsman reached the following conclusions:

1. The delay in carrying out reassessments (about 22 months) amounted to maladministration.

2. Hackney had still not completed a risk assessment at the time of the investigation; record keeping was poor, as were communications with Mr and Mrs Foster, to whom they had failed to explain the nature and purpose of the reassessment. These faults all amounted to maladministration.

3. Injustice had been caused by the maladministration. In particular, Mr and Mrs Foster had suffered anxiety and had been put to considerable time and trouble. Also, Edward and Robert had missed the opportunity of benefiting from earlier provision based on proper assessment.

It was recommended that Hackney should pay £1,500 compensation to Mr and Mrs Foster. Of general application, it was recommended that Hackney should review the needs of other people using the day centre; review provision of written information about the community care assessment process; review supervision arrangements for care managers; and implement a system to ensure that recommendations of review panels are implemented without unreasonable delay. As ombudsman decisions are often reported by the media, the 'embarrassment' factor for local authorities may have a greater impact than the relatively low compensation levels. This case provides a clear example of the damaging effect of delay relating to service provision for vulnerable adults. The full report is particularly interesting to read for the insight it gives into the extent and process of the detailed investigation carried out by the LGO.

A further LGO decision concerned services for children. In *Rochdale Metropolitan Borough Council* (03/C/18598) (2005) Mr Elliott complained that the council failed to advise him of the implications of him taking care of a young child, 'Harry', who was not related to him but who was half-brother to his own children. He complained that: he was given no financial or other support during the first 15 months he cared for Harry; the financial implications of seeking a residence order were not explained; alternatives to that residence order were not discussed with him; the council failed to provide the continuing support he needed to care properly for Harry; the council excluded him from meetings held to discuss Harry's future; and the council did not deal with his complaints properly.

The LGO found that the council had left a 17-month-old baby with Mr Elliott without undertaking even the most cursory of checks upon either him or his ability to care for a young child. For the following 12 months, largely unsupported by the council, Mr Elliott made legal decisions about Harry which he was simply not entitled to make. The ombudsman concluded that Mr Elliott was either not advised at all or advised badly concerning the options available to him. The LGO found that only when Mr Elliott complained to the council that he could no longer care for Harry was it discovered that he had, all along, been entitled to receive some financial support from the council. The LGO found that the council failed to interpret letters from Mr Elliott as formal complaints.

Mr Elliott obtained a residence order for Harry but, had he been accepted as a foster parent, he would have received a great deal more in terms of financial and general support. Fortunately for Harry, Mr Elliott proved to be an appropriate carer who had done an excellent job in looking after him.

The ombudsman found maladministration causing injustice to Mr Elliott. The council agreed to apologise to Mr Elliott and to pay him £8,000. This represented compensation plus the additional monies Mr Elliott would have received if he had been treated as a family and friends carer.

Complaints to the LGO should be made in writing and the ombudsman has a power to require access to relevant information held by the local authority. The complaint is sent to the council's Chief Executive for consideration and response. The LGO will prepare a report and can make recommendations, including compensation awards, and, whilst the local authority is not strictly bound to follow these recommendations, in practice they usually do. Advantages of complaining to the ombudsman include that the process is free, there is a possibility of informal settlement, compensation may result and the investigation is independent.

Maladministration complaints in respect of the National Health Service, including social work in hospital settings, are dealt with by the Parliamentary and Health Service Ombudsman.

Default power of the Secretary of State

The Local Authority Social Services Act (LASSA) 1970, s. 7C authorises the Secretary of State to hold an inquiry into the exercise of social services functions by a local authority (excluding duties under the Children Act 1989). The default power is limited to statutory duties and does not extend to the exercise of discretionary powers. As yet, the Secretary of State has not exercised this default power. The type of situation where it might arise would be where a local authority completely failed to provide a statutory service, or did not have a complaints procedure, or disregarded a direction. In those cases, under LASSA 1970, s. 7D, the Secretary of State could declare that the local authority is in default of its social services functions and order the authority to comply with those duties within a specified timescale.

Judicial review

Judicial review is a legal process that allows the High Court to exercise a supervisory role over the decision-making of public bodies. It is a public law remedy. Judicial review cases are focused on the process of decision-making rather than the merit of the ultimate decision. Judicial review has proved to be a useful tool for checking the actions of local authorities, as illustrated by a series of cases that related to the relevance of resources of a local authority when carrying out community care assessments. Some of the advantages of using judicial review to challenge decisions are that groups and organisations can bring cases or support individuals to bring a case provided they have a sufficient interest in the matter, and that leave is required to bring an action but, once obtained, early settlement is common. For an individual applicant 'sufficient interest' in this context would include the service user affected by the decision as well as carers. An obvious disadvantage to judicial review is expense if the complainant does not qualify for legal assistance. Proceedings are generally lengthy, though it is sometimes possible to deal with cases on an urgency basis and also to make interim injunctions prior to the final hearing. In addition, it is normally necessary first to have exhausted alternative remedies, including the local authority complaints procedure, and there are fairly strict time limits for bringing an action (within three months of the action complained of). Permission is required from the High Court before a claim for judicial review can proceed. In *R (Bhatti)* v. *Bury MBC* [2013]EWHC 3093 (Admin), the court refused to hear a claim disputing service provision and confirmed that in matters of factual dispute the complaints procedure should be used and not judicial review. (Judicial review is discussed further in Chapter 2.)

Monitoring officer

Local authorities must appoint a monitoring officer under s. 5 of the Local Government and Housing Act 1989. The officer must report to the authority any matters, including proposals, decisions or omissions, where the local authority has or is likely to contravene the law or a code of practice; or concerning any maladministration or injustice that could be investigated by the local government ombudsman. This can present a useful opportunity for a local authority to put matters in order before a complaint progresses, perhaps to a judicial review.

Action for damages

The essential legal element of professionalism is the requirement to exercise a duty of care. This is a concept drawn from negligence and if complied with, generally provides protection from liability. Case law explains the standard of the duty with reference to a professional peer group. In *ABB, BBB, CBB, DBB* v. *Milton Keynes Council* [2011] EWHC 2754 (QB) four individuals brought a claim against the local authority who were alleged to have failed to protect them from abuse as children. The case confirmed the principle established in *JD and others* v. *East Berkshire Community Health* [2003] EWCA Civ 1151, that a duty of care is owed by social workers in local authority employment, stating further:

> A social worker's duty in common with other professionals is to exercise reasonable skill and care and the test in Bolam....applies. Accordingly a social worker will not be negligent if she acts in accordance with practice accepted at the time as proper, by a responsible body of social work opinion, even though another social worker might adopt a different practice. (para 27)

As society becomes increasingly litigious, there will be circumstances when a service user decides that they are unhappy about a service or the actions of a social worker and wants to sue. In such circumstances, what is the position concerning liability? In the majority of cases where professional actions are challenged, the basis of the challenge is in negligence. An alternative route, less often relied upon, is breach of contract. The tort of negligence has three elements that must be satisfied before an action will succeed:

1. a duty of care was owed;
2. there was a breach of that duty; and
3. damage resulted as a consequence of the breach.

The first question to be addressed, then, is whether a social worker owes a duty of care to a client. A famous case, *Donoghue* v. *Stevenson* [1932] AC 562, established the principle that a general duty of care is owed to your neighbour, i.e. to any person closely affected by your conduct, and whom you should reasonably foresee might be injured by it. It is also established that if a person is considered to be a professional or expert, this duty or standard will be applied more rigorously. Vicarious liability is the principle whereby employers will be held responsible for the actions of their employees, provided they were acting in the course of their employment and not 'on a frolic of their own'.[18] For social workers it is also relevant to note that social work functions are vested in the authority rather than the individual who works as an agent of the authority. Effectively, then, an aggrieved individual will bring an action in negligence against the authority rather than the individual social worker. Certain bodies have traditionally been protected from negligence claims by 'public interest immunity', i.e. the principle that it would not be in the public interest for actions of the body to be subject to challenge because of the impact this would have on the work of the body.

A series of cases have produced contrasting decisions concerning local authority liability in tort but appear to signal a gradual erosion of the public interest immunity enjoyed by social workers (Preston-Shoot *et al.*, 2001).[19]

X (Minors) v. *Bedfordshire County Council* [1995] 3 All ER 353: the court found the authority was immune from a claim in negligence on the basis that 'general policy decisions' are not justiciable and cannot provide a basis for civil liability in negligence.

Osman v. *United Kingdom* (1998) 5 BHRC 293: the practice of English courts deciding that as a matter of law it would not be fair, just and reasonable to impose liability in particular types of cases was declared to be in breach of Art. 6, the right to a fair trial, as it precludes an individual from having the balance struck between their hardship and the public interest on the facts of the particular case. This case concerned the claim that the police owed no duty of care to the public at risk from criminal threats known to the police.

Barrett v. *Enfield London Borough Council* [1999] 3 All ER 193: this case effectively narrowed the basis for striking out claims against a local authority. Barrett brought an application alleging that Enfield LBC had looked after him negligently whilst he was in care. He based this claim specifically on the fact that he had been moved to six different residential homes, he had been fostered twice without any plans for adoption being made, he had not been provided with properly trained social workers or appropriate psychiatric advice, and proper arrangements had not been made to reunite him with his mother. The authority's application to strike out the proceedings failed. It was decided that it was not appropriate to strike out proceedings unless it was possible to give a certain answer to the question of whether the action would succeed and this was increasingly difficult to do in the developing area of negligence law. A local authority is unlikely to be found negligent for injury caused in the exercise of their statutory discretionary powers where their exercise was not wholly unreasonable or involved balancing of competing interests. The question should, however, be decided in the light of individual facts and the extent to which actions were of an operational rather than a policy nature. In practice it is not always easy to distinguish between policy and operational matters, as each one affects the other.

Phelps v. *Hillingdon London Borough Council* [1999] 1 All ER 421, CA; [2001] 2 AC 619, HL: this case signalled a significant change in approach. In an education setting, it was held that a local education authority can be liable in negligence for incompetent education, directly if it employs obviously incompetent staff, or vicariously for incompetent acts or omissions by education professionals, unless, exceptionally, it is able to establish that recognising liability would so interfere with the performance of its duties that it would be wrong to do so. The facts of the case included the failure of an educational psychologist to identify that a child was suffering from dyslexia.

W and others v. *Essex County Council and another* [2000] 2 All ER 237: claims were made by foster parents on behalf of their children, who were sexually abused by a foster child placed with them by the local authority. They claimed that the authority and their social worker knew that the boy was an abuser and had withheld that information. The court found that it was fair, just and reasonable to impose a duty of care in the circumstances.

S v. *Gloucestershire County Council; L* v. *Tower Hamlets London Borough Council* (2000) 3 CCLR 294, CA: actions in negligence were brought against the local authorities. The substance of each claim was that, when they were living in foster care as children, the foster father had sexually abused them and, in consequence, they had suffered physical and long-term psychological damage. The hearing of this case was delayed until the House of Lords gave its decision in *Barrett* v. *Enfield London Borough Council* [1999] 3 All ER 193.

The European Court of Human Rights has also played a part in this developing line of case law. The *Bedfordshire* case reached the European Court as *Z* v. *United Kingdom* (Application 29392/95) (2001) 34 EHRR 97. The House of Lords had struck out the negligence claims against the local authority. The European Court held unanimously that the United Kingdom had breached Art. 3, the right not to be subjected to inhuman or degrading treatment, by failing to protect the children from long-term abuse and neglect. The court further decided that the fact that a person, especially a child as in this case, was not able to pursue a remedy in damages against the local authority meant the United Kingdom also breached Art. 13. The children were not afforded an effective means of redress for their treatment by the council. The court awarded damages and costs. Further, in *E* v. *United Kingdom* (Application No. 33218/96) [2003] 1 FLR 348, four applicants complained that the local authority had failed to adequately protect them from physical and sexual abuse by their mother's partner over several years, and were awarded compensation.

In contrast, the courts have ruled that in relation to investigation of child abuse, no duty of care is owed to parents. Thus, in *D* v. *East Berkshire Community NHS Trust; K* v. *Dewsbury Healthcare NHS Trust; K* v. *Oldham NHS Trust* [2003] EWCA Civ 1151, claims by parents who had been the subject of unfounded accusations were not allowed. In childcare cases the interests of the child and the parents were in potential conflict, priority had to be given to the duty to investigate and no duty should be owed to parents. Also, in *D* v. *Bury Metropolitan Borough Council* [2006] EWCA Civ 1, the Court of Appeal confirmed that a local authority did not owe a duty of care to parents in the conduct of care proceedings in respect of their child, and the fact that an interim care order was conducted by agreement did not mean that a duty had arisen. An interim care order was obtained in respect of a 4-month-old baby who sustained fractured ribs thought to have been caused by non-accidental injury. The local authority then found that the child had brittle bone disease and he was returned to his parents and the care proceedings were discharged. The parents' claim for psychological harm caused by the alleged negligence of the authority was rejected.

Lawrence v. *Pembrokeshire County Council* [2007] EWCA Civ 446 confirmed the earlier decision of the House of Lords in the *East Berkshire* case, that a duty of care is not owed to parents of children who are the subject of child protection investigation. To impose such a duty in negligence could undermine effective protection of children, though an incompetent investigation could be subject to challenge under Art. 8. This line of reasoning has been subsequently followed in *RK and AK* v. *United Kingdom* [2009] 1 FLR 274.

Analysis of the above decisions suggests that it can no longer be said that local authorities enjoy an absolute immunity from liability in negligence. It probably remains easier to establish liability at operational level than policy level. In future, even if it is not possible to bring a claim in negligence against the local authority, the option remains of pursuing a claim under the Human Rights Act 1998.

Human Rights Act 1998

Provisions under the Human Rights Act 1998 (s. 7) allow victims to bring an action against a local authority if it has acted in a way which is incompatible with the terms of the Articles of the European Convention on Human Rights. (Some illustrations of this have been discussed above and Chapter 5 provides more detail on the new right of action against public authorities, including local authorities.)

Employer's duty of care to staff

As employers, local authorities owe a duty of care to their staff and may be required to pay compensation if found to be negligent. This was argued in *Colclough* v. *Staffordshire County Council* [1994] CLY 2283, where a social worker suffered injury trying to lift a 15-stone service user who had fallen out of bed. She had not received any training or information about manual handling. Similarly, in *Harvey* v. *Northumberland County Council* [2003] All ER (D) 347 (Feb), the council was found liable to its employee, a residential social worker in secure accommodation, for failing to train him in restraint techniques.

Stress-related injury has also been the subject of negligence claims. In *Walker v Northumberland County Council* [1995] 1 All ER 737, a social worker returned to work after suffering a nervous breakdown. He had been a team leader dealing with child protection cases. On his return it was foreseeable that, without further support, he could suffer a further breakdown. Appropriate support was not provided and, following a second breakdown, he took early retirement. The local authority, his employer, were found to be in breach of their duty of care and paid damages. Clearly for damages to be paid there must be foreseeable damage and the authority would be expected to take reasonable steps so as not to breach their duty. Where an authority does not respond once it is aware that an employee is suffering stress, it could be liable in negligence as above and might also have obligations under the Management of Health and Safety at Work Regulations 1999.[20]

Whistleblowing

Whistleblowing may be defined as: 'The disclosure by an employee (or professional) of confidential information which relates to some danger, fraud, or other illegal or unethical conduct connected with the workplace, be it of the employer or of his fellow employees.'[21]

In the context of social work practice, whistleblowing can in some circumstances be an appropriate response to concerns about bad practice and is a legitimate aspect of the social work role. This is recognised in the BASW Code of Ethics section, 'Being prepared to whistle-blow' which states:

> Social workers should be prepared to report bad practice using all available channels including complaints procedures and if necessary use public interest disclosure legislation and whistleblowing guidelines.

A feature of a number of inquiry reports such as Longcare (1998)[22] and the Waterhouse Report (2000)[23] has been the acknowledgement that abuse can go on undetected by outside agencies for a considerable period of time. Yet abuse cannot remain hidden from the people employed in or concerned with such establishments. Lack of employment and other protection for whistleblowers and their fear of recrimination may be partly to blame for those people not coming forward, or perhaps why, if concerns were raised, it was possible to ignore or suppress them. The Public Interest Disclosure Act 1998 amends the Employment Rights Act 1996 (**ERA** 1996) and will protect workers who disclose certain information in the public interest from being dismissed or penalised in other ways by their employer.

The advantages of responsible whistleblowing are not limited to the immediate concern of the whistleblower. Whistleblowing can cultivate an open culture in the workplace, in which constructive criticism and suggestions for improving standards will be listened to with a welcome ear. Abuse inquiries provide some of the clearest examples of why whistle-blowing is important. Speaking out about bad practice and abuse can prevent further suffering and may even be lifesaving. It can challenge environments which actually foster bad practice, notably at Winterbourne View Hospital,[24] promote proper lines of accountability, protect and enhance professional reputations by weeding out influential individuals such as Frank Beck in the Leicestershire child abuse scandal,[25] and lead to recommendations for improvements in practice which are of general application across the field. One of the recommendations of the Waterhouse report was that: 'Every local authority should establish and implement conscientiously clear whistle-blowing procedures enabling members of staff to make complaints and raise matters of concern affecting the treatment or welfare of looked after children without threats or fear of reprisals in any form' (Recommendation 8).

These advantages may not be sufficient, however, to encourage an isolated worker to make a disclosure. The most obvious deterrent is fear of the reaction of the employer and possible sanctions, which might include victimisation or dismissal. An incident which causes concern to one worker may not be viewed collectively as a clear example of bad practice. Confusion about appropriate standards may act as a further deterrent and may be particularly influential where a senior member of staff advises a newly qualified professional that this is the way things are done 'in the real world'! Clear national standards could assist here. Peer group pressure may prevent a worker from speaking out against a colleague, as may fear of reprisals from work colleagues, e.g. being 'sent to Coventry'. Junior or less qualified staff may not have the confidence to complain about the practice of those who are more senior in the workplace hierarchy. This can be further exacerbated if there is a fear that management will not listen to or respond to concerns. The existence of complaints procedures will often assist a worker who wishes to raise a concern; however, if the procedure is unnecessarily complex, this may equally act as a further deterrent.

The Employment Rights Act 1996, as amended by the Public Interest Disclosure Act 1998, sets out a framework in which Ells and Dehn[26] suggest responsible whistleblowing is possible by:

- Reassuring workers that silence is not the only safe option.
- Providing strong protection for workers who raise concerns internally.
- Reinforcing and protecting the right to report concerns to key regulators.
- Protecting more public disclosures, provided there is a valid reason for going wider and that the particular disclosure is reasonable.
- Helping to ensure that organisations respond by addressing the message rather than the messenger and resist the temptation to cover up serious malpractice.

It is a requirement under ERA 1996 that, to qualify for protection, the worker making a qualifying disclosure must reasonably believe the truth of the information and that disclosure is in the public interest. This requirement is clearly designed to deter malicious and false allegations. In *Street* v. *Derbyshire Unemployed Workers' Centre* [2004] EWCA Civ 964, the Court of

Appeal dismissed a claim where there was evidence of personal antagonism. For a statement to be made in good faith requires that the predominant motivation for making the report is public interest. A qualifying disclosure is one relating to one or more of the following categories:

- a criminal offence;
- failure to comply with a legal obligation;
- a miscarriage of justice;
- danger to the health and safety of any individual;
- damage to the environment; or
- deliberate concealment of information that would show any of the previous categories.[27]

These categories would include most, if not all, malpractice within the social sector.

Wider disclosures will be protected if there is a specific reason for the whistleblower to go wider, e.g. the whistleblower believes evidence would be concealed or destroyed, or where the worker has previously made a disclosure to his employer, which is substantially the same, and no action resulted. To be protected it must be reasonable for the disclosure to be made in the way it is made and factors determining reasonableness will include the serious-ness of the issue, to whom the disclosure is made, whether the failure disclosed is likely to continue and whether it is in breach of any duty of confidentiality owed by the employee. Disclosures to the press are unlikely to be encouraged.

Section 43J of ERA 1996 presents an important development in employment rights. It makes void any provision in an agreement that purports to prevent a worker from making a protected disclosure. In other words, 'gagging clauses' are made illegal.

If a worker who has made a disclosure does suffer any detriment by his employer, there is a right of complaint to the Employment Tribunal and compensation is payable. Detriment includes acts and omissions, and examples of behaviour could include disciplinary proceed-ings, suspension, and denial of promotion, salary increases or other benefits normally en-joyed. Where a worker is dismissed or selected for redundancy because he made a protected disclosure, this will be treated as an unfair dismissal.

A limitation of ERA 1996 is that employers are not obliged to introduce whistleblowing procedures; nor is there likely to be a great deal of consistency in the procedures that do exist. It is worthy of note that most Social Services Departments already have whistleblow-ing procedures in place. Legally, workers are under no obligation to raise concerns or draw attention to areas of malpractice, though professional codes of practice may encourage sen-sible whistleblowing. Ultimately, the legislation will have made a most significant impact if it can promote more open cultures in which whistleblowing is positively encouraged as a way of improving practice.

Record keeping

Accurate record keeping has always been an essential aspect of good social work practice and is vital in cases which reach court. The BASW Code of Ethics (2012) includes this section on maintaining clear and accurate records:

> Social workers should maintain clear, impartial and accurate records and provision of evi-dence to support professional judgements. They should record only relevant matters and specify the source of information.

In relation to statements for court proceedings it is essential that they are based on contemporaneous records, not recollections made some months later. In the case of *Surrey County Council* v. *M and Others* [2013] EWHC 2400 (fam), witnesses when confronted with the contemporaneous records repeatedly had to revise the contents of their written statements.

Recent years have seen the development of much greater rights of access by the individual to official records. Absolute confidentiality of records is unlikely to be guaranteed. The relevant law on access to records is contained in the Data Protection Act 1998 and Freedom of Information Act 2000.

Data Protection Act 1998

The Data Protection Act 1998 (**DPA** 1998) came into force on 1 March 2000. In effect it provides individuals with new rights of access to their personal data and imposes new obligations on data controllers, such as local authority social services departments, to operate good data protection practices. The general principle is that people are entitled to access information held about themselves (subject to a few exceptions). The DPA 1998 applies to both electronic and manual records. There is accompanying guidance to the Act.[28] The scheme of the legislation is contained in eight basic principles, which define how personal data can be managed. The language of DPA 1998 is rather technical, and explanation of some of the key terms is necessary before consideration of the principles.

Personal data

The term 'personal data' includes any information held either manually or electronically, which relates to a living individual and from which it is possible to identify that individual.[29] Personal data may include, e.g., National Insurance numbers or expressions of opinion about an individual. The individual is referred to as the data subject.

Data controller

The data controller is the body that manages the purposes for which information is processed. For example, the HCPC will be the data controller for the social work profession register established under the Care Standards Act 2000.

Processing

The term 'processing' covers a wide range of activities or action involving personal data. It would include opening and reading a file about an individual, collecting, storing, destroying or altering personal information.

Exempt information

There are some important categories of exempt information to which the principle of access to personal information does not apply. Exemptions include information required for the purpose of safeguarding national security; personal data processed for the prevention or detection of crime, the apprehension or prosecution of offenders or the assessment or collection of any tax where disclosure would be prejudicial; references (except where access is given by the person who holds the reference and the author is not identified); information which is likely to cause serious harm to the physical or mental health or condition of the data subject or any other person; and personal information about someone else.

For example, in *Roberts* v. *Nottinghamshire Healthcare NHS Trust* [2008] EWHC 1934 (QB), a **restricted patient** detained at Rampton Hospital made a request to access a psychology report about himself. This was denied on the ground that it would be 'likely to cause serious harm to the physical or mental health of the data subject' (Art. 5, Data Protection (Subject Access Modification) (Health) Order 2000). In supporting the refusal, the court noted that a refusal to disclose must be 'necessary and proportionate' and commented:

> The question is whether there may very well be a risk of harm to health even if the risk falls short of being more probably than not. Harm to health could arise in various ways. In the context of mental health, it could be self harm or harm to others. The issue demands a factual inquiry: taking all matters into account such as the personality of the applicant, his past history, the care regime to which he is subject and so on, might there very well be a risk of harm to health on release of the data?

Data protection principles

1. *Personal data shall be processed fairly and lawfully.* To comply with this provision, it is important that when information is obtained from an individual, the purpose for which that information is required is made clear. Before processing information, at least one of the following conditions should apply: the consent of the data subject has been obtained; processing is necessary under contract, law or for another legal obligation (e.g. an employee providing personal information to HM Revenue and Customs); processing is necessary to protect the interests of the data subject, or for the administration of justice, exercising a legal function or function of a Government department. The final condition will apply to much of the data processing carried out by Social Services Departments, such as good practice under 'Working Together' or statutory duties under the Children Act 1989.

2. *Personal data shall only be obtained for specific lawful purposes and must not be processed in any way that is incompatible with that purpose.* Under this principle it will be necessary to have policies regarding the retention and disposal of data.

3. *Personal data shall be adequate, relevant and not excessive for the purpose for which it is collected.* Organisations should not hold irrelevant information.

4. *Personal data shall be accurate and kept up to date when necessary.* Systems for checking accuracy and updating need to be in place.

5. *Personal data must be kept no longer than necessary.* If the reason for keeping the information no longer exists, it should be destroyed.

6. *Personal data shall be processed in accordance with the rights of data subjects.* Individuals have the right to access a copy of personal data held about them. Although technically it is not necessary to respond to a request unless it is received in writing, it may be good practice to respond to oral requests in some circumstances. A request does not have to be framed in technical language: e.g. 'I would like to see the information you have got on me' should be accepted as a request. If satisfied that the request comes from the data subject and a fee of £10 has been paid, then the request must be complied with within 40 days. This is the maximum period for responding to a Subject Access Request (**SAR**). Care must be taken not to release personal data that may relate to another individual, and in some circumstances the request may be refused if a disclosure would cause damage or distress to the data subject. Schedules 2 and 3 provide more detail.

7. *Appropriate security measures should be taken against any unlawful processing of personal data or accidental loss, damage or destruction of personal data.* Clear systems for accessing data need to be established. This may range from password protected access to electronic data to who has the keys for the filing cabinet.

8. *Personal data should not be transferred outside the European Economic Area unless the country to which it is transferred has an equivalent type of data protection legislation.* This applies even if the subject of the information goes to live outside the area.

Implications of the DPA 1998

Great care must be taken over the way information about individuals is recorded, and the substance of the information that is recorded must be limited to that which is essential to the carrying out of social work responsibilities. Training on good data protection practice should be available. Social work records, whether held manually or electronically, are clearly covered by the Act.

An Information Commissioner has been introduced to regulate the Data Protection Act 1998 and may bring enforcement proceedings if there has been a breach of the Act. If there is a breach, e.g. if personal information about an individual is inappropriately made public, and the individual suffers harm, then compensation can be claimed and criminal action may be taken against the data controller. It is important to note that there may be personal liability under the DPA. If, for example, an individual disclosed personal information in an e-mail to another person in an unauthorised way, the individual could be held responsible and fined up to £5,000. Inappropriate disclosure of personal information could also constitute a breach of the individual's right to respect for private and family life contained in Art. 8 ECHR.

The Information Commissioner has issued guidance, 'Subject access requests and social services records', including consideration of counselling or other support when distressing information is disclosed. The guidance notes state:

> Parents will often exercise subject access rights on behalf of their children. If a practitioner believes the child is mature enough to understand the nature of the request and the nature of the information which may be disclosed, then careful consideration must be given to any instructions received from the child. For example, has the child given some information to a practitioner and specifically asked for this to be withheld from a parent? The child's wellbeing should also be taken into account if information disclosed to the parent might have a detrimental affect on this, or might undermine the ability of a practitioner to work with the child. This is particularly important if the file contains details of a child's concerns or allegations about parental abuse. In all cases where a practitioner believes that a child is mature enough to exercise their rights, the parent should be asked to provide proof that they are acting with the child's consent.

Subject access requests must be handled properly, the guidance advises that: 'It is good practice to keep a record of exactly what information you have sent in response to a SAR, together with a note of information you have withheld.'

Freedom of Information Act 2000

Provisions of the Freedom of Information Act 2000 complement the Data Protection Act 1998.[30] Taken together, this 'right to know' legislation supports the movement for greater 'transparency' in organisations that hold information about the public, and should lead to greater care in handling and recording information, and greater accountability in public spending. The Act applies to approximately 100,000 public authorities. It is not limited to personal information held about an individual. In summary the 2000 Act provides:

- A general right of access to information that public authorities carrying out their public functions hold (subject to some exemptions). This includes organisations which contract with public authorities. Information may be requested about any aspect of the public authorities' remit.

- If the information requested falls within one of the exemptions listed in the Act, it will generally not be provided, although there is a duty to disclose exempted information where it is 'in the public interest' to do so. The authority is also excused from replying to 'vexatious or repeated' requests.

- Exempt information includes that relating to security measures; court records; personal information (this could be accessed via DPA 1998); information provided in confidence; legal privilege; personal information concerning a third party; and health and safety (see ss. 21–44 for the full list).

- An Information Tribunal to enforce rights under this Act and the DPA 1998.

- A requirement for public authorities to adopt a publication scheme, dealing with manner of publication, types of information routinely published and whether a charge will be made. For example, the Department of Health Scheme lists information it makes available as including NHS annual accounts, statistics on health and healthcare, and advice for the public. Information should normally be made available within 20 days unless an exemption applies.

- Each authority should have a designated senior member of staff responsible for records management.[31]

- The Information Commissioner has powers to enforce the Act.

Not all requests under the Freedom of Information Act will be successful. As an example, in *London Borough of Camden* v. *IC EA/2007/0021* the tribunal considered a request for the names of all persons subject to Anti-Social Behaviour Orders (**ASBOs**) (current or expired) in the local authority's area. It found that publicity long after the making of an ASBO was quite different from identification and denunciation at the time of the order, and could be seen as an unjustified humiliation taking no account of any improvements in behaviour following the making of the order. Therefore, processing such personal data, long after the making of the relevant ASBO, would be unfair and in breach of the data protection principles.

The issue of sharing information is also of great importance in the health service. Following the Caldicott review in 1997, 'guardians' of personal information were introduced into NHS organisations to ensure lawful and appropriate handling of patient information. This model was also adopted into local authorities with social services responsibilities. Guardians have the task of auditing existing systems of data handling.

Chapter summary

- Frequently, a social worker will represent the authority as the applicant for a particular order, e.g. care order, and may have to provide a report for the court.

- The children's guardian, an experienced social worker, independent of the local authority and appointed by the court to represent the best interests of the child, provides reports to the court in many applications concerning children.

- A social worker may act as an 'appropriate adult' in cases where a child or vulnerable adult is being interviewed by the police at a police station. The role is to 'advise, observe and facilitate communication'.

- As social workers will often be required to give evidence in court, it is essential to develop skills for giving evidence. The study of this topic is known as 'courtcraft'. In essence, it involves good preparation, familiarity with court venues and procedures, and clear understanding of the role in court.

- Knowledge of rules of evidence (which vary between civil and criminal matters) can be useful when preparing a case and giving evidence. Evidence must be admissible, i.e. relevant; hearsay should be avoided where possible; experts can give opinion evidence; a witness must be competent to give evidence (able to take the oath); and sometimes corroborating evidence will be required.

- Social work decisions may be challenged in seven different ways: local authority complaints procedure; local government ombudsman; default powers of the Secretary of State; judicial review; local authority monitoring officer; action for damages; and complaints under the Human Rights Act 1998.

- Law to protect people who whistleblow on bad practice is contained in the Public Interest Disclosure Act 1998.

- The Data Protection Act 1998 and Freedom of Information Act 2000 govern access to personal information that is held manually or electronically.

Exercises

Consider what action should be taken in the following circumstances and whether the Public Interest Disclosure Act 1998 would offer employment protection:

1. John is a student social worker on placement in a day centre for adults with learning disabilities. He is concerned that one of the staff has made racist remarks about two of the adults who come to the centre. He is reluctant to raise this with the manager of the day centre because of the close friendship between the manager and the staff member. He mentions it to his practice teacher and then makes a formal report to regulation and inspection.

2. Jane has worked as a care assistant at a residential home for three weeks. She has had a row with the manager because he has refused Jane's request to have Saturday night off. The next day Jane contacts a reporter for the local newspaper and claims that residents in the home suffer from neglect. The reporter visits the home and attempts, unsuccessfully, to interview the manager, who tells Jane to leave the premises and not to bother coming back.

Courtcraft

Spend some time thinking about any court experiences you may have had, or anticipate what you think it would be like to give evidence. Consider the following questions:

- What are my most important aims when giving evidence to the court?
- What impression would I like to make at court?
- Who am I accountable to when giving evidence?
- What anxieties do I have about giving evidence?

- What strategies can I adopt to ensure I say what I want to say?
- How can I translate nerves into confidence?
- What happens if we 'lose'?

Revisit the court observation guide in Chapter 3 and include in your analysis: consideration of rules of evidence and courtcraft skills.

Access to information

Consider whether the following requests for information are likely to be granted and whether the Data Protection Act 1998 or the Freedom of Information Act 2000 provides the authority:

- A wants to know how much the local parish council has spent on new 'dog fouling' signs.
- B wants to know the location of CCTV cameras in the local hospital and in the area of the town railway station.
- C wants to see the reference provided recently for a job he unsuccessfully applied for.
- D wants to see the local authority contract with the domiciliary care agency providing a service to her mother.
- E wants to know the ages of the prospective adopters of her child who was removed from her care.
- F wants to know the home address of the Director of Social Services.

Consolidation

The following exercise is designed to consolidate some of the issues discussed in the first four chapters and to reinforce the principle that social work takes place within a legal framework.[32] It is particularly valuable when used to analyse a case, perhaps experienced during placement.

Relevant legislation: Isolate the legislation relevant to the case. Was it familiar? Did you need to carry out any research or seek legal advice? Was the legislation comprehensible and clear on the relevant issues?

Accountability: What bodies were you accountable to in working with this case? Were the lines of accountability clear?

Function and role: What was your function and role in this context?

Basis of involvement: Did you have a right or a duty to be involved with the client?

Client group: What characteristics of this person allowed or required you to be involved? NB: use legal definitions.

Discrimination: Did you consider any aspects of discrimination arose in this case and were you equipped to deal with them?

Control of case: Once involved, what did you decide you could or ought to do and were you able to follow this through?

Client choice: What choices, if any, did your client have and what influenced that choice?

Appeals/complaints: What recourse did all the parties have to challenge any decisions?

Websites

The website of the Children and Family Court Advisory and Support Service (CAFCASS):
www.cafcass.gov.uk

Further information about the provision of advocacy services for children and young people making a complaint are available from the Department for Education site:
www.education.gov.uk

Summaries of cases and information about how the local government ombudsman investigates complaints are available from:
www.lgo.org.uk

The Parliamentary and Health Service Ombudsman deals with complaints about Government departments and their agents and the National Health Service. The website includes a step-by-step guide to making a complaint:
www.ombudsman.org.uk

Public Concern at Work, an independent authority, which seeks to ensure concerns about malpractice are properly raised and provides support for whistleblowers. The site includes summaries of whistleblowing cases:
www.pcaw.co.uk

Further information about the Data Protection Act 1998, the Freedom of Information Act 2000 and detail about the Information Commissioner are available from:
www.ico.gov.uk

Further reading

The role of the children's guardian is considered in:

Dickens, J. (2004) 'Risks and responsibilities – the role of the local authority lawyer in child care cases' 16 *Child and Family Law Quarterly* p. 17. (Presents findings from a study of how local authority social workers and their solicitors work together in child care cases.)

Lindley, B., Richards, M. and Freeman, P. (2001) 'Advice and advocacy for parents in child protection cases – what is happening in current practice' 13 *Child and Family Law Quarterly* p. 167. (Discussion of the particular need for advocacy of parents whose children are the subject of child protection investigations.)

Timmis, G. (2001) 'CAFCASS – A service for children or a service for the courts?' 31 *Family Law* p. 281.

Timmis, G. (2002) 'Meeting Children's Rights to Participation in Family Proceedings. The Overriding Aim for CAFCASS' *Representing Children* p. 40.

Courtcraft is explored further in:

Cooper, P (2014) *Court and Legal Skills (Focus on Social Work Law)*. Basingstoke: Palgrave Macmillan.

Davis, L. (2007) *See You in Court: A Social Worker's Guide to Presenting Evidence in Care Proceedings*. London: Jessica Kingsley Publishers.

Seymour, C. and Seymour, R. (2011) (2nd edn) *Courtroom and Report Writing Skills for Social Workers*. Exeter: Learning Matters.

Aspects of challenging social work are addressed in the following articles:

Bailey Harris, R. and Harris, M. (2002) 'Local authorities and child protection – the mosaic of accountability' 14 *Child and Family Law Quarterly* p. 117.

Hunt, G. (ed.) (1998) *Whistleblowing in the Social Services*. London: Edward Arnold. (Provides consideration of whistleblowing and examples in the specific context of social services.)

Williams, C. (2002) 'The practical operation of the Children Act complaints procedure' 14 *Child and Family Law Quarterly* p. 25.

Notes

[1] See also *Guidance from the President's Office: McKenzie Friends* [2005] Fam Law 405; L. Reed (2005) 'McKenzie Friends in Family Proceedings' 35 *Family Law* p. 820.

[2] The term 'officer of the service' is substituted for 'probation officer' by the Criminal Justice and Courts Service Act 2000, reflecting introduction of CAFCASS.

[3] National Probation Service (2005) 'National Standards'.

[4] DHSS (1974) 'Report of the Committee of Inquiry into the Care and Supervision Provided in Relation to Maria Colwell'. London: HMSO.

[5] CAFCASS Guidance on Representation of Children in Private Law Proceedings Pursuant to Rule 9.5 Family Proceedings Rules (April 2005); s. 122 of the Adoption and Children Act 2002.

[6] Department of Health (2000) *Reporting to Court under the Children Act: A Handbook for Social Services*. London: The Stationery Office.

[7] M. Haley and A. Swift (1985) 'P.A.C.E. and the Social Worker: A step in the right direction?' 6 *Journal of Social Welfare Law* pp. 355–73.

[8] J. Timms (2001) 'Advocacy Services for Children and Young People' in L.-A. Cull and J. Roche (eds) *The Law and Social Work: Contemporary Issues for Practice*. Basingstoke: Palgrave.

[9] The Advocacy Services and Representations Procedure (Children) (Amendment) Regulations 2004 (SI 2004/719); 'Providing Effective Advocacy Services for Children and Young People Making a Complaint under the Children Act 1989: Get it Sorted' (DFES): www.gov.uk/government/uploads/system/uploads/attachment_data/file/273899/providing_effective_advocacy.pdf.

[10] See critique in J. Lane and C. Walsh (2002) 'Court Proceedings', in K. Wilson and A. James (eds) (2nd edn) *The Child Protection Handbook*. Edinburgh: Bailliere Tindall.

[11] *Fallon* v. *Lancashire County Council* (1992) Decision 208.

[12] SI 1991/1115.

[13] Criminal Justice and Public Order Act 1994.

[14] M. Bell and R. Daly (1992) 'Social workers and solicitors working together?' 22 *Family Law* pp. 257–61.

[15] Provided for by Children Act 1989, s. 26 and National Health Service and Community Care Act 1990, s. 50.

[16] The Local Authority Social Services Complaints (England) Regulations 2006 (SI 2006/1861) came into force on 1 September 2006 and replace the previous framework provided by the Complaints Procedure Directions 1990. The regulations are accompanied by guidance to the new procedure, 'Learning from Complaints – Social Services Complaints Procedure for Adults'.

[17] See J. White (2006) 'Community care and the local government ombudsmen for England', 9 *Community Care Law Reports* 8.

[18] A phrase used to describe actions outside the course of employment, originates from *Joel* v. *Morrison* (1834) 6 C & P 501, p. 503.

[19] M. Preston-Shoot, G. Roberts and S. Vernon (2001) 'Values in social work law: strained relations or sustaining relationships?' 23 *Journal of Social Welfare and Family Law* p. 1.

[20] SI 1999/3242.

[21] Lord Borrie, QC (1996) *Four Windows on Whistleblowing.* London: Public Concern at Work.

[22] T. Burgner *et al.* (1998) *Independent Longcare Inquiry.* Buckinghamshire County Council.

[23] Department of Health (2000) *Lost in Care.* London: HMSO.

[24] Flynn, M. and Citarella, V. (2012) *Winterbourne View Hospital: A Serious Case Review,* South Gloucestershire Council on Behalf of South Gloucestershire Safeguarding Adults Board.

[25] Leicestershire Social Services (1993) *The Kirkwood Report.*

[26] P. Ells and G. Dehn (2001) 'Whistleblowing: Public Concern at Work' in L.-A. Cull and J. Roche (eds) *The Law and Social Work: Contemporary Issues for Practice.* Basingstoke: Palgrave.

[27] Employment Rights Act 1996, s. 43B.

[28] Department of Health (2000) *Data Protection Act: Guidance to Social Services.* London: The Stationery Office.

[29] See ICO (2007) 'Guidance on Determining What is Personal Data'.

[30] See further: P. Birkinshaw (2001) *Freedom of Information: The Law, the Practice and the Ideal.* London: Butterworths.

[31] Further information and a code of practice to the Act can be found at www.justice.gov.uk/information-access-rights/foi-guidance-for-practitioners/code-of-practice.

[32] Adapted from 'A checklist of legal issues in cases' in 'Teaching, Learning and Assessing Social Work Law. Report of the Law Improvements Project Group' (1991).

Chapter 5

The Human Rights Act 1998 and social work practice

Learning objectives

To develop an understanding of the following:

- The context in which the Human Rights Act 1998 was introduced.
- How the Articles of the European Convention are incorporated into domestic law.
- The meaning of 'public authority'.
- The terms of the Articles and their case law interpretation.
- The concepts of proportionality and margin of appreciation.
- The impact of the Act on social work practice.
- The influence of European and international law and Conventions.

Talking Point

A woman with mental health problems increasingly struggled following the death of her husband. She was placed in 24-hour supported care and her children were fostered. It was agreed that the children could visit their mother three times each week, but these visits were gradually reduced to one per week on the basis that the authority did not have enough staff to supervise the visits. Both the children and their mother were greatly distressed by this. The mother's advocate noticed that the local children's services department was not present during a care programme approach meeting and that the children's interests were not being properly represented. After attending a BIHR training session, he invoked the children's right to respect for family life and convinced the mental health team to invite children's services to the next meeting. The three visits each week were restored as a result. From this point onwards, the manager of the children's care team personally saw to it that each visit occurred. The mother and her children have remained very close and recently secured funding to enjoy an overseas holiday together.

A learning disabled couple were living in a residential assessment centre so their parenting skills could be assessed by the local Social Services Department. CCTV cameras were installed, including in their bedroom. Social workers explained that the cameras were there to observe them performing their parental duties and for the protection of their baby. The couple were especially distressed by use of the CCTV cameras in their bedroom during the night. With the help of a visiting neighbour, the couple successfully invoked their right to respect for private life. They explained that they did not want their intimacy to be monitored, and that, besides, the baby slept in a separate nursery. As a result, the social services team agreed to switch off the cameras during the night so that the couple could enjoy their evenings together in privacy.

A husband and wife had lived together for over 65 years. He was unable to walk unaided and relied on his wife to help him move around. She was blind and used her husband as her eyes. They were separated after he fell ill and was moved into a residential care home. She asked to come with him but was told by the local authority that she did not fit the criteria. Speaking to the media, she said: 'We have never been separated in all our years and for it to happen now, when we need each other so much, is so upsetting. I am lost without him – we were a partnership.' A public campaign launched by the family, supported by the media and various human rights experts and older people's organisations, argued that the local authority had breached the couple's right to respect for family life (Art. 8). The authority agreed to reverse its decision and offered the wife a subsidised place so that she could join her husband in the care home.

A woman and her children were fleeing domestic violence. The woman's husband was attempting to track the family down and they moved towns whenever he discovered their whereabouts. The family eventually arrived in London and were referred to the local Social Services Department. Social workers told the mother that she was an 'unfit' parent and that she had made the family intentionally homeless. They said that her children had to be placed into foster care. An advice worker helped the mother to challenge this claim on the basis of the right to respect for family life (protected by Art. 8). As a result, the family were told that they could remain together and that the Social Services Department would provide the deposit if they could secure private rented accommodation.

A physical disabilities team at a local authority had a policy of providing support to service users who wanted to participate in social activities. A gay man asked if a support worker could accompany him to a gay pub. His request was denied even though other heterosexual service users were regularly supported to attend pubs and clubs of their choice. During a BIHR training session, the man's advocate realised that the man could invoke his right to respect for private life and his right not to be discriminated against on grounds of sexual orientation to challenge this decision.

We hope these stories inspire you to strive for improvements in public services practice and policy. They show that the Human Rights Act is for everyone, providing the means to free all of us from injustice and allowing us to live to our full potential.

(Foreword to *The Human Rights Act – Changing Lives*.)

These case studies are taken from the British Institute of Human Rights (BIHR) publication, *The Human Rights Act – Changing Lives* (2008). They illustrate a range of situations where human rights arguments have been utilised successfully, without recourse to the courts, to improve aspects of individuals' lives. BIHR argue that their research in this field has found numerous examples which evidence an emerging culture of human rights.

Introduction

The Human Rights Act 1998 (HRA 1998) is having a real influence on the development of law in the United Kingdom. Various aspects of social work law and practice have been subject to challenge via the Act. It continues to provide an additional scrutiny of practice and its influence is apparent in official documents. For example, the working definition of adult abuse in 'No Secrets' reads: 'Abuse is a violation of an individual's human and civil rights by any other person or persons.' It is therefore essential to have a working knowledge of the principles under the Act that are likely to be asserted. Human rights will permeate all areas discussed in this book, so while the opportunity is taken here to introduce a framework of the Act, there will be further reference throughout the text to its implications in specific areas. Inevitably, some of those references will be necessarily speculative, given the relatively recent introduction of the Act and the pace of litigation. The potential long-term impact of the HRA 1998 should not be underestimated. Jack Straw, Home Secretary at the time the Act was introduced, claimed: 'The Human Rights Act 1998 is the most significant statement of human rights since the 1689 Bill of Rights'.[1]

In social work terms, the Act is at least an opportunity to promote best practice. At best it may also promote a real culture of rights, which is empowering for service users. This had been explained as follows:

A culture of respect for human rights would exist when there was a widely-shared sense of entitlement to these rights, of personal responsibility and of respect for the rights of others, and where this influenced all our institutional policies and practices. This would help create a more humane society, a more responsive government and better public services, and could help to deepen and widen democracy by increasing the sense amongst individual men and women that they have a stake in the way in which they are governed.[2]

The examples given at the start of the chapter support this position. The importance of the Act for social work is also clear from the BASW Code of Ethics (2012) section on 'Challenging the abuse of human rights', which reads:

> Social workers should be prepared to challenge discriminatory, ineffective and unjust policies, procedures and practice. They should challenge the abuse of power and the exclusion of people from decisions that affect them. Social workers should not collude with the erosion of human rights or allow their skills to be used for inhumane purposes such as systematic abuse, detention of child asylum seekers and threats to family life of those in vulnerable positions.

The Act presents opportunities to reinterpret, amend and update legislation and lessen the impact of established case law and may provide the catalyst for reform of antiquated and discriminatory laws.

The actual impact of the Act will not be apparent until it has been in force for some time. Many have made their own predictions; however, Lord Justice Sedley has commented: 'neither those idealists who hoped to see a new era of respect for individual rights and freedoms, nor those who, like the Scottish judge Lord McCluskey, foresaw "a field day for crackpots, a pain in the neck for judges and legislators, and a goldmine for lawyers" have turned out to be right.'[3] Fear that courts would be swamped by applications does not appear to have materialised. An emerging trend seems to be that human rights points are being added to existing claims, but relatively few new claims based solely on human rights issues have been lodged. One exception to this, where human rights arguments frequently feature, is in the area of immigration and asylum, e.g. *R (Ben-Abdelaziz)* v. *Haringey London Borough Council* [2001] 1 WLR 1485. In part the scarcity of cases may be due to comments urging restraint, e.g. Lord Woolf, who insisted it was essential that counsel took a responsible attitude as to when it was appropriate to raise arguments based on the HRA 1998 and judges should be robust in resisting inappropriate attempts to introduce such arguments. In *Re F (Minors) (Care: Termination of Contact)* [2000] 2 FCR 481, Wall J commented that he would be disappointed if the Convention were to be routinely paraded as a makeweight ground of appeal or if there were to be extensive citation of Strasbourg authorities in every case. It may also reflect the fact that many of the individuals whose rights are violated are themselves vulnerable and not naturally litigious. On a more positive note, Liberty urge bold and imaginative use of the Convention by lawyers and judges.

What does the HRA 1998 do?

The HRA 1998 incorporates the Convention for the Protection of Human Rights and Fundamental Freedoms (usually referred to as the European Convention on Human Rights (ECHR)) into UK domestic law. The Convention was ratified in 1951, British lawyers having made a major contribution to its drafting. It contains rights, prohibitions and freedoms arranged in sections referred to as articles.

The focus of the Act is on promoting and upholding rights. The United Kingdom, in contrast to most other democracies, has no written constitution or positive guarantees of rights. This is largely a result of the way the political and constitutional tradition has developed in the United Kingdom. '"Freedom" as it has emerged in this tradition rests largely on the (negative) freedom from government interference rather than positive human rights guarantees, enshrined in a written constitution or human rights instrument.'[4]

The long title describes the Act as one 'to give *further* effect' to the rights and freedoms of the Convention. Since 1966 it has been possible for an individual to directly petition the European Court of Human Rights in Strasbourg, bringing a claim against the United Kingdom for violation of one of the Articles. The European Court of Human Rights (**ECtHR**) was established in 1959 and the first case which found a breach of the Convention by the United Kingdom was decided in 1975.[5] There were, however, a number of disadvantages to the process of petitioning the ECtHR, including financial cost. In essence, the process was expensive, cases costing as much as £30,000. It was necessary to show that all domestic remedies had been exhausted before reaching the ECtHR. This added to the expense and also contributed to delays of around five years. These factors often proved prohibitive. The case for full incorporation of the Convention was thus, partly, practical. The emphasis in the Act is on 'bringing rights home' (incidentally the title of the consultation paper which preceded the Bill),[6] making the Convention more accessible, so that remedies which would be available in Strasbourg can be ordered by the domestic courts. It will still be possible for cases against the United Kingdom to reach Strasbourg; however, the requirement that domestic remedies are exhausted first remains. This is to ensure that the domestic courts have the first opportunity to resolve any breach. The application to Strasbourg has to be made within six months of the final decision in domestic proceedings.

Incorporation of the rights into English law

There are three principal sections that effect the incorporation of the rights (summarised in Table 5.1).

Consideration of case law

Section 2 of the HRA 1998 provides that a court or tribunal which determines a question which has arisen in connection with a Convention right must take into account any judgment, decision or opinion of the European Court of Human Rights. This imposes mandatory consideration of relevant Strasbourg jurisprudence on domestic courts. This requirement will impact on the doctrine of precedent. The Supreme Court as the superior court, will no longer simply be bound by its own decisions but must also consider European decisions

Table 5.1 Incorporation of the Human Rights Act 1998

Section 2	Section 3	Section 6
Courts must take into account any judgment, decision or opinion of the European Court of Human Rights	So far as possible, legislation must be read and given effect in a way that is compatible with the Convention rights	It is unlawful for a public authority to act in a way that is incompatible with a Convention right

as binding and not simply of persuasive authority. A criticism often directed at the system of precedent has been the fact that once a poor decision has been made it may stand for many years. In contrast, the Convention has been described as a 'living instrument which . . . must be interpreted in the light of present day conditions' (*Tyrer* v. *United Kingdom* (1978) 2 EHRR 1, para. 31). The effect of this is that case law should develop with circumstances in an organic way and reflect changes in society. It will not be necessary for existing case law to be specifically overruled where changes in society dictate the need for a different approach. As an example, the court found in *Marckx* v. *Belgium* (1979) 2 EHRR 330 that the distinction between legitimate and illegitimate children was no longer compatible with the Convention.

Compatibility of legislation

Secondly, s. 3 provides that, so far as possible, primary and subordinate legislation must be read and given effect in a way that is compatible with the Convention rights. This is referred to as the technique of 'reading down'.[7] Where a provision has a range of possible meanings, the court must give effect to the meaning that is compatible with the Convention. This principle applies to past and future legislation, and to primary and secondary legislation. It encourages the courts to develop a more purposive approach to statutory construction and is not limited to cases of ambiguity.

If it is not possible to construe legislation to give effect to the Convention, the High Court may issue a 'declaration of incompatibility'. The courts cannot quash primary legislation which in their view is not compatible; that remains the responsibility of Parliament. Absolute parliamentary sovereignty is thus retained. If a declaration is made, the Government can use a fast track process to introduce amending legislation. If the Government does not take this opportunity – and it will be under immense public and political pressure to do so – the declaration will act as a trigger for the aggrieved individual to take the case to Strasbourg. For example, in *R (H)* v. *London North and East Region Mental Health Review Tribunal* [2001] EWCA Civ 415, the court made a declaration that ss. 72 and 73 of the Mental Health Act 1983 were incompatible with Art. 5. The sections placed the burden of proof on the patient to show continued detention was unlawful, whereas to be compatible the burden should be on the tribunal to show that continued detention was lawful. Within family law, a declaration of incompatibility has been made in relation to the failure of the law to recognise transsexuals' acquired sex for the purposes of marriage: *Bellinger* v. *Bellinger* [2003] UKHL 21. The Gender Recognition Act 2004 gives effect to the required change in the law.

The obligation to interpret legislation compatibly with the Convention applies to old and new legislation. In terms of legislation passed after the Human Rights Act 1998, in theory, the interpretation requirement should present less of a difficulty. The Joint Parliamentary Committee on Human Rights considers all Bills to ensure compatibility, and can suggest any necessary amendments. There is also a requirement (s. 19) that during a Bill's passage through the Parliamentary process the relevant minister makes a 'statement of compatibility' to the effect that in his or her view the Bill is compatible with the Convention.

Public authorities

Thirdly, and of great significance for social work, a new responsibility is imposed on public authorities. Public authorities are of central importance under the Act. Under s. 6 it is unlawful for a public authority to act in a way that is incompatible with a Convention right (unless as a result of primary legislation the authority could not have acted differently).

A 'public authority' includes any court or tribunal, and any person certain of whose functions are functions of a public nature (s. 6(3)). This is likely to include local government, social services, the police, health authorities, probation, public utilities, inspection bodies and certain private bodies where they are exercising functions of a public nature, e.g. a professional regulatory body. It is possible for a person or body to have both private and public functions. For example, a general practitioner when undertaking NHS work will be a public authority but not when treating a private patient. The impact of the HRA 1998 will depend considerably on how widely the courts interpret the concept of a public function and whether it is an area where further litigation is likely. So far it appears that the courts have interpreted the term rather more restrictively than Parliament may have intended. The Court of Appeal, in *R (Heather)* v. *Leonard Cheshire Foundation* [2002] EWCA Civ 366, decided that a private charitable organisation managing a care home was not a 'public authority'. This was a disappointing decision given that the home was receiving public funding and was providing care which would otherwise have been provided by the state. Some of the argument focused on the fact that some of the residents had made private arrangements to enter the home; however, that seems a weak justification for withholding the obligation to give effect to the human rights of the residents, many of whom were vulnerable. Of some reassurance, however, in such a case is that the regulatory body is clearly a public authority. A subsequent decision, though not overruling the *Leonard Cheshire* case, adopted a wider interpretation of the term emphasising a functional approach (*Aston Cantlow and Wilmcote with Billesley Parochial Church Council* v. *Wallbank* [2003] UKHL 37). The most recent decision in this area, however, confirms the *Leonard Cheshire* position. In *YL* v. *Birmingham City Council* [2007] UKHL 27, the House of Lords decided that when providing accommodation and care under a local authority contract independent sector care providers were not carrying out a public function and were therefore not public authorities for the purposes of the Human Rights Act. Accordingly, these providers are not required by the Human Rights Act to act compatibly with the Convention rights. Section 145 of the Health and Social Care Act 2008 reverses this position. It ensures that the protections provided by the Human Rights Act apply to people receiving publicly arranged care in an independent sector care home by defining a person providing care in a care home as exercising a function of a public nature in doing so. It does not, however, extend to all contracted-out services, such as domiciliary care, or to self funded residents who make their own arrangements, or people placed in care homes as 'aftercare services' under s. 117 of the Mental Health Act 1983.

Recent case law is more positive. In *R (Weaver)* v. *L & Q Housing Trust* [2009] EWCA Civ 587, the Court of Appeal ruled that most Registered Providers of Social Housing are exercising public functions and are thus subject to the Human Rights Act. In deciding that the provision of housing by the registered provider was a public function, the court noted in particular: the Housing Trust significantly relied on public finance in allocating and managing social housing; the Trust operates closely with local government assisting it to achieve its statutory duties; and the provision of subsidised housing could be described as a public service outside private commercial activity.

Protection under the HRA is extended yet further by the Care Act 2014. Under s. 73, a registered care provider will be deemed a public authority for the purposes of the HRA where it is providing care or support to an adult or carer, be it in a care home or their own home, and that the care or support is either put in place or funded in any way by a local authority.

It is of crucial importance that public authorities, including Social Services Departments, examine policies and procedures for compliance with the rights. The Department of Health suggested in a local authority circular:[8] 'As the UK has been signed up to the ECHR since 1951, the expectation is that best practice in the services already respects the Convention.'

Such confidence may be misplaced and, while scrutiny of policy may seem an enormous task, it is not acceptable for a public authority, which has a positive duty to comply with the Convention, simply to sit back and await challenge. It is also clear that public authorities will carry liability for their agents if they outsource, for example, delivery of certain services. As a minimum, any contracting-out arrangements should include terms that require contractors to comply with the public authorities' obligations under the Articles.

It is significant that courts themselves are public authorities. Taken with the rules of interpretation it is clear that courts are obliged to decide *all* cases before them – whether they arise in connection with a statutory or common law principle, and whether they involve public authorities or private individuals' compatibly with Convention rights. Wall LJ confirmed in *Re V (A Child) (Care Proceedings: Human Rights Claims)* [2004] EWCA Civ 54: 'Every court hearing proceedings under Part IV of the 1989 Act (that is the family proceedings court (FPC) the county court and the High Court) has a duty under s. 3(1) of the 1998 Act to give effect to the provisions of the 1989 Act in a way which is compatible with convention rights.' (The 1989 Act referred to is the Children Act 1989.)

This duty on the court can lead to indirect application of the Act, in private cases sometimes referred to as the 'horizontal' effect. Actions between an individual and a public authority are referred to in terms of the direct or 'vertical' application of the Act. In a private case between two individuals, e.g. where one individual applies for a non-molestation order against the other, even though there is no suggestion that a public authority has breached an article, in reaching its decision the court (as a public authority) must act compatibly with the Convention. In this example it could be argued that the making of a non-molestation order is a violation of Art. 8, the right to respect for private and family life.

Section 7 makes clear the significance of s. 6. Failure to comply with Convention rights is a new ground for judicial review of a public authority. A new **cause of action** against public authorities is created, and Convention rights are available as a defence to actions brought by public authorities against individuals.

Section 7 provides:

---

s. 7

7. **(1)** A person who claims that a public authority has acted (or proposes to act) in a way which is made unlawful by section 6(1) may –

   (a) bring proceedings against the authority under this Act in the appropriate court or tribunal, or

   (b) rely on the Convention right or rights concerned in any legal proceedings, but only if he is (or would be) a victim of the unlawful act.

(HRA 1998)

It is clear from s. 7(1)(b) that a separate action under s. 7 is not necessary (and the practice has been strongly discouraged) where there are ongoing proceedings. For example, in care cases where parents might wish to challenge the action of the local authority, relying on the Convention, the human rights arguments should be dealt with by the court hearing the care proceedings. The arguments should be brought to the court's attention as early as possible to avoid delay and it would only be necessary in exceptional cases to transfer the case to the High Court to address the human rights arguments: *Re L (Care Proceedings: Human Rights Claims)* [2003] EWHC 665 (Fam).

It is also important to note that an individual does not have to w authority has actually acted unlawfully before bringing a claim under s. 7. for proceedings where the public authority 'proposes to act'. This could apply, to claims in respect of the content of a care plan before it is implemented, or a pr change to policy or procedures.

Reflect

The Department of Health optimistically stated, 'the expectation is that best practice in the services (NHS and Social Services) already respects the Convention since the UK has been signed up to it for 50 years', in **LAC** 2000.

Do you agree?

In the application of the Act two further principles – **proportionality** and the margin of appreciation – are of enormous importance.

Proportionality

Any interference with a Convention right must be proportionate to the intended outcome. Even if an action which interferes with a Convention right pursues a legitimate aim, the means of achieving the aim must not be excessive. To coin a phrase, 'You must not use a sledgehammer to crack a nut'. Interference with a qualified Convention right may be justified if it is:

- in accordance with law;
- for a legitimate purpose;
- proportionate.

This principle was clearly applied in *Re O (A Child) (Supervision Order: Future Harm)* [2001] EWCA Civ 16, where the Court of Appeal decided that a supervision order rather than a care order provided a proportionate response. In the case Hale LJ found that a care order would be severe in three respects: power to the local authority to remove the child from her parents; power to the local authority to have parental control and responsibility; and a long period of time for its discharge. Any intervention of the court needed to be proportionate to the aim for protection of family life in the European Convention.

Margin of appreciation

The application of Convention rights will frequently involve a balancing exercise of competing claims. In recognition of this and of the various countries signed up to the Convention, the Court of Human Rights allows a 'margin of appreciation' to each country, rather than simply substituting its own view for that of the national authority. It allows for different countries to take different approaches to the rights, reflecting their different cultures and traditions, including religion, where it is acceptable for there to be differences in interpretation, e.g. the question of abortion. The principle was described in *Handyside* v. *United Kingdom* (1976) EHRR 737: 'By reason of their direct and continuous contact with the vital forces in their country, state authorities are in a better position than the international judge to give an opinion on the exact content of requirements.'

(s. 1)

rights, prohibitions and freedoms and fall into three categories. Some
are limited or qualified (see Table 5.2).

ts (Arts. 3, 4, 7) cannot be restricted in any circumstances and violation
ot balanced against any general public interest.

ghts (Arts. 2, 4(2), 5, 6(1)) are those Articles where derogation is possible, in
ds the right is established but there are some limitations. The existence of those
ons or specific exceptions, however, is not balanced against the public interest.

ied rights (Arts. 8, 9, 10, 11) are Articles set in positive form but subject to limitation or restriction clauses, which enable the balance between individual rights and the
general public interest to be weighed. A ***prima facie*** violation of a qualified right will be
justified only if the limitation is prescribed by law, it pursues a legitimate aim, it is necessary in a democratic society, fulfils a pressing social need and is proportionate.

The Articles

It is appropriate to consider the Articles of most relevance to social work in turn, together
with case law illustrations of their application. Clearly, some Articles are already proving to
be subject to more litigation than others. It is also important to remember that in some cases
a number of Articles may be argued and the decisions shed some light on the interrelationship of the Articles. The Articles are written in quite general terms and apply universally to
all. There are no Articles that apply specifically to particular groups, e.g. children. The Articles

Table 5.2 Human Rights Act 1998

HUMAN RIGHTS ACT 1998		
European Convention on Human Rights and Fundamental Freedoms		
ARTICLES		
Absolute	**Qualified**	**Limited**
Art. 3: Prohibition against torture, inhuman or degrading treatment or punishment	Art. 8: Right to respect for private and family life, home and correspondence	Art. 2: Prohibition of forced or compulsory labour
Art. 7: Prohibition of punishment without law	Art 10: Freedom of expression	Art 5: Right to liberty
Art. 4: Prohibition against slavery	Art. 11: Freedom of assembly and association	Art. 6(1): Right to a fair trial
High threshold but any breach is a violation of the Article	Right may be breached if: • In accordance with law • Breach pursues a legitimate aim • Measures are proportional	Article contains a clear statement of circumstances which permit breach of the right

provide for basic rights, and some areas that might seem significant and where individuals would wish to assert a 'right' are excluded, for example there is no 'right to employment'.

Article 2

> **ECHR**
>
> Everyone's right to life shall be protected by law.
>
> (HRA 1998)

This Article is relevant to the debate about euthanasia, resource allocation, withdrawing treatment, and age-related treatment decisions. It relates to quality of life not simply life or death decisions. While the outcome of such cases may not change the reasons for taking a particular course of action, reasons will need to be clearly justified with reference to the Convention. In some circumstances there may be a positive obligation on a public authority to protect life. For example, in *Association X* v. *United Kingdom* (1978) 14 DR 31, a case which concerned a vaccination programme, the court stated that the Article 'enjoins the state not only to refrain from taking life intentionally but, further, to take appropriate steps to safeguard life'. Steps to protect life were taken by the court in *Venables and Thompson* v. *News Group Newspapers Ltd* [2001] 1 All ER 908, where injunctions were granted against publishing details (apart from their names) of the individuals who killed James Bulger, in response to the risk to their lives if they were found. A health authority was found in breach of Art. 2 where it negligently failed to protect a detained mental patient in *Savage* v. *South Essex Partnership NHS Foundation Trust and MIND (intervening)* [2007] EWCA Civ 1375. The court ruled that where the authority knew or ought to have known of the existence of a real and immediate risk to the patient from self harm, it should have taken steps to avoid that risk.

At appeal, *Savage* v. *South Essex Partnership NHS Trust* [2008] UKHL 74 confirms that in certain circumstances there will be an obligation on public authorities to take steps to protect life. A woman was detained in a mental hospital for treatment under s. 3, being treated for paranoid schizophrenia, having a history of admissions and absconding. She absconded and committed suicide by throwing herself in front of a train. Her daughter argued that the hospital had failed to take steps to prevent her from committing suicide. The court noted that health authorities have general obligations to protect the lives of patients such as employing competent staff. Beyond that there may be further operational obligations, which as Lord Scott described: 'arise only if members of staff know or ought to know that a particular patient presents a "real and immediate' risk of suicide. In these circumstances Art. 2 requires them to do all that can be reasonably expected to prevent the patient from committing suicide.' *Rabone & Rabone* v. *Pennine Care NHS Trust*, extended the duty to take positive steps to prevent a patient committing suicide. The principle of the duty to take steps to prevent suicide also applied to informal patients.

The right to life does not include the right to die at a time and manner of your own choosing and therefore a prosecution under the Suicide Act 1961, in respect of an individual who assists another to commit suicide, would not be in breach of the Article according to *Pretty* v. *United Kingdom* (2002) 35 EHRR 1. Unlike the House of Lords, the Court of Human Rights did concede that Art. 8 was engaged.

Article 2, the right to life, includes a requirement that an effective independent investigation is carried out in certain circumstances where a death occurs. This includes inquests into deaths in custody (*Jordan* v. *UK* (2001) 37 EHRR 52). The case of *R (Allen)* v. *HM Coroner for Inner North London* [2009] EWCA Civ 623, found that this requirement may extend to the death of a mental patient in a hospital and will always be required where it appears that a detained patient may have committed suicide.

Article 3

> ### ECHR
>
> No one shall be subjected to torture or to inhuman or degrading treatment or punishment.
>
> (HRA 1998)

Article 3 is an absolute prohibition. It follows that it will be unlawful for any public authority to treat an individual in a way that violates the Article. Challenges may be brought based on various circumstances, e.g. use of electroconvulsive therapy (ECT), experimental medical treatment, restraint, seclusion or force-feeding. It is necessary to consider existing case law to evaluate the likelihood of a finding of violation and much will hinge on the meaning of key terms used in the Article.

With regard to torture, the case of *Ireland* v. *United Kingdom* (1978) 2 EHRR 25 considered five 'techniques': wall standing; hooding; subjection to noise; sleep deprivation; food and drink deprivation. This behaviour was found not to constitute torture but did amount to degrading treatment. The term 'degrading' applied to the techniques used as they were such as to cause feelings of fear, anguish and inferiority, and were capable of humiliating and debasing the prisoners. The decision also ruled that the other factor, 'ill treatment', must attain a minimum level of severity to fall within Art. 3. That minimum level is relative and will depend on all the circumstances of the case, including duration of the treatment, its physical and mental effects, the age, sex and state of health of the victim.

In *A* v. *United Kingdom (Human Rights: Punishment of Child)* (1998) 27 EHRR 611, A was beaten by his stepfather with a stick. The stepfather was charged with assault occasioning actual bodily harm but was acquitted, having argued that the assault was permitted as 'reasonable chastisement'. It was found that the lack of clear guidelines as to what amounted to reasonable chastisement and the failure to protect A and provide a deterrent amounted to a breach of Art. 3. Further, in *Z* v. *United Kingdom* (2001) 34 EHRR 97, the Court of Human Rights found the United Kingdom in breach of Art. 3 where a local authority had failed to act to protect children who had suffered 'horrific ill treatment and neglect' by their parents. The court awarded substantial damages and stressed the positive obligation on local authorities to protect individuals from the actions of others.

A further decision of the Court of Human Rights which found a local authority in breach of Art. 3 for its failure to protect children was *E* v. *United Kingdom* [2003] 1 FLR 348. The court found that the local authority had failed in its duty to protect E and her brothers and sisters and to monitor the behaviour of a known offender who lived with the children and their mother. Damage caused to the children by the offender could have been minimised or avoided had they acted properly. As a result of the breach the children were entitled to an award in damages.

In *Renolde* v. *France* [2008] (ECHR 5608/05), the imposition of solitary confinement for 42 days was also considered inhuman treatment and a violation of Art. 3. In relation to Art. 3, the court noted that:

the assessment of whether the treatment or punishment concerned is incompatible with the standards of Article 3 has, in the case of mentally ill persons, to take into consideration their vulnerability and their inability, in some cases, to complain coherently or at all about how they are being affected by any particular treatment.

To send an individual to another country knowing that they will be likely to suffer torture or inhuman or degrading treatment, can amount to a breach of Art. 3. This is highly relevant to decisions about immigration and asylum.

Article 4

ECHR

1. No one shall be held in slavery or servitude.

2. No one shall be required to perform forced or compulsory labour.

(HRA 1998)

Article 4 is an absolute article prohibiting slavery, servitude, forced or compulsory labour. It is increasingly relevant for social work practice given recognition of the practice of human trafficking. The State must refrain from subjecting any individual to slavery, servitude, forced or compulsory labour. It also has positive obligations to prosecute acts, investigate allegations and protects victims. The Asylum and Immigration (Treatment of Claimants etc) Act 2004 includes an offence of trafficking people for exploitation, and the Coroners and Justice Act 2009 makes it an offence to hold a person in slavery or servitude or require a person to perform forced or compulsory labour. Concern remains that not all victims of trafficking are identified as such and may not receive support or protection.

Article 5

ECHR

1. Everyone has the right to liberty and security of person. No-one shall be deprived of his liberty save in the following cases and in accordance with a procedure prescribed by law:

    (a) lawful detention of a person after conviction

    (b) lawful arrest or detention of a person ...

    (c) detention of a minor ... for the purpose of educational supervision ...

    (d) lawful detention of persons for the prevention of the spreading of infectious diseases, of persons of unsound mind, alcoholics or drug addicts or vagrants.

    ...

4. Everyone who is deprived of his liberty by arrest or detention shall be entitled to take proceedings by which the lawfulness of his detention shall be decided speedily by a court and his release ordered if the detention is not lawful.

(HRA 1998)

This is not an absolute right, as deprivation of liberty is permissible in certain cases (those most relevant to social work are also set out in the box) prescribed by the Article, provided a procedure prescribed by law is followed. It is concerned with *deprivation* of liberty, rather than *restriction* of liberty, the distinction between deprivation of and restriction upon liberty being one of intensity or degree (*Ashingdane* v. *United Kingdom* (1985) 7 EHRR 528).

Article 5 is a prohibition on arbitrary detention. Arbitrary detention could apply to restraint practices, lock-door policies, sedation, etc., in residential establishments, to the use of detention under the scheme of the Mental Health Act 1983 and has been argued (unsuccessfully) in relation to the use of secure accommodation under s. 25 of the Children Act 1989: see the case of *Re K (A Child) (Secure Accommodation Order: Right to Liberty)* [2001] Fam 377 (discussed in Chapter 10). The Article was found to have been breached in the case of *HL* v. *United Kingdom* (2004) EHRR 761, the European Court judgment of the appeal of *R* v. *Bournewood Community and Mental Health Trust, ex parte L* [1998] 3 All ER 458. The case concerned informal detention of mental health patients who are mentally incapable of consenting to detention but are compliant. Under the Mental Health Act 1983 (prior to its amendment by the Mental Health Act 2007), such patients were not entitled to the safeguards provided for formally detained patients such as the right of appeal to the Mental Health Review Tribunal. In response to this case, 'Deprivation Of Liberty Safeguards' (**DOLS**) have been introduced under the Mental Capacity Act 2005. (See further discussion in Chapter 15.) The leading authority on the operation of DOLS is the Supreme Court decision *P* v. *Cheshire West and Chester Council*.

Article 6

> **ECHR**
>
> In the determination of his civil rights and obligations …, everyone is entitled to a fair and public hearing within a reasonable time by an independent and impartial tribunal established by law.
>
> (HRA 1998)

This represents an extension to the principle of 'natural justice' or 'fairness', which permeates the legal system. It encompasses the concept of 'equality of arms', which requires a degree of balance between the parties in terms of legal representation and may have an impact in terms of requiring greater access to legal assistance and representation, and where relevant assistance of interpreters. In *Re O (Children); Re W-R (A Child); Re W (Children)* [2005] EWCA Civ 759, the Court of Appeal noted that Art. 6 ECHR was engaged in any application by a litigant in person for assistance of a McKenzie friend and that there was a presumption in favour of allowing this and ensuring a fair hearing. This Article also supports the evidential requirement (included in rules and regulations) that relevant material is disclosed to the other party prior to any hearing.

A high proportion of cases before the European Court have been based on this Article, and it will often be employed in connection with another Article, e.g. where someone is a victim of restraint practices and has no means of challenge. The continued growth in numbers of administrative tribunals may be partly due to the influence of this Article. The Article would apply to conduct of case conferences and adoption panels.

The requirement of independence and impartiality has been called into question in the context of the adequacy of social services complaints procedures. This point was tested in

R (on the application of Beeson) v. *Dorset CC* [2002] EWCA Civ 1812. This case began as a judicial review of a local authority decision that an individual had deprived himself of his property before entering residential care. It was decided initially that the local authority complaints procedure panel which comprised two councillors and one independent member, was not sufficiently independent and impartial for the purposes of Art. 6. On appeal, the Court of Appeal stated that the real question was whether the addition of judicial review to the process satisfied the standard. It found that if there was no substantive reason to question the integrity of the panel decision, whatever its appearance might suggest, the added safeguard of judicial review would usually satisfy the Art. 6 standard.

This principle is likely to apply across the range of social services complaints procedure panels. The argument advanced by the Court of Appeal is that, in any case where there is a concern that the panel was not sufficiently independent or impartial, the fact that the decision can be reviewed by judicial review in the High Court is sufficient to provide that element of the Art. 6 requirement. Looked at overall this may be so; however, it pays insufficient regard to the 'bringing rights home' philosophy which underpins the Human Rights Act 1998. It is expensive and time consuming for a claimant to take a case to judicial review and this may prove to be a deterrent for some. The preferable course would have been to ensure absolute and transparent independence and impartiality at the panel stage by extending the requirement for independence to at least two members.

In *T* v. *United Kingdom*, *V* v. *United Kingdom* (2000) 30 EHRR 121, trial of children for murder in an adult court was found to be a violation of Art. 6 with regard to effective participation. In *B* v. *United Kingdom*, *P* v. *United Kingdom* (2002) 34 EHRR 19 it was found that to hear a custody case and pronounce judgment in public would frustrate the aim of protecting the privacy of children and the practice of hearing children's cases *'in camera'* did not breach Art. 6. This position has been confirmed in *Pelling* v. *Bruce-Williams* [2004] EWCA Civ 845. More recently, in *BBC* v. *Cafcass Legal* [2007] EWHC 616 (Fam) (a case concerning the public identification of third parties in a judgment concerning parents accused of injuring their child by the local authority), Munby J stated: 'There is an emerging consensus that, at least in care cases, judgments should be published, albeit in anonymised form, if not as a matter of routine then at the very least very much more frequently than in the past.' The parents' interest in seeking to protect their reputation publicly was both vindicated by Art. 8 and supported by powerful public interest in such vindication. The BBC's application to disclose the video footage shot for a documentary engaged both Art. 6 and Art. 10 of the Convention.

Recognition of the detrimental effect of delay on proceedings has led to a number of initiatives to ensure speediness in resolving disputes. It is important, however, that the pressure to promote cost efficient and speedy disposal of cases does not override the need for proper examination of the facts. In *Re Dhaliwal (A Child)* [2005] EWCA Civ 743, the Court of Appeal found that there had been a breach of the right to a fair trial in a contested contact and residence order case. Limited court time meant that issues were not fully explored and key individuals including the child's paternal grandmother, whom it was proposed would offer daily care, did not give evidence. There was as a result, an 'impression of overall unfairness within Art. 6 terms' (Wall LJ). New time limits for the conduct of care proceedings have been introduced by the Children and Families Act 2014 (discussed in Chapter 9).

The influence of Article 6 is clear in the Family Procedure Rules 2010 which govern the conduct of family cases. The 'overriding objective' is 'to deal with cases justly, having regard to the welfare issues involved', which involves, so far as is practicable, ensuring cases are dealt with 'expeditiously and fairly', and 'ensuring that the parties are on an equal footing' (rule 1).

Article 8

> ### ECHR
>
> **(1)** Everyone has the right to respect for his private and family life, his home and his correspondence.
>
> **(2)** There shall be no interference by a public authority with the exercise of this right except such as is in accordance with the law and is necessary in a democratic society in the interests of national security, public safety or the economic well being of the country, for the prevention of disorder or crime, for the protection of health or morals, or for the protection of the rights and freedoms of others.
>
> (HRA 1998)

Broad interpretation is likely regarding this Article, which has frequently been invoked, and may supplement the lack of any real privacy laws in the United Kingdom. There is potential for it to be relied on, e.g. in the context of vulnerable adults, moving from independent living in the community to residential accommodation, sharing rooms, being offered only communal meals, no provision for couples to be together, lack of after-care services, covert surveillance, physical integrity, e.g. tagging, and violations which relate to a person's dignity as an aspect of private life. Case law discussed below relates to provision of community care services.

It may be used as a defence against unwanted interference, including over-zealous investigations, because any interference by the state with a person's private and family life, home or correspondence must be justified by one of the exceptions. It is pertinent to note that the Act applies to all; it may also be argued by an alleged abuser that his or her removal from home may constitute a violation of his or her rights. It will be increasingly important to recognise the existence of rights conflicts within a family, whether as between a child and his parents or between adults.

Family life is interpreted broadly under the Convention, beyond the boundaries of married couples and immediate relatives. In *B* v. *United Kingdom* (1988) 10 EHRR 87, a contested contact case, the court stated that 'the mutual enjoyment by parent and child of each other's company constitutes a fundamental element of family life'. The prison policy of separating babies from their mothers at 18 months of age was challenged under this Article, but found not to be a breach of the mother's right to family life, in *R (P)* v. *Secretary of State for the Home Department* [2001] EWCA Civ 1151. Article 8 includes protection of physical integrity and protection from sexual abuse: *X and Y* v. *Netherlands* (1985) 8 EHRR 235. The right to privacy has applied to enjoyment of homosexual sexual relations (*Dudgeon* v. *United Kingdom* (1981) 4 EHRR 149), and in *Pretty* v. *United Kingdom* (2002) 35 EHRR 1, it was described as:

> ... a broad term not susceptible to exhaustive definition. It covers the integrity of the person. Elements such as, gender identification, name and sexual orientation and sexual life fall within the personal sphere protected by Article 8. Article 8 also protects a right to personal development and to establish and develop relationships with other human beings and the outside world.

The second part of Art. 8 expressly qualifies the right. In doing so, the Act seeks to balance rights of individuals with other public interests. This is known as proportionality, as any limitations must be proportionate to the end achieved. The question to be posed will be whether the interference is prescribed by law, serves a legitimate objective and is necessary in a democratic society. Such questions could be applied to justify the inclusion of an individual's name on the list of people unsuitable to work with vulnerable adults or children, under the Safeguarding Vulnerable Groups Act 2006. Inclusion could arguably be an interference with the right to privacy; however, it is prescribed by law, is intended to protect the rights and freedoms of others, and has been deemed necessary in UK society. Indefinite inclusion on the list without any right to challenge and other safeguards might be considered not proportionate, as the term is explained in the following quote: 'Inherent in the whole of the Convention is the search for the fair balance between the demands of the general interest of the community and the requirements of the protection of the individual's human rights' (*Soering* v. *United Kingdom* (1989) 11 EHRR 439).

Medical treatment can be an aspect of family life, as illustrated in *Glass* v. *United Kingdom* [2004] 1 FLR 1019. Here, a 12-year-old boy who was severely disabled became seriously ill following surgery. At the hospital his mother opposed the medical view that he should not be resuscitated if his heart stopped and also did not wish him to be given morphine. Despite expression of these views, a DNR (do not resuscitate) note was placed on the boy's notes and he was given diamorphine. His condition deteriorated further and at one point during an argument about treatment a fight took place on the ward between the doctors and the boy's family. The European Court found that Art. 8 had been breached. To impose treatment against the parent's wishes clearly interfered with the boy's right to respect for private and family life. The court stated that the hospital trust should have sought court intervention through a declaration as it was not a situation of necessity. This case clearly places the onus on hospital authorities to seek court intervention before administering treatment where there is a dispute.

In *G* v. *E* [2010], a local authority removed a young man with learning disabilities from the home of his long-term carer without sanction by the Court of Protection. The carer was not involved in the decision to remove the young man and had no contact with him for several months. The court noted that Art. 8 gives, 'not only substantive protection against any inappropriate interference with their family life but also procedural safeguards including the involvement of the carers in the decision-making process' (para. 88). The failure to involve the carer contributed to the court's finding that there had been a breach of the young man's Art. 8 rights.

Finally, a significant case for social services illustrates the broad interpretation of Art. 8.

Key Case

In *R (Bernard)* v. *Enfield London Borough Council* [2002] EWHC 2282 (Admin) the court found that human rights were violated by failure to provide adequate community care services. Damages were awarded.

The facts of the case are quite complex and revolve around housing needs of a family comprising husband and wife and six children aged between 3 and 20. The wife, aged 48, suffered right-side paralysis following a stroke, was largely immobile, reliant on an electric wheelchair, doubly incontinent and diabetic. Her husband cared for her and the children.

The family had lived in a house adapted by Enfield Borough Council but were forced to sell due to mortgage arrears. They held a tenancy of a second house for 15 months (not adapted). At the end of that tenancy they moved to a third house, provided by Enfield's Housing Department. They then moved to a fourth house, which had no adaptations and was provided as temporary accommodation, the family having been considered intentionally homeless in June 2000.

In September 2000 social services assessed the needs of claimants and their family and concluded that the fourth house was totally unsuitable for the following reasons:

- The wife was unable to use wheelchair in house.
- The only accessible toilet was in a lean-to in the back garden, downstairs, so she was unable to get there without her husband's help.
- The bath was also in the lean-to.
- The wife was forced to live in the lounge, where her husband and youngest two children also slept.
- The front door opened directly into the lounge.
- There were steps to the front door so the wife was unable to leave house by herself.

Enfield accepted that it needed to provide residential accommodation to meet the family's needs under s. 21 of the National Assistance Act 1948 and the current house could not be suitably adapted, but no action was taken. The family actually moved into suitably adapted accommodation the day before the hearing of their claim, some two years after the initial assessment.

The judgment makes clear that application of the HRA 1998 means that community care functions must be exercised compatibly with Convention rights. The court noted that the family had lived in deplorable conditions, but the circumstances of the case did not meet the threshold of mistreatment required for Art. 3, i.e. minimum level of severity (though the arguments were 'finely balanced'). It was relevant that mistreatment had arisen by 'corporate neglect' rather than deliberate mistreatment. The claim that Enfield had acted incompatibly with Art. 8 was successful.

The court noted that private life includes a person's physical and psychological integrity (*Botta* v. *Italy* (1998) 26 EHRR 241) and[9] that 'the fundamental element of family life is the right to live together so that family relations can develop naturally and that members of a family can enjoy one another's company'. The obligation is to do more than protect individuals from arbitrary interference with Art. 8 rights – it can require a positive act by state authorities, noting 'those entitled to care under s. 21 are a particularly vulnerable group. Positive measures have to be taken (by way of community care facilities) to enable them to enjoy, so far as possible, a normal private and family life.'

When applying Art. 8 the court will ask the following question: Is there an interference? The answer will be 'Yes': if provision would secure a person's physical and psychological integrity and development of personality in relations with others; if provision would allow family relations to develop naturally and allow family members to enjoy one another's company; if there is a direct link between the services that could be provided and the user's private/family life.

Bernard was clearly an extreme case highlighting apparent bad practice. Not every service user who is dissatisfied with the outcome of a community care assessment will be able to mount a human rights claim. Whether there has been a breach of human rights will always depend on the circumstances of the case and not all failures will equal breach. *Bernard* is, however, a significant application of the human rights philosophy and demonstrates the court's willingness to enforce the duty of public authorities to act in compliance with the Articles of the European Convention.

The following extract from the judgment in *Bernard* summarises the human rights issues in the case:

> Following the assessments in September 2000, Enfield was under an obligation not merely to refrain from unwarranted interference in the claimants' family life, but also to take positive steps, including the provision of suitably adapted accommodation to enable the claimants and their children to lead as normal a life as possible, bearing in mind the second claimant's severe disabilities. Suitably adapted accommodation would not merely have facilitated the normal incidents of family life, for example she would have been able to move around her home to some extent and would have been able to play some part … in looking after their children. It would also have secured her 'physical and psychological integrity'. She would no longer have been housebound, confined to a shower chair for most of the day, lacking privacy in the most undignified of circumstances, but would have been able to operate again as part of her family and as a person in her own right, rather than being a burden, wholly dependent upon the rest of her family. In short it would have restored her dignity as a human being.

A further decision, *Anufrijeva* v. *Southwark London Borough Council* [2003] EWCA Civ 1406, is more restrictive and suggests that a public authority in a similar position should only be liable where there is negligent culpability.

A series of questions must be considered in a systematic way in determining whether there has been a breach of Art. 8. For ease of reference these questions are set out below.

Art. 8

- Does the issue concern an aspect of the right to respect for private and family life, home and correspondence?
- Has there been an interference with the right?
- Has the interference been by a public authority, or a body exercising a public function, or the state?

If the answer to any of the above questions is NO then there is NO BREACH. Where an interference is established proceed with the following questions:

- Is the interference lawful?
- Is the interference necessary in a democratic society?
- Is the interference proportionate?

If the answer to the above is YES there is NO BREACH.

Article 9

ECHR

Everyone has the right to freedom of thought, conscience and religion; this right includes freedom … to manifest his religion or belief, in worship, teaching, practice and observance.

(HRA 1998)

The terms of Art. 9 should encourage residential homes to respect different religious ceremonies depending on their residents' beliefs. It may also apply in respect of dress codes. In *R (SB)* v. *Headteacher and Governors of Denbigh High School* [2005] EWCA Civ 199, a Muslim schoolgirl asserted her right to wear religious dress (a *jilbab*) in school. As she had missed time off school, the Court of Appeal also found an infringement of her right to education under Art. 2, Protocol 1 but the decision was later overturned by the House of Lords ([2006] UKHL 15). Reference to religious belief will not justify inappropriate behaviour that might violate other rights, e.g. chastisement of children based on religious belief, the subject of *R (Williamson)* v. *Secretary of State for Education and Employment* [2005] UKHL 15.

It was argued in *Williamson* that s. 548 of the Education Act 1996, which bans corporal punishment in all schools, interfered with the claimants' freedom to manifest their religion in accordance with Art. 9 of the European Convention on Human Rights. The claimants were a group of teachers and parents of pupils at independent schools. They sought a declaration by judicial review that s. 548 did not prevent a parent delegating to a teacher the right to administer corporal punishment. The schools provided a Christian education based on biblical observance. Various sections from the Bible were cited to support the use of corporal punishment. For example: 'Do not withhold correction from a child for if you beat him with a rod, he will not die. You shall beat him with a rod and deliver his soul from hell.' The claim was dismissed. The court held that under Art. 9 there was a difference between freedom to hold a belief and freedom to manifest a belief. Freedom to manifest a belief was qualified. Section 548 interfered with the parents' rights but it was justified as the legislature had taken the view that corporal punishment at school was unnecessary and undesirable and other non-violent methods of punishment were available.

Article 10

ECHR

Everyone has the right to freedom of expression. This right shall include freedom to hold opinions and to receive and impart information and ideas without interference by public authority . . .

(HRA 1998)

Most cases under Art. 10 have related to the freedom of the press to publish information in matters of local, national and international interest. Article 10 issues often conflict with a corresponding individual right to privacy, and the courts will carry out a balancing exercise as illustrated in the following decision.

Key Case

In *R (on the application of Stone and others)* v. *South East Coast Strategic Health Authority* [2006] EWHC 1668 (Admin), S challenged the defendants' decision to publish in full the report following an independent inquiry they had commissioned into the care, treatment and supervision of S in the years prior to his committing two murders and one attempted murder. S had cooperated with the inquiry by giving it full access to his medical, probation and other records.

The court noted that the protection of personal data, and the need for appropriate safeguards, was of fundamental importance to a person's enjoyment of the right to respect for private and family life provided by Art. 8, particularly in the case of medical data. However, Art. 10 of the Convention had also to be considered and given due weight. An ultimate balance had to be struck between those competing rights, and the court had to conduct a close and penetrating examination, because there had to be a compelling case to justify publication of the full report. In this case the decision to publish was justified and proportionate, and did not constitute an unwarranted interference with the claimant's rights under the European Convention on Human Rights, Art. 8, nor a breach of the Data Protection Act 1998.

In employment law, this Article should override any gagging clauses designed to prevent whistleblowing and supports the provisions of the Public Interest Disclosure Act 1998.

This right also extends to the right to receive information (*Open Door Counselling and Dublin Well Woman* v. *Ireland* (1992) 15 EHRR 244), and may have implications for local authorities' publications relating to available services. It is important that information the local authority may publish, about its services and also about human rights, is in an accessible format, for example, to reflect languages spoken in the locality. Information should also be accessible to people with disabilities. The British Institute of Learning Disabilities (BILD) has produced a useful guide to the HRA which considers implications for people with learning disabilities illustrated by shared experiences.[10] An accompanying poster translates the rights into more accessible language, for example:

- I should be able to say what I like as long as I respect other people, and expect people to listen to me (Art. 10).
- I should have my rights respected (Art. 6).
- I should be safe at home and have time to myself (Art. 8).
- I can speak out and complain if something is wrong (Art. 10).
- I can get married and have children (Art. 12).
- It is wrong for anyone to shout at me, call me names, hit or hurt me (Art. 3).
- It is wrong for anyone to lock me in or stop me going out (Art. 5).

Article 12

ECHR

Men and women of marriageable age have the right to marry and to found a family, according to the national laws governing the exercise of this right.

(HRA 1998)

It is apparent from the wording of Art. 12 that it is limited to heterosexual relationships and there have been cases where transsexuals have been denied the right to marry (*Rees* v. *United Kingdom* (1986) 9 EHRR 56; *Cossey* v. *United Kingdom* (1991) 13 EHRR 622). In

Goodwin v. *United Kingdom* [2002] 2 FLR 487, the ECHR found that the United Kingdom's refusal to allow people who had undergone gender reassignment the ability to alter their gender on their birth certificate was in breach of Convention rights. Legislation to remedy this position has been introduced in the form of the Gender Recognition Act 2004. The Civil Partnership Act 2004, which provides for legal recognition of homosexual relationships in a similar form to marriage, and subsequently the Marriage (Same Sex Couples) Act 2013, should also be noted. It is possible that decisions to sterilise young women with learning disabilities may be subject to closer scrutiny in future, given the application of the right to found a family under Art. 12 (*Re F* [1990] 2 AC 1). Article 12 is also relevant to adoption as a means of founding a family. However, it is unlikely to support an argument that an individual has a right to fertility treatment.

Article 14

> **ECHR**
>
> The enjoyment of the rights and freedoms set forth in this Convention shall be secured without discrimination on any ground such as sex, race, colour, language, religion, political or other opinion, national or social origin, association with a national minority, property, birth or other status.
>
> (HRA 1998)

Article 14 prohibits discrimination (based on a wide range of grounds) in individuals' enjoyment of the rights contained in Articles of the European Convention on Human Rights. It is not a freestanding Article but is directly linked to the other Articles.

Sexuality is not specifically listed in Art. 14 as a ground of discrimination but case law has shown that discrimination on the grounds of a person's sexuality does fall within the Article. This position was confirmed in the case of *Ghaidan* v. *Mendoza* [2004] UKHL 30. The issue in this case was whether Mr Mendoza was entitled to succeed to a tenancy under the Rent Act 1977, i.e. was he entitled to carry on the tenancy of the property in which he lived with his same-sex partner, when his partner died, the tenancy having been in his partner's name. The relevant paragraph in the regulations refers to a surviving spouse or 'a person who was living with the tenant as his or her wife or husband'. Applying the duty to read legislation compatibly with the Convention, the court interpreted 'as his or her wife or husband' to mean, 'as if they were his or her wife or husband', thus including homosexual couples. The court commented that issues of discrimination have 'high constitutional importance'.

First Protocol

The First Protocol contains Articles that were added to the Convention following ratification:

Article 1: Protection of property may be relevant to cases of financial and material abuse suffered by vulnerable adults and to the operation of systems whereby management of property and finances are delegated to another person or body.

Article 2: Right to education could be relevant in general terms to people with a learning disability and to provision for special educational needs, and specifically to the provision of sex education.

Challenges under the Human Rights Act will frequently include more than one of the articles as illustrated in the case of *ZH* v. *Commissioner of Police for the Metropolis [2012] EWHC 604* (QB). A 16-year-old boy with severe autism and epilepsy was taken swimming and refused to move from the poolside. His carers were unable to move him with distraction techniques. Police attended and were informed of his autism. When one of them touched the boy he jumped into the pool. He was lifted, struggling, out of the pool and the police restrained him with handcuffs and leg restraints. He was then placed in a cage in the police van. Human rights claims under Articles 3, 5 and 8 were successful. It was found that the police had inflicted inhuman or degrading treatment on the boy considering the duration of force and restraint, injuries to the boy and his age, health and vulnerability. He was deprived of his liberty as the nature and duration of the restraint amounted to more than a restriction on movement. The police actions also interfered with the boy's right to respect for his private life and could not be justified as proportionate as less intrusive action could have been taken. Damages were awarded. The court noted that, 'The case highlights the need for there to be an awareness of the disability of autism within the public services.'

Reflect

Does the Human Rights Act 1998 really address fundamental rights in modern society? Would you add to or alter the existing rights?

Using the HRA 1998

To bring a claim under the HRA 1998, the individual must be a 'victim'. This means that they are directly affected by the measure or at least at risk of being affected, or a person closely or personally related to one affected. It is not possible to complain in abstract about behaviour. This formulation is more restrictive than the existing criterion for judicial review applications of having a 'sufficient interest' in an issue. It will be possible for interest groups, e.g. MIND and BAAF, to bring an action only if their members are themselves victims. It is possible for a company or group of individuals to make a claim as a victim. In fact, case law suggests that the term 'victim' is not unduly restrictive. For example, in *Campbell and Cosans* v. *United Kingdom* (1982) 4 EHRR 293, a case which challenged the use of corporal punishment in schools, the applicants were classed as victims because their children went to state schools where corporal punishment was permitted; the applicants' children had not actually been punished.

Remedies

If a court finds that there has been a violation of one of the Articles, there are a range of possible remedies available to the person whose rights have been breached. These remedies are: injunctions, declarations, declaration of incompatibility, and an award of 'just satisfaction' in financial compensation. Damages awarded under the HRA 1998 will be assessed in a slightly different manner from the normal calculation of damages in civil cases but may nevertheless be substantial. In *Smith and Grady* v. *United Kingdom* (1999) 29 EHRR 493, the discharge of the applicants from the armed forces following an investigation into their sexual orientation was found to be a violation of their right to respect for private life (Art. 8). In the circumstances they were awarded £19,000 each. The total cost to the

Government, including costs and expenses, far exceeded the amount paid in damages. This serves as a further useful reminder of the value of local authorities' reviewing procedures in search of any areas of non-compliance. Litigation is expensive and if a local authority is found to be in breach it may be faced with a substantial bill.

Equality and Human Rights Commission

At the time the Human Rights Act 1998 was introduced there was no body equivalent to the Equal Opportunities Commission or the Commission for Racial Equality (**CRE**) to assist people who wished to bring a case under the provisions of the HRA 1998. The Parliamentary Joint Committee on Human Rights reported a compelling case for establishing a human rights commission in England and Wales. It argued that respect for human rights is not at the heart of public authorities' policies and practices, and that bodies such as local councils and hospitals act defensively, in aiming to avoid litigation but no more.[11]

The Equality Act 2006 created the Equality and Human Rights Commission which drew together the functions of equality commissions, e.g. the Commission for Racial Equality, with an extended remit to include human rights issues. One of the duties of the Commission is to promote human rights and to raise public bodies' awareness of their obligations under the HRA 1998. (The role of the Commission is considered in more detail in Chapter 6.)

The Commission has powers under s.16 of the Equality Act 2006 to make formal enquiries into particular areas of practice. Examples of recent enquiries include:

- 'Hidden in plain sight: Inquiry into disability-related harassment' (2011). This report includes an examination of ten serious cases in which disabled people died or were seriously injured, including Fiona Pilkington and Steven Hoskin.

- 'Close to home: An inquiry into older people and human rights in home care' (2011). This inquiry highlights the fact that unlike residential homes, independent homecare providers and unregulated providers such as personal assistants do not have any direct duties under the Human Rights Act, yet provide the large majority of care in individuals' own homes.

Influence of European and international law and Conventions

The discussion above explains how the European Convention on Human Rights has been fully incorporated into our domestic law. There are other European and international Conventions which it is useful to be aware of, even though they do not carry the same force of law and are best described as morally persuasive statements of intent.

Universal Declaration of Human Rights 1948

The Universal Declaration of Human Rights 1948 contains a number of Articles which are similarly worded to the ECHR, e.g. Art. 33: 'Everyone has the right to life, liberty and the security of person.' It is, however, a broader statement of rights, starting with Art. 1, which states that 'All human beings are born free and equal in dignity and rights.'

Other significant Articles include:

Article 6: Everyone has the right to recognition everywhere as a person before the law.

Article 14: Everyone has the right to seek and to enjoy in other countries asylum from persecution.

Article 16: Men and women of full age, without any limitation due to race, nationality or religion, have the right to marry and to found a family. Marriage shall be entered into only with the free and full consent of the intending spouses. The family is the natural and fundamental group unit of society and is entitled to protection by society and the state.

Article 21: Everyone has the right to take part in the government of his country, directly or through the freely chosen representatives. Everyone has the right of equal access to public service in his country.

United Nations Convention on the Rights of the Child 1989

The United Nations Convention on the Rights of the Child 1989 provides a useful guide for good practice for promoting children's rights. Whilst the rights are not enforceable in a court of law in the same way as the right within the HRA 1998, the rights are nevertheless persuasive and have been referred to in domestic judgments. The United Kingdom has experienced a high level of criticism by the UNCRC Committee on the Rights of the Child, which conducts reviews of states' compliance with the Convention. Recently, this criticism may arguably have been partly responsible for the introduction of the Children's Commissioner in England.

The Articles include a range of rights which position the child's best interest as priority, provide for children to participate in decisions affecting them, and ensure the protection from harm and provision of basic needs. The following Articles are particularly significant, starting with a commitment to anti-discrimination.

Article 1

States parties shall respect and ensure the rights set forth in the present Convention to each child within their jurisdiction without discrimination of any kind, irrespective of the child's or his or her parent's or legal guardian's race, colour, sex, language, religion, political or other opinion, national, ethnic or social origin, property, disability, birth or other status.

Article 3

1. In all actions concerning children, whether undertaken by public or private social welfare institutions, courts of law, administrative authorities or legislative bodies, the best interests of the child shall be the primary consideration.

2. States parties undertake to ensure the child such protection and care as is necessary for his or her well-being, taking into account the rights and duties of his or her parents, legal guardians, or other individuals legally responsible for him or her, and shall take all appropriate legislative and administrative measures.

3. States parties shall ensure that the institutions, services and facilities responsible for the care or protection of children shall conform with the standards established by competent authorities, particularly in the areas of safety, health, in the number and suitability of their staff, as well as competent supervision.

Article 9

States parties shall ensure that a child shall not be separated from his or her parents against their will, except when competent authorities subject to judicial review determine, in accordance with applicable law and procedures, that such separation is necessary for the best interests of the child. Such determination may be necessary in a particular case, such as one involving abuse or neglect of the child by the parents, or one where the parents are living separately and a decision must be made as to the child's place of residence.

Article 12

States parties shall assure to the child who is capable of forming his or her own views the right to express those views freely in all matters affecting the child, the views of the child being given due weight in accordance with the age and maturity of the child.

It is clear that the rights outlined in the above Conventions extend further than the rights that have been incorporated into domestic law via the Human Rights Act 1998. For example, the HRA 1998 does not include reference to the right of access to public services, nor does it specifically recognise the special status of a child.

United Nations Convention on the Rights of Persons with Disabilities 2006

Article 12

States parties reaffirm that persons with disabilities have the right to recognition everywhere as persons before the law, recognise that persons with disabilities enjoy legal capacity on an equal basis with others in all aspects of life, take appropriate measures to provide access by persons with disabilities to the support they may require in exercising their legal capacity, and ensure that all measures that relate to the exercise of legal capacity provide for appropriate and effective safeguards to prevent abuse. Such safeguards shall ensure that measures relating to the exercise of legal capacity respect the rights, will and preferences of the person, are free of conflict of interest and undue influence, are proportional and tailored to the person's circumstances, apply for the shortest time possible and are subject to regular review.

Article 19

States parties recognise the equal right of all persons with disabilities to live in the community, with choices equal to others and shall take effective and appropriate measures to facilitate full enjoyment by persons with disabilities of this right and their full inclusion and participation in the community.

Chapter summary

- The Human Rights Act 1998 will have a significant influence on the future development of vast areas of English law, but particularly on the role and responsibilities of public authorities, which includes Social Services Departments.

- The Human Rights Act 1998 incorporates the European Convention on Human Rights into domestic law, making its rights, freedoms and prohibitions more directly enforceable in the domestic courts.

- The Articles of the ECHR are incorporated in three main ways. First, courts are bound to take into account judgments of the European Court when determining any question in connection with a Convention right; second, legislation must be read and given effect in a way that is compatible with the Convention rights; third, it is unlawful for a public authority to act in a way that is incompatible with the Convention rights.

- Public authorities including central and local government, police, courts, social services, CAFCASS, regulatory bodies and others exercising functions of a public nature may be faced with compensation claims if they violate or propose to violate individual rights. This establishes a further level of accountability for social services.

- The ECHR Articles contain rights, prohibitions and freedoms which may be absolute, limited or qualified. Some interference with the rights may be permissible but must be proportionate.

- Rights which are particularly relevant to social work practice are: the prohibition against torture or inhuman or degrading treatment or punishment (Art. 3); the right to liberty and security of the person (Art. 5); the right to a fair and public hearing (Art. 6); the right to respect for private and family life (Art. 8).

- To make a claim under the HRA 1998, a person must be a 'victim', i.e. directly affected by the measure, or at risk of being affected, or closely related to such a person.

- One of the objectives of the Commission for Equality and Human Rights is to promote human rights.

- Other international and European Conventions exist which, although not carrying full force of law in this country, are nevertheless morally persuasive.

Exercise

In the following scenarios, consider which and whose human rights have been breached and how any competing rights might be balanced:

1. Julie and Adam, parents of Josie, aged 2, are regular drug users. Their neighbour, Mrs Thomas, sees Josie crying at the window one evening and assumes Julie and Adam are out when they do not answer the door to her. In fact they are in the back garden. She reports this to the police and social services. Julie and Adam are known to social services and have a history of being uncooperative. Their elder child, Jack, was born addicted to heroin and taken into care at birth. A case conference is held the next day and the health visitor expresses concern over Josie's development. Julie and Adam are not invited to attend. The local authority apply for an *ex parte* emergency protection order and Josie is removed to foster carers who live 40 miles away. Julie and Adam have no means of transport.

2. Mrs Jones has multiple sclerosis and is aged 72. She is a resident in Ferndale Nursing Home. She has lived there for four years. Her husband lives alone in the matrimonial home and is becoming increasingly frail. Mr and Mrs Jones would like to share a room in the nursing home and have been on a waiting list for a double room for 15 months. Mrs Jones' daughter is concerned that at times when she has visited the home, Mrs Jones' door has been locked from the outside. The staff say it is because she has a tendency to wander and might fall. Mrs Jones says she is happy at the home, although she does not like getting up at 7 a.m. for breakfast in the dining room and, as a Jehovah's Witness, she does not like having to join the other residents to watch 'Songs of Praise' on Sundays. The home owner has announced that his profits are down and he intends to close the home

at the end of the month. Mrs Jones had assumed she would end her days at the home and does not want to move.

3. Linda and Tony both have learning disabilities and live in a small community home with two other adults and a care worker. They enjoy each other's company and have recently become engaged. Linda is upset because her mother has told her she will not be able to get married because of her learning disability. When she asked John, the care worker, about this he agreed, saying that marriage is not really for people like Linda and Tony. Linda's mother is concerned that Linda and Tony might be having sexual relations and has been to see a consultant about a sterilisation for Linda. Neither Linda nor Tony have ever had any sex education. Before she moved into her current home Linda lived in a residential home for young people with learning disabilities. While there she was raped by another resident. Linda told Amy, her favourite care assistant, about this, around a week after it happened and they went to the police. At the station the policeman who interviewed Linda said it would not be possible to prosecute the other resident because Linda would not be able to give evidence. He said it was better to keep things like this informal. He went to the home and had a word with the resident. The home owner was furious at having the police visit the home and sacked Amy.

Websites

Information on the Human Rights Act 1998 is available from Liberty. The site gives an overview of the HRA and also considers the rights of particular groups, e.g. immigrants, travellers, children and young persons and prisoners:
www.yourrights.org.uk

Decisions of the European Court of Human Rights are available from:
www.echr.coe.int

The website of the British Institute of Human Rights includes the recent report, 'The Human Rights Act Changing Lives' (2008 2nd edn) from which the examples at the start of the chapter were taken:
www.bihr.org.uk

The Ministry of Justice is responsible for developing human rights policy. Its site includes up-to-date materials and links to other useful sites.
www.justice.gov.uk/human-rights

Information relating to the United Nations Convention on the Rights of the Child (1989) is available from:
www.unicef.org/crc/

The Commission for Equality and Human Rights website:
www.equalityhumanrights.com

Further reading

There is a wealth of information available on the Human Rights Act 1998, some of it geared specifically to particular areas of interest, such as social work. General texts include:

Choudhry, S. and Herring, J. (2009) *Human Rights and Family Law*. Oxford: Hart.

Hoffman, D. and Rowe, J. (2013) *Human Rights in the UK: An Introduction to the Human Rights Act 1998* (4th edn). Harlow: Pearson. (Very accessible and easy to understand, also including a copy of the Act.)

Wadham, J., Mountfield, H., Prochaska, E. and Brown, C. (2011) *Blackstone's Guide to the Human Rights Act 1998* (6th edn). London: Blackstone Press. (A comprehensive guide to the law, including a copy of the Act.)

With a particular focus on the impact on social work see:

Ife, J. (2008) *Human Rights and Social Work: Towards Rights-based Practice.* Cambridge: Cambridge University Press.

McDonald, A. (2001) 'The Human Rights Act and social work practice' 13(3) *Practice* p. 5. (Discussion of the implications of the Act for social work practice and the relationship between human rights and anti-oppressive practice.)

Williams, J. (2001) '1998 Human Rights Act: social work's new benchmark' 31 *British Journal of Social Work* p. 831. (This article outlines the effect of the Act illustrated by reference to examples from social work practice.)

Specific areas of social work practice are covered by:

Clements, L. and Read, J. (2003) *Disabled People and European Human Rights: A Review of the Implications of the 1998 Human Rights Act for Disabled Children and Adults in the UK.* Bristol: Policy Press.

Clements, L. and Parker, C. (2008) 'The UN Convention on the Rights of Persons with Disabilities: a new right to independent living?' 4 *European Human Rights Law Review* p. 1361.

Fortin, J. (2011) 'A decade of the HRA and its impact on children's rights' *Family Law* p. 176.

Harris-Short, S. (2005) 'Family Law and the Human Rights Act 1998: judicial restraint or revolution?' 17(3) *Child and Family Law Quarterly* p. 329.

Johns, R. (2004) 'Of unsound mind? Mental health social work and the European Convention on Human Rights' 16(4) *Practice* p. 247.

Munro, E. and Ward, H. (2008) 'Balancing parents' and very young children's rights in care proceedings: decision-making in the context of the Human Rights Act 1998' 13(2) *Child and Family Social Work* p. 227.

Watson, J. and Woolf, M. (2003) *Human Rights Act Toolkit.* London: Legal Action Group Books. (A useful practical guide to the Act designed for non-lawyers working in relevant organisations such as health and social services. Includes checklists which can be applied in order to test and demonstrate compliance with the Act.)

Notes

1. J. Wadham and H. Mountfield (2006) *Blackstone's Guide to the Human Rights Act 1998* (4th edn). London: Blackstone Press.
2. D. Lammy MP, Parliamentary Under Secretary at the Department for Constitutional Affairs. Third Anniversary of Human Rights Act Audit Commission Conference speech, 2003.
3. Sedley LJ (2003) 'The rocks or the open sea: where is the Human Rights Act heading?'. LAG Annual Lecture.
4. Ibid.
5. *Golder* v. *UK* (1975) 1 EHRR 524.

[6] Home Office (1987) 'Bringing Rights Home'.

[7] R. Edwards (2000) 'Reading down legislation under the Human Rights Act' 20(3) *Legal Studies* pp. 353–71.

[8] LAC (2000) 17.

[9] Citing from R. Clayton and H. Tomlinson (2003) *Law and Human Rights.* Oxford: Oxford University Press.

[10] A. Hughes and P. Coombs (2001) *Easy Guide to the Human Rights Act 1998: Implications for People with Learning Disabilities.* Kidderminster: BILD Publications.

[11] See 'The case for a Human Rights Commission' published by the Joint Committee on Human Rights on 19 March 2003, available at www.publications.parliament.uk.

Chapter 6

Discrimination

Learning objectives

To develop an understanding of the following:

- A range of references in legislation and guidance which support anti-discriminatory practice.
- The legal basis of the requirement for anti-discriminatory practice in social work.
- The implications of the Human Rights Act 1998 for discrimination.
- An outline of equality legislation, which outlaws discrimination on nine protected characteristics, including race, sex and disability.
- The meaning of direct, indirect and dual discrimination, victimisation and harassment.
- Ways in which the right not to be discriminated against may be enforced, including the role of the Equality and Human Rights Commission.

Talking Point

In the case of *Lewisham London Borough Council* v. *Malcolm* [2008] UKHL 43 the central question for the court related to the housing needs of a disabled adult. M was diagnosed with schizophrenia. He was a secure tenant of the local authority and had sublet his flat. When the local authority discovered he had sublet, it issued possession proceedings. There was no evidence that the local authority were aware of his schizophrenia. M argued that at the time of subletting he did not understand the consequences of his decisions because of his schizophrenia. The Court of Appeal found that the possession action constituted unlawful discrimination contrary to the Disability Discrimination Act 1995.

The House of Lords allowed the local authority's appeal, stating that it was not enough for M to show that there may have been a causal connection between the sublet and his disability; he needed to show that his disability played some motivational part in the local authority decision to recover possession. The relevant comparator would be a secure tenant with no mental disorder who had sublet. M was not treated less favourably than a tenant with no mental disorder would have been and therefore there was no discrimination.

In her judgment, Hale LJ clearly articulated the challenge facing the court:

> This raises questions about the fundamental principles underlying disability discrimination law. Is it intended simply to secure that disabled people are treated in the same way as other people who do not have their disability? Or is it intended to secure that they are treated differently from other people in order that they can play as full as possible a part in society whatever their disabilities?

She continued:

> There is little doubt what the sensible answer to the issues in this case would be. It would be to enable, in the first place the Council, and in the second place the court to balance the competing interests. On the one hand, there is the public interest in the proper use of social housing, which means that local authorities should not be required to continue to supply a home to a person who no longer needs it and merely wishes to make a profit out of it, or indeed to a person who will never be able to comply with the conditions of the tenancy. On the other hand, there is the right of people with disabilities to be treated as equal citizens, entitled to have due allowance made for the consequences of their disability. This, in essence, is the result which the Equality and Human Rights Commission would like us to be able to achieve.

Discrimination law produces a significant amount of case law, such as the case here, unpicking the complex statutory schemes. The case for a single piece of discrimination law that covers all types of discrimination has been met by the introduction of the Equality Act 2010. Its objective is to simplify and clarify the law and be better able to respond to cases of multiple discrimination. Nevertheless, case law as above will continue to be relevant in the interpretation of the new law.

Introduction

> If we are committed to anti-oppressive practice then we have a duty to ensure that the rights of users are not violated. Legislation can be used to deny rights but we need to be aware of our role in minimizing the oppressive aspects of practice and the law and we must endeavour to maximize the rights to which all people are entitled. It is for this reason that we see the law as an instrument to protect people's rights. It is a powerful instrument but it is one that we can control and we should not therefore become subservient to it.

> (Dalrymple and Burke, 1995)[1]

Discrimination issues are identified throughout this book, with an emphasis on promoting anti-discriminatory and anti-oppressive practice. The objectives of this chapter are twofold: first, to draw together the various references to discrimination in legislation and guidance, beyond specific equality legislation, some of which direct social services to act in a non-discriminatory fashion. Challenging discrimination is not confined to the use of specific anti-discrimination legislation and it is necessary to take a broad perspective and consider all options. The second objective is to outline the Equality Act 2010 which replaces most of the previous anti-discrimination legislation and outlaws extended forms of discrimination on the grounds of nine 'protected characteristics'. The Act has two main purposes: to harmonise discrimination law and to strengthen the law to support progress towards equality. The 2010 Act applies to all organisations that provide a service to the public (or section of the public) and to anyone who sells goods or provides facilities. In this chapter, the legislation is considered from two perspectives: its impact on social work practice; and as an aspect of the law which a service user may be affected by in, for example, the field of employment, or provision of services. An aspect of good social work practice is ensuring that service users are aware of their rights not to be discriminated against. There may also be circumstances where social workers experience discrimination directly, whether it is in the form of racial or sexual harassment from service users or colleagues, or discrimination in relation to training, working conditions and career opportunities. As a minimum, support from managers and colleagues should be forthcoming where discrimination is experienced. In some circumstances, just as for any employee, it may be necessary to have recourse to an employment tribunal.

Reliance on law to combat discrimination has a number of limitations. This is an area where good practice has developed ahead of legal requirements. Despite the extended characteristics protected under the Equality Act 2010, anti-discriminatory practice must extend to recognition of other forms of discrimination which are not addressed by the legislation. The aim of the early anti-discrimination legislation of the 1970s was to alter entrenched attitudes and to promote change. It is clear that, despite that intention, much systematic discrimination continues to exist. The role of law as an instrument of social change must be questioned; however, it is important to recognise that the new legislation does provide a more extensive framework for certain discriminatory practices to be challenged.

It has also been noted that the law itself can operate in a way that is discriminatory. Such discrimination may be explicitly defined by statute: for example, until recently part-time staff enjoyed lesser employment protection rights than full-time staff. Discrimination may also manifest itself as a facet of the composition of the legal workforce. Despite an increase in numbers of women and people from ethnic minorities, the profession is still dominated by white, middle-class males, and this is nowhere more evident than in the courts, where, amongst the senior judiciary (High Court, Court of Appeal and House of Lords), at the time of writing there is just one ethnic minority judge. It has also been noted that some legal terms are themselves discriminatory and direct use of the terms should be avoided unless necessary for accuracy: e.g. reference to 'blind, deaf or dumb' in s. 29 of the National Assistance Act 1948.

A useful starting point for a social worker employed in the statutory sector is to become familiar with the local authority equal opportunities policy for guidance on good practice. In addition, the British Association of Social Workers (BASW) Code of Ethics (2012), contains principles that prescribe professional responsibilities of the social worker, including:

Challenging discrimination Social workers have a responsibility to challenge discrimination on the basis of characteristics such as ability, age, culture, gender or sex, marital status, socio-economic status, political opinions, skin colour, racial or other physical characteristics, sexual orientation or spiritual beliefs.

Recognising diversity Social workers should recognise and respect the diversity of the societies in which they practise, taking into account individual, family, group and community differences.

Empowering people Social workers should promote and contribute to the development of positive policies, procedures and practices which are anti-oppressive and empowering. They should respect people's beliefs, values, culture, goals, needs, preferences, relationships and affiliations. Social workers should recognise their own prejudices to ensure they do not discriminate against any person or group. They should ensure that services are offered and delivered in a culturally appropriate manner. They should challenge and seek to address any actions of colleagues who demonstrate negative discrimination or prejudice.[2]

Recognising diversity is central to the social work role and the HCPC code of practice requires social care employers to put into place and implement written policies and procedures to deal with dangerous, discriminatory or exploitative behaviour and practice. The code also requires social care workers to protect the rights and promote the interests of service users and carers by promoting equal opportunities, and respecting diversity and different cultures and values.

In addition to domestic law, it is also relevant that the United Kingdom is a signatory to various international and European treaties which include commitment to anti-discrimination. Article 1 of the Universal Declaration of Human Rights 1948 (UDHR) provides:

Art. 1

All human beings are born free and equal in dignity and rights.

(UDHR)

Article 2 expands on this principle:

> ### Art. 2
>
> Everyone is entitled to all the rights and freedoms set forth in this Declaration, without distinction of any kind, such as race, colour, sex, language, religion, political or other opinion, national or social origin, property, birth or other status.
>
> (UDHR)

The introduction of the Human Rights Act 1998 has meant that the anti-discrimination Article of the European Convention on Human Rights is directly enforceable in domestic courts. Article 14 provides:

> ### Art. 14
>
> The enjoyment of the rights and freedoms set forth in this Convention shall be secured without discrimination on any ground such as sex, race, colour, language, religion, political or other opinion, national or social origin, association with a national minority, property, birth or other status.
>
> (ECHR 1998)

The forms of discrimination envisaged by this Article are significantly broader than those covered by The Equality Act (and previous legislation), for example the reference to political opinion. The term 'other status' would suggest that the Article would apply to forms of discrimination which have not, as yet, been widely recognised. However, the application of this Article is qualified; it is not a freestanding article, but is limited to discrimination in relation to the 'enjoyment of the rights and freedoms set forth in this Convention'. (Chapter 5 set out the Articles of the Convention.) As an example, it could be argued in relation to Art. 12, the right to marry and found a family, that a restriction on availability of fertility treatment to women above a certain age, or of a particular religion, is discriminatory. The Article could not be relied on for matters not covered by the ECHR, such as the right to employment or to welfare benefits.

In other cases, where Art. 14 is argued alongside another Convention right, if the court finds a violation of the other Convention right, it may consider it is unnecessary to make a finding under Art. 14. For example, in *Smith and Grady* v. *United Kingdom* (1999) 29 EHRR 493, the applicants had been discharged from the armed services following an inquiry into their sexual orientation. It was found unanimously by the European Court of Human Rights that their right to respect for private and family life under ECHR, Art. 8 had been violated. In addition to Art. 8, the applicants also complained under Arts. 3, 10 and 14, the latter relating to discriminatory treatment by the Ministry of Defence policy against homosexuals in the armed forces. The court decided that the Art. 14 complaint did not give rise to any issue separate to those already considered and did not therefore make a specific finding under Art. 14.

As yet, the British Government has not signed Protocol 12 of the European Convention on Human Rights, which provides: 'the enjoyment of any right set forth by law shall be secured without discrimination on any ground such as sex, race, colour, language, religion, political or other opinion, national or social origin, association with a national minority, property, birth or status.' As this Protocol applies to any rights set forth by law and is not limited to enjoyment of Convention rights, it would further enhance domestic equality legislation.

Evidence of discrimination

It is beyond the scope of this text to present detailed evidence of the many and various forms of discrimination that exist within society. A brief summary, however, serves as a reminder that, for many of the service users social workers will encounter, discrimination is an aspect of their everyday experience.

- Black children are over-represented in the care system.[3]
- Children with dual black and white parentage are over-represented among looked after children.[4]
- There is also an over-representation of black children in referrals for physical abuse.[5]
- Black children are more likely to be permanently excluded from school than white children.[6]
- The stereotypical view of the African Caribbean grandmother as ever resourceful and able to cope was in part considered to be a cause of the failure to provide adequate support by social services in the Tyra Henry inquiry.[7]
- A disproportionate number of care orders are made in respect of children whose parents have a learning disability.[8]
- A black male is more likely to be detained under the criminal provisions of the Mental Health Act 1983, to be in a secure ward and to receive higher doses of medication.[9]
- Disabled people are over six times as likely as non-disabled people to be out of work and claiming benefits.[10]

It is also important to recognise that perceptions of discrimination vary. A Home Office Citizenship Survey in 2003 found that respondents from ethnic minorities were more likely than white respondents to think organisations would treat them badly. For example, black respondents felt that police, immigration, prison, courts, CPS and armed forces were more likely to treat black respondents worse than people of other races.

Institutional racism

Racism and other forms of discrimination may be manifest at an individual level based on prejudice. It is also becoming recognised that racism may operate at an institutional level. Some of the evidence cited above would suggest that institutional racism is present in social care agencies including social work.[11] The Macpherson report defined institutional racism as: '[t]he collective failure of an organisation to provide an appropriate and professional service to people because of their colour, culture or ethnic origin. It can be seen or detected in processes, attitudes and behaviour which amount to discrimination through unwitting prejudice, ignorance, thoughtlessness and racist stereotyping which disadvantages minority people.'[12] The report stated further that 'it is incumbent on every institution to examine their policies and practices to guard against disadvantaging any section of our communities'. A clear outcome of this report was the extension of the Race Relations Act 1976 in respect of duties of public authorities, further developed in the public equality duty discussed below.

Discrimination – general

In combating discrimination, and acting in a non-discriminatory fashion, it is important to look beyond primary anti-discrimination legislation. A selection of references in other legislation, guidance and codes of practice, which are intended to prevent discrimination and promote anti-discriminatory practice, are set out below.

Legislation

- The Children Act 1989, s. 22(5) requires due consideration to be given to a child's racial origin, religious persuasion and cultural and linguistic background when making any decision about a looked after child (including placement decisions).

- The Children Act 1989, Sch. 2, Part 1, para. 6 states that local authorities are required to 'provide services designed … to minimise the effect on disabled children … of their disabilities, and to give such children the opportunity to lead lives as normal as possible'.

- The Criminal Justice Act 1991, s. 95 requires those involved in the administration of criminal justice to avoid discrimination. The Home Secretary must publish information to assist with this duty on an annual basis. Ethnic monitoring in police forces has been introduced as a result of this provision.

- The Crime and Disorder Act 1998, ss. 29–32 contains specific offences of racist violence and harassment. There is a mandatory requirement to enhance the sentence if an offence was racially aggravated. (See discussion in Chapter 18.)

- The Public Order Act 1986 contains a number of offences of racial hatred, including broadcasts, written materials, use of words and behaviour with the intent to stir up racial hatred, or, having regard to all the circumstances, with the likelihood of racial hatred being stirred up (ss. 18–22). Consent of the Attorney-General is a prerequisite for the prosecution of these offences and cases have been rare.

- The Employment Rights Act 1996 makes a dismissal automatically unfair if it is for a reason related to pregnancy, childbirth, maternity leave, parental leave or time off for dependants.

- The Protection from Harassment Act 1997 introduced a criminal offence of harassment. Racial or sexual harassment could constitute a course of conduct required under the Act.

- The Mental Capacity Act 2005 guards against stereotyping in the principles set out at the start of the Act. Section 2(3) provides that lack of capacity cannot be established merely by reference to age or appearance or a condition or aspect of an individual's behaviour which might lead others to make unjustified assumptions about his capacity.

- The Racial and Religious Hatred Act 2006 introduces an offence of incitement to religious hatred.

- The Health and Social Care Act 2008 (Regulated Activities) Regulations 2010, Regulation 17 provides that in making suitable arrangemenst to ensure dignity, privacy and independence of service users and their participation in decisions relating to their care and treatment, a registered manager of a care home must take care to ensure that care and treatment is provided to service users with due regard to their age, sex, religious persuasion, sexual orientation, racial origin, cultural and linguistic background and any disability they may have.

Guidance

- The Mental Health Act 1983 Code of Practice (2008) contains a number of guiding principles which underpin the code, including a respect principle which states: 'People taking decisions under the Act must recognise and respect the diverse needs, values and circumstances of each patient, including their race, religion, culture, gender, age, sexual orientation and any disability. They must consider the patient's views, wishes and feelings (whether expressed at the time or in advance), so far as they are reasonably ascertainable, and follow those wishes wherever practicable and consistent with the purpose of the decision. There must be no unlawful discrimination' (para. 1.4).

- 'No Secrets',[13] guidance on the development of adult protection policies and procedures, includes recognition of discriminatory abuse as a form of adult abuse, comprising racist, sexist, that based on a person's disability, and other forms of harassment, slurs or similar treatment.[14]

- 'Working Together' (2013)[15] includes the following statement: 'Every assessment should reflect the unique characteristics of the child within their family and community context. The Children Act 1989 promotes the view that all children and their parents should be considered as individuals and that family structures, culture, religion, ethnic origins and other characteristics should be respected' (para. 39).

- The Care Homes Regulations 2001[16] require homes where children are to be accommodated to include in their statement of purpose a description of the home's policy on anti-discriminatory practice in relation to children and children's rights.

- The Code for Crown Prosecutors includes a two-part test for decisions whether to prosecute: first, examination of the evidence, and second, whether prosecution is in the public interest. A factor in favour of prosecution is where the offence is motivated by any form of discrimination such as racial or sexual or hostility towards a victim based on his membership of a particular section of society. The code itself is a public document produced in 14 different languages.

- Guidance to the Sexual Offences Act 2003 notes that whilst the Act sets out new sexual offences where the victim has a mental disorder: 'It is important to appreciate that where a person with a mental disorder is able to consent freely to sexual activity, they have the same rights to engage in sexual activity as anyone else.'[17]

- The National Service Framework for Older People (LAC (2001) 12) requires that NHS services are provided regardless of age, on the basis of clinical need alone. Also, social care services must not use age in eligibility criteria or policies to restrict access to services.

- Guidance itself must comply with anti-discrimination legislation. In *R (on the application of Eisai Ltd)* v. *National Institute for Health and Clinical Excellence* [2007] EWHC 1941 (Admin), guidance published by NICE on treatment of patients with Alzheimer's disease was found to be in breach of the Race Relations Act 1976 and the Disability Discrimination Act 1995 as certain of its tests were unlikely to provide an accurate assessment of certain BME or disabled patients as to suitability for treatment. It was otherwise lawful.

- 'Valuing People' (2001), the white paper on learning disability, includes the statement: 'The Government is committed to enforceable civil rights for disabled people in order to eradicate discrimination in society. People with learning disabilities have the right to a decent education, to grow up to vote, to marry and have a family, and to express their opinions, with help and support to do so where necessary' (para 2.2).

Other responses to discrimination

Existing anti-discrimination legislation provides some avenues for challenge of discrimination. In addition, it is important to be aware that issues of discrimination may feature in other types of cases and may be challenged on a number of different levels: e.g. use of the local authority complaints procedure or through specific criminal offences.

The case of *Thomas* v. *News Group Newspapers Ltd* [2001] EWCA Civ 1233, is illustrative. Miss Thomas had received race hate mail at her place of work following articles in the *Sun* newspaper. In this case the Protection from Harassment Act 1997 was applied to provide protection to the individual from harassment by the press. It was found that publication of three newspaper articles could constitute a course of conduct and therefore amounted to harassment.

Ethnic monitoring has been introduced into statistical collections on children's services. This should enable clearer analysis of how black and ethnic minority children fare. It should produce information on the services children from ethnic minorities receive and how ethnicity relates to the reasons behind the need for services.[18]

Repeal of previous anti-discrimination legislation

An obvious limitation of the anti-discrimination laws in this country has been the scope of application. Law developed in a piecemeal fashion, contained in a range of statutes and addressing discrimination on the grounds of race, sex, disability, and more recently, religion, sexual orientation and age. The Equality Act 2010 was introduced to remove inconsistencies and simplify the law and repeals all anti-discrimination legislation including the following:

- Sex Discrimination Act 1975.
- Equal Pay Act 1970.
- Race Relations Act 1976.
- Disability Discrimination Act 1995.
- Race Relations (Amendment) Act 2000.
- Employment Equality (Religion or Belief) Regulations 2003.
- Employment Equality (Sexual Orientation) Regulations 2003.
- Disability Discrimination Act 2005.
- Employment Equality (Age) Regulations 2006.

The Equality Act 2010

The Equality Act 2010 prohibits discriminatory conduct against people who have protected characteristics as outlined below. It applies to all organisations that provide a service to the public (or section of the public) and to anyone who sells goods or provides facilities. Services include: access to and use of any public places; accommodation in hotels, etc.; facilities by way of banking or insurance or credit; facilities for entertainment, recreation or refreshment; and the services of any profession or trade or any local or other public authority.[19] Social and legal services would be included. If a provider of services treats someone less favourably for a reason relating to their protected characteristic, which cannot be justified under the Act, this is discrimination. If a service provider has a practice, policy or procedure which makes it impossible or unreasonably difficult for certain people to make use of the service, there is a duty to take reasonable steps to change that practice, policy or procedure so that it no longer has that effect. This would include, for example, ensuring that information about services is produced in a way that makes it accessible to people with disabilities, e.g. Braille translations and large print copies.

The Act introduces the term 'protected characteristic'. It offers protection from discrimination in respect of the following nine areas of protected characteristics listed in s. 4, namely:

- age;
- disability;
- gender reassignment;
- marriage and civil partnership;
- pregnancy and maternity;
- race (includes ethnic or national origins, colour or nationality);
- religion or belief;
- sex;
- sexual orientation.

Much of the case law developed in relation to previous anti-discrimination legislation will continue to be helpful. It is important to note however that the definitions of disability and gender reassignment have changed.

Race s. 9

Whilst most racial discrimination in the United Kingdom is against members of ethnic minorities, the Act applies to people of every background, race, colour and nationality and could equally be relied upon by a white person who suffers discrimination. Section 9 states that race includes colour, nationality and ethnic or national origins.

'Ethnic origins'

Interpretation of this phrase was the central issue in the leading case of *Mandla* v. *Dowell Lee* [1983] 2 AC 548, concerning a Sikh schoolboy. The House of Lords found that Sikhs are a distinct ethnic group though not of distinctive national origins. In fact, though religion was not specifically covered by the **RRA** 1976, racial identity could be centred on observance of a particular religion. Lord Fraser said that an ethnic group had to regard itself and be regarded by others as a distinct community with two essential characteristics: first, a long shared history of which the group is conscious and keeps the memory alive; and second, a cultural tradition of its own including family and social customs and manners often associated with religious observance. An earlier case, *Seide* v. *Gillette Industries* [1980] IRLR 427 ruled that Jews are a racial group. In contrast, in *Dawkins* v. *Department of the Environment, sub nom Dawkins* v. *Crown Suppliers (PSA)* [1993] **IRLR** 284, the Court of Appeal held, following the guidance given in *Mandla*, that Rastafarians did not comprise a racial group, partly because they did not fulfil the requirement of 'a long shared history'.

'National origins'

It has recently been decided that, although members of the United Kingdom, it could be possible for national origins to apply to discrimination between English, Welsh, Scottish and Northern Irish people. In *BBC Scotland* v. *Souster* [2001] IRLR 150[20] the court found that the race relations legislation could cover the situation of an Englishman discriminated against by a Scottish employer on account of his being English.

Protection will also apply to a person who is affected by discrimination targeted at someone else: e.g. if services are withheld from a white person due to their marriage to a black person. A person who refuses to act in a discriminatory way will also be protected. In *Showboat Entertainment Centre Ltd* v. *Owens* [1984] 1 All ER 836, a white person was unlawfully discriminated against when he was dismissed after refusing to carry out an instruction from his employer to exclude black people from his place of work.

Pregnancy or maternity

These terms are not defined in the Act. Dismissal on the grounds of pregnancy is illegal.

Gender reassignment s. 12

Coverage extends to those proposing to undergo, undergoing or having undergone a process to change sex. A person who has the protected characteristic of gender reassignment (**GR**) is referred to under the Act as a transsexual. Not all transgender people are legally covered because GR refers to physical sex change. However, EHRC emphasises that 'best practice' is to cover all trans people for the purposes of the Equality Act.

Disability s. 6

Disability is defined in s. 6. as a 'physical or mental impairment', which, 'has a substantial and long-term adverse effect on ability to carry out normal day-to-day activities'. It is no longer a requirement to show that an impairment affects a particular 'capacity,' such as mobility, speech, hearing or eyesight. If the person behaving in a discriminatory way did not know, and could not have been expected to know of the person's disability then it will not be unlawful.

Reasonable adjustments

Under the old law it was unlawful to discriminate against a disabled person only in relation to employment and the provision of goods and services and selling, letting or managing of land or premises and there was no recognition of indirect discrimination. Both areas are expanded under the new law.

Guidance on the definition of disability was given to employment tribunals in the case of *Goodwin* v. *Patent Office* [1999] ICR 302, in which it was recognised that merely because a person was able to cope at home did not mean that he was outside the definition of a disabled person for the purposes of the **DDA** 1995. The case concerned a man who suffered from paranoid schizophrenia and had been dismissed following complaints from employees about his, at times, bizarre behaviour. The Employment Appeal Tribunal were surprised to find that, simply because the applicant was able to cope at home, the industrial tribunal found that he fell outside the definition of disability.

The proper approach for tribunals is to adopt a purposive approach to construction of the definition, assisted by guidance and the code of practice: Disability Discrimination Act (1996). The tribunal should look at all the evidence by reference to four different conditions – impairment, adverse effect, substantiality and long-term effect – and it might be helpful to address each separately, noting that substantial is used in the sense of more than minor or trivial.

'Long-term effect'

The effect of impairment is long term if it has lasted at least 12 months or it is likely to last for at least 12 months or for the rest of the life of the person.[21]

'Normal day-to-day activities'

This phrase is broad and can include, for example, putting hair rollers in and applying makeup.[22] The employment tribunal initially stated that, as this was an activity carried out almost exclusively by women, it could not be considered a normal day-to-day activity. The Employment Appeal Tribunal found to the contrary and added that anything done by most women or most men could be considered a normal day-to-day activity.

Religion s. 10

There have been some cases where religion or belief has been addressed as an aspect of ethnicity, e.g. Sikhism in *Mandla*. The definition of religion or belief is contained in s. 10. Religion means, 'any religion, ... and ... includes a reference to a lack of religion'. Belief means 'any religious or philosophical belief ... and ... includes a reference to a lack of belief'. It is likely to include all major religions and also strongly held views such as humanism or atheism. Perception by the discriminator about religious belief, even if untrue, will also be covered if the less favourable treatment was based on that perception.

Age s. 5

Age may be defined by reference to a particular age or to a range of ages, e.g. over 21s. Ageist attitudes may operate so that older people are treated less favourably in relation to employment and other areas, and legally until the introduction of the Employment Equality (Age) Regulations 2006 there was nothing to prevent an employer rejecting a job applicant because he was 'too old'. An exception to this absence of protection is provided by *Marshall* v. *Southampton and South West Hampshire Area Health Authority* [1986] 2 All ER 584, where the different retirement ages for men and women was declared unlawful by the European Court of Justice. Age is now a protected characteristic under the Equality Act 2010.

Sexual orientation s. 12

This protected characteristic is defined as sexual orientation towards persons of the same, opposite or either sex. Previously discrimination on the grounds of sexual orientation was only prohibited in the employment field under the Employment Equality (Sexual Orientation) Regulations 2003.[23]

Forms of discrimination

The Equality Act retains pre-existing forms of discrimination, such as direct and indirect discrimination and the law is extended to include, for example the new concept (in law) of dual discrimination. The following forms of discrimination are included in the new law:

- direct discrimination;
- indirect discrimination;
- dual discrimination;
- discrimination by association;
- discrimination by perception;
- harassment;
- victimisation.

Direct discrimination (s. 13)

Discrimination may be direct, where an employer/service provider treats a person less favourably than he would treat others.

Direct discrimination may include, for example, denying training opportunities to a woman because she is pregnant, or appointing a man to a job when a female applicant is better qualified. In *Gill* v. *El Vino Company Ltd* [1983] 1 All ER 398 it was found that where a wine bar would only serve women at tables and not at the bar, this directly discriminated against women, who were denied facilities and services on an equal basis.

Indirect discrimination

There may also be *indirect discrimination* under s. 19, meaning discrimination which by means of requirements or conditions discriminates in a way that is unjustifiable and detrimental against a particular group because a considerably smaller proportion of that group will be able to comply with the condition. It is for the employer or other potential discriminator to show that a condition can be justified on the basis that it is intended to meet a legitimate objective in a fair, balanced and reasonable way.

Indirect discrimination is sometimes referred to as disproportionate impact. The Equality Act extends indirect discrimination to disability and gender reassignment.

Examples of indirect discrimination include the following:

- Requiring high standards of English language competence, which indirectly discriminates against 'non-native' English speakers, or requirements for specific UK-based examinations.
- Height requirements may discriminate against certain racial groups.
- Refusing to insure properties with certain postcodes or charging excessive rates may discriminate against certain racial groups living in a community. In the case of *Hussein* v. *Saints Complete House Furnitures* [1979] IRLR 337, indirect discrimination was found where a furniture store refused to employ people from Liverpool 8. Fifty per cent of the population of that area was black.

Examples of requirements which may have a discriminatory effect on women include:

- Redundancy criteria to select part-time workers first, where the majority of part-time staff are women.

- An upper age limit for appointment to a particular job. This was found in the case of *Price* v. *Civil Service Commission* [1977] IRLR 291[24] to discriminate indirectly against women, who were more likely to have taken time out from a career for childcare responsibilities.

- A requirement to work full-time, when part-time or job share would be suitable, may discriminate against women.

- The requirement to comply with new rostering arrangements was indirect discrimination in a case where a female train driver could not comply because of her child care commitments (*London Underground* v. *Edwards (No. 2)* [1998] IRLR 364).

Dual discrimination

Under the Equality Act victims are able to pursue claims relying on two protected characteristics at the same time. This goes some way towards recognising the complexity of discrimination. It means that a person discriminated against as a black woman or as a gay disabled man would be protected.

Discrimination by association

Discrimination by association was included in some of the previous legislation, The Equality Act extends this form of discrimination to cover disability, gender reassignment and sex.

Discrimination by perception (direct)

The Equality Act extends this form of discrimination to cover disability, gender reassignment and sex.

Harassment

Harassment includes unwanted conduct, and unwanted verbal, non-verbal or physical conduct of a sexual nature, where it has the effect of violating dignity, or creating an intimidating, hostile, degrading, humiliating or offensive environment. Marital status and pregnancy are not covered as protected characteristics for the purposes of s. 26. As a separate issue, if the harassment amounts to a course of conduct (two or more separate instances) it may also lead to criminal proceedings under ss 1 and 4 of the Protection from Harassment Act 1997.

Victimisation (s. 27)

This applies if a person is subject to a detriment because he has done a 'protected act' (or it is believed that he has or is going to). A protected act includes: bringing proceedings under the Equality Act; giving evidence or information in connection with the Act, making an allegation that a person has contravened the Act.

Permitted discrimination

In limited circumstances, behaviour which could be regarded as discriminatory will be permitted as a specific exception under the RRA 1976.

- A person who employs another individual to work in their own home may discriminate as to the person chosen.

- A genuine occupational requirement for a job may make it lawful to discriminate: e.g. employment of a Chinese person as a waiter in a Chinese restaurant, choice of a black male actor to play Othello for authenticity.

- A genuine occupational requirement defence may also apply where an employee provides persons of that racial group with personal services promoting their welfare and those services are most effectively provided by a person of that racial group: e.g. Asian care staff in a residential setting catering mainly for an Asian population whose first language is not English.

- Positive discrimination may be permitted where the objective is to rectify under-representation of a particular group in an area of employment: e.g. if black social workers are under-represented in senior posts or in a specialist field, additional training opportunities could be provided.

Positive action s. 158

These provisions enable, but do not require, organisations to take steps to help people overcome their disadvantages or meet their needs both generally (s. 158) and in relation to recruitment and promotion (s. 159). If two applicants for a position are ranked equally, the job can be given to the applicant who has a protected characteristic. Positive action is not the same as positive discrimination, the latter is not permitted under s. 13 EA.

Furthermore, there is an expectation that an employer will provide reasonable adjustments to the working environment and if they fail to do so and cannot justify the failure that is also discrimination. Reasonable adjustments include modifying equipment and arranging training.

In *Kenny* v. *Hampshire Constabulary* [1999] IRLR 76, the Employment Appeal Tribunal heard an appeal by a man who suffered from cerebral palsy whose offer of employment had been withdrawn because the necessary care assistance he required for going to the toilet could not be provided. It was recognised that he was a disabled person within s. 1 of the Disability Discrimination Act 1995 and that withdrawing the offer of employment was potentially discriminatory. It was found, however, that s. 6 did not extend to a requirement for employers to provide carers to attend to their employees' personal needs and the appeal was dismissed accordingly.

Public sector equality duty

This represents a change of emphasis from law which was reliant on individuals making complaints to a position where the public sector are required to be more pro-active in promoting equal opportunities. The Equality Act 2010 imposes two specific duties on public bodies, which includes social services authorities. First, public bodies must have due regard to socio-economic inequalities when making decisions of a strategic nature about how to exercise their functions, (s. 1). Secondly, an equality duty applies.

---

s. 149

(1) A public authority must, in the exercise of its functions have due regard to the need to –

    (a) eliminate discrimination, harassment, victimisation and any other conduct that is prohibited by this Act;

    (b) advance equality of opportunity between persons who share a relevant protected characteristic and persons who do not share it;

    (c) foster good relations between persons who share a relevant protected characteristic and persons who do not share it.

(EA 2010)

This duty applies in respect of each of the nine areas of protected characteristics whereas previously a similar duty applied only in relation to race, sex and disability. A public authority is given a wide definition under the Act. It will include public authorities such as central and local government, the National Health Service, the police and Social Services Departments. It also includes (in terms similar to those in the Human Rights Act 1998) anyone whose work includes functions of a public nature. Private or voluntary agencies would therefore be included if they carry out a public function, such as providing residential care or education. Section 149 continues to explain that advancing equality of opportunity involves having regard in particular to removing disadvantages suffered by people with a shared characteristic; taking steps to meet the needs of people with a shared characteristic and encouraging people with a shared characteristic to participate in public life or other activities where their participation is disproportionately low (s. 149(3)).

Public bodies in England, including local authorities, are obliged to publish annual information regarding their compliance with the equality duty and also set equality objectives every four years. The EHRC can enforce the provisions and individuals or organisations can seek judicial review if concerned that a public body has not complied with the duty.

The duty applies to all activities of a local authority as the case of *R (Kaur and Shah)* v. *Ealing London Borough Council* [2008] EWHC 2062 (Admin) illustrates. This case concerned the application of the race equality duty in place prior to the Equality Act 2010. The council were in breach of the duty having failed to carry out a race equality impact assessment before deciding to withdraw funding from the Southall Black Sisters, an organisation providing specialist services to Asian and Afro-Caribbean women particularly in relation to domestic violence.

'Working Together' (2013) includes a statement explaining how the duty applies in relation to safeguarding children:

> the Equality Act 2010 puts a responsibility on public authorities to have due regard to the need to eliminate discrimination and promote equality of opportunity. This applies to the process of identification of need and risk faced by the individual child and the process of assessment. No child or group of children must be treated any less favourably than others in being able to access effective services which meet their particular needs. (p. 9 para. 15)

A limited number of functions still remain outside the terms of the Act. Excluded functions are: decisions not to prosecute and judicial proceedings; security services functions; parliamentary functions; some immigration and nationality functions where discrimination is based on grounds of nationality or ethnic or national origin (not race or colour).

A number of challenges have been brought against local authorities for failure to comply with the equality duty. In *R (W)* v. *Birmingham City Council* [2011] EWHC 1147 (Admin) the authority's decision to restrict the provision of support for people with disabilities to those whose needs were assessed to be critical was unlawful. By failing to assess the practical impact on those disabled persons whose needs were substantial, the local authority had not paid due regard to the equality duty. The decision maker should consider the impact of a proposed decision and ask whether a decision with that impact would be consistent with the need to pay due regard to the principles of disability equality. Further, in *Stuart Bracking and Others* v. *Secretary of State for Work and Pensions* [2013] EWCA Civ 1345 the court found that regard must be had to different classes of disabled people who may be particularly disadvantaged by the impact of a decision.

Enforcement

For disability, race and sex discrimination, an individual can complain about discrimination relating to provision of goods and services through civil proceedings in the county court. A claim should normally be brought within six months of the last act complained of. Damages and injunctions may be ordered. Questions of discrimination in employment may be dealt with by application to an employment tribunal. The duty not to discriminate in the employment field relates to employees and job applicants and includes duties not to dismiss or refuse employment on the basis of discrimination, discriminatory advertisements, training and other benefits. Strict time limits for applications to the tribunal apply. The tribunal can award compensation and can make declarations as to the complainant's rights, order the employers to take steps to prevent further discrimination and order that an equal opportunities policy be followed.[25]

Equality and Human Rights Commission

The enforcement bodies established under earlier legislation, the Disability Rights Commission, the Commission for Racial Equality and the Equal Opportunities Commission have all been dissolved and their functions transferred to a unified Commission, the Equality and Human Rights Commission, established under the Equality Act 2006.

The Commission continues to exercise powers to carry out formal investigations into complaints of discrimination, offer assistance to individuals, negotiate with employers to ensure compliance with the Act, and issue non-discrimination notices if it finds evidence of discrimination.

Its remit extends to discrimination on the basis of the nine protected characteristics and it has an extended new role in relation to human rights.

The broader role of the new Commission includes:

- Promoting equality and diversity.
- Working towards eliminating discrimination and harassment.
- Influencing the development of law and Government policy.
- Promoting understanding of good relations between different communities.
- Encouraging good practice in the treatment of disabled people and reducing isolation.
- Promoting understanding, good practice and the protection of human rights.
- Encouraging public authorities to comply with the ECHR.
- Enforcement of the various equality laws.

The Commission has published a number of reports with relevance for social work (accessible from the EHRC website). (See suggested reading below.)

Chapter summary

- Anti-discriminatory practice is an essential cornerstone of social work and is required by the BASW Code of Ethics and HCPC.
- The law relating to discrimination provides a minimum baseline on which to develop good practice. Legislation specifically makes illegal discrimination based on nine

protected characteristics: age, disability, gender reassignment, marriage and civil partnership, pregnancy and maternity, race, religion or belief, sex, sexual orientation.

- Other legislation also contains references which support the principle of equality and the need to avoid discrimination: e.g. the Children Act 1989, s. 22(5). Policy guidance and codes of practice further support anti-discriminatory practice.

- Since the introduction of the Human Rights Act 1998, Art. 14 of the European Convention on Human Rights outlaws discrimination on any ground in relation to the enjoyment of the Articles of the Convention: e.g. the right to respect for private and family life.

- Discrimination may take different forms. The Act covers direct, indirect and dual discrimination, discrimination by association or perception, harassment and victimisation.

- Public bodies exercising their functions must have regard to the need to eliminate discrimination, harassment and victimisation, advance equality of opportunity and foster good relations between people with a protected characteristic and people who do not share that characteristic. This is referred to as the public equality duty.

- The Act is supported by a single enforcement body, the Equality and Human Rights Commission.

Exercises

In each of the following cases, consider whether there is discrimination, what action might be taken and whether existing law supports anti-discriminatory, anti-oppressive practice.

- Joan applies for a job as a fitness instructor at a newly opened sports complex. She is not offered an interview and when she queries this she is told that, because of her age, she did not meet the criteria for the position.

- An 'alternative' theatre, situated in the basement of an existing 1920s theatre, refuses access to Susan and her boyfriend Mike, who uses a wheelchair, because of 'health and safety'.

- Ranbir, aged 76, is offered a place at a day centre for elderly people. She is the only person there from an ethnic minority background and hears a member of staff and woman who attends the centre making racist comments about her.

- Jenny is a child from the travelling community. She has been attending primary school for three weeks when her teacher tells her that if she does not come to school in uniform the next day she will be given a detention.

- Josh is removed from his mother's care under an emergency protection order and placed with white foster carers. He is black.

- Jane, a recently qualified social worker, has been off sick for five months with depression. Her manager invites her in for an informal chat and suggests to Jane that she probably isn't cut out for social work and might prefer to move to administrative duties. Jane is really upset and hands in her notice.

Websites

The website for the new enforcement body, the Equality and Human Rights Commission:
www.equalityhumanrights.com

The Home Office has an Equality section:
www.gov.uk/government/topics/equality-rights-and-citizenship

Further reading

Dalrymple, J. and Burke, B. (2006) *Anti-oppressive Practice: Social Care and the Law* (2nd edn). Buckingham: Open University Press.

Dutt, R. (2001) 'Racism and social-work practice' in Cull, L.-A. and Roche, J. (eds) *The Law and Social Work: Contemporary Issues for Practice*. Basingstoke: Palgrave.

Equality and Human Rights Commission (2011) 'Close to home: An inquiry into older people and human rights in home care.' London: EHRC.

Equality and Human Rights Commission (2011) 'Hidden in plain sight: Inquiry into disability-related harassment.' London: EHRC.

Hay, D. (2001) 'The Special Educational Needs and Disability Act 2001' *Education Law Journal* p. 72.

Hepple, B. (2011) *Equality: The New Legal Framework*. Oxford: Hart Publishing.

Macpherson, W. (1999) 'The Stephen Lawrence Inquiry: Report of an Inquiry by Sir William Macpherson of Cluny *et al.*' London: The Stationery Office.

Parker, C. and Clements, L. (2008) 'The UN Convention on the Rights of Persons with Disabilities: A new right to independent living?' 4 *European Human Rights Law Review* 58.

Sewell, H. (2012) *The Equality Act 2010 in Mental Health: A Guide to Implementation and Issues in Practice*. London: Jessica Kingsley Publishers.

Wadham, J., Robinson, A., Ruebain, D. and Uppal, S. (eds) (2012) *Blackstone's Guide to the Equality Act 2010* (2nd edn). London: Blackstone Press.

Notes

[1] J. Dalrymple and B. Burke (1995) *Anti-oppressive Practice: Social Care and the Law*. Buckingham: Open University Press.

[2] BASW Code of Ethics (2012), www.basw.co.uk/codeofethics.

[3] R. Barn, R. Sinclair and D. Ferdinand (1997) *Acting on Principle: An Examination of Race and Ethnicity in Social Services Provision for Children and Families*. London: BAAF/CRE.

[4] Department of Health (2000) *The Children Act Report 1995–1999* (Cm. 4579). London: The Stationery Office.

[5] J. Gibbons *et al.* (1995) in Department of Health *Child protection: Messages from Research*. London: The Stationery Office.

[6] I. Brodie (1998) *Highlight: Exclusion from School*. London: National Children's Bureau.

[7] London Borough of Lambeth (1987) *Whose Child? A Report of the Public Inquiry into the death of Tyra Henry*. London: London Borough of Lambeth.

[8] T. Booth, W. Booth and D. McConnell (2004) 'Parents with learning difficulties, care proceedings and the family courts: threshold decisions and the moral matrix' 16 *Child and Family Law Quarterly* p. 409.

⁹ D. Browne (1995) 'Sectioning – The Black Experience' in S. Fernando (ed.) *Mental Health in a Multi-Ethnic Society: A Multi-Disciplinary Handbook.* London: Routledge.

¹⁰ DfEE Disability Briefing (November 1999) cited in A. McColgan (2000) *Discrimination Law: Text, Cases and Materials.* Oxford: Hart Publishing.

¹¹ See R. Dutt (2001) 'Racism and social-work practice' in L.-A. Cull and J. Roche (eds) *The Law and Social Work: Contemporary Issues for Practice.* Basingstoke: Palgrave.

¹² W. Macpherson (1999) *The Stephen Lawrence Inquiry: Report of an Inquiry by Sir William Macpherson of Cluny et al.* London: The Stationery Office.

¹³ Department of Health (2000) 'No Secrets: Guidance on developing and implementing multi-agency policies and procedures to protect vulnerable adults from abuse'. London: Department of Health.

¹⁴ Paragraph 2.7.

¹⁵ HM Government (2013) *Working Together to Safeguard Children.* London: The Stationery Office.

¹⁶ SI 2001/3965.

¹⁷ Home Office Circular 021/2004.

¹⁸ Department of Health (2000) *The Children Act Report 1995–1999* (Cm. 4579). London: The Stationery Office.

¹⁹ DDA 1995, s. 19(3).

²⁰ See discussion in C. Munro (2001) 'When racism is not black and white' 6973 *New Law Journal* p. 314.

²¹ DDA 1995, s. 2(1).

²² *Ekpe v. Commissioner of Police of the Metropolis* [2001] IRLR 605.

²³ SI 2003/1661.

²⁴ In *Price* an upper age limit of 28 for entry as an executive officer in the civil service was found to discriminate indirectly against women.

²⁵ RRA 1976, s. 56; SDA 1975, s. 65.

Part 2

Children and families

Chapters:

Chapter 7

Supporting children and families

Learning objectives

To develop an understanding of the following:

- The legal framework for social work practice with children and families provided by the Children Act 1989.
- Central principles of the Act, including the concepts of welfare and children's rights.
- The background to and effect of the Children Act 2004.
- The concept of a 'child in need' and range of services which may be available to support children in need and their families.
- Issues relating to children with a disability.

> ## Talking Point
>
> 'Working Together' (2013) is the leading guidance on safeguarding work with children. The introduction states that
>
> **Safeguarding children – the action we take to promote the welfare of children and protect them from harm – is everyone's responsibility. Everyone who comes into contact with children and families has a role to play.**
>
> It emphasises two key principles underpinning safeguarding. First that safeguarding is everyone's responsibility and second the need for a child-centred approach.
>
> Those principles inform and contextualise the materials in this part of the text regarding children and families.
>
> In support of a child-centred approach, the following extract outlines the views of children on safeguarding:
>
> **Children have said that they need**
>
> - **Vigilance: to have adults notice when things are troubling them**
> - **Understanding and action: to understand what is happening; to be heard and understood; and to have that understanding acted upon**
> - **Stability: to be able to develop an on-going stable relationship of trust with those helping them**
> - **Respect: to be treated with the expectation that they are competent rather than not**
> - **Information and engagement: to be informed about and involved in procedures, decisions, concerns and plans**
> - **Explanation: to be informed of the outcome of assessments and decisions and reasons when their views have not met with a positive response**
> - **Support: to be provided with support in their own right as well as a member of their family**
> - **Advocacy: to be provided with advocacy to assist them in putting forward their views**
>
> ('Working Together', 2013 p. 10)

Introduction

This chapter addresses four main areas. To begin with, the Children Act 1989 (CA 1989) is introduced, being the principal legislation providing the legal framework within which social work practice with children and families is situated. The key principles of Part I of the Act – that the welfare of the child is the court's paramount consideration (including the amendment introduced by the Children and Families Act 2013 regarding parental involvement), non-intervention and avoidance of delay – are outlined. This is accompanied by a broader discussion of some of the value positions of the Act, including welfare, children's rights and parental responsibility.

Second, the Children Act 2004 (**CA 2004**) is introduced. This legislation builds on the Children Act 1989 and places emphasis on safeguarding the wellbeing of all children. Discussion of the Climbié report provides some background to the Act, and 'Every Child Matters' documentation that set out the five aspects of children's 'well being', a term incorporated in the Act. The Act establishes the role of Children's Commissioner in England to ensure that at national level issues affecting children and young people have a high profile. It also provides for some reorganisation in delivery of childcare including Director of Children's Services posts (combining education and social services) and Local Safeguarding Children Boards replacing area child protection committees. Looking beyond the Children Act 2004, the change in Government has brought changes in policy in relation to safeguarding children, largely following recommendations of the 'Munro' report. An outline of progress on key recommendations is included.

Support for families and preventative measures to combat child abuse are provided for within the framework of the Children Act 1989 in relation to children in the local authority area and specific responsibilities towards children in need. The concept of a child in need and the range of services which may be provided to support children in need and their family are discussed in the third section of the chapter. The chapter concludes with consideration of issues relating to children with a disability.

Introduction to the Children Act 1989

The Children Act 1989 is a major piece of legislation comprising 108 sections, divided into 12 Parts, with a further 15 Schedules.

Summary of central themes and changes introduced by the Children Act 1989

Readers may not have any experience of the law relating to children that applied prior to introduction of the Children Act 1989. In order to appreciate the scale of reform which the Act introduced, a brief outline of some of the key changes is provided in this section.

The 1989 Act introduced a number of language changes. The familiar concepts of custody and access were replaced by s. 8 orders, principally residence and contact orders, now combined in the new Child Arrangements Order. Parental rights and duties became parental responsibility. In each case, although there is an obvious change in terminology, more significant conceptual changes were incorporated, as suggested by reference to responsibility rather than rights and duties.

The 1989 Act provides a single route into care. Section 31 provides a threshold for care and supervision orders. The only circumstances in which a care or supervision order will be made is on satisfaction of the s. 31 criteria, on the application of the local authority (or authorised person, e.g. the NSPCC). The system of voluntary care, which could be transformed into formal care by administrative action, was replaced by provision of accommodation, to be seen as a service for families and not a back-door route into care.

Wardship (an aspect of the High Court's inherent jurisdiction) was one way in which a child could formally enter the care of the local authority prior to the Act. It is still possible for a child to be made a ward of court; however, the opportunities for a local authority to use wardship have been limited. Certain elements of the wardship jurisdiction have been retained and made more widely available via the Specific Issue Order and Prohibited Steps Order contained in s. 8.

A range of new orders were introduced by the Children Act 1989, including the Child Assessment Order, Family Assistance Order, Specific Issue Order, Prohibited Steps Order and Education Supervision Order, as well as extending the circumstances in which interim orders could be made. Procedural changes were also made (and continue to be made) to support improvements in practice. A system of **concurrent jurisdiction** was introduced between the magistrates' family proceedings court, the county court and the High Court, with provision for transfers between different levels of court. Hale J noted in 1999: 'The whole purpose of the Children Act 1989 was to give the court flexibility to meet the needs of the particular child in the particular circumstances and to do what was best for that child.'[1]

The Act gave recognition to those children in care, whether accommodated on a voluntary basis or under care orders, as 'looked after children' and includes a range of duties to promote their welfare. The Act encouraged a longer term view of responsibilities towards children with support provisions for children after they have left care.

The 1989 Act was hailed as a charter for children's rights and certainly introduces greater opportunity for the voice of the child to be heard in some circumstances. In addition, provision is made for children's guardians to be appointed in a wider range of cases. The Act places great emphasis on the advantages of children being brought up in their own families. To further this aim there is a definition of a 'child in need' and a range of services which are to be provided to support children and families and ultimately to prevent children entering the care system, supported by the principle of working in partnership. The Act provided a comprehensive reform of law relating to children and significantly it brought together public and private law in one statute, areas which had previously been treated separately. However, it should also be noted that, despite the comprehensive nature of the reform, major areas of law relating to children remain outside the Act, notably adoption and youth justice (each of which is considered in separate chapters). A child is defined under the 1989 Act as 'a person under the age of 18' (s. 105).

Given its size, finding your way around the Children Act 1989 may seem daunting. Table 7.1 maps out the parts of the Act and provides brief summaries of the key elements in each part as an initial guide.

The Children Act 1989 incorporates a number of value perspectives, which may at times appear to be in conflict. Fox-Harding (1997)[2] describes these as: laissez-faire and patriarchy; state paternalism; defence of the birth family; and children's rights. Each perspective is reflected in particular provisions throughout the Act. Opportunities for coercive state intervention should be minimal according to the laissez-faire perspective and the presumption of non-intervention in s. 1(5), and limitations on local authority use of wardship may be interpreted as reflecting this perspective. State paternalism places greater value on the role of the state to intervene to protect children's welfare as evident in the inclusion of 'future harm' in the threshold criteria and developing policy which places greater emphasis on using adoption as a childcare resource. Defence of the birth family is reflected in the Children Act emphasis on providing support to families, including recognition of children in need and the provision of accommodation as an aspect of support to families. Finally, the increased role for children's guardians and opportunities for children to initiate proceedings and express their own views in certain circumstances would suggest that the children's rights perspective is also reflected in the Children Act 1989.

It is more than 20 years since the Act was introduced and certain parts of it have already been amended, expanded or revoked, with the introduction of further new provisions, such as the Special Guardianship Order. Research has been conducted to evaluate how well different aspects are working (see 'Messages from Research' (1996) and 'The Children Act Now' (2001)) and has contributed to policy and legislative changes. Some commentators questioned whether a new Children Act was needed, including Freeman.[3]

Table 7.1 Contents of the Children Act 1989

Part I Introductory	Welfare principle and checklist, parental involvement, delay, non-intervention, parental responsibility, guardians, welfare reports
Part II Children in Family Proceedings	Child Arrangements Orders, specific issue and prohibited steps orders (s. 8), change of name and removal from jurisdiction, family assistance orders (s. 16) Special Guardianship Orders
Part III Local Authority Support for Children and Families	Provision of services, definition of child in need, accommodation, duties to children looked after, secure accommodation, cooperation between authorities
Part IV Care and Supervision	Care and supervision orders, interim orders, discharge and variation, contact with children in care, exclusion requirements, appointment of children's guardian
Part V Protection of Children	Child assessment orders, emergency protection orders, exclusion requirements, police protection, local authority duty to investigate
Part VI, VII and VIII Community Homes, Voluntary Homes and Organisations, and Registered Children's Homes	Now covered by Care Standards Act 2000
Part IX Private Arrangements for Fostering: Children	Privately fostered children, disqualification from fostering, as amended by the Children Act 2004
Part X Childminding and Day-Care	Now covered by Care Standards Act 2000
Part XI Secretary of State's Supervisory Functions and Responsibilities	Inspection of children's homes, inquiries, default powers
Part XII, ss. 85–108 Miscellaneous – General	Includes litigation limit and local authority restriction on use of wardship jurisdiction, interpretation
Schedules 1–15 Schedule 2	Schedule 2 includes requirements for the local authority to maintain a register of disabled children; prepare children's services plans; prevent neglect and abuse; reduce the need for care proceedings or criminal proceedings against children; provide family centres

This debate continued in the face of criticism that the tragedy surrounding the death of Victoria Climbié in 2000 suggested an inadequate child protection framework. Following the inquiry, new legislation, the Children Act 2004, was introduced and key features are discussed below. The essence of these changes can be described as providing for organisational changes and new duties to promote inter-agency working. The essential features of the Children Act 1989, relating to child protection have not changed (discussed further in Chapter 9). Further amending legislation such as the Children and Young Persons Act 2008 and Children and Families Act 2014 has been introduced and no doubt further legislative activity will be discussed during the lifetime of this edition.

Central principles

Welfare

Part I of the Children Act 1989 contains a number of principles which apply throughout the Act. The first and most influential is the welfare principle.[4]

> ### s. 1
>
> When a court determines any question with respect to –
>
> **(a)** the upbringing of a child; or
> **(b)** the administration of a child's property or the application of income arising from it, the child's welfare shall be the court's paramount consideration.
>
> (CA 1989)

Section 1 of the Children Act 1989 provides that the welfare of a child is the court's paramount consideration. At first sight this might appear to be a straightforward proposition worthy of support. Closer examination prompts a number of questions as to the meaning of this phrase. Welfare is an indeterminate concept (Bainham, 1998),[5] which is open to wide-ranging interpretation, meaning different things to different people. Eekalaar (1986)[6] suggests that there are three aspects to welfare: 'basic' – general physical, emotional and intellectual care; 'developmental' – opportunity to maximise resources available through childhood; and 'autonomy' – freedom to choose one's own lifestyle and enter social relations according to one's own inclinations uncontrolled by the authority of the adult world, whether parents or institutions. It encompasses a spectrum of possible interpretation, from a paternalistic emphasis on protection to a more liberal stance which places greatest value on child autonomy. Herring (2013)[7] has provided an evaluation of the various criticisms of the welfare principle and ultimately concludes that the principle is defensible. A similarly worded welfare principle is included in the Adoption and Children Act 2002, also supported by a checklist.

Welfare of the child: parental involvement

The Children and Families Act 2014 amends s.1 including a presumption in favour of parental involvement.

> ### s. 1 (2A)
>
> **(2A)** A court, ... is as respects each parent within subsection (6)(a) to presume, unless the contrary is shown, that involvement of that parent in the life of the child concerned will further the child's welfare.
>
> **(2B)** ... "involvement" means involvement of some kind, either direct or indirect, but not any particular division of a child's time.
>
> (CA 1989)

A new subsection (6) states that a parent of the child will be included as a parent for this subsection if the parent can be involved in the child's life in a way that does not put the child at risk of suffering harm, and will be considered to be so unless there is evidence before the court in the proceedings to suggest that involvement would put the child at risk of harm. This amendment applies to private law proceedings.

The welfare checklist

Given the difficulty inherent in interpreting welfare and reaching decisions which are made in the best interest of the child, the welfare checklist contained in s. 1(3) is a valuable aid to interpretation for the court. The checklist gives some clarification and direction as to the matters that a court should consider when applying the welfare principle. It has a less direct influence on social work practice, though preparation of any case for court which did not show an awareness of its features could be criticised. The Law Commission[8] envisaged the checklist providing greater consistency and clarity and promoting a more systematic approach to decision-making. The checklist is not exhaustive, and should be considered as including a minimum range of issues to be considered. In many cases other matters absent from the checklist will be relevant, and equally other elements of the checklist will not apply in every case. The checklist is not written in order of importance, though it may be symbolic that the child's wishes and feelings are positioned first on the list (*Re J* [1992] Fam Law 229). The checklist also provides a useful framework for the preparation of evidence. If circumstances arose where an element of the checklist was not considered, this would provide good grounds for appeal.

The court must have regard in particular to:

s. 1(3)

(a) the ascertainable wishes and feelings of the child concerned (considered in the light of his age and understanding);
(b) his physical, emotional and educational needs;
(c) the likely effect on him of any change in his circumstances;
(d) his age, sex, background and any characteristics of his which the court considers relevant;
(e) any harm which he has suffered or is at risk of suffering;
(f) how capable each of his parents, and any other person in relation to whom the court considers the question to be relevant, is of meeting his needs;
(g) the range of powers available to the court under this Act in the proceedings in question.

(CA 1989)

The checklist does not apply in all proceedings. It applies to all public proceedings under Part IV of the Act, care and supervision orders, whether or not they are contested. However, the checklist applies only to private proceedings, s. 8 applications, e.g. residence applications, where contested. It does apply to Special Guardianhip Orders. Other exceptions include: applications for secure accommodation orders; leave applications under s. 10 (*Re A and W (Minors) Residence Order: Leave to Apply*) [1992] 3 All ER 872); and emergency and short-term order applications under Part V of the Act.

Each of the factors in the checklist will now be considered in more detail.

s. 1(3)

(a) the ascertainable wishes and feelings of the child concerned (considered in the light of his age and understanding);

(CA 1989)

This factor may be interpreted as a clear statement of the importance of taking a child-centred approach. It is further explained in the Children Act Guidance (vol. 1): 'The Act aims to strike a balance between rights of children to express their views on decisions made about their lives and rights of parents to exercise their responsibilities.'[9] Examination of children's rights may provide some justification as to why it is appropriate for the court to be aware of the child's wishes and feelings. A key question remains as to how the child's wishes and feelings are to be ascertained.

Usually, the wishes and feelings of the child are presented to the court via a report produced by a **children and family reporter** or children's guardian whose role is to represent the best interests of the child. The report will usually be based on a number of meetings over a period of time prior to the hearing.

It is possible for a judge to see a child privately in chambers and directly discuss the child's wishes. In *Re W (A Minor) (Residence Order: Baby)* [1992] 2 FLR 332, the judge talked to children aged 10 and 12 who wished to see him, an approach that was in line with s. 1(3). The judge, however, was not bound to adopt their wishes. This approach may be problematic, however, in terms of confidentiality. If the child says anything which influences the judge's decision, it will be necessary to inform the other parties in order that they can comment. In addition, it may be argued that such an approach could increase the stress experienced by a child when involved in court proceedings. Research in Scotland, where children and young people are more likely to participate directly in hearings, often by meeting with the judge in chambers, would suggest otherwise (Raitt, 2004).[10]

As the practice of judges meeting children has developed, guidelines have been published. The 'Guidelines for Judges meeting Children who are Subject to Family Proceedings' [2010] 2 FLR 1872 stress that the primary purpose of the meeting is to benefit the child, for the child to feel part of the process, to understand the process and to be able to express her views. It is not for the purpose of gathering evidence. The application of the guidelines are discussed fully in *Re KP (A Child)* [2014] EWCA Civ 554, a case concerning wrongful removal of a child from her home in Malta to the UK. The judge conducted an extensive meeting of an hour during the hearing which wrongly strayed into the process of gathering evidence which was then relied upon in the judge's decision.

It is clear that welfare is not synonymous with the child's wishes and feelings. In *Re P (Minor: Wardship)* [1992] Fam Law 229, Butler-Sloss LJ emphasised that the court was not bound by the wishes of children, in this case brothers aged 13 and 11, and should depart from them when their future welfare so required. Welfare has to be a decision of the court, not a preference of the child. Nevertheless, all other things being equal, in *Re P (A Minor) (Education: Child's Views)* [1992] FCR 145, the wishes of a 14-year-old boy to attend school daily rather than to reside at boarding school tipped the balance when his parents were in dispute. The age and maturity of the child is relevant to the weight to be attached to the child's views. In *Re S (A Minor) (Change of Surname)* [1999] 1 FLR 672, two children applied to change their name following allegations that their father had sexually abused the older daughter. Initially, the court granted the application for the eldest child (aged 16) but refused for the younger. The Court of Appeal overruled that decision stating that, at 15, the younger daughter was also 'Gillick competent' and weight should also be given to her wishes.

---

s. 1(3)

(b) his physical, emotional and educational needs;

(CA 1989)

The court should adopt a broad interpretation of the child's various needs and not attach great weight to material considerations. In *Re W (A Minor) (Residence Order: Baby)* [1992] 2 FLR 332, the court held that there was no presumption of law that a child of any age should be with one parent or another. The relevant legal principle to apply is paramountcy of the child's welfare. However, the court noted that the 'natural position' if other things were equal would be for a mother normally to have care of a baby of under 4 weeks of age.

---

s. 1(3)

(c) the likely effect on him of any change in circumstances;

(CA 1989)

This is sometimes referred to as the 'status quo' principle. In *Re B (Residence Order: Status Quo)* [1998] 1 FLR 368, the Court of Appeal took the view that a decision to give a residence order to the child's mother when the child was 8 years old, having been cared for by his father since the age of 2, was plainly wrong.

Delay is clearly relevant to this factor. It is crucial that the court does not allow delaying tactics by one party to strengthen their case, on the basis of the status quo principle, weakening the case of an 'absent' party seeking to care for a child.

---

s. 1(3)

(d) his age, sex, background and any characteristics of his which the court considers relevant;

(CA 1989)

Cases decided prior to the Children Act 1989 are relevant to this factor: e.g. *C v. C (Minors: Custody of Children)* [1988] 2 FLR 291 supports the principle that sibling groups should be kept together wherever possible. Under s. 22(5)(c), local authorities are bound to give due consideration to a child's religious persuasion, racial origin, and cultural and linguistic background, when making decisions, particularly relating to a child's placement. The phrase 'any characteristics of his', and reference to background would presumably incorporate such issues but it is suggested that explicit reference would reflect and support anti-discriminatory practice. Research suggests that provision of information to the courts regarding diversity is inconsistent and in some instances there is insufficient regard to families' heritage (Brophy, 2003).[11]

---

s. 1(3)

(e) any harm which he has suffered or is at risk of suffering;

(CA 1989)

Harm is defined under the Children Act 1989 to include ill treatment or impairment of health or development. The Adoption and Children Act 2002 has amended the definition of 'harm' to include 'impairment suffered from seeing or hearing the ill-treatment of another'. Significant harm is the basis of the criteria for care or supervision orders. In private law proceedings, there may be some concerns about harm that the child has suffered or is at risk of suffering, which falls short of the threshold for care proceedings but may influence a decision on where the child should live and the extent of arrangements for contact as part of a Child Arrangements Order. Where the court has concerns about harm, which has not been investigated by the local authority, it may direct the local authority to carry out an investigation with a view to commencing care proceedings, under s. 37.

---

s. 1(3)

(f) how capable each of his parents, and any other person in relation to whom the court considers the question to be relevant, is of meeting his needs;

(CA 1989)

This factor invites the court to consider the suitability of relatives, or new partners of a couple who have separated. The sexuality of new partners has been the subject of court scrutiny, as has religious conviction. In *S v. S (Custody of Children)* [1980] 1 FLR 143, the court stated that being brought up in a lesbian household would not promote the child's welfare and could cause social embarrassment for the child in the community. Subsequent cases have demonstrated a more open-minded approach. In *Re B and G (Minors) (Custody)* [1985] 15 Fam Law 127, the Court of Appeal found that the religious beliefs of a parent who belonged to the Church of Scientology could be damaging to the child.

---

s. 1(3)

(g) the range of powers available to the court under this Act in the proceedings in question.

(CA 1989)

This factor reminds the court that it is not limited to granting or denying orders applied for by the parties (in family proceedings) and is sometimes referred to as the 'menu' principle. The court may make an order of its own volition if it considers that would be the best way to promote the child's welfare. An example might be where a local authority applies for a care order for a child with a plan that the child should reside with grandparents. It may be preferable to make a Child Arrangements Order whereby the child lives with the grandparents and maintain local authority involvement through a supervision order. The court may also exercise its powers to seek further information, possibly by requiring a report under s. 7 of the 1989 Act.

Conflicting welfare claims

How is the issue of welfare determined when both the parent and the child are minors? According to *Birmingham City Council* v. *H (No. 2)* [1993] 1 FLR 883, the welfare of neither should necessarily be given priority. In that case the court was faced with an application concerning the baby of a 16-year-old girl who was in care, and the welfare of the baby, as the subject of the application to court, was paramount. If there are conflicting interests between children in the same proceedings, the court should attempt to balance their interests and find the least detrimental solution, even if as in *Re A (Children) (Conjoined Twins: Surgical Separation)* [2000] 4 All ER 961, the decision might lead to one child's death.

> ### Reflect
>
> Should any elements of the welfare checklist carry more weight than others?
>
> Can you think of any alternative to the welfare principle?

Avoidance of delay

> ### s. 1(2)
>
> In any proceedings in which any question with respect to the upbringing of a child arises, the court shall have regard to the general principle that any delay in determining the question is likely to prejudice the welfare of the child.
>
> (CA 1989)

The Act makes it clear that delay in court proceedings is generally harmful to children, because of uncertainty and harm to relationships. A statutory presumption that delay is prejudicial and to be avoided is introduced. This presumption is reinforced by a number of provisions, which move the onus of controlling progress of cases to the court and away from the parties. Section 11 requires the court in s. 8 proceedings to draw up a timetable and give directions to ensure the timetable is followed. Directions hearings have been introduced and court rules require guardians to assist and advise on progress. Witness statements are disclosed before the hearings, there are restrictions on the number of experts, and concurrent jurisdiction allows transfers of cases. In public law proceedings the 'Public Law Outline' (2014) provides a timetable to be adhered to.

The presumption against delay is rebuttable. The onus would be on the party seeking delay to argue that it is positively beneficial to the child. In *C* v. *Solihull Metropolitan Borough Council* [1993] 1 FLR 290, the court suggested that any delay must be planned and purposeful. An obvious example of delay being acceptable would be where detailed assessment was required in order to reach an informed decision.

Delay should also be distinguished from duration, as it would be expected that straightforward cases could be dealt with more speedily than complex cases. Use of experts – where necessary – invariably increases the duration of a case but (unless this causes excessive delay) should be viewed as purposeful in ensuring that the court has the best information on which to reach its decision. Unfortunately, procedural issues can be a significant source of delay, including the time taken to transfer cases between courts, e.g. transferring a case from the family proceedings court to a care centre (county court). The new Family Court may reduce this cause of delay.

The no delay principle is strengthened by Article 6(1) of the ECHR, the right to 'a fair hearing within a reasonable time.'

Non-intervention

s. 1(5)

Where a court is considering whether or not to make one or more orders under this Act with respect to a child, it shall not make the order unless it considers that doing so would be better for the child than making no order at all.

(CA 1989)

In other words, there should be a positive benefit to the child in making the order. This provision applies in public and private proceedings (and has been introduced in a similar form into adoption law by the Adoption and Children Act 2002). It aims to discourage unnecessary court orders being made as part of a standard package, and to encourage parties to reach agreement and avoid matters being litigated. Once a case reaches court the principle should ensure that careful thought is given to whether or not an order should be made. In private proceedings, this principle is backed up by the concept of parental responsibility, which may help to equalise the position of the parties and 'lower the stakes' in disputes relating to children. The principle does not equate with a practice of keeping cases out of the court system unless absolutely unavoidable, though research suggests that in the early period following implementation of the Act there was evidence of such a misinterpretation in practice.[12] Application of the **no order principle** has also been evident in practice in the greater use of accommodation compared with the previous use of 'voluntary care'.[13]

Application of the section was considered in *Re G (Children) (Residence Order: No Order Principle)* [2005] EWCA Civ 1283. Following difficult negotiations, the unmarried parents of two daughters reached agreement that the mother would have residence and the father would have contact and parental responsibility. The judge interpreted s. 1(5) as providing a presumption against making orders and decided that, since the parents were no longer in dispute, no order was necessary. At the Court of Appeal this view was rejected. The court ruled that s. 1(5) does not create a presumption. Rather it calls for courts to ask the question: 'Will it be better for the child to make the order than making no order at all?' In this case it was better for the children to have an order. It was clearly important to the mother's security of mind and would promote settled arrangements in the future, after a long period of difficult negotiation. Making an order respected the parents' views that an order would be beneficial.

Litigation limit

The power to restrict applications being made, the **litigation limit**, is not one of the Part I principles but is included here as it is a provision that applies throughout the Children Act 1989.

---

s. 91(14)

A court may order that no application for an order under the Act of any specified kind may be made with respect to the child concerned by any person named in the order without leave of the court.

(CA 1989)

This provision is designed to deter litigious people who might otherwise continually re-apply for orders whenever time limits permit. For example, it is possible to apply for revocation of a care order every six months. The section is used infrequently and is appropriate in circumstances where its use will avoid anxiety and uncertainty for the child, and avoid wasting court time. In *Re F (Contact: Restraint Order)* [1995] 1 FLR 956, the provision was described as a draconian sanction of last resort principally appropriate when there is a real fear that children might become distressed or have their security disturbed through vexatious or ill-judged or obsessive pursuit by a party to the litigation process.

Re P (A Minor) (Residence Order: Child's Welfare) [1999] 3 All ER 734 provides an example of use of the section and sets out guidelines. The case concerned an application by the child's natural parents to vary a residence order, which placed the child with foster parents. The child was born into an orthodox Jewish family. At 17 months of age, when her parents were unable through illness to care for her, she was placed with foster parents of Christian faith. She was born with Down's syndrome, had a strong attachment to her foster parents and had thrived in their care. The child's natural religious and cultural heritage was found by the court to be relevant to her welfare but not a paramount consideration.

In judgment, Butler-Sloss LJ commented that there was no guidance as to the circumstances in which a s. 91(14) restriction might be imposed. It was noted that this omission was intended to give the court a wide discretion and authorities cited suggested that it would be most likely to apply where the applicant had already made repeated and unreasonable applications with little hope of success. The section was not limited, however, to oppressive or semi-vexatious applications and could operate in circumstances where there was no criticism of the applicant's conduct but in the best interests of the child it was necessary to prevent future applications. Adding that in each case a balancing exercise between the welfare of the child and the right of unrestricted access of the litigants to court would have to be carried out, a number of guidelines were suggested:

1. Section 91(14) should be read in conjunction with s. 1(1), which makes the welfare of the child the paramount consideration.

2. The court had to balance all the relevant circumstances in exercising its discretion to restrict applications.

3. An important consideration was that the restriction was a statutory intrusion into the right of a party to bring proceedings.

4. The power was to be used with great care and sparingly: the exception and not the rule.

5. Generally it was useful as a weapon of last resort in cases of repeated and unreasonable applications.

6. On clear evidence the restriction might be imposed in cases where the welfare of the child required it, even though there was no past history of making unreasonable applications.

7. In such cases the court should be satisfied that the facts went beyond the need for time to settle into a new regime and animosity between the adults; and there was a serious risk that, without the restriction, the child or primary carers would be subject to unacceptable strain.

8. The restriction can be imposed in the absence of a request.

9. The restriction can be imposed with or without time limitations.

10. The degree of restriction should be proportionate to the harm it was intended to avoid.

11. It would be undesirable to make the order *ex parte* in all but the most exceptional cases.

Re J (A Child) (Restrictions on Applications) [2007] EWCA Civ 906 provides another example. In this case a restriction order was made in respect of a child in care. There was extensive litigation regarding the child, who was born in 1992, including ten hearings in relation to contact, residence, prohibited steps orders and alleged breaches of those orders. Following the making of a care order, the mother made applications for specific contact under s. 34(3) of the Act, for permission to appeal against the care order, for a discharge of the care order and for an increase in contact. The applications were refused and, on the application of the local authority, an order made under s. 91(14) of the Act to last for five-and-a-half years until J was 18.

It is not necessary for there to have been a history of unreasonable and repeated applications for a s. 91(14) restriction order to be made. In *RK* v. *SK* [2013] EWHC 4386 (Fam) an order was made preventing applications by a father for contact for two years where a child was settled and the effect of applications would be detrimental to his welfare, in particular because of the effect on his mother's ability to care for him. Finally, in *SMD* v. *LMD* [2014] EWHC 302 (Fam) a no contact order was made where a father had sexually abused his 8-year-old daughter. Given his sense of injustice and the likelihood of him pursuing contact applications it was also proportionate to make a s. 91(14) order requiring him to seek the court's permission before any contact applications until the child reached 16.

Children's rights

The United Nations Convention on the Rights of the Child was ratified by the United Kingdom in 1989. It states in Art. 12(1) that children capable of forming their own views should be assured of the right to express those views freely in all matters affecting them. International obligations are influential but the Convention is not actually part of UK domestic law and it is not possible to directly challenge the United Kingdom if rights in the Convention are not being upheld. To find legal recognition of the concept of children's rights it is therefore necessary to consider UK case law and legislation.

A starting point when considering the development of children's rights and their expression in the Children Act 1989 is the decision in *Gillick* v. *West Norfolk and Wisbech Area Health Authority* [1986] AC 112. The case established what has become known as the mature minor principle or '*Gillick* competency'. The case concerned whether it was lawful for a doctor to give advice and contraceptives to a person under the age of 16 without parental consent. The Family Law Reform Act 1969, s. 8(1) states that a person may give informed consent to medical treatment at 16. In *Gillick* the court ruled that if a person under the age of 16 is of sufficient understanding that person may give consent to treatment in the absence of parental consent and it is not necessary to notify the parent. Lord Scarman stated: 'A minor's capacity to make his or her own decisions depends on the minor having sufficient understanding and intelligence to make the decision and is not to be determined by reference to any judicially fixed age limit.' The case was heralded as a landmark decision that provided authority for young people who were '*Gillick* competent' to make lawful decisions in a range of areas. The courts, however, were more cautious and subsequent decisions appeared to limit application of the principle. This is particularly evident in cases concerning refusal of medical treatment. In *Re W (A Minor) (Wardship: Medical Treatment)* [1992] 4 All ER 627 the court overruled the refusal to consent to treatment of a 16-year-old girl suffering from anorexia nervosa. The court (exercising its inherent jurisdiction) decided that the welfare of the girl required that her wishes be overruled. The courts have demonstrated that they are prepared to overrule the wishes of '*Gillick* competent' minors and their parents in order to reach the decision which is in the child's best interest.

The balance between children's rights and parental rights was tested again in the case of *R (Axon)* v. *Secretary of State for Health and another* [2006] EWHC 37 (Admin) and builds on the reasoning provided some 20 years earlier in *Gillick*. Mrs Axon sought a declaration that DH Guidance for health professionals on advising young people about sexually transmitted diseases and abortion was unlawful. The court decided that the guidelines were not unlawful, noting that in a contest between children's rights and parental rights those of the child should prevail. It concluded that a doctor can provide medical advice and treatment on sexual matters as long as satisfied that: the young person understands the advice; cannot be persuaded to inform his/her parents; is likely to continue to have sexual intercourse; unless the young person receives advice or treatment his physical or mental health are likely to suffer; and the best interests of the young person require him or her to receive advice without parental consent or notification.

In the recent decision of *Re A (A Child)* [2014] EWHC 1445 (Fam) a 13-year-old girl was deemed to be '*Gillick* competent' and able to decide to terminate her pregnancy. An application was made by the NHS Trust for a declaration that if she did not have capacity to consent to continuation or termination of the pregnancy, it was in her best interests to have a termination, or a declaration that she did have capacity. The judge applied the test for competence set out in *Gillick*, i.e. sufficient understanding, heard evidence from a psychiatrist and concluded that she was able to decide herself what to do.

There is no specific provision in the Children Act 1989 that promotes 'children's rights' but a number of areas have clearly been influenced by this notion. In the first section, in applying the welfare principle the court is required to have regard to 'the ascertainable wishes and feelings of the child concerned (considered in the light of his age and understanding)' (s. 1(3)(a)). The court is not, however, bound to follow those wishes. As discussed above, there may be difficulties in ensuring the child's voice is heard by the court. In most public law proceedings a children's guardian will be appointed to represent the child's interests. If the child disagrees with the guardian's view and is of sufficient maturity, he may directly instruct a solicitor to represent him. The checklist does not apply to all proceedings, however, and in private proceedings where an agreed application for s. 8 orders is being made, it is possible for the voice of the child to be hidden behind parental agreement.

In *Re M (Children) (Abduction)* [2007] UKHL 55, the court noted that, especially in the light of Article 12 of the United Nations Convention on the Rights of the Child, courts increasingly consider it appropriate to take account of a child's views and provided some explanation as to what that means. Taking account does not mean that those views are always determinative or even presumptively so. Once the discretion comes into play, the court may have to consider the nature and strength of the child's objections, the extent to which they are 'authentically her own' or the product of the influence of the abducting parent, the extent to which they coincide or are at odds with other considerations which are relevant to welfare, as well as the general Convention considerations referred to earlier. The older the child, the greater the weight that her objections are likely to carry.

Section 22 confers a duty on the local authority to consult a looked after child (or a child the local authority proposes to look after) so far as is practicable, before making a decision with respect to the child. The local authority must give due consideration to the child's wishes and feelings having regard to his age and understanding. This duty is reinforced by the child's role in the review process.

Other examples may be drawn from the 1989 Act. A child of sufficient understanding may refuse a medical or psychiatric examination or other assessment ordered under a child assessment order, emergency protection order or interim care or supervision order. In each case an assessment of the child's ability to make an informed decision will be conducted. Even the provisions which at first sight appear to support children's rights may be questioned. For example, the child's right to apply for an s. 8 order in respect of himself is subject to the court giving prior leave, whereas a parent has an automatic right to apply. In contrast, a child of sufficient understanding may apply to vary or revoke a special guardianship order directly whereas others require leave to do so. In adoption cases, in contrast to the position in Scotland the Adoption and Children Act 2002 did not introduce a requirement that the child in question should formally agree to the adoption.

The children's rights debate embraces a spectrum of views from those who advocate the child's absolute right to self-determination to those who argue that children have the right to protection and for decisions to be taken by adults in their best interests. Whatever stance is taken, ensuring rights are upheld in practice can be problematic. Some authorities employ a children's rights officer to ensure children in care are aware of their rights and to assist them in making complaints.

Information about the existence of rights must be made available in an accessible form if children are to be enabled to exercise their rights. Greater access to advocacy schemes may prove to be the most effective strategy. In addition, at national level, in order to promote children's rights and monitor Government policy and practice, the post of Children's Rights Commissioner in England exists.[14]

Children's Commissioner

In response to a recommendation of the Waterhouse Report[15] a Children's Commissioner for Wales was appointed under Part V of the Care Standards Act 2000.[16] The Welsh Commissioner has powers of independent investigation, exercised in Clwyd into allegations of child sexual abuse in schools.[17] Subsequently, following widespread support of the notion, Children's Commissioners have also been appointed in England, Scotland[18] and Northern Ireland,[19] though the terms of reference of each varies, particularly in the extent to which they can take on individual cases.[20]

The post of Children's Commissioner in England is established by the Children Act 2004, as amended by the Children and Families Act 2014. The primary function of the Commissioner, set out in CA 2004, s. 2, is 'the function of promoting and protecting the rights of children in England'.

The Commissioner must take reasonable steps to involve children in discharging his functions, and make sure children are aware of his functions and how to contact him. He is expected to report annually to the Secretary of State on his actions. The Commissioner will mainly be concerned with broad issues affecting children, and is prohibited from investigating individual cases; however, he may provide advice and assistance to children. A new s. 2A(1) provides that the Commissioner must have regard to the **UNCRC** when considering what constitutes children's rights and interests.

Children Act 2004

The introduction of the Children Act 2004 can be traced back to events surrounding the death of Victoria Climbié in February 2000, followed by the green paper, 'Every Child Matters' (2003).[21] The delivery of fully integrated services as envisaged by the Act calls for what Lord Laming described as a 'fundamental change in the mind-set of managers'. The reforms presented by the 'Every Child Matters' agenda and the legislation aim to improve multi-disciplinary working and integrated service delivery and increase accountability. The need for this was clearly identified by Lord Laming: 'I am in no doubt that effective support for children and families cannot be achieved by a single agency acting alone. It depends on a number of agencies working well together. It is a multi-disciplinary task' (para. 130).[22]

The Act introduced duties that focus on children and young people's 'well-being' and 'welfare'. 'Well-being' is based on five outcomes. Effective safeguarding and promoting of children's welfare supports wellbeing. The Act does not introduce a range of new child protection powers, rather it sets the foundations for good practice in the use of existing powers through a holistic integrated approach to child care.

Background to the Act

Victoria Climbié died, aged 8, on 25 February 2000. Her great aunt Marie Therese Kouau and her partner Carl Manning were convicted of her murder in 2001. Victoria came to live with her great aunt, to be educated in England, in November 1998. While she lived with her great aunt in London, Victoria had contact with a range of child care agencies, specifically, four social services departments, two child protection teams of the Metropolitan police, three housing departments, two hospitals and an NSPCC family centre. She did not attend school. Following her death, the Government established three statutory inquiries, chaired by Lord Laming, known as the Victoria Climbié Inquiry. The report was published in January 2003: 'The Report of the Victoria Climbié Inquiry' (Cm. 5730). The Laming report found that Victoria had suffered extreme abuse and neglect. It is a disturbing but important report to read.

The report identified a number of failings: 'The extent of the failure to protect Victoria was lamentable. Tragically, it required nothing more than basic good practice being put into operation. This never happened.' (para. 1.17). It continues:

Not one of the agencies empowered by Parliament to protect children in positions similar to Victoria's – funded from the public purse – emerge from this Inquiry with much credit. The suffering and death of Victoria was a gross failure of the system and was inexcusable. It

> is clear to me that the agencies with responsibility for Victoria gave a low priority to the task of protecting children. They were underfunded, inadequately staffed and poorly led. Even so, there was plenty of evidence to show that scarce resources were not being put to good use. Bad practice can be expensive. (para. 1.18)

In relation to management:

> The greatest failure rests with the senior managers and members of the organizations concerned whose responsibility it was to ensure that the services they provided to children such as Victoria were properly financed, staffed and able to deliver good quality services to children and families. They must be accountable.

The legal framework was described as fundamentally sound, the gap being in its implementation:

> I recognise the fact that over the years, successive governments have refined both legislation and policy, no doubt informed in part by earlier Inquiries of this kind, so that in general, the legislative framework for protecting children is basically sound. I conclude that the gap is not a matter of law but in its implementation. (para. 130)

The report made 108 recommendations covering a wide range of issues, some of which have been taken up in the Children Act 2004 and through the 'Every Child Matters' agenda. The five outcomes for children's services introduced in 'Every Child Matters' were:

- Be healthy;
- Stay safe;
- Enjoy and achieve;
- Make a positive contribution;
- Achieve economic wellbeing.

In slightly different wording, the outcomes are included as areas for improving the wellbeing of children in s. 10(2) of the Act (see below).

Organisational changes

The Act introduces key structural changes within the organisation of children's services so that local authorities will have a Director of Children's Services covering children's social services and education (s. 18). A Director of Adult Services will also be appointed. The functions of the Director of Children's Services are set out in s. 18(2) and include: education functions; children's social services functions; functions towards young people leaving care; functions delegated by the NHS relating to children. Guidance elaborates on the roles and responsibilities of Directors.[23] A Lead Council Member for Children will be appointed to provide political leadership on children's issues.[24]

Children's services authorities are defined in s. 65 as local authorities with social services and education responsibilities, i.e. county councils, metropolitan district councils, unitary authorities and London boroughs. Integrated services are to be provided through a **children's trust**. According to the Department for Education and Skills: 'Children's trusts have been created to address the fragmentation of responsibilities for children's services.' Children's trusts draw together services for children and young people in an area, underpinned by the Children Act 2004 duty to cooperate.

Local Safeguarding Children Boards replace the previous non-statutory Area Child Protection Committees, providing direct local accountability (discussed further in Chapter 9). The key objective of a **LSCB** is to coordinate and ensure the effectiveness of the safeguarding work of the bodies represented on the Board.

The Children and Young Persons Act 2008, s. 7 places the Secretary of State under a statutory duty to promote the wellbeing of children in England. This complements the existing duty contained in s. 10 of the Education Act 1996 to promote the education of the people of England and Wales. The Secretary of State now has responsibility for promoting the wellbeing of all children and young people (and, by extension, their families and those who care for them) as well as their education.

Cooperation to improve wellbeing

Section 10 introduces a requirement to cooperate for best outcomes for children. Agencies can pool funds to facilitate this. The object of the section is to secure cooperation and facilitate joint working across a wide range of organisations described as 'relevant partners' of the children's services authority and 'other bodies or persons considered appropriate', the latter probably including voluntary organisations and schools. The children's services authority is broader than its social services and education functions and extends to other departments such as housing, planning and leisure. The following are relevant partners: district council; police authority; probation board; youth offending team; Strategic Health Authority and Primary Care Trust; persons providing services under s. 114 of the Learning and Skills Act 2000 and the Learning and Skills Council for England.

---

s. 10

(1) Each children's services authority in England must make arrangements to promote co-operation between –

   (a) the authority;

   (b) each of the authority's relevant partners; and

   (c) such other persons or bodies as the authority consider appropriate, being persons or bodies of any nature who exercise functions or are engaged in activities in relation to children in the authority's area.

...

(3) In making arrangements under this section a children's services authority in England must have regard to the importance of parents and other persons caring for children in improving the well-being of children.

(5) The relevant partners of a children's services authority in England must cooperate with the authority in the making of arrangements under this section.

(CA 2004)

Wellbeing

The five outcomes set out in 'Every Child Matters' (Be healthy; Stay safe; Enjoy and achieve; Make a positive contribution; Achieve economic well-being) are translated in the Act as aspects of wellbeing.

---

s. 10(2)

The arrangements are to be made with a view to improving the well-being of children in the authority's area so far as relating to –

(a) physical and mental health and emotional well-being;
(b) protection from harm and neglect;
(c) education, training and recreation;
(d) the contribution made by them to society;
(e) social and economic well-being.

(CA 2004)

Duty to promote welfare

Section 11 explains the duty to make arrangements to safeguard and promote welfare. It is imposed on a wide range of bodies listed in s. 11(1) to include the following: a children's service authority; district council; Strategic Health Authority; Primary Care Trust; NHS Trust; NHS Foundation Trust; police authority; British Transport Police Authority; probation board; youth offending team; governor of prison or secure training centre. The duty also applies to any privatised or contracted services. Inter-agency working is the focus of this section and much of the Act. Inter-agency working is not a new idea, but the Children Act 2004 strengthens the legal basis of the concept. Guidance on this issue has been in existence since the Children Act 1989, reinforced more recently with the 2013 version of 'Working Together'.

---

s. 11(2)

Each person and body to whom this section applies must make arrangements for ensuring that –

(a) their functions are discharged having regard to the need to safeguard and promote the welfare of children;

(CA 2004)

Section 11 does not introduce any new functions for agencies; it applies to how they carry out existing functions. It introduces a statutory requirement to carry out their existing functions in a way that takes into account the need to safeguard and promote the welfare of children.

The duty to safeguard and promote the welfare of children is broader than preventing child abuse or responding to children in need. It is defined in Guidance as:

protecting children from maltreatment; preventing impairment of children's health or development; and ensuring that children are growing up in circumstances consistent with the provision of safe and effective care; ... and undertaking that role so as to enable those children to have optimum life chances and to enter adulthood successfully.[25]

Children and young people's plans

Section 17 CA 2004 introduced the requirement for children's services authority to prepare and publish a children and young people's plan setting out their strategy for how services for children and young people will be provided (s. 17). Guidance was issued and details of the plans' content set out in regulations and covers: the period of the plan; publication arrangements; review and consultation requirements. Plans are no longer required as the relevant regulations have been revoked, however many authorities still prepare plans and publish them on their websites.

Current policy

'Every Child Matters' and the Children Act 2004 were introduced by the Labour Government. Whilst these are still influential in some respects, the Coalition Government have developed their own policies with a stronger emphasis on educational achievement, and safeguarding children falls within the remit of the Department for Education (the Department for Children, Schools and Families having been disbanded). The Coalition Government launched an independent review of safeguarding practice, led by Professor Eileen Munro. The final report of this review, 'A Child-Centred System' was published in 2011 and included 15 key recommendations to underpin an effective multi-agency child protection system, the majority of which were accepted by the Government.[26] One of the recommendations was to revise existing statutory guidance. That was given effect, after further consultation, with the latest (and considerably reduced in length) version of 'Working Together' (2013), which incorporates the Framework for Assessment. The new guidance itself gives effect to some of the other recommendations. The Munro review placed real value on the professional expertise of social workers, a theme also picked up in the Family Justice Review, on focusing on the needs of the individual child and moving away from over bureaucratisation and proceduralism in social work.

Given further high profile child deaths, questions inevitably continue to be raised about the effectiveness of the framework and operation in practice of child safeguarding under the Children Acts of 1989 and 2004.

Local authority support for children in need

Local authorities must provide a range of services and facilities to children in need and their families under Part III of the Children Act 1989. Actual provision will depend partly on whether it is provided for under a duty or power and also on levels of resources which impact on the whole area of service provision. 'Working Together' (2013) emphasises the importance of 'early help' which may precede support provided to a child identified as 'in need'. In March 2013, there were 378,600 children assessed as in need of support in England.[27]

The duty of the local authority towards children in need is contained in s. 17(1). The philosophy of the 1989 Act is that the best place for a child to be brought up is usually in the child's own family and the child in need can be helped most effectively if the local authority, working in partnership with the parents, provides a range and level of services appropriate to the child's needs.[28] For this reason, services may be made available to members of the child's family as well as the child in need (s. 17(3)). 'Family' is defined to include any person who has parental responsibility for the child and any other person with whom he has been living (s. 17(10)). It would thus include not only the child's carers but also other family members such as siblings. The Children and Families Act 2014 specifically extends s. 17 to include duties to young carers.

s. 17(1)

It shall be the general duty of every local authority (in addition to the other duties imposed on them by this Part) –

(a) to safeguard and promote the welfare of children within their area who are in need; and

(b) so far as is consistent with that duty, to promote the upbringing of such children by their families, by providing a range and level of services appropriate to those children's needs.

(CA 1989)

There is a limited range of duties owed to all children living in a local authority area, and powers to provide services to all children and families and duties towards children defined as 'in need'. Certain of the duties that apply to all children may be interpreted as operating to prevent children becoming children in need, e.g. the duty to provide family centres (Sch. 2, para. 9).[29]

Section 17(10) defines a child in need:

s. 17(10)

(a) he is unlikely to achieve or maintain, or have the opportunity of achieving or maintaining, a reasonable standard of health or development without appropriate provision for him of services by a local authority under this Part;

(b) his health or development is likely to be significantly impaired, without the provision for him or her of services by a local authority under this Part; or

(c) he is disabled.

(CA 1989)

Section 17(11) includes relevant definitions:

s. 17(11)

'development' means physical, intellectual, emotional, social or behavioural development; and 'health' means physical or mental health.

(CA 1989)

Interpretation of need

Under Sch. 2 to the 1989 Act, the responsibilities of local authorities are presented in qualified terms, such as the local authority shall take *reasonable* steps or shall make such provision as they *consider appropriate*. There is no absolute duty to meet the needs of every individual child. The assessment of need is therefore a crucial stage as the reality of service provision is based on a system of prioritisation. Each local authority sets its own priorities, linked to the range of services available. For example, authorities may identify different levels of provision: e.g. indirect provision, including advice and counselling, referral on and information; low-level direct provision which may include support groups, small-scale adaptations and irregular contact; and high-level direct provision including intensive family support, and provision of accommodation.

R v. *Lambeth LBC, ex parte K (A Child)* (2000) 3 CCLR 141 ruled on the conduct of assessments. Assessments must accord with guidance issued under s. 7(1), such as 'The Children Act Guidance'. The intended procedure is that local authorities first assess the needs of the child and, where appropriate, the carers and other family members; second, produce a care plan; and third, provide the identified services.

'The Children Act 1989 Guidance' recognises the breadth of the s. 17 definition:

> The definition of need ... is deliberately wide to reinforce the emphasis on preventive support to families. It has three categories: a reasonable standard of health or development; significant impairment of health or development; and disablement. It would not therefore be acceptable for an authority to exclude any of these three – for example, by confining services to children at risk of significant harm which attracts the duty to investigate under s. 47.[30]

In fact, early implementation of s. 17 was problematic; studies found that eligibility criteria were often linked to the concept of risk but otherwise there was great inconsistency in the way authorities interpreted 'in need'.[31] Both eligibility for services and service provision were something of a regional lottery.

Guidance on assessment was produced with a principal aim being to promote a greater level of consistency across the country in terms of the factors to be taken into account in an assessment, 'The Framework for the Assessment of Children in Need and their Families' (2000). The Framework stresses the need to have a full picture of the child's circumstances and to take a child-centred approach. It is based around principles that assessment should be rooted in child development; involve children and families; build on strengths as well as identifying difficulties; be a process and involve inter-agency working (amongst others). The Framework will be used in cases where an assessment of need leads to service provision; equally, whilst it is important that need is not interpreted in the same way as 'at risk', the assessment will also be used in child-protection investigations under s. 47. Key elements of the Framework are now incorporated into the new version of 'Working Together' (2013). Figure 7.1 illustrates the range of factors to be included in an assessment.

Three general areas are assessed: the child's development needs; parenting capacity; and family and environmental factors. Each of these areas is broken down further into specific categories to be addressed in the report.

Not all services will be provided directly by the local authority. The authority has the central role of coordinating service provision. Inter-agency cooperation in provision of services is as important as inter-agency cooperation in child-protection investigations. Section 27 of the 1989 Act imposes a duty on the local authority to consider whether public authorities providing education, health and related services can assist in the exercise of its functions

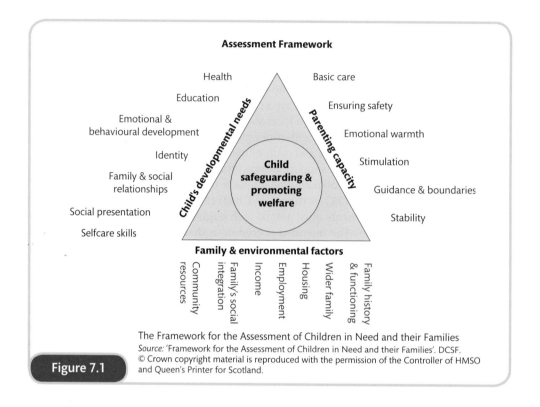

Assessment Framework

Health

Education

Emotional & behavioural development

Identity

Family & social relationships

Social presentation

Selfcare skills

Child's developmental needs

Basic care

Ensuring safety

Emotional warmth

Stimulation

Guidance & boundaries

Stability

Parenting capacity

Child safeguarding & promoting welfare

Family & environmental factors

Community resources

Family's social integration

Income

Employment

Housing

Wider family

Family history & functioning

The Framework for the Assessment of Children in Need and their Families
Source: 'Framework for the Assessment of Children in Need and their Families'. DCSF.
© Crown copyright material is reproduced with the permission of the Controller of HMSO and Queen's Printer for Scotland.

Figure 7.1

under Part III. If requested to help, an authority must provide assistance unless it is incompatible with its own duties. In addition, there is significant scope for voluntary organisations and the private sector to provide services. The above discussion on 'wellbeing' extends the statutory basis of inter-agency cooperation.

The Common Assessment Framework (**CAF**), supplements the Framework for Assessment. It provides a common approach to needs assessment that can be used by the whole children's workforce, it is common across services and may equally be completed by a health or social work or other professional. Effective use of CAF should lead to earlier holistic identification of children's needs and fewer assessments of individual children. The CAF consists of: a simple pre-assessment checklist to help practitioners identify children who would benefit from a common assessment; a process for undertaking a common assessment; and a standard form to help practitioners record, and, where appropriate, share with others, the findings from the assessment. Referral to specialist further assessment may be made following common assessment.

An amendment by the Children Act 2004 requires local authorities to ascertain children's wishes and feelings regarding provision of services (including provision of accommodation) under s. 20, giving due consideration to them having regard to age and understanding, before determining what, if any, services to provide. This puts good practice on a statutory footing (s. 17(4A) CA 1989, inserted by s. 53 CA 2004).

The services

The services, which may be provided by the local authority, include giving assistance in kind or in cash. The specific services are contained in Sch. 2 to the Children Act 1989. Table 7.2 contains duties towards children generally. Table 7.3 contains those duties that

Table 7.2 Local authority duties to support children and families

Take reasonable steps, through provision of services, to prevent children suffering ill treatment or neglect (Sch. 2, para. 4)

The authority may assist a person to obtain alternative accommodation (assistance may be in cash) where a child who is living on premises is suffering or likely to suffer ill treatment at the hands of that person (Sch. 2, para. 5)

The local authority shall take reasonable steps:

- to reduce the need to bring proceedings for care or supervision orders
- to reduce the need to bring criminal proceedings against children
- to encourage children not to commit criminal offences
- to avoid the need for children to be placed in secure accommodation (Sch. 2, para. 7)

The local authority shall provide family centres, as it considers appropriate. A family centre is a centre at which the child, his parents or anyone with parental responsibility or caring for the child, may attend for occupational, social, cultural or recreational activities, advice, guidance or counselling (Sch. 2, para. 9)

Table 7.3 Local authority services to children in need

Take reasonable steps to identify the extent of children in need (Sch. 2, para. 1(1)). Publish information about services provided by the local authority and others, including voluntary organisations, and take steps to ensure the information is received by those who might benefit from the services (Sch. 2, para. 1(2))

Where it appears a child is in need, the authority may assess his needs under the Children Act 1989 at the same time as an assessment under: the Chronically Sick and Disabled Persons Act 1970, the Education Act 1981, the Disabled Persons (Services, Consultation and Representation) Act 1986 (Sch. 2, para. 3)

Review provision of services and publish a plan (Sch. 2, para. 1A)

Where a child is living away from his family, take reasonable steps to enable him to live with them or promote contact (Sch. 2, para. 10)

The local authority shall provide, as it considers appropriate, for the following services to be available to children in need living with their families:

- advice, guidance and counselling
- occupational social control or recreational activities
- home help (including laundry facilities)
- travelling assistance to use a service
- assistance to the child and family to have a holiday (Sch. 2, para. 8)

In making arrangements for day care and to encourage people to act as local authority foster parents, the local authority shall have regard to the different racial groups to which children within the area, who are in need, belong (Sch. 2, para. 11)

The local authority shall provide day care for children in need in their area aged 5 or under and not at school, as is appropriate (s. 18)

are specific to children in need. Services in relation to disabled children are considered below. Services to children looked after by local authorities are provided for in Sch. 2 (and are discussed in Chapter 10). Many local authorities compile a 'service directory' for children, young persons and families. This should be a complete listing of services in the area, not just those provided by social services, including, for example, registered childminders, preschool facilities, teenage pregnancy services, bereavement support, toy libraries, mental health services, etc.

Challenging service provision

There is limited scope to challenge the local authority exercise of its duties towards children in need, as the following cases explain. In *Re J (A Minor) (Specific Issue Order: Leave to Apply)* [1995] 1 FLR 669, a 17-year-old boy was refused leave to seek a specific issue order that he was a child in need and required a local authority to provides services. The court held that the existence of Part III duties could not be the subject of judicial intervention other than through judicial review. However, in a subsequent case, *R v. Lambeth London Borough Council, ex parte A* [2001] EWCA Civ 1624, the court ruled that the duty owed by a local authority under s. 17 of the Children Act 1989 was a target duty owed to children in general and was not justiciable by judicial review. The case concerned an application for judicial review of the local authority's failure to meet the housing need it had identified under the section. Two children were autistic with severe learning difficulties and the family were assessed as needing appropriate housing with a garden. The court described s. 17 as a duty to strive rather than to deliver and there was no requirement to perform particular tasks or to achieve particular results. Section 17 gives a local authority discretion rather than a duty to provide accommodation in any individual case. It was described as a hybrid provision, providing more than a power but less than a specific duty to, and enforceable by, individuals. The case proceeded to the House of Lords as *R (G) v. Barnet London Borough Council; R (W) v. Lambeth London Borough Council; R (A) v. Lambeth London Borough Council* [2003] UKHL 57. The Lords confirmed that s. 17 duties were correctly classified as duties of a general character not a specific duty owed to an individual child. Housing was the primary duty of the housing authority and not the primary purpose of s. 17. The authority providing accommodation to a child were not under a duty to provide accommodation for the family as a whole. Lord Nicholls and Lord Steyn gave dissenting judgments and noted with concern the potential impact on a child of separation from his family. In such circumstances it would be difficult for the authority to argue that its actions met the needs of the child.

An amendment to s. 17 introduced by the Adoption and Children Act 2002 clarifies that authorities have the *power* to provide accommodation to children in need and their families. Children provided with accommodation under s. 17 are not included in the definition of looked after children. Under s. 17 'Provision of services for children in need, their families and others', subsection (6) now reads:

> ### s. 17(6)
>
> The services provided by a local authority in the exercise of its functions conferred on them by this section may include providing accommodation, giving assistance in kind, or in exceptional circumstances, in cash.
>
> (CA 1989)

The legal basis for provision of accommodation can be significant as illustrated in the following case. In *R (M) v. Barnet London Borough Council* [2008] EWHC 2354 (Admin) local authority accommodation was provided to a child who had a history of conflict with her parents. On approaching 18, she claimed that this accommodation was provided under s. 20 rather than s. 17. The significance of the legal basis for provision of the accommodation is that leaving care services only follow accommodation provided under s. 20. The court agreed with the authority that the accommodation was actually provided under s. 17 not s. 20. One of the elements of s. 20 is that accommodation is required as a result of her parent being prevented from caring for her. In this case her parents were willing to provide accommodation and it was only through her unreasonable refusal to return home that the authority provided accommodation. If she required accommodation after the age of 18, she would have to seek that accommodation via homelessness legislation.

The key issue of whether a young person is provided with accommodation by housing or social services and as a consequence entitled to leaving care services (only if accommodated by social services under s. 20) was considered in *R (M)* v. *Hammersmith and Fulham LBC* [2008] UKHL 14. (See discussion in Chapter 19.)

Children with disabilities

The term 'children with disabilities' will be used in this text rather than 'disabled children', in accordance with the philosophy of the Children Act 1989 that children with a disability are 'children first'[32] (and despite the fact that the Act refers to disabled children, e.g. Sch. 2, Part I, para. 6). It is also important to recognise that an argument exists in favour of using the term 'disabled children' as reflecting application of the social model of disability whereby children with disabilities experience social oppression and exclusion. A child may thus have a physical impairment but in fact is rendered disabled by a society that does not support the child to function to full potential because account is not taken of the impairment.

As seen above, a disabled child is clearly classified as a child in need for the purposes of the Children Act 1989, s. 17(10)(c). A disabled child is defined as a child who is:

s. 17(11)

Blind, deaf or dumb or suffers from mental disorder of any kind, or is substantially and permanently handicapped by illness, injury or congenital or other disability as may be prescribed.

(CA 1989)

(Note that this is the same as the definition in the National Assistance Act 1948, s. 29 relating to adults (prior to the Care Act 2014), and that it utilises oppressive language.)

Services for disabled children are provided for by the Children Act 1989 by virtue of their status as a child in need. In addition to the frameworks for assessment (discussed above), services may be accessed via other legislation, such as the Care Act 2014. Reference is made in Sch. 2, para. 3 to parallel assessments under the Children Act 1989 and other legislation.[33] It is important to be aware whether there is a duty or a power to provide services. This was evident in the case of *R* v. *Bexley London Borough Council, ex parte B* [2000] 3 CCLR 15. The court held that if a local authority is satisfied that a child needs a service which can be provided under the Chronically Sick and Disabled Persons Act **(CSDPA)** 1970, s. 2, then the authority is under a duty to provide that service and cannot avoid a specific duty owed to a child with a disability by purporting to act under the more general provisions of the Children Act 1989.

Service provision is not the sole responsibility of social services, and good levels of inter-agency cooperation with other agencies, specifically health and education, is central to effective provision of services. Some of the barriers to this objective include lack of agreement on definitions and priorities, and confusion about responsibilities for children with disabilities.

As a preliminary point, social services have a duty to provide advice, guidance and counselling services (CA 1989, Sch. 2, Part I, para. 8a). This may include advice on welfare benefits that disabled children and their families are entitled to, and referral to advocacy services so that an advocate may (amongst other things) assist the family in obtaining appropriate services.

A local authority can take resources of parents into account when deciding whether to provide services for disabled children. *R (Spink)* v. *Wandsworth London Borough Council* [2005] EWCA Civ 302 concerned provisions under the CSDPA 1970, s. 2, which applied to disabled children as well as to disabled adults (replaced by the Care Act 2014). The parents of two profoundly disabled boys were not eligible for a Disabled Facilities Grant to cover the adaptations required (these are means tested), which included a powered step lift and an adapted bathroom. The Court of Appeal found that the authority did not need to provide a service where it was reasonable to expect the parents, using their own resources, to meet those needs. It applied the three-stage approach to s. 2 set out in *R* v. *Gloucestershire County Council, ex parte Barry* [1997] 2 All ER 1, namely, there must be an assessment of need, the authority then considers whether it is necessary to meet those needs and, thirdly, if it decides it is necessary to meet those needs then services must be provided. At the second stage, the court ruled that when deciding whether it is necessary to provide a service, the authority can have regard to the parents' means.

Local authorities are required to 'provide services designed ... to minimise the effect on disabled children ... of their disabilities, and to give such children the opportunity to lead lives as normal as possible' (Sch. 2, Part I, para. 6). The provision of services needs to be flexible in order to meet the variety of needs of disabled children and their families.

The local authority should maintain a register of disabled children (Sch. 2, Part I, para. 2). There is no duty to register; it is a voluntary process and service provision is not dependent on registration. Registration can help with service planning.

A significant proportion of looked after children are disabled. If a disabled child is looked after by the local authority, and provided with accommodation, s. 23(8) requires that the local authority must, as far as is reasonably practicable, ensure that the accommodation is not unsuitable for his particular needs. Care plans for disabled children should demonstrate that the proposed plan is the best way to meet the assessed needs of the particular child. In terms of education, the policy of the Department for Education is to promote the inclusion of disabled children in mainstream education and this should be reflected in the care plan.

Taken together, these responsibilities support work with children with disabilities in the context of the Children Act 1989, following the principle that children with disabilities are children first. In reality, because the law in this area is framed in terms of powers or qualified duties, children in need and their families, including children with disabilities, often experience limited support. (The impact of the Equality Act 2010 in relation to disability is discussed in Chapter 6.)

The Children and Young Persons Act 2008 introduces further provisions to strengthen support for disabled children and their families. There is a duty imposed on local authorities to consider the welfare needs of disabled children in their area who are placed in education or health settings away from home, and then provide services to meet those needs. The Act also requires local authorities to help parents caring for disabled children by giving them breaks from their caring responsibilities (**CYPA**, s. 25). According to the explanatory notes: 'The intention is that breaks should not only be provided to those struggling to care for disabled children but also to those for whom a break from their caring responsibilities will improve the quality of the care they provide.'

Young carers and parent carers

The Children and Families Act 2014 inserts a new s. 17Z into the Children Act 1989 relating to young carers. A young carer is a person under 18 who provides or intends to provide care for another person (other than under a contract or as voluntary work).

The local authority must conduct a 'young carer's needs assessment' if if it appears to them that a young carer may have needs for support or they receive a request from the young carer or young carer's parent (s. 17ZA(1)). The assessment must consider whether it is appropriate for the young carer to provide care and will take into account the young carer's wishes to participate in education, training, recreation and work. The assessment may (with their agreement) be combined with an assessment of the cared for person's needs. From the assessment, the local authority must decide whether the young carer has needs in relation to care and if so whether they could be met by services under s.17. The young carer may also be identified as a child in need.

Parent carers are defined as people over 18 who provide or intend to provide care for a disabled child for whom they have parental responsibility. Where the local authority are satisfied that the disabled child is a child in need, the parent appears to have support needs and requests an assessment, then a 'parent carer's needs assessment' will be carried out (s. 17ZD). The assessment must have regard to the wellbeing of the parent carer and the need to safeguard and promote the welfare of the disabled child and any other child for whom the parent has parental responsibility.

In both cases the assessment is triggered by a request from the young carer or parent carer. It is disappointing therefore that a duty to provide information about the right to request an assessment was not included in the Act.

The Child Poverty Act 2010

The Child Poverty Act 2010 creates a framework to monitor progress towards the Government target to eradicate child poverty by 2020. The Act establishes a Child Poverty Commission to advise on child poverty strategies, and four targets are set by which success in eradicating poverty can be measured. The targets are to reduce the number of children experiencing relative poverty, combined low income and material deprivation, absolute poverty and persistent poverty. Local authorities must produce a child poverty needs assessment and cooperate with key agencies (district councils, police and health) to reduce poverty.

Chapter summary

- The Children Act 1989 introduced a number of themes including: parental responsibility; a new threshold for state intervention; greater opportunities to hear the voice of the child; a preference for children to be brought up by their families with appropriate service input; and some new orders such as the specific issue and prohibited steps order.

- The central principles of the Act are mainly contained in Part I and include the principle that the child's welfare shall be the court's paramount consideration. This principle is supported by a welfare checklist, which guides the court as to a range of factors to be taken into account.

- There is a presumption that delay is prejudicial and to be avoided unless it can be shown to be planned and purposeful (CA 1989, s. 1(2)).

- Courts should not make orders unless there is a positive benefit in doing so, the principle of non-intervention (CA 1989, s. 1(5)).

- It is possible to impose a restriction that no application for an order in respect of a child can be made by a named person without leave of the court (CA 1989, s. 91(14)).

- The Children Act 2004 was introduced following the Victoria Climbié Inquiry and includes duties on local authorities and other relevant agencies to cooperate to improve children's wellbeing, and to make arrangements to safeguard and promote welfare. It also established the role of Children's Commissioner in England.

- Local authorities must provide a range of services and facilities to children and their families. In addition to general duties owed to all children, a number of services are designed for children in need, defined by CA 1989, s. 17 and including disabled children.

Exercises

Consider whether in any of the following cases there is a child in need. If so what, if any, support and services might be provided.

- Teachers at a primary school are concerned about Julie Anne, a 6-year-old child who has recently moved to the area. She often arrives at school dirty and dishevelled and hungry. She did not attend school at her previous address and cannot write, but she is a bright child who enjoys school.
- Lorna, aged 8, has asthma. She lives with her mum who has a mild learning disability. The local surgery have written to Lorna's mum three times asking her to bring Lorna in to their asthma clinic for a check-up but she has failed to do so.
- Althea's husband Jason died in an industrial accident. Following Jason's death, Althea moved with her daughter Janine, aged 3, to live with her elderly mother who has severe arthritis. Althea spends a lot of her time caring for her mother, who has consistently refused to consider getting any help from social services or any other body. Janine is very withdrawn and spends most of her time watching children's videos. Althea knows very few people in the area and is becoming increasingly depressed.
- Jonathan has Down's syndrome. His parents both work full-time and they enjoy a good standard of living. Jonathan has a full-time nanny who cares for him during the day and takes him to a private preschool. The nursery teacher has expressed some concerns that Jonathan can be quite aggressive with other children.
- Susan and Peter have three children, twin boys aged 9 and a daughter, Simone, who is 7 and has a learning disability. The boys have been selected to play for a football academy 40 miles away, on Thursday evenings when Peter is at work. After a couple of sessions, Susan decides she cannot manage the journey with all three children and the boys told her that some of the other footballers were laughing at Simone. Peter has been unable to change his work shift and, as a keen footballer himself, wants the boys to continue. They have no relatives close by and have never felt able to leave Simone with a babysitter. Susan overheard one of the twins saying that Simone spoils everything for them. The tension about this issue is causing arguments between Susan and Peter.

Websites

United Nations Convention on the Rights of the Child:
www.unicef.org/crc/

The Children's Legal Centre produces a range of useful guides with an emphasis on children's rights:
www.childrenslegalcentre.com

The Advisory Centre for Education (ACE) provides independent and confidential advice on all aspects of the education service:
www.ace-ed.org.uk

Every disabled child matters:
www.edcm.org.uk

Further reading

For this chapter and the following chapters relating to children and families it will be useful to refer to a number of specialist textbooks and key documents:

Allen, N. (2010) *Making Sense of the Children Act 1989 and Related Legislation for the Social and Welfare Services.* London: John Wiley.

Bainham, A. and Gilmore S. (2013) *Children the Modern Law* (4th edn). Bristol: Family Law.

Davies, C. and Ward H. (2012) *Safeguarding Children Across Services: Messages from Research.* London: Jessica Kingsley.

Davis, L. (2008) *The Social Worker's Guide to Children and Families Law.* London: Jessica Kingsley.

Herring J, (2013) *Family Law* (6th edn). Harlow: Pearson.

Williams, J. (2008) *Child Law for Social Work: Policy and Practice.* London: Sage.

In relation to children's rights see:

Fortin, J. (2009) *Children's Rights and the Developing Law* (3rd edn). Cambridge: Cambridge University Press.

Fortin, J. (2011) 'A decade of the HRA and its impact on children's rights' *Family Law* p. 179.

Franklin, B. (ed.) (2001) *The New Handbook of Children's Rights, Comparative Policy and Practice.* London: Routledge.

Freeman, M. (2000) 'The future of children's rights' 14(4) *Children and Society* pp. 277–93.

Lyon, C. (2007) 'Children's participation and promotion of their rights' 29(2) *Journal of Social Welfare and Family Law* p. 99.

Sawyer, C. (1999) 'International developments: one step forward, two steps back, the European Convention on the Exercise of Children's Rights' 11(2) *Child and Family Law Quarterly* pp. 151–70.

Aspects of welfare are debated in:

Herring, J. (2005) 'Farewell welfare?' 27(2) *Journal of Social Welfare and Family Law* p. 159.

Herring, J. (2014) 'The welfare principle and the Children Act: presumably it's about welfare?' 36 (1) *Journal of Social Welfare and Family Law* p. 14.

James, A., James, A. and McNamee, S. (2003) 'Constructing children's welfare in family proceedings' *Family Law* p. 889. (Discusses the ways in which children's guardians and children and family reporters incorporate the principle of ascertaining the child's wishes and feelings into their working practices.)

In relation to children in need see:

Broach, S., Clements, L. and Read, J. (2010) *Disabled Children: A Legal Handbook.* London: Legal Action Group.

Murphy, J. (2003) 'Children in need: the limits of local authority accountability' 23 *Legal Studies* p. 103.

Preston-Shoot, M. (2005) 'Mapping the needs of children in need' 35(2) *British Journal of Social Work* p. 255.

Read, J., Clements, L. and Ruebain, D. (2006) *Disabled Children and the Law: Research and Good Practice* (2nd edn). London: Jessica Kingsley. (A specialist text covering children with disabilities.)

Westwood, J. (2014) *Children in Need of Support.* Basingstoke: Palgrave Macmillan.

Notes

1. *Re M (Leave to Remove Child from Jurisdiction)* [1999] 2 FLR 334 at 340.
2. L. Fox Harding (1997) *Perspectives in Child Care Policy* (3rd edn). London: Longman.
3. M. Freeman (1998) 'The next Children's Act?' 28 *Family Law* pp. 341–8. He suggests that any new legislation should be entitled the Children's Act rather than the Children Act, the latter title positioning the child as object rather than subject. The welfare principle should be extended to all decisions taken in court and beyond the courtroom to tribunals dealing with education issues and cases where one parent is trying to oust the other from the family home. 'The next Act should contain an interpretational presumption that, unless specifically excluded, all court and tribunal decisions relating to children should be governed by the paramountcy principle' (p. 343). He advocates following Scots legislation, which states that a child of 12 years of age or more shall be presumed to be of sufficient age and maturity to form a view and participate in decision-making. Again, following the Scottish model, a list of parental responsibilities should be specified in legislation. Corporal chastisement should be made unlawful and the defences providing for reasonable chastisement removed. Finally, new institutional structures are required, including a statutory duty to appoint children's rights officers, a network of Children's Legal Centres and a Children's Ombudsperson.
4. The welfare of the child is the paramount consideration in decisions taken by the court. In other circumstances a different position may apply: notably, under s. 17(4) the local authority must safeguard and promote the welfare of a child in need.
5. A. Bainham (1998) *Children – The Modern Law* (2nd edn). Bristol: Family Law, Jordan Publishing.
6. J. Eekelaar (1986) 'The emergence of children's rights' 6(2) *Oxford Journal of Legal Studies* p. 161.
7. J. Herring (2013) *Family Law* (6th edn). Harlow: Pearson.
8. Law Commission Report No. 172 'Review of Child Law: Guardianship and Custody' (1988).
9. Department of Health (1991) 'The Children Act 1989 Guidance and Regulations', vol. 1. London: HMSO.
10. Raitt, F. E. (2004) 'Judicial discretion and methods of ascertaining the views of a child' 16(2) *Child and Family Law Quarterly* p. 151.
11. J. Brophy (2003) 'Diversity and child protection', *Family Law*, pp. 674–8.

[12] J. Hunt, A. Macleod and C. Thomas (2001) 'The last resort: child protection, the courts and the 1989 Children Act' in Department of Health, *The Children Act Now: Messages from Research*. London: The Stationery Office.

[13] J. Packman and C. Hall (2001) 'From care to accommodation: support, protection and control in child care services' in Department of Health, *The Children Act Now: Messages from Research*. London: The Stationery Office.

[14] See M. Rosenbaum and P. Newell (1991) *Taking Children Seriously: A Proposal for a Children's Rights Commissioner*. London: Calouste Gulbenkian Foundation.

[15] R. Waterhouse (2000) 'Lost in care – Report of the Tribunal of Inquiry into the Abuse of Children in Care in the Former County Council Areas of Gwynedd and Clwyd since 1974', HC 201. London: The Stationery Office.

[16] As amended by the Children's Commissioner for Wales Act 2001. See further discussion in K. Hollingsworth and G. Douglas (2002) 'Creating a children's champion for Wales? The Care Standards Act 2000 (Part V) and the Children's Commissioner for Wales Act 2001' 65(1) *Modern Law Review* pp. 58–78.

[17] Children's Commissioner for Wales (2004) 'Clwyd: Report of the Examination of the Children's Commissioner for Wales into allegations of child sexual/abuse in a school setting'.

[18] Commissioner for Children and Young People (Scotland) Act 2003.

[19] Commissioner for Children and Young People (Northern Ireland) Order 2003 (SI 2003/439 (NI 11)).

[20] See detailed discussion of the respective roles in J. Williams (2005) 'Effective government structures for children?: The UK's four Children's Commissioners' 17 *Child and Family Law Quarterly* p. 137.

[21] (Cm. 5860) (Chief Secretary for the Treasury).

[22] Secretary of State for Health, Home Secretary (2003) 'The Victoria Climbié Inquiry: Report of an Inquiry by Lord Laming', Cm 5730. Norwich: The Stationery Office.

[23] DfE (2013) *Directors of Children's Services: Roles and Responsibilities*. London: DfE.

[24] See *The Role and Responsibilities of the Director of Children's Services and the Lead Member for Children*. London: DfES.

[25] Statutory guidance on making arrangements to safeguard and promote the welfare of children under s. 11 of the Children Act 2004, para. 2.8.

[26] DfE (2011) *A Child-Centred System: The Government's response to the Munro Review of Child Protection*. London: The Stationery Office.

[27] DfE (2013) *Characteristics of Children in Need 2012-13*. London: The Stationery Office.

[28] See further Department of Health (1991) 'The Children Act 1989 Guidance and Regulations', vol. 2 'Family support, day care and educational provision for young children'. London: HMSO.

[29] See discussion in A. Bainham (1998) *Children: The Modern Law* (2nd edn). Bristol: Family Law, Jordan.

[30] Department of Health (1991) 'The Children Act 1989 Guidance and Regulations', vol. 2 'Family support, day care and educational provision for young children' (para. 2.4). London: HMSO.

[31] See Department of Health (2001) *The Children Act Now: Messages from Research*. London: The Stationery Office (in particular studies 1, 8 and 23).

[32] Department of Health (1991) 'The Children Act 1989 Guidance and Regulations', vol. 6 'Children with disabilities'. London: HMSO.

[33] Chronically Sick and Disabled Persons Act 1970; Education Act 1981; Disabled Persons (Services, Consultation and Representation) Act 1986; or any other enactment.

Chapter 8

Children and family breakdown

Learning objectives

To develop an understanding of the following:

- The meaning of parental responsibility.
- Private law provisions which regulate the exercise of parental responsibility.
- Child arrangements orders.
- Representation of children in private law disputes.
- Domestic violence.
- Marriage and civil partnership.
- Divorce and relationship breakdown.

Talking Point

Two women, A and B lived together in a civil partnership. They wanted to have a child and the brother of one of them provided sperm for artificial insemination. It was agreed that the child would grow up with the women and that the man would have no role in the family. Later he decided that he wanted to be recognised as the child's father and he sought orders for contact and parental responsibility. These applications were opposed by the women.

The High Court made an order for him to have contact with the child four times a year, one occasion of which would be as a family gathering with the women. The court explained that in this case the purpose of contact was to enable the child to have the opportunity to ask questions about her heritage, from what the court describes as the 'kind man who enabled him to be'. The court also made a s. 91(14) order for five years prohibiting any further applications by any of the three adults concerning the child, the court commenting that the family needed a break from litigation. The court refused the application for parental responsibility, though it recognised that the man was the child's biological father. It also recognised that the man fulfilled the essential criteria for a grant of parental responsibility: he showed commitment, attachment and motivation, yet it was reasoned that to grant parental responsibility would be contrary to the child's best interests as the child lived in a settled nuclear family with the two women.

This case is reported as *Re B (Role of Biological Father)* [2007] EWHC 1952. It is included here as an illustration of the increasingly complex cases facing the courts today. It questions the concept of 'family' from biological, social and psychological perspectives. Courts are facing a range of family set-ups beyond what might be described as the traditional nuclear family, and having to make appropriate legal orders, ultimately for the benefit of the child. It also raises some interesting practical questions. What does a child call a man who is actually her biological father, but also her uncle?

The role of social services in such cases is really dependent on the level of concern for any children. As the application was opposed, the court would apply the welfare checklist. It would also have the benefit of reports prepared by CAFCASS. It is important as practitioners to be aware, just as the courts have to be, of the range of family arrangements, legally regulated or not, that exist in society and to approach these in a non-discriminatory fashion. The status of the women's relationship as civil partners is considered in this chapter, as is the concept of parental responsibility sought by the father and contact orders.

Introduction

The focus of this chapter is children and family breakdown. Whilst social workers have major responsibilities in child protection, where the local authority may intervene in the private life of a family, it is also necessary to have an awareness of the law which operates to regulate aspects of private family life. Consideration of the orders that formalise arrangements made for children following divorce or separation of their parents, and the role of law in domestic violence, are included in this chapter. Failure to hear the child's voice in private disputes is a criticism often directed at the English legal system and the chapter therefore considers the circumstances when independent representation of children is permitted in private law cases.

The legal status of adult relationships, marriage, divorce, cohabitation, civil partnership and dissolution is examined, as is the relationship of adults to children with a focus on parental responsibility. As illustrated above, the family is an ever-changing concept[1] and whilst much family law is embedded in traditional concepts of the married, nuclear family, recently legal recognition has been given to broader notions of family life, including same-sex partnerships in the Civil Partnership Act 2004, marriage of same sex couples under the Marriage (Same Sex Couples) Act 2013, and adoption by unmarried couples (discussed in Chapter 11). It is an area where the balance between respecting privacy and protecting the (sometimes competing) interests of members of the family is a constant challenge and the rights enshrined in ECHR, Art. 8 (the right to respect for private and family life) and Art. 12 (the right to marry and found a family) are keenly debated.

Campaigning groups, such as Fathers for Justice, have attracted a high level of media attention to the area of private law. Actions such as 'batman' scaling Buckingham Palace, and the tipping of powder paint on to the Prime Minister in the House of Commons, have helped to publicise their more serious concern, which is their view that there is an inherent gender bias in the legal system which works against fathers in family disputes. They argue for a presumption in favour of shared parenting and mandatory mediation within a more transparent system of justice. An amendment to the welfare principle and mediation requirements introduced by the Children and Families Act 2014 partially address their concerns.

Parental responsibility

Parental responsibility is a central tenet running through the Children Act 1989. It is defined as:

> ### s. 3(1)
>
> All the rights, duties, powers, responsibilities and authority which by law a parent of a child has in relation to the child and his property.
>
> (CA 1989)

In terms of the philosophical position of the Children Act 1989, the Law Commission considered that the law failed to recognise parenthood in terms of responsibility and concentrated on parental rights. This position had become outdated and misleading, particularly in view of the *Gillick* case, which builds on the previous case law[2] and makes it clear that any rights and powers of parents exist only for the benefit of the child and dwindle as the child reaches maturity. Whilst it may be argued that changing the wording away from rights to responsibility is largely symbolic, it was hoped that this would begin to reflect the everyday reality of being a parent.

The concept of parental responsibility is easier to understand in relation to a range of issues over which decisions about a child may be made, i.e. the exercise of parental responsibility. Parental responsibility covers: determination of the child's religion and education; choosing the child's name; appointing a guardian for the child; consenting to the child's medical treatment and adoption; representing the child in legal proceedings; lawfully correcting the child; protecting and maintaining the child; and having physical possession of the child.

Who has parental responsibility?

If married, both parents of a child will have parental responsibility (s. 2(1), (3)). If the parents are not married, only the mother will have automatic parental responsibility and the father is classed as a parent without parental responsibility (and may also be referred to as the unmarried father). This position has changed somewhat under the Adoption and Children Act 2002, applicable since December 2003. Under s. 111, which amends s. 4 of the Children Act 1989, where parents are not married but jointly register the birth of a child[3] and the father's name appears on the birth certificate, then the father will also have parental responsibility.[4] If an 'unmarried father' does not jointly register the birth, it would still be possible to use the existing Children Act options, i.e. parental responsibility order or agreement. This amendment was introduced because few unmarried fathers appear to have been aware of their status as a parent without parental responsibility or how to obtain it.

Further, in 2008 the Government announced, in the white paper 'Joint birth registration: recording responsibility', its intention to promote child welfare and parental responsibility by ensuring, where possible, that unmarried parents jointly register the birth of their children. When the provisions of the Welfare Reform Act 2009 are implemented, there will be further options for joint registration affecting unmarried couples who are not cooperating with each other. In such cases the mother will be required to provide the father's details to the registrar, in order to enable the registrar to contact the father and ascertain and include his details on the birth register. The unmarried father will have a corresponding right to provide his details to the registrar independently of the mother, and to have his name entered on the register subject to acknowledgement by the mother that he is the child's father. There will, however, be some cases where a mother will be exempt from the duty to provide the father's details, for example if the mother does not know the identity of the father (or his whereabouts), or where she fears her or her child's safety might be put at risk if the father is contacted.

The Children Act 1989 provides two ways for a father without parental responsibility to take steps to acquire it. The first is by way of a **recorded agreement** with the mother in the prescribed form (a parental responsibility agreement (s. 4(1)(b)). A degree of formality reflects the significance of the agreement. In *Re X (Parental Responsibility: Children in Care)* [2000] 2 All ER 66 the fact that children were subject to interim care orders did not prevent their mother from entering into a parental responsibility agreement with their unmarried father.

The second way to acquire parental responsibility is by *application to the court* (s. 4(1)(a)). An application is most likely to occur where there is a level of disagreement between the parents, often following separation. In *Re H (Minors) (Local Authority: Parental Rights) (No. 3)* [1991] Fam 151 the court established a three-point test to be applied in parental responsibility applications. The courts should consider: the degree of commitment shown by the father to the child; the degree of attachment between father and child; and the reasons for applying for the order.

In *Re S (A Minor) (Parental Responsibility)* [1995] 2 FLR 648, the Court of Appeal indicated that, where possible, an order should be made to a 'committed' father, but noting that any interference with the child's welfare could be addressed by use of s. 8 orders. *Re C and V (Minors) (Contact: Parental Responsibility)* [1998] 1 FLR 392 stressed the importance for a child's self-esteem of having a positive image of the absent father, when determining applications for parental responsibility. In *Re P (Minors) (Parental Responsibility: Change of Name)* [1997] 2 FLR 722, however, a father who was serving a long prison sentence for robbery was unsuccessful in his application for a parental responsibility order. The court recognised that, realistically, he would be unable to exercise parental responsibility.

The Adoption and Children Act 2002 introduced new ways for step-parents to acquire parental responsibility (s. 112, introducing a new s. 4A into the Children Act 1989). In a similar way to unmarried fathers the court may give parental responsibility by order or the step-parent may acquire parental responsibility by agreement with the other parent (who does not lose parental responsibility), for example a step-father would need the agreement of the birth father, unless he was not married to the child's mother and had not acquired parental responsibility. Agreement of both parents of the child is required where they were married and where the unmarried father had acquired parental responsibility, but not of the unmarried father without parental responsibility. In the absence of agreement, the section also allows for the court to make a parental responsibility order. The other parent does not lose parental responsibility. This option is not available to an unmarried step-parent.

Parental responsibility may also be acquired by the holder of a residence order (s. 12), a person who is appointed as the child's guardian (s. 5), and a local authority with a care order in respect of a child (s. 33(3)). When a child is adopted, the adoptive parents acquire parental responsibility, and the birth parents lose their parental responsibility.

More than one person may share parental responsibility and it is not lost by virtue of another acquiring it (except in adoption). Where more than one person has parental responsibility, each may act alone and without the others in meeting that responsibility (s. 2(7)). This is consistent with the aim of encouraging both parents to feel responsible for their children. Practically, as there is no duty to consult the absent parent, the responsibility may prove to be symbolic only. If a care order or placement order is in force, the local authority has parental responsibility for the child and may determine the extent to which a parent may meet his parental responsibility for the child (s. 33(3)). There are some important limitations on the local authority's exercise of parental responsibility. It cannot change the child's name or religion, appoint a guardian or consent to an adoption order (s. 33(6)).

Margaret Thatcher once famously stated that 'parenthood is for life'. Parental responsibility for parents ends on the death or adoption of the child or when the child reaches 18.[5] Exceptionally, in *Re DW (A Child) (Termination of Parental Responsibility)* [2014] EWCA Civ, an unmarried father's parental responsibility was removed by the court. This was described as a proportionate response in a case where the father's sexual abuse of the child's half-sisters had caused devastating emotional harm on the whole family.

Parental responsibility gained by others, e.g. the local authority, may be brought to an end by a court order. Parental responsibility may not be surrendered or transferred but it can be delegated. There are numerous circumstances when a child will be in the care of someone aged 16 or over who does not have parental responsibility for that child. An obvious example is the child's teacher, who is often described as being *in loco parentis*, or a foster carer. Statutory authority for this position is provided by s. 3(5), which states that:

---

s. 3(5)

A person who –

(a) does not have parental responsibility for a particular child; but
(b) has care of the child,

may do what is reasonable in all the circumstances of the case for the purpose of safeguarding or promoting the child's welfare.

(CA 1989)

This would include obtaining urgent medical attention and arranging food for the child. If a child is placed with foster carers, an 'unmarried father' without parental responsibility would have no legal right to remove the child and the foster carers could rely on the *in loco parentis* provision to retain the child.

Other legislation may impact on the aspects of parental responsibility that may be delegated. A useful example is the issue of lawful chastisement. Corporal punishment was banned in state schools under the Education Act 1996. Foster carers may not resort to physical punishment[6] but in a controversial decision it was held that childminders may do so. In the case of *Sutton London Borough Council* v. *Davis* [1995] 1 All ER 53, the judge stated that a parent had a right to chastise his or her child to a reasonable extent and a parent could delegate this right to another person. This position has altered under the Children Act 2004, which removes most defences that could formerly be relied on to justify reasonable chastisement or punishment. Section 58(2) states that: 'Battery of a child causing actual bodily harm to the child cannot be justified in any civil proceedings on the ground that it constituted reasonable punishment.'

The ability to exercise parental responsibility may be limited in reality. If a child is in care, the local authority can determine the extent to which parents exercise their parental responsibility. Even where a looked after child is provided with accommodation on a voluntary basis (under s. 20), though parental responsibility is not acquired by the local authority, the extent to which a non-resident parent can exercise parental responsibility is limited by practical circumstances. The same position applies to a parent with parental responsibility who is not living with the child. As more than one person, who may not be in a position to take all decisions jointly, may hold parental responsibility, it is exercisable severally so long as it is not inconsistent with any court orders.

Parental responsibility may be obtained by the grant of a Child Arrangements Order. This order, discussed below, settles with whom the child is to reside and have contact and confers parental responsibility on the person with residence. Where the order is granted to a parent without parental responsibility, parental responsibility is acquired and is retained up to the child's sixteenth birthday even if the residence element of the Child Arrangements Order is revoked. In all other cases, e.g. if a residence within a Child Arrangements Order was granted to a grandparent, parental responsibility is retained for the duration of the order.

Under an emergency protection order, parental responsibility is conferred upon the local authority but limited to 'such action in meeting his responsibility for the child as is reasonably required to safeguard or promote the welfare of the child' during the order. The court must separately provide for important issues such as examination of the child and contact. (See Chapter 9 for full discussion.)

Where there is a dispute between persons holding parental responsibility, it may become necessary to resolve it by recourse to a prohibited steps order or a specific issue order.

Finally, parental responsibility may be acquired by a guardian, a person appointed by a parent to be the child's guardian in the event of the parent's death (s. 5(3)). Table 8.1 summarises the various ways in which parental responsibility can be acquired.

Private law orders (s. 8)

Section 8 orders are orders introduced by the Children Act 1989. Roughly speaking, the orders of residence and contact replaced custody and access, and the orders of specific issue and prohibited steps are drawn from wardship. Under the Children and Families

Table 8.1 Who has parental responsibility?

Mother	• CA 1989, s. 2(2)(a)
Mother and father, if married	• CA 1989, s. 2(1)
Father	• Parental responsibility order (CA 1989, s. 4(2)(a))
	• Parental responsibility agreement (CA 1989, s. 4(2)(b))
	• Under Child Arrangements Order
	• Where the parents jointly register the birth (ACA 2002, s. 111)
Step-parent	• Adoption and Children Act 2002, s. 112
	• Agreement or court order
Civil partner	• Civil Partnership Act 2004, s. 75(2)
Relative/other	• For the duration of the Child Arrangements Order (CA 1989, s. 12(2))
Special Guardian	• CA 1989, s. 14C(1)(a)
Guardian	• CA 1989, s. 5(6)
Local Authority	• Care order (CA 1989, s. 33(3)(a))[†]
	• EPO[§] (CA 1989, s. 44(4)(c))[*]
Prospective adoptive parents with whom child is placed	• Placement order or placement with parental consent (ACA 2002, s. 25)

Notes: [†]Parental responsibility limited: LA cannot change the child's religion, consent/refuse adoption, appoint a guardian, change name, remove from the UK.

[§]Emergency protection order.

[*]Shall only take such action in meeting his parental responsibility for the child as is reasonably required to safeguard or promote the welfare of the child (having regard in particular to the duration of the order).

Act 2014 residence and contact orders are replaced by a single 'Child Arrangements Order'. The orders represent more than changes in terminology; there are conceptual changes and a clear link to parental responsibility. Section 8 orders are used to control the exercise of parental responsibility and have provided a wider range of options to the courts in both public and private proceedings. The orders concentrate on practical questions relating to children's lives – where they live, who they have contact with, etc. – and, in the context of parental responsibility and the 'no order' principle, are less reliant on proprietorial connotations of ownership. The expression 'section 8 orders' includes any order varying or discharging an order (s. 8(2)). Conditions may be attached to the orders under s. 11(7).

The orders

s. 8(1)

In this Act –

'child arrangements order' means an order regulating arrangements relating to any of the following –

(a) With whom a child is to live, spend time or otherwise have contact, and
(b) When a child is to live, spend time or otherwise have contact with any person

> 'a prohibited steps order' means an order that no step which could be taken by a parent in meeting his parental responsibility for a child, and which is of a kind specified in the order, shall be taken by any person without the consent of the court;
>
> 'a specific issue order' means an order giving directions for the purpose of determining a specific question which has arisen, or which may arise, in connection with any aspect of parental responsibility for a child.
>
> (CA 1989)

Mediation

Before making a family application to the court (including applications for Child Arrangements Orders), the applicant and respondent are expected to attend a Mediation Information and Assessment Meeting (**MIAM**). Section 10(1) of the Children and Families Act 2014 states: 'Before making a relevant family application, a person must attend a family mediation information and assessment meeting.'

Parents may be exempt from the expectation to attend a MIAM in cases of urgency and where there is evidence of domestic violence or child protection concerns. Non-court dispute resolution is encouraged generally and in addition to the MIAM expectation, the court may adjourn proceedings at any point for mediation to take place. Parents may be advised to attend a Separated Parents Information Programme (SPIP). A Parenting Plan may be produced as a useful way to work, put practical aspects of the arrangements for the child, and reflect shared commitment to the child. CAFCASS have produced a useful guide and template for a Parenting Plan available at www.cafcass.gov.uk/media/190788/parenting_plan_final_web.pdf.

Child Arrangements Order

The Child Arrangements Order deals with the questions of where and with whom the child is to live (formerly addressed by residence orders) and when and with whom the child is to spend time or otherwise have contact (formerly addressed by the contact order). In other words, the Child Arrangements Order brings together the elements of residence and contact into one order.

Much of the case law on residence and contact orders will continue to be relevant to Child Arrangements Orders, as will the philosophy as articulated by Sir Stephen Brown in an early decision: 'it must be remembered that a residence order under the Children Act 1989 is not an order which connotes possession or which in any sense excludes the other parent. It is an order of the court which regulates where children live during a particular period.'[7]

As the new order enables the court to specify with whom a child is to live and when a child is to live with a person, it will continue to be possible to make an order whereby the child spends time living with both parents. This was specifically provided for under s. 11(4) of the Children Act and referred to as shared care or **shared residence arrangements**.

Applying the 'no order' principle, there will still need to be some positive benefit to the child in making the order (*Re A (A Minor) (Shared Residence Orders)* [1994] 1 FLR 669. *Re WB (Minors: Residence)* [1993] Fam Law 395 provided that a shared residence order should not be made simply as a means of investing parental responsibility in the father, the same principle would apply in relation to a Child Arrangements Order where the effect is to invest parental responsibility. The Court of Appeal guidance on the use of shared residence orders in *Re D (Children) (Shared Residence Orders)* [2001] 1 FLR 495 is also relevant as to how Child Arrangements Orders are made. The court held that, where a child was spending a substantial amount of time with both parents, a shared residence order could be appropriate despite the existence of a high degree of animosity between the parents. It was not necessary to demonstrate exceptional circumstances or a positive benefit to the child; it was sufficient to show that the order would be in the child's interests. In this case there would be positive benefits from the close relationship the children had with both parents being recognised by a shared residence order, which simply reflected the reality of the situation. A shared residence order could also be made when the parents lived some distance apart and the arrangements for the children involved them spending term times with one parent and most of the holidays with the other parent: *Re F (Children) (Shared Residence Order)* [2003] EWCA Civ 592. *Re K (A Child) (Shared Residence Order)* [2008] EWCA Civ 526 confirms that the division of time in shared residence cases need not be 50/50. In this case it was more like 60/40 and the proper course is for the court to rule on the division first and then determine the appropriate order. Availability of shared residence should apply equally to same-sex parents according to the Court of Appeal in *Re G (Children) (Residence: Same-Sex Partner)* [2006] EWCA Civ 372. The lesbian co-parent had separated from the biological mother of two children conceived by anonymous donor insemination. A CAFCASS report recommended shared residence following a series of specific issue orders about aspects of the exercise of parental responsibility. The court gave a strong message that shared residence confirms equality of parents and that there was no presumption in favour of the biological mother in such a case, Thorpe LJ noting the 'evolution of the judicial acceptance of the diversity of the family in modern society'.

The grant of shared residence may have other consequences. In *Holmes-Moorhouse* v. *Richmond-upon-Thames London Borough Council* [2007] EWCA Civ 970, the question for the court was whether a person with shared residence was a person with whom dependent children, 'might reasonably be expected to reside' for the purposes of establishing a priority need for housing under the Housing Act 1996. The court held that the order was not determinative in itself, but it is clear that if more shared residence orders are made this could have an impact on housing need and allocation. Again, these principles would apply to Child Arrangements Orders.

In practice, shared care arrangements are most likely to work well where the parties are on good terms, in which case application of the 'no order' principle should negate the need for an order. It is difficult, therefore, to gauge how common such arrangements are.

Conditions may be attached to a Child Arrangements Order as applied to residence orders. For example, in *Re S (A Child) (Residence Order: Condition)* [2002] EWCA Civ 1795, the mother of a child with Down's syndrome wanted to move from London to Cornwall. The child enjoyed a close relationship with her father and grandmother in London. The court made a residence order to the mother on condition that she remained living in London.

The holder of a Child Arrangements Order providing for the child to live with them acquires parental responsibility. In the case of *B* v. *B (Grandparent: Residence Order)* [1992] 2 FLR 327, it was agreed that a child would reside with grandparents and, although application of the 'no order' principle might suggest that a residence order was not necessary, an order was made in order to vest parental responsibility in the grandparents and provide greater legal security.

When introduced by the Children Act 1989, the duration of a residence order was until the child reached the age of 16. Amendments by the Adoption and Children Act 2002 and Children and Young Persons Act 2008 mean that a residence order (**CAO** relating to residence) will last until the age of 18 unless the court directs that it should end earlier.

Local authorities have a power to make payments to a person (not a parent) with whom a child is living under a residence order (CA 1989, Sch. 1 para. 15). Authorities are likely to have a policy on when such payments might be made. As an example, in *R (M)* v. *Birmingham City Council* [2008] EWHC 1863 (Admin), the authority considered making payments where the child had been looked after for more than three months, and where the residence order was made during care proceedings or as a direct alternative to care proceedings.

Enforcement

Section 11J Children Act 1989 enables the court to make an enforcement order for non-compliance with a court order under section 8. The order may include a requirement to carry out unpaid work. There is also a power to order one person to pay compensation to another for a financial loss caused by a breach.

Change of child's name or removal from jurisdiction

Where a Child Arrangements Order/residence order is in force, no person may change the child's surname or remove the child from the United Kingdom without written consent of every person who has parental responsibility for the child or leave of the court (s. 13). An exception exists for the person with whom the child is to live, who may take the child out of the United Kingdom for up to one month without leave or consent, for holidays.

Contact

The following discussion relates to the other element of the Child Arrangements Order, namely, when and with whom a child is to spend time or otherwise have contact. As with the discussion relating to residence for a transitional period, contact orders made before the introduction of the Child Arrangements Order will continue to run.

This element of the order may also be made for persons other than parents, e.g. grandparents. The emphasis in the order is different from the old access orders in that contact is seen primarily as the right of the child. Case law has recognised contact as an aspect of 'family life' under ECHR, Art. 8 and has positioned contact as a right of the adult also, though one which is qualified. For example, in *Payne* v. *Payne* [2001] EWCA Civ 166, the father argued that if the mother was allowed to take their 4-year-old child to live in New Zealand, this would infringe his right to contact as an aspect of his Art. 8 rights. The court nevertheless found that interference by allowing removal was necessary and proportionate in protecting the child's best interests.

The wording 'or otherwise have contact' makes clear that the court can order any form of contact, including letters, phone calls, supervised contact and overnight stays. Conditions may be attached to a Child Arrangements Order via s. 11(7); however, a direction for a local authority to supervise contact between parent and child should be made by a family assistance order, rather than s. 11(7), according to *Leeds County Council* v. *C* [1993] 1 FLR 269.

Decisions of the court have demonstrated a clear commitment to ongoing contact between parents and children.[8] This position has been reinforced at policy level. A 2004 green paper, 'Parental Separation: Children's Needs and Parents' Responsibilities' stated: 'a child's welfare is best promoted by a continuing relationship with both parents, as long as it is safe to do so'. Problems have arisen in a number of cases where mothers did not support contact between child and father, for reasons of fear of violence. The judiciary have coined the term 'implacable hostility' to describe such cases. It is unfortunate that this term implies a degree of unreasonableness or irrationality where the refusal may be grounded in genuine concerns for safety. The decision of *A v. N (Committal: Refusal of Contact)* [1997] 1 FLR 533 helpfully stated that where a mother had justification for refusing contact, due to fear of violence, this should not be regarded as implacable hostility.

Re O (Contact: Imposition of Conditions) [1996] 1 FCR 317 set out a number of principles relating to contact. (It was a case where the child's mother was described as displaying irrational repugnance to an indirect contact order.)

1. The welfare of the child is paramount and interests of the parents are relevant only if they affect the welfare of the child.

2. It is almost always in the interest of the child to have contact with the non-resident parent. There are long-term advantages to the child in keeping in touch.

3. Where direct contact is not possible there should be indirect contact.

4. The court should take a medium-term and long-term view of the child's development and not give excessive weight to short-term problems.

5. No parent should be allowed to think that the more intransigent, unreasonable, obdurate and uncooperative they are, the more likely they will be to get their own way.

6. Section 11(7) confers the power to require a parent to provide a progress report and to read communications from the other parent to the child.

In exceptional cases, parental refusal of contact has been found a contempt of court resulting in the mother's imprisonment, although this power should be used only as a last resort in urgent and exceptional cases (*Re M (Minors) (Breach of Contact Order: Committal)* [1999] 2 All ER 56). In the balancing exercise, the violent parties' willingness to change and understanding of the consequences of their violence are important factors according to *Re M (Minors) (Contact: Violent Parent)* [1999] 2 FLR 321. Also, in *Re C (A Child) (Residence)* [2007] EWCA Civ 866, where a mother had failed to comply with contact orders, including orders with penal notices attached, the judge ordered an immediate transfer of residence to the father. The judge ruled that sending the mother to prison was not the way forward, as she had recently had a baby with her new partner. In the circumstances the judge felt he had no option other than to take the draconian step of ordering an immediate transfer of residence. The option to make no order was an option of abdication that was all too frequently resorted to by the courts and led to appeals from fathers protesting that the courts failed to enforce their orders.

The effect of domestic violence allegations on contact applications was the central issue in a Court of Appeal decision, which is now the leading authority on the matter. Four appeals, which raised similar issues, were heard jointly in the case of *Re L (A Child) (Contact: Domestic Violence); Re V (A Child) (Contact: Domestic Violence); Re M (A Child) (Contact: Domestic Violence); Re H (Children) (Contact: Domestic Violence)* [2000] 4 All ER 609. Dame Butler-Sloss, President of the Family Division, gave judgment. In each of the cases a father's application for direct contact had been refused against a background of domestic violence. Butler-Sloss commented on a report, 'Contact between Children and Violent Parents' (1999),[9] which was produced to the court. She stated that family judges and magistrates needed to have a heightened awareness of the existence and consequences on children of exposure to domestic violence. Decisions about contact should be child-centred and there should be no automatic assumption that contact with a violent parent was in the child's interests. The court always had to apply s. 1 of the Children Act 1989 (the welfare of the child is paramount) and should also take into account Art. 8 of the European Convention for the Protection of Human Rights. In each case the court had to balance the need to safeguard the child and promote his best interests with other issues, such as providing knowledge of religious and cultural background. Domestic violence is one material factor among many which might offset the assumption in favour of contact and this difficult balancing exercise is to be carried out. These good practice guidelines were confirmed in *Re H (A Child) (Contact: Domestic Violence)* [2005] EWCA Civ 1404 and by *Practice Direction (Residence and Contact Orders: Domestic Violence and Harm)* [2008] All ER (D) 132 (May). The practice direction applies in any family proceedings concerning contact and/or residence where a child has experienced domestic violence or is at risk of doing so. The courts should consider:

- The effect of the violence on the child and the parent with whom the child lives.
- The extent to which the parent seeking contact is motivated by the best interests of the child or as a means of continuing a process of violence or intimidation of the other parent.
- Likely behaviour during contact.
- Capacity of the parent to appreciate the effect of past violence.
- The attitude of the parent to past violent conduct and capacity to change and act appropriately.

If direct contact is considered to be in the best interest of the child the court should consider whether it should be supervised and whether any conditions should be imposed.

Some concerns about the way the judicial system has dealt with contact cases were evident in the judgment of Munby J in *Re D (Intractable Contact Dispute: Publicity)* [2004] EWHC 727 (Fam), in which, he observed, 'a wholly deserving father left my court in tears having been driven to abandon his battle for contact with his seven-year-old daughter'. The case was one that illustrated the 'appalling delays of the court system … the court's failure to get to grips with the mother's (groundless) allegations; and the court's failure to get to grips with the mother's defiance of its orders, the court's failure to enforce its own orders'. Over a period of five years the case had 43 hearings conducted by 16 different judges, numerous adjournments and 905 pages of experts' evidence. The judge described delay as the scourge of the system and called for guidance in a comparable form to the Protocol for Judicial Case Management in Public Law Children Act Cases (2003) to be introduced. He expressed dissatisfaction with the frequent judicial response to contact problems, i.e. to list the matter for further directions with a reduction in contact in the meantime, and obtain experts' reports and further evidence that produced further delays and exacerbated difficulties.

The Children and Adoption Act 2006 introduced a range of provisions intended to ensure safety of children during contact, facilitate contact in the face of obstruction and provide enforcement measures. The Act inserts new provisions into the Children Act 1989 after s. 11. These include, powers to impose 'contact activity directions' (s. 11A) and 'contact activity conditions' (s. 11B). Contact activities include attending an information session, or taking part in a programme, class, counselling or guidance session or other activity for 'assisting a person to establish, maintain or improve contact' and which may facilitate contact with a child by addressing a person's violent behaviour (s. 11E). A contact activity direction cannot require a person to undergo medical or psychiatric examination, assessment or treatment. A CAFCASS officer may be ordered to monitor compliance with activities with a power to report back to the court. The orders have been renamed 'activity directions' and activity conditions' (i.e. the reference to contact is removed) to reflect the change in emphasis regarding involvement of a person in a child's life and the Child Arrangements Order.

Re L-W (Enforcement and Committal: Contact); CPL v. *CH-W and others* [2010] EWCA Civ 1253 addressed the question of the obligations of a parent to ensure a child attends contact. The court confirmed that the obligation is to allow contact and to make the child available for contact. The parent is not obliged to ensure the child actually goes on a contact visit if the child does not wish to.

Re W (Children: Domestic Violence) [2012] EWCA Civ confirms that courts must follow Practice Direction 12J when considering applications for residence or contact where there are allegations of domestic violence. The Practice Direction has developed from the guidance in the case of *Re L, Re V, Re M, Re H.* It states,

> In every case where a finding of domestic violence is made, the court should consider the conduct of both parents towards each other and towards the child; in particular, the court should consider –
>
> **(a)** the effect of the domestic violence which has been established on the child and on the parent with whom the child is living;
> **(b)** the extent to which the parent seeking residence or contact is motivated by a desire to promote the best interests of the child or may be doing so as a means of continuing a process of violence, intimidation or harassment against the other parent;
> **(c)** the likely behaviour during contact of the parent seeking contact and its effect on the child;
> **(d)** the capacity of the parent seeking residence or contact to appreciate the effect of past violence and the potential for future violence on the other parent and the child;
> **(e)** the attitude of the parent seeking residence or contact to past violent conduct by that parent; and in particular whether that parent has the capacity to change and to behave appropriately.

Re A (Intractable Contact Proceedings: Human Rights Violations) [2013] EWCA Civ 1104 is a reminder that human rights violations may arise from a refusal of contact. The case reached the Court of Appeal after a decade of litigation including around 100 hearings regarding a mother's implacable hostility towards contact between an unimpeachable father and their daughter. The court commented on the systematic failure of the family justice system evident in the history of the case. It found that the family life rights of father and daughter to have an effective relationship had been violated and that the proceedings as a whole violated the procedural requirements enshrined in Art. 8.

Contact centres

There are 270 Child Contact Centres in England and Wales. They are predominantly staffed by volunteers. The centres aim to provide a neutral and safe place for contact to take place or for handovers. Referrals tend to be made by solicitors, court welfare officers and social services.

Specific issue

Specific issue and prohibited steps orders are orders introduced by the Children Act 1989, modelled on aspects of wardship, where the High Court enjoyed wider powers than the lower courts. These orders were intended to reduce the need to resort to wardship proceedings and are particularly suitable in cases concerned with a single issue or dispute as to exercise of parental responsibility. As the orders are available from the lower courts, they are more accessible, cheaper and quicker to obtain.[10]

Specific issue orders are designed for situations where people with parental responsibility do not agree about an aspect of the child's upbringing, e.g. surname disputes, education issues such as choice of school, religion and medical treatment. The following case law examples are illustrative.

Dawson v. *Wearmouth* [1999] 2 WLR 960 concerned the issue of whether one parent can unilaterally change a child's surname and was dealt with by an application for a specific issue order. The choice of a child's name is an exercise of parental responsibility. A key issue, therefore, where there is a dispute between parents, will centre on whether the father has parental responsibility. In this case the father issued an application for a parental responsibility order and a specific issue order as to the child's surname. Applying the criteria in s. 1 (welfare principle and checklist), the House of Lords found that in this case it would not be in the interests of the child's welfare to change the surname. The test to be applied in name change cases is, 'welfare, pure and simple', according to Ryder LJ in *Re W (Change of Name)* [2013] EWCA Civ 1488.

In *Re C (A Child) (HIV Testing)* [1999] 2 FLR 1004, the local authority applied for a specific issue order to obtain a blood test to determine whether a child was infected with HIV. There was a concern that, as the child was being breastfed by her mother, who had HIV, she could become infected. The court was prepared to override the wishes of the parents and order the blood test; however, the law could not make an order that breastfeeding should cease. In *M* v. *M (Specific Issue: Choice of School)* [2005] EWHC 2769 (Fam), the court made an order permitting the child's father to take him for a voice test at a cathedral school. If the child was successful, he might be awarded a scholarship to attend a cathedral school. The child's mother had previously refused to allow him to attend, as she did not want him to change schools.

In applications for specific issue orders, infringement of Art. 8 of the European Convention on Human Rights may be argued and under the Human Rights Act 1998 the court is of course obliged to reach a decision which is compatible with the Articles of the ECHR. For example, in *Re C (A Child) (Immunisation: Parental Rights)* [2003] EWCA Civ 1148, fathers applied for specific issue orders asking the court to order immunisation of their daughters. The Court of Appeal found that immunisation was in the girls' best interests but noted that courts invited to override parental wishes had to move extremely cautiously. The court could interfere with the rights of both the children and parents under Art. 8, in this instance on the exception permitting interference to protect the health of a child. *F* v. *F* [2013] EWHC 2683 (Fam) provides a further example. Here the court ordered two daughters aged 15 and 11 to receive the MMR vaccination against their own and their mother's wishes. In *Re F (Children) (Declaration of Paternity)* (2007) *The Times*, 6 August an order was made requiring the mother to inform her children of the identity of their natural father.

It may be possible for a specific issue order to be made to vest a particular area of decision-making (in the exercise of parental responsibility) in a named individual. For example, in *Re H (A Child: Parental Responsibility)* [2002] EWCA Civ 542, a specific issue order was made giving the mother sole responsibility for decisions relating to the child's medical treatment.

There are limits, however, to the use of specific issue orders. In *Re J (A Minor) (Specific Issue Order: Leave to Apply)* [1995] 1 FLR 669, a specific issue order could not be used to determine whether a child was a 'child in need'. Such determination was a matter for the local authority alone and not an exercise of parental responsibility. In another decision the court would not make a specific issue order to compel a local authority to supervise contact

(*Re DH (A Minor) (Child Abuse)* [1994] 1 FLR 679). Section 9 of the Children Act 1989 prohibits the court from making a specific issue order in respect of a child who is in the care of a local authority and this has been extended by the Adoption and Children Act 2002, where a local authority is authorised by the court to place a child for adoption.[11]

Prohibited steps

A prohibited steps order presents a specific restriction on the exercise of parental responsibility towards a particular child. In *Re J (Child's Religious Upbringing and Circumcision)* [2000] 1 FCR 307, a prohibited steps order was made prohibiting the child's father from making arrangements for his son, aged 5, to be circumcised without the permission of the court. Circumcision was described as an irrevocable step in a child's life and, in the event of a dispute between people exercising parental responsibility, it was for the High Court to resolve the matter. A prohibited steps order was made to prevent a step-father visiting a child in *Re H (Minors) (Prohibited Steps Order)* [1995] 4 All ER 110. In *Re A (Prohibited Steps Order)* [2013] EWCA Civ 1115, a prohibited steps order was granted preventing a mother taking her child to Kenya on holiday where the father claimed a real risk of the child being abducted and retained in Kenya.

Neither a specific issue nor a prohibited steps order should be made if this would achieve a result that could have been achieved by making a residence order, e.g. a specific issue order that a child attends a particular school which would involve a change of residence.

Who may apply for an order?

Section 10 sets out varying levels of eligibility to apply for s. 8 orders. As of right, any parent, guardian, civil partner in relation to whom the child is a child of the family, or person in whose favour a residence order is in force may apply for any s. 8 order. Note that this right is given to a parent rather than a parent with parental responsibility. It follows that a father who does not have parental responsibility is entitled to apply for a s. 8 order. Any other person, including the child, and other relatives, must obtain leave of the court to apply for an order.

The criteria for granting leave is contained in s. 10(9), which directs the court to have regard to:

> ### s. 10(9)
>
> **(a)** the nature of the proposed application;
> **(b)** the applicant's connection with the child;
> **(c)** any risk of the application disrupting the child's life to such an extent that he would be harmed by it;
> **(d)** when the child is being looked after by the local authority, the authority's plans for the child's future and the wishes and feelings of the child's parents.
>
> (CA 1989)

Leave will be granted to a child if the court is satisfied that he has sufficient understanding to make the proposed application (s. 10(8)). If a child makes an application it will be heard in the High Court, as, for example, in *Re AD (A Minor) (Child's Wishes)* [1993] 1 FCR 573, where a child applied for a residence order to be made to her boyfriend's parents enabling her to leave home and reside there. In *Re J (Leave to Issue Application for Residence Order)* [2002] EWCA Civ 1346, Thorpe LJ noted the need to 'recognise the greater appreciation that has developed of the value of what grandparents have to offer, particularly to children of disabled parents' and it has been argued (strongly by the Grandparents Association) that grandparents should not be required to seek prior leave of the court before making an application.

A s. 8 order can be made on application or the court may make an order of its own volition in any family proceedings. The court will hold an informal hearing before it lists a contested s. 8 application for trial, to ascertain whether conciliation is possible.[12] A number of restrictions on the court's power to make s. 8 orders are set out in s. 9.

(a) No s. 8 orders may be made in respect of a child in care, except for a Child Arrangements Order specifying with whom the child is to reside (previously a residence order), which then discharges the care order. To provide otherwise could lead to private orders being used to control local authorities' statutory responsibilities in conflict with the principle established by *A* v. *Liverpool City Council* [1981] 2 All ER 385.

(b) No Child Arrangements Order (previously no residence order or contact order) may be made in favour of the local authority. This issue was debated in *Nottinghamshire County Council* v. *P* [1993] 3 All ER 815. In this case the local authority sought a prohibited steps order which required that the father should not live in the same household or have any contact with his children. On analysis, it was held that the local authority was in effect seeking residence and contact orders, which it is debarred from doing, and the application for the prohibited steps order was refused.

(c) A s. 8 order will not be made for a child over the age of 16 unless there are exceptional circumstances.

(d) Local authority foster parents can apply for residence and contact orders only if they have the consent of the local authority, are a relative, or have cared for the child for one year out of the last five.

(e) If a care order is made, this discharges any s. 8 order.

Two other orders are closely linked to s. 8 orders:

- Section 37 – Investigation of the child's circumstances.
- Section 16 – Family assistance order.

Investigation of the child's circumstances (s. 37)

It is not possible to apply for a s. 37 direction. A direction will be made by the court of its own motion in appropriate circumstances, i.e. where it appears that a public law order might be required (*Re L (A Minor) (Section 37 Direction)* [1999] 3 FCR 642), although it would be possible for parties in family proceedings to suggest this to the court. If a direction is given, then the local authority must consider whether it should apply for a care or supervision order or provide services to the child or his or her family or take any other action (s. 37(2)). If the local authority decides not to apply for a care or supervision order it must inform the court of its reasons and whether any other service has been provided or any other action taken (s. 37(3)). The local authority has eight weeks in which to investigate and provide a report to the court. During this period the court can make an interim order. In addition the court may request a welfare report under s. 7 at any time. In *Re M (Intractable Contact Dispute: Interim Care Order)* [2003] EWHC 1024 (Fam), a s. 37 direction was made in circumstances where children whose contact with the non-resident parent was being denied, were suffering harm as a result.

> ## s. 37(1)
>
> Where, in any family proceedings in which a question arises with respect to the welfare of any child, it appears to the court that it may be appropriate for a care or supervision order to be made with respect to him, the court may direct the appropriate authority to undertake an investigation of the child's circumstances.
>
> (CA 1989)

Family assistance order

The family assistance order is provided by the Children Act 1989, s. 16. An order may be made in any family proceedings where the court has power to make a s. 8 order; and consent must be obtained from every person named in the order, other than the child. The effect of the order is to require an officer of CAFCASS or a local authority officer to be available to advise, assist and befriend any person named in the order. The persons who may be named in the order are set out in s. 16(2): any parent or guardian of the child, person the child is living with or who has a contact order or Child Arrangements Order in respect of the child, and the child himself. Guidance draws a contrast between the family assistance order and supervision order, the latter being designed for more serious cases where there is an element of child protection, whereas, 'a family assistance order aims simply to provide short-term help to a family, to overcome the problems and conflicts associated with their separation or divorce. Help may well be focused more on the adults than the child'.[13] The order is made by the court 'of its own motion' and cannot be directly applied for, though it is possible for a party to suggest to the court that an order would be appropriate. Orders for supervision of contact by the local authority should be made by way of a family assistance order rather than imposition of a condition under s. 11(7): see *Leeds County Council* v. *C* [1993] 1 FLR 269. However, the local authority cannot be required to take on a family assistance order if it does not have the resources to do so: see *Re C (A Minor) (Family Assistance Order)* [1996] 1 FLR 424.

The order has been little used. Research on the use of family assistance orders indicates that the majority of orders are made in response to issues arising over contact arrangements, and may be made alone or in combination with a s. 8 order. Family assistance orders tend to be made to the Court Welfare Service rather than the Social Services Department. In the area where the research was carried out, a high number of family assistance orders were made, the reason being that judges considered the order a useful and supportive means of promoting parental responsibility, and enabling more input to a case than is given in those cases where the court welfare officer's role is to produce a report. Equally, the Court Welfare Service supported the order as providing an opportunity for more sustained therapeutic work with families (Trinder and Stone, 1998).[14]

The Children and Adoption Act 2006 made some changes to the order, aiming to make it more effective. The original requirement that family assistance orders be made only in exceptional circumstances is removed, and the maximum duration of such orders is extended from 6 to 12 months.

Domestic violence

A revised definition of domestic violence was issued by the Home Office in 2013. Domestic violence is:

> Any incident or pattern of incidents of controlling, coercive, threatening behaviour, violence or abuse between those aged 16 or over who are, or have been, intimate partners or family members regardless of gender or sexuality. The abuse can encompass, but is not limited to the following types of abuse –
>
> - psychological
> - physical
> - sexual
> - financial
> - emotional.
>
> Controlling behaviour is: a range of acts designed to make a person subordinate and/or dependent by isolating them from sources of support, exploiting their resources and capacities for personal gain, depriving them of the means needed for independence, resistance and escape and regulating their everyday behaviour.
>
> Coercive behaviour is: an act or a pattern of acts of assault, threats, humiliation and intimidation or other abuse that is used to harm, punish, or frighten their victim.[15]

The significant difference from the previous definition is the inclusion of coercion and extension to include 16- and 17-year-olds.

Domestic violence is included in this chapter because the legal remedies available operate between individuals and are often associated with issues surrounding divorce and separation and applications for s. 8 orders. The effect of domestic violence in the context of contact applications has been discussed above. The law relating to domestic violence is essentially an aspect of private law. Nevertheless, the impact of domestic violence between adults upon children is increasingly being recognised in the context of child protection. This recognition is clear in the amended definition of 'harm' in the threshold criteria to include 'impairment suffered from seeing or hearing the ill-treatment of another'.[16] In addition, under the Children Act 2004, authorities have a duty to ensure local cooperation to improve wellbeing and a duty to make arrangements to safeguard children in their area and this will include children who are living in households where there is domestic violence.

In court the dispute in domestic violence proceedings is essentially between adults and there may be cases where views of children are not made known to the court. There have been calls for s. 64 of the Family Law Act 1996 to be implemented. This section would allow for regulations to be made providing for separate representation of children in proceedings under Part IV of the 1996 Act, dealing with family homes and domestic violence.

Remedies for domestic violence are now provided principally by the Family Law Act 1996, Pt IV. The Domestic Violence, Crime and Victims Act 2004 (DVCVA 2004) strengthens the rights of victims and witnesses, introduces new offences and includes tougher sanctions for perpetrators.

Relief, in the form of non-molestation orders and occupation orders, can be sought against an 'associated person'. This term encompasses a wider range of people than previous domestic violence legislation, which was limited in its application to spouses and cohabitees. Section 62(3) defines the term as including parties: who are or have been married to each other; who are cohabitants or former cohabitants; who live or have lived in the same household (other than as employees or lodgers); who are relatives, including relatives of their spouse or cohabitee (or former); who have agreed to marry; who are parents of the child or have parental responsibility for the child. The definition is extended by the DVCVA to specifically include same-sex couples within the term 'cohabitants'. As cohabiting couples are already associated persons, the significance of this is that property owners, spouses and cohabitants are the only associated persons that can apply for an occupation order. The list of associated persons is also amended to include people who have not married or cohabited but nevertheless 'have or had an intimate personal relationship with each other which is or was of significant duration'.

Case law suggests that the courts will give a wide, purposive interpretation to the definition. In *G* v. *F (Non-molestation Order: Jurisdiction)* [2000] 3 WLR 1202, justices initially refused to hear an application on the grounds that the parties were not associated persons. The parties had a joint bank account and a sexual relationship existed. The Family Division found that the justices should have found that the parties were former cohabitants, and noted that cohabitation can take many forms. The case of *JH* v. *RH (A Child)* [2001] 1 FLR 641 illustrates the extension of the use of the occupation order beyond spouses and cohabitees. A 17-year-old, described as a truculent and violent teenager, was directed to vacate his parents' home and excluded from returning there. The meaning of domestic violence was considered in *Yemshaw* v. *London Borough of Hounslow* [2011] UKSC 3. The judgment confirms that domestic violence under s. 177(1) of the Housing Act 1996, is not limited to physical contact. It should be interpreted in the same sense as the *Practice Direction (Residence and Contact Orders: Domestic Violence) (No 2)* [2009] 1 WLR 251 and includes physical and threatening or intimidation behaviour and any other forms of abuse which directly or indirectly, may give rise to the risk of harm.

The DVCVA includes a range of further relevant provisions. Breach of a non-molestation order is made a criminal offence punishable by five years' imprisonment on indictment (s. 1) and common assault becomes an arrestable offence (s. 10). The courts are given a power to impose a restraining order for the protection of a victim, even where a defendant has been acquitted of an offence relating to her, but the court believes an order is necessary to protect the victim (s. 12). Structural changes include the introduction of a new code of practice for the support and protection of victims which will apply across all criminal justice agencies (s. 32). A Commissioner for Victims and Witnesses is created (s. 48) with a role including monitoring and promoting good practice, ensuring the interests of victims and witnesses are heard in Government and keeping the code of practice under review. If the code is not observed, it will be possible for a victim or witness to complain to the Parliamentary Commissioner (Ombudsman) (s. 42).

From March 2014, following pilot studies, a domestic violence disclosure scheme and domestic violence protection orders (**DVPOs**) have been implemented. An individual has the right to ask the police to check for information about their partner. The police may disclose information that suggests the person may be at risk of violence from a partner if it is legal, proportionate or necessary (Clare's law). An agency may also make the request. A Dometic Violence Protection Order enables the police to ban a perpetrator in the immediate aftermath of a domestic violence incident from returning to a residence or having contact with the victim for up to 28 days. This is intended to be a short-term interim solution during which time the victim may seek court injunctions.

Social work and local authority involvement in domestic violence cases

The main statutory duty for social workers to become involved in domestic violence cases is triggered by the presence of children who may need protection or support. The role otherwise can be described as one of liaison and support and may include the following tasks: contacting the police; organising a refuge place; contacting a lawyer; arranging medical attention; arranging accommodation for the children; providing support at court hearings; giving evidence to the court; assisting with benefits claims; acting as an advocate to the housing authority; assisting with a criminal injuries compensation claim and generally acting as a coordinator ensuring that accurate advice and appropriate referrals are made, including referrals to an Independent Domestic Violence Adviser.

There is a wider responsibility for local authorities in relation to domestic violence in their area. Local authorities must work with other agencies to reduce crime and disorder in their area. Domestic violence will be included in local crime reduction strategies and action plans, as required by the Crime and Disorder Act 1998.[17] Local authorities are responsible for the delivery of a wide range of services to people affected by domestic violence, including housing, and have duties to individuals accepted as homeless for domestic violence reasons. A Best Value Performance Indicator for domestic violence issued in 2005 (BVPA 225) provides a useful guide to action an authority can take: produce a directory of local services that can help victims; ensure a minimum of one refuge place per 10,000 population; employ or fund a voluntary sector based domestic violence coordinator; adopt a multi-agency strategy to tackle domestic violence; support and facilitate a multi-agency domestic violence forum; develop an information sharing protocol; promote a 'sanctuary' scheme that enables victims and children to remain safely in their own homes; reduce the number of homeless cases rehoused in the previous two years as a result of violence; include a specific clause in the council's tenancy agreement stating that perpetration of domestic violence can be a ground for eviction; develop a domestic violence education pack; and conduct multi-agency training of staff.

Reflect

Do you think law and practice fully recognises the impact of domestic violence on children?

Family Court Welfare Service

The Family Court Welfare Service is provided under the auspices of CAFCASS (established by the Criminal Justice and Courts Services Act 2000).[18] In private law proceedings, including s. 8 applications and domestic violence cases, a children and family reporter (formerly known as a court welfare officer) may be involved as court reporter. Section 7(1) provides that any court when considering any question with respect to a child under the 1989 Act may ask an officer of CAFCASS or local authority to report to the court 'on such matters relating to the welfare of that child as are required to be dealt with in the report'. In contrast to the role of the children's guardian in public proceedings, the children and family reporter is not specifically the child's representative as children are not normally parties to the application. (There is an exception relating to s. 8 applications commenced by the child with leave of the court – in these cases a guardian would be appointed.) In addition, the children and family reporter is not always appointed in private law proceedings.[19] The following case may present a significant development in terms of representation of children in the private law: in *Re A (A Child) (Separate Representation in Contact Proceedings)* [2001] 1 FLR 715, a boy aged 14, who was concerned about his younger half-sister, aged 4, wanted to inform the judge that he believed it was dangerous for his sister to see her father. He had not been spoken to by the Court Welfare Service or social services. The Court of Appeal gave permission for the National Youth Advisory Service to intervene in the contact proceedings and act as guardian for the younger child. The court held that where there was a conflict of interest between the parents and child it could be necessary for a guardian to be appointed in private family law proceedings, bearing in mind the impact of the European Convention and that children were not always sufficiently seen and heard by the use of a court welfare officer's report.

In private cases the emphasis of the guardian's work (in the absence of any allegations of significant harm) is to be on intensive dispute resolution and a shared parenting approach.

A practice direction provides some clarity as to the circumstances where separate representation is likely to be appropriate, *Practice Direction 16A (Family Proceedings: Representation of Children)*. The Direction states that, before making a child party to proceedings, the court should give consideration to an alternative route such as asking an officer of CAFCASS to assist, referring the case to social services or obtaining an expert's report.

Circumstances that would merit making a child a party would include:

- where a CAFCASS officer had notified the court of his opinion that the child should be made a party;
- where the child had an interest which was inconsistent with or incapable of being represented by the adult parties;
- where there was an intractable dispute over residence and where all contact had ceased, or where there was irrational but implacable hostility to contact or where the contact dispute might be causing the child to suffer harm;
- where the child's views or wishes could not adequately be communicated to the court in a report;
- where an older child opposed a proposed course of action;
- where there were complex medical or mental health issues;
- where there were international complications outside questions of child abduction which required discussion with overseas authorities;
- where there were serious allegations of abuse or domestic violence; and
- where there was a contested issue as to blood testing.

When directing whether to make the child a party the court would consider the risk that to do so would cause delay to the proceedings. The primary consideration would be the welfare of the child. If a child was made a party and a guardian was appointed, consideration should be given to appointing an officer of CAFCASS as guardian. A county court dealing with such a case would also consider whether the case was sufficiently complex or important to merit transfer to the High Court.

Mabon v. *Mabon* [2005] EWCA Civ 634 concerned a residence order application where three boys aged 13, 15 and 17 sought separate representation. The court noted the need to recognise the right to freedom of expression and the risk of emotional harm that might be caused by denying participation in proceedings.

Section 122 of the Adoption and Children Act 2002 establishes the right to a children's guardian in complex residence and contact cases. Under the same legislation, separate representation for children placed for adoption has been implemented.

Divorce

It is necessary to have an awareness of divorce law, as it clearly affects a considerable number of families. Existing service users may ask questions of social workers about the law of divorce and the court's role in making orders consequent to divorce and wish to discuss their circumstances. In addition, at the time of divorce social workers may be directly involved in emergency work to protect children where separation follows violence, or in providing services for children and families, or supervising contact.

A brief consideration of marriage is necessary before turning to the law of divorce. It is important to note, however, that there has been a long-term downward trend in the number of marriages taking place each year, with more and more couples preferring to cohabit. There is also a tendency for couples to marry later in life.

Marriage

The legal definition of marriage is drawn from *Hyde* v. *Hyde* (1866) LR 1 P&D 130. It is:

The voluntary union for life of one man and one woman to the exclusion of all others.

Taking each element of this definition: first, the union must be voluntary; therefore, if there is no true consent it is possible to have the marriage annulled. Given the high divorce rate it is questionable whether reference to 'for life' remains a valid part of the definition.

A marriage which purports to be opposite-sex will be void if the parties are not respectively male and female. This issue has been raised in a number of transsexual cases, where the national and European courts consistently stated that a person's sexual attribution is fixed conclusively at birth. In *Rees* v. *United Kingdom* (1986) 9 EHRR 56, the court found no violation of ECHR, Art. 8, the right to respect for private life, or Art. 12, the right to marry, when the United Kingdom refused to amend the birth certificate from female to male. That position was challenged recently in *Bellinger* v. *Bellinger* [2003] UKHL 21.[20] Legislation has subsequently been introduced to rectify the position. Now, under the Gender Recognition Act 2004, the acquired gender of transsexuals is recognised. Further, since March 2014, same-sex couples have been able to marry in civil ceremonies under the Marriage (Same Sex Couples) Act 2013 (see below).

Reference to the exclusion of all others is reflected in adultery being included as one of the possible facts required to be proven before divorce.

Forced marriage

The issue of 'forced marriage' is becoming more widely recognised and new legislation, the Forced Marriage (Civil Protection) Act 2007 has been introduced, which came into force in November 2008. Previous case law confirmed that a marriage entered into under duress would be annulled.

In *NS* v. *MI* [2006] EWHC 1646 (Fam), the facts were that when N was 16 years old, her parents had taken her from the United Kingdom, where she had been born and brought up, to Pakistan purportedly for a holiday. While she was there, she realised the real purpose for her visit was that she was going to marry her cousin. N begged the respondent husband (M) not to marry her and to let her return to the United Kingdom, but he refused. N's family told her the only way she would be returning to the United Kingdom would be if she married M, and her parents threatened to kill themselves if she did not marry him. N's passport had been kept by her mother during her time in Pakistan and was only returned to her upon her return to the United Kingdom. The marriage went ahead, but was not consummated, and N returned to the United Kingdom five months later. The court accepted the evidence that N had been lured to go to Pakistan on a false pretence, and had been subjected to continued emotional pressure and moral blackmail. Her will had been overborne by duress. Forced marriages were utterly unacceptable and intolerable and the court had to use all its powers to prevent them. The court had to be careful not merely to distinguish between arranged marriage and forced marriage but also to guard against the risk of stereotyping.

The Forced Marriage (Civil Protection) Act 2007

This Act provides civil remedies for those faced with forced marriage and for victims of forced marriage. It introduces a new Part 4A into the Family Law Act 1996.[21] The Act states that a forced marriage is one that is entered into without the person's free and full consent. Force can be verbal, physical or mental. The force may be directed against another person, for example if the perpetrator threatened to commit suicide if the person did not submit to the marriage. A marriage with an incapacitated person who is unable to consent is a forced marriage within the the FMA 2007, as in *YLA* v. *PM and NZ* [2013] EWHC 3622 (Fam).

When deciding whether to make a forced marriage protection order, the court must consider the health, safety and wellbeing of the person to be protected, including their wishes and feelings, as far as it is possible to ascertain them. The court has a wide discretion to make an order containing any appropriate measures to protect a person from being forced into marriage; or to protect a person who has been forced into a marriage. The orders may prohibit or restrict certain activity or they may require a person to do something, such as produce their passport.

An order may be made in family proceedings or as a separate application. *Ex parte* orders may be made and it is possible to attach a power of arrest to an order. *Re P (Forced Marriage)* [2010] EWHC 3467 (Fam) confirms that force includes physical coercion but also 'threats or other psychological means'.

The law relating to forced marriage has developed further. Local authorities may apply direct to court for a protection order on behalf of a suspected victim of forced marriage, without seeking prior approval of the court to make the application (Family Law Act 1996 (Forced marriage) (Relevant Third Party) Order 2009 (S.I. 2009/2023)).

Key Case

The case of *A v SM and HB (Forced Marriage Protection Orders)* [2012] EWHC 435 (Fam) illustrates the use of this legislation: A and her siblings travelled with their parents, SM and HB to Bangladesh. A returned to the UK with the assistance of the Forced Marriage Unit at the British High Commission in Bangladesh, having realised that it was the intention of her parents to force her to marry. Her younger sister did enter into a marriage in Bangladesh. A obtained interim forced marriage protection orders for herself and her six siblings on an *ex parte* application. The siblings were made wards of court and on return from Bangladesh all passports were seized. B initially denied that she had been married but following an incident where she was seen being dragged into a car by her mother, the police enabled her to move to a confidential address and she stated that she had in fact been married and that her parents had told her that if she didn't marry she wouldn't be able to return to the UK and her younger siblings would be taken into care. At the final hearing the court renewed the forced marriage orders and directed the local authority to prepare reports under s. 37 Children Act 1989 with a view to seeking care orders in respect of the younger siblings.

Forced marriage and breach of a forced marriage order have become criminal offences under the Anti-Social Behaviour, Crime and Policing Act 2014.

Ground for divorce

The sole ground for divorce is irretrievable breakdown of marriage, contained in the Matrimonial Causes Act 1973, s. 1(1). Irretrievable breakdown must be established or evidenced by one of five facts. The first three facts are referred to as 'fault' grounds and the latter two as 'no fault' grounds. A **petition** (application) for divorce cannot be brought during the first year of marriage, though subsequent petitions may rely on events which occurred during that first year. In divorce proceedings the parties are referred to as the petitioner (the person applying for divorce) and the respondent.

s. 1(2)

(a) that the respondent has committed adultery and the petitioner finds it intolerable to live with the respondent;

(MCA 1973)

Adultery means voluntary heterosexual intercourse (a relationship with a person of the same sex does not count as adultery). It is not possible to rely on this ground if the petitioner has lived with the respondent for six months or more following disclosure of the adultery. There are two elements to this fact: there must have been adultery; and the petitioner must find it intolerable to live with the respondent, but that does not have to be as a consequence of the adultery (*Cleary* v. *Cleary* [1974] 1 All ER 498).

s. 1(2)

(b) that the respondent has behaved in such a way that the petitioner cannot reasonably be expected to live with the respondent;

(MCA 1973)

This fact is commonly referred to as unreasonable behaviour. That phrase is misleading, as it is not the behaviour that has to be unreasonable; rather it is the expectation that the petitioner should live with the respondent. The principle to be applied was enunciated in *Livingstone Stallard* v. *Livingstone Stallard* [1974] 2 All ER 766, where Dunn J stated: 'Would any right-thinking person come to the conclusion that this husband has behaved in such a way that this wife cannot reasonably be expected to live with him taking into account the whole of the circumstances and the characters and personalities of the parties.' This is the most widely relied upon fact.

> ### s. 1(2)
>
> **(c)** that the respondent has deserted the petitioner for a continuous period of at least two years immediately preceding the presentation of the petition;
>
> (MCA 1973)

This fact is rarely used and desertion has a technical legal definition.

> ### s. 1(2)
>
> **(d)** that the parties of the marriage have lived apart for a continuous period of at least two years immediately preceding the presentation of the petition … and the respondent consents to a decree being granted;
>
> (MCA 1973)

Facts (d) and (e) are based on separation, which is perhaps the best evidence of the breakdown of marriage. The separation facts were introduced in 1969 in an attempt to move away from a fault-based divorce system. There are two elements to fact (d): the parties must have lived apart and the respondent must consent. The two years must be a continuous period; however, it will not be broken by periods of reconciliation totalling less than six months. In order to be living apart, the spouses must not be in the same household, sharing any aspect of domestic life (*Fuller* v. *Fuller* [1973] 2 All ER 650).

> ### s. 1(2)
>
> **(e)** that the parties to the marriage have lived apart for a continuous period of at least five years immediately preceding the presentation of the petition …
>
> (MCA 1973)

For this fact, the fact of separation for five years must be proved but there is no requirement for the respondent's consent.

It is extremely rare to have a defended divorce. Most divorces are in fact straightforward, and it is the associated disputes relating to children and property that are complex. In an average case the decree nisi will be granted eight to twelve weeks after the petition is lodged, followed by the decree absolute, which may be applied for six weeks after decree nisi.

As an alternative to divorce, some couples prefer a judicial separation. This follows the same procedure as divorce up to decree nisi stage, but there is no actual termination of the marriage. There is no need to show irretrievable breakdown of the marriage for a separation; the five facts are themselves grounds for an order of judicial separation.

Civil partnership and same-sex marriage

The Civil Partnership Act 2004 enabled the first same-sex civil registrations to take place in December 2005.[22]

The purpose of the Act is to enable same-sex couples to obtain legal recognition of their relationship by forming a civil partnership provided:

- they are of the same sex;
- they are not already in an existing civil partnership or lawfully married;
- they are not within the prohibited degrees of relationships;
- they are both over the age of 18 or are over 16 and have consent of the appropriate people or bodies (in England and Wales and Northern Ireland) or are 16 or over in Scotland.

The partnership is formed when the civil partnership document is signed by the partners in the presence of each other, the registrar and two witnesses in non-religious premises. The partners must give notice of their intention to enter into a partnership to the registrar, then after a 15-day period the partnership may be registered. A civil partnership provides the same rights and responsibilities as a civil marriage: e.g. rights to occupy property of the partner; protection from domestic violence; the same rights as widows and widowers for a surviving civil partner, including succession rights to tenancies; equal treatment regarding social security and tax.

A civil partnership ends only on death, dissolution or annulment. A dissolution order (similar to divorce) will be made on the ground that the civil partnership has irretrievably broken down as evidenced by 'behaviour', two-year separation with consent or five-year separation without consent, or desertion (s. 44). These facts mirror those in divorce proceedings except that there is no adultery fact, though this might be included in the behaviour fact. The court may adjourn dissolution proceedings if it considers there is a reasonable prospect of reconciliation (s. 42). As with marriage, financial relief (lump sum, periodical payments, property adjustment, etc.) may be ordered following dissolution for the civil partner and any child of the family.

Children and civil partnership

Where there are children, a civil partner can acquire parental responsibility in a similar way to acquisition of parental responsibility by step-parents, and may apply for residence and contact orders. Parent is redefined in the Children Act 1989 to include any civil partner in a civil partnership (whether or not subsisting) in relation to whom the child concerned is a child of the family. It is possible for civil partners to adopt jointly, as a couple, recognised under the Adoption and Children Act 2002 as 'two people (whether of different sexes or the same sex) living together as partners in an enduring family relationship' (ACA 2002, s.144(4)(b)).

Same-sex marriage

Same-sex marriage was introduced under the Marriage (Same Sex Couples) Act 2013. A marriage has the same effect in relation to same-sex couples as it has to opposite-sex couples.

Married people of the same sex will not be able to divorce on grounds of adultery or have their marriage annulled on grounds of non-consummation. Parties to a civil partnership may convert their civil partnership to a marriage.

The future of the Civil Partnership Act is to be reviewed.

Openness in the family courts

There has been building pressure for greater openness to public scrutiny in the family courts. Following a number of consultations, the Ministry of Justice published a report, 'Family Justice in View'[23] in which the Government promised new legislation which will allow media access to family proceedings unless the court decides otherwise (excluding the media may be for the interests of the children or safety and protection of the parties or witnesses); pilots to be undertaken to improve public information by publishing some anonymised judgments online, giving the parties a copy of their case judgment, retaining court judgments to be accessed by children on reaching 18; some disclosure of information for the purposes of mediation or training. Various groups, including the Association of Lawyers for Children opposed these changes, arguing that the Government has lost sight of the needs of children in its efforts to respond to pressure to uphold the credibility of the family courts.

The Children, Schools and Families Act 2010 allows for greater media reporting of certain family proceedings. Accredited media representatives have been allowed to attend family proceedings since 2009 and are only able to report limited information about the proceedings they attend. Sections under this legislation introduce new arrangements for the publication of information from family proceedings. There is a general restriction on publication of information relating to proceedings, subject to three exceptions which allow publication of:

- court orders or judgment,
- publication allowed by rules of court, and
- 'authorised news publications'.

Authorised news publications will permit extended reporting by media representatives who have attended the proceedings. Publication of information likely to identify children, parties or witnesses (except professional witnesses), sensitive personal information, restricted adoption information and restricted parental order information is prohibited. Publication of all other information is allowed subject to the court's power to restrict: *Re J (Reporting Restriction: Internet: Video)* [2013] EWHC 2694 (Fam).

Reflect

What do you think are the advantages and disadvantages of making family courts more open. Is this in the child's best interest?

Chapter summary

- The concept of parental responsibility is introduced by the Children Act 1989. It may be held by a number of people in respect of a child and is defined as 'all the rights, duties, powers, responsibilities and authority which by law a parent of a child has in relation to the child'.

- Section 8 orders for Child Arrangements Orders, prohibited steps and specific issues control the exercise of parental responsibility. The residence element of a Child Arrangements Order determines where a child is to live and may be made to more than one person, and the contact element controls the type and level of contact which the child will enjoy with a range of adults. Case law and a Practice Direction lay down guidelines on contact where there has been domestic violence. Specific issue and prohibited steps orders are modelled on aspects of wardship and can be used to determine disputes over the exercise of parental responsibility.

- In family proceedings the court may make an order for the local authority to investigate a child's circumstances and determine whether it is appropriate for a care or supervision order to be made (CA 1989, s. 37).

- The family assistance order can provide support to families following separation or divorce and can be used to facilitate supervision of contact.

- Social work involvement in domestic violence cases may be triggered by statutory child care responsibilities and extend to coordinating support and providing information. Non-molestation and ouster orders are provided by the Family Law Act 1996.

- New legislation has been introduced to prevent forced marriage.

- The Civil Partnership Act 2004 provides for same-sex partnerships to be registered and to have the same legal effect as marriage, and the Marriage (Same Sex Couples) Act 2013 has introduced same-sex marriage.

Exercises

Consider what order, or combination of orders, if any, would be appropriate in the following circumstances. In each case consider the role of social services.

1. Sarah, aged 11, spends alternate weeks with each of her parents. They are in the process of an amicable divorce.

2. Tom and Louise are aged 6 and 4. They live with their mother during the week, spending weekends and part of the school holidays with their father. Their parents were not married. This arrangement has worked well until recently, when their father cancelled a couple of weekend visits at short notice and brought the children back early on another occasion. He recently announced his intention to marry his partner, who moved in with him two months ago.

3. Adam, aged 8, has been cared for by his grandparents since he was a baby. His mother is a drug user and has been unable to care for him. She sees him regularly but does not wish to care for him on a full-time basis. His grandparents want to plan for the future and would like some legal security.

4. Following his parents' acrimonious divorce, James, aged 5, has weekly contact with his father. He always returns distressed and has become enuretic. His parents regularly argue about contact in his presence.

5. Raymond and Eleanor have been married for six years. They have a 3-year-old son called Tom. Eleanor has been unhappy lately and finds Raymond irritating and insensitive to her needs. She would like another baby but he refuses to contemplate the idea. The couple lead increasingly separate lives. Raymond works away in London for much of the week and has a flat there. In an attempt to improve their relationship, Eleanor arranges for Tom to stay with his grandparents and drives to London to surprise Raymond. She lets herself in to the flat and finds Raymond in bed with another man. Eleanor wants to divorce Raymond and says if he is gay he can have no role as a father for Tom.

Websites

For further information about the work of contact centres, see the website of the National Association of Child Contact Centres:

www.naccc.org.uk

The Family Mediation Council provides information on mediation and a directory of local trained mediators

www.familymediationcouncil.org.uk

The Women's Aid website provides information to support women suffering violence including guides to the law:

www.womensaid.org.uk

Information on forced marriage is available from

www.gov.uk/forced-marriage

Further reading

Bainham, A. (2013) 'Public and private children law: an under-explored relationship' 25(2) *Child and Family Law Quarterly* p.138.

Bainham, A., Lindley, B., Richards, M. and Trinder, L. (eds) (2003) *Children and Their Families: Contact, Rights and Welfare*. Oxford: Hart Publishing. (A useful collection of essays.)

Kaganas, F. (2007) 'Grandparents' rights and grandparents' campaigns' 19(1) *Child and Family Law Quarterly*, p. 17.

Kaganas, F. (2013) 'A presumption that "involvement" of both parents is best: deciphering law's messages' 25(3) *Child and Family Law Quarterly* p. 270.

Potter, G. and Williams, C. (2005) 'Parental responsibility and the duty to consult – the public's view' 17(2) *Child and Family Law Quarterly* p. 207. (An interesting analysis of views of the public on whether there should be a duty to consult others with parental responsibility before making decisions.)

Private law orders have been considered in a range of articles:

Fortin, J., Ritchie, C. and Buchanan, A. (2006) 'Young adults' perceptions of court-ordered contact' 18(2) *Child and Family Law Quarterly*, p. 211.

George, R. H. (2010) 'Parental responsibility and shared residence orders: parliamentary intentions and judicial interpretations' 22(2) *Child and Family Law Quarterly*, p. 151

Gilmore, S. (2006) 'Court decision-making in shared residence order cases: a critical examination' 18(4) *Child and Family Law Quarterly*, p. 478.

Kaganas, F. and Piper, C. (2001) 'Shared parenting – a 70% solution?' 14(4) *Child and Family Law Quarterly*, p. 365.

Keeling, J. and Mason, T. (2008) *Domestic Violence: A Multi-professional Approach for Health Professionals.* Oxford: Oxford University Press.

May, V. and Smart, C. (2004) 'Silence in court? – hearing children in residence and contact disputes' 16(3) *Child and Family Law Quarterly*, p. 305. (Considers the extent to which children are consulted about their wishes and feelings, with examples of cases.)

Murray, C. (2004) 'Same sex families: outcomes for children and parents' 34 *Family Law*, p. 136.

Neale, B., Flowerdew, J. and Smart, C. (2003) 'Drifting towards shared residence?' 12 *Family Law*, p. 904.

Seden, J. (2001) 'Family assistance orders and the Children Act 1989: ambivalence about intervention or a means of safeguarding and promoting children's welfare?' *International Journal of Law, Policy and the Family*, p. 226.

Smart, C. and May, V. (2004) 'Why can't they agree? The underlying complexity of contact and residence disputes' 26(4) *Journal of Social Welfare and Family Law*, p. 347.

Notes

1. See A. Diduck (2003) *Law's Families.* London: LexisNexis UK.
2. *Hewer* v. *Bryant* [1969] 3 All ER 578: Lord Denning described the parental rights and duties of a parent with custody as a bundle of ever-dwindling rights and powers, which starts with a right of control and ends with little more than advice.
3. Births and Deaths Registration Act 1953.
4. This idea can be traced to a consultation paper issued by the Lord Chancellor's Department in 1998, 'Procedures for the Determination of Paternity and on the Law on Parental Responsibility for Unmarried Fathers'.
5. In limited circumstances the Human Fertilisation and Embryology Act 1990, s. 30 also provides for relinquishment of parental responsibility.
6. Foster Placement (Children) Regulations 1991 (SI 1991/910).
7. *Re W (Minors) (Residence)* (1992) *The Times*, 3 March, CA.
8. For example, in *Re R (A Minor) (Contact)* [1993] 2 FLR 762, Butler-Sloss LJ stated: 'It is the right of a child to have a continuing relationship with both parents wherever possible. This principle has been stated again and again in the appellate courts. It is underlined in the United Nations Convention on the Rights of the Child and endorsed in the Children Act 1989.'
9. Children Act Sub-Committee of the Lord Chancellor's Advisory Board on Family Law (1999) 'Contact between Children and Violent Parents'.
10. S. Gilmore (2004) 'The nature, scope and use of the specific issue order' 19(4) *Child and Family Law Quarterly*, p. 367.
11. Adoption and Children Act 2002, s. 21.
12. Practice Direction (Family Division: Conciliation) [2004] 1 WLR 1287.
13. Department of Health (1991) 'The Children Act 1989 Guidance and Regulations', vol. 1 'Court Orders'. London: HMSO, p. 15.

14 L. Trinder and N. Stone (1998) 'Family assistance orders – professional aspirations and party frustration' 10(3) *Child and Family Law Quarterly*, pp. 291–302.

15 Home Office (2013) 'Cross-Government Definition of Domestic Violence: A consultation Summary of Responses, September 2012'.

16 Amendment to the Children Act 1989 introduced by the Adoption and Children Act 2002, s. 120.

17 See: Home Office Violent Crimes Unit (2004) 'Developing domestic violence strategy – a guide for partnerships'.

18 It was previously provided by the Probation Service, actually the responsibility of the Home Office.

19 J. Timms and J. Harris-Hendriks (1999) 'The separate representation of children in private law proceedings – which children need representation under section 64 of the Family Law Act 1996?' 12(1) *Representing Children*, pp. 53–67.

20 See further discussion in A. Bradney (2003) 'Developing human rights? The Lords and transsexual marriages' *Family Law*, p. 585.

21 The Act was introduced following a consultation process which produced the reports: 'A Choice by Right' (2000) and 'Forced Marriage, A Wrong Not a Right', a consultation document issued by the Government in December 2005 and the response to that consultation dated June 2006.

22 The Act can be traced back to June 2003, when the Government published 'Civil Partnership – a framework for the legal recognition of same-sex couples in England and Wales (a consultation document)'.

23 Cm. 7502 (December 2008).

Chapter 9

Child protection

Learning objectives

To develop an understanding of the following:

- Local authority responsibilities in child protection work.
- Current definitions of forms of child abuse.
- The duty to investigate referrals and concerns that a child might be suffering or at risk of suffering significant harm.
- The role of child protection conferences and reviews.
- The range and effect of short-term and emergency orders.
- The interpretation of the threshold criteria for intervention in family life, including leading case law.
- Care and supervision orders and interim orders.
- Procedural issues including the Public Law Outline.
- The content and role of care plans.
- Independent representation for the child and the role of the children's guardian.
- The role of expert witnesses in care proceedings.
- The inherent jurisdiction and wardship.
- Types of inquiries, their purpose and influence.
- The criminal law and child abuse and special measures for child witnesses.

Talking Point

In the case *Re X (Emergency Protection Orders)* [2006] EWHC 510 (Fam), McFarlane J made the following statement which recognises the failures in the particular case but also recognises the wider challenges social workers face working in child protection.

The facts of this case have led me to produce a judgment which is highly critical of the social workers and the social services department who became involved within this family. I wish to record at the outset of this reported version of the judgment that, in my experience, failures of this degree are rare indeed. The ordinary experience of the family courts is of social workers and social services departments whose professional work is both valuable and appropriately targeted to meeting the particular needs of children and their families. Often that work is undertaken within the context of limited resources and consequential stress upon the social services organisation and the individuals who work within it.

The child protection system depends upon the skill, insight and sheer hard work of front-line social workers. Underlying those key features, there is a need for social workers to feel supported and valued by the courts, the state and the general populace to a far greater degree than is normally the case. Working in overstretched teams with limited resources, social workers frequently have to make crucial decisions, with important implications, on issues of child protection; often of necessity these decisions must be based upon the available information which may be inchoate or partial. There are often risks to a child flowing from every available option (risk if the child stays at home, risk of emotional harm at least if the child is removed). It is said that in these situations, social workers are 'damned if they do, and damned if they don't' take action. Despite these difficulties, it is my experience that very frequently social workers 'get it right' and take the right action, for the right reasons, based upon a professional and wise evaluation of the available information. Such cases sadly do not hit the headlines, or warrant lengthy scrutiny in a High Court judgment. I say 'sadly' because there is a need for successful social work, of which there are many daily examples, to be applauded and made known to the public at large.

In addition to reported case law which comments on the effectiveness of child protection work, this is an area where there is a high level of Government and policy interest. Key recent developments impacting on child protection include publication of the Munro Report, the Family Justice Review, a revised and much reduced version of 'Working Together', a new Family Court and the Children and Families Act 2014.

Introduction

Child protection is a high-profile area of work where social work as a profession and, at times, individual social workers have become the subject of much criticism. Inquiry reports published after child deaths or other situations of concern have identified individual and institutional culpability and repeatedly stated the importance of inter-agency work and good record keeping. There are examples of children who have been removed from their families where they suffered abuse only to be further abused in residential or foster placements, which were provided as a safe environment. Case law decisions are gradually removing the immunity from actions in negligence that local authorities enjoyed on public policy grounds.[1] In addition, the Human Rights Act 1998 has emphasised a clear duty on local authorities to protect children from abuse and enables compensation to be paid if a local authority fails in this duty.[2] As a result of the above it would be easy for a culture of defensive practice to develop in child protection and to forget the many success stories. It is essential that practice in this area continues to develop in line with research findings and that processes and procedures are rigorous and robust. The legal framework for intervention in child protection is largely contained in the Children Act 1989. The principles (outlined in Chapter 7) are applicable and there is a body of guidance that should be adhered to.

The judgment in a further decision specifically points out that social services can and should learn lessons from difficult cases and apply them to future similar cases. In *Re E (Care Proceedings: Social Work Practice)* [2000] 2 FCR 297, there was a history of social work intervention accompanied by a family's failure to cooperate with professionals, resulting in a pattern of abusive parenting over a long period. Lessons to be learnt included: the need to keep an up-to-date running chronology of significant events on the front of a social work file; recognition that lack of parental cooperation was never a reason to close the file or remove a child from a protection register; information given by health visitors and teachers in referrals is valuable and should be thoroughly investigated; a decision to take no action on a case should never be made without full knowledge of the file and consultation with the professionals who know the family; children who were part of a sibling group should always be considered in the context of the family history; and, in order to avoid drift, work with families had to be time-limited. In the particular case, Bracewell J commented that, had those matters been followed, effective intervention to protect the children would have occurred much earlier.

Child protection is properly viewed as an aspect of the duties in respect of 'Safeguarding and promoting the welfare of children'. The new 'Working Together' Glossary clarifies that safeguarding and promoting the welfare of children means:

- protecting children from maltreatment;
- preventing impairment of children's health or development;
- ensuring that children are growing up in circumstances consistent with the provision of safe and effective care; and
- taking action to enable all children to have the best life chances.

Whereas Child Protection is:

Part of safeguarding and promoting welfare. This refers to the activity that is undertaken to protect specific children who are suffering, or are likely to suffer significant harm.

This chapter begins with a brief outline of current definitions of child abuse. A discussion of the local authority duty to investigate where there are concerns follows, and includes consideration of the important role of child protection conferences and reviews in the investigative process. The next section outlines a range of short-term and emergency orders, which support the process of investigation and offer immediate protection to the child, followed by a section on care proceedings incorporating care and supervision orders, the significance of care plans, the role of the children's guardian and the expert witness in child protection proceedings. The inherent jurisdiction and wardship are explained next, followed by an evaluation of the role of inquiries. Finally, to consider child protection in a broad sense, the chapter continues with a section on the arrangements for screening child care workers; and guidance on interviewing the child; the position of the child as a witness and the role of criminal proceedings concludes this chapter.

Definitions of child abuse

It is difficult to offer a precise definition of child abuse, as knowledge and understanding and research findings mean that this is an evolving concept. 'Working Together to Safeguard Children' (2013) notes the variable circumstances stating that abuse is 'A form of maltreatment of a child. Somebody may abuse or neglect a child by inflicting harm, or by failing to act to prevent harm. Children may be abused in a family or in an institutional or community setting by those known to them or, more rarely, by others (e.g. via the internet). They may be abused by an adult or adults or another child or children' (Glossary).

It is commonly agreed that there are different types of abuse, namely emotional, physical and sexual abuse and neglect. Beyond these categories it has been argued that other forms of abuse should be recognised, such as institutional abuse, satanic or ritual abuse and medical abuse. Clearly, any professional working in the field of child protection needs to be alert to new research and open to the recognition of new or previously unidentified forms of abuse. In law the term 'significant harm' is central to any understanding of the state's powers to intervene in cases of child abuse. The term is explored fully in relation to s. 31, the threshold criteria, later in this chapter but it should be noted that it also features in other sections: e.g. applications for a child assessment order or emergency protection order.

The following extract from the 'Working Together' (2013) Glossary provides a description of each of the four major types of abuse:

Physical abuse
A form of abuse which may involve hitting, shaking, throwing, poisoning, burning or scalding, drowning, suffocating, or otherwise causing physical harm to a child. Physical harm may also be caused when a parent or carer fabricates the symptoms of, or deliberately induces illness in a child.[3]

Emotional abuse
The persistent emotional maltreatment of a child such as to cause severe and persistent adverse effects on the child's emotional development. It may involve conveying to a child that they are worthless or unloved, inadequate, or valued only insofar as they meet the needs of another person. It may include not giving the child opportunities to express their views, deliberately silencing them or 'making fun' of what they say or how they communicate. It may feature age or developmentally inappropriate expectations being imposed on children. These may include interactions that are beyond a child's developmental capability, as well as overprotection and limitation of exploration and learning, or preventing the child participating in normal social interaction. It may involve seeing or hearing the ill-treatment of another. It may involve serious bullying (including cyber bullying), causing children frequently to feel frightened or in danger, or the exploitation or corruption of children. Some level of emotional abuse is involved in all types of maltreatment of a child, though it may occur alone.

Sexual abuse

Sexual abuse involves forcing or enticing a child or young person to take part in sexual activities, not necessarily involving a high level of violence, whether or not the child is aware of what is happening. The activities may involve physical contact, including by penetration (for example, rape or oral sex) or non-penetrative acts such as masturbation, kissing, rubbing and touching outside of clothing. They may also include non-contact activities, such as involving children in looking at, or in the production of, sexual images, watching sexual activities, encouraging children to behave in sexually inappropriate ways, or grooming a child in preparation for abuse (including via the internet). Sexual abuse is not solely perpetrated by adult males. Women can also commit acts of sexual abuse, as can other children.

Neglect

The persistent failure to meet a child's basic physical and/or psychological needs, likely to result in the serious impairment of the child's health or development. Neglect may occur during pregnancy as a result of maternal substance abuse. Once a child is born, neglect may involve a parent or carer failing to:

- provide adequate food and clothing, shelter (including exclusion from home or abandonment);
- protect a child from physical and emotional harm or danger;
- ensure adequate supervision (including the use of inadequate care-takers); or
- ensure access to appropriate medical care or treatment.

It may also include neglect of, or unresponsiveness to, a child's basic emotional needs.

Neglect and emotional maltreatment have been found to be the most common ground of harm to children (Brophy, 2006).[4]

'Working Together to Safeguard Children – A Guide to Inter-Agency Working to Safeguard and Promote the Welfare of Children' (2013)

The original 'Working Together', was published in 1991, and updated versions published in 1999, 2006 and 2010. Further documents supplemented these versions including, 'Safeguarding Children Involved in Prostitution' (2000), and 'Safeguarding Children in Whom Illness is Fabricated or Induced' (2002). The current version, published in 2013,[5] replaces the previous 2010 version and also replaces the 'Framework for the Assessment of Children in Need and their Families' (2000) and statutory guidance on making arrangements to safeguard and promote the welfare of children under s. 11 of the Children Act 2004. The guidance is issued under s. 7 of the Local Authority Social Services Act 1970, ss. 11(4) and 16 of the Children Act 2004 and, as such, 'should be complied with unless local circumstances arise' (p. 5). Although much reduced in length the new version of 'Working Together to Safeguard Children' describes how agencies should work together and gives guidance on assessing need investigations and conduct of case conferences and reviews and the role of Local Safeguarding Children Boards, Serious Case Reviews and Child Death Reviews. Much of the material is presented in accessible tabular and flow chart form.

Family Justice Review

The Family Justice Review (FJR) reported in 2011, the Government response was published in 2012 and a number of the recommendations have achieved statutory recognition in the

Children and Families Act 2014. The major concern of the FJR in the public law field was delay, with care cases taking on average over a year to complete, despite earlier attempts to reduce delay in the form of the Protocol on Judicial Case Management in Public Law Children Act cases, (2003) and the Public Law Outline (2008). A requirement that public law cases should not exceed 26 weeks is introduced in the Act. The review also recommended introduction of the single family court.

Local Safeguarding Children Boards (LSCBs)

The Children Act 2004 introduced Local Safeguarding Children Boards (LSCBs), replacing Area Child Protection Committees (**ACPCs**). The boards are established by s. 13 and their functions described in s. 14. The board will comprise representatives of the Children's Services Authority and each partner and include CAFCASS. Following consultation within the board it is also possible to add representatives of other bodies, 'of any nature exercising functions or engaged in activities relating to children in the area of the authority' (Children Act 2004 s. 13(6)). Senior representatives of agencies are likely to constitute an executive board with subcommittees to deal with specific areas, e.g. training. It is possible for two or more Children's Services Authorities to establish a LSCB for their combined area (Children Act 2004 s. 13(8)). The function of the LSCB is to coordinate and ensure the effectiveness of each body represented on the board in safeguarding and promoting the welfare of children. Within that remit boards will produce their own policies and procedures, be consulted in the development of the Children's Services Plan, communicate best practice and hold serious case reviews where a child died or was seriously harmed (previously the ACPC would conduct a review (Part 8)).[6] Section 31 of the Children and Young Persons Act 2008 places a duty on registrars to provide the LSCB with the particulars of the death of any child within seven days of registering the death.

The Chair of the LSCB was frequently the Director of Social Services. However, 'Working Together' (2013) requires that, 'In order to provide effective scrutiny, the LSCB should be independent' (12) and able to, 'hold all agencies to account' (13) though working closely with the Director of Children's Services. An annual report must be published that deals with effectiveness of safeguarding and promoting welfare of children in the local area, including lessons from reviews.

Duty to investigate

Local authorities receive referrals from a wide variety of sources, including the professional and lay person (though there is no legal duty on a private individual to report concerns). Almost all referrals will require some level of investigation but a relatively small proportion will lead to statutory intervention. Referrals come from a variety of sources. Research by Gibbons[7] identified the following sources of referral: education – 23 per cent; health visitors, GPs and other health professionals – 17 per cent; household/lay – 17 per cent; social services professionals – 13 per cent; police and probation – 12 per cent; anonymous – 6 per cent; and others – 12 per cent. 'Working Together' notes that referrals may also come from children themselves. The nature of any concerns, how they have arisen and the child's needs should be clarified with the person making the referral. If that person is a professional the referral should be confirmed in writing. There must be clarity about any action to be taken and by whom, and all decisions should be recorded in writing. There is a clear emphasis on timeliness in 'Working Together', 'Within one working day of a referral being received, a local authority social worker should make a decision about the type of response that is required and acknowledge receipt to the referrer.' A referral may lead to no further action, provision of support or further investigation and the possibility of an emergency short-term order. The LSCB are expected to publish a threshold document that details processes for early help assessment and the criteria for assessment and for statutory services under s. 17 (children in need), s. 47 (investigation), s. 31 (care order application) and s. 20 (duty to accommodate a child) (para 18). Where an assessment follows the referral it should be completed within 45 days. If there is reasonable cause to suspect the child is suffering or likely to suffer significant harm a strategy discussion will be held involving social services, the police, health and other bodies as appropriate. The emphasis of strategy meeting is to plan immediate future action.

The local authority's duty to investigate is established under CA 1989, s. 47, which provides:

s. 47

(1) Where a local authority –

    (a) are informed that a child who lives, or is found, in their area –

        (i) is the subject of an emergency protection order; or

        (ii) is in police protection; or

    (b) have reasonable cause to suspect that a child who lives, or is found, in their area is suffering, or is likely to suffer, significant harm, the authority shall make, or cause to be made, such inquiries as they consider necessary to enable them to decide whether they should take any action to safeguard or promote the child's welfare.

(CA 1989)

Further subsections elaborate on that central duty to make inquiries. When inquiries are being made, the local authority must take steps to obtain access to the child themselves or by a person authorised for that purpose, unless they are satisfied that they have sufficient information already (s. 47(4)). If issues arise in the course of inquiries relating to education, the local authority is directed to consult the relevant local education authority (s. 47(5)). Central to inquiries is the need for the local authority to see the child. If access to the child is denied or the local authority is denied information as to the child's whereabouts, the local authority shall apply for an emergency protection order, a child assessment order, a care order or a supervision order unless they are satisfied that the child's welfare can be satisfactorily safeguarded without doing so (s. 47(6)). If the local authority, on the conclusion of inquiries, decides not to apply for an order, it is directed to consider whether it would be appropriate to review the case at a later date and, if so, to set a date (s. 47(7)). The principle of working together is given statutory footing in s. 47(9), which provides for various persons to assist with the local authority's inquiries unless to do so would be unreasonable in all the circumstances of the case. The specified persons are: any local authority; any local education authority; any local housing authority; any health authority; and any other person authorised by the Secretary of State (s. 47(11)).

In addition to the above provision, s. 15 of the Crime and Disorder Act 1998 amends s. 47 by introducing a new subsection (1)(a)(iii), which reads: 'has contravened a ban imposed by a curfew notice'. In those circumstances the local authority is directed to commence inquiries as soon as practicable and, in any event, within 48 hours of the authority receiving the information. In relation to this subsection there is no reference to risk of harm. (The Crime and Disorder Act 1998 is discussed fully in Chapter 13.)

It is good practice for local authorities to refer parents to independent advice and advocacy agencies as soon as inquiries commence under s. 47.

The duty to investigate imposed on social services is distinct from any responsibility the police may have to conduct a criminal investigation, though a joint approach to some aspects such as interviewing the child may be appropriate. In *R (S)* v. *Swindon Borough Council* [2001] EWHC Admin 334, a man challenged a local authority's decision to continue its child protection investigation after he had been acquitted of indecent assault. The judge found that, as s. 47 required the local authority to have only 'reasonable cause to suspect' significant harm, not reasonable cause to believe, the duty to investigate was not removed by the acquittal. The judge also stated that the local authority duty to investigate remained the same before and after the coming into force of the Human Rights Act 1998. The threshold for investigation is thus quite low.

The investigation must be carried out 'properly'. In another recent case, a father and child claimed damages from the local authority after inquiries were pursued beyond the point required by s. 47 and damage resulted. Interviews had been held improperly with the child and information was wrongly withheld from the father (*L* v. *Reading Borough Council* [2001] EWCA Civ 346).

Case conferences and reviews

The first major recognition of the child protection case conference can be found in a 1974 DHSS letter following the Colwell inquiry.[8] Its recommendations were for area review committees to be formed in every local authority, child protection registers to be established and child abuse manuals to be drawn up. Case conferences were recognised as an invaluable tool for coordinating investigations into child abuse.

Case conferences are non-statutory bodies and, whilst occupying a central role in the child-protection process, neither their role nor their composition is set out in legislation. Due to the multi-disciplinary make-up of the case conference, it is not possible for conferences to make decisions about the conduct of cases; rather, recommendations are formulated which must be ratified by the Social Services Department with responsibility for child protection. The purpose of the initial child protection conference is to bring together and analyse in an inter-agency setting all relevant information and plan how best to safeguard and promote the welfare of the child. A range of tasks for the conference may include: appointing a lead social worker; identifying membership of a core group of professionals and family members to implement the child protection plan; setting timescales for core group meetings, production of a child protection plan and reviews; agreeing an outline child protection plan.

All initial child protection conferences should take place within 15 working days of the strategy discussion. Within that time band, there is a need to balance the urgency of the case and the need for adequate preparation and the initial assessment. The core group should meet within 10 working days of the initial child protection conference. A first review of progress since the initial case conference will be held within 3 months and thereafter every 6 months as long as the child remains subject to a child protection plan.

Levels of attendance will vary according to the circumstances of the case but previous versions of 'Working Together' acknowledged that very large conferences can inhibit discussion

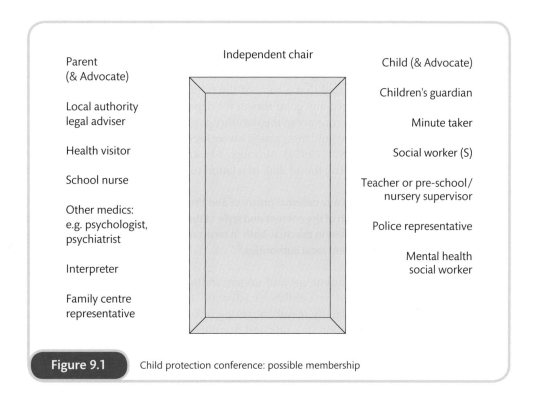

Figure 9.1 Child protection conference: possible membership

Parent (& Advocate)

Local authority legal adviser

Health visitor

School nurse

Other medics: e.g. psychologist, psychiatrist

Interpreter

Family centre representative

Independent chair

Child (& Advocate)

Children's guardian

Minute taker

Social worker (S)

Teacher or pre-school/ nursery supervisor

Police representative

Mental health social worker

and be intimidating for the family. It thus recommended that those attending 'should be there because they have a significant contribution to make, arising from professional expertise, knowledge of the child or family or both'. The LSCB should specify the required quorum. Written reports should be provided by agencies that are invited but unable to attend. In each case a written report should be provided to the conference by social services, summarising the information obtained through initial assessment and s. 47 inquiries, including a chronology of significant events and agency contact with the child. Figure 9.1 illustrates the range of potential members.

The conference will be chaired by a professional who is independent of operational or line management responsibilities for the case under discussion. The responsibilities of the chair include outlining the purpose of the conference, or setting an agenda, ensuring confidentiality, enabling full contributions to the discussion from all members and ensuring decisions are taken systematically. A chair should have appropriate skills including knowledge and understanding of anti-discriminatory practice.

Involvement of the child and family

The chair should meet the child and parents in advance of the conference to ensure they understand the purpose and process. Parents should normally be invited to attend the conference and helped fully to participate with the option of bringing an advocate, friend or supporter. An early decision of the European Court of Human Rights found breaches of Arts. 6 and 8 of the European Convention through failure to involve parents in decision-making regarding children in care (*R v. United Kingdom* [1988] 2 FLR 445). According to *R v. Cornwall County Council, ex parte LH* [2000] 1 FLR 236, the parents' solicitor cannot be refused attendance at the conference. In that case a blanket ban of solicitors attending child protection conferences and the withholding of minutes from a parent who had attended the conference was found to be unlawful. The decision relied on the status of guidance contained in 'Working Together', which envisaged a parent being accompanied by a friend or lawyer and stated that a copy of the minutes should be sent to all parties. The council had not articulated any good reason for departing from the guidance, and the practice was thus found to be contrary to the statutory guidance and unlawful. (NB This case was decided when the relevant guidance, issued under LASSA 1970, s. 7 was 'Working Together under the Children Act 1989' (1991)). Although advocacy services are developing across the country, Lindley *et al.* (2001) found that, in relation to advocacy for parents in child protection cases:

> the absence of any national protocol and theoretical framework underpinning this service has led to much of the content and style of the work being developed 'on the hoof' resulting in wide variations in practice, both in terms of the service delivered, and how it is responded to by different local authorities.[9]

The child of sufficient age and understanding should also have the opportunity to attend and be supported by a children's advocate. Each conference will need to plan the level of involvement of family members, taking into account the need for professionals to be able to share information in a safe and non-threatening environment and for family members to speak to the conference in the absence of other family members. The chair may decide in exceptional circumstances to exclude a parent or carer from the child protection conference, perhaps where there is a risk of violence or intimidation or if the parent is subject to criminal prosecution in respect of the child. A full minute should be taken of the decision to exclude parents alongside everything else discussed at the conference (*Re X (Emergency Protection Orders)* [2006] EWHC 510 (Fam)).

Family group conferences

Family group conferences were described in the 2010 'Working Together' as 'a decision making and planning process whereby the wider family group makes plans and decisions for children and young people who have been identified either by the family or by service providers as being in need of a plan that will safeguard and promote their welfare' (para. 10.2). Family group conferences do not replace child protection conferences and they are more likely to be utilised to develop a plan for a child in need.[10]

Part V of the Children Act 1989 deals with orders for the protection of children. Where an application is made to court concerning a child, the proceedings will be conducted in private. This position has been upheld by the European Court in *B* v. *United Kingdom* [2001] 2 FLR 261.

Short-term and emergency orders

Child assessment orders

The child assessment order (CAO) was introduced by the Children Act 1989 broadly in line with a recommendation of the report 'A Child in Mind; Protection of Children in a Responsible Society' (1987) (the Kimberley Carlile Report).[11] It is designed to cover those situations where there are concerns about a child, and lack of cooperation from the child's carers is preventing full assessment. The order is not intended to be used in obvious emergency situations. The court may treat an application for a CAO as an application for an emergency protection order if it feels the grounds for an emergency protection order exist.

Section 43 provides that a CAO will be made on the application of a local authority or authorised person (NSPCC) where the court is satisfied that all three limbs of the section must be satisfied:

---

s. 43

(a) the applicant has reasonable cause to suspect that the child is suffering, or is likely to suffer, significant harm;

(b) an assessment of the state of the child's health or development, or of the way in which he has been treated, is required to enable the applicant to determine whether or not the child is suffering, or is likely to suffer, significant harm; and

(c) it is unlikely that such an assessment will be made, or be satisfactory, in the absence of an order under this section.

(CA 1989)

The effect of the order is to require the child to be produced for assessment under the terms of the order. Directions can be included in the order relating to any aspect of assessment, such as the type of assessment and where and by whom it will be carried out. If the child is of sufficient understanding to make an informed decision, he may refuse a medical or psychiatric examination or other assessment (s. 43(8)). The order lasts for seven days, a relatively short period in which to carry out anything other than a primarily medical assessment. The seven-day period may commence at a specified start date later than the date of the court hearing, which would enable appropriate involvement of other professionals.

The guidance describes the CAO as: 'A lesser, heavily court controlled order dealing with the narrow issue of examination or assessment of the child in specific circumstances of non co-operation by the parents and lack of evidence of the need for a different type of order or other action.'[12] An example is provided of a child who is failing to thrive, whose parents are unwilling or unable to face the child's condition.

The order does not authorise the child's removal from home unless directions are included in the order and it is necessary for the assessment (s. 43(9)). In exceptional circumstances, for example, this may include overnight stays if 24-hour monitoring is considered a necessary part of the assessment. The local authority does not acquire parental responsibility when a child assessment order is made.

It was anticipated that this order would rarely be used and research supports that hypothesis. Dickens (1993)[13] suggests that reasons for a lack of use in the immediate period after implementation of the Act included: lack of knowledge about the order; the fact that it is rare for parents not to be persuaded to cooperate, even if the threat of legal action has to be used; and that seven days is a very limited period for an assessment.

Emergency protection orders

Emergency protection orders (**EPOs**) were introduced by the Children Act 1989 to provide immediate protection for a child. An application may be made to a single justice but in most cases will be made to the family proceedings court. The grounds for an application for an EPO are contained in s. 44 of the Children Act 1989.

---

s. 44

(1) Where any person ('the applicant') applies to the court for an order to be made under this section with respect to a child, the court may make the order if, but only if, it is satisfied that –

   (a) there is reasonable cause to believe that the child is likely to suffer significant harm if –

   (i) he is not removed to accommodation provided by or on behalf of the applicant; or

   (ii) he does not remain in the place in which he is then being accommodated;

   (b) in the case of an application made by a local authority –

   (i) inquiries are being made with respect to the child under section 47(1)(b); and

   (ii) those inquiries are being frustrated by access to the child being unreasonably refused to a person authorised to seek access and that the applicant has reasonable cause to believe that access to the child is required as a matter of urgency; or

   (c) in the case of an application made by an authorised person –

   (i) the applicant has reasonable cause to suspect that a child is suffering, or is likely to suffer, significant harm;

   (ii) the applicant is making inquiries with respect to the child's welfare; and

   (iii) those inquiries are being frustrated by access to the child being unreasonably refused to a person authorised to seek access and the applicant has reasonable cause to believe that access to the child is required as a matter of urgency.

(CA 1989)

The EPO operates as a direction to produce the child and gives authority to the applicant to retain or remove the child (s. 44(4)(a), (b)). Under an EPO the applicant acquires parental responsibility (s. 44(4)(c)) but this is limited to what is necessary to safeguard the welfare of the child having regard to the duration of the order. In other words, parental responsibility may be exercised in relation to day-to-day matters but long-lasting changes would not be authorised. In addition, specific directions will be included in an EPO in relation to contact with a child (s. 44(6)(a)), and to medical or psychiatric examination or other assessment of the child (s. 44(6)(b)). As with the CAO, a child of sufficient understanding to make an informed decision may refuse to submit to an examination or other assessment (s. 44(7)). Subject to any specific directions given by the court, the applicant (usually the local authority) must allow the child reasonable contact with his parents, any person with parental responsibility or with whom the child was living immediately before the order, and any person who has a contact order (s. 44(13)). The inclusion of this provision can be directly traced to events in Cleveland, where parents whose children had been removed under place of safety orders (in some cases for 28 days) were denied any contact.

There is a power to return the child home if it appears safe to do so and to remove the child again if there is a change of circumstances. For example, if an EPO is made in respect of a child where sexual abuse is suspected, and the alleged perpetrator is charged and initially remanded in custody, it may be possible to return the child home provided that there is an individual who can care for the child. If the alleged perpetrator is granted bail and allowed to return home, it would be possible to move the child again, during the order (s. 44(12)).

Duration of the order

An emergency protection order lasts for eight days (s. 45(1)). It is possible for the order to be extended, once only, for a further seven days. Given the action that must be taken during an EPO the limited duration imposes significant pressure on the professionals involved in the case. An application for the EPO to be discharged may be made by the child, his parents, a person with parental responsibility or a person with whom the child was living immediately before the order. Under the original Children Act provisions, it was only possible to apply to discharge the order after 72 hours (s. 45(8)). This right of challenge does not apply if the person was given notice of the application and was present at the hearing. Applications for discharge were therefore normally made in cases where the initial application was made *ex parte* (i.e. where notice was not given, because to do so would have placed the child in danger).

This position changed under the Children and Young Persons Act 2008 (**CYPA**), following a judgment given in the Northern Ireland High Court, which held that Art. 64(8) of the Children (Northern Ireland) Order 1995, which is identical to s. 45(9) of the 1989 Act and provides that 'no application for discharge of an emergency protection order shall be heard for 72 hours beginning with the making of the order', is contrary to Arts. 6(1) and 8 of the European Convention on Human Rights (ECHR). That decision would be persuasive in the courts in England and Wales, so s. 30 CYPA 2008 repeals s. 45(9) of the 1989 Act to ensure provisions for the discharge of emergency protection orders are compatible with Arts. 6 and 8 of the ECHR. The section allows the court to hear an application to discharge an emergency protection order as soon as it is made.

The applicant for an EPO may be any person, the local authority or the NSPCC as an authorised person. The grounds for the application are slightly different in each case. For any person the court must be satisfied that the applicant has reasonable cause to *believe* the child is likely to suffer significant harm. An example might be a doctor who wishes to prevent a child's removal from hospital or a youth worker who is concerned that a young person may be sexually abused on return home from a youth club. For the local authority there is an additional ground that where s. 47 inquiries are being made and are being frustrated by access to the child being unreasonably denied then an EPO application may be made. For the NSPCC the court must find that the applicant has reasonable cause to *suspect* that a child is suffering or likely to suffer significant harm.

It may be necessary to apply for an EPO very shortly after receiving an initial referral, or the need may arise due to a change in circumstances or exacerbation of events in ongoing involvement with a family.

Key Case

An important decision has considered the impact of the Human Rights Act on emergency protection orders. Munby J gave the judgment in *X Council* v. *B (Emergency Protection Orders)* [2004] EWHC 2015 (Fam).[14] In this case the local authority were granted *ex parte* (without notice) EPOs in respect of three children (all of whom suffered severe illness) of a family with whom they had a long involvement. The authority's concerns centred on mother's failure to follow medical advice, engage with medical services and inappropriate management of medicines. An assessment of the children was required and the authority did not consider this was possible whilst the children were with their parents. The authority were criticised for seeking EPOs rather than child assessment orders, which would have been a more proportionate response. Munby J gave a full and detailed judgment within which he summarised 14 key points of guidance in relation to emergency protection orders, recited below given their importance for good practice and emphasis on proportionate responses in child protection:

(1) An EPO, summarily removing a child from his parents, is a 'draconian' and 'extremely harsh' measure, requiring 'exceptional justification' and 'extraordinarily compelling reasons'. Such an order should not be made unless the FPC is satisfied that it is both necessary and proportionate and that no other less radical form of order will achieve the essential end of promoting the welfare of the child. Separation is only to be contemplated if immediate separation is essential to secure the child's safety; 'imminent danger' must be 'actually established'.

(2) Both the local authority which seeks and the FPC which makes an EPO assume a heavy burden of responsibility. It is important that both the local authority and the FPC approach every application for an EPO with an anxious awareness of the extreme gravity of the relief being sought and a scrupulous regard for the Convention rights of both the child and the parents.

(3) Any order must provide for the least interventionist solution consistent with the preservation of the child's immediate safety.

(4) If the real purpose of the local authority's application is to enable it to have the child assessed then consideration should be given to whether that objective cannot equally effectively, and more proportionately, be achieved by … a CAO under section 43 of the Act.

(5) No EPO should be made for any longer than is absolutely necessary to protect the child. Where the EPO is made on an ex parte (without notice) application very careful consideration should be given to the need to ensure that the initial order is made for the shortest possible period commensurate with the preservation of the child's immediate safety.

(6) The evidence in support of the application for an EPO must be full, detailed, precise and compelling. Unparticularised generalities will not suffice. The sources of hearsay evidence must be identified. Expressions of opinion must be supported by detailed evidence and properly articulated reasoning.

(7) Save in wholly exceptional cases, parents must be given adequate prior notice of the date, time and place of any application by a local authority for an EPO. They must also be given proper notice of the evidence the local authority is relying upon.

(8) Where the application … is made ex parte the local authority must make out a compelling case for applying without first giving the parents notice. An ex parte application will normally be appropriate only if the case is genuinely one of emergency or other great urgency – and even then it should normally be possible to give some kind of albeit informal notice to the parents – or if there are compelling reasons to believe that the child's welfare will be compromised if the parents are alerted in advance to what is going on.

(9) The evidential burden on the local authority is even heavier if the application is made ex parte. Those who seek relief ex parte are under a duty to make the fullest and most candid and frank disclosure of all the relevant circumstances known to them. This duty is not confined to the material facts: it extends to all relevant matters, whether of fact or of law.

(10) Section 45(7)(b) permits the FPC to hear oral evidence. But it is important that those who are not present should nonetheless be able to know what oral evidence and other materials have been put before the FPC … The FPC must 'keep a note of the substance of the oral evidence' and must also record in writing not merely its reasons but also any findings of fact.

(11) The mere fact that the FPC is under the obligations imposed by rules … is no reason why the local authority should not immediately, on request, inform the parents of exactly what has gone on in their absence. Parents against whom an EPO is made ex parte are entitled to be given, if they ask, proper information as to what happened at the hearing and to be told, if they ask, (i) exactly what documents, bundles or other evidential materials were lodged with the FPC either before or during the course of the hearing and (ii) what legal authorities were cited to the FPC. The local authority's legal representatives should respond forthwith to any reasonable request from the parents or their legal representatives either for copies of the materials read by the FPC or for information about what took place at the hearing. It will therefore be prudent for those acting for the local authority in such a case to keep a proper note of the proceedings, lest they otherwise find themselves embarrassed by a proper request for information which they are unable to provide.

(12) Section 44(5)(b) provides that the local authority may exercise its parental responsibility only in such manner 'as is reasonably required to safeguard or promote the welfare of the child'. Section 44(5)(a) provides that the local authority shall exercise its power of removal under section 44(4)(b)(i) 'only … in order to safeguard the welfare of the child.' The local authority must apply its mind very carefully to whether removal is essential in order to secure the child's immediate safety. The mere fact that the local authority has obtained an EPO is not of itself enough. The FPC decides whether to make an EPO but the local authority decides whether to remove. The local authority, even after it has obtained an EPO, is under an obligation to consider less drastic alternatives to emergency removal. Section 44(5) requires a process within the local authority whereby there is a further consideration of the action to be taken after the EPO has been obtained. Though no procedure is specified, it will obviously be prudent for local authorities to have in place procedures to ensure both that the required decision making actually takes place and that it is appropriately documented.

(13) Consistently with the local authority's positive obligation under Article 8 to take appropriate action to reunite parent and child, sections 44(10)(a) and 44(11)(a) impose on the local authority a mandatory obligation to return a child who it has removed under section 44(4)(b)(i) to the parent from whom the child was removed if 'it appears to [the local authority] that it is safe for the child to be returned.' This imposes on the local authority a continuing duty to keep the case under review day by day so as to ensure that parent and child are separated for no longer than is necessary to secure the child's safety. In this, as in other respects, the local authority is under a duty to exercise exceptional diligence.

> (14) Section 44(13) requires the local authority, subject only to any direction given by the FPC under section 44(6), to allow a child who is subject to an EPO 'reasonable contact' with his parents. Arrangements for contact must be driven by the needs of the family, not stunted by lack of resources.

The well-publicised case of *R (G)* v. *Nottingham City Council* [2008] EWHC 152 serves as a reminder that a child can never be removed from a parent without the authority of an EPO or care order. G, who was 18, had been in the care of the local authority. She gave birth and two hours later her son was removed to another room in the hospital on the basis of a 'birthplan' produced following a case conference, which instructed hospital staff to remove the baby and prevent any unsupervised contact. This was unlawful and an order was made to reunite G with her baby.

Reflect

Consider in the following scenarios whether an EPO, CAO or no order would be appropriate.

1. Julie is the mother of 3-year-old twins who live with her during the week and stay with their father, Ron, at weekends. Julie's older two children, Sam, aged 9, and Louise, aged 11, were removed from her care after their stepfather John was found guilty of sexual and physical assaults of them. He was imprisoned for six years. Julie began a short relationship with Ron, the twins' father, and agreed with social services that she would have no more contact with John. Since she separated from Ron, Julie has secretly resumed letter contact with John and social services have been informed that he will be moving in with Julie on release, expected next week.

2. Hopeshire Social Services have received several reports from neighbours of Jane and Peter, claiming to have heard persistent screaming from the house, which is believed to be their daughter Geraldine. They also say that Geraldine has not been seen going to nursery for several days but when they saw her in the back garden she had a black eye and bruises to her legs. A social worker goes to the house at 10.30 a.m. but is told by Jane that Geraldine is unwell, asleep and cannot be disturbed. When the social worker asks if she can come in for a chat, Peter comes to the door with their Rottweiler dog and tells the social worker in no uncertain terms to go away and stay away.

3. Joan, a health visitor, contacts Hopeshire Social Services to relay her concerns about Susie, a 3-year-old girl who lives with her mum, Amy, and her grandmother, Rosie. Her father, Jack, is currently in prison having breached an ouster and non-molestation order in respect of violence towards Amy. Amy appears very depressed and Joan suspects she is drinking heavily. Susie has a squint in one eye and appears under-nourished. She has very little speech and is clingy and withdrawn. Joan obtained a place for Susie at the local pre-school but Amy says it is too far to walk. Three appointments at the eye hospital have been missed and the hospital are reluctant to arrange any more. Joan arranged to collect and take Amy and Susie to the last appointment but they were out. Amy said at a later visit that she forgot. Rosie is schizophrenic and occasionally is verbally abusive to Joan and refuses to let her in.

Police protection

The police are able to remove and detain a child without reference to the court. Under s. 46:

> ### s. 46
>
> **(1)** Where a constable has reasonable cause to believe a child would otherwise be likely to suffer significant harm, he may –
>
> **(a)** remove the child to suitable accommodation and keep him there; or
> **(b)** take reasonable steps to ensure the child's removal from any hospital, or other place, in which he is being accommodated is prevented.
>
> (CA 1989)

Police protection is a short-term remedy of no more than 72 hours' duration. The police must inform the local authority as soon as is reasonably practicable after taking a child into police protection. It may then be appropriate for the local authority to apply for an EPO in respect of the child. In that case the eight-day period runs from the start of police protection. The police must also take steps to inform the child's parents, any person with parental responsibility, or any person with whom the child was living immediately before being taken into police protection (s. 46(4)).

The Children Act 1989 does not give the police authority to enter property by virtue of s. 46; however, a warrant may be obtained under s. 48. There may be obvious emergency situations where obtaining a warrant will cause delay. For example, if a child can be seen at an upstairs window and appears to be at risk of falling, and the police cannot raise anybody to open the door, then reliance on s. 17 of the Police and Criminal Evidence Act 1984 enables the police to enter premises without a warrant, to save life or limb.

Recovery orders

It is a criminal offence to remove a child who is the subject of a care order, EPO or police protection, from the responsible person, or to keep the child away from the responsible person, e.g. by failing to return the child after a contact visit (s. 49). The responsible person is the person who had care of the child by virtue of the order. If a child has been taken away or is being kept away from the responsible person, has run away or is missing, the court may make a recovery order (s. 50). A person with parental responsibility (under an EPO or care order) or the designated officer, where the child is in police protection, may apply for a recovery order. Where an order is in force it is a direction to produce the child; it authorises removal of the child and it requires anybody with information as to the child's whereabouts to disclose that information to the police or an officer of the court. In addition, it authorises the police to enter specified premises and search for a child, using reasonable force where necessary, in addition to their general authority under the Police and Criminal Evidence Act, s. 17.

Children's refuges

Certain children's homes and also foster carers may be classed as providing a refuge for children who appear to be at risk of harm. A certificate will be issued by the Secretary of State to recognised refuges. A refuge can provide temporary accommodation to a child and, provided a certificate is held, the person providing the refuge will be exempt from prosecution for abduction or harbouring a child. A refuge can prove to be a vital resource, given some of the problems of institutional abuse that have been highlighted in recent years.[15]

Power of exclusion

Under s. 38A and s. 44A of the Children Act 1989 the court may exclude an alleged abuser from the home rather than having to remove the child. An exclusion order may be attached to an EPO or an interim care order.

The court must be satisfied of three criteria:

(a) that there is reasonable cause to believe that if a person (the relevant person) is excluded from a dwelling-house in which the child lives, the child will cease to be likely to suffer significant harm, and enquiries will not be frustrated; and

(b) another person living in the same house, whether or not the parent, is able and willing to give to the child the care which it would be reasonable to expect a parent to give; and

(c) that person consents to the inclusion of the exclusion requirement.

A power of arrest may be attached to the order so that in the event of breach – for example, if the excluded person returns to the home – an arrest can take place without warrant. In *Re L (Children)* [2001] EWCA Civ 151, a case where an exclusion order had been breached repeatedly, a sentence of four months' imprisonment was given. The judge noted that the person in breach (the father) was unable to appreciate that orders had to be obeyed and needed to come to terms with the fact that the family situation had changed.

The exclusion order is available only if the person at home gives consent. In many cases this may be the mother, whose partner would be the subject of the exclusion order. There may be many reasons why she might not be able or willing to give consent, perhaps due to fear or unwillingness to recognise the possibility that her partner may have abused her child. It is most likely that the person being excluded will be a member of the household, e.g. stepfather. It is also possible to exclude a person from without the household from entering the house or a defined area, e.g. a neighbour suspected of abuse whilst babysitting. The person remaining in the home must also be able to provide the standard of reasonable parenting. In many cases it will not be possible to clearly identify one person only as the abuser. If there were additional concerns relating to the standard of care the remaining parent would be able to provide, an exclusion order would not be appropriate.

Where an application for an exclusion order is made, a statement must be served on the relevant party (i.e. person to be excluded) in order that he is made aware of the evidence upon which the order is based so that he can make an informed decision as to whether to apply to vary or discharge the order. The statement must set out the facts on which the application for exclusion is based and evidence supporting an application for an interim care order or EPO. It must make clear what the person is required to do, e.g. leave the dwelling-house, not enter the dwelling or a defined area (*W v. A Local Authority (Exclusion Requirement)* [2000] 2 FCR 662). If the child is removed for more than 24 hours by the local authority, the exclusion order will lapse.

Prior to introduction of the exclusion order, local authorities utilised a power contained in Sch. 2, para. 5. Where it appeared that a child was suffering or likely to suffer significant harm at the hands of a person living at the same premises, the local authority could assist that person to move from the premises. Assistance could be given in cash and often involved

CARE AND SUPERVISION ORDERS

the local authority paying for bed and breakfast accommodation. The key difference between this power (which remains available to the local authority) and the exclusion order relates to the consent of the alleged abuser. In the former power the local authority could only assist an individual who was willing to move. The power to assist with alternative accommodation may be persuasive but the provision has no force if the individual wishes to stay in the premises. If that were the case the only alternative would be to remove the child. It appears that, despite its apparent advantages, the new power has been used infrequently.[16]

Care and supervision orders

The law relating to care and supervision orders is contained in Part IV of the Children Act 1989. It is possible for a care or supervision order to be made on the application of the local authority only in respect of a child under the age of 17.

'significant harm'

The grounds which must be satisfied before an order can be made are set out in s. 31 and are commonly referred to as the threshold criteria. 'Significant harm' is the threshold justifying compulsory intervention. The Lord Chancellor described the criteria as the 'minimum circumstances which should always be found to exist before it can be justified for a court to even begin to contemplate whether the state should be enabled to intervene compulsorily in family life'. The phrase was intended to be broad and flexible in order to incorporate a wide range of circumstances; in fact it has caused major interpretational problems and a succession of case law decisions. 'Working Together' (2010) provides further explanation (this section is not included in the new reduced version):

> There are no absolute criteria on which to rely when judging what constitutes significant harm. Consideration of the severity of ill-treatment may include the degree and the extent of physical harm, the duration and frequency of abuse and neglect, and the extent of premeditation, degree of threat and coercion, sadism, and bizarre or unusual elements in child sexual abuse. Each of these elements has been associated with more severe effects on the child, and/or relatively greater difficulty in helping the child overcome the adverse impact of the maltreatment. Sometimes, a single traumatic event may constitute significant harm, e.g. a violent assault, suffocation or poisoning. More often, significant harm is a compilation of significant events, both acute and longstanding, which interrupt, change or damage the child's physical and psychological development. Some children live in family and social circumstances where their health and development are neglected. For them, it is the corrosiveness of long-term emotional, physical or sexual abuse that causes impairment to the extent of constituting significant harm. In each case, it is necessary to consider any maltreatment alongside the family's strengths and supports. (para. 1.24)

It was anticipated when the Children Act 1989 was introduced, with its emphasis on partnership, prevention and provision of services and the 'no order' rule, that there would be fewer care proceedings. In fact judicial statistics showed an increase in both the applications for and care orders made, a trend described as a 'care proceedings explosion'.[17] Nevertheless, research suggests that the Children Act 1989 has raised the threshold for intervention, and the children subject to care order applications have very serious problems. The impact of the **Public Law Outline** (first version), introduced in April 2008 must also be considered, as it requires much greater assessment and preparation before issuing applications. In response it appears that greater use is being made of voluntary s. 20 accommodation.

The relevant section is set out below:

> ### s. 31
>
> **(2)** A court may only make a care order or supervision order if it is satisfied –
>
>   **(a)** that the child concerned is suffering, or is likely to suffer, significant harm; and
>   **(b)** that the harm, or likelihood of harm, is attributable to –
>   **(i)** the care given to the child, or likely to be given to him if the order were not made, not being what it would be reasonable to expect a parent to give to him; or
>   **(ii)** the child's being beyond parental control.
>
> (CA 1989)

In hearing cases it is necessary for all allegations to be determined, not just sufficient to meet the threshold criteria.

Certain of the terms used in the threshold criteria are further defined in subsection (9) and case law decisions have provided further clarification.

> ### s. 31(9)
>
> 'Harm' means ill-treatment or the impairment of health or development; including, for example, impairment suffered from seeing or hearing the ill-treatment of another;
>
> 'Development' means physical, intellectual, emotional, social or behavioural development;
>
> 'Health' means physical or mental health; and
>
> 'Ill-treatment' includes sexual abuse and forms of ill-treatment which are not physical.
>
> (CA 1989)

The definition of the meaning of 'harm' in the Children Act 1989 (s. 31) was extended to include 'impairment suffered from seeing or hearing the ill-treatment of another' by the Adoption and Children Act 2002, s. 120.

Subsection (10) introduces the concept of the similar child:

> ### s. 31(10)
>
> Where the question of whether harm suffered by a child is significant turns on the child's health or development, his health or development shall be compared with that which could reasonably be expected of a similar child.
>
> (CA 1989)

There are three stages to the process of satisfying the threshold criteria and obtaining a care or supervision order. The first stage is to find 'significant harm'. 'Significant' is not defined. A single act of abuse may constitute significant harm or there may have been a series of acts which taken together cause significant harm. Guidance suggests that 'the significance could exist in the seriousness of the harm or the implication of it'.[18] In *Humberside County Council* v. *B* [1993] 1 FLR 257, 'significant' was described as, 'considerable, or noteworthy or important'. In *Re L (Care: Threshold Criteria)* [2007] 1 FLR 2050, the court noted that 'significant harm must be something unusual, more than commonplace human failure or inadequacy'.

The following brief examples illustrate the difficulty in assessing significant harm.

- A child aged 4 months has a broken rib.
- A child aged 6 months has faint fingermark bruising around the mouth.
- A child aged 2 years has 20 random bruises of differing ages around the knees and lower leg.

In the first case the injury is both substantial and significant. In the second case the harm caused may not be considered a substantial injury but it is significant in that the injury is unlikely to have been caused accidentally and may suggest that the child has been force-fed or a dummy has been forced into the child's mouth to stop crying. In the third case, 20 bruises is a substantial injury; however, given the age of the child and the position of the bruises it is likely that they are attributable to the usual tumbles and bumps that a 2-year-old child experiences. It is clearly not sufficient to look simply at the extent of an injury, but also to consider what the injury signifies.

'is suffering'

Re M (A Minor) (Care Order: Threshold Conditions) [1994] 3 WLR 558, a House of Lords decision (overruling the Court of Appeal), confirmed that the phrase 'is suffering' in s. 31(2) relates to the period immediately before the child protection process was implemented in respect of the child. In that case, at the time of the hearing, as the child was placed with a member of his wider family, it could not be said that he was suffering significant harm, nor that he was likely to suffer significant harm. The child had suffered significant harm when his father murdered his mother. The House of Lords ruled that it is incorrect to apply the words 'is suffering' literally as the present tense, to be applied at the date of the hearing. If that were the case, very few care orders would be made because the local authorities will have made arrangements to safeguard the child in the period before the final hearing. The correct interpretation is to apply 'is suffering' to the date of the initial statutory intervention. This may be the date of the initial care order application or the date of an EPO application. This interpretation clearly follows the spirit rather than the letter of the law.

In *Re G (Children) (Care Order: Evidence)* [2001] EWCA Civ 968, the Court of Appeal held that in determining whether the criteria were made out the court can take into account information later acquired, relating to the state of affairs at the relevant date (i.e. the point of initial intervention) and later events where they could help prove the state of affairs at the relevant date.

'likely'

Before the Children Act 1989 was introduced, it was possible to take action in respect of likely future harm only via the inherent jurisdiction. Inclusion of the word 'likely' in the threshold criteria has reduced the need to have recourse to wardship. Unfortunately, there is no indication of the degree of likelihood required, but it clearly invites risk assessment. In *Newham London Borough Council* v. *Attorney-General* [1993] 1 FLR 281, the court stated that it would be wrong to equate the phrase with 'on the balance of probabilities'. This part of the criteria may be relied upon in respect of newborn babies where there is a concern that parents will not be able to offer adequate care, and cases where harm arose during pregnancy, as in *Re D (A Minor)* [1987] AC 317, where the mother was a drug addict. It is not possible for a care order to be made simply on the basis that harm occurred in the past but, as in *Re D*, it may be possible to infer likelihood of future harm based on previous behaviour. It may also be used to retain a child being looked after when parents indicate that they want the child returned to them, if the local authority argues that the child is likely to suffer significant harm because of the state of affairs at home, perhaps due to the presence of an unsuitable adult. Likelihood of harm is linked to the ability of the parent to meet the emotional needs of the child for the years ahead: *Re H (A Minor) (Section 37 Direction)* [1993] 2 FLR 541, where Scott-Baker J stated: 'the likelihood of the harm is not confined to present or near future but applies to the ability of a parent or carer to meet the emotional needs of a child for years ahead.'

The application of 'likely' was further examined in the leading case of *Re H and R (Child Sexual Abuse: Standard of Proof)* [1996] 1 All ER 1. In this case a 15-year-old girl alleged that her step-father had sexually abused and had raped her on four occasions, over a period of seven years. He was prosecuted but acquitted of rape. The local authority applied for care orders in respect of three younger children on the basis that, as a result of the allegations of abuse made by their older sister, they were likely to suffer significant harm. In deciding whether the threshold criteria were satisfied, the House of Lords in a majority judgment (3:2) held that the question was whether there was a 'real possibility' that the child would suffer significant harm. This position has been followed in *Re U (Serious Injury: Standard of Proof); Re B* [2004] EWCA Civ 567, which also confirmed that responsibilities of local authorities and the applicable standard of proof in care order cases had not changed as a result of the Cannings case (*R* v. *Cannings* [2004] ECWA Crim 1).

Potential confusion over the standard of proof which *Re H and R* may have caused has been addressed by the House of Lords in *Re B (Children) (Sexual Abuse: Standard of Proof)* [2008] UKHL 35. In this appeal it was contended that 'likelihood' should be satisfied where there was a 'real possibility' rather than on a balance of probability. That was rejected. The court confirmed that:

> the standard of proof in finding the facts necessary to establish the threshold under section 31(2) or the welfare considerations in section 1 of the 1989 Act is the simple balance of probabilities, neither more nor less. Neither the seriousness of the allegation nor the seriousness of the consequences should make any difference to the standard of proof to be applied in determining the facts.

Whether a child 'is suffering' or 'is likely to suffer' significant harm, in each case the court must be satisfied on the balance of probabilities.

'similar child'

Where concerns relate to the child's health and development, in determining whether the harm suffered is significant, the court must compare the child's health or development with that of a similar child (s. 31(10)). There is a danger that use of the similar child concept may provide a rather crude comparison. The court must compare the particular child before it with a hypothetical similar child. To illustrate, consider how in the following scenario a comparison with a white English 3-year-old child might lead to the wrong conclusions.

There are concerns about a 3-year-old child, who was born in England; her parents are from Pakistan. The health visitor is concerned that her development is slower than might be expected and mentions failure to thrive, describes the child as small and underweight for her age, listless and with limited language. In assessing the child as small and underweight, it is possible that development or centile charts have been used which may be Eurocentric and misleading when applied to different physiques. There are different expectations of development in different cultures, for example, as to potty-training or sleeping arrangements. English may not be the first language spoken at home and, if the child does not attend a pre-school, she may not encounter spoken English on a regular basis. In addition, experience of racism and possible unequal access to services may be a factor.

The similar child test may also be difficult to apply in respect of children with disabilities. A child who has Down's syndrome is not necessarily comparable with a notional child with Down's syndrome because the nature of the condition is so individualised.

In the case of *Re O (A Minor) (Care Proceedings: Education)* [1992] 4 All ER 905, a girl aged 15 had persistently truanted from school for three years. A care order was made on the basis that her intellectual and social development was suffering and was likely to suffer, and the harm was significant, as compared with a similar child. The judge stated that a similar child, in this context, meant 'a child of equivalent intellectual and social development, who has gone to school, and not merely an average child who may or may not be at school'.

The second stage of the process, once the court has found harm in s. 31(2)(a), is to find the cause for the harm.

'attributable to an absence of reasonable care'

Ground (b)(i) looks at standards of care and asks whether the harm or likelihood of harm is attributable to an absence of reasonable care which has been, or is likely to be, offered to the child. In other words, it questions whether the standard of care is below that which it would be reasonable to expect the parent of such a child to give to him. The phrase has both a subjective and an objective element. It is subjective in the sense that the care must meet the required standard for the particular child, a subjective test which will vary depending on the child's particular needs. The objective element requires the care to be reasonable in relation to the child's needs, not what is reasonable for the particular parent to provide (*a* parent not *the* parent). It is a child-focused test which addresses the particular needs of the child but makes little allowance for the characteristics of the particular parent.

For example, the care that a parent must give to meet the needs of a child with special needs, who is disabled or has suffered abuse, may be greater than that required for a child who does not have any special needs. The care given by the parent, however, may be that which the parent is able to give with the assistance of any support services to which the parent is entitled. The fact that the care which will be given in the future might be provided by another person and be adequate is not relevant at this stage. The court will look at the actions of the carer at the time the concerns became evident. So, in *Northamptonshire County Council* v. *S* [1993] Fam 136, it was not relevant that the grandmother would be likely to care for the child in the future, where significant harm had been caused by neglect by the mother.

Difficulties may arise where it is not possible to attribute the harm caused. This was precisely the issue in *Lancashire County Council* v. *B* [2000] 1 FLR 583,[19] where a 7-month-old baby suffered at least two episodes of shaking and it was not possible to determine whether this harm had been caused by the child's mother or father or the childminder. The House of Lords found that it was not necessary to exactly attribute the care or absence of care to a particular parent. If that were so, it would invite cases where parents collude to deny that either has caused harm. The court ruled that where care for a child was shared it was sufficient that the court was satisfied that the harm was attributable to any of the primary carers. Lord Nicholls stated that to decide otherwise could lead to 'the prospect that an unidentified and unidentifiable carer might otherwise be free to inflict further injury on a child he or she had already severely damaged'. This is an important and useful decision, as there may be many reasons why it is not possible to identify with certainty the perpetrator of abuse. Hayes (2000)[20] suggests the following reasons: child abuse is often met with denial; inaccurate information about the circumstances leading to abuse is often provided; it is common for there to be no witnesses to abuse; there may be a number of people who have had contact with the child who could be possible perpetrators; there may be evidential difficulties surrounding the child's account of abuse or a very young child may not be able to communicate at all.

The *Lancashire* interpretation was adopted in *Re O and N (Children) (Non-accidental Injury); Re B (Children) (Non-accidental Injury)* [2003] UKHL 18, a conjoined appeal in the House of Lords. In 'uncertain perpetrator' cases, the phrase 'care given to the child' included the care given by any of the carers and it was not necessary to identify the perpetrator exactly in order to satisfy the threshold. The correct test is to ask whether there is a likelihood or real possibility that X, Y or Z was the perpetrator. At the welfare stage, the court has to proceed on the basis that each carer was a possible perpetrator. *Re A-C; Re A (Fact-finding: Possible Perpetrators)* [2013] EWCA Civ 132, confirms that the test is whether there is a real possibility that a person may be the perpetrator and there may be a 'pool of perpetrators' where one or more people may have caused injury.

Successful criminal prosecutions are unlikely in uncertain perpetrator cases, in part due to the higher standard of proof required by the criminal law. In response to this predicament, a new offence of 'causing or allowing the death of a child' was been introduced by the Domestic Violence, Crime and Victims Act 2004, and extended by an amending Act to include causing or allowing serious injury.

'beyond parental control'

This element of the criteria originates from the Children and Young Persons Act 1969, which provided the law on care proceedings before the Children Act 1989. It is a question of fact whether a child is beyond parental control and is not linked to parental culpability. In *M v. Birmingham City Council* [1994] 2 FLR 141, a 13-year-old girl was described as wayward and uncontrollable, sometimes violent and demonstrating a disturbed pattern of behaviour, including absconding and taking drug overdoses. Her mother was a caring parent who had attempted to obtain help for the child's problems. The girl in *Re O*, the truanting case mentioned above, was also found to be beyond parental control.

More recently in *Re K (A Child) (Post Adoption Placement Breakdown)* [2013] 1 FLR 1, an application for a care order as made in respect of a 15-year-old girl who had been adopted at the age of 6. K was found to be beyond parental control as a manifestation of reactive attachment disorder. Section 20 accommodation as an alternative was not an option due to the lack of cooperation between her parents and the local authority.

At the third stage, the court, having found that the child is suffering or likely to suffer significant harm which is attributable to care not being reasonable or the child being beyond parental control, must decide whether it is appropriate to make an order and, if so, which order. It has jurisdiction to make a care or supervision order if the threshold criteria are satisfied, but it is not *bound* to make an order.

In the Children Act 1989, Part I principles of welfare, non-intervention and the menu of orders come into play. In deciding whether the care order will provide a positive benefit to the child, the court will need to consider the local authority's plans for the child in the form of the care plan. The court also needs to consider the children's guardian's recommendations and give reasons if it decides not to follow those recommendations. The order must be proportionate.

In *C* v. *Solihull Metropolitan Borough Council* [1993] 1 FLR 290, the local authority applied for a care order, but the court actually made a residence order to the parents, with a supervision order to the local authority. In *Re D (A Minor) (Care or Supervision Order)* [1993] 2 FLR 423, the local authority was satisfied that a supervision order would allow proper monitoring of a situation but the court held that a care order was more appropriate. The case centred on risk assessment of a father towards his baby with a new partner, when he was thought to be responsible for serious injuries to a 2-month-old baby with his first wife and had served a prison sentence for cruelty to children.

In *Re O (A Child) (Supervision Order: Future Harm)* [2001] EWCA Civ 16, the Court of Appeal considered whether a supervision order or care order was most appropriate in the case in question in the context of the Human Rights Act 1998. The court stated that cases decided before the 1998 Act might not be appropriate to current and future care order applications. Hale LJ stated that a care order in this case would be severe in three aspects: power to the local authority to remove the child from its parents; power to the local authority to have parental control and responsibility; and a long period of time for its discharge. Any intervention by the state between parents and children should be proportionate to the aim of protection of family life in the European Convention.

Convention rights come into play when the judge decides which, if any, order to make, not on determination of whether the threshold is crossed: *Re B (A Child)* [2013] UKSC 33. Once the court has to consider which of one or more options would be proportionate, it must approach the exercise by taking a 'global, holistic, evaluation of each of the options', not a linear process by which options having been dismissed the court is left with the option at the end of the line as the remaining choice.

To summarise, the court must work through three stages, as illustrated by Figure 9.2, before it can make a care or supervision order: it must find that significant harm occurred or is likely to occur; it must be satisfied as to the cause of that actual or likely harm; and it must apply the central principles of the Children Act 1989 before making an order.

Effect of a care order

The local authority has parental responsibility for the child whilst a care order is in force, has authority to remove the child from home and to decide where he is to live (s. 33). The child's parents retain parental responsibility but the local authority has the power to determine the extent to which a parent may meet parental responsibility towards the child. A care order revokes any residence order/Child Arrangements Order, previously in force.

Interim care orders

During the investigation period, while appropriate assessments are carried out, the child can be protected via an interim care order. To obtain an interim care order the applicant must satisfy the court that there are reasonable grounds for believing the threshold criteria apply, for which evidence will be presented to the court at the final hearing. The first interim

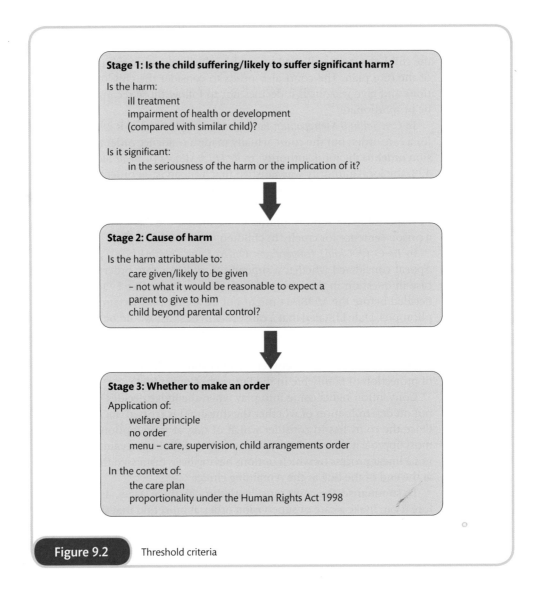

Stage 1: Is the child suffering/likely to suffer significant harm?

Is the harm:
    ill treatment
    impairment of health or development
    (compared with similar child)?

Is it significant:
    in the seriousness of the harm or the implication of it?

Stage 2: Cause of harm

Is the harm attributable to:
    care given/likely to be given
    – not what it would be reasonable to expect a
    parent to give to him
    child beyond parental control?

Stage 3: Whether to make an order

Application of:
    welfare principle
    no order
    menu – care, supervision, child arrangements order

In the context of:
    the care plan
    proportionality under the Human Rights Act 1998

Figure 9.2   Threshold criteria

order is normally made for eight weeks (s. 38(4)), after which it may be renewed for further periods of four weeks (s. 38(5)). Evidence at interim care order applications may be limited to changes of circumstances and the impact of those changes on whether there should be an interim order: *Re B (Interim Care Orders: Renewal)* [2001] 2 FLR 1217. During an interim order the court has a wide jurisdiction to make directions for assessment to obtain necessary information for its decision (s. 38(6)). In *Re B (A Child: Interim Care Order)* [2002] EWCA Civ 25, this included a direction as to residence in a mother and baby unit. Directions for treatment alone would not be permissible under s. 38(6); however it is recognised that the line between assessment and treatment can be rather blurred (*Re G (Interim Care Order: Residential Assessment)* [2005] UKHL 68; *Re L and H (Residential Assessment)* [2007] EWCA Civ 213). The Children and Families Act 2014 amends s.38 so that the court may direct the assessment or expert evidence only if it is 'necessary' to assist the court to resolve the proceedings.

The court can also make directions as to contact, for example in *Kirklees Metropolitan District Council* v. *S* [2006] 1 FLR 333, an order was made by the family proceedings court for daily supervised contact between a 1-month-old baby and her mother. It was noted that this level of contact was unusual but appropriate in the circumstances as a short-term order.

It has been generally understood that an interim order should not be used to enable the court to keep the case under review whilst postponing the final hearing, nor where there is disagreement over the care plan (*Re L (Minors) (Sexual Abuse: Standard of Proof)* [1996] 1 FLR 116). Such use would extend the court's involvement and control over the local authority. This position was questioned in *Re W and B (Children: Care Plan)* [2001] EWCA Civ 757, a Court of Appeal judgment which ruled that the trial judge should have a wider discretion to make an interim care order or defer final care order. The parts of the judgment in relation to care plans were overturned by the House of Lords (in *Re S (Children: Care Plan); Re W (Children: Care Plan)* [2002] UKHL 10) and are now addressed by amendments to the Children Act, discussed below. As to extended use of interim care orders, Lord Nicholls noted that it is not possible to provide a precise test as to when a court should continue interim relief and when it should proceed to make a care order, but it should always bear in mind the delay principle. If the uncertainty before the court needs to be resolved before the court can decide whether to make a care order, interim relief would be appropriate. In other cases if the uncertainty relates to an aspect of the care plan that is suitable for immediate resolution, a limited period of 'planned and purposeful' delay provided by interim relief can be justified. Beyond that, Lord Nicholls observed that 'when deciding to make a care order the court should normally have before it a care plan which is sufficiently firm and particularised for all concerned to have a reasonably clear picture of the likely way ahead for the child for the foreseeable future'. Such an analysis provided judges with a 'degree of flexibility' and appears to partially accept the stance of the Court of Appeal. The Court of Appeal clarified the basis for removal of a child on an interim basis pending determination of a care order application, in *In the Matter of L-A* [2009] EWCA Civ 822. In the earlier decision, *Re L* [2008] 1 FLR 575, Ryder J suggested that for a child to be removed there must be 'an imminent risk of really serious harm'. The Court of Appeal clarified that that is not the test and that the established position is simply that removal is required because the child's safety requires interim protection.

Care plans

The court cannot make a care order with respect to a child until it has considered a s. 31A care plan.

---

s. 31A

(1) Where an application is made on which a care order might be made with respect to a child, the appropriate local authority must, within such time as the court may direct, prepare a plan ('a care plan') for the future care of the child.

(2) While the application is pending, the authority must keep any care plan prepared by them under review and, if they are of the opinion some change is required, revise the plan, or make a new plan.

(CA 1989)

It will normally be the responsibility of the social worker to prepare a plan; however, this must be done in consultation with the child, his or her parents, others likely to have a significant input into the child's life, and the children's guardian.

Guidance about planning for children is included in 'The Children Act 1989: Guidance and Regulations', vol. 2, accompanying the Care Planning, Placement and Case Review (England) Regulations 2010 (in particular regulation 5).

The care plan should contain the following key elements:

1. Overall aim: A brief summary of the case and summary of timetables.

2. Child's needs in line with the developmental needs domain of the Assessment Framework including: contact; needs arising from race, culture and religion or language, special education, health or disability; the extent to which the wishes and views of the child had been obtained and acted upon; arrangements for and purpose of contact including sibling contact and arrangements for promoting and maintaining contact with a parent and anyone else with parental responsibility.

3. Views of others: the extent to which wishes and views of the child's parents and others with a sufficient interest in the child had been obtained and acted upon.

4. Placement plan details and timetable: the proposed placement; likely duration; arrangements for health care (the health plan), education (the personal education plan) and reunification; other services to be provided; details of the parents' role in day-to-day arrangements. Where adoption is a possible option the authority should adopt a **twin track** approach.[21]

5. Management and support by local authority: who is responsible for implementing the overall plan and specific tasks; the name of the child's **IRO**, contingency plan; arrangements for input by parents, child and others into ongoing decision-making process; arrangements for making representations or complaints.

A separate care plan is required for each child who is the subject of proceedings, although large parts of the plan may be similar for sibling groups. This supports the court's duty to consider the individual needs of each child and make orders accordingly, as for example in *Re F (Children) (Interim Care Order)* [2007] EWCA Civ 516, where the court made a care order in respect of a child who has ADHD and had been struck by a belt. The court was not satisfied in respect of two other children that the mother could not cope with them and refused the care orders. The care plan should be specific to the particular child, not simply based on general policy considerations, as was challenged, for example, in *Berkshire County Council* v. *B* [1997] 1 FLR 171, where the local authority plan was adoption for all children under the age of 10. For a teenage child, the care plan will also need to consider the arrangements for leaving care. If the court is not satisfied with the care plan, it should not make the final care order. In *Re S and W (Care Proceedings)* [2007] EWCA Civ 232, the court invited the director of social services to reconsider a care plan, which stated that children were to be placed for adoption outside the family, when in fact the local authority had changed its view and planned to make family placements.

Where an application for a care order has been made, the care plan is of great significance when the court, satisfied that the threshold criteria have been met, comes to decide whether or not an order should be made (applying the non-intervention principle of s. 1(5)). The court must determine whether the care plan is in the best interests of the child and will be better than making no order and returning the child to his former circumstances.

Under the Children Act 1989 as originally implemented, once a care order was made the court lost any power to control the arrangements for the child or ensure compliance with the terms of the care plan. Furthermore, the guardian's involvement would also end when a care order was made, there being no power to direct the guardian to continue to be involved (*Kent County Council* v. *C* [1993] 1 FLR 308). The court, however, had an important role, with which the guardian should assist in subjecting the care plan to 'rigorous scrutiny'.[22] The extent to which the courts could control aspects of the care plan was questioned in a Court of Appeal decision, *Re W and B (Children: Care Plan)* [2001] EWCA Civ 757, and its judgment (briefly) placed a clear duty on the local authority and/or guardian to return failing care plans to court, having 'starred' essential milestones in the care plan. The case was appealed to the House of Lords, as *Re S (Children: Care Plan); Re W (Children: Care Plan)* [2002] UKHL 10, whose judgment rejected the reasoning of the Court of Appeal, arguing the introduction of starred care plans went beyond the interpretation allowed under the Human Rights Act, stating: 'Under the proposed starring system courts would effectively exercise a newly created supervisory function.' The House of Lords did, however, give a clear indication in the following statement that this was an issue requiring further consideration:

> I cannot stress too strongly that the rejection of this innovation on legal grounds must not obscure the pressing need for the Government to attend to the serious practical and legal problems identified by the Court of Appeal ... One of the questions needing urgent consideration is whether some degree of court supervision of local authorities' discharge of their parental responsibilities would bring about an overall improvement in the quality of child care provided by local authorities.

Parliament responded to these concerns with a further amendment to the Children Act 1989 (by the ACA 2002). Once a care order is made, there is now a provision for review of care orders and possible return to the court. Section 26 of the Children Act 1989, which deals with reviews for looked after children, is amended to require that the s. 31A plan is kept under review, and if some change is required, to revise the plan or make a new one. Local authorities are required to appoint a person (known as an Independent Reviewing Officer) in respect of each case to: participate in reviews; monitor the performance of the authority's functions in respect of the review; and refer the case to CAFCASS Legal if he considers it appropriate (s. 26(2A)). CAFCASS may then return the case to court for judicial directions in appropriate cases, most obviously where the local authority does not adhere to the care plan and this is not in the best interests of the child.

The Children and Families Act 2014 signals a change of emphasis in the required scrutiny of the care plan by the court. Under s.15, inserting a new s. 31(3A) into the Children Act 1989, when a court is deciding whether to make a care order it is required to consider the permanence provisons of the plan, i.e. whether the plan is for the child to live with parent, family or friends, to be adopted or other long-term care arrangement such as foster care. The court is not required to consider the remainder of the plan.

Procedure

Either the local authority or authorised person (NSPCC) can apply for a care order in respect of a child. If the NSPCC make the application the order will actually be made to the relevant local authority. Every person with parental responsibility for the child has automatic party status and must receive at least three days' notice of the application. The father of the child must also be notified, or reasonable steps taken to trace him, even if he does not have parental responsibility. The child has party status and a children's guardian will be appointed.

The principle of avoidance of delay will apply throughout care proceedings. Delay in children's cases has been acknowledged as a problem for some time and was considered in

'A Scoping Study on the Causes of Delay' (2002).[23] This study found that common reasons for delay included: unrealistic timetabling and poor enforcement of timetables, inadequate preparation time, more than one judge in a case and inadequate disclosure. In response to these and earlier concerns,[24] the *Protocol for Judicial Case Management of Public Law Children Act Cases* [2003] 2 FLR 719[25] was published with a view to achieving a significant reduction in delay. The aim of the protocol was to achieve more effective case management, address over-reliance on experts and ensure effective use of resources with target of completing cases within 40 weeks[26] but in *Re G (Protocol for Judicial Case Management in Public Law Children Act Cases: Application to Become Party in Family Proceedings)* [2004] EWHC 116 (Fam), the court cautioned that: 'The protocol is a tool to improving applying family justice and not, in the quest for speed and consistency to impair it.'

A Government review in 2006, found ongoing difficulties with court proceedings, including delay, despite the protocol and suggested further improvements, some of which were given effect by replacement of the protocol by a new Practice Direction, the *Public Law Outline: Guide to case management in Public Law proceedings* (**PLO**) (2008). The PLO introduced a more streamlined court process with four key stages in public law proceedings and was accompanied by a revised version of 'The Children Act 1989 Guidance and Regulations', Vol. 1, 'Court Orders: A Framework for the Care and Upbringing of Children' (**DCSF**, 2007).

Concerns continued beyond implementation of the PLO and, following the Family Justice Review and introduction of the Children and Families Act 2014, revised versions have been introduced of both the Public Law Outline (2014) and 'The Children Act 1989 Guidance and Regulations', Vol. 1, now entitled 'Court orders and pre-proceedings: For local authorities' (DfE, 2014).

The main elements at each of the stages are summarised below.

Pre-proceedings

The emphasis of the PLO is on much greater preparation before proceedings are issued. The local authority will complete a pre-proceedings checklist which shows the work done before proceedings. With the application the local authority should include the following materials:

- previous court orders;
- assessment materials relevant to the key issues including capacity to litigate, section 7 and s. 37 reports;
- social work chronology;
- social work statement and genogram;
- Care Plan;
- current assessments to which the social work statement refers and on which the local authority relies.

STAGE 1 *Issue and Allocation*

On Day 1 the Local Authority files the application with the court and copies to CAFCASS.

On Day 2 the court allocates the case to a specified level of judge, serves documents on the parties and gives directions including:

- appointing children's guardian;
- appointing solicitor for the child if necessary;
- appointing a litigation friend if necessary;

- directions to file documents including a LA case summary, case analysis by the children's guardian, parent's response;
- requests for disclosure, e.g. to the police;
- arranging an advocates' meeting and setting a date for the Case Management Hearing (**CMH**);
- consider any requests for urgent preliminary CMH contested interim order.

STAGE 2 *Case Management Hearing*

An advocates' meeting must be held not later than 2 days before the CMH.

The CMH is held between day 12 and day 18, at which the court gives further directions, including:

- Drawing up the timetable for the child (taking into account important dates for the child, such as, significant educational steps, proposed placement changes), and timetable for the proceedings, with a view to dealing with the application without delay and within 26 weeks of the date the application was issues.
- Identifying any additional parties.
- Identifying the key issues.
- Identifying evidence necessary for the court to determine key issues including whether it is necessary for any expert witnesses to be instructed.
- Giving directions for any concurrent placement order proceedings.
- Listing the Issues Resolution Hearing and Final Hearing.

STAGE 3 *Issues Resolution Hearing* (**IRH**)

A further advocates' meeting is held no later than 7 days before the IRH.

Key issues to be determined by the court are identified at the IRH and may be resolved or narrowed by hearing evidence.

Final directions are given including filing the final care plan and setting a date for the final hearing.

The Children and Families Act 2014 (amending s. 32 Children Act 1989) gives statutory effect to a 26-week limit for the completion of care proceedings (see Figure 9.3). In one of a series of commentaries on the Family Justice Reforms; the President of the Family Division, Sir James Munby stated: 'My message is clear and uncompromising: this deadline can be met, it must be met, it will be met. And remember, 26 weeks is a deadline, not a target; it is a maximum, not an average or a mean. So many cases will need to be finished in less than 26 weeks'.

Nevertheless, there may be circumstances where it is necessary for an extension beyond 26 weeks to be granted. In the context of an application for a care and placement order, *Re B-S (Children)* [2013] EWCA Civ 1146:

> If despite all, the court does not have the kind of evidence we have identified, and is therefore not properly equipped to decide these issues, then an adjournment must be directed, even if this takes the case over 26 weeks. Where the proposal before the court is for non-consensual adoption, the issues are too grave, the stakes for all are too high, for the outcome to be determined by rigorous adherence to an inflexible timetable and justice thereby potentially denied.

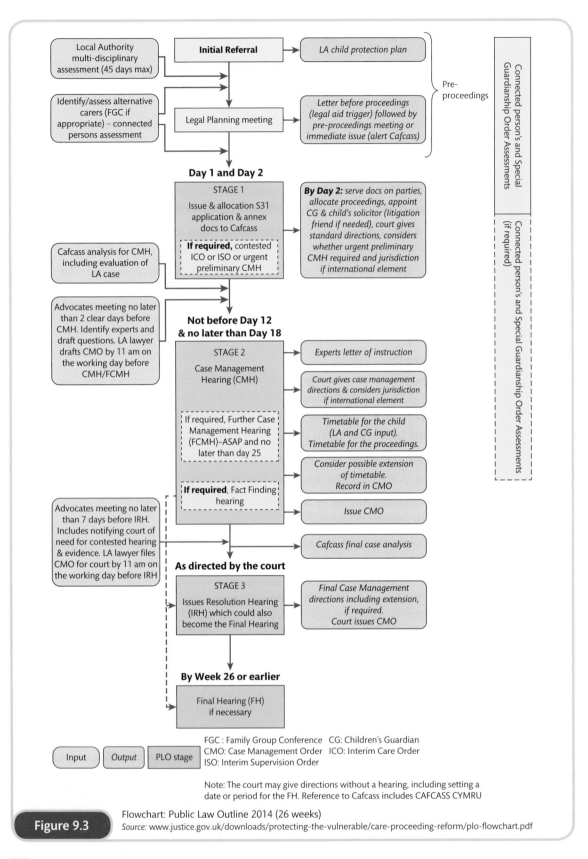

Local Authority multi-disciplinary assessment (45 days max)

Initial Referral → *LA child protection plan*

Identify/assess alternative carers (FGC if appropriate) – connected persons assessment

Legal Planning meeting → *Letter before proceedings (legal aid trigger) followed by pre-proceedings meeting or immediate issue (alert Cafcass)*

Pre-proceedings

Connected person's and Special Guardianship Order Assessments

Connected person's and Special Guardianship Order Assessments (if required)

Day 1 and Day 2

STAGE 1
Issue & allocation S31 application & annex docs to Cafcass

If required, contested ICO or ISO or urgent preliminary CMH

By Day 2: *serve docs on parties, allocate proceedings, appoint CG & child's solicitor (litigation friend if needed), court gives standard directions, considers whether urgent preliminary CMH required and jurisdiction if international element*

Cafcass analysis for CMH, including evaluation of LA case

Advocates meeting no later than 2 clear days before CMH. Identify experts and draft questions. LA lawyer drafts CMO by 11 am on the working day before CMH/FCMH

Not before Day 12 & no later than Day 18

STAGE 2
Case Management Hearing (CMH)

→ *Experts letter of instruction*

→ *Court gives case management directions & considers jurisdiction if international element*

If required, Further Case Management Hearing (FCMH)–ASAP and no later than day 25

→ *Timetable for the child (LA and CG input). Timetable for the proceedings.*

→ *Consider possible extension of timetable. Record in CMO*

If required, Fact Finding hearing

→ *Issue CMO*

Advocates meeting no later than 7 days before IRH. Includes notifying court of need for contested hearing & evidence. LA lawyer files CMO for court by 11 am on the working day before IRH

→ *Cafcass final case analysis*

As directed by the court

STAGE 3
Issues Resolution Hearing (IRH) which could also become the Final Hearing

Final Case Management directions including extension, if required. Court issues CMO

By Week 26 or earlier

Final Hearing (FH) if necessary

Input   Output   PLO stage

FGC : Family Group Conference   CG: Children's Guardian
CMO: Case Management Order   ICO: Interim Care Order
ISO: Interim Supervision Order

Note: The court may give directions without a hearing, including setting a date or period for the FH. Reference to Cafcass includes CAFCASS CYMRU

Flowchart: Public Law Outline 2014 (26 weeks)
Source: www.justice.gov.uk/downloads/protecting-the-vulnerable/care-proceeding-reform/plo-flowchart.pdf

Figure 9.3

Robust judicial case management will be the key. It is clear that extensions beyond 26 weeks should not often be granted, however the President indicated three possible contexts where this might be necessary, namely,

- Cases where it is obviously not possible to conclude in 26 weeks (heavy medical evidence with a separate fact-finding hearing, FDAC type cases, international cases or cases where special measures are required for the purposes of meeting the parental disabilities)
- Cares where something unexpected happens (late allegations or the emergence of a potential family carer late in the day)
- Cases where litigation failure by a party makes it unjust to conclude (as in *Re B-S (Children)*).

In *Re C (A Child)* [2014] EWCA Civ 128, the Court of Appeal provided guidance on the approach in cases involving parents with disabilities, in this instance a hearing disability. McFarlane LJ advised that 'Courts should not simply be driven by the 26-week deadline by which cases should be concluded. If there are aspects of a case that indicate the timescale for assessment cannot provide an effective and meaningful process because of the disabilities of one or more of the individuals involved, it is better to extend the timetable by a modest degree.'

Split hearings

Some cases will be dealt with as split hearings. The case is effectively split into a fact-finding hearing to establish whether the threshold criteria are met, followed by a 'welfare' hearing at which the court exercises its discretion as to what will be in the best interests of the child. Active case management and timetabling is essential to avoid delay, which has sometimes been a feature of split hearing cases (*Re Y and K (Children) (Care Proceedings: Split Hearing)* [2003] EWCA Civ 669).

The case of *Re H (Children) (Summary Determination of Issues)* [2002] EWCA Civ 1692 recognises that, in the course of care proceedings, negotiations will take place between the local authority and the parents as to findings of fact the court needs to make in order to determine whether the threshold criteria are met. It is understandable that parents will wish to avoid adverse findings where there are allegations of serious risk. The case concerned a girl, aged 5 at the time of the hearing. The local authority case was that she had suffered significant harm as a result of the fictitious accounts of epilepsy made by her mother which led to unnecessary anti-convulsive medication being prescribed and administered, at a higher dosage than prescribed, by her mother. In addition, the local authority stated that the mother had failed to keep medical appointments for the child and the unruly behaviour of her brother had harmed her. The local authority were prepared to rely on the latter allegations which the mother conceded and, at first instance, findings were not made as to whether the mother had fabricated the epilepsy and overdosed the medication. The child's guardian appealed and the Court of Appeal found that it was in the child's best interest for there to be findings as to the fabrication of epilepsy and overdose. Such findings were necessary in anticipation of future questions regarding access to the mother.

Human rights and child protection

The duty to protect children is reinforced by a number of European decisions. The United Kingdom has been found in breach of the European Convention on Human Rights for failure to protect children in the case of *Z* v. *United Kingdom* (2001) 34 EHRR 97. This case was an appeal from the House of Lords decision in *X (Minors)* v. *Bedfordshire County*

Council [1995] 3 All ER 353, where claims in negligence against the local authority were struck out. In this case four children suffered serious psychological disturbance and physical neglect by their parents. The European Court of Human Rights found the United Kingdom to be in breach of Art. 3, the right not to be subjected to inhuman or degrading treatment, by failing to protect the children from serious, long-term neglect and abuse. The local authority had a duty to protect the children from the time they first became aware of their treatment, in October 1987, but the children were not taken into care until April 1992. The court did not consider the application under Art. 8 (right to respect for family life), having found an Art. 3 breach. The court found, further, that as the children in these applications were unable to pursue a remedy in damages against the local authority, the United Kingdom was in breach of Art. 13, in not providing an effective remedy. The court therefore awarded damages and costs to the applicants. This decision limits further the extent to which claims against the local authority will be barred on grounds of public policy.

Procedural aspects of a case may also be challenged under the Human Rights Act 1998, as in the case of *TP* v. *United Kingdom* (2002) 34 EHRR 42. It was found that the local authority had failed to respect the family life of the mother (TP), contrary to Art. 8, as she was not properly involved in the decision-making process regarding her child who was taken into care. The local authority had failed to disclose all the information about the child's allegations of sexual abuse (in the form of a video).

In *P, C and S* v. *United Kingdom* (2002) 35 EHRR 1075, the court found that lack of legal representation in care proceedings violated the guarantee of effective access to courts under Art. 6 and the procedural guarantees of Art. 8.

The case concerned the newborn child of a mother who had been charged in the United States of cruelty to a previous child (induced illness syndrome). The child was removed at birth. The mother represented herself in four-week care proceedings. Issues of contact were not dealt with in those proceedings. The court commented that the 'procedures adopted not only gave the appearance of unfairness but prevented the applicants from putting their case in a proper and effective manner on the issues that were important to them'. It also warned that:

> ... the taking of a new born baby into public care at the moment of its birth is an extremely harsh measure. There must be extraordinarily compelling reasons before a baby can be physically removed from its mother against her will ... as a consequence of a procedure in which neither she nor her partner had been involved.

The courts must always ensure that orders made are no more intrusive than necessary and a proportionate response. So, for example, in *T (A Child)* [2009] EWCA Civ 121, the local authority successfully appealed against the making of a care order in a case where it had applied for a supervision order and was supported by the guardian in this. The court did not have good reason to impose the more draconian order.

Human rights complaints arising before the final care order should normally be dealt with in the context of the care proceedings by that court. There is no need for a separate application and any human rights claims should be brought to the court's attention at the earliest opportunity. If necessary, the whole case may be transferred for the attention of a High Court judge (*Re L (Care Proceedings: Human Rights Claims)* [2003] EWHC 665 (Fam), confirmed in *Re V (A Child) (Care Proceedings: Human Rights Claims)* [2004] EWCA Civ 54).

Contact with children in care

There is a statutory presumption in favour of contact, contained in s. 34:

s. 34

(1) Where a child is in the care of a local authority, the authority shall … allow the child reasonable contact with –

(a) his parents;

(b) any guardian of his;

(c) where there was a residence order in force with respect to the child immediately before the care order was made, the person in whose favour the order was made; and

(d) where, immediately before the care order was made, a person had care of the child by virtue of an order made in the exercise of the High Court's inherent jurisdiction with respect to children, that person.

(CA 1989)

The local authority must apply to the court if it wishes to terminate contact, unless under s. 34(6) it is necessary to refuse contact in order to safeguard and promote the child's welfare. This power of refusal lasts for a maximum period of seven days, after which approval of the court is required. The arrangements for contact must be considered by the court and the purpose of contact must be clear. Section 34 may be used to achieve phased rehabilitation between parent and child or to enable a level of ongoing contact even if rehabilitation is unlikely. Subject to the restriction on terminating contact, after a care order is made, the contact arrangements are largely a matter for local authority discretion. The Court of Appeal held, in *Re W (A Minor) (Parental Contact: Prohibition)* [2002] 1 FCR 752, that the court could not prohibit a local authority into whose care a child had been placed from permitting parental contact with the child.

Re F (Minors) (Care Proceedings: Termination of Contact) [2000] 2 FCR 481 is a case which tested the human rights compliance of s. 34. The High Court found that nothing about s. 34(4) of the Children Act 1989, which gave the court power to authorise a local authority to terminate contact with children in its care, was not human rights compliant when used in appropriate cases as part of a care plan approved by the court. In this case, where there was no prospect of returning children to their mother, and the local authority care plan proposed adoption, leave to terminate contact had been granted. The mother claimed that this was an infringement of her rights under Arts. 6(1) and 8 of the ECHR. It was held that the court had correctly balanced the respective rights of the mother and the children to reach a conclusion which was in the children's best interests and had acted proportionately. A further decision on s. 34(4) gives guidance on its use and warns that 'a s. 34(4) order should not be made … merely against the possibility that circumstances may change in such a way as to make termination of contact desirable' (*Re S (Children) (Termination of Contact)* [2004] EWCA Civ 1397). In *Re K (Contact)* [2008] EWHC 540 (Fam), a s. 34(4) order was made authorising refusal of contact. Supervised contact between the mother and her baby had been poor and the baby's safety prompted the order following one occasion where the parents had a physical fight in which the mother threw the baby to the contact supervisor.

Supervision orders

The same threshold criteria must be satisfied for a supervision order as for a care order (s. 31). However, the effect of a supervision order is different from that of a care order. Under a supervision order the local authority does not acquire parental responsibility. The focus of a supervision order is ensuring that local authorities can provide certain services for the child and family and monitor the situation whilst the child remains with parents. The reasons for a supervision order being made rather than a care order were considered in the case of *Re O (A Child) (Supervision Order: Future Harm)* [2001] EWCA Civ 16, discussed above. It is crucial that the choice of order reflects a proportionate interference by the state with the right to family life. It was also noted in *Re D (Care or Supervision Order)* [2000] that 'courts should not saddle local authorities with care orders if it really is not necessary to do so, when they have so many demands on their resources'.[27]

A supervisor will be appointed to 'advise, assist and befriend' the child and to take steps to ensure the supervision order is complied with (s. 35). The supervision order may include a variety of requirements such as where the child is to live, for the child to take part in specified activities or present himself to a particular person at a specified place, for the parents' attendance at courses and for the local authority to supervise parental contact. However, the only real sanction for failure to comply with any of the requirements is for the supervisor to seek a variation or discharge of the supervision order. A supervision order initially lasts for up to one year; it can be extended by the courts for a maximum period of three years. It is possible for an interim supervision order to be made in the period prior to the full hearing of an application for a care or supervision order.

The role of the guardian during the operation of a supervision order was considered in *Re MH (A Child) (Supervision Orders); Re SB (Children) (Supervision Orders)* [2002] 1 FCR 251. The court held that s. 12 of the Criminal Justice and Courts Services Act 2000 (CJCSA 2000), which defines the function of CAFCASS, alters the position established in *Re G (A Minor) (Social Worker: Disclosure)* [1996] 2 All ER 65. In the latter case the court found that the guardian had no function once proceedings were completed. Section 12 states:

---

s. 12

(b) … where a supervision order is made, the proceedings are not to be treated as concluded until the order has ceased to have effect.

(CJCSA 2000)

The judge interpreted this provision so that the guardian's functions will continue after the order, effectively expanding the role of the guardian. This decision has major resource implications for CAFCASS, although it should be noted that the court retains the power to terminate the guardian's appointment.

Discharge and variation

Section 39 of the Children Act 1989 deals with discharge of a care or supervision order and variation, substitution or extension of a supervision order. It is possible for the child, local authority or any person with parental responsibility to apply for the discharge of a care order, or to substitute the order with a supervision order. An application to vary or discharge a supervision order can be made by the child, his supervisor or any person with parental responsibility, or the person with whom the child is living.

Discharge and variation of care orders

If a Child Arrangements Order with a residence element (previously a residence order) is made, this will discharge a care order (CA 1989, s. 91(1)). (See Chapter 8.) The range of people who may apply for a Child Arrangements Order is wider than those entitled to apply for the discharge of a care order. In particular, only fathers with parental responsibility can apply for the discharge of a care order, whereas a parent, including fathers without parental responsibility, can apply for a Child Arrangements Order. There are no specific conditions to be met for discharge or substitution; the court will simply consider the welfare of the child. A children's guardian will be appointed, preferably the guardian who acted in the previous proceedings because prior knowledge of the case is likely to reduce delays.

Variation, extension or discharge of supervision orders

Supervision orders will initially be made for up to one year and may be extended to a maximum of three years on the application of the local authority (Children Act 1989, Sch. 3, para. 6). An application to extend a supervision order should not normally be made until the order is at least nine months old. In *Wakefield District Council* v. *T* [2008] EWCA Civ 199, the court purported to make a supervision order for three years by making a 12-month order and at the same time extending it for a further two years. The Court of Appeal confirmed that the clear purpose of the Children Act 1989 is for the initial supervision order to be made for 12 months with the possibility of extension by a separate application if further supervision is required.

Supervision orders may be varied or revoked in relation to any specific obligation imposed on the supervisor, directions dealing with psychiatric and medical examination and treatment, where the requirements of the supervisor are not met. A supervision order cannot be varied to a care order. The child's welfare is the paramount consideration in any application to vary, extend or discharge a supervision order.

Reflect

Consider the factors that would suggest a court is more likely to make:

- a care order; or
- a supervision order.

The role of the children's guardian

In 1984 the guardian *ad litem* service was established. Its origins can be traced to the Maria Colwell inquiry report, published in 1974, which stated: 'It would have been of assistance to the court to have had the views of an independent social worker.'[28] In addition, Art. 12 of the United Nations Convention on the Rights of the Child states:

> ## Art. 12
>
> **(2)** ... the child shall in particular be provided the opportunity to be heard in any judicial or administrative proceedings affecting the child either directly or through a representative or an appropriate body in a manner consistent with the procedural rules of national law.
>
> (UNCRC 1989)

The children's guardian (previously the guardian *ad litem*) is now one of three services, together with the Court Welfare Service and functions of the Official Solicitor in representing children, amalgamated into the Children and Family Court Advisory and Support Service (CAFCASS).

The role of the guardian was extended by the Children Act 1989, as was the range of circumstances in which a guardian will be appointed. Section 41 of the Children Act 1989 provides that, in specified proceedings, the court shall appoint a children's guardian for the child concerned unless satisfied that it is not necessary to do so in order to safeguard his interests. Once appointed, the guardian is under a duty to safeguard the interests of the child (s. 41(2)(b)). Guidance and rules expand on the duties of the guardian, which include: assisting the court with timetabling and avoidance of delay; ensuring that the child has an effective voice in court by representing the ascertainable wishes and feelings of the child; attending court and directions hearings; and preparing a report advising the court on matters including the child's level of understanding, the child's wishes, the order to be made, if any, and any other matter on which the court requests an opinion.

The guardian is a skilled professional, usually a professionally qualified social worker with at least five years' post-qualifying experience. Dale-Emberton (2001) describes the role as including: investigating the background to a case; accessing information and analysing and evaluating documents; gathering information through interviews with the child in a way that is sensitive and age appropriate, and also with the parents, other relatives and professionals; managing a case to avoid delay; and ensuring people with parental responsibility are aware of the proceedings.[29]

From the child's perspective, the guardian can provide the means to ensure that the child's own views are presented to the court and enable the child to feel part of the process, even if the child does not attend any court hearings. In research, where children were asked to name the most important characteristics of a guardian, 71 per cent said it was the ability to listen to children and 43 per cent said it was the guardian's role in explaining things to children.[30]

The guardian will also appoint a solicitor for the child. The solicitor will normally be appointed from the Law Society's Children Panel, being one with special expertise in childcare cases. The solicitor's role is to give legal advice to the guardian and to present the case to court, instructed by the guardian. Even if the child is not likely to be present at any court hearings, it would be good practice for the solicitor to meet the child. There are some cases where the guardian's instructions to the solicitor are in conflict with the child's expressed wishes. In these circumstances, if the child is assessed as competent to give instructions, then the solicitor will take instructions direct from the child and advocate the views of the child, not a recommendation as to what is in the child's best interests. If the guardian requires legal representation, another solicitor will be appointed. The court ultimately decides whether the child is competent to give instructions, but will be advised by the guardian on this point (*Re M (Minors) (Care Proceedings: Child's Wishes)* [1994] 1 FLR 749).

The specified proceedings in which a guardian must be appointed are:

- applications for a care order or supervision order;
- family proceedings where the court has directed the local authority to investigate a child's circumstances under s. 37(1);
- applications for discharge of a care order or variation or discharge of a supervision order;
- an application to substitute a supervision order for a care order;
- proceedings where the court is considering making a Child Arrangements Order for a child subject of a care order;
- applications for contact with a child subject of a care order;
- associated appeals;
- applications for secure accommodation orders;
- applications to change a child's surname or remove a child from the jurisdiction, in respect of a child subject to a care order;
- applications to extend a supervision order;
- applications for parental orders (Human Fertilisation and Embryology Act 1991, s. 30);
- contested applications for adoption or placement.

In carrying out any of the above roles, the guardian has a right of access to local authority records. Section 42 of the Children Act 1989 provides that the guardian shall have the right at all reasonable times to examine and take copies of records held by the local authority relating to the child in question.

The guardian's report is an important document in care and other child-related proceedings. It will be read by the parties, including the child in some cases, their legal representatives, local authority social workers, the magistrates or judge, and any expert witnesses who may be called upon to comment on its contents.

The PLO introduces some changes to the role of the children's guardian in care proceedings. The guardian has a key role in providing information to the court at an earlier stage and throughout the duration of the proceedings, rather than the previous practice of preparing a single lengthy report for the final hearing. Guardians will be expected to provide a case analysis at an earlier stage for the court (an initial case analysis by Day 10 in time for the advocates' meeting) with relevant updates. The exact format of the report will vary depending on the nature of the application but since the PLO, in care proceedings it is likely to be presented as a highly focused 'Case Analysis' with evidence presented under the following key headings:

- Significant harm threshold analysis
- Case Management requirements
- Analysis of parenting capacity to meet child's needs
- Child impact analysis
- Early permanence analysis including proposed placement and contact framework
- Updates since last filed analysis
- Recommendations.

Research suggests that guardians make a significant contribution to the formulation of care plans (McCausland, 2000).[31]

Expert witnesses

The expert witness has had a significant role in child care cases. In cases where sexual, physical or emotional abuse is suspected, medical evidence may be determinative. Other types of experts may give evidence (e.g. addressing the effect of addictive behaviour or mental health problems, risk assessments and relationship assessments) and over recent years it seemed that the courts were becoming increasingly reliant on expert evidence.[32] Changes introduced by the Children and Families Act 2014, s.136, are likely to reverse that trend as experts will only be instructed where 'necessary'.

Expert evidence in care proceedings, which should have a less adversarial tone than other proceedings, is adduced to assist the court in reaching its decision. An expert may be requested by one or other party or by joint request and the opinion given should not show bias towards any party. There is an expectation that the parties will use an 'agreed' expert where possible. As it would be contempt of court to disclose confidential documents to a person beyond the parties to the case, an expert can become involved only with the approval of the court, and will usually be appointed and terms of enquiry specified at a directions hearing. Specifically, an expert cannot examine or assess the child without leave of the court.[33] As expert evidence will include opinion, it is essential that professional integrity is established and can withstand cross-examination. Opinion may be required as to whether a particular injury is consistent with the claim as to how it occurred. The judgment in *Re R (A Minor) (Expert Evidence)* [1991] 1 FLR 291 provides guidance on opinion evidence in family proceedings and suggests that expert opinion evidence should be objective, properly researched and based on consideration of all material facts.[34] In *Re A (Family Proceedings: Expert Witness)* [2001] 1 FLR 723, the court had the opportunity to comment on the role of the expert. In this case, a father who was having supervised contact with his two children at a contact centre surreptitiously videoed a session; the video was sent via his solicitors to a child psychologist, who was asked to provide a report on the father's interaction with the children. No permission had been sought from the court and no notice was given to the mother or her legal representatives. The judgment stated that in family proceedings it was wholly inappropriate for an expert witness to be instructed without the knowledge of the court; nor should experts accept instructions in the absence of court authority and awareness of the court order relating to their instructions.

The courts clearly have high expectations of experts. In *Re X (Non-Accidental Injury: Expert Evidence)* [2001] 2 FLR 90, an expert gave the opinion that a 20-month-old child's fractures were caused by temporary brittle bone disorder, a condition which other experts contested the existence of. Singer J was critical of the expert's evidence and his conduct and ruled that future applications to seek a report from him should not be granted without the sanction of a High Court judge.[35]

Human rights arguments were raised in the case of *L v. United Kingdom (Disclosure of Expert Evidence)* [2000] 2 FCR 145. The court in care proceedings ordered the mother to disclose an adverse expert's report. She argued that this was a breach of Arts. 6 and 8 of the ECHR. The court found that the obligation to disclose the report did not deprive the mother of her right to a fair trial, as she had legal representation and was able to present her case. The court did find a breach of Art. 8 (right to respect for private and family life), but held that this was justified by Art. 8(2) because it was necessary for protection of the child's interest.

Further guidance on the role of expert witnesses was given in *Oldham Metropolitan Borough Council v. GW and PW* [2007] EWHC 136 (Fam), where the court warned against the expert straying into the role of decision-maker. The court directed that: local authorities should always write a letter of instruction when asking a potential witness for a report or opinion;

once instructed, experts in their advice to the court should conform to the best practice of their clinical training. They should identify the range of opinion on the question to be answered, giving reasons for the opinion held. The use of a balance sheet approach to the factors that supported or undermined an opinion could be of great assistance.

In *Re L (Care: Threshold Criteria)* [2007] 1 FLR 2050, a retrial took place because the expert had acted outside of the letter of instruction and given an opinion on the question of harm which she had not been asked for. It was a case where concerns for the children arose from the learning difficulties of the parents. The judgment gives a reminder that compulsory powers can only be used when the threshold criteria are met and not on the basis that substitute parents might provide greater intellectual stimulus for the children. 'Such social engineering was wholly impermissible.'

In *Re TG (Care Proceedings: Case Management: Expert Evidence)* [2013] EWCA Civ 5, a father claimed his baby had sustained injuries from being tipped out of a bouncy chair by his sibling. The court was right to refuse permission to instruct an expert biomechanical engineer to give evidence on tipping and impact forces as that went into the realms of speculation and could not be described as 'reasonably required' evidence.

In *Re H-L (A Child) (Care Proceedings: Expert Evidence)* [2013] EWCA Civ 655 the new test for instructing an expert was considered. Expert evidence must be 'necessary to assist the court to resolve the proceeding' under the Family Procedure Rules 2010 r. 25.1. Sir James Munby endorsed a quote from another judgment (*Re P (Placement Orders: Parental Consent)* [2008] EWCA Civ 535, [2008] 2 FLR 625), which said necessary 'has a meaning lying somewhere between "indispensable" on the one hand and "useful", "reasonable" or "desirable" on the other hand', having 'the connotation of the imperative, what is demanded rather than what is merely optional or reasonable or desirable'. National Standards for Expert Witnesses in family courts have been introduced (**MJ**, 2013) to ensure that the expert:

- has knowledge appropriate to the case,
- has been active in the area of work or practice and have sufficient experience of the issues relevant to the case,
- is regulated/accredited to a regulatory body where appropriate,
- has relevant qualifications and training,
- complies with safeguarding requirements.

Wardship and the inherent jurisdiction

The vast majority of family and child law cases are now considered by a judge at the appropriate level in the new Family Court. However, the Family Division of the High Court has retained the exercise of the inherent jurisdiction and may make a child a ward of court. Wardship and the inherent jurisdiction are not one and the same. Wardship is in fact an exercise of the inherent jurisdiction under which the court obtains parental responsibility for the child and no major step in the child's life can be taken without the consent of the court. Prior to the Children Act 1989, local authorities were able to apply to make a child a ward of court and obtain a care order in respect of that child as part of the wardship jurisdiction.

Section 100 of the Children Act 1989 imposed restrictions on local authority use of wardship. This section provides that the High Court can no longer place a ward of court in the care or under supervision of a local authority, cannot require a child to be accommodated by a local authority, cannot make a child who is subject to a care order a ward of court or give the local authority the power to determine questions relating to the exercise of parental responsibility for a child. As a balance to this restriction, other provisions in the Act were designed to reduce the need for local authorities to have recourse to wardship. Elements of the wardship jurisdiction were introduced in the form of specific issue orders and prohibited steps orders (s. 8) (see discussion in Chapter 8) and the breadth of the threshold criteria covered situations where wardship would have been utilised to supplement the old grounds for intervention (e.g. in cases where concerns relate to future harm). It remains possible for local authorities to have recourse to the inherent jurisdiction in limited circumstances, having first obtained leave of the court (s. 100(3)). The court will grant leave only if the local authority could not achieve its objective through any other order available to the court, and there is reasonable cause to believe the child will suffer significant harm if the court does not act. So, in *C* v. *Salford City Council* [1994] 2 FLR 926, a wardship application by foster parents was dismissed because an application for a residence order gave the court all the powers it needed in the particular case.

The inherent jurisdiction lends itself to situations where a one-off major decision is required rather than cases where ongoing involvement of the court is required. Case law has produced examples of the types of circumstances that may justify leave being granted. Declarations may be made by the court in relation to the lawfulness of medical treatment and surgery. In *Re C (A Minor) (Detention for Medical Treatment)* [1997] 2 FLR 180, the inherent jurisdiction was exercised to authorise treatment of a 16-year-old child suffering from anorexia nervosa; and in *Re A (Children) (Conjoined Twins: Surgical Separation)* [2000] 4 All ER 961, a declaration was made by the court against the wishes of the parents. Wardship may be used in threatened child abduction cases where the court wishes to retain a child in this country because it automatically makes removal of the child from the jurisdiction illegal.

If there are concerns about a child having contact with an adult (not a parent), then wardship may be used to prevent the contact, as, for example, in *Re R (A Minor) (Contempt: Sentence)* [1994] 2 All ER 144, where a 14-year-old girl was having a relationship with a married man. An injunction prohibited contact and on breach he was sentenced for contempt of court.

Screening child care workers

It has been possible for some time for criminal record checks to be made in respect of prospective workers who will work with children.[36] This area is now addressed in the Safeguarding Vulnerable Groups Act 2006, which establishes a vetting and barring scheme. This legislation was introduced partly in response to the Bichard Report. Recommendation 19 states:

> New arrangements should be introduced requiring those who wish to work with children, or vulnerable adults, to be registered. The register would confirm that there is no known reason why an individual should not work with these client groups.

It replaces the previous register established by the Protection of Children Act 1999.[37]

The scheme operates in the same way in respect of those working with children and vulnerable adults, but information will be held on two separate lists. Inclusion on the list prevents an individual from working with children. (The scheme is discussed in more detail in Chapter 17.)

Sex offenders

The names of sex offenders are held on the Sex Offender Register established under the Sex Offenders Act 1997. In addition to existing offences such as rape, the Sexual Offences Act 2003 includes a range of 'abuse of trust' offences where a person engages in sexual activity with a child in relation to whom they are in a position of trust. A Criminal Records Bureau check will reveal convictions under this Act and also whether a person is named on the Sex Offender Register. It is possible for parents, carers and guardians to ask the police if a person known to them is a child sex offender under the child sex offender disclosure scheme (sometimes referred to as Sarah's law).

The Criminal Justice and Courts Services Act 2000 provides additional remedies to restrict unsuitable people from working with children. It is possible to add a disqualification order to the sentence of certain offenders who have abused children. The effect of this order is to ban the person from applying for paid or unpaid work, accepting or carrying out work with children for a period of at least ten years. Breach of the order is a criminal offence. The offences that can lead to a ban are contained in Sch. 4 and, in addition to sexual offences, include murder, assault or cruelty to a child. The disqualification order can be added only to a custodial sentence of 12 months or more.

Child abuse inquiries

The first major child abuse inquiry was held in 1945, following the death of Denis O'Neill, a child in foster care. It prompted the Children Act 1948 and the formation of children's departments. Since the 1970s the number of inquiries appears to have gradually increased and in many cases the media have seized the opportunity to scapegoat individuals named in the reports and discredit Social Services Departments. Such an approach does little to instil public confidence in social services and can be very damaging to morale. In fact, inquiries can have a significant positive influence on both professional practice and the law. The positioning of law as a key element in social work training is partly attributable to the influence of inquiries. This section will consider the types of inquiries that may be held, their functions and the key findings of (a selection of) inquiries which have directly shaped the law.[38]

Types of inquiries/reviews

Inquiries will be held following the death or serious injury of a child. The inquiry may be an internal case review, an external inquiry with an independent chair (which may be held in public or private), or an inquiry commissioned by the Secretary of State. It is possible for a public inquiry to be held following an internal case review of the same case. An inquiry may be conducted in either an inquisitorial or adversarial style. Chapter 5 of the new 'Working Together' deals with child death review processes, and Chapter 4 addresses serious case reviews in the context of learning and improvement. Serious case reviews must be led by an independent person and must be published.

The functions of an inquiry are to:

- ascertain the facts of the case;
- critically outline the role and functions of relevant agencies;
- make recommendations for legislation, guidance and practice;
- learn lessons for the future;

- meet public concern; and
- establish responsibility.[39]

Key findings from public inquiries

The most consistent findings of inquiry reports have been the failure of inter-agency work and cooperation, and the need for better training. Specific findings in particular reports have led directly to changes in professional practice and the law. A selection of examples are cited below.

Maria Colwell (1974)[40]

- Maria, aged 7, was killed by her step-father. She had been returned to her mother after a five-year period living with her aunt, following concerns over general neglect. Her care order was revoked and replaced with a supervision order. She was undernourished and severely beaten.
- DHSS instigated the system of Area Child Protection Committees, case conferences and at risk registers. The Children Act 1975 introduced the requirement for a guardian *ad litem* to act in cases where revocation of a care order was sought.

Jasmine Beckford (1985)[41]

- Jasmine died, aged 4, having been beaten over a period of time by her step-father and severely undernourished. He had previously been convicted of causing injuries to Jasmine and her sister in 1981. The children were home on trial when Jasmine died. She had been seen by her social worker only once in the ten-month period before her death. The report claims that her death was both predictable and preventable.
- DHSS placed greater emphasis on 'protection' and child abuse registers were renamed child protection registers.

Kimberley Carlile (1987)[42]

- Kimberley, aged 4, was killed by her step-father, who was subsequently convicted for her murder. She had multiple bruising and had scars and had previously been beaten and starved.
- The report recommended the introduction of a child assessment order, subsequently included in the Children Act 1989.

Tyra Henry (1987)[43]

- Tyra, aged 22 months, was killed by her father while a care order was in force. The report found that Tyra's mother was the main focus of social services work, rather than Tyra. The report addressed the issue of cultural stereotyping and noted that there was an assumption that Tyra's Afro-Carribean grandmother would find a way to cope.
- The introduction of 'care plans' can be traced back to this report.

The Cleveland Report (1988)[44]

- In 1987, 121 children were removed from their families in Cleveland under place of safety orders on suspicion of sexual abuse. Heavy reliance was placed on the use of the anal reflex dilatation test as a diagnosis of sexual abuse. Many of the parents were denied access to their children while under place of safety orders.
- The report made the notable statement that 'a child is a person not an object of concern'. It recommended greater rights for parents and children including statements that

children should not be subjected to unnecessary medical examinations. Recommendations were incorporated into 'Working Together' guidelines including a policy change in favour of parents attending case conferences.

- A number of provisions of the Children Act 1989 may be traced to the Cleveland report, including: child's right of refusal of medical examination; local authority ability to make provision for an alleged abuser to be accommodated so that the child could remain at home; reduction in duration of emergency protection order (EPO) compared with longer place of safety order; presumption that parents will have access to their child during an EPO.

Pin-down (1991)[45]

- The Pin-down report found that physical and emotional abuse of children and young people in homes in Staffordshire masqueraded as accepted practice for the control and discipline of the young people.

- Following the Pin-down report, the Department of Health set up a general inquiry into the provision of residential care. The 'Utting Report'[46] ensued and contained recommendations designed to raise standards in residential care, many of which have been incorporated into the Care Standards Act 2000.

Victoria Climbié (2003)

- The report of the Victoria Climbié inquiry, chaired by Lord Laming, was set up following Victoria Climbié's tragic death on 25 February 2000. The report details a catalogue of administrative, managerial and professional failure. It outlines a number of occasions upon which the most minor and basic intervention on the part of the staff concerned could have made a material difference to the eventual outcome.

- Lord Laming made the following statement:

  … the legislative framework is fundamentally sound. The gap is in its implementation. Having considered all the evidence it is not to the often hapless front-line staff that I direct most criticism for the failure to protect Victoria. True their performance often fell well short of an acceptable standard of work. But the greatest failure rests with the senior managers and members of the organisations concerned whose responsibility it was to ensure that the services they provided to children such as Victoria were properly financed, staffed and able to deliver good quality services to children and families. They must be accountable.

- The report contains 108 recommendations. Key recommendations have been implemented by the Children Act 2004 and the 'Every Child Matters: Change for Children' policy and include organisational changes for social services, establishment of Local Safeguarding Children Boards and a duty to cooperate to safeguard and promote welfare.

'Baby Peter' (2009)

- Lord Laming was asked to produce a report on the progress being made to implement effective safeguarding arrangements for children since implementation of the 'Every Child Matters' agenda. Specifically, 'the task was to evaluate the good practice that has been developed since the publication of the report of the Independent Statutory Inquiry following the death of Victoria Climbié' to identify the barriers that are now preventing good practice becoming standard practice, and recommend actions to be taken to make systematic improvements in safeguarding children across the country'.[47] He calls for a 'change in culture' and a 'step change in the arrangements to protect children from harm'.

- A key recommendation is the revision of 'Working Together to Safeguard Children', to set out clear expectations at all points where concerns about a child's safety are received, ensuring intake/duty teams have sufficient training and expertise to take referrals and that staff have immediate, on-site support available from an experienced social worker.

Child protection and the criminal law

In addition to the civil structure for child protection provided by the Children Act 1989, in many cases of child abuse a criminal offence will be committed. These offences range from indecent assault through to rape and murder. The decision on whether to prosecute a perpetrator of abuse rests with the police and ultimately the Crown Prosecution Service. The possibility of a criminal trial does impact on the civil child protection process, however, particularly in relation to good practice in interviewing children (discussed further below), and inter-agency work with the police. The courts have consistently stated that the existence of criminal proceedings should not delay the civil proceedings, where the primary objective is to protect the child. Wilson LJ noted that it was 'generally unwise for the family court to await the outcome of criminal proceedings in the hope that either a conviction or … an implosion of the prosecution case would in effect resolve matters for the purposes of the family proceedings' in *Re F-H (Dispensing with Fact-Finding Hearing)* [2008] EWCA Civ 1249.

A list of offences against children is contained in Sch. 1 to the Children and Young Persons Act 1933, and the term 'Schedule One Offender' has been used to refer to a person who has committed such an offence. Following a 2005 review of the Schedule, a Home Office Circular[48] to the police and social services (amongst others) states that the term 'is ill-defined and, to a certain extent, unhelpful'. It suggests that the term should be replaced by 'a person identified as presenting a risk, or potential risk, to children'.

Some of the criminal offences that may be committed against a child are outlined below:

- Any person over the age of 16 who has responsibility for a child, who wilfully assaults, ill treats, neglects, abandons, or exposes him, or causes or procures him to be assaulted, ill treated, neglected, abandoned, or exposed, in a manner likely to cause him unnecessary suffering or injury to health, shall be guilty of an offence (Children and Young Persons Act 1933, s. 1).

- To unlawfully abandon or expose any child, under the age of 2, whereby the child's life is endangered or health is likely to be permanently injured (Offences Against the Person Act 1861, s. 27).

- A range of specific child sexual offences are contained in the Sexual Offences Act 2003,[49] including: sexual activity with a child (s. 9); causing or inciting a child to engage in sexual acitivity (s. 10); engaging in sexual activity in the presence of a child (s. 11); meeting a child following sexual grooming; abuse of position of trust offences (ss. 16–24); familial child sexual offences replace incest (ss. 25–29); abuse of children through prostitution and pornography; rape and assault of a child under 13 (ss. 5–8).

- Sexual intercourse with a girl under 16 unless the man is under 24, believes her to be over 16 and it is a first offence (Sexual Offences Act 1956, s. 6).

- Assault, grievous bodily harm or wounding (Offences Against the Person Act 1861, ss. 47 and 20).
- Causing or allowing the death of a child (or vulnerable adult) also referred to as familial homicide (Domestic Violence, Crime and Victims Act 2004, s. 5).[50] The offence carries a maximum sentence of 14 years. It will apply in circumstances where it is unclear who in the household actually caused a child's death. It will be possible to charge more than one person with causing or failing to protect the child. The mother of a 4-month-old child was convicted of this offence in *R v. Stephens; sub nom R v. Mujuru* [2007] EWCA Crim 1249. The mother's partner had assaulted the child on one occasion and the mother did not seek treatment for the child. A further assault by the partner caused the child's death. The mother was convicted under s. 5 on the basis that she knew that her partner posed a significant risk of harm to her child and she had failed to take steps to prevent harm. The Court of Appeal ruled that the word 'significant' had no special meaning under the Act and whether the risk was significant was a matter for the jury to determine. As a further example, the parents of 'Baby Peter' were convicted of this offence.
- The Domestic Violence, Crime and Victims (Amendment) Act 2012 amends s. 5 of the Domestic Violence Crime and Victims Act 2004 by introducing a new offence of causing or allowing a child or vulnerable adult to suffer serious harm. This is in addition to the existing offence in s. 5 of causing or allowing the death of a child or vulnerable adult. The new offence of causing or allowing a child or vulnerable adult to suffer serious harm is punishable with up to 10 years' imprisonment. 'Serious harm' in this context is equivalent to grievous bodily harm.

Evidence of children[51]

In many cases of child abuse (particularly of a sexual nature) there will be no witnesses to the abuse. The child's account of what has happened can be the principal evidence relied upon. However, the allegation of abuse initially came to light (e.g. the child made a comment to a teacher), it will need to be fully investigated and this process will entail interviewing the child. The chapter on interviewing children in the Cleveland report remains pertinent and valuable reading. Enduring messages from chapter 12 of the report include:

- undesirability of referring to 'disclosure' interviews which prejudge the situation;
- interviews should be undertaken only by those with appropriate training and skills, and approached with an open mind;
- open-ended questions should be utilised;
- interviews should be at the child's pace and not be too long;
- the interview should take place in a suitable setting;
- the interview should be carefully recorded.

Where there is a possibility of legal proceedings (civil and/or criminal), it is essential that the purpose of any interview is clear. Due to rules of evidence, it is unlikely that a 'therapeutic' interview will be admissible as evidence in a criminal trial (*Re D (Minors) (Child Abuse: Interviews)* [1998] 2 FLR 11). In civil proceedings, as hearsay evidence is admissible, it is less likely that the child will be required to give evidence. This does not mean, however, that the above caution as to the purpose of the interview can be forgotten. Hearsay evidence of an interview which was carried out inappropriately, perhaps by excessive use of leading questions, will be of little value to the court.

Guidance as to the conduct of investigative interviews of children who are victims of abuse where a criminal prosecution is likely to be brought against the perpetrator, is contained in 'Achieving Best Evidence in Criminal Proceedings: Guidance on interviewing victims and witnesses, and guidance on using special measures (MJ 2011). The interview will be carried out jointly by officers from the police and social services who have received specialist training. The guidance extends beyond interviewing to pre-trial witness support and preparation at court stage. The guidance includes general principles for interviewing children which include: establishing rapport; truth and lies; establishing the purpose of the interview; raising issues of concern; obtaining a free narrative account; questions thereafter and closure.

The Youth Justice and Criminal Evidence Act 1999 makes further provision in the form of 'special measures' relating to the evidence of vulnerable and intimidated witnesses, including children. The court can exercise a degree of discretion as to the 'special measures' that may be made available to a witness but children under the age of 17 are automatically eligible for assistance (s. 16). Special measures include: use of screens so that the child cannot see the accused (s. 23); giving evidence by live link (s. 24); removal of wigs and gowns while the witness testifies (s. 26); giving evidence in private (in sexual offences cases), i.e. the press are removed (s. 25); video recording of evidence-in-chief (s. 27); video recording of cross-examination and re-examination (s. 28); examination of witness through an intermediary – this could be an interpreter or person with particular communication skills or a social worker (s. 29); and use of communication aids (s. 30). The case of *R (D)* v. *Camberwell Youth Court* [2005] UKHL 4 confirms that the use of special measures for child witnesses is compatible with Art. 6 ECHR, the right to a fair trial.

The most important of the new measures is, arguably, the new facility of video recording cross-examination and examination-in-chief, which answers the deficiency identified in the old law.[52] It has been noted that an advantage of pre-recorded cross-examination is that it may be possible for therapy for the child to start earlier as the risk of contaminating the child's evidence and undermining credibility is diminished.[53] Guidance, 'Provision of Therapy for Child Witnesses Prior to a Criminal Trial' (2001), clarifies the position on provision of therapy prior to criminal trial, including evaluation of different therapeutic techniques.[54]

The practice of children giving evidence has differed between the criminal and civil courts. Children as young as 4 have given evidence in criminal cases (*B* [2010] EWCA Crim, 4),but in civil care proceedings a presumption has operated that such involvement in the court process was likely to have a detrimental effect on the child's welfare. The Supreme Court in *Re W* [2010] UKSC 12, held that there was no longer a presumption or even a starting point against children giving evidence in such cases. The case involved care proceedings which were initiated following allegations of a 14-year-old child against her step-father. The court had to decide whether the step-father's application for the girl to give evidence should be granted.

Subsequently in response to that case, a Working Party of the Family Justice Council produced, 'Guidelines in relation to children giving evidence in family proceedings' [2012] 2 FLR. The guidelines confirm that the principal objective of the court when deciding whether a child should give evidence is to achieve a fair trial. The court must balance the possible advantage that the child's evidence will provide to determining the truth, against the possible damage to the child's welfare in giving evidence. To carry out that balancing exercise the guidance lists 22 factors for the court to consider, including the child's willingness to give evidence and the age, maturity, vulnerability, understanding, capacity and competence of the child. The court should also consider alternatives to the child giving live evidence at the hearing and, if the decision is made that a child should give evidence, steps to reduce the risk of harm should be taken including: the use of special measures and an intermediary, a familiarisation visit before the hearing, and a supporter present during the evidence. The guidance clearly states that a child should not be questioned directly by an alleged perpetrator. There are also suggestions about the conduct of the hearing and the appropriate style of advocacy to be adopted, with no 'Old Bailey' style cross examination.

Chapter summary

- Child protection is a high profile area of work; it is crucial to be alert to new research, developments in recognition of abuse, changes in the law, and to learn from the findings of inquiry reports. The main types of child abuse are physical, emotional and sexual abuse, and neglect.

- The duty to investigate concerns relating to possible child abuse is clearly imposed on social services under s. 47 of the Children Act 1989. However, other bodies, such as the housing and health authorities, are required to assist with those inquiries.

- The child protection conference is a crucial part of the investigative stage. At the conference recommendations will be made as to the future action to be taken to safeguard the child and promote his welfare. The child's family, and the child if of a sufficient age, should normally be involved in the conference.

- Short-term orders introduced by the Children Act 1989 include the child assessment order (CAO) and emergency protection order (EPO). The CAO is designed to cover situations where there are concerns about a child and lack of cooperation is preventing full assessment. The EPO can provide immediate protection for a child, for a period of eight days (extendable in exceptional circumstances to 15 days). The applicant for an EPO may be any person, the local authority or the NSPCC. In addition, the police have a power to remove and detain a child for a maximum period of 72 hours.

- The Family Law Act 1996 includes a power of exclusion, which enables the court to exclude an alleged abuser from the home, rather than removing the child. The order may be attached to an emergency protection order or an interim care order.

- Care and supervision orders may be made on the application of the local authority, where the threshold criteria are satisfied. There are three stages that must be completed before an order will be made: first, significant harm must be established; secondly, the harm must be attributable to the care the child has received or his being beyond parental control; and thirdly, the court will apply the welfare and 'no order' principle and the menu of orders before deciding which, if any, order to make. Aspects of the criteria are defined in the legislation and a body of case law has developed, which defines further terms. Interim care or supervision orders may be made while the investigation continues.

- Expert witnesses will provide evidence in child care cases if such evidence is considered 'necessary' to assist the court.

- Care proceedings must be completed within 26 weeks. The Public Law Outline sets out procedural steps.

- The local authority is obliged to prepare a care plan for a child it is proposing to look after, including children for whom an application for a care order is made. Its implementation will be kept under review by an Independent Reviewing Officer.

- There is a presumption in favour of contact between the child and significant others after a care order is made.

- In order that the child is independently represented in proceedings, a children's guardian, (CAFCASS), will be appointed. The guardian has a right of access to local authority records and must produce a report to court. If the child does not agree with the guardian's recommendation, and is of sufficient age and understanding, a separate solicitor may be appointed to represent the child.

- The High Court exercises the inherent jurisdiction and may make orders in respect of children according to their best interests, e.g. in relation to the lawfulness of proposed medical treatment. The wardship jurisdiction is also exercised by this court. Local authority access to wardship was restricted by the Children Act 1989.

- The Safeguarding Vulnerable Groups Act 2006 establishes the vetting and barring scheme to prevent unsuitable people from being engaged in child care positions.

- There is a range of criminal offences against children that may be committed in child abuse cases. 'Achieving Best Evidence in Criminal Proceedings' provides guidance on how joint interviews of a child by the police and social services are to be conducted where there is the possibility of a prosecution. Special measures may be utilised to make the witness experience less stressful for children.

Exercises

1. David and Julie are married with one child, Lucy, aged 4. The health visitor has noted that Lucy appears uncomfortable with strangers, is clingy, underweight and has a slight hearing impairment. She passed on these concerns to social services three weeks ago and a social worker is planning to visit the family this week. When the social worker visits, Julie tells her that David has left after a violent incident, which she refuses to discuss in any detail. Julie tells the social worker that, after he left, Lucy said she was glad he had gone and she 'didn't like the way that he touches me at night'. Julie says she does not want him to see Lucy ever again. Later that day a senior social worker visits and Julie retracts her earlier comments, saying it was all a misunderstanding and that David is expected home shortly. The social worker is concerned that Lucy may be at risk. What action should be taken?

2. Richard and Helen are a married couple in their mid-thirties. They have two daughters – Anne, aged 14, and Clare, aged 6. They recently separated. Their relationship has deteriorated dramatically since Richard became unemployed and he now believes that Helen is having an affair with a woman. The children are currently living with Helen, but Richard wishes to care for them full time. Helen has petitioned for divorce and Richard has applied for a residence order. At the same time, Anne and Clare's teachers have become concerned about both the girls' behaviour. Anne's schoolwork is deteriorating and she has been involved in bullying. Clare's teacher is particularly concerned because she has noticed that Clare has become increasingly withdrawn whereas previously she was very lively. One day the teacher notices that Clare has bruises on her thighs, but she refuses to explain their cause. The teacher passes this information to social services. When the social worker contacts the parents, Helen claims that Richard must have caused the bruises when he took the girls out at the weekend. Richard denies the allegation. Anne has told the school nurse that her father smacks her and her sister but does not want the nurse to tell anybody about this. Consider how this case should progress.

Websites

The Department of Health and Department for Education sites include many of the official publications referred to in this chapter, Circulars and Local Authority Social Services letters, and have useful 'What's New' sections:

www.doh.gov.uk
www.education.gov.uk

The CAFCASS website provides further information about the service and the role of the guardian:

www.cafcass.gov.uk

The National Society for the Prevention of Cruelty to Children (NSPCC):

www.nspcc.org.uk

Further reading

Department for Education (2011c) *The Munro Review of Child Protection: Final Report: A Child Centred System* (Cm 8062). London: DfE.

Detailed textbooks with a particular focus on child protection:

Lyon, C. (2003) *Child Abuse* (3rd edn). Bristol: Family Law, Jordan Publishing.
Holt, K. (2014) *Child Protection*. Basingstoke: Palgrave Macmillan.

A selection of articles provide critiques of various aspects of the child protection process. In relation to short-term intervention, see:

Lavery, R. (1996) 'The child assessment order – a reassessment' 8(1) *Child and Family Law Quarterly*, p. 41.
Masson, J. (2002) 'Police protection – protecting whom?' 24(3) *Journal of Social Work*, p. 72.
Masson, J. (2005) 'Emergency intervention to protect children: using and avoiding legal controls' 17(1) *Child and Family Law Quarterly*, p. 1.

Aspects of the child protection process and perspectives of professionals and parents are considered in:

Booth, T., Booth, W. and McConnell, D. (2004) 'Parents with learning difficulties, care proceedings and the family courts: threshold decisions and the moral matrix' 16(4) *Child and Family Law Quarterly*, p. 409.
Cobley, C. (2004) '"Working Together?" – Admissions of Abuse in Child Protection Proceedings and Criminal Prosecutions' 16(2) *Child and Family Law Quarterly*, p. 175.
Corby, B. (2004) 'Towards a new means of inquiry into child abuse cases' 25(3) *Journal of Social Work Law*, p. 229.
Hann, J. and Owen, M. (2003) 'The implementation of care plans and its relationship to children's welfare' 15(1) *Child and Family Law Quarterly*, p. 71.
Iwaniec, D., Donaldson, T. and Allweis, M. (2004) 'The plight of neglected children – social work and judicial decision making and management of neglect cases' 16(4) *Child and Family Law Quarterly*, p. 423.
Larkin, E., McSherry, D. and Iwaniec, D. (2005) 'Room for improvement? Views of key professionals involved in care order proceedings' 17(2) *Child and Family Law Quarterly*, p. 231.

Lindley, B., Richards, M. and Freeman, P. (2001) 'Advice and advocacy for parents in child protection cases – an exploration of conceptual and policy issues, ethical dilemmas and future directions' 13(3) *Child and Family Law Quarterly*, p. 311.

The following address the role of the guardian:

Clark, A. and Sinclair, R. (1999) *The Child in Focus: The Evolving Role of the Guardian* ad Litem. London: National Children's Bureau.
McCausland, J. (2000) *Guarding Children's Interests.* London: The Children's Society.
Masson, J. and Winn Oakley, M. (1999) *Out of Hearing: Representing Children in Care Proceedings.* Chichester: NSPCC/Wiley.

Guidance on roles and responsibility in child protection are helpfully covered in:

Davies, C. and Ward, H. (2012) *Safeguarding Children Across Services: Messages from Research.* London: Jessica Kingsley Publications.
Jones, J. (2012) 'Human trafficking in the UK: a focus on children' 24(1) *Child and Family Law Quarterly* p. 77.
Walsh, E. (2006) *Working in the Family Justice System. A Guide for Professionals* (2nd edn). Bristol: Family Law, Jordan Publishing.
Wilson, K. and James, A. (eds) (2002) *The Child Protection Handbook* (2nd edn). Edinburgh, Bailliere Tindall.

The effectiveness of provisions in the Youth Justice and Criminal Evidence Act 1999 for child witnesses is considered in:

Burton, M., Evans, R. and Sanders, A. (2006) 'Protecting children in criminal proceedings: parity for child witnesses and child defendants' 18(3) *Child and Family Law Quarterly*, p. 397.

Notes

[1] See discussion in Chapter 4, and *Z* v. *United Kingdom* (2001) 34 EHRR 97.

[2] *A* v. *United Kingdom (Human Rights: Punishment of Child)* (1998) 27 EHRR 61; *Z* v. *United Kingdom* (2001) 34 EHRR 97.

[3] There is a supplement to 'Working Together' specifically addressing fictitious illness: (2002) 'Safeguarding Children in Whom Illness is Induced or Fabricated by Carers with Parenting Responsibilities – Supplementary Guidance to Working Together to Safeguard Children', London: Department of Health.

[4] DCA (2006) 'Research Review: Childcare Proceedings under the Children Act 1989'.

[5] The pdf is available to download on HM Government website www.gov.uk.

[6] Often referred to as 'Part 8' Reviews, due to their introduction in Part 8 of the 1991 version of 'Working Together'.

[7] Department of Health (1995) 'Child Protection: Messages from Research'. London: HMSO, p. 29.

[8] Department of Health and Social Security (1974) 'Report of the Committee of Inquiry into the Care and Supervision Provided in Relation to Maria Colwell'.

[9] B. Lindley, M. Richards and P. Freeman (2001) 'Advice and advocacy for parents in child protection cases – an exploration of conceptual and policy issues, ethical dilemmas and future directions' 13(3) *Child and Family Law Quarterly*, p. 311.

[10] P. Nixon (2001) 'An Introduction to Family Group Conferences' in L.-A. Cull and J. Roche *The Law and Social Work: Contemporary Issues for Practice.* Basingstoke: Palgrave.

[11] Department of Health and Social Security. London: HMSO.

[12] 'The Children Act 1989 Guidance and Regulations', vol. 1 'Court Orders'. London: HMSO, para. 4.4.

[13] J. Dickens (1993) 'Assessment and control of social work: an analysis of the reasons for the non-use of the child assessment order' 15(2) *Journal of Social Welfare and Family Law*, p. 188.

[14] For further analysis of this case see: J. Masson (2004) 'Emergency protection, good practice and human rights' 34 *Family Law*, p. 882.

[15] See, e.g. the Waterhouse Report: R. Waterhouse (2000) 'Report of the tribunal of inquiry into the abuse of children in care in the former county council areas of Gwynedd and Clwyd since 1974'. London: The Stationery Office.

[16] A. Pack (2001) 'Most efficacious, in every case? Exclusion requirements – an overview' *Family Law*, p. 217.

[17] C. Beckett (2001) 'The great care proceedings explosion' 31(3) *British Journal of Social Work*, p. 493; Department of Health (2001) 'The Children Act Now: Messages from Research', London: The Stationery Office (pp. 55–6).

[18] 'The Children Act 1989 Guidance and Regulations', vol. 1 'Court Orders', London: HMSO (p. 24).

[19] Discussed further in A. Perry (2000) 'Section 31 – threshold or barrier? The implications of *Lancashire County Council v B*' 12(3) *Child and Family Law Quarterly*, p. 301.

[20] J. Hayes (2000) 'The threshold test and the unknown perpetrator' *Family Law*, p. 260.

[21] See *Re D and K (Care Plan: Twin Track Planning)* [1999] 2 FLR 872.

[22] As discussed in *Re J (Minors) (Care Proceedings: Care Plan)* [1994] 1 FLR 253.

[23] Department for Constitutional Affairs: available at www.dca.gov.uk/family/scopestud.htm.

[24] See also M. Booth (1996) *Avoiding Delay in Children Act Cases*. London: Lord Chancellor's Department.

[25] See E. Saunders (2003) 'The New Care Protocol' *Family Law*, p. 774.

[26] DCA SR 2004 Technical Notes for PSA Targets.

[27] (2000) 30 Fam Law 600.

[28] Department of Health and Social Security (1974) 'Report of the Committee of Inquiry into the Care and Supervision Provided in Relation to Maria Colwell'. London: HMSO.

[29] A. Dale-Emberton (2001) 'Working with children: a guardian ad litem's experience' in L.-A. Cull and J. Roche (eds) *The Law and Social Work: Contemporary Issues for Practice*. Basingstoke: Palgrave.

[30] J. McCausland (2000) *Guarding Children's Interests: The Contribution of Guardians ad Litem in Court Proceedings*. London: The Children's Society.

[31] Ibid.

[32] For a full discussion of the role, see J. Wall (2000) *A Handbook for Expert Witnesses in Children Act Cases*. Bristol: Family Law, Jordan Publishing.

[33] Family Proceedings Rules 1991 (SI 1991/1247), r. 4.18(1).

[34] Further guidance on the appointment and role of expert witnesses is given in *Re G (Minors) (Expert Witnesses)* [1994] 2 FLR 291.

[35] See also Expert Witness Group (1997) *The Expert Witness Pack for Use in Children Act Proceedings*. Bristol: Family Law, Jordan Publishing.

[36] Home Office (1993) 'Protection of children: disclosure of criminal background of those with access to children', Circular No. 47/93.

[37] This Act established a protection of children register, which combines and places on a statutory footing the Department of Health's consultancy service index and the Department for Education and Skills' 'List 99'.

[38] Useful analysis of child abuse inquiries is presented in P. Reder, S. Duncan and M. Gray (1993) *Beyond Blame: Child Abuse Tragedies Revisited*. London: Routledge.

[39] See C. Lyon and P. De Cruz (1993) *Child Abuse* (2nd edn). Bristol: Family Law, Jordan Publishing.

[40] Department of Health and Social Security (1974) 'Report of the Committee of Inquiry into the Care and Supervision Provided in Relation to Maria Colwell'. London: HMSO.

[41] Department of Health and Social Security (1985) 'A Child in Trust: Jasmine Beckford'. London: HMSO.

[42] Department of Health and Social Security (1987) 'A Child in Mind: Protection of Children in a Responsible Society'. London: HMSO.

[43] Department of Health and Social Security (1987) 'Whose Child?'. London: HMSO.

[44] Butler-Sloss, LJ (1988) 'Report of the Inquiry into Child Abuse in Cleveland' (1987, Cmnd. 412). London: HMSO.

[45] Staffordshire County Council (1991) 'The Pindown Experience and the Protection of Children: The Report of the Staffordshire Child Care Inquiry 1990'. Staffordshire County Council.

[46] Sir W. Utting (1991) *Children in Public Care: A Review of Residential Care*. London: HMSO; followed by a further report, Sir W. Utting (1997) *People Like Us. The Report of the Review of Safeguards for Children Living Away from Home*. London: HMSO.

[47] Introduction to Lord Laming (2009) 'The Protection of Children in England: a Progress Report', London: The Stationery Office, p. 3.

[48] Home Office (2005) Guidance on Offences Against Children, 16/2005.

[49] See J. Spencer (2004) 'The Sexual Offences Act 2003: Child and Family Offences' *Criminal Law Review*, p. 347.

[50] Follows Law Commission proposals in their September 2003 publication, 'Children – their non-accidental death or serious injury'.

[51] See generally on child witnesses in criminal proceedings, J. R. Spencer and R. Flin (1993) *The Evidence of Children: the Law and the Psychology* (2nd edn). London: Blackstone Press.

[52] For details of the Act and further information on special measures, see D. Birch and R. Leng (2000) *Blackstone's Guide to the Youth Justice and Criminal Evidence Act 1999*. London: Blackstone Press.

[53] See discussion in P. Bates (1999) 'The Youth Justice and Criminal Evidence Act' 11(3) *Child and Family Law Quarterly*, p. 289.

[54] Home Office, Crown Prosecution Service, Department of Health. London: The Stationery Office.

Chapter 10

Looked after children

Learning objectives

To develop an understanding of the following:

- The term 'looked after children'.
- The duties owed by local authorities towards looked after children.
- The duty to provide accommodation as an aspect of service provision.
- Outcomes for looked after children
- Local authority and private fostering.
- Residential accommodation and secure accommodation.
- The role of the independent visitor.
- Support for young people leaving care.

> ## Talking Point
>
> The responsibilities of the Independent Reviewing Officer were considered in detail in *A and S (Children)* v. *Lancashire County Council* [2012] EWHC (Fam) 1689, a case which unfortunately demonstrates how the review process failed to protect the interests of two children, described as profoundly damaged by the care system. The Court found violations of the rights guaranteed by Articles 3, 6 and 8 and damages were awarded.
>
> Two brothers were freed for adoption as infants but no adoptive placement was ever found for them. By the time their case was heard by the High Court they were aged 16 and 14. Their care history comprised experience of multiple placements, 77 and 96 respectively. They suffered physical and sexual abuse in at least two placements and were described as becoming increasingly unsettled and disturbed. The boys had lost contact with their birth family despite requests for contact, no substitute permanent family was found and nobody held parental responsibility for them.
>
> Between 1999 and 2011, 35 Looked After Children Reviews were held for each boy. One Independent Reviewing Officer identified in the case had chaired 16 reviews and accepted that he had not carried out his monitoring role effectively in providing a safeguard for the boys. It was noted that he had at times a caseload which was three times good practice guidance and that he lacked training and recourse to legal advice. The court noted that, 'These were children with increasingly complex needs, but there is no record of any serious consideration being given to important questions such as whether keeping them together was in their interests, nor an acknowledgement of the possible value and purpose of family contact.'
>
> A and S successfully brought proceedings against the local authority and the IRO (as its employee) under the Human Rights Act 1998
>
> The case clearly highlights concerns that the IRO role was not effective in providing an independent safeguard for looked after children. Similar concerns were found by Ofsted in a report in 2013 which found the role was underdeveloped and IROs needed to be more effective in challenging drift and delay.

Introduction

Looked after children (**LAC**) are those children who are accommodated by the local authority, away from their family, in a residential or foster placement, placed or authorised to be placed for adoption, and all children who are the subject of a care order, even if they are living with their parents. The term includes some short-term arrangements such as children under an emergency protection order or police protection and also children subject to a criminal supervision order with residence or detained under the grave crimes provision of the Children and Young Persons Act 1933, s. 53. From the implementation of **LASPO** all children and young people remanded in youth detention accommodation will have LAC status.

The accommodation (provided for a continuous period of more than 24 hours[1]) may be provided on a voluntary basis, or under the authority of a care order or other court order. Accommodation may be provided on a long-term basis or a series of planned short-term placements, including support foster care (formerly referred to as 'respite care') and fostering for adoption.

The local authority is often described as the 'corporate parent' of looked after children and has a range of responsibilities towards them.[2] Improving the role of the corporate parent and outcomes for looked after children was considered in 'Care Matters: Time for Change' (2007)[3] with some of those recommendations given effect in the Children and Young Persons Act 2008.

There are a significant number of looked after children. On 31 March 2013, 68,110 children were looked after. About 42 per cent of those children return home within eight weeks but many will need to be looked after in a planned way with a degree of permanence for a substantial part of their lives. The majority (75 per cent) live with foster carers. The legal status of LAC includes children accommodated under s. 20 and children under a care order (59 per cent). Five per cent lived with their parents with social services input, five per cent were placed for adoption, and nine per cent were is secure units, children's homes and hostels.[4] There were 1,860 looked after unaccompanied asylum-seeking children in England in 2013.

This chapter will consider the duties towards looked after children, including the obligation to provide suitable accommodation. The material is structured to reflect the child's journey through placement leading to independence. For those looked after children for whom rehabilitation with their families is not possible, security and stability may be achieved through adoption (see Chapter 11). A clear preference has emerged from official publications for greater use of adoption for looked after children. A total of 3,980 looked after children were adopted during the year ending 31 March 2008.[5]

The chapter moves on to consider a range of alternative options for looked after children offering some degree of permanence, namely fostering and residential accommodation, and includes discussion of secure accommodation. Finally, the responsibilities of local authorities towards looked after children who cease to be looked after, under the Children (Leaving Care) Act 2000 (**C(LC)A** 2000) are considered.

Duties towards looked after children

A local authority has certain duties towards all looked after children. These duties are set out in the Children Act 1989, s. 22. The Children and Young Persons Act 2008 replaced s. 23 of the Children Act 1989 with new provisions 22A–F. The new provisions emphasise that the local authority has a duty to provide a child in its care with accommodation and to maintain the child in other respects.

---

s. 22(3)

It shall be the duty of a local authority looking after any child –

(a) to safeguard and promote his welfare; and
(b) to make such use of services available for children cared for by their own parents as appears to the authority reasonable in his case.

(CA 1989)

Local authorities have a duty of consultation before making decisions regarding looked after children. Specifically, they are directed to ascertain the wishes and feelings of the child, his parents, and any person with parental responsibility, and any other person whose wishes and feelings are considered relevant to the matter in hand (s. 22(4)). The authority is then directed to give due consideration to the views ascertained. In exceptional circumstances this duty of consultation may be limited, as in *Re P (Children Act 1989, ss 22 and 26: Local Authority Compliance)* [2000] 2 FLR 910, where restricted consultation was permitted because of the continuing risk the father posed to the children in placements outside the family. In addition, before making the decision, under s. 22(5) the local authority must also give due consideration to the child's racial origin and cultural and linguistic background. This factor is likely to be most relevant to placement decisions and would suggest that, where possible, a child's placement should be able to meet the child's cultural needs and be with a family of similar religious persuasion, racial origin and cultural and linguistic background. Where adoption is proposed for the child, the duty in ACA 2002, s. 1(5) applies, namely: 'In placing the child for adoption, the adoption agency must give due consideration to the child's religious persuasion, racial origin and cultural and linguistic background.'

There is a duty to promote contact between the child and his parents, any other person who has parental responsibility, and relatives and friends. This is not an absolute duty and is qualified in circumstances where it would not be reasonably practicable or is not consistent with the child's welfare. To enable contact, the local authority *may* make payments to assist with travelling and subsistence costs incurred in visits to the child or by the child visiting his family, if undue financial hardship would be caused without the assistance. The regulations recognise the importance of sibling relationships and, if not living together, requires the care plan to detail arrangements for the child to have sibling contact. The local authority must also ensure that parents (and others with parental responsibility) are kept informed of the child's whereabouts, unless this would prejudice the child's welfare.

The accommodation should normally (if reasonably practicable and consistent with the child's welfare) be near to the child's home and be able to provide accommodation for siblings to stay together. The accommodation must be suitable to the child's needs if he is disabled. The placement should be within the local authority's area and should not disrupt the child's education (s. 22C).

There is an ongoing monitoring role and the local authority is under a duty to ensure the looked after child is visited and seen alone by a representative of the authority (s. 23ZA).

Provision of accommodation

Perhaps the most important decision the local authority will take with respect to a looked after child is where the child is to be accommodated. Section 22 imposes a duty on the local authority to provide accommodation and maintain a looked after child and outlines a range of possible placements. Wherever possible a child should be placed with a parent (in which case the LA should consider whether the care order is still required), a person who is not a parent but has PR, a person who had a residence order before the making of a care order. If that is not possible the key message from the section (as amended by the CYPA 2008) is the emphasis on kinship or connected persons placements as the preferred placement, defined as 'placement who is a relative, friend or other person connected with C and who is also a local authority foster parent' (s. 22C (6)(a)). If and only if that is not possible other appropriate placements are listed as: local authority foster parents, who may be relatives or who are unconnected; children's homes; or other arrangements, which might include for example living independently with support.

Provision of accommodation on a voluntary basis is intended to be seen as a service to support parents and it is significant that s. 20, which deals with provision of accommodation for children in need, is contained in Part III of the Act: 'Local Authority Support for Children and Families'. The local authority must accommodate children in need who appear to require accommodation as a result of:

> ## s. 20(1)
>
> **(a)** there being no person who has parental responsibility for him;
>
> **(b)** his being lost or having been abandoned; or
>
> **(c)** the person who has been caring for him being prevented (whether or not permanently, and for whatever reason) from providing him with suitable accommodation or care.
>
> (CA 1989)

The duty is to provide accommodation for a child, not for a parent and child. In *R (G)* v. *Barnet London Borough Council* [2003] UKHL 57, a mother and her 1-year-old child had come to the United Kingdom from Holland. The local authority were of the view that the child's best interests would be served by remaining in the care of his mother and they offered to pay their fare to return to Holland. This was rejected. The local authority therefore was found to have acted within the terms of the Children Act 1989 by offering to accommodate the child only, under s. 20. The local authority may be considered to be accommodating a child where it plays a major role in making arrangements even if the accommodation is provided by a known carer. For example, in *Southwark London Borough Council* v. *D* [2007] EWCA Civ 182, social services asked a father's former girlfriend to look after his 14-year-old daughter following an allegation that he had attacked her. The local authority argued that it had facilitated a private fostering arrangement but this was not accepted by the court.

According to *R (RO)* v. *East Riding of Yorkshire Council* [2011] EWCA Civ 196, many children in residential special schools will be classed as looked after children, meaning that duties under the Children Act 1989 apply and they are likely to be entitled to leaving care services. The basis for the decision was that the placement was not wholly or mainly to meet educational needs (as provided under Education legislation), it also met the boy's care needs and was therefore provided under s. 20.

A person may be prevented from providing suitable accommodation in a variety of circumstances, including housing difficulties, hospital admission, illness, etc. The arrangement is voluntary and is an obvious area where the local authority must work in partnership with parents. A child cannot be accommodated under s. 20 if there is opposition from a person with parental responsibility who would himself be able to provide accommodation for the child. In such circumstances the only way the local authority could provide accommodation would be under the authority of a care order. Where a child is accommodated with the consent of the parents, the local authority does not have the power to move the child to live with foster carers against the parents' wishes. In *R* v. *Tameside Metropolitan Borough Council, ex parte J* [2000] 1 FCR 173, a 13-year-old girl with severe disabilities and autistic tendencies had lived in a residential home near to her parents' home for two years. Judicial review found that the local authority decision to move J against her parents' wishes was unlawful.

To reinforce the voluntary nature of s. 20 accommodation, there is no requirement for a person who wishes to remove the child to give notice to the local authority (s. 20(8)). Any question of notice and arrangements for the appropriate circumstances in which a child should be returned will be covered by negotiated agreement with parents. Such agreements are covered by the Care Planning Placement and Case Review Regulations 2010. It is important to note that an agreement is not a binding contract and any notice provision it contains is unenforceable by the local authority. It may be argued that this renders such agreements pointless. Their value, however, rests on the fact that they should be negotiated with parents and relied upon in the spirit of partnership.

On occasion s. 20 may be employed in preference to intervention under a care order. The following key case emphasises the need for true consent to s. 20 and recognises that in some cases this will require children's social workers to have a working knowledge of the law relating to capacity.

Key Case

Re CA (A Baby) [2012] EWHC 2190 (Fam)

This case illustrates the need for social workers in child protection to have an understanding of capacity law. It involved an application by the local authority for a final care and placement order for a child. The mother had significant learning difficulties and was described as being 'devoid of parenting instinct or intuition'. Three older children were already the subject of placement orders.

CA was removed from her mother on 1 February 2012, the day she was born, under a s. 20 agreement. The mother knew of the plan and had 'demonstrated submission but not consent to it'. On the day of CA's birth, the mother had the trauma of deciding to have life-sustaining surgery, had significant pain for which she received morphine, and was repeatedly faced with the decision to consent to CA's removal. She initially refused her consent to the s. 20 agreement but consented later after she was medicated with morphine.

Hedley J gave judgment and included guidance for social workers when seeking s. 20 consent from a parent immediately or soon after birth.

Every social worker has a personal duty to be satisfied the person giving consent has capacity to do so. To determine whether the person has capacity the social worker should consider s. 3 of the Mental Capacity Act 2005. If the social worker has doubts about capacity she should make no further attempts to obtain consent at that time.

If the social worker believes the person has capacity, she must also be satisfied that the person is fully informed of the consequences and refusal of consent, the choices available and the facts relevant to giving of consent.

The social worker should also be satisfied that removal is fair and proportionate.

Finally Hedley J confirmed that, '*willingness to consent cannot be inferred from silence, submission or even acquiescence. It is a positive stance*' (para 44).

Local authorities are under a general duty (s. 22G) to take steps to secure sufficient accommodation that is appropriate for the needs of children they look after within their authority area.

Care plans

The Care Planning, Placement and Case Review Regulations 2010, require the local authority to set out the arrangements for a looked after child in a care plan, which should be written in such a way that it can be understood by the child (subject to age and understanding) and family. Key elements of the plan include: a description of the child's needs and required services, details of the placement and why it has been chosen for the child, measures to safeguard and promote the child's welfare, with specific, measurable outcomes, roles and responsibilities of family and practitioners, contact, decision-making arrangements, contingency plans and a named IRO.

Each child will also have a health plan and a personal education plan.

Reviews

The circumstances of looked after children should be reviewed regularly. Regulations prescribe the detail.[6] An Independent Reviewing Officer (IRO) (who will be a registered and experienced social worker) will chair the reviews and monitor the s. 31A care plan and may refer the case to CAFCASS if there are concerns; the CAFCASS officer may then return the case to court. A review should be held within 20 days of the initial placement, followed by a further review in three months' time and thereafter every six months (as a minimum). The issues to be considered at reviews are set out in Schedule 7 of the regulations and include the child's progress and whether his needs are being met in the placement, any changes that might need to be made to the plan and contact arrangements and the child's legal status. The child (of sufficient age and understanding) will normally attend the review and parents are entitled to attend reviews unless given a specific reason as to why they should not, e.g. fear of violence. Also, health reviews of looked after children should be conducted every six months for children under 5 and at least once a year for children over 5. This follows an initial health assessment of the child's physical and mental health, to be carried out as soon as practicable after the children become looked after. The effectiveness of the IRO role was questioned in the green paper 'Care Matters' and in the case of *S (A Child Acting by the Official Solicitor)* v. *Rochdale Metropolitan Borough Council and the Independent Reviewing Officer* [2008] EWHC 3283 (Fam). Some reforms to the scheme followed in the Children and Young Persons Act 2008 (introducing section 25A–C Children Act 1989).

When a child first becomes looked after, a named individual must be appointed by the local authority as the IRO for the child, the intention being that each looked after child should have a named IRO, to provide continuity in the oversight of the case and to enable a relationship to develop between the child and the IRO. Under s. 25B the IRO must: monitor the local authority's performance of its functions in relation to the child's case, beyond the review; ensure that the local authority give due consideration to any views expressed by the child; chair the review meetings; and keep a written record of each review. The local authority is specifically placed under a duty to cooperate with the IRO and take all reasonable steps to enable the IRO to perform his functions.

Outcomes for looked after children

In comparison with other children in society, looked after children appear to fare less well on a number of levels. This includes levels of educational attainment, e.g. 15.3 per cent obtained at least five GCSEs (or equivalent) at grades A*–C compared with 58 per cent of all children, although it is noted that 67.8 per cent of looked after children have special educational needs. The DfE statistical release on outcomes notes that LAC face significant challenges:

> During the year ending 31 March 2013, 6.2% of looked after children aged 10–17 had been convicted or subject to a fine, warning or reprimand and 3.5% of all looked after children had a substance misuse problem. Looked after children are twice as likely to be permanently excluded from school and nearly three times more likely to have a fixed-term exclusion than all children. Around half of all children aged 5–16 were considered to be 'borderline' or 'cause for concern' in relation to their emotional and behavioural health.[7]

Mental health needs of looked after children also raise concern. In a study of 1,039 looked after children Meltzer *et al.* (2003)[8] found that 50 per cent of boys and 33 per cent of girls aged 5–10 had an identified disorder; for children aged 11–15, it rose to 55 per cent of boys and 43 per cent of girls. Also, conduct disorder was found in 42 per cent of boys and 31 per cent of girls.

Given the circumstances in which some children become looked after, having suffered neglect or abuse, and coming from disadvantaged backgrounds, these outcomes may not be a great surprise. Nevertheless, it is not appropriate simply to accept the inevitability of such outcomes, and the Government has adopted a position whereby it has set targets to significantly improve outcomes for looked after children.

The primary vehicle for this initiative is the 'Quality Protects' programme ('Children First' in Wales). Associated initiatives have come out of the 'Modernising Social Services' agenda and include new systems of regulation under the Care Standards Act 2000, the 'Sure Start' programme and 'Connexions'. The objectives of these initiatives should be seen in the context of the 'Every Child Matters: Change for Children' programme, which aims to improve outcomes for all children.

Aspects of the Quality Protects strategy relate to all children likely to come into contact with social services but it is particularly targeted at children in need (discussed in Chapter 6) and looked after children. There are 11 main objectives, each accompanied by sub-objectives and performance indicators, published in 'The Government's Objectives for Children's Social Services' (1998).[9] The Quality Protects objectives clearly call for greater use of adoption for looked after children. The Prime Minister's Review of Adoption leant further support to this, with the following quote drawn from the introduction: 'It is hard to overstate the importance of a stable and loving family life for children. That is why I want more children to benefit from adoption.'[10]

Two particular aspects of outcomes for looked after children have been priortised by Government: improving the stability of placements for looked after children, and improving their educational achievement. The stated objective is to narrow the gap in educational achievement between looked after children and other children and to reduce the number of placement moves experienced by looked after children. All looked after children should have a personal education plan covering achievement, development and educational needs, short-term targets, long-term plans and aspirations. Statutory guidance expects social workers to be 'effective advocates in dealing with school admissions, issues arising from behavioural problems and school discipline and school exclusions'.[11] (The education of looked after children is considered further in Chapter 12.)

In relation to stability, in 2005 a **DfES** study[12] found that 65 per cent of looked after children had been in the same placement for at least two years, but there was wide variation between different authorities. Factors which were most likely to lead to improvements in stability were improvements in placement choice and placement support.

Fostering

The term 'foster carer' is used in this text in preference to foster parent. It was acknowledged in the Children Act 1989 Guidance that although 'foster parent' is the term used in legislation and regulations, and is understood by the general public, the term 'foster carer' is more commonly used by professionals.[13] Fostering is a term that applies to a great variety of arrangements. It may be short- or long-term, provided in emergencies, as part of a planned provision of 'respite' care, by local authority, or private carers, and increasingly by relatives, friends and other connected persons. There are some 'specialist' foster carers who cater, for example, for children who have been abused in a particular way, or for gay teenagers.

Foster carers do not acquire parental responsibility by virtue of the fostering arrangement. They are **de facto** carers acting '*in loco parentis*', a situation which lacks legal security. If faced with a parent who wishes to resume care of their child, or a local authority who plans to move the child, there is little that the foster carers can do to prevent removal, other than to rely in the short term on s. 3(5) of the Children Act 1989 or to seek an emergency protection order (EPO). If foster carers wish to continue to care for a child on a long-term basis, they may seek a residence order, where the child has been living with them for one out of the last five years (CA 1989, s. 9(3)), or they have the consent of those with parental responsibility, or the consent of the local authority if they are relatives of the child. Where a foster carer wishes to adopt a foster child, the foster parent must give notice of intention to adopt under s. 44 at least three months before the application to adopt. During the three-month period the local authority will prepare a report for the court.

Despite the legally insecure position of foster carers, their profile has been raised and there is a greater emphasis on the training and professionalism of foster carers. Foster carers frequently provide reports to case conferences and reviews, and may have to give evidence to court and keep records relating to a child. A Department of Health publication includes a useful checklist for foster carers to assist with the preparation of statements to be used in court.[14]

Local authority foster carers

A significant proportion of children looked after by the local authority are placed with local authority foster carers. A local authority foster carer may include a relative but not a parent. The foster carer's role is described in the regulations as being: 'to care for any child placed with him as if the child were a member of the foster-parent's family and to promote his welfare having regard to the long and short term plans for the child.'

Fostering arrangements are governed by the Fostering Services (England) Regulations 2011 which provide for the approval process of foster carers and written placement agreements. Foster carers must be approved under the Fostering Services (England) Regulations 2011 and Fostering Services National Minimum Standards (2011) are in place.

'The Children Act 1989 Guidance and Regulations', volume 4 'Fostering Services' 2011, provides further guidance on practice issues. Some local authorities have difficulty recruiting sufficient foster carers to provide choice when placing looked after children. In particular, some local authorities have regular recruitment drives for ethnic minority foster carers. Paragraph 11 of Sch. 2 to the Children Act 1989 directs a local authority to have regard, in publicising and recruiting for the fostering service, to the different racial groups to which children in need in the area belong. This is important because a local authority must be satisfied that a particular placement is the most suitable way of performing its duty to safeguard and promote the child's welfare, and the child's cultural background and racial origin is an important consideration.

Prospective foster parents must provide references and be assessed by the local authority or fostering agency before approval can be given. The assessment is comprehensive and includes consideration of health, age, marital status, religious persuasion, racial origin and cultural background, family members, employment record, accommodation, etc. In *R (Johns and Johns)* v. *Derby City Council* [2011] EWHC 375, a couple who were members of the Pentecostalist church and disapproved of homosexual relationships applied to be approved as foster carers. The High Court found that such views could be taken into account as part of the fostering approval process and the couple could not complain of unlawful religious discrimination under the equality legislation. As to Art. 9 rights in relation to religion, the couple had the absolute right to hold religious beliefs but the right to manifest beliefs is not absolute.

Following approval, a 'foster placement agreement' (reg. 27(5)) will be drawn up concerning the foster carer's relationship with the authority and information about arrangements for the child including financial support. The agreement includes details of the training and support to be given to the foster carer, review and placement procedures, and the duties expected of the foster carer. The foster carers should care for the child as if he were a member of the foster carers' family, not administer corporal punishment, and notify the authority of significant changes in the household or serious illness of the child. The agreement should contain all the information the authority considers necessary to enable the foster parents to care for the child. This information should include details of the child's personal history, religion, cultural and linguistic background and racial origin, health needs and education needs. If adoption is being considered for a looked after child, the local authority must place the child with a local authority foster carer who is also approved as a prospective adopter (Fostering for Adoption, Children and Families Act 2014).

Information given to foster carers was found to be inadequate in the case of *W and others* v. *Essex County Council* [1998] 3 All ER 111. Here, children of foster carers were given leave to sue the council and social worker for negligence on the grounds that they were not told that the foster child who was placed with them had previously sexually abused his sister.

A fostering allowance is paid to local authority foster carers. An enhanced rate may be payable to specialist foster carers. The National Foster Care Association recommends a minimum allowance based on the age of the child and the location. The Children Act 2004 introduces a power for the Secretary of State to set the level of payments made to foster carers caring for looked after children. In *R (L)* v. *Manchester City Council* [2001] EWHC Admin 707, the council had a policy of financially assisting foster carers who were relatives or friends on a considerably smaller scale than other foster carers. This was found to be unlawful. The policy was '*Wednesbury*' irrational, fundamentally discriminatory and in breach of Arts. 8 and 14 of the European Convention on Human Rights. This position has been confirmed in guidance: 'Criteria for calculating fees and allowances must apply equally to all foster carers, whether the foster carer is related to the child or unrelated, or the placement is short or longterm' (2011); and also by the Court of Appeal in *London Borough of Tower Hamlets* v. *The Queen on the Application of X* [2013] EWCA Civ 904.

The local authority is not vicariously liable for the acts of foster carers. However, in *Barrett* v. *Enfield London Borough Council* [1999] 3 All ER 193, a claim was allowed for damages to be paid in respect of a child who suffered harm whilst placed with foster carers. Foster carers should take out their own insurance to cover their fostering role.

Local authority fostering services are subject to inspection under the Care Standards Act 2000.

In addition to the system for review of adoption determinations, the Independent Review of Determinations (Adoption and Fostering) Regulations 2009 (made under powers of the Children and Young persons Act 2008), provides a new system for the independent review of fostering determinations. An independent panel may review determinations made, refusing an individual's approval as a foster carer, terminating approval as a foster carer, or altering the terms of approval as a foster carer.

The Children and Families Act 2014 amends the Children Act 1989, inserting s. 23CZA regarding arrangements for certain former relevant children to continue to live with foster parents, in a 'staying put arrangement' until the age of 21. The local authority must continue to provide financial and other support during this extended time.

Private foster carers

At 31 March 2013, 1,780 children were reported as being cared for and accommodated in private fostering arrangements in England, although this is thought to be an underestimate due to under reporting. Private foster carers are those who foster a privately fostered child, defined in s. 66 of the Children Act 1989. A privately fostered child is under the age of 16 (18 if disabled); is accommodated by someone who is not a parent, does not have parental responsibility and is not a relative; and is accommodated for more than 28 days. A privately fostered child is not a looked after child under s. 22 of the Children Act 1989 and the local authority are not involved in making the arrangement.

The local authority has responsibilities under Part IX of the Children Act 1989 and the Children (Private Arrangements for Fostering) Regulations 2005[15] to regulate and support private fostering. A person who is privately fostering a child or proposes to privately foster a child (and any person involved (whether directly or not) in arranging for the child to be fostered privately, and a parent of the child or other person with parental responsibility for the child) should notify the local authority and an officer will visit and report back to the local authority. Within the first year of the arrangement the child should be visited every six weeks, then every 12 weeks in subsequent years, and unless considered inappropriate the officer should speak to the child alone.

A person may be disqualified from private fostering under s. 68 of the Children Act 1989 and the Disqualification for Caring for Children Regulations 1991.[16] The grounds are: if a child of the individual has been the subject of a care order or otherwise removed from his care; the person has been convicted of a specified offence; or the person has been concerned with a registered home which has been deregistered or has had an application for registration refused; or the person has been prohibited from being a private foster parent. The local authority should be notified of private fostering arrangements.

The local authority must be satisfied that the welfare of privately fostered children is satisfactorily safeguarded and promoted. It may impose a fostering prohibition where: a prospective foster parent is not a suitable person; the premises intended to be used for fostering are not suitable; or it would be prejudicial to the welfare of the child to be accommodated by that foster parent in those premises (Children Act 1989, s. 69).[17]

The Children Act 2004 responds to the criticisms directed at the law on private fostering in the Climbié inquiry and strengthens the scheme for registration and monitoring of private fostering. The relevant guidance is, 'The Replacement Children Act 1989 Guidance on Private Fostering', DfES, 2005.

Usual fostering limit

A foster parent, whether private or local authority, may not foster more than three children, the 'usual fostering limit', unless the children are siblings or the foster parent has been exempted from the usual limit. Local authorities may impose a lower limit. If a foster parent exceeds the usual limit, he will be treated as a person carrying on a children's home and subject to the conditions governing the operation of children's homes.

Residential care

The Utting Report (1997) defined residential care as: 'Continuous residence in permanently staffed accommodation for more than three children, which provides or enables access to the care and services normally available to children and such additional measures of care, control and treatment as resident children require.' The report noted that residential care has a crucial role in the range of services available to children and should not be seen as a last resort. The number of children in residential care has steadily decreased, however. In providing residential care, the report emphasised the need for a planned approach, proper management, inspection and monitoring of the service, and the need for more professionally qualified staff.[18]

Practice and standards and the legal framework for residential care have been consistently challenged by successive inquiry reports, which have revealed the abuse of children and young people living in residential accommodation. A selection of those inquiry reports are listed below:

- Report of the inquiry into the conduct of Leeways children's home (1985).
- The Pin-down inquiry (1991).
- The Leicestershire inquiry (1992).
- Ty Mawr Community Home inquiry (1992).
- The Aycliffe Centre for children (1993).
- Report of the tribunal of inquiry into the abuse of children in care in the former county council areas of Gwynedd and Clwyd since 1974: 'Lost in care' (2000).

Guidance has been produced as a result of the findings of inquiry reports: e.g. following Pin-down, which was described as a 'regime intrinsically dependent on elements of isolation, humiliation and confrontation', the Department of Health published guidance on permissible forms of restraint in children's residential care. The key elements of that guidance provided that physical restraint, the positive application of force with the intention of overpowering the child, should only be used within the following framework:

- necessary to prevent the child significantly injuring him or herself, others or causing damage to property;
- dialogue and diversion to avoid need for a warning;
- minimum force necessary;
- the presence of other staff as assistance and witnesses;
- gradually relax restraint once safe;
- act of care and control, not punishment;
- not used purely to enforce compliance with staff instructions if no other risks involved.

Regulation of children's homes

The Care Standards Act 2000 defines a children's home as an establishment which provides care and accommodation wholly or mainly for children (Care Standards Act 2000, s. 1(2)). Health service hospitals, independent hospitals and clinics, residential family centres and schools (other than boarding schools providing 295 days' or more accommodation in a year) are exempt from the definition, as is accommodation provided by a foster carer, parent or relative, i.e. a domestic household. The Children's Homes (Amendment) Regulations 2011, Children Act Guidance and Regulations, Volume 5 'Children's Homes' and National Minimum Standards' apply to children's homes, and Ofsted are responsible for inspections.

The National Minimum Standards (NMS) for Children's Homes deal with planning for care, quality of care, complaints and protection, care and control, environment, staffing, management and administration, specialist provision including secure accommodation and refuges. Within each grouping there are a number of sub-groups, e.g. quality of care includes standards relating to consultation; privacy and confidentiality; provision and preparation of meals; personal appearance, clothing and pocket money; good health and wellbeing; treatment and administration of medicines; education; leisure and activities. They are intended to specify the minimum standard and many homes are likely to exceed the standards.

Managers of children's homes must be registered under the Care Standards Act 2000 based on compliance with requirements in the regulations and legislation. The standards will also be taken into account. Registration may be cancelled if conditions of registration are not complied with. An appeal may be made to the Care Standards Tribunal (part of the First-tier Tribunal) against cancellation of registration or refusal of registration. The case of *William Mitchell* v. *Commission for Social Care Inspection* [2004] 0369, EA provides an example.[19] Mitchell unsuccessfully appealed against the CSCI decision to refuse his application to become the registered manager of a children's home. The criteria for managing a home are contained in the Children's Homes Regulations 2001[20], and stipulate that a person shall not manage a children's home unless he is fit to do so, and he will not be fit unless he is of integrity and good character, and he has the qualifications, skills, and experience necessary for managing the children's home (reg. 8). Standard 22.7 of the National Minimum Standards for Children's Homes was also relevant to the case, and states: 'Physical restraint is only used to prevent likely injury to the child concerned or to others, or likely serious damage to property.' The burden of proof is on the applicant to prove that he is 'fit'. Mitchell became employed in residential social work after he left the army. Concerns were raised and became subject of a disciplinary hearing, about physical intervention and restraint being used in a way that was not reasonable and appropriate. Evidence was produced concerning eight incidents including the following:

- A resident appeared to be encouraging another resident to cause damage by punching the walls. When she refused to leave the room she was physically restrained by the appellant and a co-worker and removed.

- A resident was found to have cigarettes in her room. She refused the appellant's request to hand them over and was physically restrained.

- A resident was being noisy and abusive. She appeared to be bleeding from her arm and had a history of self-harm. She was physically restrained for seven minutes on her bed.

- A resident was asked to leave the room of another resident as she was preventing her from getting ready for school. The appellant told her he would 'extract her from the room using non-violent intervention'. As he approached her, she began to throw punches, so the appellant placed his hand either on her lower throat or her breastbone, placed her on the bed, then grasped both her hands.

The regulation inspector gave evidence that, in her view, restraint had been used as a means of enforcing compliance and therefore inappropriately. A further expert witness was critical of the appellant's methods and expressed his opinion that the appellant failed to use effective de-escalation techniques and there was no indication that the use of physical intervention was a last resort. The tribunal found the appellant to be a sincere, honest man who had done well to gain the required paper qualifications in residential care following retirement from the army. He had, however, failed to discharge the burden to show he was a fit person, and the tribunal concluded: 'Whilst his use of physical restraint was well intended and at the time believed by him to be an appropriate intervention in difficult situations, critical analysis revealed lack of judgment and inadequate skills and training.'

Each child accommodated in a children's home should have a 'child placement plan', which should address day-to-day care arrangements for the child, arrangements for health and accommodation and arrangements for contact (reg. 12).

A number of cases have ordered payment of compensation to adults who were abused in residential accommodation as children and this is a further demonstration of the removal of the blanket immunity from actions in negligence formerly enjoyed by local authorities. In *C* v. *Flintshire County Council* [2001] EWCA Civ 302 the claimant was bullied by other residents in her first placement without staff intervention and in the second home she suffered physical, emotional and sexual abuse by staff and was illegally detained in a secure unit. She was awarded a total of £70,000 in damages for the local authority's negligence. In *KR* v. *Bryn Alyn Community (Holdings) Ltd* [2003] EWCA Civ 85, 14 adults were awarded damages for long-term psychiatric or psychological injury caused by sexual, physical and emotional abuse suffered whilst resident in children's homes in North Wales.

Secure accommodation

There are times when it is considered necessary for a child to be placed in secure accommodation, i.e. accommodation provided for the purpose of restricting liberty. There are 298 approved places in the 17 secure children's homes open in England and Wales.[21] A decision that a child needs to be in secure accommodation will often necessitate a move.

Section 25 of the Children Act 1989 provides:

---

s. 25

(1) . . . a child who is being looked after by a local authority may not be placed, and, if placed, may not be kept, in accommodation provided for the purpose of restricting liberty ('secure accommodation') unless it appears –

  (a) that –
   (i) he has a history of absconding and is likely to abscond from any other description of accommodation; and
   (ii) if he absconds, he is likely to suffer significant harm; or
  (b) that if he is kept in any other description of accommodation he is likely to injure himself or other persons.

. . .

(4) If a court determines that any such criteria are satisfied it shall make an order authorising the child to be kept in secure accommodation and specifying the maximum period for which he may be so kept.

(CA 1989)

Secure accommodation is defined in the Children (Secure Accommodation) Regulations 1991,[22] reg. 2(1) as: 'Accommodation which is provided for the purpose of restricting the liberty of children to whom section 25 of the Act applies.'

A secure accommodation order may be made in respect of a child who is the subject of a care order or, providing there is parental consent, any other child to whom the criteria apply. If the child is not subject to a care order, the s. 20(8) provision applies to secure accommodation in the same manner as it does to any other accommodation for a looked after child. The effect of this is that a person with parental responsibility could remove a child (not subject to a court order) from a secure accommodation without notice.

It is possible for a child to be kept in secure accommodation for a total of 72 hours before an application is made to court. The 72 hours may be consecutive, or not consecutive within a period of 28 days. The court may make a secure accommodation order for a maximum initial period of three months, or it may make a 28-day interim secure order. A six-month order may be made if it is the second application for a child.

The local authority has a duty to avoid the need for children to be placed in secure accommodation (CA 1989, Sch 2, para. 7(c)). The court must make an order if the criteria are satisfied but it will require detailed information about absconding patterns, what happens when the child absconds (e.g. any offences that are committed), where the child goes and with whom. In addition, the aims of a secure placement for the particular child, in the context of a care plan, should be presented to court. The local authority should not detain the child in secure accommodation if the criteria for detention cease to apply. As s. 25 applications are 'specified proceedings' under the Children Act 1989, a children's guardian should be appointed and the child must be legally represented. The child is able to attend the secure accommodation order hearing if she wishes as in *A City Council* v. *T, J and K (by her Children's Guardian)* [2011] EWHC 1082 (Fam).

The question whether human rights are breached by the imposition of secure accommodation orders under the Children Act 1989, s. 25 was considered in *Re K (A Child) (Secure Accommodation Order: Right to Liberty)* [2001] 1 Fam 377. Here the court refused an application for a declaration of incompatibility. It was accepted by the court that the purpose of s. 25 was to restrict liberty and it therefore fell within ECHR, Art. 5 as a deprivation of liberty. Article 5 is, however, a qualified article and the court held that detention under a secure accommodation order fell within the exception at Art. 5(1)(d):

Art. 5(1)(d)

... the detention of a minor by lawful order for the purpose of educational supervision or his lawful detention for the purpose of bringing him before the competent legal authority.

(ECHR)

A secure placement that did not involve educational or therapeutic provision might not subsequently be upheld, however.

Secure accommodation was the subject of a further Human Rights Act 1998 challenge in the case of *Re M (A Child: Secure Accommodation)* [2001] EWCA 458. In this case the Court of Appeal considered whether the procedure for obtaining a secure accommodation order was compatible with Art. 6(3) of the Convention. Article 6(3) concerns those charged with a criminal offence. It was decided that secure accommodation is protective in nature and therefore criteria applicable to criminal cases do not apply, even though there is a loss of liberty. The court found that the procedure for obtaining secure accommodation orders was compatible with Art. 6(3) but that any application should comply with the minimum requirements of Art. 6(3) relating to notice of the nature of the charge, adequate time to prepare a defence, the ability to defend oneself through legal assistance of one's own choosing, free assistance of an interpreter if required, and the opportunity to cross-examine witnesses.

Independent visitors

The Children Act 1989[23] introduced the role of the independent visitor. It is stated in para. 17 of Sch. 2 to the Act that:

> ## Sch. 2, para. 17
>
> Where it appears to a local authority in relation to any child they are looking after that –
>
> **(a)** communication between the child and –
>   **(i)** a parent of his,
>   **(ii)** any other person who … has parental responsibility, has been infrequent, or
> **(b)** he has not visited or been visited by (or lived with) any such person during the preceding 12 months and it would be in the best interests of the child for an independent person to be appointed, they shall appoint an independent visitor.
>
> (CA 1989)

The duty of the independent visitor is to visit, advise and befriend the child. The independent visitor may also have a role in helping to prepare the young person for leaving care. An independent visitor will not be appointed (or an appointment can be terminated) if the child objects and the local authority is satisfied that his objection arises from the child's sufficient understanding to make an informed decision.[24]

An Ofsted survey (2012) of children's and young people's views on independent visitors found that 71 per cent of the young people did not have an independent visitor, in many cases because they had not been offered one; those with independent visitors wanted them to give help and support and be there to talk to; and half of the care leavers interviewed had kept in touch with their visitor. It seems that there is potential for independent visitors to have a much greater impact than is presently the case.[25]

In addition to the independent visitor, advocates and children's rights officers are available in some areas and present a potential safeguard against institutional abuse.

Section 16 CYPA 2008 extends the group of looked after children for whom an independent person must be appointed, to include all those for whom an appointment would be 'in their best interests'. The Act also provides for additional visiting requiring local authorities to ensure that all looked after children and children who were looked after, but ceased to be looked after as they have been taken into custody, are visited by a representative of the local authority and that appropriate advice, support and assistance is made available to them.

Leaving care

Children leaving care tend to do so at an earlier age than children living with their own families and often experience multiple disadvantage. The Children Act 1989, s. 24 introduced a duty towards looked after children to advise, assist and befriend with a view to promoting their welfare when they cease to be looked after. The duty was owed to young people between the ages of 16 and 21. In support of this duty, guidance called for local authorities to act as 'corporate parent' for young people leaving care. Leaving care services and projects, however, proved to be provided in a patchy and under-resourced fashion, often failing to meet the needs of young people leaving care. Research continued to highlight the plight of children leaving care, with poor levels of educational achievement and high levels of pregnancy amongst young women.[26]

The unsatisfactory picture emerging regarding children leaving care is partly attributable to the weakness of the Children Act 1989 provisions. This area is now covered by the Children (Leaving Care) Act 2000 (**C(LC)A** 2000). Central to the Act is the role of personal advisers for young people and pathways planning. The following is a summary of provisions:

- Local authorities must meet the needs of eligible 16- and 17-year-olds in care (eligible children) or care leavers (relevant children), those who were eligible or relevant before reaching 18 (former relevant children), and former relevant children pursuing further education or training (under 25).[27]
- There is a duty on local authorities to keep in touch with their care leavers until at least the age of 21.
- At the age of 16, each young person in care must have a comprehensive written pathway plan mapping out a clear route to their independence. The plan leads on from the care plan and should include information on education, health, accommodation and any contingency plans. The content specified by the guidance is set out in Table 10.1. The

Table 10.1 Pathway plans

Pathway plans

---

1. The nature and level of contact and personal support to be provided, and by whom, to the child or young person.
2. Details of the accommodation the child or young person is to occupy.
3. A detailed plan for the education or training of the child or young person.
4. How the responsible authority will assist the child or young person in relation to employment or other purposeful activity or occupation.
5. The support to be provided to enable the child or young person to develop and sustain appropriate family and social relationships.
6. A programme to develop the practical and other skills necessary for the child or young person to live independently.
7. The financial support to be provided to the child or young person, in particular where it is to be provided to meet his accommodation and maintenance needs.
8. The health needs, including any mental health needs, of the child or young person, and how they are to be met.
9. Contingency plans for action to be taken by the responsible authority should the pathway plan for any reason cease to be effective.

The pathway plan must also record key details such as the name, age and contact details of the young person, the name and contact details of the personal adviser and those of any other people who will be actively involved in delivering aspects of the plan. It will note the date due for review.

Children (Leaving Care) Act 2000 Regulations and Guidance.
(paras. 21–22)

---

plan is described by the guidance as 'pivotal to the process whereby children and young people map out their future' (para. 7.2). It should be reviewed at least every six months.

- Personal and practical support must be provided by local authorities to 16- and 17-year-olds in care or care leavers to meet the objectives of their pathway plan.

- An adviser will be allocated to each young person to participate in implementation and review of the pathway plan, coordinate provision of support and assistance to meet the needs of the young person, and to be kept informed of his wellbeing. This may include helping the young person find training, employment or education opportunities and acting as the 'Connexions' adviser. *R (A)* v. *Lambeth LBC* [2010] EWHC 1652 (Admin) confirms that a personal adviser should not produce a young person's pathway plan. The personal adviser is a separate role to that of the social worker and the functions of the personal adviser include participating in the preparation of the plan and its review but not its actual preparation and production.

- Assistance for care leavers aged 18–21 with education, training and employment shall be continuous.

- Accommodation should be suitable in relation to health and other needs and bed-and-breakfast accommodation should only be used in an emergency for 16- and 17-year-olds.

- In place of the current system of benefits, a new financial regime will be introduced and administered by the Social Services Department. Most care leavers will no longer be entitled to claim welfare benefits.

- All young people covered by the C(LC)A 2000 will have access to the Children Act 1989 complaints procedure.

- Unaccompanied asylum-seeking children are covered by the C(LC)A 2000.

A High Court case has emphasised the importance of pathway plans. In *R (J) Caerphilly County Borough Council* [2005] EWHC 586 (Admin), Munby J gave guidance to local authorities as to what is expected in drawing up a pathway plan. The case concerned a 17-year-old, J, who had been in care for four years, having suffered abuse and disruption in his home life and with a number of criminal convictions. The local authority and other agencies had attempted to help J but he was uncooperative and unwilling to engage. Supported by the Howard League, J sought a declaration that the local authority has acted unlawfully in failing to assess his needs, prepare a pathway plan, appoint a personal adviser and provide accommodation. The court ordered the authority to produce a lawful assessment and a plan and gave the following guidance:

The child's personal adviser may be an employee of the local authority but it must be clear to the adviser and the local authority that the adviser was acting in the role of adviser to the child and not some other conflicting role. The personal adviser should not prepare the assessment and plan, the role being to liaise with the authority and focus on its implementation. The court described the personal adviser as a go-between between the child and the authority. In this case the local authority had failed to involve J in the process, which it had embarked on far too late. The plan had failed to specify key dates or identify specialist support. It was not a detailed operational plan. It failed clearly to identify the child's needs, what was to be done about them, by whom and by when. Where a child is unwilling to cooperate, this is not a reason for the authority not to carry out its obligations under the Act and regulations. The child's lack of engagement should be clearly documented in the plan with the steps the authority has taken to engage the child, and proper thought should be given to contingency plans.

The Children and Young Persons Act 2008 places a duty on local authorities to pay a bursary to former relevant children who go on to higher education. It also extends the entitlements of former relevant children to the appointment of a personal adviser and other assistance in connection with education or training. The framework of different responsibilities and support for each category of young people is explained further in DfE guidance, 'Planning Transition to Adulthood for Care Leavers' (2010).

Chapter summary

- Looked after children are those children who are accommodated by the local authority, away from their family, in residential or foster placements, and all children who are the subject of a care order, even if they are living with their parents. There are approximately 68,000 looked after children on any one day.

- It is the duty of a local authority to safeguard and promote the welfare of all looked after children. Local authorities must consult the child, his parents, any person with parental responsibility and others whose wishes and feelings are relevant, before making decisions regarding a looked after child and give due consideration to the child's racial origin, cultural and linguistic background.

- The local authority must provide accommodation and maintain looked after children under CA 1989, s. 23. The accommodation should normally be near to the child's home and contact between the child and their family should be promoted. Accommodation provided on a voluntary basis is an aspect of service provision to families.

- Fostering covers a wide range of situations including short- and long-term arrangements and provision of respite care. There are private and local authority foster carers.

- Residential care continues to have a role to play in the provision of security and stability for some children. Standards in residential care have been challenged in a number of reports and a new regulatory framework is provided by the Care Standards Act 2000 and Children's Homes Regulations 2011. An independent visitor will be provided to advise, assist and befriend certain looked after children. Sometimes a child will need to be placed in secure accommodation.

- The local authority has responsibilities towards young people leaving care, under the Children (Leaving Care) Act 2000, which develops earlier provisions of the Children Act 1989.

Exercises

The Beeches, a local authority children's home, provides accommodation for 15 young people. Consider whether any action should be taken in respect of the following incidents and what form it should take.

- A 17-year-old male resident and a 13-year-old female resident are discovered having sexual intercourse. They have not used any contraception and it is not an ongoing relationship. The girl later tells a member of staff that she was being bullied by other girls in the home who called her frigid.

- A 16-year-old male resident has been out shopping with a male member of staff in preparation for leaving the home. On the way back to the Beeches, they call at the member of staff's own home, drink a can of lager each and look at pornographic magazines.

- A 14-year-old girl returns to the Beeches at 2 a.m., four hours after the agreed time. She is abusive to staff when they ask where she has been and tries to assault a female member of staff when she asks if the girl has been taking drugs. She is restrained by a male member of staff by twisting her arm behind her back, thereby sustaining a strained wrist. She is taken to her room and locked inside. The following morning she is prevented from telephoning her social worker and is told she has nothing to complain about.

Websites

Many of the relevant official publications relating to looked after children and adoption issues can be accessed via the Department for Education website:
www.education.gov.uk/childrenandyoungpeople/families/adoption

British Agencies for Adoption and Fostering (BAAF) provides a wide range of information and research publications:
www.baaf.org.uk

BAAF also host a website focusing on private fostering
www.privatefostering.org.uk

The Fostering Network (formerly known as the National Foster Care Association) is an organisation that aims to promote improvements in foster care through involvement with agencies and foster carers. It is also a useful resource for information on fostering, producing a range of publications and reports:
www.fostering.net/

Voice for the Child in Care is a national organisation which provides independent advocacy and advice for children in care, care leavers, in custody and in need:
www.voiceyp.org

Carelaw is an information site for children and young people in care in England and Wales, providing accessible information in a question and answer format:
www.carelaw.org.uk

The Catch 22 National Care Advisory Service (NCAS) works to improve young people's transition from care to adulthood.
www.leavingcare.org/

Further reading

Texts which focus on looked after children:

Ball, C. (2014) *Looked After Children: Social Work Law Focus Series*. Basingstoke: Palgrave Macmillan.

Cocker, C. and Allain, L. (2008) *Social Work with Looked After Children*. Exeter: Learning Matters.

Schofield G. and Simmonds J. (2009) (eds) *The Child Placement Handbook* (London: BAAF).

Relevant Government documents include:

Department of Health (1997) 'People Like Us: The Report of the Review of Standards for Children Living Away from Home' (the Utting Report). London: The Stationery Office.

Department of Health (1998) 'Caring for Children Away from Home: Messages from Research'. London: The Stationery Office.

Department of Health (1998) 'Quality Protects: Transforming Children's Services'. London: Department of Health.

Department of Health (1999) 'The Government's Objectives for Children's Social Services'. London: Department of Health.

Department for Education and Skills (2004) 'Get It Sorted: Guidance on Providing Effective Advocacy Services for Children and Young People Making a Complaint Under the Children Act 1989'. London: DfES.

Department for Education and Skills (2005) 'The Replacement Children Act 1989 Guidance on Private Fostering'. London: DfES.

Department for Children, Schools and Families (2010) 'The Children Act 1989 Guidance and Regulations Volume 2: Care Planning, Placement and Case Review'. Nottingham: DCSF Publications.

Department for Children, Schools and Families (2010b) 'Sufficiency: Statutory Guidance on Securing Sufficient Accommodation for Looked After Children'. London: DCSF.

Department for Children, Schools and Families (2010c) 'IRO Handbook: Statutory Guidance for Independent Reviewing Officers and Local Authorities on their Functions in Relation to Case Management and Review for Looked After Children'. Nottingham: DCSF.

Department for Children, Schools and Families and Department for Communities and Local Government (2008) 'Provision of Accommodation for 16 and 17 Year Olds Who May Be Homeless and/or Require Accommodation'. Nottingham: DCSF.

Department for Education (2010) 'Family and Friends Care: Statutory Guidance for Local Authorities'. London: DfE.

Department for Education (2010) 'Guidance and Regulations Volume 3: Planning Transition to Adulthood for Care Leavers'. London: DfE.

Department for Education (2011) 'Guidance and Regulations Volume 4: Fostering Services'. London: DfE.

Department for Education (2013) 'Improving Permanence for Looked After Children'. London: DfE.

Department for Education (2013) 'The Children Act 1989 Guidance and Regulations Volume 5: Children's Homes'. London: DfE.

Department for Education (2014) 'Looked-after children: contact with siblings', update to 'The Children Act 1989 Guidance and Regulations Volume 2: Care Planning, Placement and Case Review'. London: DfE.

In relation to leaving care:

Broad, B. (2005) 'Young people leaving care: Implementing the Children (Leaving Care) Act 2000?' 19(5) *Children and Society* p. 343.

Morgan R. and Lindsay, M. (2006) *Young People's Views on Leaving Care: What Young People in and Formerly in Residential and Foster Care Think About Leaving Care*. London: CSCI. (A comprehensive report written by the Children's Rights Director for England.)

Stein, M. (2012) *Young People Leaving Care: Supporting Pathways to Adulthood*. London: Jessica Kingsley Publishers.

Wheal, A. (ed.) (2005) *The Leaving Care Handbook*. Lyme Regis: Russell House.

Residential care and secure accommodation are specifically addressed in:

Butler, I. and Drakeford, M. (2005) *Scandal, Social Policy and Social Welfare.* Bristol: BASW/ Policy Press. (Analyses the concept of 'scandal' with chapters on residential care of children and 'Pin-down'.)

Dunnett, K *et al.* (eds) (2006) *Health of Looked After Children and Young People.* Lyme Regis: Russell House Publishing.

Stather, J. (2013) *Secure Accommodation Handbook.* Bristol: Family Law.

Stein, M. (2006) 'Missing Years of Abuse in Children's Homes' 11 *Child and Family Social Work* p. 11.

Waterhouse, R. (2000) 'Report of the Tribunal of Enquiry into the Abuse of Children in Care in the Former County Council Areas of Gwynedd and Clwyd since 1974'. London: House of Commons.

Other aspects of law relating to planning and placement of looked after children:

Knowles, G. and Sharp, M. (2012) 'IRO service: still a work in progress?' (Parts 1 and 2) *Family Law* (November) p. 1258 and (December) p. 1377.

Schofield, G., Thoburn, J., Howell, D. and Dickens, J. (2007) 'The search for stability and permanence: modelling the pathways of long stay looked after children' 37(4) *British Journal of Social Work* p. 619.

Sinclair, I. (2005) *Fostering Now: Messages from Research.* London: Jessica Kingsley. (Sixteen research studies.)

Talbot, C. and Williams, M. (2003) 'Kinship care' *Family Law* p. 502. (Considers outcomes for the increasing number of children living in kinship care arrangements.)

Thomas, N (2011) 'Care planning and review for looked after children: fifteen years of slow progress?' 41 *British Journal of Social Work* p. 387.

Notes

[1] Children Act 1989, s. 22(2).

[2] See DfES (2003) 'If This Were My Child'.

[3] Cm. 7317.

[4] DfE Statistical First Release SFR 36/2013.

[5] Ibid.

[6] Care Planning, Placement and Case Review Regulations 2010 (replacing the Review of Children's Cases Regulations 1991). See also the IRO Handbook: 'Statutory guidance for independent reviewing officers and local authorities on their functions in relation to case management and review for looked after children' (DCSF, 2010).

[7] SFR 50/2013

[8] Meltzer, H., Gatward, R., Corbin. T., Goodman, R. and Ford, T. (2003) *The Mental Health of Young People Looked After by Local Authorities in England.* London: The Stationery Office.

[9] Department of Health. London: HMSO. See also Department of Health (1998) 'Quality Protects: Transforming Children's Services'. London: Department of Health.

[10] Tony Blair: Prime Minister's Review of Adoption (2000). Performance and Innovation Unit.

[11] DfES 'Statutory Guidance on the Duty on Local Authorities to Promote the Educational Achievement of Looked After Children under s 52 Children Act 2004'. p. 23.

[12] DfES (2005) *Qualitative Study: The Placement Stability of Looked After Children.* London: DfES.

[13] 'The Children Act 1989 Guidance and Regulations', vol. 8 'Private fostering and miscellaneous', London: DfES, p. 1.

[14] J. Plotnikoff and R. Woolfson (2000) *Reporting to Court under the Children Act: A Handbook for Social Services*. London: Department of Health/The Stationery Office.

[15] SI 2005/1533.

[16] SI 1991/2094.

[17] See, further, 'The Children Act 1989 Guidance and Regulations', vol. 8 'Private fostering and miscellaneous', London: DfES.

[18] Department of Health (1997) 'People Like Us: The Report of the Review of Standards for Children Living Away from Home' (The Utting Report). London: The Stationery Office.

[19] Further decisions of the Care Standards Tribunal can be accessed on its website: www.carestandardstribunal.gov.uk.

[20] SI 2001/3967.

[21] SFR 14/2014.

[22] SI 1991/1505.

[23] See also Definition of Independent Visitors (Children) Regulations 1991 (SI 1991/892).

[24] *Hereford and Worcester County Council* v. *S* [1993] 2 FLR 360. See also 'The Children Act Guidance and Regulations', vol. 4 'Residential care'. London: DfES.

[25] www.ofsted.gov.uk/resources/independent-visitors.

[26] See B. Broad (1999) 'Young people leaving care: moving towards "joined up" solutions?' 13 *Children and Society* p. 81.

[27] The exact definitions are:

Eligible children: Children aged 16 and 17 who have been looked after for at least 13 weeks since the age of 14 and who are still looked after.

Relevant children: Children aged 16 and 17 who have been looked after for at least 13 weeks since the age of 14, and have been looked after at some time while 16 or 17, and who have left care.

Former relevant children: Young people aged 18–21 who have been either *eligible* or *relevant children*, or both.

Qualifying children and young people over 16: Any person under 21 (24 if in education or training) who ceases to be looked after or accommodated or privately fostered after the age of 16.

Chapter 11

Adoption

Learning objectives

To develop an understanding of the following:

- The current law of adoption embodied in the Adoption and Children Act 2002.
- Background to the reforms introduced by the Adoption and Children Act 2002.
- National Standards for Adoption.
- Particular issues within adoption, including the question of who can adopt, placement, the role of parental consent and the development of 'open adoption'.
- Issues surrounding the adoption process, including the role of the adoption panel.
- Alternative routes to security and stability,[1] including use of and special guardianship.

Talking Point

An important Supreme Court decision reinforces the need for adoption agencies to give proper consideration to alternative placements before the court will approve an adoptive care plan.

A mother (M) appealed against refusal of her application for leave to oppose the making of an adoption order (under s. 47(5)), in relation to her children who had been made subject of care and placement orders. The children were placed with prospective adopters and an application for adoption was made. The mother's new circumstances were described as 'astonishingly different'. The judgments of both the Supreme Court and Court of Appeal provide guidance on the proper approach in adoption applications and the analysis of applications under s. 47(5). The Supreme Court emphasised a number fundamental principles for adoption cases (reinforcing points made in the earlier decision of *Re B (A Child) (Care Proceedings: Threshold Criteria)* [2013] UKSC 33.

Key points:

- The court cannot give leave to oppose an adoption order application unless there has been a change in (the mother's) circumstances. If leave is granted then the parent can oppose the adoption order and is also entitled to fresh consideration of whether parental consent should be dispensed with.

- 'Orders contemplating non-consensual adoption – care orders with a plan for adoption, placement orders and adoption orders – are "a very extreme thing, a last resort", only to be made where "nothing else will do", where "no other course [is] possible in [the child's] interests",' [22]

- '… although the child's interests in an adoption case are paramount, the court must never lose sight of the fact that those interests include being brought up by the natural family, ideally by the natural parents, or at least one of them, unless the overriding requirements of the child's welfare make that not possible'. [26]

- '… the court "must" consider all the options before coming to a decision…. They range, in principle, from the making of no order at one end of the spectrum to the making of an adoption order at the other.' [27]

- '… the court's assessment of the parents' ability to discharge their responsibilities towards the child must take into account the assistance which the authorities would offer.' [28] 'It is the obligation of the local authority to make the order which the court has determined is proportionate work. The local authority cannot press for a more drastic form of order, least of all … adoption, because it is unable or unwilling to support a less interventionist form of order.' [29]

- 'We have real concerns, shared by other judges about the recurrent inadequacy of the analysis and reasoning put forward in support of the case for adoption, both in the materials put before the court by local authorities and guardians and also in too many judgements. This is nothing new. But it is time to call a halt.' [30]

Re B-S [2013] EWCA Civ 1146 may be described as a landmark ruling from the Court of Appeal on adoption law and practice. It has subsequently been applied in a series of cases, including *Re E* [2013] EWCA Civ 1614, *Re HA (A Child)* [2013] EWCA Civ 3634 and *Re L* [2013] EWCA Civ 1481.

One of the practice implications of this judgment is that evidence from the local authority will increasingly be presented following a balance sheet model, analysing placement options, weighing up advantages and disadvantages in depth in order to evidence that nothing less than adoption will meet the needs of the child. The Supreme Court applies existing law but emphasises the need to apply the principle of proportionality in arriving at decisions, and the need for rigorous, evidence-based practice by local authorities and reasoned judgements by the courts 'where the issues are so grave and the stakes, for both child and parent, so high' [40].

Introduction

Adoption may be described as the process whereby the legal relationship between the child and her birth parents is severed and a new relationship is created between the child and her adoptive parents. Adoption terminates parental responsibility and is permanent and irrevocable. The law on adoption is contained in the Adoption and Children Act 2002 (**ACA** 2002), which replaced and revoked the old law contained in the Adoption Act 1976 (**AA**). The main provisions of the Act are considered throughout this chapter following discussion of the context and background to the reforms. Towards the end of the chapter the amendments made to the Children Act 1989 are outlined with more detailed consideration of special guardianship, an order introduced by the Act as one of a number of alternatives to adoption providing varying degrees of stability and legal certainty. The order is compared with both adoption and residence (as an element of the Child Arrangements Order).

The opportunity was missed to reform adoption law and incorporate adoption into the Children Act 1989, despite the fact that a Department of Health review of adoption was ongoing at the time the Children Act was introduced; and a subsequent Adoption Bill in 1996 never became law. To a certain extent this defeated one of the objectives of the Children Act, which was to provide a comprehensive piece of legislation dealing with all aspects of childcare, as a significant body of child law remained outside the Act. The Children Act did make some changes to adoption, which were described as minor and inconsequential by the guidance. In fact their impact has been significant.

Children Act 1989 changes to adoption

The following changes to adoption occurred as a result of the Act:

- The term 'parental responsibility' replaced parental rights and duties in the Adoption Act 1976.
- Adoption proceedings were designated family proceedings and hence the menu of orders principle applies. The effect of this is that, in proceedings where an adoption order is sought, it is possible for the courts to select an alternative order from the menu if it is considered appropriate. For example, if an adoption order is sought by a relative of the child, the court might consider that a Child Arrangements Order would be more appropriate determining the child's place of residence and contact.
- The Children Act 1989 established an Adoption Contact Register, whereby an adopted person, on reaching majority, could make contact with any birth relatives who had placed their names on the register.

Background to the Adoption and Children Act 2002

History suggests that some form of informal adoption has always been practised; however, there was no formal legal adoption in England and Wales until the Adoption Act 1926 was introduced. This Act did little to regulate the process, simply giving legal recognition to *de facto* transfers. In 1927 there were 3,000 adoptions. The next significant piece of adoption legislation was the Adoption Act 1958. In subsequent years a number of reports found levels of dissatisfaction with the absence of a clear legal framework to regulate the practice of adoption. The Houghton Committee reported in 1972, its recommendations leading to the Children Act 1975, the adoption provisions of which became the Adoption Act 1976. Over that period there were significant changes in society, which affected the numbers of children available for adoption. In 1968 adoptions were at a peak, with 27,000 adoptions registered. Since that time the numbers of children available for adoption have consistently fallen, contributory factors include the increased availability of contraception and abortion and less stigma surrounding single parenthood. At the same time, different children started to be considered available for adoption, with fewer and fewer newborn babies available. An influential report, 'Children Who Wait' (1973)[2] identified significant numbers of children languishing in care without appropriate plans for permanency. The emphasis of the Children Act 1975 was to position adoption as a local authority resource to provide permanency for children in care and to encourage greater long-term planning.

A steady drop in the number of children leaving care through adoption had been identified through the 1990s[3] and concerns were expressed that the adoption system has been characterised by delays, with a quarter of children waiting more than three years for placement. These issues were taken up at the highest level in the Prime Minister's Review of Adoption, published in 2000. In the foreword, the Prime Minister (Tony Blair) states:

> it is hard to overstate the importance of a stable and loving family life for children. That is why I want more children to benefit from adoption. We know that adoption works for children. Over the years many thousands of children in the care of local authorities have benefited from the generosity and commitment of adoptive families, prepared to offer them the security and wellbeing that comes from being accepted as members of new families. But we also know that many children wait in care for far too long. Some of the reasons are well known. Too often in the past adoption has been seen as a last resort. Too many local authorities have performed poorly in helping children out of care and into adoption.

This determination and commitment to adoption reform was reflected in a number of developments introduced prior to the new legislation. In October 2000 an 'Adoption and Permanence Task Force' was established, its aim being to 'support local councils in improving their performance on maximising the use of adoption as an option for meeting the needs of looked after children'. A white paper, entitled 'Adoption: a new approach' followed in December 2000 and included a national target of increasing by 40 per cent the number of looked after children adopted from care. In order to help agencies to identify matches of children and prospective adopters, a National Adoption Register was established in April 2001. The clear focus of the Adoption and Children Act 2002 reflected previous publications on the adoption of looked after children. It is essential to recognise that looked after children do not present as a homogeneous group: there are different reasons for becoming looked after; there are differing legal statuses of being looked after; looked after children have different individual characteristics including age, disability and ethnic origin. This was acknowledged in the Prime Minister's Review which noted: 'adoption from care is not about providing couples with trouble free babies. It is about finding families for children of a range of ages, with challenging backgrounds and complex needs.'

Critiques of the ACA inevitably emerged (see Further reading) and the legislation is complex and not very accessible. It is supplemented by a daunting amount of secondary legislation which contains much of the detail and procedure in the form of rules and regulations (at least 25 types identified in the Act). Further developments have included publication of 'An Action Plan for Adoption: Tackling Delay' (2012), new Statutory Guidance in 2013, and a considerable body of case law.

Current law on adoption

Introduction

Adoption is a complex area of law and practice. Current legislation, the Adoption and Children Act, has been in place since December 2005.[4] The Act updated adoption law, aligned adoption law more closely with the Children Act 1989 and included the objectives of improving performance of adoption services and promoting greater use of adoption for looked after children. The Act introduced the special guardianship order, adding to the range of possibilities for permanence for a child. Recent case law has emphasised the need to consider the full range of permanency options and that due to the absolute severance of the parent–child relationship, adoption may properly be seen as a 'last resort'. The Act is supported by National Minimum Standards (2013) and Statutory Guidance (2014).

The adoption service

Adoption services are provided by approved **adoption agencies**. All local authorities are required by s. 2 of the Adoption and Children Act 2002 to provide a comprehensive adoption service in order to meet the needs of children who have been, or may be, adopted, their parents, guardians and prospective adopters (the elements of what is sometimes referred to as 'the adoption triangle'). This comprehensive service includes provision of adoption support services (discussed below). Each local authority must prepare a plan for the provision of adoption services (s. 3). In addition to local authorities directly acting as adoption agencies, there are a number of registered adoption societies (previously known as voluntary adoption agencies, e.g. Barnardo's) in England and Wales providing services including recruitment of adopters, assessment and matching. Under the Education and Inspection Act 2006 local authority and voluntary adoption agencies are regulated by Ofsted. Each local authority is required to provide a 'children's guide' to its adoption service, for children and prospective adopters.

Social workers involved with adoption cases will usually be experienced members of family placement teams specialising in adoption work. Regulation 10 of the Adoption Service (England) Regulations 2003 (SI 2003/370) requires there to be a 'sufficient number of suitably qualified, competent and experienced persons working for the purposes of the adoption service'. The statutory guidance stipulates that adoption reports may only be prepared by social workers with appropriate qualifications and direct experience of adoption work and that, 'Reports must be succinct and accurate. There should be robust social work analysis with strong evidence that distinguishes between fact, opinion and third party information' (para 8.7).

If the child concerned has been the subject of care proceedings, adoption may have been identified in the care plan as the proposed plan for the child. In other cases the decision to place the child for adoption may follow unsuccessful attempts at rehabilitation with the child's family. Statutory childcare reviews provide the focus for decisions following the care order. Once the decision is made to plan for adoption there may be a change of social worker, reflecting the different areas of expertise. The social worker in an adoption case is likely to have to work with the child, the birth family and the prospective adopters, each of which are likely to have a different perspective on the proposal and different needs (standards do provide for the birth family to have their own support worker). Adoption and placement orders can only be made by the court, and the local authority legal adviser should work closely with the social worker in preparing the application and associated documentation.

National Standards

The legislation is underpinned by National Minimum Standards (2013, DfE), the purpose of which is to ensure that all those involved in the adoption process have an understanding of what to expect and that there is consistency in adoption services across the country. A number of principles underpin the standards, which are expressed as values at the beginning of the document. For example:

- The child's welfare, safety and needs are at the centre of the adoption process.
- Children are entitled to grow up as part of a loving family that can meet their developmental needs during childhood and beyond.
- Children's wishes and feelings are important and will be actively sought and fully taken into account at all stages of the adoption process.
- Delays should be avoided as they can have a severe impact on the health and development of the children waiting to be adopted.
- A sense of identity is important to a child's wellbeing. To help children develop this, their ethnic origin, cultural background, religion, language and sexuality need to be properly recognised and positively valued and promoted.
- The particular needs of disabled children and children with complex needs will be fully recognised and taken into account.
- Adoption is an evolving life-long process for all those involved – adopted adults and birth and adoptive relatives. The fundamental issues raised by adoption may reverberate and resurface at different times and stages throughout an individual's life.
- Agencies have a duty to provide services that consider the welfare of all parties involved and should consider the implications of decisions and actions for everyone involved.
- Adopted adults have their adoptive identity safeguarded and the right to decide whether to be involved in contact or communication with birth family members.

Standards are likely to have a significant impact on good practice of the adoption service and the courts as they are used by Ofsted in their inspection process. The standards are arranged in themes with application to children; prospective adopters; adoptive parents; birth parents and birth families; councils (corporate and management responsibilities) and agency functions and voluntary adoption agencies. Each section begins with a key standard, an outcome and further detailed elaboration of the key standard.

A selection of the standards are included below:

National Adoption Standards for England

- Prospective adopters are prepared and supported to promote the child's social and emotional development, and to enable the child to develop emotional resilience and positive self-esteem.

- Initial contact arrangements are focused on the child's needs with the views of the prospective adopters and birth family members taken into account.

- Children, prospective adopters, adopters, birth parents and members of the birth family are helped to understand the harm unauthorised or unmediated contact, including through online social networks, can have and are supported if unauthorised contact is made. The child's need for a permanent home will be addressed at the four-month review and a plan for permanence made.

- The adoption agency implements an effective strategy to recruit and assess prospective adopters who can meet most of the needs of those children for whom adoption is the plan.

- Birth parents are given access to, and are actively encouraged to use, a support worker from the time adoption is identified as the plan for the child.

- The consent of the birth parents to their child being placed for adoption is sought, or an application for a placement order is made as part of the care proceedings, immediately after the decision of the agency's decision-maker that the child should be placed for adoption, bearing in mind that any delay is likely to prejudice the child's welfare.

- The adoption panel makes a considered recommendation on the proposed placement of a child with particular prospective adopters within six months of the adoption agency's decision-maker deciding that the child should be placed for adoption.

- The prospective adopters are helped to fully understand the child's background, health, emotional and developmental needs and the practical implications for parenting that child before they agree for the match to be passed to the adoption panel.[5]

Guidance

Statutory guidance supports the Adoption and Children Act 2002 (DfES, 2014, replacing 2005, 2011 and 2013 versions). It is issued under s. 7 of the Local Authority Social Services Act 1970, and as such should be complied with unless there are exceptional local circumstances which justify a variation in practice. The chapter in the 2013 version 'Adoption Agency and Local Authority Responsibilities in Court Proceedings' is now incorporated into the Children Act 1989 Statutory Guidance, Volume 1: Court Orders and Pre-proceedings (vol. 1, 2014). 'Guidance on Fostering for Adoption' is included in Volume 2: Care Planning, Placement and Case Review.

Principles

Part 1 of the Act introduces a set of principles in the section entitled 'Considerations applying to the exercise of powers'. The aim is to achieve consistency between the Children Act

1989 and the Adoption and Children Act 2002 through alignment of principles which put the child at the centre of the adoption process. (Similar principles contained in Part 1 of the Children Act 1989 are discussed in Chapter 7.)

Welfare

> ### s. 1
>
> **(1)** This section applies whenever a court or adoption agency is coming to a decision relating to the adoption of a child.
>
> **(2)** The paramount consideration of the court or adoption agency must be the child's welfare, throughout his life.
>
> (ACA 2002)

Use of the word 'paramount' is a departure from the previous welfare provision in the 1976 legislation, where reference was made to 'first consideration being given to the need to safeguard and promote the welfare of the child throughout his childhood' (Adoption Act 1976, s. 6). Under the old law, welfare did not necessarily prevail over other considerations, including the birth parents' interests. It was the single most important factor but not overriding all other considerations, as paramountcy suggests. The section applies whenever a court or agency is coming to a decision. This is an area of difference between the Acts: in the Children Act 1989, the paramountcy principle applies to decisions of the court only, though of course agencies have this in mind in those cases which reach court. The test applies throughout the child's life, clearly recognising that the decision must reflect the long-lasting impact of an adoption order and extending beyond the previous test where consideration applied throughout childhood. The phrase 'coming to a decision' applies where orders that might be made include adoption or placement or granting leave.

Welfare checklist

The welfare principle is supported by a checklist, in similar but not identical terms to the checklist in the Children Act 1989. It is not intended to be exhaustive, nor in any order of priority. Every aspect of the checklist should be addressed in reports to court.

Children Act case law may be relevant to interpretation and application of aspects of the checklist.

> ### s. 1(4)
>
> **(4)** The court or adoption agency must have regard to the following matters (among others) –
>
>   **(a)** the child's ascertainable wishes and feelings regarding the decision (considered in the light of the child's age and understanding),
>
>   **(b)** the child's particular needs,
>
>   **(c)** the likely effect on the child (throughout his life) of having ceased to be a member of the original family and become an adopted person,

➡

> **(d)** the child's age, sex, background and any of the child's characteristics which the court or agency considers relevant,
>
> **(e)** any harm (within the meaning of the Children Act 1989) which the child has suffered or is at risk of suffering,
>
> **(f)** the relationship which the child has with relatives, and with any other person in relation to whom the court or agency considers the relationship to be relevant, including –
>
> > **(i)** the likelihood of any such relationship continuing and the value to the child of its doing so,
> >
> > **(ii)** the ability and willingness of any of the child's relatives, or of any such person, to provide the child with a secure environment in which the child can develop, and otherwise to meet the child's needs, and
> >
> > **(iii)** the wishes and feelings of any of the child's relatives, or of any such person, regarding the child.
>
> (ACA 2002)

Each factor in the checklist is worthy of fuller discussion.

s. 1(4)

> **(a)** the child's ascertainable wishes and feelings regarding the decision (considered in the light of the child's age and understanding)
>
> (ACA 2002)

The 1992 review of adoption suggested that a child of 12 plus should have to give consent to his or her own adoption, as is the case in Scotland. This position did at least recognise the need for a child's formal input during the process but was rejected and the familiar phrase 'considered in the light of the child's age and understanding' is included as preferable to a fixed age. Such an omission regarding a major life-changing decision is in flagrant disregard of children's rights. The judge in any particular case has discretion as to the weight to attach to the child's ascertainable wishes and feelings. Whilst actual consent of the child is not required, it is unlikely that adoption would proceed were the child to express a wish not to be adopted. Given the increase in older children being adopted, and the range of alternatives to adoption, this is a particularly important element of the checklist.

s. 1(4)

> **(b)** the child's particular needs
>
> (ACA 2002)

This factor incorporates the child's physical, emotional and educational needs as expressed in the Children Act 1989 checklist and is likely to extend to other needs including social, psychological and health. The case of *Re M (Contact: Welfare Test)* [1995] 1 FLR 274 may be relevant here. It noted the fundamental emotional need of every child to have an enduring relationship with both of his parents. Emotional needs are also relevant when considering any continuing relationship with siblings as looked after children are often adopted apart from their siblings.

> ### s. 1(4)
>
> **(c)** the likely effect on the child (throughout his life) of having ceased to be a member of the original family and become an adopted person
>
> (ACA 2002)

There are two important aspects of this factor: both ceasing to be and becoming a member of a family. The United Nations Convention on the Rights of the Child states that it is the fundamental right of every child to belong to a family, and Art. 8 of the ECHR, the right to respect for family life, is also relevant. In ceasing to become a member of the original family, there are risks to the child in terms of his sense of identity and possible feelings of abandonment. Becoming a member of the adoptive family may provide a sense of permanence and security for the child (and the adopters) and removes the uncertainty of possible further applications and moves. The comparable section in the Children Act 1989 considers the likely effect of any change in the child's circumstances. The provision here is clearly more focused on the effect of adoption. As with the welfare principle, the court must consider the effect on the child throughout his life, not just his childhood. By implication succession rights and interests and nationality could be a relevant consideration.

> ### s. 1(4)
>
> **(d)** the child's age, sex, background and any of the child's characteristics which the court or agency considers relevant
>
> (ACA 2002)

The child's age is specified and this may be particularly relevant to issues of contact. Given the lifelong benefits, adoption of older children is clearly anticipated. The child's characteristics would extend to consideration of any disability or special health needs and may include racial and cultural issues. The opportunity to consider these characteristics in the checklist is particularly important since the previous specific direction to the court to their consideration has been revoked. Section 1(5), which stated 'In placing the child for adoption, the adoption agency must give due consideration to the child's religious persuasion, racial origin and cultural and linguistic background' has been repealed by the Children and Families Act 2014.

The role of ethnic origin and culture had become a significant feature of discussion of adoption placements and the ACA 2002 included a specific requirement to give due consideration to religious persuasion, racial origin and cultural and linguistic background as one of the principles (in the same terms as the duty on local authorities when considering making a decision about a looked after child (including placement) in CA 1989, s. 22(5)). The debate focused on whether it is good practice to place a black child with a white family and various terms have been employed, including trans-racial adoption and same-race placement. A limited amount of case law presents inconsistency in the way in which the law has approached the issue. For example, in *Re P (A Minor)* [1990] FCR 260, a mixed-race baby was placed with a white foster mother at 5 days old. It was intended to be a short-term placement but the child remained there for over a year. At the time of the hearing, the foster mother was not in a position to adopt the child, and the judge supported a move to a black adoptive family who could meet his cultural and identity needs; any trauma felt by the child in having to move could be limited by sensitive handling. In *Re O (Transracial Adoption: Contact)* [1995] 2 FLR 597, a black child of Nigerian parents had been in the care of white foster carers at the time of the hearing of the foster carers' application for adoption. The court made an adoption order to provide security for the family and an end to social work intervention. The parents' consent was dispensed with as being unreasonably withheld, despite the argument that adoption was anathema to Nigerian culture. A condition for contact with the mother was attached to the order.

Guidance in a circular entitled 'Adoption – Achieving the right balance' (now repealed) recognised the importance of a child's ethnic origin, culture and religion as significant factors to be taken into account, noting that 'placement with a family of similar ethnic origin is most likely to meet the child's needs as fully as possible'. It guards against agencies waiting indefinitely for a new family, and states: 'it is unacceptable for a child to be denied loving adoptive parents solely on the grounds that the child and adopters do not share the same racial or cultural background'.

The emphasis of the formal guidance was to find a family of similar ethnic background if possible but if that was not possible, the child should not be kept waiting. A family should be found which may not share the same characteristics as the child but is committed to assisting the child to understand his background and culture and be proud of his heritage. It is also important for the family to be able to deal with racism that the child might encounter, and this is a strong argument in favour of placing the child with a black family even though (particularly with children of mixed race) the family may not exactly match the child's ethnic background. This stance has clearly been influenced by concerns about the effect that delay has on a child waiting for an adoptive family, and a shortage of prospective adoptive parents (and foster carers) from ethnic backgrounds. The repeal of s.1 (5) is based on the Government's view that consideration of ethnicity is an important, but should not be an overriding, consideration in adoption placements. In fact as s.1 (5) was considered alongside the range of factors in the welfare checklist it did not amount to an overriding consideration and it is regrettable that this important provision has been removed from the legislation.

---

s. 1(4)

(e) any harm (within the meaning of the Children Act 1989) which the child has suffered or is at risk of suffering

(ACA 2002)

This factor refers to any harm, not just significant harm. Harm is as defined under the Children Act, which includes the amendment introduced by the ACA to 'impairment suffered from seeing or hearing the ill-treatment of another'.

s. 1(4)

(f) the relationship which the child has with relatives, and with any other person in relation to whom the court or agency considers the relationship to be relevant, including –
  (i) the likelihood of any such relationship continuing and the value to the child of its doing so,
  (ii) the ability and willingness of any of the child's relatives, or of any such person, to provide the child with a secure environment in which the child can develop, and otherwise to meet the child's needs,
  (iii) the wishes and feelings of any of the child's relatives, or of any such person, regarding the child

(ACA 2002)

This factor is one of the provisions in the Act that calls on the court to consider contact. The term 'relationship' is not confined to legal relationships (s. 1(8)(a)), but allows the views of other important people in the child's life to be taken into account, such as foster carers. It also includes the child's birth parents (without reference to parental responsibility). It is a factor that may be especially relevant to the older child with existing links to their birth family. It refers to 'ability and willingness' to meet the child's needs rather than 'capability', as in the Children Act 1989. Article 8 arguments are particularly important here in terms of continuation of some form of 'family life'.

Delay

s. 1(3)

The court or adoption agency must at all times bear in mind that, in general, any delay in coming to the decision is likely to prejudice the child's welfare

(ACA 2002)

Again, the delay principle is drawn from the Children Act. The court will draw up a timetable for the avoidance of delay. The Public Law Outline will also have an impact on the overall timescales for a child between care proceedings and final placement.

There is also a close link to time limits set out in the National Standards, for example the commitment to make decisions about permanency at each looked after child's four-month review.

The Department of Education published, 'An Action Plan for Adoption: Tackling Delay', in March 2012. The intention is to introduce new timescales to reduce delays in the adoption process. Adoption scorecards will measure performance of adoption agencies, including key indicators, such as: time from entering care to being placed with an adoptive family; speed of the matching process.

No order

> ### s. 1(6)
>
> The court or adoption agency must always consider the whole range of powers available to it in the child's case (whether under this Act or the Children Act 1989); and the court must not make any order under this Act unless it considers that making the order would be better for the child than not doing so
>
> (ACA 2002)

This principle incorporates the 'menu' principle of the Children Act and the 'no order' principle. The court is reminded of its obligation to consider whether other orders such as residence, care and supervision, contact and special guardianship might be appropriate instead of adoption, or in the case of contact, alongside an adoption order. This is particularly important given the courts' obligations under the Human Rights Act, the obvious interference with family life that an adoption order would effect and the need to act proportionately.

The court was faced with such an exercise in the case of *Re M (A Minor) (Adoption or Residence Order)* [1998] 1 FLR 570. Justice Ward identified two distinct and separate questions for the court. First, should the child live with the applicants or someone else and second, should the child live with that person under the aegis of adoption, care, residence alone, residence and s. 91(14) restriction, or no order at all. In reaching a decision it was necessary to have regard to the nature and effect of each order and the advantages and disadvantages each brings to the safeguarding and promotion of the welfare of the child.

The menu principle is supported by the requirement that the court must not make any order unless it considers that making the order would be better for the child than not doing so, the 'no order' principle. This again reflects the least interventionist approach and the need for proportionality. Whilst it may be argued that, in following that approach, adoption will be seen as a last resort, it does not mean that other 'least interventionist' orders have to be exhausted first. At planning stages the range of options should be considered for the individual child (not under a policy umbrella; e.g. all children under 8 are placed for adoption) and there should be evidence of such consideration.

Who can adopt?

Section 49 states that an application for adoption can be made by a couple, or one person (as long as certain conditions as to domicile and minimum age are satisfied: ss. 50–51).

Various factors beyond the basic legal requirement will actually determine whether an applicant(s) is considered suitable to adopt; this issue has been the subject of much controversy. A white paper issued in 1993[6] implored Social Services Departments to make 'common-sense and objective professional assessment and avoid reliance on ideology' (para. 4.28) in their judgments on suitability and not to be bound by dogmatic policies driven by ideas of political correctness.[7] The use of such a subjective term as 'common sense' is of little improvement. The reference is unhelpful and serves to undermine the skills required to assess suitability for adoption. It should be noted, however, that there has been considerable regional variation in the approach taken by different authorities, often driven by preferences of adoption panel members as well as authority policies. A number of specific cases are considered.

Step-parents

Adoptions by step-parents constitute about one-half of the total number of adoptions each year. Under the old law, in order to adopt it was necessary for the step-parent to apply jointly with his spouse. In most cases, therefore, where it is the step-father who wishes to adopt, his wife (the birth mother) had to adopt her own child. The adoption order extinguished the parental responsibility of the child's natural father (where he held parental responsibility), and may not always be appropriate for that reason. It has been suggested that in some cases there may be a *'quid pro quo'* aspect to the adoption, in that motivation for the adoption may be that the child can take on the step-parent's surname and the birth parent is relieved of any continuing financial obligations.[8]

The 2002 Act changes the position on adoption by step-parents. Adoption is permitted by one person, under s. 51, where that person is the partner of a parent of the person to be adopted. The applicant, i.e. the step-parent, must have lived with the child for six months minimum. This change in the law means that the parent of the child is no longer required to adopt her own child.

It should also be noted that as the term 'partner' is used, it is not necessary for the step-parent to be married to the child's parent. They may be in a cohabiting heterosexual or same-sex relationship. This is consistent with the late amendment to the Act which allowed unmarried couples to adopt jointly. However, it is inconsistent with the amendment to the Children Act (below), where a step-parent may acquire parental responsibility only if married to the child's parent.

The step-parent must give three months' notice to the local authority of his intention to apply for an adoption order and the authority will prepare a report for the court dealing with suitability and following the s. 1 principles.

Single person

Policy documents have tended to refer to adoption by single persons as particularly suitable to the adoption of children with special needs against a preference in favour of married couples. Under the old law an adoption application was sometimes made by one person, who was part of a cohabiting or homosexual couple, with an application for joint residence to both of the couple. This was clearly the case in *Re W (A Minor) (Adoption: Homosexual Adopter)* [1997] 2 FLR 406.

Couples

A late amendment to the Act (following much debate) removed the previous restriction that only married couples could apply jointly to adopt a child. The preference for married couples rather than cohabitees was based on the argument that couples who have committed themselves legally to their relationship are more likely to be able to provide long-term stability for the adopted child. High divorce rates and the trend for more couples to cohabit both undermine this presumption and potentially limit the number of available prospective adoptive couples.

The legislation allows adoption by single people or couples (s. 49) as defined by s. 144(4):

> ## s. 144(4)
>
> ... a couple means –
>
> **(a)** a married couple, or
>
> **(b)** two people (whether of different sexes or the same sex) living as partners in an enduring family relationship.
>
> (ACA 2002)

In the assessment of suitability of adopters, regulations require that, 'in determining the suitability of a couple to adopt a child, proper regard is to be had to the need for stability and permanence in their relationship'. This change to the law will considerably widen the pool of prospective adopters.

Sexuality

The restriction against adoption by unmarried couples was also pertinent to the consideration of homosexual couples who wish to adopt. There was no specific reference to sexuality in the Adoption Act 1976 but early case law showed a judicial reluctance to approve adoption or other permanency options where the applicant was gay. For example, in *S v. S (Custody of Children)* [1980] 1 FLR 143, an application for custody by a lesbian mother was unsuccessful. In *Re P (A Minor) (Custody)* (1983) 4 FLR 401, the judge stated that there is disadvantage to a child of a homosexual parent, as 'a lesbian household would quite likely be the subject of embarrassing conduct or comment' (p. 405).[9] More recently, a less homophobic attitude can be detected from cases such as *Re W (A Minor) (Adoption: Homosexual Adopter)* [1997] 2 FLR 406, where the court stated the accurate position that there is nothing in law which prevents a single applicant for adoption being homosexual.

Age and health

The actual legal restrictions as to who may adopt are quite limited. In practice, other issues may effectively present a barrier to approval by the adoption panel. Most agencies have developed guidelines on the maximum age of prospective adopters, to ensure that the parents of adopted children will not be significantly older than non-adoptive parents of children of the same age, and so that there is a reasonable prospect of them being fit and healthy. Any age limit is most likely to apply to couples who wish to adopt a baby or young child. In practice, some couples who have exhausted fertility treatments before considering adoption may find that they are 'too old'. It may still be possible for an older individual or couple to adopt an older child. The guidance explains:

> The age of the prospective adopter must also be considered in the light of the gap in age between them and the child to be placed with them. Too large a gap may have an adverse effect upon the child and possibly upon their relationship with the adoptive parents. Where a child has already suffered change, deprivation and loss in their early years, demands on adoptive parents, both physical and emotional, are likely to be considerable, particularly as the child grows older. (para 3.22)

In practice, the medical member of the adoption panel can also influence agency policy on the extent to which health issues such as obesity or smoking should be taken into account in the assessment process.

> **Reflect**
>
> What restrictions would you place on people suitable to adopt? Does the legal framework reflect your view?

Who can be adopted?

A child under the age of 18 can be adopted. Consent of the child is not required, although her wishes and feelings will be ascertained by the children's guardian or reporting officer and will also be covered in the child's permanence report prepared by the agency social worker.[10]

A child must have been placed with the prospective adopters for a continuous period of at least ten weeks before the application is made (s. 42). In step-parent adoptions the child must have lived with the step-parent for a continuous period of six months preceding the application. A child must have lived with local authority foster parents for a year before they can apply to adopt. This 'probationary period' allows the relationship between the prospective adopters and the child to start to develop and allows the agency to see the child with the applicants. An order will not be made if the local authority has not had sufficient opportunities to see the child with the applicants in the home environment.

Conditions for making an adoption order – placement and consent

An adoption order may not be made in England and Wales[11] unless one of two conditions is satisfied as set out in s. 47.

The first condition is that the court is satisfied that each parent or guardian consents to the adoption order, has consented under s. 20 (and has not withdrawn the consent) and does not oppose the making of the adoption order, or the parent's or guardian's consent should be dispensed with.

The second condition is that the child has been placed for adoption by an adoption agency with the prospective adopters in whose favour the order is proposed to be made, either with parental consent or under a placement order, and no parent or guardian opposes the making of the adoption order.

Placement and consent are considered in more detail below.

Placement

A new system of placement and placement orders prior to adoption is introduced by the Act. This system replaces freeing (now abolished), a feature of some but not all adoption cases under the old law.

The placement regime alters the timing of the courts' involvement in the process by formalising the placement stage. The idea is that an earlier court decision on the child's placement avoids a *fait accompli* in circumstances where a child might have become settled with prospective adopters before the birth parents had an opportunity to challenge. Placement is one of the most difficult aspects of the new legislation, rather technical and legalistic and dealt with in ss. 18–29.

The agency will be able to place a child for adoption, or allow a child who has been placed with another carer to stay with them as prospective adopter, only where the parents of the child have given consent or a placement order has been obtained. In the situation which was common under the old law, where a child was placed with prospective adopters following a care order, placement under the new provisions would inevitably be delayed if the birth parents did not consent, as obtaining a placement order from court would be a prerequisite. In fact practice has developed so that courts will often deal with the care order and placement order at the same time where adoption has been identified as the plan for the child.

The exact procedure depends on whether parental consent to placement is forthcoming, so there are two possible routes: placement with consent and placement by court order (see below). Placement applies to all adoptions, including relinquishment cases, but it most obviously fits with adoption of looked after children.

Placement with consent (s. 19)

Where the adoption agency is satisfied that each parent or guardian of a child has consented to the child being placed for adoption, the agency is authorised to place the child for adoption. The consent may be to specific adopters or any who may be chosen by the agency. The parent may also state that he does not wish to be informed of any application for an adoption order. This is particularly relevant to cases where children are relinquished for adoption and the parent does not want any involvement in the process after giving consent.

Where a parent (with parental responsibility) agrees to a placement, they retain parental responsibility though exercise is subject to the control of the agency. The agency acquires parental responsibility and this is shared with the prospective adopters with whom a child is placed. The parent can ask for the child to be returned to her at any point up to the adoption application being made. Once an application is made, the court must sanction the child's removal. Having agreed to the placement, the parent cannot oppose the final adoption order without leave of the court, which will be given only if there has been a change of circumstances.

In *Sandwell Metropolitan Borough Council* v. *GC* [2008] EWHC 2555 (Fam) the High Court provided some clarification on the legal position for consensual placement of a child under the age of 6 weeks. In such cases, the mother who wishes to relinquish her baby should initially sign a written consent which allows the agency to place the baby. On reaching 6 weeks, if the plan is still for adoption, then the mother should be asked to sign the standard s. 19 parental consent to placement for adoption form. At the same time, it may be appropriate to seek s. 20 advance consent to an adoption order.

Placement orders (s. 21)

The placement order authorises the agency to place a child for adoption with any prospective adopters. The order will be made only if the child is subject to a care order or the court is satisfied that conditions for making a care order have been made out. Parents' consent is required unless the court is satisfied that their consent should be dispensed with. If parents do not agree to placement, a placement order must be sought. If the local authority plan is for adoption of a child under a care order or in (voluntary) accommodation (CA 1989, s. 20), it must apply for a placement order (s. 22). Where there are care proceedings and the care plan is for adoption, the local authority will often apply for care order and placement order at the same time. The placement order authorises the local authority to place the child with any adopters it chooses.

An adoption agency should not seek a placement order until it is clear that adoption is suitable for the child. This issue was the focus of *Re T (Children: Placement Order)* [2008] EWCA Civ 248:

Key Case

The Court of Appeal heard a case concerning two boys, aged 5 and 7. Their parents had severe learning difficulties and the boys had had a difficult upbringing, to the extent that two independent social workers described them as the most damaged children they had ever worked with. Their attachments to their parents had been very weak and, in a year with foster parents, they had also failed to form proper attachments, both remaining 'detached and angry'. The local authority planned a specialist therapeutic foster placement for at least six months, as it was not certain that adoption was viable. The aim of the placement was to help the boys form attachments. Otherwise a successful adoption was unlikely and, as a result, would probably not be attempted.

Nevertheless, the authority applied to the courts and was granted a placement order, as well as a care order. The father appealed.

The court found that the authority had been premature in applying for a placement order as it was not known at that stage whether the boys would ever be suitable for adoption. It therefore could not yet be said whether adoption was in the boys' best interests and the placement order should not have been made. The court stated:

> Plainly a placement order can be, and perhaps usually should be, made at the same time as a care order is made on a plan for adoption which the judge approves, even though at that stage a good deal of investigation and preparation is needed before the child can actually be placed, and it is not known whether a suitable family will be found or not.

The difference in this case was that the authority could not be sure that adoption was in the boys' best interests. The court also noted the significant impact on parents once a placement order is made. It becomes extremely difficult to raise any further objections afterwards, as the court's permission is required. In this particular case the court felt this was especially difficult for these parents because of their learning difficulties. On a practical note it was also relevant that publicly funded legal help might become more difficult to obtain after a placement order was made (*Re T (Placement Order)* [2008] EWCA Civ 248).

The case clearly shows that an adoption agency should not seek a placement order until it is clear that adoption is suitable for the child and that packages of care and adoption orders will not routinely be made in cases even where rehabilitation with the birth family has been ruled out.

The agency acquires parental responsibility when authorised to place by consent or placement order. Parental responsibility is given to prospective adopters while the child is placed with them. The birth parents retain parental responsibility but the agency may restrict the exercise of parental responsibility of any parent or of prospective adopters. When a placement order is made, any care order is suspended and s. 8 orders and supervision orders are revoked. The placement order ends when the child is adopted, reaches 18 or marries. The order may be revoked by the court on application of the local authority or the child or others with leave of the court. The person seeking leave to apply for revocation of a placement order has to establish a change of circumstances. Having done so, the court still has a discretion whether to grant leave and this is exercised based on the welfare of the child and prospect of success (*M* v. *Warwickshire County Council* [2007] EWCA Civ 1084). A placement order cannot be revoked once the child is actually placed with the prospective adoptive family. This means prospective adopters that the child is actually matched with. In *Re S (Placement Order: Revocation)* [2008] EWCA Civ 1333, the court found that a child who was living with a foster carer after a potential placement with prospective adopters had fallen through, could not be said to be placed.

Re F (A Child) (Placement Order) [2008] EWCA Civ 439 confirmed that placement for adoption should not be accelerated in order to deprive a parent of the opportunity to seek revocation of a placement order, noting that: 'local authorities and adoption agencies must understand that it is the court which is in control, and which has been given by Parliament the responsibility for making these decisions. The courts are not a rubber stamp for local authority/agency actions, however reprehensible.'

The local authority were severely criticised by the court for its failure to respond to a father's requests for information about his daughter, and placing the child the day before the father's application for permission to apply for revocation. Once the child was placed, the court had no power to hear the father's application.

Parental consent

An adoption order cannot be made unless the court is satisfied that each parent or guardian of the child: consents to the making of the adoption order; has consented under CA 1989, s. 20 (and has not withdrawn the consent) and does not oppose the making of the adoption order; or that the parent's or guardian's consent should be dispensed with (s. 47).

A parent is the mother or married father or father with parental responsibility, i.e. not the unmarried father (without PR). Steps should be taken to contact the unmarried father of a child, counsel him and seek his views on adoption, even though he does not have to give his consent. The courts have found that there needs to be justification for excluding a natural parent from a child's life. These issues were examined in an appeal against the decision to make an adoption order to the natural father: *Re B (A Child) (Adoption by One Natural Parent)* [2001] UKHL 70.

The issue of involvement of natural fathers without parental responsibility was also considered in *Re H, Re G (Adoption: Consultation of Unmarried Fathers)* [2001] 1 FLR 646, in which the mother wished to conceal the existence of her baby from the father and her family. The court will consider whether the father has 'family life' with the child under ECHR, Art. 8, and in this case found that he did not. It will usually be appropriate to give notice of adoption proceedings to the natural father, however, and a mother's desire for confidentiality will normally not prevail over the requirement to give notice to the father. A further case, *Re J (Adoption: Contacting Father)* [2003] EWHC 199 (Fam), provides a further example of circumstances where it was considered lawful not to notify the father. In this case it was significant that the young mother had concealed her pregnancy from the community, she had split up with the father who had moved away from the area shortly after she became pregnant and she had only given the name of the father on an assurance from the social worker that he would not be informed.

Consent must be given unconditionally and with full understanding of what is involved (s. 52). A mother cannot give a legally binding consent until after six weeks from the date of birth of the child concerned.

In cases where parental consent is an issue, the court should adopt a two-stage test. First, it will determine whether adoption is in the child's best interests; if so, secondly, it will consider the issue of agreement and, specifically, whether grounds for dispensing with parental consent exist at the time of the hearing: *Re D (A Minor) (Adoption: Freeing Order)* [1991] 1 FLR 48.

There were six grounds for dispensing with parental consent in the Adoption Act 1976, s. 16(2). The most widely used ground was that 'the parent is withholding his agreement unreasonably'. Under the new law there are only two grounds:

---

s. 52

(1) The court cannot dispense with the consent of any parent or guardian of a child to the child being placed for adoption or to the making of an adoption order in respect of the child unless the court is satisfied that –

   (a) the parent or guardian cannot be found or is incapable of giving consent, or

   (b) the welfare of the child requires the consent to be dispensed with.

(ACA 2002)

Whilst removal of connotations of 'unreasonable' parents is a positive change, this is nevertheless a significant erosion of the birth parents' position on such an important issue.

Ground (a), that the parent cannot be found or is incapable of giving consent, is reproduced from the 1976 Act. Every reasonable effort should be made to trace the parent, as it would be possible to set aside an adoption order if a parent came forward at a later date. Incapacity relates to mental or physical condition, e.g. parent in a coma.

Adoption application

After placement, when the child has lived with prospective adopters for ten weeks (in an agency placement), the prospective adopters may apply for an adoption order. As consent from birth parents will have been dealt with earlier, this should be relatively straightforward. It will only be possible for birth parents to oppose the adoption order if they obtain leave of the court on the basis that there has been a change in circumstances since the making of a placement order. This was the issue for the court in *Re B-S*, the Talking Point case at the beginning of the chapter. It is important to remember that there are two stages to the analysis – a change in circumstances and an evaluation of whether leave should be given. Part of that evaluation will relate to the prospect of success of the parent's application. Here it must be remembered that the issue is, 'the prospect of resisting the making of an adoption order, *not* … the prospect of ultimately having the child restored to the parent's care' (*Re B-S* [74]).

Effect of an adoption order

The effect of an adoption order under the new legislation is the same as the previous law. An adopted person is to be treated in law as if born as the child of the adopter(s) (s. 67). Parental responsibility is obtained by the adoptive parents; parental responsibility of the birth parents (and any other holder of parental responsibility) is extinguished. Any duties relating to maintenance payments and any liabilities under the Child Support Act 1991 cease to have effect. The case of *Re PW (Adoption)* [2011] EWHC 3793 (Fam) confirmed the public policy importance of finality of adoption orders. An application for an adoption order to be revoked was not successful, the court confirming that only in rare cases will this happen where there has been a fault in the process.

Open adoption

Adoption has gradually moved on from the days when it was 'shrouded in secrecy' and there is now more openness about the process, operating on a number of levels. The concern and initial resistance to openness in adoption, particularly where the child has face-to-face contact with the birth family, was that it would impede the attachment process[12] and lead to placement breakdown. It is very difficult to assess the impact of contact, due to the variety in its nature, and the various research projects present an inconclusive picture.[13] However, the suggestion that contact weakens placements does not appear to be supported (Fratter, 1996).[14]

Adopted adults (adopted before commencement of the 2002 Act) have the right to access their birth records from the Registrar General and to be provided with counselling support. The position is different for an adult adoptee who was adopted after commencement of the Act. That person cannot access information direct from the Registrar General, he must do so through an intermediary of the adoption agency. The Children Act 1989 introduced the Adoption Contact Register,[15] a register which is used to match up those adopted adults who wish to have contact with members of their birth family with any relatives who have registered their names.

Openness during adoption before the child reaches maturity has also increased in practice and gained legal recognition. Fratter (1996) describes openness in adoption as 'a range of options which depart from the exclusive, closed model of adoption'. Triseliotis[16] identifies three varieties of open adoption. Adoption with contact involves maintaining meaningful links, determined according to the child's needs, between the child and members of the birth family. Open adoption refers to the process in which the birth parent is actively involved in selecting prospective adopters. Semi-open adoption is the process where the agency provides full but non-identifying information about the birth and adoption families to each other, but they do not meet.

The advantages of contact have been summarised by Ryburn[17] in relation to the child, the birth parents and the adoptive parents. Contact enables the child to come to terms with difficult issues in their past, avoids speculation and fantasy, and provides reassurance that the birth family support the placement. Birth parents are helped to resolve the grief of their loss, and to move on; and adoptive parents gain a sense of security and permanence.

There has been an increase in case law where some form of open arrangement is recognised. The practice of open adoption has no doubt been influenced by the Children Act 1989 presumption of continued contact between the child and members of the birth family following care orders. In *Re E (A Minor) (Care Order: Contact)* [1994] 1 FLR 146, the Court of Appeal refused a local authority's application to terminate contact between two young children and their birth parents in order to move towards closed adoption, stating that 'the emphasis is heavily placed on the presumption of continuing parental contact'.[18] An order for contact may be achieved by adding a Children Act 1989, s. 8 contact order.

Re C (A Minor) (Adoption: Conditions) [1988] 2 FLR 159 was a landmark decision in which contact was ordered between siblings after adoption. Lord Ackner stated:

> In normal circumstances it is desirable that there should be a complete break, but ... each case has to be considered on its own particular facts. No doubt the court will not, except in the most exceptional case, impose terms or conditions as to access to members of the

child's natural family to which the adopting parents do not agree. To do so would be to create a potentially frictional situation which would be hardly likely to safeguard or promote the welfare of the child.

Clearly, formalised contact arrangements were envisaged by the judiciary as being appropriate only in exceptional circumstances and where the adoptive parents agreed.

Since the Children Act 1989, s. 8 contact orders could be made alongside an adoption order, as in *Re T (A Minor) (Adoption: Contact Order)* [1995] 2 FLR 251 (now as an aspect of a Child Arrangements Order). If a birth parent applies for s. 8 contact, the application should be notified to the Official Solicitor and the local authority: *Re E (Adopted Child: Contact: Leave)* [1995] 1 FLR 57.

In many cases contact arrangements will be agreed informally and no order made. In *Re T (Minors) (Adopted Children: Contact)* [1995] 2 FLR 792, where there was no formal order relating to contact and the adopters had offered suitable indirect contact, the Court of Appeal stated that it would not allow adoptive parents to resile from agreed contact arrangements without good reason. Some form of contact will frequently be arranged and adoption agencies are beginning to use written contact agreements, which can help to clarify expectations and remove conflict.[19] In *Re G (Adoption: Contact)* [2002] EWCA Civ 761, Ward LJ gave a significant statement on the benefit of contact:

> … in a case like this the benefit is the benefit that comes from the children simply knowing who the natural parental figures are. It is to remove the sense of the ogre, as they reach adolescence and begin to search for their own identity … That is why the current research is in favour of some contact in adoption.

In most cases contact is an issue that must be agreed between the birth parents and the adoptive parents if it is to be workable, and increasingly prospective adopters are being prepared for adoption with some level of contact. In an exceptional case, *Re O (Transracial Adoption: Contact)* [1995] 2 FLR 597, a contact order was made on adoption without the consent of the adopters.

In *Re R (Adoption: Contact)* [2005] EWCA Civ 1128 Wall, LJ stated, 'The imposition on prospective adopters of orders for contact with which they are not in agreement is extremely, and remains extremely, unusual.' Nevertheless in *MF v. LB of Brent and Ors* [2013] EWHC 1838 (Fam), a case where the adoptive parent expressed some reservations about contact, Ryder LJ made an order for contact between a 7-year-old boy and his grandmother stating that the child's 'welfare … requires the maintenance of a relationship with his maternal grandmother and sister'.

It is possible for a contact order to be made after the adoption order, but this will be limited to fairly exceptional circumstances. After an adoption order has been made, the birth parent is no longer a 'parent' under the Children Act 1989. He must therefore initially obtain leave of the court under s. 10(4) to make an application for contact. In considering whether leave should be granted, the court must consider the extent to which the proposed application would disrupt the child's life, and it is unlikely to be granted unless there has been a fundamental change in circumstances: *Re E (Adopted Child: Contact: Leave)* [1995] 1 FLR 57. This may, however, be a possible avenue where an informal arrangement for contact has not been honoured after the adoption order and the birth parent seeks to formalise the original agreement. In *Re J (A Child) (Adopted Child: Contact)* [2010] EWCA Civ 581 birth parents applied for annual provision of a photograph of their former child. The local authority, adoptive parents and Children's Guardian all opposed the application. The adoptive parents feared that the birth mother would use the photo-graph to locate the child and possibly disrupt the adoption. The local authority success-fully appealed against the first instance judgment to allow the application. In the Court of Appeal there was significant reliance on the premise that it is unusual to grant a contact order contrary to the adoptive parents' wishes and the final order allowed for annual let-terbox contact facilitated by the local authority where a photograph could be viewed but not retained. As the adoption order had been made, the application for contact was made under s. 8 of the Children Act 1989.

Contact under the Adoption and Children Act 2002

The Adoption and Children Act 2002 does not introduce a presumption in favour of contact with adoption. It does, however, introduces provisions which oblige the court to consider arrangements for contact. Where an agency is authorised to place a child with prospective adopters, existing contact orders under the Children Act 1989 are extinguished. Before mak-ing a placement order the court must consider arrangements which the adoption agency has made, or proposes to make, for contact, and invite the parties to comment, and may make an order for contact under s. 26. Short-term refusal of contact is permitted by s. 27.

At the adoption application stage, s. 46(6) requires that, before making an adoption or-der, the court must consider whether there should be arrangements for allowing any person contact with the child; and for that purpose the court must consider any existing or pro-posed arrangements and obtain any views of the parties to the proceedings.

Contact will also be considered as an aspect of subsection (f) in the welfare checklist as an element of the relationship which the child has with relatives, the likelihood of the relation-ship continuing and the value to the child of its doing so, and the wishes and feelings of any of the child's relatives, or of any such person, regarding the child.

The Children and Families Act 2014 changes the mechanism for making post-adoption contact orders with the introduction of s. 51A ACA 2002. The section applies where a child has been placed or the agency is authorised to place the child and when the court is mak-ing an adoption order or has made an adoption order. The court can make an order which requires the adoptive parent to allow the child to have contact with a named person. It can also prohibit a person from having any contact with the child. Named persons (those who can either have contact or be prohibited) are those who would be related to the child but for the adoption (i.e. birth family), former guardians, anyone who had PR for the child or with whom the child has lived for at least a year within the last 5 years (that would include foster carers). The child and the adoptive parents can apply as of right, anyone else, includ-ing members of the birth family, needs leave of the court. Section 8 orders will not be made for post adoption contact anymore.

Reflect

Consider the advantages and disadvantages of contact with adoption for:

- the child;
- the birth parents;
- the adoptive parents.

Should contact be arranged informally or by court order?

Concurrent planning

The continually evolving practice around adoption and placement, which openness signifies, is also apparent in the development of concurrent planning[20] (also referred to as twin tracking and parallel planning). Its use is usually limited to particular children: those who are identified as at greatest risk of delay and repeated placements. The child will be placed with carers who are approved both as foster carers and prospective adopters. The birth family have a final opportunity to work towards rehabilitation of the child. It is made clear to all concerned that there are two plans:

1. The child will be returned home following the birth parents' satisfactorily working through the problems which led to the child entering care. The foster carers assist with this rehabilitation work.

2. If option 1 is not possible, the carers will adopt the child.

Guidance confirms that, 'Concurrent planning is usually used in cases where the local authority is still attempting rehabilitation with the birth family, but expects that adoption will become the plan should rehabilitation with the birth family be not successful' (p. 15, 2014).

The whole process is time limited and involves intensive work, with suitable rehabilitation or education programmes. Early evaluation suggests that concurrent planning can be highly beneficial for the children concerned, who are protected from repeated moves and may be adopted sooner. Recruitment of sufficient carers may limit its availability in practice.[21]

Fostering for adoption

Concurrent planning principles have informed the development of 'Fostering for Adoption' (**FfA**). The difference is that the decision will have been made that the child is not likely to return to the biological family and permanency is to be achieved by adoption. The Children and Families Act 2014 provides statutory recognition of FfA. A new s. 22C is introduced into the Children Act 1989 so that when the LA is considering adoption or is satisfied that a child ought to be placed for adoption but that is not yet authorised then they must consider placing the child with 'a local authority foster parent who has also been approved as a prospective adopter'. The idea behind the new provision is to promote early permanence for children.

The adoption panel

The Adoption Agencies Regulations 2005[22] require adoption agencies (usually the local authority) to establish an adoption panel. In a 2002 consultation, the Department of Health stated: 'In broad terms ... the role of the adoption panel is: to provide an independent perspective, informed by a broad range of expertise to monitor and quality assure social work recommendations on adoption cases.'[23]

The adoption panel makes recommendations on three principal issues:

1. the suitability of prospective adoptive parents; and

2. whether a prospective adopter is suitable for a particular child, i.e. matching child and adoptive parents.

3. Recommendations about adoption support.

The panel no longer makes a recommendation as to whether adoption is in the best interests of a child – as this duplicates the role of the court when making a placement order and is properly a matter for the court.

To make the above recommendations the panel will need to ensure that it has received all relevant information and that the correct steps have been taken by the agency. There is clearly a 'quality assurance' aspect to the panel's role. The panel must keep a written record of the reasons for its recommendations, including any serious areas of dissent. The adoption panel will receive reports from the local authority social worker and its medical adviser will provide a medical report in relation to the child and the adoptive parents.

Membership of the adoption panel is specified by regulations. Since 1997, panel membership requirements have altered to shift the balance between professional and independent members, with a view to enabling panels to give more independent and informed advice and to be more representative of the local community.[24] Membership will include: an independent chairperson; an adviser; two social workers (each having at least three years' post-qualifying experience in childcare social work including adoption work experience); an elected member of the local authority; a medical adviser; and at least three independent people with relevant experience (if possible including an adoptive parent and a person who has been adopted), up to a maximum of 11 people. As far as possible panels should be gender balanced and reflect the composition of the community.

All panel recommendations are reported to the agency for a decision to be made (within seven days of the panel recommendation).

Representations to the panel

In *R* v. *Wokingham District Council, ex parte J* [1999] 2 FLR 1136, the court considered whether the mother of a child the local authority proposed to place for adoption should be able to make representations to the panel. The mother was not permitted to attend the panel, provide written representations or read the reports. Her claim that this amounted to a breach of natural justice was dismissed. The court suggested that it would be desirable to allow her to make written representations but held that a refusal was not unlawful. The panel was not making a final decision and she would be able to participate in any court hearing.

The position is different for prospective adopters, who are entitled to make representations to the panel after seeing their assessment report. Written observations will be considered by the panel or, because under the National Standards prospective adopters must be invited to attend panel, they may make oral representations. This position can be distinguished from the case above because, if prospective adopters are refused by the panel, there will not be any court proceedings in which they could make representations.[25]

The Adoption and Children Act 2002 establishes the **independent review mechanism** under s. 12, as a form of external appeal. It provides an opportunity for the independent review of qualifying determinations, including decisions on prospective adopters' suitability to adopt. If prospective adopters are not approved for adoption, they have 40 days in which to decide whether to make representations to the agency or to apply to the independent review mechanism for fresh consideration of their application by an independent review panel (which will effectively 'mirror' adoption panels in their composition). So far, there have been few applications for reviews. The case of *R (A, T and S)* v. *Newham London Borough Council* [2008] EWHC 2640 provides an example. Here, the adoption panel refused to approve a couple for adoption, although they had already adopted another child. They exercised their right to an independent review, which recommended approval. The High Court ruled that the authority could only depart from the review recommendation if it had 'good reasons' for not following it.

Information to prospective adopters

A v. *Essex County Council* [2003] EWCA Civ 1848 is a further decision which addresses 'liability' of social services. A local authority was found to be vicariously liable for losses that arose from the failure of its social workers to ensure that prospective adopters were given full and relevant information concerning a child prior to placement.

In February 1996 two children were formally placed with A and B for adoption and on 1 May 1997 the court made adoption orders. The boy was subsequently diagnosed as suffering from Attention Deficit Hyperactivity Disorder (ADHD). A and B expected behavioural problems, their complaint was they were not prepared to accept the degree of disturbed behaviour that they were faced with. A and B alleged that the male child proved impossible to control to such an extent that he damaged A and B's home, health and family life. In press reports he was described as a 'wild child'. They claimed that the social workers had failed to give relevant information that they had to A and B or to ensure that it was given to them.

The court applied the precedent of *Phelps* v. *Hillingdon London Borough Council* [2001] 2 AC 619, and ruled that a local authority could be vicariously liable notwithstanding that the 'professional' was acting in furtherance of the authority's performance of a statutory duty, breach of which did not of itself result in damages. It was clearly in the public interest that professionals who are paid to offer their services to the public act to the appropriate standard. The court also noted that it was a cavalier attitude to the agency's own forms that permitted the lack of proper information for A and B to arise and continue undetected. The Form E did not give a full or fair picture of the male child. A and B were entitled to damages for such injury, loss and damage that they may prove they sustained during the placement but not thereafter. In effect, once the adoption order was made, the adoptive parents were taken to have accepted the child, whereas during the placement period they could have terminated the arrangement.

Adoption proceedings

Adoption proceedings will take place in the Family Court. Adoption proceedings are included in the definition of family proceedings under the Children Act 1989 and it is therefore possible for the court to exercise its powers under the Children Act 1989, s. 10 and make a range of orders. It will sometimes be necessary to consolidate the proceedings with other applications concerning the child, such as an application for a care order or applications for s. 8 orders. New court rules were introduced alongside the Act and include as r. 1 an overriding objective of enabling the court to 'deal with cases justly, having regard to the welfare issues involved'.[26] This includes a requirement to deal with each case fairly and expeditiously in a way that is proportionate to its nature and complexity, consistent with the delay principle. The rules provide the court with powers of case management including the power to extend or reduce time limits. The rules build on guidance for good practice issued in 2001[27] applicable to cases dealt with under the old law, which provided for all hearings and directions to be dealt with by an adoption judge and for each court to have a special adoption officer with a significant role in active case management, including tasks such as liaising with CAFCASS and the adoption agency.

To ensure confidentiality for the prospective adopters, a serial number may be applied for before commencing proceedings and the proceedings will then be conducted so as to ensure the prospective adopters are not seen by or made known to the birth parents.

The court will also receive an independent report from a reporting officer or a children's guardian. A reporting officer will be appointed where the application for adoption is not contested. It is the reporting officer's role to obtain the child's parents' written consent. In addition, the reporting officer will briefly report on whether the adoption is considered to be in the best interests of the child. In contested cases a children's guardian will be appointed and will carry out a full investigation and make a report to the court as to whether adoption is in the best interests of the child. The guardian may also make other recommendations, e.g. that a residence order would be more appropriate than an adoption order, or as to orders for contact.

Expectations of good practice in evaluating all possible permanency options were highlighted from the Court of Appeal judgment, *Re B-S (Children)* [2013] EWCA Civ 1146, in the opening 'Talking Point'. Here it is important to stress again the court's position that nonconsensual adoption should only be considered when all other options have been evaluated and simply 'nothing else will do', effectively placing adoption as a matter of last resort only. The case for adoption must be supported by clear evidence that it will be in the child's best interests throughout his lifetime and not implicitly or explicitly linked to local authority resources (or lack of).

Adoption support services

The Adoption Support Services Regulations 2005 provide the detailed framework for provision of support in line with the duty imposed on social services authorities to make arrangements to provide adoption support services, including financial support. Availability of support may increase willingness of prospective adopters to take on what may be a challenging task. The local authority must prepare and publish a plan for provision of adoption services (s. 5) and all local authorities must appoint an Adoption Support Services Adviser. Registered adoption societies may provide many support services and the need for a coordinated effort is noted by s. 3(5): 'The facilities of the service must be provided in conjunction with the local authority's other social services and with registered adoption societies in their area, so that help may be given in a co-ordinated manner without duplication, omission or avoidable delay.'

Adoption support services may be provided to:

- children who may be adopted, their parents, siblings and guardians:
- persons wishing to adopt a child;
- adopted persons, their parents, natural parents and former guardians (s. 3).

The local authority is under a duty to carry out an assessment of need for adoption support services at the request of any of the people named above (s. 3). If the authority decides that a person has needs for adoption support services, it must then decide whether to provide any. If the authority decides to provide services, it must plan the provision and keep the plan under review.

The framework for adoption services includes: counselling, advice and information; a system for financial support; support groups for adoptive families; assistance with contact arrangements between adopted children and their birth relatives; therapeutic services for adopted children; an Adoption Support Services Adviser to help those affected by adoption to access support services; and development of adoption support plans for adoptive families.

The Children and Families Act 2014 introduces a right for an adopted person or parent of an adopted person to receive adoption support in the form of a personal budget (s. 4A ACA 2002). The Act also introduces a duty on the local authority to provide information about adoption support services (s. 4B ACA 2002)

Adoption or residence?

The irrevocable nature of adoption and the degree of permanence it provides may be described as adoption's key features. Adoption does more than determine where a child is to live; it both creates and extinguishes parental responsibility. Whilst there are other ways of providing a degree of legal permanence, any order other than an adoption order may be perceived as less than ideal. It is clear, however, that the range of children requiring some form of security and stability has changed drastically since adoption in its current form was introduced, and there may be reasons in some cases why an adoption order is not the most appropriate way of providing that security and stability. This was precisely the issue the Court of Appeal had to consider in a complex case, *Re M (A Minor) (Adoption or Residence Order)* [1998] 1 FLR 570. In circumstances where the child had initially stated that she wanted to live with, but did not want to be adopted by, her long-term foster carers, a residence order (rather than an adoption order) was made, with a s. 91(14) restriction against further applications by the mother, for added security.[28]

Special guardianship

A new order, known as special guardianship, is introduced as an alternative order to adoption, providing a high level of legal security (ACA 2002, Part 2, s. 115).[29] It may be particularly suitable for older children who do not want the legal links to their birth family to be severed, but who need the security of a permanent alternative placement. The Prime Minister's Review of Adoption (PIU, 2000) envisaged special guardianship being appropriate for: 'Local authority foster parents, relatives, older children who do not wish to be legally separated from their birth family, children cared for on a permanent basis by their wider family, and certain minority ethnic communities with religious and cultural objections to adoption.' Early case law has stated the need to view each case on its own particular facts, with an obligation on judges to give full reasons and explain their decisions with care. In *Re AJ (Adoption Order or Special Guardianship Order)* [2007] EWCA Civ 55, the court clarified that although special guardianship orders might be appropriate in intra-familial placements, the order had not replaced adoption for those situations where a child is placed permanently with wider family, rather it is an additional option to consider. In the particular case the child needed the added security that an adoption order provided. In some situations a special guardianship order might be preferred on the basis that it does not skew existing relationships in the way that an adoption order does, where the placement is with family members, in this case grandparents (*S v. B and Newport City Council; Re K* [2007] 1 FLR 1116).

A new s. 14A is inserted into the Children Act 1989 creating the new order. A 'special guardianship order' is an order appointing one or more individuals to be a child's **special guardian(s)**. A special guardian must be 18 or over and must not be a parent of the child (it is not therefore an order that could be made to parents who have separated in respect of their child). It is perhaps unfortunate that the term 'guardianship' has been chosen because this may cause some confusion with guardianship under the Children Act 1989, s. 5.

> ### s. 14A
>
> **(1)** A 'special guardianship order' is an order appointing one or more individuals to be a child's 'special guardian' (or special guardians).
>
> **(2)** A special guardian –
> - **(a)** must be aged eighteen or over; and
> - **(b)** must not be a parent of the child in question.
>
> (CA 1989, as amended)

Special guardianship is a private law order. Some individuals have an automatic entitlement to make an application for special guardianship, namely:

- Any guardian of the child.
- Any holder of a residence order in respect of the child.
- A local authority foster parent with whom the child has lived for at least one year immediately preceding the application.
- Any person the child has lived with for three years.
- Any person with consent of holders of residence order; the local authority where child is in care; those with parental responsibility (alternatives).

Others falling outside that list require leave of the court. The court has the power to make the order in family proceedings of its own motion (i.e. it is not dependent on an application for special guardianship being made). It is not possible for a local authority to apply for special guardianship on another's behalf. When making a special guardianship order the court must also consider whether a contact order should be made, whether any s. 8 order be varied or discharged, and it may give leave for change of surname, as for example in *Re L (A Child) (Special Guardianship: Surname)* [2007] EWCA Civ 196, where a special guardianship order was made to the maternal grandparents with an order relating to contact between the mother and child and an order refusing permission to change the child's surname.

A person who intends to apply for special guardianship must give three months' notice to the local authority. This triggers a duty on the local authority to prepare a report which addresses the suitability of the applicant, the child's wishes and feelings and anything else it considers relevant. Regulation 21 of the Special Guardianship Regulations 2005[30] sets out the details that must be covered in the report. Guidance[31] reminds those preparing reports that: 'The safety of the child is of paramount concern and it is vital that the background of the prospective special guardian is checked rigorously. The special guardian (with an appropriate support package) should be considered able to meet the child's needs at the time of the making of the order and in the future' (para. 106).

The court cannot make an order unless it has received a report from the local authority. These requirements inevitably draw the local authority into private law cases where it might otherwise not have had any involvement. It is a new area of responsibility with obvious resource implications. Even if a report had been prepared by the local authority with a view to adoption, containing the bulk of the information required by s.14A(8), the local authority needed at least to supply any missing information, and cross-refer to the rest. This was the situation in *Re S (A Child) (Adoption Order or Special Guardianship Order) (No. 2)* [2007] EWCA Civ 90, where the court had attempted to make a special guardianship order of its own motion in place of the adoption order applied for.

Each local authority must also make arrangements for provision of special guardianship support services, to include counselling, advice and information. Support services may include financial assistance to the special guardian similar to a fostering allowance, and can include payment of legal fees associated with making the application. A local authority was found to have acted unlawfully in aligning its special guardianship allowance scheme rigidly with lower adoption allowances than fostering allowances (*B* v. *Lewisham Borough Council* [2008] EWHC 738 (Admin)). Authorities must also establish procedures to consider representations about special guardianship support services.

Effect of a special guardianship order

The order discharges any care order, contact order or other s. 8 order in respect of the child. The special guardian acquires parental responsibility and has the right to act exclusively in exercising parental responsibility. The birth parent retains parental responsibility but their ability to exercise it is constrained. Maintenance liability does continue alongside the order. The special guardian can appoint a person to be the child's guardian in the event of his death.

The order may be distinguished from adoption as it does not terminate birth parents' parental responsibility and it is revocable. It provides greater security than residence as there are restrictions in place on applications for variation.

Variation or discharge

To apply to vary a special guardianship order an applicant, including a birth parent, requires leave of the court, whereas to vary residence a parent can apply as of right.

Variation and discharge can be applied for by the special guardian, a parent or guardian of the child; an individual who has residence in respect of the child; an individual who has or had parental responsibility for the child immediately before the special guardianship order; the child (if he has sufficient understanding); a local authority with a care order in respect of the child. Other than in applications by the special guardian, leave of the court is required to make an application and with the exception of applications by the child, leave will normally only be granted if there has been significant changes in circumstances since the original order was made.

The court may vary the order itself in any family proceedings where the welfare of the child arises; for example, in child protection proceedings, or where the special guardians are divorcing and there is a dispute as to the arrangements for the child.

If the court is faced with a choice between special guardianship and adoption, Thorpe J advises that: 'the key question which the court will be obliged to ask itself in every case in which the question of adoption as opposed to special guardianship arises will be: what order will better serve the welfare of this particular child' (*Re S (A Child) (Adoption Order or Special Guardianship Order)* [2007] EWCA Civ 54).

Table 11.1 summarises the key differences between adoption, special guardianship and residence.

Table 11.1 Key differences between adoption, special guardianship and residence

Order	Parental Responsibility (PR)	Duration	Permanence	Local authority (LA) support
Adoption	Acquired by adoptive parents (including step-parent adoption). Birth parents lose PR.	For life.	Irrevocable. Severs previous legal relationship.	Range of adoption support services available.
Special Guardianship	Acquired by special guardian (SG) and exercisable to the exclusion of others. Retained by birth parents but exercise is constrained.	Until 18.	May be varied or discharged by court. Leave required by all except SG and only granted if significant change in circumstances.	Range of special guardianship support services available.
Residence (S.8 CA 1989, now within the Child Arrangements Order)	PR to holder of order. PR retained by those with PR before order. Discharges care order and PR of LA.	Until the child is 16. May be extended to 18.	May be varied or discharged by court. Parents and child may apply as of right. Leave required by others, s. 10(9).	LA *may* make contributions to child's maintenance.

Chapter summary

- The Adoption and Children Act 2002 has reformed adoption law and replaced the previous law contained in the Adoption Act 1976. The Act is supported by National Standards and statutory guidance.

- The 2002 Act includes a set of principles applying to decisions about adoption: the paramount consideration of the court or adoption agency must be the child's welfare throughout his life; a welfare checklist supports the welfare principle; delay is likely to prejudice the child's welfare; the court must consider the whole range of powers available to it and apply the no order principle.

- Adoption agencies (local authority) must provide a comprehensive adoption service in order to meet the needs of children who have been adopted or may be, their parents, guardians and prospective adopters (the elements of what is sometimes referred to as 'the adoption triangle'). The service includes provision of adoption support services. Registered adoption societies also provide services.

- Adoption applications may be made in respect of a child under the age of 18, by a single person or a couple, married or unmarried. Step-parents may adopt or acquire parental responsibility.

- Adoption panels make recommendations about the suitability of prospective adoptive parents; and whether a prospective adopter is suitable for a particular child, i.e. matching child and adoptive parents.

- An adoption order may not be made unless each parent or guardian consents to the adoption order, or their consent should be dispensed with and the child has been placed for adoption by an adoption agency with the prospective adopters in whose favour the order is proposed to be made.

- There is increasing openness about the adoption process. Adopted adults are entitled to have access to their birth records and there is an Adoption Contact Register. Many adopted children will have some level of contact with their birth family throughout the adoption.

- A new order known as special guardianship is introduced as an alternative to adoption and provides a higher degree of legal security than residence as there are strict limitations on its variation.

Exercise

John is 8 years old. He lives with his mother, Julie, and his step-father, David. Julie and David have been married for 18 months. John's father, Ian, is serving a 14-year prison sentence. He writes to John occasionally and sends birthday and Christmas presents. John has not seen his father for four years. Since they married, David has said to Julie that he would like to adopt John, so that they can 'be a real family'. Ian will not agree to this as he believes it will mean he loses touch with John and John's surname will be changed. Julie is very anxious about any court proceedings because her divorce from Ian was very traumatic, and is nervous about a social work assessment of her relationship with David. He was also married previously and has no contact with his child from that marriage. John knows that David is not his real dad, but thinks that if he is adopted he will not be teased as much about his father being in prison. Which (if any) orders would be appropriate in this scenario?

Websites

British Agencies for Adoption and Fostering (BAAF) provides a wide range of information and research publications:
www.baaf.org.uk

Barnardo's:
www.barnardos.org.uk

There is a guide to adoption at:
www.gov.uk/child-adoption

Further reading

Specialist texts include:

Allen, N. (2007) *Making Sense of the New Adoption Law: A Guide for Social and Welfare Services*. Lyme Regis: Russell House Publishing. (Provides an excellent contextual account of the Act placing its discussion in the wider social and political context and is written primarily for practitioners.)

Bridge, C. and Swindells, H. (2003) *Adoption: The Modern Law*. Bristol: Family Law, Jordan Publishing.

McFarlane, A. and Reardon, M. (2010) *Child Care and Adoption Law: A Practical Guide*. Bristol: Jordan Publishing.

For background to the Act and on development of its provisions see Department of Health publications:

Department of Health (1999) *Adoption Now: Messages from Research*. Chichester: Wiley.
Department of Health (2000) 'Adoption: a new approach' (Cm. 5017). London: The Stationery Office.

Further analysis of the legislation and implications for practice is covered in a range of articles including:

Ball, C. (2005) 'The Adoption and Children Act 2002: A critical examination' 29(2) *Adoption and Fostering* p. 6.
Cullen, D. (2005) 'Adoption – a (fairly) new approach' 17(4) *Child and Family Law Quarterly* p. 475.
Harris-Short, S. (2008) 'Making and breaking family life – Adoption, the State and Human Rights' 35(1) *Journal of Law and Society* p. 28.
Lowe, N. (1997) 'The changing face of adoption – the gift/donation model versus the contract/services model' *Child and Family Law Quarterly* p. 371.
Masson, J. (2003) 'The impact of the Adoption and Children Act 2002: Part 2 – The provision of services for children and families', *Family Law* p. 644. (Part 1 deals with parental responsibility and is at (2003) *Family Law* p. 580.)

Safda, M. (2004) 'Adoption and Children Act 2002: where are we so far?' 34 *Family Law* p. 449.
Sagar, T. and Hitchings, E. (2007) '"More adoptions, more quickly": A study of social workers' responses to the Adoption and Children Act 2002' 26(3) *Journal of Social Welfare and Family Law* p. 199.
Sloan, B (2013) 'Conflicting rights: English adoption law and the implementation of the UN Convention on the Rights of the Child' 25(1) *Child and Family Law Quarterly* p. 39.

Particular practice issues of contact, concurrent planning, partnership and adoption of looked after children are considered in:

Fratter, J. (1996) *Adoption with Contact – Implications for Policy and Practice*. London: BAAF.
Masson, J. (2000) 'Thinking about contact – a social or a legal problem?' 12(1) *Child and Family Law Quarterly* p. 15.
Smith, C. (2005) 'Trust v. law: promoting and safeguarding post-adoption contact' 27(4) *Journal of Social Welfare and Family Law* p. 315.
Thoburn J. (2003) 'The risks and rewards of adoption for children in public care' 15(4) *Child and Family Law Quarterly* p. 391.
Wigfall, V., Monck, E. and Reynolds, J. (2006) 'Putting programme into practice: the introduction of concurrent planning into mainstream adoption and fostering services' 36 *British Journal of Social Work* p. 41.

A number of publications have considered the likely impact of special guardianship, as an alternative to adoption for some children.

Bainham, A. (2007) 'Permanence for children: special guardianship or adoption' 66 *Cambridge Law Journal* p. 520.
Bond, A. (2007) 'Adoption orders: special guardianship orders' 37 *Family Law* p. 321.
Eddon, G. (2006) 'Placing children with family members' 36 *Family Law* p. 948.

Eddon, G. (2007) 'Special guardianship – imaginative use?' 37 *Family Law* p. 169.

Hall, A. (2008) 'Special guardianship and permanency planning: unforeseen consequences and missed opportunities' 20(1) *Child and Family Law Quarterly* p. 359.

Jordan, L. and Lindley, B. (ed.) (2006) *Special Guardianship: What Does it Offer Children who Cannot Live with Their Parents?*. London: Family Rights Group.

Simmonds, J. (2011) *The Role of Special Guardianship in Permanency Planning for Children in England and Wales*. London: BAAF.

Notes

1. The terms 'security' and 'stability' are preferred to 'permanence'.

2. J. Rowe and L. Lambert (1973) *Children Who Wait: A Study of Children Needing Substitute Families*. London: ABAA.

3. J. Triseliotis (1998) 'Is permanency through adoption in decline?' 22(4) *Adoption and Fostering* p. 41.

4. A few provisions were implemented earlier than December 2005, for example the changes to parental responsibility for unmarried fathers.

5. Department for Education (2011) 'Adoption: National Minimum Standards' (DfE-00028-2011).

6. Department of Health, Welsh Office, Home Office, Lord Chancellor's Department (1993) 'Adoption: The Future' (Cm. 2288). London: HMSO.

7. See also S. Jolly and R. Sandland (1994) 'Political correctness and the adoption white paper' *Family Law* p. 30.

8. Justice Heald (1992) 'Whither adoption' *Family Law* p. 29.

9. Cited in R. Sandland (1993) 'Adoption, law and homosexuality: can gay people adopt a child?' 5 *Journal of Social Welfare and Family Law* p. 321.

10. See J. Selwyn (1996) 'Ascertaining children's wishes and feelings in relation to adoption' 20(3) *Adoption and Fostering* p. 14.

11. In Northern Ireland and Scotland a third condition applies, that the child must be freed for adoption. Freeing in England and Wales is abolished by the Act.

12. J. Goldstein, A. Freud and A. Solnit (1980) *Before the Best Interests of the Child*. London: Burnett Books.

13. See discussion in Department of Health (1999) *Adoption Now: Messages from Research*. Chichester: Wiley.

14. J. Fratter (1996) *Adoption with Contact – Implications for Policy and Practice*. London: BAAF.

15. Adoption Act 1976, s. 51A.

16. J. Triseliotis (1991) 'Open adoption' in A. Mullender (ed.) *Open Adoption: The Philosophy and Practice*. London: BAAF.

17. M. Ryburn (1998) 'In whose best interests? Post-adoption contact with the birth family' 10(1) *Child and Family Law Quarterly* p. 53.

18. [1994] 1 FLR 146 at 151e, per Sir Stephen Brown.

19. Social Services Inspectorate (1995) 'Moving Goalposts'. London.

20. And, more recently, the Coram project in London.

21. See L. Katz and B. Clatworthy (1999) 'Innovation in care planning for children' *Family Law* p. 108; and N. Wall (1999) 'Concurrent planning – a judicial perspective' 11(2) *Child and Family Law Quarterly* p. 97.

22. SI 2005/389.

23 DoH (2002) *A Fundamental Review of the Operation of Adoption Panels*. London: DoH, p. 36.

24 LAC (97) 13.

25 See S. Pepys and J. Dix (2000) 'Inviting applicants, birth parents and young people to attend adoption panel. How it works in practice' 24(4) *Adoption and Fostering* p. 40.

26 Family Procedure (Adoption) Rules 2005 (SI 2005/2795).

27 'Adoption Proceedings – A New Approach', by the President of the Family Division, from the Lord Chancellor's Department (2001).

28 See further discussion of this case: D. Savas and S. Treece (1998) *Re M (Adoption or Residence Order)* 'Adoption or Residence? Too many parents …?' 10(3) *Child and Family Law Quarterly* p. 311.

29 See also the Special Guardianship Regulations 2005 (SI 2005/1109).

30 SI 2005/1109.

31 DfES (2005) Special Guardianship Guidance.

Chapter 12

Education

Learning objectives

To develop an understanding of:

- The legislative framework which underpins the provision of school education in England and Wales.
- The duty to ensure children receive efficient, full-time education.
- Some current areas of debate in educational provision, in particular attendance, truancy and exclusion.
- The role of the social worker with children and families as it touches on issues in education and schooling.
- The education of looked after children.

> ## Talking Point
>
> The following description by an experienced head teacher of what makes for a good Education Welfare Officer (**EWO**) also offers an insight into the satisfaction and interest a social worker can derive by specialising in education related work:
>
> As individuals, **EWOs** see the whole picture of the child and work to address their social care needs. They are warm, positive and energetic people able to relate to and respect all adults and children ...
>
> Effective EWOs are able to empathise with families and their difficulties ...
>
> Similarly, they understand and are sympathetic to the school's perspective and form good relationships with teachers and other staff. They are ready to question senior staff and challenge practices which may be creating a barrier to the inclusion of a child or family in the class or school. EWOs are efficient communicators ...
>
> A good EWO is very firm and consistent but sympathetic, always ready to praise and positively reinforce improvement, however small.[1]

Introduction

The law of education is complex primarily because of the amount of legislation that impacts upon schooling. It may reasonably be observed that education law inevitably reflects the political importance of education as a social policy issue. The consequence is frequent change and new legislation. This chapter provides an overview of the framework and basic principles of education law as issues which affect children; in particular, matters of admission, exclusion and discipline. It continues with consideration of the role of social workers in mainstream schools, including the education of looked after children, special educational needs, and the Education Supervision Order.[2] Throughout the chapter there are references to more detailed and explanatory information available on various websites, very often at the Department for Education ('DfE').

The role of the social worker in education-related law has become more important over recent years. For example, the emphasis in the Children Act 2004 is upon inter-agency working (particularly in Part 2, Children's Services) where there is recognition of the interlinking of education and social welfare for children. The Education and Inspections Act 2006, s.1 inserted a new s. 13A into the Education Act 1996 which provides:

> ## s. 13A
>
> A local education authority shall ensure that their functions relating to the provision of education ... are ... exercised by the authority with a view to –
>
> **(a)** promoting high standards,

> **(b)** … ensuring fair access to educational opportunity, and
> **(c)** promoting the fulfilment by every child concerned of his educational potential.
>
> (EA 1996)

And, most recently, the Children and Families Act 2014, s. 19 calls on the local authority to have regard to:

> ### s. 19
>
> **(d)** the need to support the child and his or her parent, or the young person, in order to facilitate the development of the child or young person and to help him or her achieve the best possible educational and other outcomes.
>
> (CAFA 2014)

However, so far as social work practice is concerned, there is an increased emphasis on child protection in schools and the revised version of 'Working Together' (2013) places this responsibility firmly at the heart of a school's activities, reminding local authorities (at p. 49) of their duty under Section 175 of the Education Act 2002 to exercise their functions with a view to safeguarding and promoting the welfare of children who are pupils at a school. Additionally, current policy concern with a failure of children to attend school and receive education means that there is considerable attention paid to truancy. Thus local authorities are expected to:

- promote good attendance and reduce absence, including persistent absence;
- ensure every pupil has access to full-time education to which they are entitled; and,
- act early to address patterns of absence.[3]

While there is a tension between these elements of aspiration, protection and control (and while it is accepted that education law is complex) social work practitioners can, by exercising their own professional skills, do a great deal for the education of the children for whom they are responsible. The following information seeks to clarify this rather dense area of law and for more detail there is ample, easily obtained, information on the websites of the Department of Education and the Office for Standards in Education ('Ofsted') (and in the other resources listed in Further reading.)

Framework of education law

Until 2013 the law (the Education Act 1996, s. 8) required that all children received an education up to the age of 16, the position that had prevailed since 1972. However, the Education and Skills Act 2008 implement the recommendations of the Leitch *Review on Adult Skills* and, by s. 1, imposes a duty on anyone who:

(a) has ceased to be of compulsory school age;
(b) has not reached the age of 18; and
(c) has not attained a level 3 qualification

to participate in appropriate full-time education or training.

This provision has been implemented in stages. From 2013, young people have been required to continue in education or training to the end of the academic year in which they turn 17; and from summer 2015 they will be required to do so until their 18th birthday

The 1944 Education Act, s. 6, established Local Education Authorities (**LEAs**) and for nearly 70 years these have been responsible for the provision of public education. However, the Education and Inspections Act 2006, s. 162, permits the Secretary of State to remove reference to 'LEAs' and replace it with reference to 'local authorities'. The rationale seems to be related to the current policy to diversify the structure of schools. As the Government comments, 'we recognise that the very rapid development of the academy programme since the last election raises a number of questions about how that role [of the LEA] will be fulfilled'.[4]

The last twenty years have seen particularly extensive legislation. The Education Act 1996 (**EA 1996**), which consolidated earlier education legislation, provides an essential framework for much law relating to schools. It is worth noting that the Act includes amongst other overarching aims, s. 13:

s. 13

A local education authority shall (so far as their powers enable them to do so) contribute towards the spiritual, moral, mental and physical development of the community by securing that efficient primary education and secondary education are available to meet the needs of the population of their area.

(EA 1996)

The 1996 Act has since been supplemented by a plethora of additional legislation of which the most important are probably the School Standards and Framework Act 1998 (**SSFA**) and the Education Act 2002 (**EA 2002**). These two Acts provide detailed provision for local authority relations with maintained schools, covering such matters as governance, finance, curriculum and admissions. The EA 2002 imposes some wider and less specific responsibilities, for example to safeguard the welfare of pupils (s. 175) and to consult with pupils on matters which may affect them (s. 176).[5] Both the 1996 and 2002 Acts must now be read subject to some further changes introduced by the Education Act 2011 (**EA 2011**).

Other relevant statutes include The Children Act 2004, for example s. 2(3)(c) which specifically requires the Children's Commissioner to be particularly concerned with 'education, training and recreation' as an aspect of children's wellbeing. The Education Act 2005 is largely concerned with arrangements for the inspection and organisation of schools and is to an extent superseded by the 2006 Education and Inspections Act. The 2011 Education Act makes further amendment to matters of governance, finance and curriculum and provides (in Part 6) detailed arrangements for academies.

School governance may not seem immediately relevant to social workers but the variety of arrangements now available may influence how social work is carried out. Thus, the familiar 'maintained schools' (community, foundation or voluntary) are funded by central government via the local authority which has control over the school management. 'Academies', on the other hand, are not under direct control of the LEA and, strictly, are independent though publicly funded (funds are paid via central government, not the local authority). Academies may, for example, set their own pay and conditions for staff, change the date of terms and school days and their teaching is not confined to the National Curriculum (though they must still provide a 'broad-based' curriculum compliant with the Education Act 2002, s. 78).

However, academies must follow the law and guidance on admissions, special educational needs and exclusions just as maintained schools. The current Coalition Government encourages schools to consider converting to academy status and there are detailed provisions in Part 6 of the Education Act 2011. Schedule 11 of the 2011 Act inserts a new s.6A (1) into the Education and Inspections Act 2006 (the so-called 'academy presumption'):

> ### s. 6A
>
> **(1)** If a local authority in England thinks a new school needs to be established in their area, they must seek proposals for the establishment of an Academy.
>
> (EA 2011)

Local authorities should consider the DfE policy.[6] Such process inevitably impacts on local authority finances.

School attendance

The corollary of the duty of local authorities to provide education is the legal obligation on parents (a 'parent' is anyone who has parental responsibility for, or care of, the child, EA 1996, s. 576(1)) to secure their child's education. The principal statement of this requirement is in the Education Act 1996, s. 7, which provides that:

> ### s. 7
>
> The parent of every child of compulsory school age shall cause him to receive efficient full-time education suitable:
>
> **(a)** to his age, ability and aptitude and
> **(b)** to any special educational needs he may have
>
> either by regular attendance at school or otherwise.
>
> (EA 1996)

Famously, this means that in England, education is compulsory but school is not. Thus, it is possible for parents to educate their child at home, and an increasing number do so. The term applied by the DfE is 'elective home education'. A 'suitable' education means one that 'primarily equips a child for life within the community of which he is a member, rather than the way of life in the country as a whole, as long as it does not foreclose the child's options in later years to adopt some other form of life if he wishes to do so', *R* v. *Secretary of State for Education and Science, ex p Talmud Torah Machzikei Hadass School Trust, The Times*, London, 12 April 1985.[7] There is a 2007 DfE guide for local authorities.[8]

There is no requirement to seek permission from the local authority to educate at home (unless the child is at a special school)[9] or to have regular contact with the authority or to follow the National Curriculum (which applies only to registered pupils, EA 2002, Part 6). However, the authority is under a duty (EA 1996, s. 436A) to make arrangements to identify children not receiving an education (whether at school or otherwise) and if 'it appears' to an authority that a child of compulsory school age is not receiving a suitable education, it may issue a notice to the parent requiring him to satisfy the authority that the child is indeed receiving a satisfactory education (EA 1996, s. 437(1)).

The exercise of the choice to home educate gives rise to some debate. In 2009, the then Minister for Education received *A Review of Elective Home Education*.[10] This review suggested the number of home-educated children could be anything between 20,000 and 89,000, though other researchers have estimated higher numbers. Significantly for social workers, the report debated the question of the child's right to an education and also to be free from harm, and discussed whether home education may prioritise the parents' rights over those of the child. Most controversially, perhaps, the Review highlighted the contested debate about the extent to which home-educated children may be at risk of harm because they are not subject to the 'conventional' scrutiny naturally arising from being in the public place that is the school. In evidence to the Review, the NSPCC called for increased monitoring of home-educated children and the Chief Inspector of Social Work said:

> Current DCSF guidelines for local authorities on elective home education place insufficient emphasis on safeguarding the welfare of children. In a small number of cases, our evaluation of serious case reviews has identified that a lack of oversight of children receiving home education contributed to a serious incident or the death of a child. Schools have an important responsibility to monitor children's safety and welfare but this safety net is missing for children educated at home. (para. 8.9)

In 2010, Ofsted reported on home education[11] and recorded similar concerns about the lack of recording for those children educated at home. However, it also noted that one third of the parents the researchers spoke to reported bullying of their child as the reason why they had decided to elect for home education. This is a difficult area of practice for social workers; you may wish to reflect on the impact of s. 175 Education Act 2002 referred to earlier and look at Articles 12 and 28 of the *United Nations Charter on the Rights of the Child*, together with Monk's (2009) discussion on the subject.[12]

Most parents, however, send their children to a school provided by the State. Assuming a parent wishes to use conventional schooling, she should register the child at a school and ensure his attendance. If a child is not registered (and the parents cannot satisfy the LEA that the child is receiving suitable education) sanctions may apply.

As indicated earlier, school attendance (or more accurately a failure of attendance) has become a central issue of education policy.[13] DfE statistics for the school year 2012–13[14] show overall absenteeism to be 5 per cent of the school population. Although this figure has declined somewhat over the last five years, it is still a significant number of absent children and the raw data hide notable differences in cohorts.

The rate of *overall* absence for those pupils who were known to be eligible for and claiming free school meals was 7.6 per cent compared to 4.7 per cent for non-**FSM** pupils. The rate for *persistent* absenteeism was almost three times greater amongst those eligible for FSM when compared with their fellow pupils. The comparable figures for absences amongst children with a statement of Special Educational Needs are remarkably similar. Absences increase as children grow older (absence is 1.5 times more likely in Year 11 than Year 7) and the highest rate of absence (over 20 per cent) is in respect of Irish Traveller/ Roma Gypsy children. Unsurprisingly, persistent absentees are more likely to come from lone parent households and those where the principal adult is unemployed. There is a more detailed analysis in the statistical bulletin and the DfE (2011) research paper, *A profile of pupil absence in England*.[15]

Whatever the reasons for absence, having identified those children who are not attending school, what happens next? Social workers need to be aware of these remedies for absence:

- Case work, advice and support.
- **School attendance order**, EA 1996, s. 437.
- Prosecution under EA 1996, s. 444.
- Parenting contracts under Anti-social Behaviour Act 2003.
- Parenting orders under Crime and Disorder Act 1998.
- Penalty notice, EA 1996, s. 444A.
- **Education supervision order**, Children Act 1989, s. 35.

Perhaps the more important practical remedies lie in case work and support as delivered by EWOs and generalist social workers but if such methods fail then there are available legal sanctions.

EA 1996, s. 437 provides for School Attendance Orders (**SAOs**):

---

s. 437

If it appears to a local education authority that a child of compulsory school age in their area is not receiving suitable education, either by regular attendance at school or otherwise, they shall serve a notice in writing on the parent requiring him to satisfy them within the period specified in the notice [15 days] that the child is receiving such education.

(EA 1996)

Non-compliance with the order is a criminal offence (EA 1996, s. 443); only the local authority may bring a prosecution (s. 446). Before instituting proceedings for an offence under s. 443 or s. 444 (below), a local authority must consider whether it would be appropriate (instead of, or as well as, instituting the proceedings) to apply for an education supervision order (below) with respect to the child (s. 447).

Even if the child is not subject to a school attendance order, the parent still commits an offence under s. 444 (punishable by a fine of up to £1,000) if a registered pupil 'fails to attend regularly at school', or, under s. 444(1A) (punishable by a fine of up to £2,500 or imprisonment for up to three months), if the parent *knows* that his child is failing to attend regularly at school and fails to cause him to do so. In practice, fines are usually modest (an average of £165 in 2010[16]). The offence is one of strict liability[17] unless one of the statutory excuses applies, namely:

- absence with leave;
- sickness or other avoidable cause (which must relate to the child);
- religious observance;
- the school is not within walking distance (two miles for a child under the age of 8 and three miles for a child over 8) and there are no suitable authority arrangements for transport;
- the child has no fixed abode.

It is for the parent to show, on a balance of probabilities, that s/he has a reasonable justification for the child's absence and this 'reverse burden of proof' was confirmed by the Education and Inspections Act 2006, s. 109, which amends s. 444 of the 1996 Act. There is no defence where the parent fails to ensure attendance because he cannot control the teenage child or even, as in this case, where she is in fear of violence from him, *Hampshire County Council* v. *E* [2007] EWHC 2584 (Admin).

In 2012 nearly 12,500 parents were prosecuted[18] and a few were imprisoned because of their children's truancy from school. It has been observed that while the procedure for court process may provide an opportunity for dialogue, prosecutions are likely to be 'both inappropriate and ineffective when the underlying cause and resolution of non-attendance issues [lie] beyond the immediate and direct control of the parent'.[19]

If parents fail to ensure the attendance at school of their child, the matter is likely to be taken up by the local authority as a matter of concern for safeguarding. Prior to 1989 it was possible for care orders to be made in respect of 'truancy'. This route into care was abolished by the Children Act 1989 and in its place the education supervision order (ESO) was introduced in s. 36 of that Act:

---

s. 36

(1) On the application of any local education authority, the court may make an order putting the child with respect to whom the application is made under the supervision of a designated local education authority.

(2) In this Act 'an education supervision order' means an order under subsection (1).

(3) A court may only make an education supervision order if it is satisfied that the child concerned is of compulsory school age and is not being properly educated.

(4) For the purposes of this section, a child is being properly educated only if he is receiving efficient full-time education suitable to his age, ability and aptitude and any special educational needs he may have.

(CA 1989)

In practice, failure to comply with a school attendance order will be good evidence to meet the criteria required in ss. 3 and 4 so as to justify the making of a supervision order. An order cannot be made in respect of a child in care. An education welfare officer will usually act as supervisor and it is his responsibility to 'advise, assist and befriend' the child. Additionally, he may give directions to the child and parents to ensure the child's proper education and it is an offence for parents not to comply with these directions. The supervision order is of one year's duration but may be extended to a maximum of three years. In any event, it will end when the child reaches school leaving age or if a care order is made. The local authority, parents and the child can apply for discharge of the order.

The application for a supervision order constitutes 'family proceedings' so the paramountcy principle applies. *The Children Act 1989 Guidance* suggests that a supervision order will be more effective in circumstances where parents experience difficulty in exercising proper influence over children, but if parents are 'hostile', a prosecution may be the more appropriate course. There is some good guidance from the National Children's Bureau.[20]

Parenting contracts, parenting orders and penalty notices are permissive powers available to school governing bodies, local authorities and head teachers. They apply only to pupils of compulsory school age who are registered at a school though parenting contracts and parenting orders for misbehaviour can be applied to pupils outside compulsory school age, e.g. in a sixth form.

The Anti-social Behaviour Act 2003, s. 19, introduced parenting contracts which, although voluntary, result in an agreement by parents to undergo a guidance programme. Such contracts may arise through non-attendance or misbehaviour of the pupil but breach of the agreement does not give rise to any legal liability. The **EA 2005** extended provision for dealing with referrals for alternative provision for excluded pupils and the use of parenting contracts in general.[21]

More punitive in nature than the parenting contract is the parenting order. This is available when a parent breaches a school attendance order, or fails to secure the regular attendance of a registered child at school, or where a child safety order has been made or an ASBO imposed. This power was introduced by the Crime and Disorder Act 1998, s. 8, and allows the court to impose an order for up to 12 months. Failure to comply with a parenting order (which is a civil order) is itself a criminal offence, and may result in a fine of up to £1,000 or other community punishment. Parents will be expected to attend parenting or counselling classes.

In 2012–13, under these provisions, about 13,000 parenting contracts were entered into, but fewer than 300 parenting orders made.[22]

As an alternative to formal prosecution, s. 23 of the Anti-social Behaviour Act 2003 permits a headteacher, local authority or the police to serve a 'penalty notice' which imposes an immediate fine on parents for 'unauthorised absence' of the child, i.e. failing to ensure that their child of compulsory school age regularly attends the school where he is registered. The fine is £60 but if unpaid within 21 days rises to £120. In the period September 2012 to August 2013, some 52,000 penalty notices were issued but very many fines (almost one fifth) went unpaid.[23] Research suggests that fines produce short-term improvement in attendance but thereafter the effect tails off.[24]

Social work responsibilities

Knowledge of the education system will enable social workers to provide better support to children and families or young adults. In addition direct intervention by social workers in the education sphere is no longer limited to the work of Education Welfare Officers. Schools now sometimes provide social workers based within the school and paid out of the school budget. These will be generalist trained workers, offering not specialised education-related advice but a support service to children and families in need.[25] One trainee social worker involved in such an innovative scheme commented:

> Working with young people, families, teaching staff, support staff and senior managers enabled a holistic, whole-system approach to meeting young people's needs. Interventions ranged from developing individual action plans to adding to the school's personal and social education programme and developing staff resources on accessing other agencies. This approach allowed us to respond in a way that was person-centred and knowledge- and values-based, unconstrained by the managerial agendas, bureaucratic procedures and heavy caseloads of traditional statutory working.[26]

Pending further development of these innovations, however, significant statutory responsibilities towards children in education remain to be discharged by Education Welfare Officers. The National Careers Service[27] suggests work as an EWO may include:

- identifying attendance problems and possible solutions;
- explaining to parents their legal responsibility for their children;

- taking action through the magistrates' court if necessary;

- helping families get benefits for school meals, transport or clothing;

- referring to other agencies and professionals, such as social services and educational psychologists, when necessary;

- giving support by home visits or meeting parents and pupils in school;

- finding ways for parents to build good relationships with the school;

- helping to arrange other education for pupils who are excluded;

- writing case notes and letters to parents, and preparing court reports.

The EWO may carry out 'attendance sweeps' with the police pursuant to the CDA 1998 and may also advise on home education and child protection issues, prepare reports in cases of **SEN** and will usually be the supervisor under an Education Supervision Order. In addition, social workers will frequently have direct contact with education professionals when working to support children in need and their families. A substantial amount of the child protection referrals to social services are from teachers and other education professionals. Inter-agency cooperation between social services and education is therefore essential on a number of levels.

A right to education?

The Standards in Scotland's Schools etc. Act 2000 provides in s. 1 that: 'It shall be the right of every child of school age to be provided with school education by, or by virtue of arrangements made, or entered into, by, an education authority.' There is no corresponding statement in English law. The claim to the 'right of the child to education' contained in the United Nations Convention on the Rights of the Child, Art. 28 (1), is not endorsed by domestic legislation. Instead, England has a markedly weaker statement in Article 2 of the First Protocol to The European Convention on Human Rights (now incorporated into domestic law by the Human Rights Act 1998), which provides:

> ### Art. 2
>
> No person shall be denied the right to education. In the exercise of any function which it assumes in relation to education and to teaching, the State shall respect the rights of parents to ensure such education and teaching in conformity with their own religious and philosophical convictions.
>
> (ECHR, Protocol 1)

The 'right' to parental preference is articulated but there is no direct reference to the wishes and feelings – or the voice – of the individual child. All too often, it is assumed that the child's interests and the parents' will coincide.[28]

As is evident, the 'right' pursuant to Article 2 of the First Protocol is phrased in negative rather than positive terms but arguably is upheld by the principle of compulsory education. However, there is no 'right' to education of a particular level or quality *(Belgian Linguistics (No. 2) Case (1968) 1 EHRR 252)* nor, necessarily, to one in compliance with parents' beliefs *(Valsamis v. Greece (1996) 24 EHRR 294)*. Article 2 was accepted by the United Kingdom subject to a reservation (initially contained in s. 9 of the Education Act 1996 but maintained in the HRA 1998) that pupils will be educated in accordance with their parents' wishes 'only so far as that is compatible with provision of efficient instruction and avoidance of unreasonable public expenditure'. One practical result of this qualification is the annual round of appeals by parents who do not secure a place for their child at their preferred school.

Key Case

The leading English case remains *A* v. *Headteacher and Governors of Lord Grey School* [2006] 2 AC 363 where Lord Bingham said:

[Art 2, Protocol 1] was intended to guarantee fair and non-discriminatory access to that system [of state education] by those within the jurisdiction of the respective states. The fundamental importance of education in a modern democratic state was recognised to require no less. But the guarantee is, in comparison with most other Convention guarantees, a weak one, and deliberately so. There is no right to education of a particular kind or quality, other than that prevailing in the state. There is no Convention guarantee of compliance with domestic law. There is no Convention guarantee of education at or by a particular institution. There is no Convention objection to the expulsion of a pupil from an educational institution on disciplinary grounds, unless (in the ordinary way) there is no alternative source of state education …

In *A* v. *Essex County Council* [2010] UKSC 33, a child with acute special educational needs was left without any schooling for 18 months because the local authority could not secure a suitable place due to financial constraints. The Supreme Court held that the child had not been denied the limited right to education contained in Article 2, Protocol 1.

Articles of the Convention (other than Article 2 of the First Protocol) which are most likely to arise for consideration in education law cases are: Articles 3, 6, 8, 9, 10 and 14. (The detail of these Articles and the operation of the Act generally are dealt with elsewhere in this book and should be referred to accordingly.)

There are many examples of litigated cases on human rights aspects of education. Some of the more important are: *R (Begum)* v. *Headteacher and Governors of Denbigh High School* [2006] UKHL 15 (refusing to allow a pupil to wear a jilbab was not a breach of Art 9); *R (Playfoot)* v. *Governing Body of Millais School* [2007] EWHC 1698 (Admin) (the decision of the school not to permit the pupil to wear a 'purity' ring as a symbol of her commitment to celibacy before marriage was not unlawful or in breach of Articles 9 or Article 14); and *A* v. *Headteacher and Governors of the Lord Grey School* [2004] EWCA Civ 382, mentioned above.

It is interesting and important to note that domestic law still plays a significant role in disputes of this broad type relating to discipline. In contrast to *Begum* and *Playfoot*, in the case of *R (Watkins-Singh)* v. *The Governing Body of Aberdare Girls' High School* [2008] EWHC 1865 (Admin), Sarika Watkins-Singh successfully challenged her school's refusal to permit her to wear the Sikh *Kara* bangle, not primarily on Human Rights Act grounds but under the Race Relations Act 1976 and the Equality Act 2006 (now superseded by the Equality Act 2010). The 2010 Act proscribes discrimination in education specifically in relation to admission, access to facilities and exclusion.

Local authority liability

It was claimed in *X (Minors)* v. *Bedfordshire CC* [1995] 2 AC 633 that the local authority had negligently failed to provide for the claimant's special needs. The House of Lords decided that it was not fair, just or reasonable to impose a duty of care on the local authority in respect of these statutory duties (i.e. public law functions), for example how to exercise its powers and discretions in relation to pupils with SEN. However, if an authority offers a service (e.g. an educational psychologist) it is under a duty to exercise reasonable care in the manner in which it runs that service and if it does so negligently, a claim may arise. This is what happened in *Phelps* v. *Hillingdon LBC* [2001] 2 AC 619. The psychologist employed by the LEA failed to diagnose the claimant's dyslexia in circumstances where the court found the psychologist to be in breach of her duty of care and the LEA to be vicariously liable as employer for that negligence.

It seems unlikely that there will be a flood of claims based on this principle given the necessity to identify an individual who breached a duty of care to the claimant. See for example, *Crowley* v. *Surrey CC* [2008] EWHC 1102 where there was no finding of negligence in relation to an allegation of a failure to identify and diagnose a child's speech defect. However, in the remarkable case of *Connor* v. *Surrey CC* [2010] EWCA Civ 286, the Court of Appeal confirmed that there was a duty of care to an employee, a head teacher, who suffered illness when the employing local authority failed to take action to protect her from extreme bullying behaviour by her own school's governors.

School structures and the role of governors

The SSFA 1998 details the classification of 'maintained' schools (those maintained by local authorities) into community, foundation, voluntary or special schools. Most are community schools and those which are voluntary are either voluntary controlled or aided and are familiar as the former 'church schools'.

Governing bodies have overall responsibility for the governance and management of schools, SSFA 1988, s. 38 and see also EA 2002, Part 3, Chapter 1 and Part 11. Note that s. 175(2) of the 2002 Act specifically charges governors to exercise their functions so as to safeguard and promote the welfare of children. Over recent years governing bodies have acquired many areas of responsibility which were previously the domain of local authorities. In particular, their role entails: determining and monitoring areas of the curriculum; ensuring the National Curriculum is delivered and daily worship takes place; appointing and dismissing staff; determining how the school budget is spent; developing policies (including policies on discipline, sex education and special needs); and reporting annually to parents on all of these issues.

As mentioned earlier, academies are not controlled by the local authority and in that sense are 'independent'. However, unlike conventional independent schools (where there is a direct contract between parent and school) academies' proprietors have a direct contract with the Secretary of State. Academies are, therefore, 'independent' charitable companies whose trustees are the school governors. They have the power to employ staff, appoint the Principal and administer the academy's finances. 'Free' schools are effectively newly created academies and otherwise have no distinct legal status. The primary advantage to the governors of an academy is that they have freedom to depart from the National Curriculum and to control their own budget.

Academies were originally created by the previous Labour Government as 'all ability state schools with a mission to transform education ... set up where the local status quo in secondary education is simply not good enough'.[29] However, the present (2014) Coalition Government has a policy of 'increasing the number of academies and free schools to create a better and more diverse school system' and this has led to serious debate as to the merit of school organisation and what some see as its fragmentation; see the overview by Wolfe (2013).

There is extensive guidance for governors available from the DfE and a good starting point is the 2014 'Governors' Handbook'.[30] The School Governance (Roles, Procedures and Allowances) (England) Regulations 2013 provide a comprehensive set of regulations by reference to which governors should carry out their duties. The primary and over-arching duties of the governing body are clearly stated:

> 6.–(1) The functions of the governing body include the following core functions –
>
> (a) ensuring that the vision, ethos and strategic direction of the school are clearly defined;
>
> (b) ensuring that the head teacher performs his or her responsibilities for the educational performance of the school; and
>
> (c) ensuring the sound, proper and effective use of the school's financial resources.

Discipline

One of the central concerns of school governors is to ensure good discipline in their school. The purpose of discipline in school is to create an environment which is suitable for education and learning. Poor behaviour (often including bullying of fellow pupils) by a few children may in practice impact negatively on the right of the majority of pupils to an effective education and a happy schooling.[31] The Education and Inspections Act 2006 (**EIA 2006**), s. 88, requires a governing body to promote good behaviour and discipline among pupils and to make a written statement of general principles to guide the head teacher. It also requires governing bodies to have regard to guidance from the Secretary of State for Education (or, in the case of Wales, the Welsh Assembly) in making and reviewing the written statement of general principles on school discipline; such guidance has been issued.[32]

Corporal punishment has been banned in the state sector since 1987 and is now illegal in all schools, including independent schools, EA 1996, s. 548. Any other action that teachers take to enforce discipline must be reasonable and proportionate and exceeding that limit could lead to action against the teacher for assault or battery. The Education Act 1997, s. 4, amended the 1996 Act to provide some clarification in this difficult area through provision of a power for staff to use 'such force as is reasonable in the circumstances' to prevent a pupil committing an offence, causing personal injury or damage to property, or behaving in a way which prejudices the maintenance of good order and discipline at the school.[33] Otherwise, disciplinary sanctions must be 'reasonable in all the circumstances' (EIA 2006, s. 91) and in practice are likely to be limited to detention (provided for by s. 5 of the 1997 Act – there are extensive rules about the arrangements to be made) and confiscation of 'inappropriate items'.[34]

Exclusions

So that a school can successfully pursue its aim to provide effective learning and teaching it is necessary that the school may, if all else fails, exclude disruptive pupils. The head teacher has power, by EA 2002, s. 52, to exclude a pupil, either permanently or for one or more fixed periods of up to a total of 45 days in any school year.

Within a school's policy on discipline, exclusion should be the last resort. Over the last few years there has been a decline in the number of pupils excluded. Nevertheless, the figures for 2011–12[35] show that:

- There were 5,170 permanent exclusions from all schools (down from 8,680 in 2008) representing 0.07% of all pupils.

- There were 304,370 fixed period exclusions from state-funded secondary schools.

- The most common reason for exclusion was persistent disruptive behaviour – about a third of all cases.

- The permanent exclusion rate for boys was three times higher than that for girls.

- Boys are more likely to be excluded (both permanently and for a fixed period) at a younger age than girls, with very few girls being excluded during the primary years.

- The most common point for both boys and girls to be excluded is at ages 13 and 14; around 52 per cent of all permanent exclusions were of pupils from these age groups.

Certain children are disproportionately likely to be excluded. Children with special educational needs (with or without a statement) are significantly (between five and ten times) more likely to be excluded than other children and looked after children about four times more. Boys of Afro-Caribbean origin are three times more likely than their peers to be permanently excluded, and traveller children are also significantly more likely to be excluded than children from other groups.

The governors and head teacher must follow statutory requirements contained in the School Discipline (Pupil Exclusions and Reviews) (England) Regulations 2012. There are separate sections for maintained schools and academies (and for pupil referral units). Detailed guidance is available in the DfE's publication, *Exclusion from maintained schools, Academies and pupil referral units in England* and this should be consulted.[36]

The head teacher must inform the 'relevant person' (the child's parents or, if over 18, the pupil) of the reason for and period of the exclusion (or if it is permanent) and of the right to make representations to the governing body and request reinstatement. The governors must consider the interests of both the excluded pupil and other pupils at the school. There is no further avenue of appeal in respect of a *fixed-term* exclusion. Note that the pupil, if under 18, does not have any right to make representations – he is entirely dependent on his parent doing so – though he should be encouraged to attend any hearing, *R* v. *Governors of Dunraven School, ex p B* [2000] LGR 494. At least three governors should consider the representations and they must act independently, *R (on the application of DR)* v. *Headteacher and Governing Body of St George's Catholic School* [2002] EWCA Civ 1822. The governors must give a written note of the outcome of their deliberations and, where the exclusion is permanent and is upheld, the pupil must be advised of his right to seek a review of that decision.

Parents of children who have been *permanently* excluded may appeal within 15 days of receipt of the governors' decision to an independent review panel. The panel, which is arranged by the local authority (for a maintained school) or by the 'proprietor' (in the case of an academy), consists of three or five members but will include one head teacher, one governor and one lay member. A parent may request, for the purpose of the review, that a SEN expert be appointed to provide impartial advice on how special educational needs may be relevant to the decision to exclude the pupil permanently.

Under EA 2002, s. 51A (4) the panel may:

---

s. 51A

(a) uphold the decision of the responsible body,

(b) recommend that the responsible body reconsiders the matter, or

(c) if it considers that the decision of the responsible body was flawed when considered in the light of the principles applicable on an application for judicial review, quash the decision of the responsible body and direct the responsible body to reconsider the matter.

(EA 2002)

This represents a change from the appeal regime that existed prior to 2012 and is a result of changes introduced by the Education Act 2011.

A local authority is under a duty to provide suitable full-time education for excluded pupils from the sixth day of exclusion (EA 1996, s. 19 and Education and Inspections Act 2006, s. 100). This may be achieved by placement in Pupil Referral Units (PRUs). These are effectively small schools (about 420 of them) run by LEAs and providing (in 2012) for about 14,000 pupils.[37] PRUs are relieved of many statutory obligations and take the bulk of pupils permanently excluded from mainstream schools. Their educational success rate is low, about 1 per cent of pupils earning five GCSE passes at Grade A–C, and about 75 per cent of pupils have SEN.

Overall, exclusion is a complex and contentious area of school practice. There is ample information on the detail of the process from the DfE in the publications referred to and a considered discussion of exclusion in the wider context of increasing social diversity in Harris (2007). Exclusion is central to the question of 'social justice' in education; for example, there is evidence of a correlation between exclusion and adult criminal activity.[38]

Sex education

Sex and relationship education has a vital role to play in reducing the number of sexually transmitted infections contracted by young people and the number of conceptions among girls below the age of 16. Current statutory guidance dates back to 2000[39] though another government enquiry into sex education has been announced in April 2014.[40] Fortunately, additional non-governmental (but approved) guidance is now available from the **PSHE** Association.[41]

The law in this area attempts to strike a balance in order to provide adequate education without undermining the role of parents. All secondary schools are required to provide sex education within the National Curriculum, EA 2002, s. 80, which must give due regard to moral considerations and the values of family life, EA 1996, s. 403. In primary schools, sex education is *not* compulsory but the governors must at least address the question and have a policy on the subject, EA 1996, s. 404. Under s. 405, there is a statutory right for parents to withdraw their child from sex education classes without the need to give reasons (but this does not extend to national curriculum science lessons that teach biological reproduction). Strictly, academies and free schools do not have to offer **SRE** as they are exempt from following the national curriculum. However, Ofsted inspections are required to consider all 'social, cultural and moral provision' in the school which would necessarily include provision for SRE. In 2013, Ofsted produced its own report on PSHE, entitled 'Not Yet Good Enough'.[42] It included this comment (at p. 4):

> Sex and relationships education required improvement in over a third of schools, leaving some children and young people unprepared for the physical and emotional changes they will experience during puberty, and later when they grow up and form adult relationships. This is a particular concern because … failure to provide high quality, age-appropriate sex and relationships education may leave young people vulnerable to inappropriate sexual behaviours and exploitation, particularly if they are not taught the appropriate language, or have not developed the confidence to describe unwanted behaviours, do not know who to go to for help, or understand that sexual exploitation is wrong.

In 2013, at bill stage of the now enacted Children and Families Act 2014, an amendment was put down seeking compulsory sex and relationship education for all children but it was defeated by government vote.[43] The reluctance to limit the parent's right to remove a child from sex education and the emphasis on giving discretion to schools and teachers to decide exactly how and what to teach in SRE apparently trumped any 'right' of children to be educated against the risks attached to ignorance in sexual matters; some may consider this a question of safeguarding.

Looked after children

In recent years the educational under-achievement of looked after children ('LAC') has been highlighted. The level of under-achievement should not be underestimated and raw statistics paint a depressing picture. Each year, the Office of National Statistics publishes *Outcomes for Children Looked After by Local Authorities* and the figures for 2013,[44] though showing some improvement over earlier years, still demonstrate a marked deficit when comparing academic results in the LAC cohort with their non-looked after peers. In the case of the 'gold standard' of five GCSE passes at grade A–C (including English and Maths), the success level for LAC is 15.3 per cent as against 58 per cent for non-LAC.

There are other markers of potential difficulty in terms of educational achievement, not least that 68 per cent of LAC have a designated special educational need (mostly 'behavioural, social and emotional difficulty') compared with 19 per cent in the general school population. Some 29 per cent of LAC have a formal 'statement' of SEN (effectively requiring the provision of additional help – see below) under the existing legislation. This compares with 3 per cent for other children. As mentioned earlier, a looked after child is also significantly more likely to be excluded from school. Research in this area has improved latterly; see Jackson (2013).

Social services are under a duty under s. 22(3)(a) of the Children Act 1989 to safeguard the welfare of looked after children. The Children Act 2004 added s. 22(3A):

> ### s. 22(3A)
>
> The duty of a local authority under subsection (3)(a) to safeguard and promote the welfare of a child looked after by them includes in particular a duty to promote the child's educational achievement.
>
> (CA 2004)

Now, the Children and Families Act 2014 has inserted two additional sub-sections:

> ### ss. 3(B), 3(C)
>
> (3B) A local authority in England must appoint at least one person for the purpose of discharging the duty imposed by virtue of subsection (3A).
>
> (3C) A person appointed by a local authority under subsection (3B) must be an officer employed by that authority or another local authority in England.
>
> (CAFA 2014)

This amendment now encapsulates in legislation the requirement for local authorities to appoint a 'virtual school head' to take responsibility for all LAC in that authority's area. These children are on a single 'virtual' school register regardless of where they may be physically. The hope is that the virtual head teacher will have the specialist knowledge to work with social and health professionals while also providing extra support to designated teachers in individual schools. 'Designated teachers' are provided for by the Children and Young Persons Act 2008, 20, which requires the governing body of a maintained school to 'designate a member of the staff at the school ... as having responsibility for promoting the educational achievement of registered pupils at the school who ... are being looked after by a local authority ...'.

Other provisions relating to LAC include: the introduction of Personal Education Plans for each child (to cover achievement, development and educational needs, short-term targets, long-term plans and aspirations); the use of Independent Reviewing Officers to monitor the local authority's effectiveness in its role of 'corporate parent'; and Joint Area Reviews to examine just how schools are meeting the needs of looked after children. EA 2005, s. 106 specifically requires maintained schools to give priority to LAC in respect of admission policies. Current initiatives include payment by central government of 'pupil premium plus' funding of £1,900 per LAC from April 2014. As ever, there is statutory guidance.[45]

Special educational needs (SEN)

In 2011, the Government published a green paper, 'Support and Aspiration: A new approach to SEN and Disability'. This resulted in a report of the same name[46] which introduced 20 'pathfinder areas' to trial and pilot new arrangements for SEN provision. These pathfinder projects will run until late 2014 and, at the time of writing, the outcome of the work is unknown. However, that has not stopped the Children and Families Act 2014 making radical change to arrangements for provision of education to those children with special needs. There has long been a *SEN and Disability Code of Practice* but this is currently (May 2014) under review. A new draft code has been published[47] (some 253 pages long) but is still subject to consultation. Readers should check the DfE website to learn when the final version is issued. In practice, the code is probably the most important document to access as it sets out how local authorities should meet their obligations under the Act.

Most of the provisions relating to SEN in the 2014 Act came into force in September 2014. The most overt change will be that the current 'statement' of SEN will be replaced by a single 'Education, Health and Care Plan' (**EHC**) and such plans will apply up to the age of 25. Local authorities will be required to work with health services to plan and commission support across education, health and social care.

The initial concept of special educational needs arose largely out of the Warnock report[48] which concluded that, where possible, children with learning difficulties should be educated in mainstream schools. This approach was adopted by the Education Act 1981 which introduced the term of 'special educational need' and endorsed the overriding principle of inclusivity. The general principle of inclusivity continues to be endorsed by the Children and Families Act 2014 in s. 33(2). However, Warnock herself has since aired doubts about the wisdom of this approach[49] and, in any event and more practically, the key to successful inclusion for most schools relates primarily to funding.

However it is dealt with, the question of SEN is a significant one in school education. The definition of SEN is now in the Children and Families Act 2014, s. 20:

---

s. 20

(1) A child or young person has special educational needs if he or she has a learning difficulty or disability which calls for special educational provision to be made for him or her.

(2) A child of compulsory school age or a young person has a learning difficulty or disability if he or she —

  (a) has a significantly greater difficulty in learning than the majority of others of the same age, or

  (b) has a disability which prevents or hinders him or her from making use of facilities of a kind generally provided for others of the same age in mainstream schools or mainstream post-16 institutions.

(CAFA 2014)

For educational purposes, SEN is likely to mean in practice that the child has needs in the areas of communication and interaction, cognition and learning, emotional and social behaviour, and sensory and/or physical needs.

Under the current regulations, if a child has SEN then a 'statement' (made after an assessment of the child's educational needs and usually at the request of a parent (EA 1996, s. 329)) gives a child an enforceable entitlement (as against the local authority) to the special educational provision recorded in the statement as being necessary for that child. Hence, statements are a 'much sought after prize for children with SEN and their parents'.[50] (About 230,000 pupils, 2.8 per cent of all schoolchildren, have a statement of SEN.)[51] Local authorities, on the other hand, because of limited resources, are, perhaps understandably, not always keen to incur the expenditure required to meet those perceived needs.[52] The inevitable result is litigation in which parents, for equally understandable reasons, challenge the decisions of the local authorities in an effort to secure the provision sought for their child.

It appears that the existing broad structure of application and possible challenge will be followed under the 2014 Act. The parent or young person may request 'an EHC needs assessment' under s. 36 (1). If, in the light of that assessment, the local authority considers that the child or young person needs 'special educational provision' then under s. 37 (1) it must prepare and maintain an EHC plan and under s. 42 it is thereafter under a duty to secure that specified provision for the child. An appeal may be brought under s. 51 against a local authority decision not to undertake a needs assessment or (if one has been undertaken) a decision that an EHC plan is not necessary. The appeal is to the Health, Education and Social Care (HESC) Chamber of the First-tier Tribunal (SEN and disability).[53] The number of appeals over the last seven years or so has been remarkably consistent at between about 3,000 and 3,500 per annum.[54]

Reflect

Birmingham City's webpage for its Education Welfare Service (www.birmingham.gov.uk/education-welfare) states that 'The work of the Education Welfare Service (EWS) focuses on these key areas: School Attendance [and] Child Employment and Entertainment Licensing.' Do you think these are or should be the only 'key' areas of activity for the EWS? The page contains no reference to safeguarding: should it?

Chapter summary

- Significant statutory responsibilities towards children in education law are discharged by education welfare officers. Social workers will be directly involved with education professionals when working in child protection and with children in need and looked after children whose educational attainment may have been poor. There is a duty to promote educational attainment of all children.

- There is a large amount of statute law which governs the management of schools and pupils and various 'initiatives' from the Department for Education. The basic legal framework is contained in the Education Act 1996.

- The law requires all children to receive an education. Local education authorities are obliged to provide education and parents are obliged to ensure their children receive efficient full-time education. This may be provided at home.

- If a child is registered at a school, the parents must ensure his/her attendance. Failure to do so may result in a school attendance order.

- Schools may exclude pupils in limited circumstances. It is possible to appeal against permanent exclusion, and reinstatement of the pupil may be ordered.

- All secondary schools are obliged to provide sex education; parents have a right to withdraw their child from sex education lessons.

- Special educational needs are defined in legislation. Most children with SEN will be educated in mainstream education with some additional support.

- Education supervision orders may be made where a child is not being properly educated.

Exercises

1. Tommy is aged 12 and lives with his mother, Jean, and his two siblings. Tommy is coming to the end of his first term of secondary school. His attendance record is poor, with 18 days' unauthorised absence out of a possible attendance of 52 days. Jean says that she can no longer control Tommy and, though she does try to encourage him to attend school, if he does not want to go she accepts there is nothing she can do.

   When Tommy is at school, he is frequently involved in fights with other boys, who accuse him (often with justification) of being dirty and smelly.

   Tommy's form teacher has prepared a brief report, saying that Tommy is not a malicious child but he is large for his age, frequently clumsy, occasionally aggressive to his peers, and significantly behind his expected age-related attainment in reading and writing.

   What action do you consider taking to improve Tommy's current educational underachievement?

2. You are the supervising social worker for Ruth, an 11-year-old girl who has been in the care of your local authority for three years since there was a finding of sexual abuse by her father. Until the care order was made, Ruth lived in a 'traveller' community.

   Ruth has been placed in long-term foster care. She displays significant behavioural problems and has already suffered two brief, fixed-term exclusions from her junior school. She is due to start secondary school next term.

   The foster carer has reported to you that she has visited the headteacher of the new school to discuss Ruth's impending transfer. The head was frankly hostile. She commented that 'kids in care always drag down the exam results' and 'these traveller children are a particular nuisance'.

   What support could you provide to Ruth in these circumstances, especially to deal with the transition to secondary school? Do any Human Rights Act considerations arise?

Websites

Department for Education:
www.gov.uk/government/organisations/department-for-education

Ofsted:
www.ofsted.gov.uk

Advisory Centre for Education:
www.ace-ed.org.uk

British Dyslexia Association:
www.bdadyslexia.org.uk/

Home education:
www.educationotherwise.net/

Independent Parental Special Education Advice:
www.ipsea.org.uk

Special Needs advice:
www.specialneedsjungle.com/

Further reading

Ford, J., Hughes, M. and Ruebain, D. (2009) *Education Law and Practice*. Bristol: Jordan Publishing.

Harris, N. (2007) *Education, Law and Diversity*. Oxford: Hart Publishing.

Harris, N. (2009) 'Playing catch-up in the school yard? Children and young people's "voice" and education rights in the UK' 23(3) *International Journal of Law Policy and Family*, pp. 331–66.

Horner, N. and Krawczyk, S. (2006) *Social Work in Education and Children's Service*, Exeter: Learning Matters.

Jackson, S. (ed.) (2013) *Pathways through education for young people in care: ideas from research and practice*. London: British Association for Adoption and Fostering.

Oliver, S. and Clements, P. (2007) *Special Educational Needs and the Law*. Bristol: Jordan Publishing.

Wolfe, D. (2013) 'Schools: The legal structures, the accidents of history and the legacies of timing and circumstance' *Education Law Journal*, pp. 100–13, available free at: www.davidwolfe.org.uk/ELJ_2013_02_Articles_Wolfe.pdf.

Notes

[1] Pauline Doidge in *Community Care* 3.10.07 accessed at: www.communitycare.co.uk/Articles/2007/10/03/106011/education-welfare-officers-and-social-work-in-schools.html.

[2] The Government of Wales Act 2006 devolved to the Welsh Assembly power to legislate on various matters including education. Readers who practice in Wales should check that there is no local legislation that impacts on matters discussed here. Scotland, of course, has long had a separate education system.

[3] DfE (2013) *School attendance: Departmental advice for maintained schools, academies, independent schools and local authorities* (DFE/00257/2013).

[4] www.education.gov.uk/a0063423/local-authorities-faqs

[5] See the guidance in: *Safeguarding Children in Education* (DfES/0027/2004) and *Safeguarding Children: Safer Recruitment and Selection in Education Settings* (DfES/1568/2005).

[6] www.gov.uk/government/policies/increasing-the-number-of-academies-and-free-schools-to-create-a-better-and-more-diverse-school-system.

[7] See Gabb, S. (2004) *Home Schooling: A British Perspective* available at: www.seangabb.co.uk/academic/homeschooling.htm.

[8] *Elective Home Education Guidelines for Local Authorities* available at: www.dcsf.gov.uk/localauthorities/_documents/content/7373-DCSF-Elective%20Home%20Education.pdf.

[9] Regulation 9(2), Education (Pupil Registration) Regulations 1995 (SI 1995/2089).

[10] *Report to the Secretary of State on the Review of Elective Home Education in England*, Graham Badman: www.kscb.org.uk/pdf/HC-610_Home-ed.pdf.

[11] Ofsted (2010) *Local authorities and home education* at: www.ofsted.gov.uk/resources/local-authorities-and-home-education

[12] D. Monk (2009) 'Regulating home education: negotiating standards, anomalies and Rights' *CLFQ* 21(2), p. 155.

[13] There is a vast amount of guidance on behaviour and attendance on the DfE page: www.gov.uk/schools-colleges/behaviour-attendance.

[14] SFR 09/2014 at: www.gov.uk/government/uploads/system/uploads/attachment_data/file/295132/SFR09_2014_Text.pdf.

[15] DfE (2011) *A profile of pupil absence in England* at: www.gov.uk/government/uploads/system/uploads/attachment_data/file/183445/DFE-RR171.pdf.

[16] Taylor, C. (2012) *Improving Attendance at School*, London: DfE.

[17] *Hampshire CC v. E* [2007] EWHC 2584 (Admin).

[18] www.publications.parliament.uk/pa/cm201314/cmhansrd/cm140124/text/140124w0001.htm.

[19] Kendall, S. *et al.* (2004) *School attendance and the prosecution of parents: Effects and effectiveness*, NFER, available at: www.nfer.ac.uk/publications/PPT01/PPT01_home.cfm.

[20] Newvell, J. (2008) *Multi-agency Interventions with Poor School Attenders: Education Supervision Orders Developing effective practice*, NCB, available at: www.ncb.org.uk/media/580484/multi_agency_interventions.pdf.

[21] There is good general guidance in DCSF (2007) 'Guidance on Education-Related Parenting Contracts, Parenting Orders and Penalty Notices' (00530-2007BKT-EN).

[22] DfE (2014) *Parental responsibility measures: academic year 2012 to 2013*, available at: www.gov.uk/government/publications/parental-responsibility-measures-academic-year-2012-to-2013.

[23] See note 22.

[24] Crowther, K. and Kendall, S. (2010) *Investigating the Use of Parental Responsibility Measures for School Attendance and Behaviour*. London: DfE.

[25] See this example: www.communitycare.co.uk/2010/01/21/good-practice-a-social-worker-operates-on-site-at-a-school/#.U2y78FfDXWs.

[26] Heather Phillips (2008) 'Multidisciplinary social work in schools' *Community Care*, 5 March 2008, accessed at: www.communitycare.co.uk/Articles/2008/03/05/107507/multidisciplinary-social-work-in-schools.html.

[27] See www.nationalcareersservice.direct.gov.uk/advice/planning/jobprofiles/Pages/educationwelfareofficer.aspx.

[28] For a full discussion of the 'right to education', see Harris (2007), chapter 2.

[29] DCSF (2008) *Academies and Trusts: Opportunities for schools, sixth form and FE colleges*, ref: 00929-2007DOM-EN.

[30] DfE (2014) *The Governors' Handbook: For governors in maintained schools, academies and free schools* at: www.gov.uk/government/uploads/system/uploads/attachment_data/file/270398/Governors-Handbook-January-2014.pdf.

[31] DfE (2012) *Pupil behaviour in schools in England*, at: www.gov.uk/government/uploads/system/uploads/attachment_data/file/184078/DFE-RR218.pdf.

[32] DfE (2014) *Behaviour and discipline in schools: Advice for headteachers and school staff*, at: www.gov.uk/government/uploads/system/uploads/attachment_data/file/277894/Behaviour_and_Discipline_in_Schools_-a_guide_for_headteachers_and_school_staff.pdf

[33] DfE (2013) *Use of reasonable force: Advice for headteachers, staff and governing bodies* at: www.gov.uk/government/uploads/system/uploads/attachment_data/file/268771/use_of_reasonable_force_-_advice_for_headteachers_staff_and_governing_bodies__-_final_july_2013_001.pdf.

[34] See note 32.

[35] www.gov.uk/government/publications/permanent-and-fixed-period-exclusions-from-schools-in-england-2011-to-2012-academic-year.

[36] DfE (2012) *Exclusion from maintained schools: Academies and pupil referral units in England: A guide for those with legal responsibilities in relation to exclusion*, at: www.gov.uk/government/uploads/system/uploads/attachment_data/file/269681/Exclusion_from_maintained_schools__academies_and_pupil_referral_units.pdf.

37 DfE (2012) *Improving Alternative Provision* (Charlie Taylor) at: www.gov.uk/government/ uploads/system/uploads/attachment_data/file/180581/DFE-00035-2012.pdf.

38 Williams, K. *et al.* (2012) *Prisoners' childhood and family backgrounds: Results from the Surveying Prisoner Crime Reduction (SPCR) longitudinal cohort study of prisoners*, MJ, available at: www. gov.uk/government/uploads/system/uploads/attachment_data/file/278837/prisoners-childhood-family-backgrounds.pdf.

39 DfE (2000) *Sex and Relationship Education Guidance* at: www.gov.uk/government/uploads/ system/uploads/attachment_data/file/283599/sex_and_relationship_education_ guidance.pdf.

40 Commons select committee on Personal, Social, Health and Economic education and Sex and Relationships Education in schools; www.parliament.uk/business/commit-tees/committees-a-z/commons-select/education-committee/inquiries/parliament-2010/ pshe-and-sre-in-schools/.

41 PSHE Association (2014) *Sex and relationships education (SRE) for the 21st century* at: www. pshe-association.org.uk/uploads/media/17/7910.pdf.

42 Ofsted (2013) *Not yet good enough: personal, social, health and economic education in schools* at: www.ofsted.gov.uk/resources/not-yet-good-enough-personal-social-health-and-economic-education-schools.

43 House of Commons Debates, 11 June 2013, col. 270.

44 *Outcomes for Children Looked After by Local Authorities in England*, as at 31 March 2013 at: www. gov.uk/government/uploads/system/uploads/attachment_data/file/264385/SFR50_ 2013_Text.pdf.

45 DFE (2010) *Promoting the Educational Achievement of Looked After Children: Statutory Guid-ance for Local Authorities* at: www.gov.uk/government/uploads/system/uploads/attach-ment_data/file/276468/educational_achievement_of_looked_after_children.pdf.

46 www.gov.uk/government/uploads/system/uploads/attachment_data/file/180836/DFE-00046-2012.pdf.

47 www.gov.uk/government/uploads/system/uploads/attachment_data/file/304534/Code_ of_Practice_Draft.pdf.

48 *The Warnock Report: Report of the Committee of Enquiry into the Education of Handicapped Children and Young People* (1978) Cmnd. 7212.

49 Warnock, M. (2005) *Special Educational Needs: A new look*, Impact No. 11, London: Phi-losophy of Education Society of Great Britain.

50 O'Mahoney, C. (2008) 'SEN: balancing the interests of children and parents in the state-menting process', *Child and Family Law Quarterly*, p. 199.

51 www.gov.uk/government/uploads/system/uploads/attachment_data/file/225699/ SFR30-2013_Text.pdf.

52 For a reasoned view from a local authority, see: Ranson, R. (2008) 'Making provision for children and young people with SEN and disabilities – a LA perspective', *Education Law* p. 100.

53 www.justice.gov.uk/downloads/tribunals/special-educational-needs-and-disability/ HowToAppealAgainstSENDdecision_Jan11.pdf.

54 www.gov.uk/government/uploads/system/uploads/attachment_data/file/265148/ quarterly-tribs-q2-2013-14.pdf.

Chapter 13

Youth justice

Learning objectives

To develop an understanding of the following:

- The context in which youth justice operates.
- The role of the social worker in the youth justice system.
- The structural framework for dealing with youth justice issues, including Youth Offending Teams and provision of youth justice services.
- The duty imposed on the police and local authorities to prevent youth crime.
- Orders, which are designed to help prevent youth offending, including parenting orders, child safety orders and child curfew schemes.
- The age of criminal offending and abolition of *doli incapax*.
- The role of the appropriate adult.
- The range of disposal options available to the court, i.e. reprimands and warnings; reparation orders; action plan orders; anti-social behaviour orders; curfew orders; supervision; sex offender orders; community orders; detention and training orders; parenting orders; and referral orders.

Talking Point

In *Hills* v. *Chief Constable of Essex Police* [2006] EWHC 2633 (Admin) an ASBO made in respect of a 12-year-old boy required him not to:

1. act in any way that causes or is likely to cause harassment, alarm or distress to any other person not of the same household as himself. This includes (a) not spitting or making any rude sign in any public place; (b) not hitting, pushing, kicking, threatening, abusing or insulting any person in a public place to which the public have access;

2. carry any knife or bladed article in any public place;

3. enter the area known as Harvesters, Tolleshunt D'Arcy as shown and marked on [an] attached map ...;

4. associate with Chantelle Allen in any public place;

5. damage, hit, kick or otherwise interfere with any property not belonging to [him] in a manner that causes or is likely to cause harassment, alarm or distress to any other person;

6. kick footballs or other balls at any dwelling or property, except in his own home or garden.

The court noted that the terms of any ASBO should be clear, enforceable and necessary. It is questionable whether the terms of the order or the following examples fulfil those requirements.[1]

- In any public place, wearing, or having with you anything which covers, or could be used to cover, the face or part of the face. This will include hooded clothing, balaclavas, masks or anything else which could be used to hide identity, except that a motorcycle helmet may be worn only when lawfully riding a motorcycle (*R* v. *Boness* [2005] EWCA Civ 2395).

- Not to be a passenger in or on any vehicle, whilst any other person is committing a criminal offence in England or Wales *R (W)* v. *Acton Youth Court* [2005] EWHC 954 (Admin).

- A 13-year-old was banned from using the word 'grass' for six years.[2]

The Anti-social Behaviour Order (ASBO) was one of the most controversial orders introduced by the Crime and Disorder Act 1998. It has been used extensively in respect of juveniles in various situations as illustrated, in ways which arguably bring the law into disrepute, are unlikely to alter behaviour, or represent threats to society, to the extent that it has been described as a 'badge of honour' for some young people.

The procedure for responding to anti-social behaviour is modified by the Anti-social Behaviour, Crime and Policing Act 2014, which introduces Injunctions and Criminal Behaviour Orders in place of ASBOs but similar in substance.

Introduction

Youth justice is an area that has been characterised by swings in policy and practice between a 'welfare' and a 'justice' approach, each reflected in a variety of legislation. Youth justice has always been and continues to be a live political issue.[3]

The statutory framework for youth justice is largely contained in two major pieces of legislation – the Crime and Disorder Act 1998 (CDA 1998) and the Youth Justice and Criminal Evidence Act 1999 (**YJCEA** 1999). In addition, the Powers of Criminal Courts (Sentencing) Act 2000 (**PCC(S)A** 2000) consolidates a number of provisions relating to orders initially introduced in the Crime and Disorder Act 1998. Further changes to community and custodial sentencing are introduced by the Criminal Justice and Immigration Act 2008, LASPO 2012 and the Anti-social Behaviour Crime and Policing Act 2014.

The Introductory Guide to the Crime and Disorder Act 1998 states that 'action must be taken quickly to nip youth offending in the bud'. This appears to contradict the view that most children and young people simply grow out of offending behaviour and should not be introduced to the formal youth justice system if avoidable. Whilst it is true that a disproportionate amount of crime is committed by young people (e.g. in 2009–2010, 23 per cent of known offenders were under the age of 18),[4] the Act appears to have been driven by a profound error of judgment in terms of identifying groups. There is a significant difference between juvenile nuisance and juvenile crime, which the Act does not reflect. Whilst the focus is on orders that respond to the very young and the perceived threat to society from children, between 1986 and 1994 the peak age of offending in fact rose from 15 to 18.

The impetus for the CDA 1998 may be traced back to an Audit Commission report which identified a number of criticisms of the youth justice system.[5] Two further factors, were significant: the murder of Jamie Bulger and the arrival of the 'persistent offender'. Media interest in both issues suggested a social crisis in which children frequently and increasingly committed the most serious crimes against other children, and marauding gangs of young people made our streets unsafe to walk around in. Research does not support either position as accurate.

The reforms were based on the principles underlying the concept of restorative justice, explained in the white paper as follows:

Restoration: young offenders apologising to their victims and making amends for the harm they have done;

Re-integration: young offenders paying their debt to society, putting their crime behind them and rejoining the law-abiding community; and

Responsibility: young offenders – and their parents – facing the consequences of their offending behaviour and taking responsibility for preventing further offending.

'Breaking the Cycle' a green paper issued in 2010 by the Coalition Government indicates a commitment to increased use of restorative justice.

The Crime and Disorder Act 1998 enmeshes civil and criminal law, a feature which is particularly important with regard to disposal and sentencing. For example, the anti-social behaviour order is a civil order made in civil court but, if breached, criminal sanctions may follow. This poses an inherent contradiction, in that an order which is granted on satisfaction of the civil standard of proof, balance of probabilities, carries a criminal sanction if breached, whereas criminal sanctions would ordinarily follow only if the court had initially been satisfied beyond reasonable doubt. Criticism has also been levied at the Act to the effect that it criminalises certain behaviour in children before the age of criminal responsibility.

Youth justice and 'Every Child Matters'

'Every Child Matters' (2003) set out five key outcomes for children's wellbeing, with an emphasis on early intervention and prevention and coordinated services. Criminal justice agencies are envisaged as having a role in securing the five outcomes for children and young people. The Children Act 2004 provided legal underpinning to the structural changes required for the delivery of child care services. The Act names police authorities, chief constables, probation boards and **youth offending teams** (YOTs) in the s. 10 duty to cooperate to improve wellbeing of children in the area. In addition, Local Safeguarding Children Boards will include chief constables, probation boards, YOTs and governors to secure training centres in their membership. The implications of the 'Every Child Matters' programme are addressed in a number of documents specific to particular services, including 'Every Child Matters: Change for Children in the Criminal Justice System' (2004). It notes that the key focus of the criminal justice system is on two of the outcomes:

- Making a positive contribution. A key element of this is encouraging young people to choose to engage in law-abiding and positive behaviour.

- Staying safe. Ensuring children and young people are safe from crime, exploitation, bullying, discrimination and violence is one of the major responsibilities of the criminal justice system.

More recently the DCSF is emphasising the need for a preventive response to problems caused by young people's anti-social behaviour in 'Aiming High for Young People: A Ten Year Strategy for Positive Activities' (2007).[6]

Social worker's role in youth justice

In youth justice terms a 'child' is defined as under the age of 14 and a 'young person' as 14–17 years inclusive (CDA 1998, s. 117). The term 'juvenile' is used in this chapter to include children and young persons unless it is necessary to specify child or young person.

There are a variety of ways in which a social worker may be involved with youth justice issues. For example:

- Social workers are among the groups of professionals who will be represented on youth offending teams.

- Social workers may be the designated responsible officer under a child safety order and provide supervision of community sentences.

- Social workers frequently act as the appropriate adult under the Police and Criminal Evidence Act 1984 during police interviews of young people.

- Writing reports and attending court to present reports as an 'officer of the court'. (See report writing section in Chapter 4.)

- The local authority will be notified by the police if the decision is taken to prosecute a young person.

- The local authority must provide support for a child or young person awaiting trial or disposal.

- Social workers may be involved with the families of prisoners and have direct responsibility for children of prisoners, taking decisions about their long-term welfare and interim placement for the duration of the prison sentence.

- Under the Children Act 1989 the local authority has a responsibility to reduce the need to bring criminal proceedings against children in its area.[7]

- Research indicates that children living away from home are a particularly vulnerable group and may come into contact with the criminal justice system. Social workers have responsibilities towards children who have left care under the Children (Leaving Care) Act 2000.

- Social workers working in residential establishments, which provide secure and non-secure accommodation, may be responsible for young people who are placed on remand until their criminal trial takes place.

- The case of *R (Howard League)* v. *Secretary of State for the Home Department* [2002] EWHC 2497 (Admin) confirms that provisions of the Children Act 1989 apply to those under 18 in prison establishments. In this judicial review application brought by the Howard League for Penal Reform the court made a declaration that the statement that the Children Act 1989 did not apply to people under the age of 18 in prison establishments (contained in Prison Service Order No. 4950) was wrong in law. As a result it will be necessary for Social Services Departments to become more involved in meeting the needs of children in custody. Specifically, the judgment confirms that the duty to investigate under CA 1989, s. 47 and the duty to support children in need under CA 1989, s. 17 apply to children detained in prisons. Munby J in the High Court stated that the case:

    … on the face of it ought to shock the conscience of every citizen … if it really be the case that children are still being subjected to the degrading, offensive and totally unacceptable treatment described and excoriated by the chief inspector … then it can only be a matter of time … before an action is brought under the Human Rights Act 1998.

The key provisions of the Crime and Disorder Act 1998 may be grouped into three areas:

- institutional arrangements within the criminal justice system (Part III);
- measures for the prevention of crime and disorder (Part I);
- options for dealing with young offenders (Part IV).[8]

Institutional arrangements

The Crime and Disorder Act 1998 imposes responsibilities on local authorities as corporate bodies, not on the Social Services Department, as might have been expected. It follows that all local authorities, including district, county, metropolitan and unitary authorities, have responsibilities under the Act. The implications of the Act are central to each authority's community safety strategy,[9] on which audits take place. Responsibilities fall into three areas:

1. to create youth offending teams (YOTs);
2. to develop **youth justice plans**;
3. to provide and coordinate **youth justice services**.

Within the youth justice system, all individuals and organisations must have regard to the aim of preventing offending set out in s. 37:

s. 37

(1) It shall be the principal aim of the youth justice system to prevent offending by children and young persons.

(2) In addition to any other duty to which they are subject, it shall be the duty of all persons and bodies carrying out functions in relation to the youth justice system to have regard to that aim.

(CDA 1998)

Section 5 imposes a responsibility on the local authority and the police to create crime and disorder reduction strategies in their area; s. 6 calls on the local authority and the police to implement the strategy. Prior to formulation of the strategy, a crime and disorder audit will take place, which reviews levels and patterns of crime and disorder.

Youth offending teams

Youth offending teams (YOTs), required by CDA 1998, s. 39 have a multi-agency membership and are intended to provide the opportunity for agencies to work in partnership. Certain agencies are specified and must participate but others may be invited at discretion, e.g. housing, justice's clerks. They will consist of police, social workers, probation officers and representatives from education and health, at the very least.

Section 115 is an important provision relating to sharing information. It provides that:

s. 115

(1) Any person who, apart from this subsection, would not have power to disclose information –

(a) to a relevant authority; or

(b) to a person acting on behalf of such an authority,

shall have power to do so in any case where the disclosure is necessary or expedient for the purposes of any provision of this Act.

(CDA 1998)

A relevant authority includes the police, local authorities, probation and health authorities. This is a wide-ranging provision and, in practice, agencies in each area produce information-sharing protocols. It is perhaps surprising that the prison service was not included in the list of those bodies that are required to share information with YOTs.

Section 38 stipulates that there must be at least one YOT for each county council or unitary area. The main function of the team is to provide youth justice services in the framework of the youth justice plan.[10]

YOT responsibilities have extended to include the operation of youth inclusion and support panels (**YISPs**); these are multi-agency panels intended to provide support to young people between the age of 8 and 13 who are at risk of offending.

Youth justice plan

Each Social Services Department must produce a youth justice plan every year (CDA 1998, s. 40) with its strategy and local targets designed to meet national objectives. This remains a separate requirement from the statutory children and young people's plans required by the Children Act 2004.

Youth justice services

Local authorities must ensure youth justice services are available. Youth justice services may include:

- provision of appropriate adults when children and young persons are detained or questioned by the police;

- assessment of children and young persons for rehabilitation programmes to prevent reoffending, where the young person receives a reprimand or final warning;

- provision of support for children and young persons remanded or committed on bail awaiting trial or sentence;

- placement in local authority accommodation when remanded or committed to the care of the local authority;

- provision of court reports for criminal proceedings;

- allocation of responsible officers for parenting orders, child safety orders, reparation orders and action plan orders;

- supervision for young persons sentenced to supervision, community rehabilitation or community punishment/community punishment and rehabilitation orders;

- supervision of children and young persons sentenced to detention and training orders or supervision orders;

- post-release supervision;

- any other functions assigned in the youth justice plan.

Youth Justice Board

A National Youth Justice Board has been established under CDA 1998, s. 41 and Sch. 2. The Board is now based in the Ministry of Justice, comprising 10 or 12 individuals representing a wide-ranging membership. The role of the Board is stated to be: to oversee the delivery of youth justice services; work to prevent offending and re-offending; and ensure custody is safe, secure and addresses the causes of offending behaviour. The Board publishes an annual report and other materials and its website is a useful source of information.[11]

Prevention of youth crime

Section 17 of the CDA 1998 imposes a duty on local authorities and police authorities in exercising their various functions to consider the crime and disorder implications and the need to do all they reasonably can to prevent crime and disorder in their area. It is questionable whether this actually adds anything to the existing provisions contained in the Children Act 1989, Sch. 2, para. 7, which requires the local authority (though in practice this has often been confined to social services) to take steps to reduce the need to bring criminal proceedings against children in its area.

Particular provisions, which are relevant to prevention of youth crime, are contained in Part I of the CDA 1998 and include:

- child curfew schemes – a curfew may be set for a particular area and the police have powers to return home any child who is in breach of the curfew;

- local authority duty of investigation;

- child safety orders – available for children under the age of 10 who are at risk of becoming involved in crime or already involved in anti-social or criminal behaviour;

- parenting orders – an order designed to reinforce parental responsibility;

- anti-social behaviour orders to protect people from harassment, alarm or distress.

Child curfew schemes

s. 14

A local authority may make a scheme … if … the authority considers it necessary to do so for the purpose of maintaining order.

(CDA 1998)

The use of the word 'may' suggests that this is a permissive rather than a mandatory option for the local authority. A local authority can develop a child curfew scheme, following a requirement to consult with the police and other local bodies. It must then be submitted to the Secretary of State and, if confirmed, the local authority is then free to implement the child curfew scheme. It is obliged to publicise the scheme by posting the notice in a conspicuous place and other ways the authority views as appropriate (CDA 1998, s. 14(7)).

A curfew scheme may be made for a specified period up to 90 days. It is a ban on children of specified ages (under 10) being in a public place within a specified area, during specified hours within the period from 9.00 p.m. until 6.00 a.m. Different time limits may be set for different ages of children: e.g. 10.00 p.m. may be considered appropriate for 9-year-olds (CDA 1998, s. 14(6)). The scheme applies to all children of the specified age unless they are under the effective control of a responsible person over the age of 18. The objective of the order is to prevent criminal tendencies from developing. Application of a blanket scheme fails to recognise that there may be legitimate reasons for a young child to be in breach of the curfew. The most obvious example is where a child is effectively escaping from violent or abusive behaviour in their home.

The order formalises the surveillance role of the police and is unlikely to promote positive relations between children and the police. A police officer is required to take a child in breach of a curfew to his or her home, unless he has reasonable cause to believe that the child would, if removed to that place, be likely to suffer significant harm (CDA 1998, s. 15(3)). If there is no responsible adult at home, it is expected that the child will be taken to the police station temporarily.

Where a child has been found unsupervised during the operation of a curfew, the police will inform the local authority (s. 15(2)), who must then visit the child's family within 48 hours to determine whether there is any need for intervention or support (s. 15(4)). The Children Act 1989 is amended to incorporate this requirement. A new provision is inserted regarding local authority investigations. Section 15 of the Crime and Disorder Act 1998 amends s. 47 of the Children Act 1989, introducing the following provisions:

s. 47

(iii) has contravened a ban imposed by a curfew notice … and … the inquiries shall be commenced as soon as practicable and, in any event, within 48 hours of the authority receiving the information.

(CA 1989, as amended)

Contravention of a ban therefore becomes an additional trigger in the s. 47 criteria for investigation. In contrast to the other aspects of s. 47, there is a specific time period for the investigation written into the Act (48 hours); however, there is no enforcement provision should a local authority fail to meet this requirement. Significantly, in this new limb of s. 47 there is also no reference to risk of harm as justification for state investigation. It is clear, therefore, that failure to comply with a curfew notice has the potential to lead to much greater state intervention.

The Criminal Justice and Police Act 2001 extends the scheme to those under 16 and allows the police as well as the local authority to establish schemes (ss. 48–49) though there has been limited take up of curfew schemes.

Reflect

Consider how a police officer might react on finding the following children in breach of a curfew order set in respect of children aged between 5 and 10 years old from 9 p.m.

- John, aged 9, is out with a group of four boys of similar ages. All but John run out of sight when the police officer approaches. John has a spray paint can in his pocket and fresh paint on his hands.
- Lucy, aged 7, is with her 13-year-old sister, on their way to fetch fish and chips. Their mother gave them the money to fetch a takeaway because she did not have time to cook any tea and has now gone out with her boyfriend for 'a quick drink'.
- Jane and Susan, sisters aged 8 and 9, are walking to their grandmother's house which is about half a mile away from their home. They have to walk past the local shopping centre, where youths have a tendency to congregate in the evening. It is 10.30 p.m. and they are concerned that they cannot wake their mother, who is diabetic.

Anti-social Behaviour Act 2003

The Anti-social Behaviour Act 2003 (**ASBA** 2003) introduced further powers which have a similar aim to curfew powers. Section 30 provides for designation of an area where the behaviour of young people has been problematic. The grounds are:

s. 30(1)

(a) that any members of the public have been intimidated, harassed, alarmed or distressed as a result of the presence or behaviour of groups of two or more persons in public places in any locality in his police area, and

(b) that anti-social behaviour is a significant and persistent problem in the relevant locality.

(ASBA 2003)

The police have the power to designate an area but are required to obtain the consent of the local authority. The designation must be publicised and can be of up to six months' duration. Designation triggers two further powers: dispersal and removal to place of residence.

A police officer can order a group to 'disperse' in a designated area if he has reasonable grounds to believe their presence has resulted or is likely to result in any member of the public being 'intimidated, alarmed or distressed' (s. 30(3)). It then becomes an offence for a person to knowingly contravene that order. The police also have the power to remove a person, believed to be under 16, from a designated area, between the hours of 9 p.m. and 6 a.m. and take them to their place of residence. The power applies only where the child or young person is not under the effective control of a parent or adult and would not apply where the police officer has reasonable grounds to believe that if removed to the place of residence the child would 'be likely to suffer significant harm' (s. 30(6)).

Child safety order

Child safety orders (CDA 1998, ss. 11–13) tackle an issue in the family court, which would appear to be part of the criminal law. There is an overlap in the remit of the order with emergency protection orders and interim supervision orders. The child safety order is made on the application of a local authority (with social services responsibilities) in respect of a child under 10. As applications for child safety orders are family proceedings, the welfare of the child will be paramount in these proceedings (i.e. the welfare test of the Children Act 1989 applies). Other aspects of the Children Act 1989 do not, however, apply. A children's guardian will not be appointed as these are not specified proceedings under CA 1989, s. 41, nor will the child receive separate legal representation. An order can be made for a child less than 10 years of age where one of the following conditions applies:

s. 11(3)

(a) the child has committed an act which, if he had been aged 10 or over, would have constituted an offence;
(b) a child safety order is necessary for the purpose of preventing the commission of an act as mentioned in paragraph (a) above;
(c) the child has contravened a ban imposed by a curfew notice;
(d) the child has acted in a way that caused or was likely to cause harassment, alarm or distress to one or more persons not of the same household as himself.

(CDA 1998)

There are procedural requirements that the court must take into account before making an order. These are explained in the introductory guide:

> before a court makes a child safety order it will be required to obtain and consider information about the person's family circumstances; explain the effect of the order, the requirements imposed and the consequences which may follow if the child fails to comply with those requirements; and avoid, as far as practicable, any potential conflict with a parent's religious beliefs and any interference with the child's attendance at school.

The order lasts for a maximum of 12 months. The child is placed under the supervision of a responsible officer and is required to comply with specified requirements. The requirements are any: 'which the court considers desirable in the interests of – (a) securing that the child receives appropriate care, protection and support and is subject to proper control; or (b) preventing any repetition of the kind of behaviour which led to the child safety order being made'. Examples of requirements that may be set are: preventing the child being in certain places, e.g. a shopping centre; preventing the child associating with certain children; or requiring involvement in a particular activity, such as a homework club. The order can require the child to be home at a certain time and may in effect provide a curfew for a specific child.[12] A responsible officer may be a member of the YOT or may be a social worker in the Social Services Department. Before the court can make an order, s. 12 sets out a number of preliminary requirements. The court must obtain and consider information about the child's family circumstances and likely effect of an order on those circumstances. The court must explain to the parents, in ordinary language, the effect of the order and any requirements, the consequences of non-compliance and the court power to review the order. In considering any requirements to be imposed, the court must avoid any that would conflict with the parent's religious beliefs or interfere with school attendance.

Concern has been raised that the use of child safety orders could criminalise children before the age of criminal responsibility and introduce them at an early stage into the youth justice and care systems.[13]

The child safety order can be varied, or it may be discharged on application of the parent or responsible officer or if the child fails to comply with any requirements of the order. If the child fails to comply with the order, the court can make a parenting order. The Children Act 2004 removed the power of the court to make a care order on breach of a child safety order. This provision had been widely criticised as introducing a further route into care which was not based on satisfaction of the threshold criteria.

Parenting order

The parenting order (CDA 1998, s. 8) is a free-standing order, which the court can make in conjunction with a range of other orders. It is an order designed to help and support parents or guardians in addressing their child's anti-social or offending behaviour. The order can be made in the family court or other civil work of the magistrates' court, or in criminal courts including the youth court, adult magistrates' court and Crown Court. Section 8 provides that the order may be made in the following circumstances:

s. 8(1)

… where in any court proceedings –

(a) a child safety order is made in respect of a child;

(b) an anti-social behaviour order or sex offender order is made in respect of a child or young person;

(c) a child or young person is convicted of an offence; or

(d) a person is convicted of an offence under section 443 or section 444 of the Education Act 1996.

(CDA 1998)

Section 443 of the Education Act 1996 is the offence of failing to comply with a school attendance order and s. 444 is the offence of failing to secure regular attendance at school of a registered pupil.

There are two aspects to the order:

1. Compulsory attendance by the parents at counselling or guidance sessions.

2. The order may contain specific requirements, which the parent must comply with. This aspect of the order may last for up to a year.

The effect of the parenting order is to require parents to attend counselling or guidance sessions once a week for up to 12 weeks. The court is obviously limited to making orders where such facilities are available. It may include other requirements, e.g. specific to that child's behaviour, and these requirements may extend for up to 12 months. Examples include the parent ensuring that the child avoids visiting certain areas unsupervised, is at home during certain hours, or attends certain extra-curricular activities. Parents may be subject to a fine or probation order if they fail to comply with requirements in a parenting order. A responsible officer will be appointed by the court to ensure the order is carried out effectively. There is a tension between the objectives of an order that purports to provide support to parents but is formally enforceable. It also seems to imply that children offend because their parents have not acted responsibly, when often it is clearly not the case. The order may present a further burden on a dysfunctional family, which invites breach of the order.

The High Court had the opportunity to consider parenting orders in the case of *R (M)* v. *Inner London Crown Court* [2003] EWHC 310 (Admin) and confirmed that parenting orders comply with the Human Rights Act. The facts were that a mother appealed against the making of a parenting order and a compensation order, following conviction of her 13-year-old daughter for wounding. The court stated that the decision whether to make a parenting order was an exercise of judgment, not a finding of fact, and there was no applicable guidance for magistrates to follow. In response to the mother's claim that the order breached her Art. 8 rights, the court found that there was no breach. It applied the test of proportionality and noted that there is a pressing social need to address problems of juvenile crime, that parenting orders were introduced to confront juvenile crime, and that such orders are necessary in a democratic society. The decision to make the order in this particular case had, however, been irrational and it was quashed.

Reflect

Are parenting orders, parenting contracts and child curfew laws consistent with the idea that young people should be responsible for their actions?

Parenting contracts

The Anti-social Behaviour Act 2003 has made it possible for parents to enter voluntarily into parenting contracts, in specified circumstances. Where a child has been excluded from school or failed to attend school regularly, or the child has been referred to a YOT and a member of the team has reason to believe the child has engaged or is likely to engage in criminal conduct or anti-social behaviour, schools, local authorities and YOTs may enter into a parenting contract with parents. The parenting contract contains an agreement from the parent to comply with the contract requirements for a specified period and a commitment from the school, LA or YOT to support the parent to help him comply with the requirements. If a parent refuses to enter into a parenting contract or breaches its terms then it is likely that a parenting order would be sought.

Removal of truants

Section 16 CDA 1998 allows the police to remove truants from a public place to premises that have been designated to receive them (e.g. a school or local authority office), or the school from which they are absent. This provision relates to children and young persons of compulsory school age. The provision was suggested by the Schools Exclusion Unit. Its justification is the suggestion that truanting children in public places may be tempted to commit crimes or anti-social behaviour.

Acceptable behaviour contracts

Acceptable behaviour contracts (**ABCs**) developed out of practice in Islington, in response to problems on certain housing estates. ABCs are not provided by statute but have been promoted by the Government as an initiative applicable to young people involved in low-level anti-social behaviour which falls short of behaviour which requires an ASBO. The need for an ABC, under which the young person agrees to stop the behaviour and may undertake activities, is identified by the local authority and YOT. Breach may prompt an application for an ASBO.

Anti-social behaviour orders

The Anti-social Behaviour Crime and Policing Act 2014 will repeal s. 1 of the Crime and Disorder Act 1998, and introduce instead, Injunctions and Crime Behaviour Orders. The new orders are considered below. For the interim period until implementation of the **ABCPA** 2014 the following section on ASBOs applies.

Some examples of the use of the anti-social behaviour order (ASBO) established under s. 1 of the Crime and Disorder Act 1998, were given at the start of the chapter. It is considered in this section because, although it is a court order responding to anti-social behaviour, it is an order made in the civil court rather than a disposal in the youth court, and is intended to prevent further anti-social behaviour. It may be made in respect of a child over the age of 10 or an adult. The responsible authority (i.e. the police or district council in consultation with each other), registered social landlords (housing associations), housing action trusts and British Transport Police may apply for the ASBO. In either case the relevant Social Services Department and the YOT must also have been consulted. It is also possible for magistrates to make an ASBO following conviction of a criminal offence.

The order may be made in respect of an individual or a group, e.g. a family. The Introductory Guide to the Act states: 'It is intended that the order will be targeted at criminal or sub-criminal behaviour, not minor disputes between neighbours, or matters which can be dealt with effectively under existing legislation.' Between 2000 and 2012, 37 per cent of all ASBOs were imposed on 10–17 year olds.[14]

The ASBO is something of a hybrid order, being made in civil proceedings on the balance of probabilities, yet breach of the order being a criminal offence (carrying a maximum penalty of five years' imprisonment) and the guidance referring to criminal or sub-criminal behaviour. A House of Lords ruling, *R (McCann)* v. *Crown Court at Manchester; Clingham* v. *Kensington and Chelsea Royal Borough* [2002] UKHL 39, has confirmed that anti-social behaviour order proceedings are civil. It follows that they cannot be challenged under the fair trial provisions of the Human Rights Act 1998 (ECHR, Art. 6(2) and (3)) and are not subject to the strict rules of evidence applied in criminal cases. In this case police officers gave evidence of allegations of anti-social behaviour made by members of the public who were too frightened to give evidence or could not be identified.

The House of Lords also considered the standard of proof to be applied in ASBO applications. Precedents exist for civil standard of proof – the balance of probabilities – to be heightened in cases where the matters alleged have a particularly serious bearing on the reputation of the person. This heightened standard of proof, which equates to the criminal standard of proof, is to apply in ASBO applications when deciding whether the defendant acted in an anti-social way.

Anti-social behaviour is not defined in the CDA 1998; however, guidance[15] refers to harassment, alarm and distress. These terms are very similar to those employed in the Protection from Harassment Act 1997. It is designed to be a lengthy order, for not less than two years' duration (CDA 1998, s. 1(7)). It is possible to attach specific prohibitions to the order, necessary for the purposes of protecting people in the local government area from anti-social acts by the defendant, for example not entering a particular shop. The examples at the start of the chapter would suggest that not all conditions are likely to be effective or enforceable. It is only possible to attach negative prohibitions to ASBOs, the order cannot include a positive requirement, for example participating in activities.

The grounds for an application for an anti-social behaviour order are:

---

s. 1(1)

(a) that the person has acted … in an anti-social manner, that is to say, in a manner that caused or was likely to cause harassment, alarm or distress to one or more persons not of the same household as himself; and

(b) that such an order is necessary to protect persons in the local government area in which the harassment, alarm or distress was caused or was likely to be caused from further anti-social acts by him;

(CDA 1998)

For example, an ASBO might be appropriate in the following cases.

- Three men with learning disabilities live together in a terraced house and attend a nearby day centre. Regularly, when they walk home, two youths aged 15 and 17 shout abuse at them, leave litter on their doorstep and try to trip them up.

- A man in his early thirties drives around very slowly following groups of children walking to and from school, staring at them and occasionally pulling up in front of them. He is known to the police but has not committed any criminal offence. Many parents have started walking with older children to school as the children are becoming frightened of this man.

- A 20-year-old man has committed acts of physical and financial abuse of his grandmother and shown threatening behaviour towards her and other elderly residents in a sheltered housing scheme.

An ASBO should not be imposed on a defendant who lacks the capacity to understand the order: *Cooke* v. *DPP* [2008] EWHC 2703 (Admin).

Key Case

R (M) v. *Sheffield Magistrates' Court* [2004] EWHC 1830 (Admin) deals with the situation where the child who is subject of an application for an ASBO is in care and the Social Services Authority are the applicant. The facts of the case are set out in full, as the case illustrates a range of youth justice issues.

The claimant (M) sought judicial review of the imposition of an interim anti-social behaviour order (ASBO) against him. M was made subject to a care order at the age of 6 under the Children Act 1989, s. 31. Parental responsibility was shared by the local authority and M's mother. M lived in a series of residential care homes, but was ultimately placed temporarily with his maternal grandmother. An ASBO panel held a conference, which concluded that anti-social behaviour involving M had been proved. Following a report from social services, which suggested that M might be suffering from a disability and that an ASBO would not solve his problems, the panel nevertheless agreed that an ASBO was necessary. Following allegations that he had been involved in an attempt to steal a motor vehicle, the magistrates' court placed M on an intensive supervision and surveillance programme (**ISSP**) attached to a supervision order. The local authority issued a summons, which alleged that M had behaved in an anti-social manner, and the orders were revoked following M's conviction of two offences and breaching the conditions of the order. At the same time, M was made subject to a curfew order and sentenced to a further ISSP programme. The application for an ASBO was made by the local authority. M's social worker declined to be a witness for M, as he wished to be a witness for his employer the local authority. M was unable to call anybody from the local authority as a witness discharging parental responsibility on his behalf. The local authority was granted a without notice interim ASBO and M was granted permission to apply for judicial review.

The issues for the court were: (1) how the interests of a child in care could be protected when the authority responsible for a child's care made an application for an ASBO against the child; and (2) whether it had been appropriate to apply for an interim ASBO.

The court ruled that a conflict of interest would arise when a local authority, having parental responsibility for a child under the 1989 Act, exercised its power under the Crime and Disorder Act 1998 to apply for an ASBO. The conflict had prejudiced M, but had not precluded the authority from making an application under the 1998 Act against a child in its care. The 1989 Act contemplated the local authority remaining empowered to act to fulfil its duty to the public. The problem areas were as follows:

- a decision to apply for an ASBO was a decision within s. 22(4) of the 1989 Act, which required the authority to ascertain the wishes and feelings of the child and any person having parental responsibility for that child. In this case the wishes and feelings of M, his grandmother and his social workers had not been obtained;

- the relevant social worker should not participate in the decision to apply for an ASBO;

- the social services/workers for the authority should be available to assist and be witnesses at court, if requested, for the child in question;

- no court should, save in exceptional circumstances, make an order against a child in care, without someone from the social services who could speak to the issue;

- once a decision had been taken to apply for an ASBO, there should be no contact between the ASBO team and social services without the consent of the child's legal representative.

As to the interim ASBO, the court stated that the order should not have been granted without notice and where there was no one present from social services. The ASBO should have had regard to the existing ISSP and prevailing curfew. There could be no further progress in the ASBO application until the steps above had been completed. In all the circumstances, and as the interim order had expired, no relief was necessary.

Individual support orders

Individual support orders were introduced under ss. 322 and 323 of the Criminal Justice Act 2003 to provide support to young people subject to ASBOs in the interests of preventing any repetition of the kind of behaviour which led to the making of the ASBO. The orders will be run by YOTs and may require the young person to take part in activities and education. ISOs will be repealed by the Anti-social Behaviour, Crime and Policing Act 2014.

Anti-social Behaviour, Crime and Policing Act 2014

Injunctions (Part 1)

An injunction (for up to 12 months) may be made against a person over the age of 10 who has engaged or threatened to engage in anti-social behaviour, to prevent the person from engaging in anti-social behaviour.

Anti-social behaviour is defined in s. 2 as

(a) conduct that has caused, or is likely to cause, harassment, alarm or distress to any person,

(b) conduct capable of causing nuisance or annoyance to a person in relation to that person's occupation of residential premises, or

(c) conduct capable of causing housing related nuisance or annoyance to any person.

A power of arrest may be attached to the injunction if the anti-social behaviour included use or threat of violence or there is a significant risk of harm to others from the person (s. 4). Applications may be made by local authorities, housing providers, the police, Transport for London, the Environment Agency and others.

The local YOT must be consulted before any application for an injunction.

Criminal Behaviour Orders (Part 2)

A criminal behaviour order may be made where a person is convicted of an offence and: the court is satisfied beyond reasonable doubt that the offender has engaged in behaviour that caused or was likely to cause harassment, alarm or distress to anyone; and the court considers that making the order will prevent the offender from engaging in such behaviour. The order can include prohibitions and requirements.

It may be made in addition to a sentence being imposed for an offence or a conditional discharge. The prosecution must apply for the criminal behaviour order – the court cannot make the order of its own volition. The prosecution must seek the views of the local YOT before applying for the order. For a juvenile the order must be made for between 1 and 3 years. Breach of an order is an offence.

Gang injunctions

The Crime and Security Act 2010 introduced the power to take out a gang injunction against a young person aged between 14 and 17. Gang injunctions for adults are also available under the Policing and Crime Act 2009. The police and local authorities may apply for a gang injunction but must consult with YOTs and other partners prior to application. The purpose of the injunction is to prevent gang-related violence. The Policing and Crime Act 2009 defines gang-related violence as:

> Violence or a threat of violence which occurs in the course of, or is otherwise related to, the activities of a group that: consists of at least 3 people; uses a name, emblem or colour or has any other characteristic that enables its members to be identified by others as a group; and is associated with a particular area.

Requirements and prohibitions may be attached to the injunction but must not conflict with the young person's religious beliefs or interfere with work or education. Prohibitions may include: not associating with named gang members; exclusion zones; not wearing particular colours or types of clothing that identify them as a gang member; not having dangerous dogs; restricting the use of the internet for, for example, uploading of gang-related videos or social networking; curfews. Requirements may include: participating in particular activities; attending mediation with rival gang members; attending anger management sessions.

A power of arrest may be attached to prohibitions. In addition, failure to comply with the injunction can result in breach proceedings as a civil contempt of court. Breach of a gang injunction may also be enforced (against 14–17-year-olds) with new civil orders – a civil supervision order and a civil detention order. YOTs will be required to supervise young people who are given the civil supervision order, which may last for up to six months and contain supervision, activity and curfew requirements. Where a respondent has failed to comply with a gang injunction or a subsequent civil supervision order, the court can impose a detention order, detaining the young person for a maximum of three months in a secure training centre, young offender institution, or secure accommodation.

Offending and orders

However commendable the aims of orders that seek to prevent young people engaging in criminal behaviour, there will inevitably be those who do commit offences, are discovered by the police and a decision is taken to prosecute their behaviour. The remainder of this chapter will consider in chronological order the stages in the youth justice system, culminating in discussion of the range of disposal orders, some of which were introduced by the CDA 1998 (mostly consolidated into PCC(S)A 2000).

At this point it is useful to remember that Art. 37 of the United Nations Convention on the Rights of the Child states that the 'arrest, detention or imprisonment of the child ... shall be used only as a measure of last resort and for the shortest appropriate time' and to evaluate the following provisions of the youth justice system in the light of that Article.

Offending behaviour

The age of criminal responsibility in England and Wales is 10.[16] Under that age there is an irrebuttable presumption that a child cannot be guilty of an offence.[17] From that age a child is presumed capable of committing and being held responsible for a criminal act. The Crime and Disorder Act 1998 abolishes the *doli incapax* (incapable of evil) rule for those aged 10–14 years. This rule covers the age at which criminal responsibility is acquired. For those aged under 10 the *doli incapax* rule applies and a child is considered incapable of evil and is immune from prosecution. For those aged 10–14 before the Crime and Disorder Act 1998, the *doli incapax* rule applied but was a rebuttable presumption. The prosecution therefore had to prove that the child appreciated the seriousness of his wrongdoing. This more flexible approach allowed for different levels of maturity within that age band. All children will now acquire criminal responsibility at the age of 10. This is arguably at odds with the approach elsewhere of the law relating to children that they develop autonomy and responsibility gradually and at different rates, as the familiar phrase 'considered in the light of his age and understanding' suggests. This is significantly lower than most other European countries. For example, it is 12 in Greece, 13 in France, 14 in Germany, 16 in Spain and 18 in Belgium.

There are no offences that are specific to juveniles. A person aged between 10 and 17 may be charged with any of the offences for which an adult may be charged. In addition, the process for dealing with juveniles charged with a criminal offence is broadly the same as for an adult, with a few notable differences, which are discussed below. (Chapter 18 deals in detail with adult offenders.)

Pre-court measures

Three measures are available in cases where it appears an offence has been committed but it is a proportionate and appropriate response, taking into account the views of the victim, even for a juvenile with a previous conviction: 'community resolution', 'youth conditional caution' and 'youth caution'. In each case the YOT must be notified.

Community resolution

A 'community resolution' is intended to resolve a minor offence or anti-social behaviour incident through informal agreement between the parties involved. Police officers will assess the offence, taking into account the wishes of the victim and the offender's history, in order to reach an outcome which best meets the needs of the victim and of the public. YOTs will be notified and a community resolution may be disclosed as police information if relevant to an enhanced disclosure and barring service report.

Youth caution

The youth caution and youth conditional cautions are out-of-court disposals which replace Final Warnings and Reprimands. The aim is to reduce the number of juveniles prosecuted for low level offences.

A youth caution may be given for any offence when the young person admits the offence and there is sufficient evidence for a realistic prospect of conviction, but it is not in the public interest to prosecute.

Youth conditional caution

In similar circumstances to the youth caution, the juvenile signs a document which details: the offence; admission of the offence; consent to the caution; any conditions attached to the caution. It is appropriate where the public interest can best be served by the young person complying with suitable conditions rather than a prosecution.

Arrest and charge

If a juvenile is arrested, he should not be detained in a police cell unless there is no other secure accommodation available and the custody officer believes that it is not practical to supervise the child unless he is in a cell, or that the child will be more comfortable in a cell than any other secure accommodation at the station (PACE 1984, Code of Practice C, para. 8.8). The juvenile should not come into contact with adult suspects.

If the juvenile is charged with an offence, the custody officer will have to consider the question of bail. If police bail is refused, the child must be remanded to appear before the youth court at the earliest opportunity. Until then, the child should be accommodated by the local authority (PACE 1984, s. 38(6)). If the child is over the age of 12 this may be in secure accommodation. LASPO ss. 91–92 provides that the court shall remand a child committed for trial or sentence to the local authority and may attach conditions such as electronic tagging. Under CDA 1998, s. 97 the court can make the remand for 12–16-year-olds direct to secure accommodation, provided the criteria in CYPA 1969, s. 23(5) are satisfied. Section 67(1) of the Criminal Justice Act 1967 provides for the period spent in custody while waiting for trial sentence to be taken into account when calculating a custodial sentence. To apply to a juvenile, the remand must have been in accommodation provided for the purpose of restricting liberty. In *R* v. *Secretary of State for the Home Department, ex parte A* [2000] 2 AC 276, the House of Lords found that this provision was not triggered in circumstances where a juvenile's liberty had been restricted by use of a curfew; it was limited to periods in secure accommodation.

Section 98 of the CDA 1998 amends the provision for remand of 15- and 16-year-old boys. At present they may be remanded to prison as an alternative to local authority secure accommodation; this happens increasingly as a result of the lack of local authority secure places. Now, if a boy of 15 or 16 is defined as vulnerable (CDA 1998, s. 98(3)), he will be remanded to local authority secure accommodation. Other boys of that age will be remanded to a remand centre or prison. Girls will not be remanded to prison until aged 17.

Section 58 of PACE 1984 provides that, if a child is detained at the police station, he is entitled to have someone informed of his whereabouts and is entitled to free legal advice under the duty solicitor scheme or provided by a solicitor of the child's choice.

The appropriate adult

In addition to a solicitor, an appropriate adult should be present during any interview of a juvenile under the age of 18.[18] The appropriate adult can exercise the child's right to legal advice. It is important to distinguish the role of the appropriate adult from that of the solicitor. PACE 1984, Code C, para. 11.16 provides:

> Where the appropriate adult is present at an interview, he shall be informed that he is not expected to act simply as an observer; and also that the purposes of his presence are, first, to advise the person being questioned and to observe whether or not the interview is being conducted properly and fairly, and secondly, to facilitate communication with the person being interviewed.

The Crime and Disorder Act 1998, s. 38(4)(a) further describes the role of the appropriate adult as to 'safeguard the interests' of children and young persons detained by the police. At the interview, but not before, the police have a responsibility to inform the appropriate adult of what the role entails. This is unhelpful, as the appropriate adult should be pro-active and take certain action before the interview. This would include looking at the custody record, making sure that the young person knows why they are detained and that they are aware of their rights, for example to make a phone call and to require legal advice.

The appropriate adult for a child or young person will be drawn from the following list (PACE 1984, Code C, para. 1.7):

1. the parent or guardian (or local authority or voluntary organisation if the juvenile is in care);

2. a social worker or a member of a local youth offending team;

3. failing either of the above, another responsible adult aged 18 who is not a police officer or employed by the police.

In most cases the juvenile's parents, or a person with parental responsibility for the juvenile, will act as appropriate adult. There may be circumstances, however, when that person is not available or is not considered suitable to act as the appropriate adult (for example, in *DPP* v. *Blake* [1989] 1 WLR 432 the confession of a juvenile was found to be inadmissible, as it was obtained in the presence of her estranged father with whom she had a poor relationship). In those cases a social worker will frequently be called upon to act as appropriate adult. A social worker should not act as appropriate adult if he called the police or is a witness, as he may not be perceived as independent (*DPP* v. *Morris*, 8 October 1990, unreported).[19] One of the youth justice services that a local authority (in cooperation with the police, probation committee and health authority) is required to provide is sufficient people to act as appropriate adults.

Recently there has been an increase in the number of volunteer schemes that provide appropriate adults. This is specifically endorsed in a Home Office circular, which suggests that volunteers may take the role of appropriate adult, possibly through partnership arrangements with local voluntary organisations.[20] Clearly, if volunteer appropriate adult schemes are to be successful, the volunteers will require a level of training and support. In a case where a volunteer appropriate adult claimed compensation for post-traumatic stress disorder suffered as a result of sitting in interviews related to the Frederick West trial, the court held that the police had no duty of care to prevent psychological harm to the applicant.[21] Such a decision may deter future volunteers.[22] The desire for training is not confined to volunteers and it is imperative that if social workers are to fulfil this role they should also receive appropriate training.

If a parent does not act as appropriate adult, it is now open to question whether this might be in breach of their right to family life under the Human Rights Act 1998. On a wider level, the role of the appropriate adult may be questioned as part of the suspect's right to a fair trial under Art. 6 of the European Convention on Human Rights. The duty imposed on public authorities, which includes the police and the local authority, to comply with the terms of the Convention reinforces the responsibilities to provide appropriate adults and to ensure that the appropriate adult is always present and is informed of the terms of the role.

If a young person is not provided with an appropriate adult, this would probably be considered a significant and substantial breach of PACE rules and the court then has the power to exclude any evidence obtained (PACE 1984, s. 78). As well as being present during any interviews, the appropriate adult should be present when the young person is informed of his or her rights, is charged, takes part in an identification parade or is searched, and where the police issue a warning or reprimand. (Police powers are considered further in Chapter 18.)

Code C was revised in 2013 to extend availability of appropriate adults to 17-year-olds following the case of *R (on the application of HC)* v. *Secretary of State for the Home Department & Anor* [2013] EWHC 982 (Admin). The practice of treating 17-year-olds as adults rather than children, denying the right to contact parents and have an appropriate adult present during questioning, was held to be inconsistent with the UN Convention on the Rights of the Child.

Reflect

Should the role of appropriate adult always be filled by a qualified social worker?

The youth court

The youth court deals with the majority of criminal cases taken against juveniles. It is part of the magistrates' court and was formerly known as the juvenile court. There are a number of features that distinguish the youth court from the adult criminal court. The magistrates who sit in the youth court are drawn from a special panel based on particular relevant experience and having received appropriate training. A district judge (formerly known as a stipendiary magistrate) may hear a juvenile case alone but normally the bench will consist of three magistrates, including both sexes. The proceedings are not open to the public[23] and, although the press are entitled to be present, any reports must not contain information that would identify the accused. There is a power in s. 49(4A) of the Children and Young Persons Act 1933 to dispense with reporting restrictions in criminal proceedings concerning a juvenile, thereby identifying the juvenile. This power should be exercised with great care, caution and circumspection, according to the Divisional Court in *McKerry* v. *Teesside and Wear Valley Justices* [2000] Crim LR 594. The Lord Chief Justice stated that the reporting restrictions provisions should be read against the background of international law and practice, which the European Court had considered in the Thompson and Venables (Bulger) case. It was noted that there was a tension in this case, where a newspaper wished to publish the name of a 15-year-old found guilty of theft, between the competing principles of Art. 8 (the right to privacy) and Art. 10 (freedom of expression). The court found that the power to dispense with anonymity had to be exercised with great care and it would be wrong to dispense with this right as an additional punishment. The Lord Chief Justice continued that '[i]t was also extremely difficult to see any place for "naming and shaming"'.

In addition, s. 44 of the Youth Justice and Criminal Evidence Act 1999 prohibits the publication of information relating to any person under the age of 18 who is involved in any offence, in the period prior to proceedings being commenced. This section has a wide remit, relating not only to offenders but also to witnesses and victims, and it is hoped that it will encourage more young people to come forward as witnesses.

Access to court is limited to the people who are directly involved in the case. This will involve the magistrates and court staff, the parties and the young person's parents, legal representatives, social workers and probation officers. The proceedings are intended to be less formal than in adult court and the layout of the court should reflect this. Magistrates should sit at a table rather than a raised dais. The young person sits in front of the magistrates, not in a dock, and his parent(s) and social worker sit next to or behind him. The magistrates and the clerk address the juvenile by his first name and should explain the charge and other matters in ordinary language. Where the juvenile and other witnesses give evidence, they will promise rather than swear to tell the truth. At the outcome of the case the magistrates make a 'finding of guilt' rather than a 'conviction' and make a 'disposal on a finding of guilt' rather than a 'sentence'. The court must have regard to the welfare of the child under s. 44 of the Children and Young Persons Act 1933.

A juvenile may be tried in the adult magistrates' court where he is jointly charged with an adult. In the serious cases outlined below, a juvenile will be tried in the Crown Court.

Serious offences

Certain serious offences defined by s. 90 of the Powers of Criminal Courts (Sentencing) Act 2000 (formerly Children and Young Persons Act 1933, s. 53) will be tried and sentenced in the Crown Court. Commonly, reference has been made to 'section 53s'. Section 90 refers to murder. Section 91 refers to a range of offences including manslaughter and offences that carry a maximum penalty of 14 years' imprisonment or more where committed by an adult. Where the youth court considers that, if the case is proven, a term of detention is the likely disposal, then the case will be heard in the Crown Court.

Dangerousness

The concept of 'dangerousness' and the dangerous offender was introduced by the Criminal Justice Act 2003. It provides a further method by which the youth court can commit a youth to the Crown Court on satisfaction of certain criteria. An offender is 'dangerous' if the court considers there is a 'significant risk to members of the public of serious harm occasioned by the commission by him of further specified offences' (**CJA** 2003, s. 225). There is a presumption (rebuttable if unreasonable) that an adult offender who has previously been convicted of a relevant offence, is dangerous. For youths the presumption does not apply, the court will take into account information about the nature and circumstances of the offence, and pattern of behaviour and information about the offender, in deciding on dangerousness. The court will assess serious risk in each case.

The CJA introduced indeterminate sentences of imprisonment for public protection and extended sentences for public protection. LASPO (Legal Aid, Sentencing and Punishment of Offenders Act) 2012 has replaced both by the extended determinate sentence for specified violent and sexual offences. The sentence comprises a custodial term followed by an extended licence period, which together cannot exceed the maximum term for the offence.

Disposal

Youth courts must follow the principle of proportionate sentencing contained in the Criminal Justice Act 2003, as amended by the Criminal Justice and Immigration Act 2008. Effectively, this means that the court will consider how serious the offence is, taking into account any aggravating and mitigating factors, and reflect the level of seriousness in the choice of sentence. Furthermore, CDA 1998, s. 80 requires the Court of Appeal to consider producing sentencing guidelines in suitable cases, and CDA 1998, s. 81 established a Sentencing Advisory Panel to provide advice on sentencing to the Court of Appeal. Section 153 of the Powers of Criminal Courts (Sentencing) Act 2000 specifically provides for sentences to be increased where an offence is racially aggravated. The judge is required to impose a higher sentence and state in open court that the offence is racially aggravated. This provision is relevant to all offenders, whatever the sentence. There are also a number of specific racially aggravated offences created by the Crime and Disorder Act 1998, which provide for enhanced maximum penalties for existing offences (e.g. criminal damage) where racial aggravation is proved. This applies to juveniles and adults.

Welfare is relevant as the court has to take account of s. 44 CYPA 1933 when sentencing:

---

s. 44

Every court in dealing with a child or young person who is brought before it, either as an offender or otherwise, shall have regard to the welfare of the child or young person...

(CYPA 1933)

In addition to the orders that can be made in respect of the juvenile, the court can make a range of orders affecting parents. It is usual for the court to require the attendance of parents at the hearing. In addition, it can impose **parental bindovers**, compensation orders and fines.

In summary, the disposal options available since the Crime and Disorder Act 1998 reforms are:

- reparation order – reparation may be made to the victim of a crime, a person otherwise affected or the community at large;
- referral orders – a referral is made to a YOT for assessment and participation in a programme to prevent reoffending;
- sex offender orders;
- detention and training orders – replace a variety of custodial options;
- youth rehabilitation orders.

Referral orders (PCC(S)A 2000, ss. 16–20)

A new sentencing disposal was introduced by the Youth Justice and Criminal Evidence Act 1999 in the form of the referral order, now consolidated in ss. 16–20 PCC(S)A 2000. It is a compulsory sentence for children and young persons aged 10–17 who plead guilty and are convicted for the first time by a court. The court can make a referral order for a minimum period of three months and no longer than one year, the actual period depending on the seriousness of the crime. The young offender is referred to a Youth Offender Panel (**YOP**). Panels should be convened within 15 days of the court hearing and are intended to offer a less formal meeting than court, where the young offender and his/her family and the victim can consider the circumstances of the offence and draw up a 'contract'. It is an expectation that a parent(s) will attend panel meetings with the young offender (if under the age of 16) and, to reinforce this expectation, if parents fail to attend without reasonable excuse, contempt proceedings may result. When the order is made, it will be usual practice for the court to order parents to attend. If the young offender does not attend the panel, and cannot give an acceptable reason for non-attendance, then the offender will return to court for re-sentencing. Also, if the young offender will not agree to a contract, he or she will return to court for re-sentencing. The panel will reconvene for interim progress reports, after one month and then every three months. As the conviction is spent as soon as a referral order has been completed, this may in practice prove to be the incentive for offenders to agree and comply with contracts.

Youth Offender Panels should be made up of a representative group of the community, though early indications are of a majority of women, and few unemployed members. In their work, YOPs should be guided by the principles of 'restoration, reintegration and responsibility', which underlie restorative justice (Home Office (1997) pp. 31–2).

Success of the referral order must depend in large part on the range of programmes of activities that are available to be included in a contract. Contracts may include an element of reparation (e.g. a written apology to the victim), and the programme should be designed to prevent further offending. Contracts may include educational activities, intensive work with a YOT officer, sporting activities, involvement in a support group, family group conferences and curfews.

Reparation order (PCC(S)A 2000, ss. 73–75)

As the name suggests, where a reparation order is made, the offender is involved in supervised direct reparation. The order may be made for a juvenile over the age of 10. Reparation orders provide for the offender to make reparation to the victim of the crime, any person otherwise affected, or the community at large (the victim's consent must be obtained). A maximum of 24 hours' reparation is permitted, to be completed within three months. Reparation conditions can also be attached to supervision orders. The Introductory Guide suggests that reparation might include writing a letter of apology or apologising to the victim in person, cleaning graffiti or repairing criminal damage. Again, before making an order, the court must consider a written report by a probation officer, social worker or member of the YOT, outlining the type of reparation proposed, availability of appropriate work, and the attitude of the victim to the proposed reparation. The order will be supervised by a social worker, probation officer or member of a YOT. Pilot studies conducted prior to full implementation of the CDA applied a range of methods of reparation, for example, distributing crime leaflets, designing a leaflet outlining help available to young drug users, voluntary work at a hospice.[24]

Sex offender orders (CDA 1998, ss. 2–3)

Sex offender orders were introduced by CDA 1998, s. 2. The police are the applicants for an order, which is made by the magistrates' civil court after there has been a conviction for a sexual offence. The order will be made where a person is a sex offender (defined in the Sex Offenders Act 1997) and there is a risk of serious harm to the public. The order is intended to be preventative and requires sex offenders to register under the Sex Offenders Act 1997. An order will last for a minimum period of five years and will contain prohibitions designed to protect the public from harm by the defendant (e.g. staying away from particular premises), but it cannot require treatment of the individual. Breach of the order is a criminal offence. In the majority of cases it is anticipated that sex offender orders will be made in respect of adults; however, they can be made for anyone over the age of criminal responsibility.

Custodial sentences

The **UNCRC** clearly states that custodial sentences should be considered as a last resort for juveniles. The principle of 'proportionality' discussed above applies to custodial sentences and under the PCC(S)A 2000, s. 79 the court must be satisfied that:

> ### s. 79
>
> **(a)** the offence, or the combination of the offence and one or more offences associated with it, was so serious that only such a sentence can be justified for it; or
> **(b)** that the offence is a violent or sexual offence, and that only such a sentence would be adequate to protect the public from serious harm from the offender.
>
> (PCC(S) A 2000)

A pre-sentence report is required before a custodial sentence can be imposed (s. 156 CJA 2003). The Youth Justice Board National Standards include guidance on the required content of reports and Standard 5 provides:

> Reports prepared by the YOT are balanced, impartial, timely, focused, free from discriminatory language and stereotypes, verified, factually accurate, understandable to the child or young person and their parents/carers, and provide the required level of information and analysis to enable sentencers to make informed decisions regarding sentencing.

Detention and training order (PCC(S)A 2000, ss. 100–107)

Section 73 of CDA established the detention and training order, followed by supervision. It is a generic custodial sentence replacing the sentences of a secure training order and detention in a young offender institution. An order may be made in respect of juveniles aged between 12 and 17. A child under the age of 15 must be a persistent offender to become the subject of an order. The maximum period of detention is reduced from two years to three months by **LASPO**. The period of detention will be spent in a secure training centre, a young offender institution, a youth treatment centre or local authority (or other) secure accommodation. Supervision will be provided after release, in the community, normally after 50 per cent of the detention element is complete.

Powers of Criminal Court (Sentencing) Act 2000, s. 90

Where a child is found to have committed a grave crime (e.g. murder), he or she must be detained during Her Majesty's pleasure, the exact place and period to be directed. Under s. 60 of the Criminal Justice and Courts Services Act 2000, in the case of a murder committed by a person under the age of 18 the trial judge will now fix the **tariff** in open court. Tariff is the minimum period that must be served before first consideration for an early release. This change was occasioned by the European Court of Human Rights ruling in *T* v. *United Kingdom; V* v. *United Kingdom* (2000) 30 EHRR 121 (the 'Bulger case'). Previously, the judge would make a private recommendation to the Lord Chief Justice, who could adjust the tariff;

the papers were then passed to the Home Secretary, who could make a further adjustment. In the Bulger case, the trial judge recommended that Venables and Thompson serve a minimum period of eight years; this was raised to 15 years by the Home Secretary at the time, Michael Howard. The case was taken to the European Court of Human Rights, which found breaches of the European Convention on Human Rights in terms of sentencing practice and also that the defendants did not receive a fair hearing in accordance with Art. 6(1).

A Practice Direction followed the case.[25] The Practice Direction is an important development in youth justice, which tackles many of the difficulties apparent in the Bulger case and suggests changes necessary to ensure compliance with the European Convention on Human Rights as required by the Human Rights Act 1998. The Practice Direction provides for special measures to be introduced to ensure a fair hearing at trial. The measures required will vary depending on the particular child's needs, assessed by the trial judge, 'the steps which should be taken to comply with the direction should be judged, in any given case, taking account of the age, maturity and development (intellectual and emotional) of the young defendant on trial' (para. 2). The added pressure of being tried with an adult is acknowledged by the Practice Direction and it states that a court should order separate trials for juveniles and adults, unless it is in the interests of justice to do otherwise. It also recommends that young defendants should visit the court out of hours to become accustomed to the setting. The level of formality of the trial should be reduced, including removal of wigs and gowns, changes to the courtroom and limitations on access. Many of these features are already present in the youth court. Of course, a murder trial will always be conducted in the Crown Court, whatever the age of the defendant. The Practice Direction suggests that, in the court, everyone should sit at the same level, and the defendants should be able to sit next to their family and near the lawyers. (In the Bulger trial the defendants actually sat in a raised dock so that they could view the proceedings.) The Practice Direction suggests that only people with a direct interest in the outcome of the trial should be allowed into the court, but if press access is restricted, a provision should be made for the trial to be viewed through a TV link into another area. The Practice Direction raises a number of issues that have been addressed in the Youth Justice and Criminal Evidence Act 1999 in respect of child witnesses. (These provisions are discussed in Chapter 9.)

Youth rehabilitation order

The youth rehabilitation order (**YRO**) is the standard community sentence to be used for juveniles. As a range of requirements can be attached to the order, it should offer a flexible way to respond to the the juvenile's circumstances by a menu of interventions.

The requirements that can be attached to a YRO are:

- activity requirement for up to 90 days;
- curfew requirement;
- exclusion requirement for up to three months;
- local authority residence requirement;
- education requirement;
- mental health requirement;
- unpaid work requirement for between 40 and 240 hours (16–17 year olds);
- drug testing requirement;
- intoxicating substance requirement;

- supervision requirement;
- electronic monitoring requirement;
- prohibited activity requirement;
- drug treatment requirement;
- residence requirement, where the offender was 16 or over at the time of sentence;
- programme requirement;
- attendance centre requirement;
- intensive supervision and surveillance requirement;
- intensive fostering, where the court is satisfied that the offending behaviour was significantly due to the juvenile's living circumstances and fostering will assist with rehabilitation. Parents and the local authority must be consulted.

For the court to sentence a person to a YRO it must be satisfied that the offence is sufficiently serious and that any restriction of liberty is proportionate to the seriousness of the offence. If the YRO is breached, the court may order a fine, amend the YRO or revoke the YRO and re-sentence. Further detail on each requirement of the YRO is contained in Practice Guidance (2010).[26]

Chapter summary

- The law relating to youth justice is substantially contained in the Crime and Disorder Act 1998, the Youth Justice and Criminal Evidence Act 1999 and the Powers of Criminal Courts (Sentencing) Act 2000. There is an increasing emphasis on the prevention of youth crime.
- The role of a social worker in youth justice is varied and may include: membership of a youth offending team; acting as designated responsible officer on a child safety order; advising, assisting and befriending a young person under a supervision order; acting as an appropriate adult; and contact with young people in secure accommodation.
- The Crime and Disorder Act 1998 introduced new structures for youth justice. Institutional arrangements are underpinned by s. 37, which introduces a statutory aim to prevent offending by children and young persons. Youth offending teams with multi-agency membership have been introduced and every Social Services Department must produce a youth justice plan.
- Youth justice services may include: assessment of children and young persons for rehabilitation programmes; provision of support whilst children and young persons are remanded on bail; placements in local authority secure or non-secure accommodation; provision of court reports; supervision of young persons and post-release supervision. A National Youth Justice Board is established to oversee the delivery of youth justice services.
- Section 17 of the CDA 1998 imposes a duty on local authorities and police authorities to do all they reasonably can to prevent crime and disorder. Parenting orders, child safety orders, child curfew schemes and an enhanced local authority duty of investigation are particularly relevant orders in respect of preventing youth crime.
- The anti-social behaviour order is a civil order to prevent harassment, alarm or distress, breach of which is a criminal offence. It is due to be replaced by Injunctions and Criminal Behaviour Orders.

- Since the abolition of the *doli incapax* rule, all children will now acquire criminal responsibility at the age of 10.

- Targets have been introduced for reducing delays in the youth justice system, with particular emphasis on persistent young offenders, defined as: 'a young person aged 10–17 who has been sentenced by a criminal court in the United Kingdom on three or more separate occasions for one or more recordable offences, and within three years of the last sentencing occasion is subsequently arrested or has an information laid against them for a further recordable offence'.

- If a child is interviewed at the police station, he should be accompanied by an appropriate adult, whose role is to safeguard the interests of children and young persons detained by the police, and 'not … to act simply as an observer; … the purposes of his presence are, first, to advise the person being questioned and to observe whether or not the interview is being conducted properly and fairly, and secondly, to facilitate communication with the person being interviewed'.

- Most criminal cases taken against juveniles will be heard in the youth court in which magistrates drawn from a special panel hear cases. Proceedings are not open to the public and there are restrictions on press reporting. Certain serious offences (murder and offences carrying a maximum penalty of 14 years' imprisonment) will be tried in the Crown Court.

- If the court makes a finding of guilt, disposal options include detention and training orders and youth rehabilitation orders with conditions.

Exercises

1. Jeannie, aged 15, has recently started going out with James, who is 28. Her parents are very unhappy about the relationship and think she may also be taking drugs. She has failed to attend school today and is picked up by the police in an area of town known for prostitution, in possession of £100 cash and £50-worth of cosmetics. Just as the police are about to drive off, James rushes over, shouting at Jeannie not to talk, and damages the police car with an iron bar. At the police station the custody officer calls Jeannie's parents, who state that 'she is no longer our daughter' and refuse to come to the station. A social worker is called to be with Jeannie and notices injection marks on her arm. Jeannie admits to theft of the cosmetics but denies any knowledge of the money. She has no previous convictions. Initially she claims not to know James, but after a four-hour period of questioning she breaks down and states that he is her pimp, the money is for him, but she is frightened that he will beat her up if he finds out she has told the police.

    Consider the responsibilities of the social worker called to the station. If the social worker fulfils the role adequately, what changes to the above scenario might occur. What are the options for responding to Jeannie's situation?

2. Michael, a 15-year-old, has had a turbulent childhood; he has been living in a residential children's home for the last two years and frequently fails to attend school. He has received cautions from the police for criminal damage. Recently he has become friendly with Joe, who is aged 19 and lives in a bedsit near Michael. Joe has had three appearances before the youth court for shop theft, criminal damage and public order matters. One night Michael is stopped on the street by two police officers who have been notified of a break-in at a local off-licence store. The police had been informed that two youths were seen running

away from the store and suspect that Michael is one of them. Michael denies any knowledge or involvement in the break-in. The police are still suspicious and take Michael to the police station to assist them with their inquiries. After two hours of questioning, Michael confesses and tells the police where Joe lives; the police then contact Michael's social worker. At Joe's flat the police find ten bottles of gin and, on further searching, discover a quantity of cannabis. Joe is charged with burglary and possession of drugs and Michael is charged with assisting burglary.

Were the correct procedures followed at the police station? If the offences are prosecuted, which court will hear the case against Michael? If the case is proven, what is the likely disposal?

Websites

The Home Office site provides a mass of information on the Crime and Disorder Act 1998 and associated youth justice reforms. The introductory guide to the Act, and guidance on each of the new orders is available. Criminal statistics and research publications are also available: **www.homeoffice.gov.uk**

The Youth Justice Board website provides a wealth of information on youth justice issues: **www.justice.gov.uk/youth-justice**

The National Association for Youth Justice is a campaigning organisation for the rights of children and young people in the criminal law and the website includes useful briefing notes: **www.thenayj.org.uk**

The national Appropriate Adult Network website includes useful information about the role: **www.appropriateadult.org.uk**

Further reading

The Youth Justice Board has issued National Standards and Guidance for Youth Justice:

HMCS and YJB (2010) *Making it Count in Court* (2nd edn). London: YJB and HMCS.
YJB (2010) 'The Youth Rehabilitation Order and Other Youth Justice Provisions of the Criminal Justice and Immigration Act 2008: Practice Guidance for youth offending teams'. London: YJB.
YJB (2013) *National Standards for Youth Justice Services*. London: YJB.

The journal *Youth Justice* includes a range of relevant articles.

A number of specialist texts consider youth justice in more detail:

Goldson, B. (ed.) (2000) *The New Youth Justice*. Lyme Regis: Russell House Publishing.
Leng, R., Taylor, R. and Wasik, M. (1998) *Blackstone's Guide to the Crime and Disorder Act 1998*. London: Blackstone Press.
Moore, T. and Wilkinson, T. (2001) *Youth Court Guide*. London: Butterworths.
Muncie, J (2005) *Youth and Crime: A Critical Introduction* (3rd edn). London: Sage.
Pickford, J. and Dugmore, P. (2012) *Youth Justice and Social Work* (2nd edn). London: Sage.
Stephenson, M., Giller, H. and Brown, S. (2011) *Effective Practice in Youth Justice* (2nd edn). London: Routledge.

Critical examination of the youth justice system features in the following articles:

Arthur, R. (2005) 'The Youth Justice System in England and Wales: complying with international human rights law' 3 *International Family Law* p. 3.

Ball, C. (2004) 'Youth justice? Half a century of responses to youth offending' *Criminal Law Review* p. 167.

Fionda, J. (1999) 'New Labour, old hat: youth justice and the Crime and Disorder Act 1998' *Criminal Law Review* p. 36.

Gelsthorpe, L. and Morris, A. (1999) 'Much ado about nothing – a critical comment on key provisions relating to children in the Crime and Disorder Act 1998' 11(3) *Child and Family Law Quarterly* p. 209.

Hollingsworth, K. (2012) 'Youth Justice in the Big Society' 34 *Journal of Social Welfare and Family Law* p. 241.

Parry, G. (2005) 'Protecting the juvenile suspect: What exactly is the appropriate adult supposed to do? *Child and Family Law Quarterly* p. 373.

Smith, R. (2005) 'Welfare versus justice – again!' 5(1) *Youth Justice* p. 3.

For further information and discussion of anti-social behaviour see:

Anderson, J., Falkowski, D., Greatorex, P. and Tankel, B. (2011) *Anti-Social Behaviour Law* (2nd edn). Bristol: Jordan Publishing.

Ashworth, A. (2004) 'Social control and "anti-social behaviour"' 120 *Law Quarterly Review* p. 263.

MacDonald, S. (2006) 'A suicidal woman, roaming pigs and a noisy trampolinist: refining the ASBO's definition of "anti-social behaviour"' 69(2) *Modern Law Review* p. 183. (Suggests that ASBOs have been employed for social control at the expense of more constructive forms of intervention.)

Notes

1 For a full discussion of this case see S. Macdonald (2007) 'ASBO prohibitions and young people – *Hills* v *Chief Constable of Essex Police*' 19(3) *Child and Family Law Quarterly* p. 374.

2 Examples taken from S. Macdonald and M. Telford (2007) 'The use of ASBOs against young people in England and Wales: lessons from Scotland' 27(4) *Legal Studies* p. 604.

3 For a full review of changes in policy see: C. Ball (2004) 'Youth justice? Half a century of responses to youth offending' *Criminal Law Review* p. 167.

4 Home Office Research Report 64 (2012) 'An estimate of youth crime in England and Wales: Police recorded crime committed by young people in 2009–10'.

5 Audit Commission (1996) 'Misspent Youth: Young People and Crime: A Consultation Paper', identified a number of criticisms, including: delay in processing young offenders through the courts; little being done to address offending behaviour; lack of preventive work with potential offenders; and uncoordinated work between the agencies involved in youth justice. These deficiencies were taken up in the white paper published by the (then) newly elected Labour Government, 'No More Excuses: A New Approach to Tackling Youth Crime in England and Wales' (1997) and was followed by the Crime and Disorder Act 1998.

6 HM Treasury and DCSF (2007).

7 Children Act 1989, Sch. 2, para. 7.

8 This classification is adopted by A. Bainham (1998) *Children: The Modern Law*, Bristol: Family Law, Jordan Publishing.

9 The term 'community safety' is increasingly used in preference to crime prevention.

[10] Home Office (1998) 'Establishing Youth Offending Teams' provides some guidance on the role of YOTs.

[11] See www.youth-justice-board.gov.uk.

[12] See discussion by L. Gelsthorpe and A. Morris (1999) 'Much ado about nothing – a critical comment on key provisions relating to children in the Crime and Disorder Act 1998' 11(3) *Child and Family Law Quarterly* pp. 209–21.

[13] C. Piper (1999) 'The Crime and Disorder Act 1998: child and community "safety"' 62(3) *Modern Law Review* pp. 397–408.

[14] Home Office and Ministry of Justice (2013) 'Anti-social behaviour order statistics: England and Wales 2012'.

[15] Home Office (1998) 'Introductory Guide to the Crime and Disorder Act 1998'. London: Home Office.

[16] UNCRC, Art. 40(3) requires establishment of a minimum age below which children shall be presumed not to have the capacity to infringe the penal law.

[17] Children and Young Persons Act 1933, s. 50.

[18] For further discussion of this role see: B. Littlechild (1998) 'Appropriate adult services' 144 *Childright* pp. 8–9, and H. Pierpoint (1999) 'Appropriate practice? Young suspects' rights under UNCRC' 162 *Childright* pp. 8–10.

[19] Cited in T. Moore and T. Wilkinson (2001) *Youth Court Guide*. London: Butterworths.

[20] Home Office (1998) 'Inter-departmental circular on establishing youth offending teams.

[21] *Leach* v. *Chief Constable of Gloucestershire* [1999] 1 All ER 215.

[22] For the evaluation of a volunteer scheme, see T. Nemitz and P. Bean (1998) 'The effectiveness of a volunteer appropriate adult scheme' 38(3) *Medicine, Science and the Law* pp. 251–6.

[23] Children and Young Persons Act 1933, s. 47(2).

[24] P. Tain (1999) 'Youth Justice' *Solicitors Journal* 18 June, p. 581.

[25] Practice Direction (Crown Court: Trial of Children and Young Persons) [2000] 2 All ER 285.

[26] YJB (2010) *The Youth Rehabilitation Order and Other Youth Justice Provisions of the Criminal Justice and Immigration Act 2008: Practice Guidance for youth offending teams*. London: YJB.

Part 3

Vulnerable adults

Chapters:

Chapter 14

Adult social care

Learning objectives

To develop an understanding of the following:

- The legal context to work with adult service users.
- The legal framework for adult social care provided by the Care Act 2014.
- The concept of 'wellbeing'.
- Personalisation.
- The duty to assess for care and support services, provision of services and implications of resources.
- The principles of charging for services.
- Avenues for complaints in respect of assessment and provision.
- The role of carers and provision of support for carers.
- The provision and regulation of domiciliary and residential services.

Talking Point

The Care Act represents the most significant reform of care and support in more than 60 years, putting people and their carers in control of their care and support. For the first time, the Act will put a limit on the amount anyone will have to pay towards the costs of their care.

And, crucially, the Act delivers key elements of the Government's response to the Francis Inquiry into the awful events at Mid Staffordshire hospital, increasing transparency and openness and helping drive up the quality of care across the system.

Care and support is something that nearly everyone in this country will experience at some point in their lives; even if you don't need care yourself, you will probably know a family member or friend who does, or you may care for someone. And many more of us will need care in the future so it is important for us to have a modern system that can keep up with the demands of a growing ageing population.

Until now it's been almost impossible for people who need care, carers, and even those who manage the care system, to understand how the previous law affecting them worked. Over nearly 70 years it has been added to again and again and is out of date and confusing. The Care Act has created a single, modern law that makes it clear what kind of care people should expect.

To help make things clearer we have introduced a minimum eligibility threshold across the country – a set of criteria that makes it clear when local authorities will have to provide support to people. Until now, local authorities have been able to decide this threshold themselves, meaning decisions varied from place to place. And, in the face of financial pressures, a number of councils have raised their threshold level in recent years. In future, councils will not be allowed to tighten their thresholds beyond this minimum threshold, giving those who are eligible peace of mind that they won't have their care taken away from them because of some arbitrary change to the criteria.

This isn't just about making things easier to understand – it's also about changing the way we care for people. Central to the Act is the concept of wellbeing. First and foremost councils will now have a duty to consider the physical, mental and emotional wellbeing of the individual needing care. They will also have a new duty to provide preventative services to maintain people's health.

Until now, we've had a one size fits all approach to care. The focus has been on what disabilities someone has, or what services local authorities can provide, rather than on the individual. That's disempowering. So for the first time the system will be built around each person – what they need, how they can best be cared for, and what they want. By providing and legislating for Personal Budgets in the Care Act we are giving people the power to spend money on tailored care that suits their individual needs as part of their support plan.[1]

The above passages are an extract from the statement by Care and Support Minister Norman Lamb introducing the scope of the law reform provided by the Care Act 2014. The reforms, based on the work of the Law Commission, are significant and whilst some elements inevitably require clarification, an accessible single piece of legislation for adult social care is welcome.

Introduction

This chapter is divided into three sections: introducing the legal framework for work with adult service users; assessment for services; and two particular areas of service provision – domiciliary care and residential accommodation.

Social work with adult service users is the focus of the next four chapters. The law in this area is complex and has attracted much criticism over the years. It is encouraging that this area has been subject to various reviews which recognise the changing context to adult social care. Changes to policy were evident in the green paper, 'Independence, Well being and Choice' (2005), the white paper, 'Our Health, Our Care, Our Say' (2006), 'Putting People First' (2007), and 'The case for change – why England needs a new care and support system' (2008), amongst others. Further, the Coalition Government published 'A Vision for Adult Social Care: Capable Communities and Active Citizens' (2010) and established the Dilnot Commission which reported in 2011 on the funding system for care and support, recommending an absolute cap on any individual's contribution to their own social care costs. In terms of law reform, the work of the Law Commission on adult social care law is most significant and forms the basis of the new Care Act 2014. With over £20 billion annual expenditure by local authorities on adult social care, and 1.77 million people in receipt of services, this is an area of great social and economic significance. The need for reform was evident on a number of levels. The relevant law developed in a piecemeal fashion, since the National Assistance Act 1948 resulting in a framework both extensive and complex which contains overlapping and conflicting obligations. There are concerns that some of the language used is outdated and oppressive and further that elements of the law might conflict with human rights principles.

The aim of the Law Commission was to make recommendations which would provide a clearer and more coherent legal framework for adult social care, with emphasis on simplification, consistency, transparency and modernisation. Ultimately, these objectives may be achieved by the resulting single consolidated statute, the Care Act 2014. It is important to remember that, for a complete understanding of the law relating to adults, other legislation such as the Mental Capacity Act 2005 and the Mental Health Act 2007 must also be considered.

The chapter commences with an outline of the range of adult service users to whom the new Act will apply, recognising that this range will present a variety of needs and dilemmas for the social work practitioner. It is important that this diversity is fully recognised and that generalised assumptions are not made. The law, however, has tended to operate in relation to particular categories of people or particular needs or scenarios. That approach was evident in previous legislation which tended to focus on, for example, older people or people with physical disabilities. As a preliminary issue, therefore, a consideration of the categories of service users that the law recognised and the former legislation, now repealed by the Care Act 2014, is set out by way of reference for understanding ongoing cases and for comparison. Throughout the chapter, case law decided under the previous legal framework is included where it establishes principles which are likely to continue to have application. At the time of writing, the Care Act 2014 has received Royal Assent but the guidance and regulations which will inevitably follow have not been finalised.

Adult service users

Whilst the law can separate individual characteristics of adults, and organisational teams may also reflect these categories, the reality of the individuals encountered in everyday practice is less clear cut. For example, some elderly people will also have a physical disability, which may or may not be associated with old age; equally, people with mental illness grow older and other elderly people may suffer from a mental illness associated with increasing years.

Older people

The term 'older people', rather than elderly people, will be adopted in this text following acceptance of this term in the field of gerontology as a value-free description of later life, i.e. persons over the age of 65.[2] In legal terms there is no clear definition of an old person (in contrast, a child is clearly defined as a person under the age of 18 (Children Act 1989, s. 105)). Even in respect of specific legal duties, different terms are used without definition, such as 'aged', or 'by reason of old age'. What is clear is that, given increasing longevity (and with more people reaching 100 years of age each year), it is inappropriate to speak collectively of the needs of older people. It is worth noting that there are more women than men in the older age bracket. In the context of community care, there will be people who are being cared for by carers who are themselves older people. Older people will increasingly come to the attention of mental health services, given that the incidence of depression and dementia in older people is high (approximately one in five of those aged over 85). A significant number of older people live in residential settings, though the majority retain independence living in the community. There is an increasing awareness of the law relating to older people, particularly concerning issues surrounding management of financial affairs and mental capacity. The Equality Act 2010 prohibits direct or indirect age discrimination. Article 14 of the European Convention on Human Rights is relevant if an older person is discriminated against in terms of enjoyment of the other Articles in the Convention: e.g. if different practices exist in respect of older and younger residents relating to the privacy enjoyed in a residential setting.

People with a mental disorder

The legal framework for social work with people with a mental disorder is provided by the Mental Health Act 1983 (discussed fully in Chapter 15). The Act contains a definition of the term 'mental disorder'. Many people with mental disorders are able to live in the community. Others may spend time in hospitals or mental nursing homes as informal patients, or, in limited circumstances, may be compulsorily detained in a hospital for a fixed period of time. The criminal law may make specific orders with regard to mentally disordered offenders (discussed in Chapter 18). People with a mental disorder may be entitled to a range of services to enable them to live in the community under a care plan, they may be supported by a guardianship order, or in receipt of after-care services following a period of formal detention.

People with a learning disability

People with learning disabilities will occasionally fall under the compulsory detention provisions of the Mental Health Act 1983 where their learning disability is accompanied by 'abnormally aggressive or seriously irresponsible behaviour'. Guidance states that services for adults with learning disabilities should be arranged on an individual basis, taking account of 'age, or needs, degree of disability, the personal preferences of the individual and his or her parents or carers, culture, race and gender'.[3] A white paper, 'Valuing People – A New Strategy for Learning Disability' (2001), provides the framework for provision of services for people with learning disability. Many people with learning disabilities live in the community with their families or in supported group homes and some may live in residential accommodation. Considerable research has shown that people with learning disabilities are particularly vulnerable to sexual exploitation.[4] (A range of specific sexual offences against people with 'mental disorder' is outlined in Chapter 17.)

People with a physical disability

People with a physical disability may receive services to reduce the impact of their disability. The Disability Discrimination Act 1995 (DDA 1995) made it unlawful to discriminate against disabled people in the provision of goods and services. Disability (physical and mental) is now included as one of the protected characteristics in the Equality Act 2010.

People with a physical disability may register on the register of disabled persons compiled by social services but are not obliged to do so, and registration is not a prerequisite for service provision. Registration data is held under the following categories: very severe handicap; severe or appreciable handicap; and other persons.[5] Children with disabilities will normally be entitled to support as 'children in need' (Children Act 1989, s. 17). (This is discussed in Chapter 7.)

Legal framework pre Care Act 2014

A summary of the legal provisions relating to adult service users in place before the implementation of the Care Act 2014 is given in Table 14.1.

Table 14.1 Summary of legal provisions relating to adult service users in place prior to implementation of the Care Act 2014

Legislation	Section	Summary
National Assistance Act 1948	29	Local authority power to promote the welfare of people 'aged 18 and over who are blind, deaf or dumb or who suffer from mental disorder of any description and other persons who are substantially and permanently handicapped by illness, injury or congenital deformity'
	21	Duty to provide residential accommodation for persons who by reason of age, illness, disability or other circumstances are in need of care or attention which is not otherwise available to them
	47	Power of removal from home (see Chapter 17)
Health Services and Public Health Act 1968	45	Local authority may make arrangements for promotion of welfare of old people
Chronically Sick and Disabled Persons Act 1970	1	Local authorities to inform themselves of number of people within NAA 1948, s. 29
	2	Duty to assess needs and provide specified services to disabled people, e.g.adaptations
National Health Service Act 1977 (2006)	Schedule 8	Duty to provide home helps for households where help is required owing to the presence of a person who is suffering from illness, lying in, an expectant mother, aged, handicapped as a result of having suffered from illness or by congenital deformity

Table 14.1 (Continued)

Legislation	Section	Summary
Mental Health Act 1983	117	After-care services (see further Chapter 15)
Health and Social Services and Social Security Adjudications Act 1983	17	Local authority power to make reasonable charges for non-residential community services
Disabled Persons (Services, Consultation and Representations) Act 1986	4	Right to an assessment
	9	Duty to provide information about services
National Health Service and Community Care Act 1990	46	Requirement for community care plans
	46(3)	Definition of community care services
	47	Assessment of need for community care services
	47(5)	Services may be provided pending assessment
	48	Inspection of premises where community care services provided
	50	LA Complaints procedure
Disability Discrimination Acts 1995 and 2005	1 and 19	Unlawful to discriminate on the grounds of disability in the provision of goods and services. Replaced by Equality Act 2010
Carers (Recognition and Services) Act 1995	1	Assessment of a carer's ability to provide and continue to provide care for a person
Community Care (Direct Payments) Act 1996	1	Power to make direct payments
Carers and Disabled Children Act 2000	1	Carer entitlement to assessment independent of assessment of person cared for
	2	Definition of care services
Carers (Equal Opportunities) Act 2004	1	Obligation on LA to inform carer of right to assessment
	2	Assessment to include carer's wishes as to work, education, training and leisure
	3	Cooperation between local authority and other bodies
Health and Social Care Act 2008	145	Extended availability of direct payments to a 'suitable person' to manage the payment on behalf of an adult lacking capacity

The Care Act 2014

The Care Act 2014 begins with a section on 'General responsibilities of local authorities' in relation to care and support. The primary principle is promoting individual wellbeing, (s. 1). Further important principles are: preventing needs for care and support (s. 2); integrating care and support with health services (s. 3); providing information and advice (s. 4); promoting diversity and quality in provision of services (s. 5); and cooperation in general and in specific cases (ss. 6

and 7). Throughout the Act there are references to matters that will be dealt with by Regulations and it will be necessary to consider those once published and implemented. It is disappointing that the government have ignored the recommendation of the Law Commission to issue a code of practice in support of the Act, in similar fashion to the codes supporting the Mental Capacity Act 2005 and Mental Health Act 2007, and rather more accessible for practitioners.

The wellbeing principle

s. 1(1)

The general duty of a local authority, in exercising a function under this Part in the case of an individual, is to promote that individual's well-being.

Care Act 2014

This general duty is followed by an elaboration of the meaning of wellbeing in s. 1(2). Different elements may have more or less significance to a particular individual's circumstances and the draft guidance notes 'There is no hierarchy, and all should be considered of equal importance when considering "wellbeing" in the round' (Draft Guidance 1.5).

s. 1(2)

'Well-being', in relation to an individual, means that individual's well-being so far as relating to any of the following –

(a) personal dignity (including treatment of the individual with respect);
(b) physical and mental health and emotional well-being;
(c) protection from abuse and neglect;
(d) control by the individual over day-to-day life (including over care and support, or support, provided to the individual and the way in which it is provided);
(e) participation in work, education, training or recreation;
(f) social and economic well-being;
(g) domestic, family and personal relationships;
(h) suitability of living accommodation;
(i) the individual's contribution to society.

(Care Act 2014)

The framework set out in the Care Act 2014 of a key principle – wellbeing – followed by a range of relevant factors has parallels with the approach in the Children Act 1989 regarding welfare.

The reference to dignity in the statute is welcome, although it may be considered a highly subjective term, and it is to be hoped that practitioners and the courts will take a pro-active stance in promoting dignity. The approach of both the local authority and the court to an obvious issue of dignity was disappointing in the Supreme Court case of *R (on the application of McDonald)* v. *Kensington and Chelsea RLBC* [2011] UKSC 33. The decision also demonstrates the limits to choice and control within the law. The original needs assessment in this case referred to a *need for assistance to use the commode during the night*; the council had originally supplied a night carer, but subsequently proposed replacement of that service with incontinence pads, which the user, who was not incontinent, referred to as an affront to her dignity. However, in a later needs review the council had rephrased the need, referring to the *need to urinate safely at night*. The Supreme Court judgment confirmed the Court of Appeal view that the provision of continence pads was a legitimate way of meeting the revised need. It rejected the claim that the council had interfered with the service user's rights to private and family life under Article 8 (ECHR) and that, even had they done so, such interference would have been justified because the change of provision represented a proportionate response to the individual's needs, ensured her safety and independence, and (in securing cost savings) promoted the equitable allocation of limited care resources. Equally, the council's action did not constitute unlawful disability discrimination. LJ Hale gave a powerful dissenting judgment. If decided under the new law, paragraph (d) 'control by the individual over day-to-day life (including over care and support, or support, provided to the individual and the way in which it is provided)', would also be relevant.

Other principles

The next section of the Act includes a range of principles which the local authority must have regard to when exercising its functions. Again, this inclusion of principles is similar to the approach taken in the Mental Capacity Act 2005. The principles outlined in section 1(3) are:

---

s. 1(3)

Principles

(a) the importance of beginning with the assumption that the individual is best-placed to judge the individual's well-being;

(b) the individual's views, wishes, feelings and beliefs;

(c) the importance of preventing or delaying the development of needs for care and support or needs for support and the importance of reducing needs of either kind that already exist;

(d) the need to ensure that decisions about the individual are made having regard to all the individual's circumstances (and are not based only on the individual's age or appearance or any condition of the individual's or aspect of the individual's behaviour which might lead others to make unjustified assumptions about the individual's well-being);

(e) the importance of the individual participating as fully as possible in decisions relating to the exercise of the function concerned and being provided with the information and support necessary to enable the individual to participate;

(f) the importance of achieving a balance between the individual's well-being and that of any friends or relatives who are involved in caring for the individual;

(g) the need to protect people from abuse and neglect;

(h) the need to ensure that any restriction on the individual's rights or freedom of action that is involved in the exercise of the function is kept to the minimum necessary for achieving the purpose for which the function is being exercised.

(Care Act 2014)

The clear intention is that practice in this area must be informed by the principles in s. 1(3) and must develop in a way that promotes individual decision-making and participation, avoids discrimination and stereotyping and is the least restrictive intrusion on individual rights.

Prevention, integration, information and diversity

Local authorities are expected to provide or arrange for services, facilities or resources to prevent, delay and reduce needs for care and support (s. 2). This duty applies both to adults who might need care and support and to carers. The duty involves the authority identifying available services in their area and also identifying adults with unmet needs for care and support and carers with unmet needs for support.

Section 3 requires local authorities to ensure integration of care and support provision with health provision where this is likely to promote the wellbeing of adults and carers; contribute to prevention or delay of needs; or improve the quality of care and support for adults and carers.

Section 4 requires local authorities to provide information and advice relating to care and support. Provision must be comprehensive, including information on the types of care and support that is available, e.g. residential care; reablement; the range of services available and different providers; the process to access care and support; access to independent financial advice; and how to raise any concerns about safety or wellbeing of an adult with needs for care and support. The information must be provided in an accessible format and proportionate to the needs of those for whom it is provided.

Publishing information has always been the first step in **care management**; and under the previous framework (**NHSCCA** 1990, s. 46) local authorities were required to publish community care plans as public documents, including a list of available services. Consumer surveys, however, suggest that service users are often ill-informed. Article 10 of the European Convention on Human Rights (the right to freedom of expression) may be relevant to this issue. The right extends to the right to receive information (*Open Door Counselling and Dublin Well Woman Centre* v. *Ireland* (1992) 15 EHRR 244) and may have implications for local authorities' publications relating to available services. Questions about, for example, whether there are sufficient leaflets, in accessible places, in different languages, become relevant.

The introduction of the National Health Service and Community Care Act 1990 signalled a policy change in delivery of services. Local authorities were to become the lead agency for coordinating community care services through arranging and purchasing in a mixed economy of care, but would not have a monopoly on providing services. The emphasis on providing individuals with choice was evident and that policy became more explicit with greater roll out of direct payments and the advent of personalisation. Section 5 of the new Act, 'Promoting diversity and quality in provision of services' explicitly affirms this approach.

s. 5

(1) A local authority must promote the efficient and effective operation of a market in services for meeting care and support needs with a view to ensuring that any person in its area wishing to access services in the market –

(a) has a variety of providers to choose from who (taken together) provide a variety of services;

(b) has a variety of high quality services to choose from;

(c) has sufficient information to make an informed decision about how to meet the needs in question.

(Care Act 2014)

Cooperation

Sections 6 and 7 set out general and specific duties of cooperation.

Section 6 requires the local authority and its relevant partners to cooperate with each other in the exercise of their functions relating to adults with needs for care and support and carers. Relevant partners are: district councils, NHS bodies, police, prisons, probation and others as specified. The local authority must also cooperate with others it considers appropriate engaged in activities relating to adults with needs for care and support (s. 6(2)), such as: a person providing care and support; dental, ophthalmic and pharmaceutical services; private hospitals and private housing providers (s. 6(3)).

The authority must also ensure internal cooperation between officers with responsibility for adults with care and support needs and carers; housing officers; children's services and the director of public health (s. 6(4)). It is significant that housing and children's services are listed, as one of the named objectives for cooperation is ensuring smooth transition for children to adult care and support. In addition, as lack of cooperation and poor information sharing has been identified as a failing in numerous serious case reviews, another named objective is 'identifying lessons to be learned from cases where adults with needs for care and support have experienced serious abuse or neglect and applying those lessons to future cases' (s. 6(6)(e)).

Under s. 7 if the local authority requests cooperation of a relevant partner or another local authority it must cooperate unless that would be incompatible with its own duties. Equally, the local authority, if requested to, must cooperate with a partner or other local authority.

Assessment and eligibility

In assessment, procedural fairness and reasoned decision-making is essential and will be subject to closer scrutiny since the advent of the Human Rights Act 1998. The National Health Service and Community Care Act 1990, assessment for community care services provision (s. 47) is replaced by s. 9 of the Care Act 2014, which provides for a 'needs assessment':

---

s. 9

(1) Where it appears to a local authority that an adult may have needs for care and support, the authority must assess –

   (a) whether the adult does have needs for care and support, and
   (b) if the adult does, what those needs are.

(Care Act 2014)

As was the case under the old law, there is a low threshold for an assessment to be triggered – i.e. the appearance of need.

Refusal to assess may be challenged by judicial review, and the local authority should give reasons if it is not going to carry out an assessment. Given the breadth of the phrase 'where it appears', the scope to decline an assessment is extremely limited. This aspect of the former provision was tested in *R v. Bristol City Council, ex parte Penfold* [1998] 1 CCLR 315. In this case the council refused to assess a woman for community care services because it had decided she had no real prospect of eventually being provided with services. The court described the first step in the assessment process as providing a very low threshold test. The duty to assess was triggered by the appearance of need for any service which could be provided, not which was actually likely to be provided. The effect of the judgment is to prevent councils screening out individuals prior to assessment and, in all but the most extreme cases, if an individual requests a needs assessment, he or she should be provided with one. Scott-Baker LJ, giving judgment in the *Bristol* case, also made the point that, even if it is unlikely that needs identified in the assessment will be met, the assessment is still useful in terms of identifying unmet needs, which will be useful for future strategic planning. Unmet need recorded as such is lawful if outside the eligibility criteria. The emphasis is firmly placed on the local authority to assess people who might be eligible for services, rather than on the individual to request an assessment.

The authority is specifically directed not to pre-judge any assessment or screen out assessments as s. 9(3) stipulates that the authority must carry out its duty to assess regardless of its view of the level of the adult's needs or the adult's financial resources.

Once that threshold is crossed, i.e. the 'appearance' of need is established, the use of the word 'must' in (1) indicates a mandatory obligation or duty on the local authority to carry out an assessment of whether the adult has needs for care and support and if so, what those needs are. A specific time limit in which assessments should be carried out is not included in the legislation (it may feature in regulations or guidance) but by implication an assessment should be completed within a reasonable time. Timescales may be stipulated by a local authority to prioritise the most urgent cases, where an identifiable risk is apparent before assessment. Where there is unreasonable delay it would be appropriate to utilise the complaints procedure or complain to the local government ombudsman (see ombudsman decision below as an example).

The section continues to prescribe the content of the needs assessment. It must include assessment of the impact of the adult's needs for care and support on their wellbeing, the outcomes that the adult wishes to achieve in day-to-day life, and whether, and if so to what extent, care and support could contribute to the achievement of those outcomes (s. 9(4)).

The authority is directed to involve the adult, any carer and anyone else the adult asks the authority to involve or, if the adult lacks capacity, anyone the authority identifies as interested in the adult's welfare (s. 9(5)).

Assessments should be carried out in a multi-disciplinary fashion with the individual and carers participating fully. The assessment should provide and support choices and self-determination and allow an element of measurable risk. The procedure should be flexible and supported by individual and central case management and monitoring of the assessment process and outcome.

It is essential that all agencies and professionals involved with the individual are brought into the assessment procedure as necessary in order for the multi-disciplinary object of assessment to be realised. Statutory support for this principle is provided in the cooperation principles outlined above. A multi-disciplinary assessment could include an extensive range of individuals and agencies, such as social workers from hospital or the community, community nurses, general practitioners, community psychiatric nurses, physiotherapists, occupational therapists, home-care assistants, housing agencies, sheltered housing wardens, hospital consultants (e.g. geriatricians), members of the family and social network, interpreters and, of course, the service user.

The assessment should be comprehensive, focused on wellbeing and the outcomes the adult wishes to achieve in day-to-day life, and is likely to include the following issues: biographical details, self-perception of needs, physical health, mental health, use of medicines, abilities, aptitudes, transport, social networks and support, care services and needs of carers, housing, finance, risk, race and culture.

The authority must also consider whether alternatives to care and support could contribute to the achievement of the outcomes that the adult wishes to achieve in day-to-day life, particularly existing preventative services under s. 2 or information and advice under s. 4.

The final subsection (7) is important. The adult has the right to refuse an assessment. If the adult refuses assessment that local authority will have discharged its duty unless circumstances in section 11 apply, namely:

---

s. 11

(2) But the local authority may not rely on subsection (1) (and so must carry out a needs assessment) if –

(a) the adult lacks capacity to refuse the assessment and the authority is satisfied that carrying out the assessment would be in the adult's best interests, or

(b) the adult is experiencing, or is at risk of, abuse or neglect.

(Care Act 2014)

This provision may be increasingly significant where there are adult safeguarding concerns.

It is possible that after an initial refusal, an adult may then decide they would like an assessment. In that case the duty to assess applies once more.

Eligibility

Under the old law, having carried out an assessment and identified a need for services the local authority then had a discretion, 'having regard to the results of that assessment, shall then decide whether his needs call for the provision by them of any such services' (s. 47(1)(b). The link between this discretion and limited resources has been subject to challenge in a number of cases. *R* v. *Gloucestershire County Council, ex parte Barry* [1997] 2 All ER 1 remains the leading decision in this area. This decision appeared to suggest that resources could be a relevant factor for councils to take into account when assessing need for all community care services. The case came to court as a judicial review application in the following circumstances. In 1995, Gloucestershire County Council, facing funding cuts of £2.5 million, withdrew or cut provision of home care services to 1,500 service users and changed its eligibility criteria. Mr Barry challenged the decision of the authority to withdraw services provided to him under s. 2 of the Chronically Sick and Disabled Persons Act 1970 (for assistance with laundry and cleaning), on the basis that, although the authority's funding position might have changed, his needs had not. In the House of Lords' judgment there was recognition of the difficulties faced by local authorities in managing resources to fulfil duties in the complex area of community care. The court held, by a majority, that resources might be taken into account when assessing or reassessing whether an individual is in need of services. The concept of need has to be considered in the context of other relevant factors, including an authority's own resources. Since the *Gloucestershire* decision, it is clear that local authorities are justified in using eligibility criteria as a means of rationing resources. Eligibility criteria must be satisfied by an individual before his needs will be met. Local authorities would not be justified, however, in failing to provide services to an individual with an established need simply because the end of a financial year is looming and resources have run out. Eligibility criteria have to be set so as to anticipate such situations and operate to identify what levels of need will attract services. Eligibility criteria may be reset periodically and resources taken into account when setting new criteria. As a result, those in receipt of services under the old criteria would need to be reassessed before any reduction in services.

Guidance was issued following the *Gloucestershire* decision.[6] In response to concerns over the judgment, the guidance confirmed that the judgment did not provide authority for decisions to be taken on the basis of resources alone and that resource pressures were not an excuse for taking arbitrary or unreasonable decisions.

In 2003 the Department of Health published guidance on assessment and eligibility criteria in 'Fair Access to Care Services?' LAC (2003) 12. Implementation of that was intended to lead to fairer and more consistent eligibility decisions across the country. The guidance is issued under s. 7(1) of the Local Authority Social Services Act 1970 and, as such, councils risk breaching the law if (in the absence of a good reason) they do not follow the guidance. The guidance is clearly a response to the disparate arrangements that have existed around the country and challenges to community care decisions often based on judicial review and leading to a body of case law. The guidance identifies four eligibility bands – critical, substantial, moderate and low – which relate to individuals' needs and risks to independence. The bands should include consideration of immediate needs as presented and also longer-term risks including needs which are likely to worsen without help, as identified through risk assessments. The guidance emphasises that councils should operate only one set of criteria based on the eligibility bands outlined. Separate criteria relating, for example, to the depth and type of assessment and for specific services should be abolished. The guidance draws a distinction between presenting needs, as those issues that are identified when social care support is sought, and eligible needs as those needs that fall within the council's eligibility criteria. Presenting needs which do not fit into eligibility criteria have been known as 'unmet needs', a term which is implicitly discouraged by the new guidance. Many authorities have set a threshold for meeting need between the 'moderate' and 'substantial' band, i.e. those with presenting needs falling into the critical or substantial risk to independence bands will be eligible for services whereas those whose needs present a moderate or low risk to independence will not.

In most cases the bands are differentiated by the degree to which each factor is affected by the risk to independence, as indicated by the words in bold, for example, vital/the majority of/several/one or two family roles cannot be sustained. Additional factors are included in the more serious bands, e.g. life will be threatened. See for example the extract in Table 14.2.

Whilst one of the objectives of the guidance is fairer and more consistent eligibility decisions, it will still be possible for councils to take account of their adult social care resources when setting eligibility criteria. Councils do need to be able to respond to the needs of their particular adult population and a measure of flexibility is welcomed; however, there will still

Table 14.2 Examples of eligibility criteria

Critical risk to independence	Substantial risk to independence	Moderate risk to independence	Low risk to independence
Serious abuse or neglect has occurred/ will occur	Abuse or neglect has occurred/will occur		
There is/will be an inability to carry out **vital** personal care or domestic routines	There is/will be an inability to carry out **the majority of** personal care or domestic routines	There is/will be an inability to carry out **several** personal care or domestic routines	There is/will be an inability to carry out **one or two** personal care or domestic routines

inevitably be regional variation in the services provision for people with similar needs living in different parts of the country.[7]

A **CSCI** report in 2008[8] found that 62 per cent of councils in England operated only at the highest bands of 'critical' and 'substantial'. Three councils only provided support to individuals whose needs fell into the critical band. A High Court judgment has confirmed that it is lawful only to fund services to meet 'critical needs' (*R (Chavda)* v. *Harrow London Borough Council* [2007] EWHC 3064 (Admin)).

In response to the CSCI review the 'Fair Access to Care Services' guidance was reviewed and replaced by: DH (2010) 'Prioritising Need in the Context of Putting People First: A whole system approach to eligibility for social care – guidance on eligibility criteria for adult social care in England 2010'. This guidance continued to apply the same eligibility criteria but within the policy of personalisation.

The Care Act 2014 includes a section on eligibility criteria (s. 13). Where the local authority has carried out an assessment and is satisfied that an adult has needs for care and support, the next stage is to determine whether the needs meet the eligibility criteria. Rather than including eligibility criteria in guidance as under the old, new Regulations will set out the new eligibility criteria. It is expected that the criteria will reflect previous practice with 'critical' and 'substantial' needs being eligible for support.

Whenever a local authority makes a determination about whether needs meet eligibility criteria it must provide the adult with a written record and reasons.

Once it is established that an individual has eligible needs for care and support, s. 18 provides that the LA must meet those needs, providing the individual is resident in the area, and has resources below the financial limit. The local authority must also meet the eligible needs of those who ask the authority to meet their needs even though their means are above the financial limit, in other words self-funders.

Reflect

Can community care services properly be described as supportive and preventative if they are only allocated to those whose needs are substantial or critical?

Personalisation

Provision of adult social care in recent years has been subject to an approach which the Department of Health have termed the 'personalisation agenda'. The approach is explained in guidance (LAC(DH)(2008)1):

> The direction is clear: to make personalization, including a strategic shift towards early intervention, the cornerstone of public services. In social care, this means every person across the spectrum of need, having choice and control over the shape of his or her support, in the most appropriate setting. For some, exercising choice and control will require a significant level of assistance either through professionals or through independent advocates.

This policy is effectively endorsed by the Care Act 2014. An independent personal budget, defined as a statement, 'which specifies what the cost would be to the local authority concerned ... of meeting the adult's eligible needs for care and support' must be set. Budgets must be kept under review and if the circumstances of an individual have changed a needs assessment must be carried out and the independent budget revised as necessary.

The case of *R (Broster & Others)* v. *Wirral* MBC [2010] EWHC 3086 (Admin), which found that there is no duty on a local authority to provide a personal budget and a refusal to do so does not breach of Article 8, ECHR or equality legislation, would no longer stand. Personal budgets were not provided to 16 people with learning disabilities, living as tenants of an organisation providing accommodation and services under contract to the council. The court was concerned that the tenants would be unduly influenced by the organisation in deciding to spend their budget allocation with the organisation even after the council withdrew from the contract.

In setting a personal budget it is likely that local authorities will continue to use the RAS (Resource Allocation System), a national framework employed by local authorities, which sets indicative allocations for the cost of meeting specific need. In *R (Raphaela Savva)* v. *Kensington and Chelsea* [2010] EWCA Civ 1209, a disabled woman challenged the lawfulness of the council's calculation method for her personal budget and complained that the council had not provided adequate reasons for its allocation to her. The Court of Appeal found that it was not unlawful for the council to use the RAS. The RAS must, however, only be a starting point, used together with work by assessors who must decide in each individual case whether the amount is sufficient. The court also ruled that the local authority was, in the interests of fairness, required to give an adequate explanation of how a personal budget allocation is determined, although they could in future consider this duty discharged by an offer of the provision of reasons on request and the court did not anticipate this being an onerous duty. For example, in the particular case it was suggested that it would be '... adequate to list the required services and assumed timings ... together with the assumed hourly cost' (para 21).

The use of RAS as a starting point for budget allocation was confirmed in *R (KM)* v. *Cambridgeshire CC* [2010] EWHC 3065 (Admin).

Direct payments may be made under ss. 31–33. Where a personal budget specifies an amount that the local authority must pay towards meeting an individual's eligible needs, part or all of that amount may be provided as a direct payment. As was the case under the old law, a direct payment may be managed directly by the individual with or without some help. If the person lacks capacity, an authorised person may both request the local authority to make direct payments and may manage the payment in the person's best interests.

Direct payments may continue to be used by the individual to choose how best to meet their own needs, including by employment of a personal assistant. The personal assistant may be someone already known to the individual or a person specifically recruited for that purpose.

Where direct payments are used to employ an individual, as a carer for example, the service user becomes an employer bound by employment legislation. Such a situation was illustrated in the case of *Roberts* v. *Carlin* [2010] UKEAT 612 where a personal assistant made a complaint of sex discrimination to the Employment Tribunal after her apparent dismissal due to her pregnancy.

Care and support plan

Where the local authority is going to meet an individual's needs it must prepare a care and support plan (s. 24). This is a document which specifies the identified needs, which needs meet the eligibility criteria, how the local authority is going to meet those needs, the impact on wellbeing and desirable outcomes, includes the personal budget, any needs that are to be met by direct payments and the amount and frequency of those payments. The local authority must involve the individual, any carer(s) and any other person the adult asks to be involved or appears to have an interest in the adult's welfare if lacking capacity. Through this process the objective is to reach agreement as far as possible as to how the authority should meet needs; if it is not possible to reach agreement about an aspect of the plan, any points of difference should be recorded.

The adult (and carer) must have a copy of the plan. The plan may be combined with the plan of another person, including a child or young carer, if the individual agrees. Plans must be kept under review and may be revised if circumstances change (s. 27) , e.g. where a physical disability worsens or a person who has provided a substantial amount of care can no longer do so. A reassessment must take place before any reduction in services and the case of *R* v. *Birmingham City Council, ex parte Killigrew* [1999] 3 CCLR 109 states that services can be reduced only if the person would not be left in 'serious physical risk'. In this case services were reduced from twelve hours to six hours daily. The decision was quashed because reassessment failed to address why services, which she had been assessed as needing, were no longer needed. In other words, there is a level below which service provision cannot be reduced, no matter what the financial circumstances of the authority, if the result would be unacceptable risk.

A complaint about the content of a care plan would initially be dealt with through the Complaints and Representations Procedure. In *R (Lloyd)* v. *Barking and Dagenham London Borough Council* [2001] EWCA Civ 533, the Court of Appeal held that judicial review should be the last resort as a means of challenging the local authority's care plan, in this case made in respect of a disabled person.

How to meet needs

Section 8 sets out examples of what may be provided to meet needs. This consolidated list replaces the many and various references to different types of services that featured in previous legislation.

---

s. 8

(a) accommodation in a care home or in premises of some other type;
(b) care and support at home or in the community;
(c) counselling and other types of social work;
(d) goods and facilities;
(e) information, advice and advocacy.

(Care Act 2014)

The ways in which those services may be provided are also specified: the local authority may arrange for another person to provide the service, it may provide the service itself, or it may make direct payments to the individual.

In relation to (a) 'accommodation in a care home or in premises of some other type', the fact that the housing authority has responsibilities to provide housing should not remove from Social Services Departments the responsibility to arrange and provide accommodation in some circumstances. For example, in *R* v. *Islington London Borough Council, ex parte Batantu* (2001) 33 HLR 76, the community care assessment of need included the need for more spacious ground-floor accommodation. In this case the assessment found that the existing accommodation (a small twelfth-floor flat for B, his wife and four children) contributed to his mental health problems. There was a duty to provide appropriate accommodation and not to treat this as a pure housing issue, which would have left B waiting several years for more appropriate accommodation. Housing and accommodation needs may thus be included as part of the care package.

Government policy to make direct payments available to as many eligible people as possible in order to 'give recipients control over their own life by providing an alternative to social services provided by a local council'[9] continues under the Care Act 2014. A possible disadvantage of direct payments may be greater susceptibility to abuse and lesser regulation of certain services. Direct payments can provide greater control to the individual and guidance suggests that local authorities 'should seek to leave as much choice as possible in the hands of the individual, and allow people to address their own needs in innovative ways, whilst satisfying themselves that the person's assessed needs are being met, and that public funds are being spent appropriately and with best value'.[10] Direct payments cannot be used where the individual is subject to guardianship under the Mental Health Act 1983, or to pay for services that the National Health Service should provide, or for permanent (more than four weeks in a year) residential care. The local authority may make the payment subject to appropriate conditions, e.g. financial procedures. A person using direct payments to arrange care services should be advised to go to a reputable agency and to draw up a contract of employment.[11]

Choice, preference or need?

The Care Act 2014 includes s. 30 'cases where adult expresses preference for particular accommodation'. The section provides for regulations to be made which may provide that where a local authority is going to meet needs by providing accommodation and the adult expresses a preference for a particular type of accommodation and specified conditions are met (in the regulations), then the authority must provide the preferred accommodation. There may be an additional cost for the individual.

Previously decided case law may provide insight into how this is likely to apply and establishes that the question of preference or need is more than simply a matter of semantics. In the case of *R* v. *Avon County Council, ex parte M* [1994] 2 FCR 259, the local authority was under a duty to make arrangements for residential accommodation for a 22-year-old man with Down's syndrome. The man's preference, which was described as 'entrenched', to go to a particular home was rejected by the council – it wished to place him in a home which it claimed would meet his needs but which was cheaper. In fact it was found that the entrenched position of this man was a psychological need, rather than a preference, and the authority were obliged to meet that need.

A move to another part of the country, perhaps to be closer to relatives, has also been recognised as a possible aspect of individual need. If the preferred area was typically more expensive than the accommodation costs the placing authority would normally pay, to meet the need of such an individual the authority would pay the normal rate in the more expensive area.[12]

Further case law limited the reality of individual choice in community care provision. In *R* v. *Lancashire County Council, ex parte Ingham* (1995) 5 July QBD: CO/774, the court upheld the local authority's decision to provide for an assessed need for 24-hour care in a nursing home rather than in the elderly woman's own home. The local authority could take resources into account in deciding which service to provide to meet her needs. This position was confirmed when the case was consolidated with another appeal. In practice, local authorities often set a financial 'ceiling' as the maximum amount of care that they will provide to an individual at home. Provided that the alternative way of providing care (usually in a care home) will meet the individual's need, and the decision has been taken following an individual reassessment, this is lawful practice. In practice, if high levels of care at home will cost more than an appropriate type of residential care, the latter is likely to be offered as the means of meeting individual need. The Choice of Accommodation Directions 1992[13] provided that an individual has the right to choose a home, subject to it being suitable, there being a room available in the home, and it being available at a price which is no more than the authority will normally pay for that level of need. If no accommodation were available at that cost, the local authority would have to pay a higher rate.

Home closures

There have been a number of cases where residents have sought to challenge local authority decisions to close care homes. In *R (on the application of Dudley, Whitbread and others)* v. *East Sussex County Council* [2003] EWHC 1093 (Admin), the High Court found that closing a home is not necessarily incompatible with residents' rights under Art. 8, a person's right to respect for his home. Any interference with residents' rights must be proportionate and the court stressed the need for the process leading to closure to be managed properly including a consultation exercise. In times where authorities are having to deal with scarce resources and closing homes may result in cost savings the court showed a reluctance to interfere with the authority's decision.

The court rejected evidence that care home closures and associated transfer of residents lead to increased mortality, describing the statistical evidence as 'massively overstated'. It also rejected arguments under Art. 3, which provides that no one shall be subject to inhuman or degrading treatment. The court stated that closure of the centre and subsequent transfer of residents did not come close to the threshold required for treatment to be inhuman or degrading.

Anti-discriminatory practice and assessment

Adherence to principles of anti-discriminatory practice is an essential aspect of any type of assessment process carried out by social services. The characteristics of many adult service users make them especially vulnerable to discrimination, and an awareness of the relevance of anti-discrimination law can help to promote good practice in this area. (Fuller discussion of discrimination law can be found in Chapter 6.)

The Care Act 2014 and its predecessor the NHSCCA 1990 (in contrast to the Children Act 1989) does not make specific reference to race, religion, language and culture. It is perhaps not surprising that particular problems relating to community care for black and ethnic minority people have been identified, including under-use of services and restricted choice of services,[14] and assumptions being made about extended family networks of support, despite changing employment patterns and reduction in family size in the Asian community.[15] Service provision must, however, comply with the provisions of the Equality Act 2010. This legislation places a duty on all public bodies,[16] including local authorities, to promote equality of opportunity and good relations between persons who share a protected characteristic and persons who do not, in all of its functions. In community care this duty will extend to the assessment process, planning, publishing information and provision of services. The measures taken to ensure equality of opportunity in community care should be addressed in each authority's equality scheme.

Delay

Timescales for carrying out assessments are not stipulated in the legislation and, in the absence of a clearly identified period, the law expects that assessments should be carried out within a reasonable time. This will vary dependent on the circumstances and most authorities include timescales and priority groups in their own policies. Excessive waiting times have featured in many local government ombudsman decisions, and local authority complaints, and generally staff shortages, have not been found to justify delays.[17] A case which reached the courts was *R (J)* v. *Newham London Borough Council* [2001] EWHC Admin 992, in which the court decided that 35 days was too long a delay. Having carried out an assessment, delay in implementing the care plan should also be minimised. Again, the expectation is that the duty to meet needs by implementing the care plan will be carried out within a reasonable time, that time varying depending on the circumstances of the case.

Advocacy

Section 67 of the Care Act 2014 introduces a right to independent advocacy in certain circumstances. The authority must arrange for an independent advocate to represent and support and facilitate involvement of the individual where the requirements in sub-section (4) are met, namely:

s. 67(4)

... the local authority considers that, were an independent advocate not to be available, the individual would experience substantial difficulty in doing one or more of the following –

(a) understanding relevant information;
(b) retaining that information;
(c) using or weighing that information as part of the process of being involved;
(d) communicating the individual's views, wishes or feelings (whether by talking, using sign language or any other means).

(Care Act 2014)

An advocate need not be involved if there is another appropriate person who can represent and support the individual. This might, for example, be a friend or family member, it cannot be a person providing care or treatment for the individual. The individual must consent to the involvement of that appropriate person. If the individual lacks capacity to consent the local authority must be satisfied that being supported by that person will be in the individual's best interests. Regulations will set out more detail of the advocate's role, including the right to have access to relevant health, local authority, care home and other records.

The circumstances in which the advocate may be involved include carrying out a needs assessment (including child's, child carer's and young carer's assessments), preparing and revising the care and support plan.

Adult social care and human rights

Challenges within the field of adult social care have been brought under the Human Rights Act 1998. For example the case of *R (Bernard)* v. *Enfield London Borough Council* [2002] EWHC 2282 (Admin), where failure to provide community care services was found to be a violation of Art. 8. (This is discussed fully in Chapter 5.) In *Anufrijeva* v. *Southwark London Borough Council* [2003] EWCA Civ 1406, similar arguments about the positive obligations arising from Art. 8 were rejected. The court's decision reflects a concern to discourage HRA claims based on failures to provide services. Where such claims are made, they should be linked to an application for judicial review or, preferably, dealt with by the local government ombudsman. The court approved the *Bernard* decision but suggested that it would be unusual to find circumstances where failure to provide services would breach Art. 8 and not Art. 3, except that a breach under Art. 8 alone may arise where the family life aspect of Art. 8 was significant. In cases where it is alleged that Art. 8 has been breached through failure to provide services, *Anufrijeva* rules that the claimant needs to demonstrate 'culpability' on the part of the authority and serious consequences for the individual arising from the failure.

The case of *A* v. *East Sussex County Council* [2003] EWHC 167 (Admin) centred on a dispute about manual handling for two severely disabled sisters. The judgment includes a number of statements about the application of Art. 8 (right to respect for private and family life) to disabled people:

> The other important concept embraced in the 'physical and psychological integrity' protected by Art. 8 is the right of the disabled to participate in the life of the community and to have what has been described as 'access to essential economic and social activities and to an appropriate range of recreational and cultural activities'. This is matched by the positive obligation of the state to take appropriate measures designed to ensure to the greatest extent feasible that a disabled person is not 'so circumscribed and so isolated as to be deprived of the possibility of developing his personality'.

Section 73 of the Care Act 2014 designates provision of regulated care or support a public function. As a consequence the provider is bound under s. 6 of the Human Rights Act 1998 to act compatibly with the Articles of the European Convention. This provision extends the position under the Health and Social Care Act 2008 (s.145) which defined a person providing care in a care home as exercising a function of a public nature. The new section applies to registered care providers providing care and support to an adult (or support to a carer) in the course of providing personal care in the adults home, or residential accommodation together with nursing or personal care. The care or support must have been arranged by or paid for by an authority. A self-funder would have to have their care arranged by a local authority to benefit from this protection.

Charging for services

Reform of the provisions on charging implements proposals of the 'Dilnot' report ('Fairer Care Funding: Report of the Commission on Funding of Care and Support' (2011)). The local authority has a power to charge for meeting needs (s. 14), and will carry out a financial assessment (s. 17). The power to charge is subject to the introduction of a care cap in s. 15. Application of the care cap provisions will mean that an individual will only pay contributions to their care and support up to a maximum limit in their lifetime. The amount of the care cap will be specified in regulations, likely to be introduced at around £70,000 and adjusted annually. These provisions are unlikely to be introduced until 2016.

After-care services provided under s. 117 of the Mental Health Act 1983 are excluded services and cannot be charged for (confirmed in *R* v. *Richmond London Borough Council, ex parte W* [1999] 2 CCLR 402).

Complaints procedure

In assessment, procedural fairness and reasoned decision-making is essential. An avenue for challenge is equally important if a level of accountability is to be achieved. Article 6 of the European Convention on Human Rights may have some application here. The Article provides for fair determination of a person's civil rights and a person probably has a civil right to a service, having passed through eligibility criteria. Failure to provide a service, or to cut it without a lawful reassessment, might amount to a breach of human rights, if the decision has been taken unfairly. A fair decision-making process should involve a chance to make representations, proper reasons being given for a decision based on close consideration of individual needs rather than general application of policy. All relevant matters should be taken into account in an assessment and all irrelevant matters disregarded.

Section 50 of the NHSCCA 1990 amends s. 7 of the Local Authority Social Services Act 1970, giving the Secretary of State the power to order Social Services Authorities to establish a complaints procedure. The local authority must establish a procedure for considering representations (including complaints) made by qualifying individuals relating to the discharge or failure to discharge any of their social services functions in respect of that individual.[18] There are three stages to the process: an informal stage; the formal or registration stage; and the review stage. A complainant may go direct to the formal stage. At the review stage a panel is convened, which must include a person who is independent of the authority.[19] It may be helpful for an individual who wishes to make a complaint (and to participate fully in the community care process outlined in this chapter) to have the support of an advocate.

Carers will often effectively take on the role of advocate, though there can be conflicts between the carer and the person cared for, in which case an independent advocate is preferable. There is also a significant growth of self-advocacy groups such as 'People First', who define self-advocacy as speaking for yourself, standing up for your rights, making choices, being independent and taking responsibility for yourself.[20] (Complaints are discussed further in Chapter 4.)

Financial compensation is not provided for under the complaints process.

Local government ombudsman

A reported decision illustrates the role of the local government ombudsman as providing a useful means of challenging the actions of local authorities in the field of community care. The role of the ombudsman is to consider whether there has been maladministration in a case. *Investigation into Complaint No. 97/A/2959 against Hackney London Borough Council* [1998] 2 CCLR 66 concerned two brothers aged 41 and 39, both with learning difficulties. They had been attending a day centre for about ten years. In 1995, Hackney transferred management of the centre to a charity as part of reorganisation of services for people with learning difficulties and reorganisation of the community care division. The transfer took place on the understanding that Hackney and the charity would reassess the needs of all users of the centre within six months. Despite reminders from the charity and Edward and Robert's parents, Mr and Mrs Foster, the assessment did not commence until 1997. Mrs Foster lodged a complaint, which was upheld in January 1997 by the Social Services Complaints Review Panel, concluding that Hackney had been negligent and recommending that the reassessment be carried out within three months. The Director of Social Services wrote explaining that the cause of the delay was lack of resources. By November 1998, Hackney had still not completed risk assessments or a care plan for Edward or Robert.

The local government ombudsman reached the following conclusions:

1. The delay in carrying out reassessments (about 22 months) amounted to maladministration.

2. Hackney had still not completed a risk assessment at the time of the investigation; record keeping was poor, as were communications with Mr and Mrs Foster, to whom they had failed to explain the nature and purpose of the reassessment. These faults all amounted to maladministration.

3. Injustice had been caused by the maladministration. In particular, Mr and Mrs Foster had suffered anxiety and had been put to considerable time and trouble. Also, Edward and Robert had missed the opportunity of benefiting from earlier provision based on proper assessment.

It was recommended that Hackney should pay £1,500 compensation to Mr and Mrs Foster. Of general application, it was recommended that Hackney should review the needs of other people using the day centre; review provision of written information about the community care assessment process; review supervision arrangements for care managers and implement a system to ensure recommendations of review panels are implemented without unreasonable delay. This case provides a clear example of the damaging effect of delay relating to service provision for vulnerable adults. The full report is particularly interesting to read for the insight it gives into the extent and process of the detailed investigation carried out by the local government ombudsman.

In *R (Ireneschild)* v. *Lambeth London Borough Council* [2006] EWHC 2354 (Admin) the court commented in relation to a community care assessment: 'It is an assessment prepared by a social worker for his or her employers. It is not a final determination of a legal dispute by a lawyer which may be subjected to over-zealous textual analysis. Courts must be wary of expecting so much of hard pressed social workers that we risk taking them away, unnecessarily, from their front-line duties.' The Court of Appeal also stressed that disputes of this sort should not normally end up in the courts. The statutory social services complaints procedure and the local government ombudsman should be used instead.

Other avenues for complaint include: the role of the monitoring officer, judicial review, default powers of the Secretary of State and action for damages. (These are all discussed in Chapter 4.)

Carers

Carers play a vital role in adult social care, providing most support.[21] There are approximately 7 million carers throughout Britain, including some carers providing care for a few hours a week and others providing literally 24-hour care. Women are more likely to be carers than men and carers are most likely to be aged 45–64 (although there are a significant number of 'young' carers who may be caring for their parents). Carers may also have their own care and support needs.

One of the NHSCCA 1990 objectives was to ensure that service providers make practical support for carers a high priority. Building on this provision, the Carers (Recognition and Services) Act 1995 (**C(RS)A** 1995) was introduced.[22] Two further statutes were introduced, the Carers and Disabled Children Act 2000 (**CDCA** 2004) and the Carers (Equal Opportunities) Act 2004 (**C(EO)A** 2004) to strengthen provision for carers.

One of the more positive features of the Care Act 2014 is the way it aligns assessment of carer's needs with asessments of the person being cared for. Carers are entitled to an assessment under s. 10 in substantially the same terms as adults under s. 9, i.e. the appearance of need for carer support. The previous requirement that carers provide a substantial amount of care on a regular basis in order to be assessed has been removed. Carer's needs for support are assessed under s. 10 as a 'carer's assessment'. A carer is an adult who provides or intends to provide care for another adult. Care includes practical or emotional support (11). Carers who are engaged under a contract or as voluntary work are generally excluded subject to local authority discretion in sub section (10). A carer may refuse an assessment. The number of carer assessments are likely to increase under the new legislation.

The cared for person must agree to any services to be delivered direct to him. The detail of how any services provided to the carer will assist the person being cared for should be contained in the care plan. Carers may receive direct payments to purchase services. For example, this might enable a carer to pay somebody to carry out shopping and other chores, or free up more of the carer's time to provide care.

Young carers and parent carers

A large number of young people have caring responsibilities. The Social Care Institute for Excellence (**SCIE**) offers the following definition of a young carer, 'children or young people under 18 who provide, or intend to provide, care, assistance or support to another family member'.[23] The assessment of young carers under the Care Act 2014 is provided for in ss. 63 and 64 and focus on the likely needs of the young carer on reaching 18.

In addition, young carers may be assessed as entitled to services and support under the Children Act 1989 as a child in need (see Chapter 7).

Whilst there is an expectation that all parents will care for their children, the Care Act recognises that some parents will need support to continue to care after the child reaches 18. Assessment of a child's carer's needs for support is provided for in ss. 60–62. The local authority has a power not a duty to provide care to a child's carer.

Meeting need: particular services

Section 8 of the Care Act 2014 lists examples of what may be provided to meet needs. This section of the chapter will describe the provision and regulation of two particular services: residential care and domiciliary services. At the outset, however, it is important to remember that services cannot be imposed on someone against their will. This may prove to be a crucial issue in adult safeguarding cases.

A decided case confirms that, in limited circumstances, a person's refusal of care may allow a local authority to consider that it has discharged its statutory duty even where no services have been provided. In *R* v. *Kensington and Chelsea Royal London Borough Council, ex parte Kujtim* [1999] 4 All ER 161, an asylum seeker was twice evicted from hotel accommodation for threatening behaviour. The local authority accepted that the person was in need of care and attention not otherwise available and they were under a duty to provide him with accommodation. The Court of Appeal noted, however, that services could not be imposed on a person against their will. If someone refuses to comply with reasonable conditions (in this case good behaviour in multi-occupancy establishments) then the authority is entitled to regard such a stance as 'unequivocal and persistent rejection' of the service offered. The statutory duty is then regarded as discharged. (Note that if anti-social behaviour is an aspect of need, this case would not apply. There must be a rejection by a service user who is responsible for his own actions.)

If a person responsible for his own actions makes it impossible for the local authority to purchase appropriate care, then the person is rejecting appropriate offers of help. This is not, therefore, a case about the exercise of discretion; it is about not being able to coerce people into accepting services against their wishes.

Residential accommodation

At first sight, consideration of residential accommodation does not sit easily in a chapter on adult social care with a focus on living independently in the community, and could be described as the very antithesis of care in the community. It is included here because residential accommodation may be provided for short periods of time as part of a care package, in circumstances where the individual will return to the community. Also, residential accommodation may be arranged for an individual through the assessment or reassessment process and may follow a period of care and support in the community.

Local authorities can provide residential care themselves or make arrangements with private and voluntary sector organisations.[24] In making the arrangements, the authority must have regard to the need for providing accommodation of different types suited to the different types of people who might need residential care through age, illness, disability or other circumstances. Provision of residential care will follow the s. 9 single assessment provision. Under the previous law there were different requirements for residential care under the National Assistance Act 1948.

Accommodation provided must be suitable for the person's needs. There are human rights dimensions to the question of suitability. For example, ECHR, Art. 9 provides that 'everyone has the right to freedom of thought, conscience and religion; this right includes freedom … to manifest his religion or belief, in worship, teaching, practice and observance'. The terms of this Article should encourage residential homes to respect different religious ceremonies depending on their residents' beliefs.

Regulation of residential accommodation

A system of regulation of residential and nursing care with a view to upholding standards has been in place since 1986. The Care Standards Act 2000 (CSA 2000) reformed the regulatory system for care services in England and Wales with a wider remit than the former legislation, the Registered Homes Act 1984 (RHA 1984). The CSA 2000, supported by National Standards, set out to address these areas and provide protection for vulnerable people from abuse and neglect and to promote high standards in quality of care.

The legislation is supported by national minimum standards and regulations. Central to the regulation of residential accommodation is the requirement that an individual is registered as the proprietor of a care home, possibly with a manager also registered; that individual must be a fit person and has responsibility to fulfil the requirements of the regulations and national standards.

Care Quality Commission

In relation to adult services, there is a single regulatory body for Health and Social Care, the Care Quality Commission (**CQC**). This body was introduced by the Health and Social Care Act 2008 and combines the former functions of the Commission of Social Care Inspection, the Healthcare Commission and the Mental Health Act Commission (all of which are abolished). The new Commission has responsibility for registration, inspection and regulation of regulated services.

Under s. 3(1) of the Health and Social Care Act 2008, 'the main objective of the Commission is to protect and promote the health, safety and welfare of people who use health and social care services'. It is a public body and hence required to act compatibly with the European Convention Articles contained in the Human Rights Act 1998.

Providers who were required to register under CSA 2000 will continue to be regulated under the new framework. In addition, most NHS and PCT community services will be registered, as will mental health services under the direction or supervision of a psychiatrist (inpatient, outpatient or community). Areas not due to be covered include: personal assistants directly employed by service users; counselling and advocacy; day care services.

Regulations govern regulated activity and breach may lead to enforcement action (e.g. cancelling registration) or constitute a criminal offence. The Commission's duty to regulate must be exercised in a way that is proportionate to the risks to service users of a particular setting. The CQC has enforcement powers. It may issue warning notices prior to further enforcement action setting out what action needs to be taken to avoid further enforcement action. Penalty notices for fixed fines as an alternative to prosecution may be issued where there has been a breach of regulations. It will also be possible to suspend a person's registration.

Domiciliary services

Domiciliary services may be provided to an individual as part of their community care package or may be arranged independently of any social services assessment. Domiciliary services may include home helps or meals on wheels and help with bathing and dressing. Prior to implementation of the CSA 2000, there had been no formal regulation of domiciliary agencies. It was possible for any person, regardless of qualifications and expertise, to set up an agency without any external scrutiny. The exception was if a local authority chose to contract with an agency to provide community care services as part of an individual's care plan. In that situation, a local authority would have to have been satisfied with regard to the standards of care provided and could stipulate standards through its contracting arrangements. The CSA 2000 now requires all domiciliary care agencies to register and be inspected annually if they provide personal care services.

Chapter summary

- The Care Act 2014 provides the statutory basis for the assessment and provision of adult social care and support. A raft of previous community care legislation has been repealed following recommendations of the Law Commission for a single statute.
- The general duty of the local authority under the Care Act 2014 is to promote an individual's wellbeing, a term that is further defined to include personal dignity, protection from abuse and neglect and other matters.

- An individual who is assessed as eligible for care and support will be provided with a care plan, which should be reviewed regularly.

- Many people in receipt of care and support services will also have a carer. Carers are entitled to assessment of their needs in order to provide care.

- There is a body of case law dealing with judicial review applications relating to the provision of care services under the old legal framework. It is also possible to raise concerns about community care services via the complaints procedure or to the local government ombudsman or monitoring officer.

- Short periods of residential accommodation may be included in a care plan, or an individual may move to residential accommodation on a permanent basis when no longer able to live at home. The provision of residential accommodation is regulated by the Care Standards Act 2000.

Exercises

1. Surinder is an 18-year-old woman with Down's syndrome. She lives at home with her parents; her two older brothers left home some years ago and have their own families. She attended a local comprehensive school until she reached the age of 16 and has stayed at home with her parents since then. The family have not received any support from social services. Her parents are very protective of Surinder and she is always accompanied by them if she goes out, even to the local shop. Surinder would like to go to college and meet up with her old school friends but her parents will not allow her to travel alone. Her parents are growing older and her father, who drove until recently, has lost his driving licence due to poor eyesight. Surinder's sister-in-law, Jasmin, has said that Surinder could move in with her family and help to look after her children but Surinder's parents will not allow this. They have a row with Jasmin and tell Surinder not to have any further contact with her. Surinder is becoming depressed and is eating very little. Jasmin contacts social services to see if they can help Surinder to gain more independence.

   What steps might a social worker take, once contacted by Jasmin?

2. Annie is 88 years old and cared for by her daughter, Dorothy, aged 66. They live in a third-floor flat, which Annie bought from the council. Annie is losing her sight and suffers from arthritis. She is on a waiting list for a hip replacement. She cannot use the stairs and the lift at the flats is often out of order. She does not want to go out much in any case, as she is anxious about falling. She has recently become incontinent and needs attention at night. They have no washing machine and the laundry is a bus ride away.

   Dorothy is finding caring for her mother very stressful and feels unable to leave her for more than a short time. She has not been able to do any of the things she had planned on retirement. She contacted social services and explained their situation. Three months later, a social worker visited. She spent approximately half an hour at the flat. She offered Annie a place at a day centre for elderly people, four miles away, one day a week but said she could not help with transport to get her there. She said that at the moment she could not offer any help such as meals on wheels or home help but she would come back in six months' time, at the start of the next financial year. In response to Dorothy's concerns that she was finding it hard to care for her mother, the social worker said Annie could move to a residential home but that the flat would have to be sold to pay for it.

   What are the legal and practice issues raised in this scenario?

Websites

Information about carers may be found at the Carers UK website:
www.carersuk.org

For information relating to carers, see:
www.gov.uk/government/policies/helping-carers-to-stay-healthy

The website of the British Council of Disabled People:
www.bcodp.org.uk/

The website of the Disability Alliance provides advice and useful publications:
www.disabilityalliance.org

The British Institute of Learning Disabilities (BILD) website includes a wide range of information and research about learning disability:
www.bild.org.uk/

Association for Real Change, for service providers in the learning disability sector:
www.arcuk.org.uk

Age Concern is a national organisation with regional offices providing a wide range of information and advice relating to older people:
www.ace.org.uk

A guide to the scheme for direct payments is available from the Department of Health website:
www.gov.uk/apply-direct-payments

Further reading

Most texts relating to adults focus on community care law before the introduction of the Care Act 2014 but may nevertheless continue to be useful, particularly for case law which may continue to influence application of the new law:

Clements, L. and Thompson, C. (2014) *Community Care and the Law* (5th edn). London: Legal Action Group. (A detailed text, including guidance and case law.)

Mandelstam, M. (2008) *Community Care Practice and the Law* (4th edn). London: Jessica Kingsley.

Williams, J., Roberts, G. and Griffiths, A. (2014) *Adult Social Care Law in England*. Basingstoke: Palgrave Macmillan (The most recent text.)

A critical perspective on personalisation and on the Care bill is provided in two articles:

Clements, L. (2013) 'Reform of adult social care law' 3(3) *Elder Law Journal* p. 252.

Clements, L. (2011) 'Social care developments: a sideways look at personalisation and tightening eligibility criteria' 1 *Elder Law Journal* p. 47.

With a particular focus on older people:

Ashton, G. (2005) *Elderly People and the Law* (2nd edn). London: LexisNexis Butterworths.

Fenge, L.-A. (2001) 'Empowerment and community care – projecting the voice of older people' 23(4) *Journal of Social Welfare and Family Law* pp. 427–39.

Herring, J. (2009) *Older People in Law and Society.* Oxford: Oxford University Press.

On carers:

Carers UK (2003) *Missed Opportunities: The Impact of New Rights for Carers*. London: Carers UK. (This report publishes the findings of a survey of 2,000 carers as to the extent to which the Carers National Strategy, and carers legislation, have improved their lives.)

Clements, L. (2011) *Carers and their Rights: The Law Relating to Carers*. London: Carers UK.

In relation to disability see also:

Cooper, J. (ed.) (2000) *Law, Rights and Disability*. London: Jessica Kingsley.

Gray, B. and Jackson, R. (2002) *Advocacy and Learning Disability*. London: Jessica Kingsley.

A useful insight to complaints procedures is provided in:

Gulland, J (2009) 'Independence in complaints procedures: lessons from community care' 31(1) *Journal of Social Welfare and Family Law* p. 59.

Notes

1 www.gov.uk/government/speeches/care-bill-becomes-care-act-2014.

2 See discussion in A. Brammer and S. Biggs (1998) 'Defining elder abuse' 20(3) *Journal of Social Welfare and Family Law* p. 285.

3 Department of Health LAC (92) 15 'Registered Homes Act 1984: I. Small residential care homes. II. Inspection'. London: Department of Health.

4 See the Bulletin 'NAPSAC' produced by the National Association for the Protection from Sexual Abuse of Adults and Children with learning disabilities, and the work of H. Brown, including H. Brown, J. Stein and V. Turk (1995) 'The sexual abuse of adults with learning difficulties: report of a second two-year incidence survey' 8(1) *Mental Handicap Research* p. 3.

5 Department of Health LAC (93) 10 'Approvals and directions for arrangements from 1 April 1993 made under Schedule 8 to the National Health Service Act 1977 and sections 21 and 29 of the National Assistance Act 1948'. London: Department of Health.

6 LASSL (97) 13 'Responsibilities of local authority social services departments; implications of recent legal judgments'.

7 The guidance is issued as a local authority circular, LAC (2002) 13, and is accompanied by practice guidance in the form of frequently asked questions.

8 Commission for Social Care Inspection (2008) *The State of Social Care in England 2007–08*. London: CSCI.

9 Department of Health (2003) 'Direct payments guidance: community care, services for carers and children's services (direct payments)'. London: Department of Health.

10 Department of Health (1997) 'Community Care (Direct Payments) Act 1996: policy and practice guidance'. London: Department of Health.

11 Note the role of the National Care Standards Commission to regulate domiciliary care agencies.

12 Department of Health LAC (92) 27 'National Assistance Act 1948 (Choice of Accommodation) Directions 1992'. London: Department of Health.

13 As note 12.

14 M. Butt (1996) 'Social Care and Black Communities: A review of recent research studies'. London: HMSO. See also W. I. U. Ahmad and A. Atkin (eds) (1996) *Race and Community Care*. Buckingham: Open University Press.

15 H. Cowen (1999) *Community Care, Ideology and Social Policy*. London: Prentice Hall Europe.

[16] The definition of public authority is based on that contained in the Human Rights Act 1998 (discussed in Chapter 2).

[17] See M. Mandelstam (2005) *Community Care Practice and the Law* (3rd edn). London: Jessica Kingsley, pp. 152–9 for a full discussion of such cases.

[18] Local Authority Social Services (Complaints Procedure) Order 1990 (SI 1990/2244).

[19] See further guidance on this area, Department of Health (1991) 'The right to complain'. London: HMSO.

[20] People First (1993) 'Self-Advocacy Starter Pack'. London: People First.

[21] See: www.carers.gov.uk; www.carersuk.org; www.carersinformation.org.uk.

[22] See policy guidance: Department of Health (1996) 'Carers (Recognition and Services) Act 1995: policy guidance'. London: Department of Health.

[23] Social Care Institute for Excellence (2007) Practice Guide J: 'Implementing the Carers (Equal Opportunities) Act 2004'. London: SCIE.

[24] NHSCCA 1990, s. 42(2).

Learning objectives

To develop an understanding of the following:

- The legal framework for practice in the area of mental health provided by the Mental Health Act 1983, as amended by the Mental Health Act 2007.
- The legal definition of mental disorder.
- The role of the approved mental health professional, the nearest relative and Independent Mental Health Advocacy Services.
- Powers of compulsory detention and guardianship.
- Patients' rights and treatment in hospital.
- Arrangements for discharge, including the role of the Mental Health Review Tribunal.
- Provision for after-care and for community treatment orders.
- Mental health and children and young people.
- The distinction between mental disorder and mental incapacity.

Talking Point

The following is an extract from the code of practice to the Mental Health Act 1983.

RECALL OF A SUPERVISED COMMUNITY TREATMENT PATIENT TO HOSPITAL

Mary has a long-standing bipolar disorder. She has been on **SCT** for the past 12 months following an initial two months' detention in hospital. Mary's condition has been managed successfully by a care plan which includes oral medication. However, it has transpired that Mary has missed taking a significant amount of her medication over the past couple of weeks. One of the conditions of Mary's CTO is that she regularly attends a named clinic to review her treatment and progress. For the first time since her discharge from hospital, she fails to attend. The responsible clinician meets with members of the multi-disciplinary team to decide whether Mary needs to be recalled to hospital for treatment.

When the multi-disciplinary team members meet, they are required to consider the principles. Among the questions they might wish to consider in making a decision in these circumstances are the following.

Purpose principle

- What are the risks to Mary and others if she does not receive her medication? How soon might those risks arise and in what circumstances?
- What will be best for Mary's wellbeing overall?

Least restriction principle

- What are the possible alternatives for managing Mary's care? For example, the multi-disciplinary team contacting Mary, or arranging a home visit to see her.
- Would varying the conditions of the CTO assist Mary to comply with her treatment programme?
- Might Mary be prepared to accept another treatment regime if there is an alternative which would be as clinically effective?
- Have alternative options been explored with Mary before?

Respect principle

- What is Mary's view of why she has stopped taking her medication?
- Is Mary's failure to attend clinic anything to do with a conscious decision to refuse medication, or is there some other reason? Have all possible reasons been considered?
- Are there any social, cultural or family-related factors, which may have led Mary to miss her appointment?
- Taking into account Mary's history and known past and present wishes, are there any particular reasons why Mary may not have presented at the clinic?
- Has Mary expressed any views about what she would like to happen if she stopped taking her medication?

Participation principle

- Is Mary willing to discuss what is going on?

- What might be the best way of approaching Mary to discuss the current situation?
- Are Mary's family or carers involved in her day-to-day care aware that she is on SCT, and if so should their views be sought on the best way to help Mary to re-establish contact with services?
- What is Mary's view about her family being contacted?
- Have Mary's family or carers expressed any views about what they think may help Mary?
- Does Mary's GP have any ideas about engaging Mary?

Effectiveness, efficiency and equity principle

- Mary has said in the past that she enjoys her contact with the team's community psychiatric nurse (CPN) – would giving her more time with the CPN be an effective way of tackling the current situation? Could it be done without other patients with the same or greater clinical needs being disadvantaged?

The scenario illustrates two particular aspects of the law: first, the operation of supervised community treatment order; and, second, the application of the guiding principles of the code to a particular scenario.

Introduction

Mental health is a significant area of social work practice. A statutory framework is provided by the Mental Health Act 1983 (**MHA 1983**), as amended by the Mental Health Act 2007 (**MHA 2007**) but it remains something of an ethical minefield. Tension abounds in the form of conflicting claims and wishes of the patient, the safety of the patient and the protection of members of the wider community, and the position of the nearest relative. In resolving these various issues, the social worker is often at the forefront of decision-making but must work alongside a range of other professional groups. It is perhaps not surprising that many aspects of social work practice in mental health have, until the recent reforms, been invested in a specially qualified social worker, the approved social worker (**ASW**) (now, a role undertaken by a broader range of practitioners including social workers and renamed the **approved mental health professional** (**AMHP**)). Nevertheless, *all* social workers are likely to encounter service users with mental health difficulties at some point and it is useful therefore to have an overview of the relevant law. For example, a child protection social worker may have concerns about the care being provided to a child by his parent who has enduring mental health problems.

The extent of mental health problems in society is surprisingly high. One in four people suffer from some form of mental health problem at some point in their lives and a substantial amount of sickness absence from work is attributable to some form of mental or emotional disturbance, including depression. The extent of mental illness is likely to increase further with demographic changes, given that approximately one in five people over the age of 85 suffer from some form of dementia. The range of mental health problems is extensive. There is an unfortunate perception in society that people with mental health problems are dangerous. This has no doubt been fuelled by media attention given to exceptional cases such as Christopher Clunis,[1] and the Government's original proposals to reform the MHA 1983[2] lent some support to that position. In fact, research suggests that there is no significant increase in the risk of homicide posed by people with a mental illness.[3]

The key legislation is the MHA 1983; however, this must be viewed in the context of broader adult social care law and policy. Many people with mental health problems will receive community care services under a care plan (as discussed in Chapter 14). The current law has been the subject of extensive review process and long anticipated reform has been presented in the MHA 2007. Rather than presenting a completely new legal framework for mental health, it amends the MHA 1983, many of the original provisions of which remain intact.[4] There are, however, some fundamental changes. This chapter therefore covers the existing law, in the form of the amended MHA 1983, with some reference to the former law by way of comparison and to emphasise significant developments.

Key changes introduced by the Mental Health Act 2007

- Changing professional roles – AMHP, responsible clinician, independent mental health advocacy.
- New definition of mental disorder.
- New community treatment order.
- Right of patient to displace the nearest relative.
- Introduction of deprivation of liberty safeguards (inserted into Mental Capacity Act 2005).

Code of practice

The Mental Health Act 1983 is accompanied by a Code of Practice (2008), which adds detailed guidance on the application of the Act. In addition, a 'Reference Guide' has been produced which explains legal provisions of the Act. Both documents are complementary and written in an accessible style.

The code commences by setting out five key principles to underpin practice. It was hoped by many that principles would be contained in the Act (as with the Mental Capacity Act 2005) rather than in the code. There is, however, an obligation for certain professionals to 'have regard' to the code. In relation to the previous code, the House of Lords explained the meaning of the term to 'have regard' in R (Munjaz) v. Mersey Care NHS Trust [2005] UKHL 58. The court said that the code was more than 'mere advice', rather it was guidance 'which any hospital should consider with great care and from which it should depart only if it has cogent reasons for doing so'.

The five principles are:

1. The purpose principle.
2. The least restriction principle.
3. The respect principle.
4. The participation principle.
5. The effectiveness, efficiency and equity principle.

The code includes illustrations of the application of these principles, such as the 'talking point' example.

The term 'patient' is used throughout the MHA 1983 to refer to 'a person suffering or appearing to suffer from mental disorder' (s. 145) (within the definition provided by the Act), even where the person is not residing in hospital, e.g. a person who is the subject of a guardianship order and living in the community. For consistency the same approach will be taken in this chapter. The Act applies to adults and children.

Mental health and mental capacity

Mental capacity (considered separately in Chapter 16) has been subject of major law reform with the introduction of the Mental Capacity Act 2005 (MCA). Mental incapacity and mental illness are commonly confused, though they are quite different in nature and in legal terms. A person with a mental illness as defined by the Mental Health Act 1983 may also lack mental capacity. For many people, however, the mental illness will not have a significant impact on the ability to make a range of decisions, including consent to medical treatment. For other individuals, capacity to make complex financial decisions may be limited but the majority of other more routine decisions may be still be within their capacity. There are other individuals who lack capacity to make a range of decisions but who would not fall within the definitions of mental illness under the Act. An obvious example would be an individual with a mental impairment or learning disability who does not display any 'abnormally aggressive or seriously irresponsible conduct'. The consequences in terms of any legal interventions will vary depending on whether the key issue is one of mental capacity or mental illness and further on the type of mental illness and associated behaviour. Proposals to reform the law on mental health and mental capacity were introduced at around the same time but a separate approach has been retained in the legislative framework provided by the MCA 2005 and the MHA 1983 (as amended). The Mental Health Act 2007 also makes some amendments to the MCA 2005, most notably in respect of the deprivation of liberty safeguards. The interface between the Mental Health Act and the Mental Capacity Act is complex and at times a person may be subject to provisions of both Acts in relation to care and treatment. Where there are alternative routes to provide support to an individual, the emphasis under both areas of law (together with the Codes of Practice) is on the least intrusive route and might therefore suggest a preference for the MCA. It is also important to remember that the MCA only applies to people aged 16 and over, whereas the MHA applies to adults and children.

The Codes of Practice accompanying each Act give guidance on this interface in practice.

Professionals may need to think about using the MHA to detain and treat somebody who lacks capacity to consent to treatment (rather than use the MCA), if:

- it is not possible to give the person the care or treatment they need without doing something that might deprive them of their liberty;

- the person needs treatment that cannot be given under the MCA (for example, because the person has made a valid and applicable advance decision to refuse an essential part of treatment);

- the person may need to be restrained in a way that is not allowed under the MCA;

- it is not possible to assess or treat the person safely or effectively without treatment being compulsory (perhaps because the person is expected to regain capacity to consent, but might then refuse to give consent);

- the person lacks capacity to decide on some elements of the treatment but has capacity to refuse a vital part of it – and they have done so; or

- there is some other reason why the person might not get treatment, and they or somebody else might suffer harm as a result.

> Before making an application under the MHA, decision-makers should consider whether they could achieve their aims safely and effectively by using the MCA instead.
>
> (Chapter 13 MCA Code of Practice)
>
> In deciding whether it is necessary to detain patients, doctors and approved mental health professionals must always consider the alternative ways of providing the treatment or care they need.
>
> The fact that patients cannot consent to the treatment they need, or to being admitted to hospital, does not automatically mean that the Act must be used. It may be possible to rely instead on the provisions of the Mental Capacity Act 2005 to provide treatment in the best interests of patients who are aged 16 or over and who lack capacity to consent to treatment.
>
> (Chapter 4 MHA Code of Practice)

Reflect

Think about how you might explain the concepts of mental capacity and mental health to a service user, how they differ and how they relate to each other.

Government strategy for mental health

In place of the previous National Service Framework, the government has published a mental health strategy applicable to all agencies engaging with mental health issues. An overriding theme is that mental health problems should be treated as seriously as physical health problems. The strategy contains six shared objectives with outcome indicators:

1. More people will have good mental health.
2. More people with mental health problems will recover.
3. More people with mental health problems will have good physical health.
4. More people will have positive experiences of care and support.
5. Fewer people will suffer avoidable harm.
6. Fewer people will experience stigma and discrimination.[5]

The fourth objective is particularly relevant to social work and is explained further:

> Care and support, wherever it takes place, should offer access to timely, evidence-based interventions and approaches that give people the greatest choice and control over their own lives, in the least restrictive environment, and should ensure that people's human rights are protected.

Anti-oppressive practice

It is important to be aware that many people with mental health problems will experience discrimination in various areas of life. This discrimination may be intensified if the person is also a member of an ethnic minority. There is evidence that, in practice, race is considered an index of dangerousness in the mental health field. In comparison to a white man, a black man is more likely to be detained under the criminal provisions of the MHA 1983, to be in a secure ward and to receive higher doses of medication.[6] A further mental health and ethnicity census in 2005 found that black African and Caribbean people are three times more likely to be admitted to hospital and up to 44 per cent more likely to be detained under the Mental Health Act.[7]

Definitions

The key term under the Act is 'mental disorder', which is defined as 'any disorder or disability of the mind'. This replaces the previous definition of mental disorder as 'mental illness, arrested or incomplete development of mind, psychopathic disorder and any other disorder or disability of mind'. In addition, the separate classifications of mental impairment, severe mental impairment, mental illness and psychopathic disorder are removed.[8]

Learning disability is defined as 'a state of arrested or incomplete development of mind which includes significant impairment of intelligence and social functioning' (s. 1(4)). A person will not be considered to be suffering from a learning disability for some sections of the MHA 1983 (including long-term admission and guardianship) unless their learning disability is 'associated with abnormally aggressive or seriously irresponsible behaviour'. This effectively restates the old position in relation to people with learning disabilities' inclusion in the terms mental impairment and severe mental impairment. These are legal definitions and may appear to contrast with medical or social understanding of mental health.

As before, dependence on alcohol or drugs is not considered to be a mental disorder under the new definition. The previous exclusion, however, relating to promiscuity, sexual deviancy and other immoral conduct, has not been retained. This brings certain disorders of sexual preference, such as paedophilia, which are now clinically recognised as mental disorders, within the scope of the legislation.

Chapter 3 of the code of practice provides guidance on the definition of 'mental disorder'. Some examples are given of conditions which would fall within the new term:

> Affective disorders, such as depression and bipolar disorder.
>
> Schizophrenia and delusional disorders.
>
> Neurotic, stress-related and somatoform disorders, such as anxiety, phobic disorders, obsessive compulsive disorders, post-traumatic stress disorders and hypochondriacal disorders.
>
> Organic mental disorders such as dementia and delirium.
>
> Personality and behavioural changes caused by brain injury or damage.
>
> Personality disorders.
>
> Mental and behavioural disorders caused by psychoactive substance use.
>
> Eating disorders, non-organic sleep disorders and non-organic sexual disorders.
>
> Learning disabilities.
>
> Autistic spectrum disorders.
>
> Behavioural and emotional disorders of children and adolescents.

The Code notes that this is not an exhaustive list. Many of the code of practice examples set out in the box above would previously have been included in the term 'mental illness', which was a subcategory of mental disorder under the previous framework. It was not specifically defined in the legislation or in the code of practice. It was a question for the professionals involved (including approved social workers) to identify its presence. That remains so in relation to the many forms of mental disorder which may be covered by the wide term 'mental disorder' in the new framework.

The Court of Appeal declined the opportunity precisely to define mental illness in the case of *W v. L* [1974] 3 WLR 859. This case concerned a patient, aged 23, whose behaviour included putting a cat in a gas oven, making another cat inhale ammonia, hanging a puppy, threatening his wife with a knife and threatening to push her downstairs to cause a miscarriage. At the time, prior to the MHA 1983, his behaviour was considered sufficient for him to be classified as having a psychopathic disorder, but in order to be detained for longer than 28 days it was necessary to determine whether his condition also fell within the definition of mental illness. The court found him both psychopathic and mentally ill. Lawton LJ provided the following statement on the meaning of mental illness:

> [The words 'mental illness' are] ordinary words of the English language. They have no particular medical significance. They have no particular legal significance. How should the court construe them? The answer in my judgment is … that ordinary words of the English language should be construed in the way that ordinary sensible people would construe them. That being in my judgment the right test, then I ask myself, what would the ordinary sensible person have said about the patient's condition in this case if he had been informed of his behaviour? In my judgment such a person would have said: 'well, the fellow is obviously mentally ill'.

Such an approach is less than helpful to those seeking a precise definition. The lack of precision may be advantageous in accommodating expanding knowledge of different types of mental health problems; for example, anorexia nervosa has been recognised as a mental illness (*Re KB (Adult) (Mental Patient: Medical Treatment)* (1994) 19 BMLR 144). Conversely, it also permits inclusion of those with eccentric or unconventional behaviour.

Learning disability

The new legislation includes the term 'learning disability' in preference to the term 'severe mental impairment', which replaced 'severe subnormalities' in previous legislation. The term refers to handicap rather than illness, conditions which are less likely to be cured and which would currently be referred to as 'learning disabilities'. The arrested or incomplete development of mind must be associated with abnormally aggressive or seriously irresponsible conduct to come within the terms of the MHA 1983 for certain provisions. This provision was introduced in the original 1983 Act in response to concern that compulsory detention would not normally be appropriate for people with learning disabilities and could be stigmatising. Incorporation of the requirement for abnormally aggressive or seriously irresponsible conduct was intended to include only those people with mental impairment who need hospital detention for their own safety or that of others. A legal loophole remains, however, which became evident in the Beverley Lewis case, where a 23-year-old, deaf, blind, black woman died wrapped in newspaper and weighing only 5 stone. The authorities were at a loss to act where a woman with learning disabilities exhibited passive behaviour. It is questionable whether or not her self-neglect in that case could have been interpreted as seriously irresponsible conduct.[9] There is no clear legal guidance as to what is meant by abnormally aggressive or seriously irresponsible conduct. The code of practice suggests:

> Abnormally aggressive behaviour. Any assessment of this category should be based on observations of behaviour which lead to a conclusion that the actions are outside the usual range of aggressive behaviour, and which cause actual damage and/or real distress occurring recently or persistently or with excessive severity.
>
> Irresponsible conduct. The assessment of this characteristic should be based on an observation of behaviour which shows a lack of responsibility, a disregard of the consequences of action taken, and where the results cause actual damage or real distress, either recently or persistently or with excessive severity. (para. 30.5)

Case law has taken a restrictive approach to the term irresponsible conduct. For example, in *Re F (Mental Health Act: Guardianship)* [2000] 1 FLR 192, the fact that a person with a learning disability wanted to return to live in a situation where there was a possibility of abuse was not considered evidence of 'seriously irresponsible conduct'. Again, in *Newham London Borough Council* v. *S (Adult: Court's Jurisdiction)* [2003] EWHC 1909 (Fam), the adult concerned had a tendency to rush into the road without looking but this was not found to be seriously irresponsible conduct. A later case found that past history of irresponsible conduct could be sufficient in finding severe mental impairment as indicating a propensity to such conduct (*Lewis* v. *Gibson* [2005] EWCA Civ 587).

The role of the approved mental health professional

The role of the approved social worker (ASW) has been taken on by an approved mental health professional (AMHP). The majority of social work functions under the MHA 1983 are invested in this role. It is intended that a wider range of professionals (beyond social workers) may become AMHPs. Essentially the role is the same, with the additional responsibilities in relation to community treatment orders. All ASWs automatically became AMHPs when the 2007 legislation was implemented. Local authorities will continue to be responsible for providing training, approving and providing a sufficient number of AMHPs for 24-hour cover. AMHPs do not have to be directly employed by the local authority but will be accountable to a specific local authority. To be approved as an AMHP, a person must have 'appropriate competence in dealing with persons who are suffering from mental disorder'.[10] To satisfy this requirement the person must have a professional qualification as one of the following:

- a social worker registered with the HCPC;
- a first level nurse registered with the Nursing and Midwifery Council, whose field of practice is mental health or learning disability;
- a registered occupational therapist;
- a chartered psychologist.

It is not possible for a doctor to be approved as an AMHP. The person must also be able to satisfy a number of key competences, including application of values to the AMHP role, working in partnership and knowledge of the legal and policy framework. Approval lasts for five years.

This is currently the only aspect of social work that legally requires a further qualification. Nevertheless, it appears that, historically, there has been substantial variation in the arrangements for training and supervision of ASWs and ratios of ASWs to population, across the

United Kingdom.[11] Huxley *et al.*[12] conducted a national survey of ASW numbers in England and Wales in 1992 and 2002 and suggest that there had been a decline in the ratio of ASWs per 100,000 population of over 50 per cent.[13]

Perhaps the most significant aspect of the work of the AMHP is their statutory role in arranging compulsory admission to hospital; however, it is important to note that the everyday work of a mental health social worker is much broader than this. The AMHP is under a duty, set out in s. 13(1A), to make an application for admission to hospital or reception into guardianship in respect of any patient if he is satisfied that such an application ought to be made and having regard to any wishes expressed by relatives of the patient or other relevant circumstances that it is necessary or proper for the application to be made by him. This is an individual duty invested in the AMHP to be exercised on the basis of their own judgment rather than at the behest of others. Protection against liability is offered by the MHA 1983, s. 139. An AMHP will not be liable to civil or criminal proceedings for any act done under the Act, rules or regulations, unless the act was done in bad faith or without reasonable care.

It will be important for AMHPs to establish good working relationships with other professionals, including psychiatrists and the police. Many AMHPs are employed in multidisciplinary Community Mental Health Teams. It is vital for the AMHP to keep a full record of their reasons for making (or not making) an application. Failure to keep such records might be found to be maladministration.

Where guardianship is arranged, the AMHP may be involved as the patient's guardian in some cases. Prior to an application for admission to hospital (where this is being considered), the approved mental health professional must interview the patient in a suitable manner and be satisfied that detention in hospital is the most appropriate way of providing care and treatment. In some cases it is difficult to satisfy this requirement and the code notes (at para. 2.11f): 'It is not desirable for a patient to be interviewed through a closed door or window except where there is serious risk to other people.' A genuine attempt to interview should be made, whatever the extent of communication difficulties or particular circumstances of the case. This may involve the use of trained interpreters or an AMHP with appropriate communication skills.

The AMHP will often work closely with the patient's nearest relative and must consult the nearest relative before making an application for treatment or guardianship. It is crucial that the AMHP can ascertain the identity of the nearest relative, as any subsequent detention may be unlawful if the correct nearest relative was not consulted (*Re S-C (Mental Patient) (Habeas Corpus)* [1996] QB 599).

The emphasis of an AMHP's assessment of an individual will be on the social effects of mental illness and consideration of community-based alternatives. In carrying out an assessment, the AMHP will obtain appropriate information to enable a decision to be made as to the least restrictive way to offer appropriate help to the individual. The options will be dependent on the range of community-based resources available, which may, for example, support an individual who is willing to take prescribed medication at home as well as consideration of the community treatment order (**CTO**). In addition, as an alternative to a section, the AMHP should consider whether the individual would agree to admission as an informal patient. If an application for formal admission is made, the AMHP should arrange the conveyance of the patient to hospital, accompany the patient and remain with him until medical examination can take place. The AMHP should clearly explain his role to the patient and also explain the rights of the patient.

Other responsibilities of the approved mental health professionals include providing social enquiry reports for the hospital or mental health tribunal; and making arrangements for aftercare upon a patient's discharge. The AMHP is not involved with decisions relating to treatment of the patient once in hospital. The AMHP has no power to seek discharge of a patient.

> **Reflect**
>
> Why do you think the AMHP is the only social work position that requires additional training?

A report of the Workforce Action Team on the mental health National Service Framework proposed the recruitment of non-qualified staff, to be known as support, time, recovery (STR) workers, to release ASWs from basic tasks. Their role is envisaged as promoting independent living, encouraging service users to take responsibility for practical needs and giving support with daily living activities.[14] According to the Department of Health: 'an STR worker is someone who works as part of a team which provides mental health services and focuses directly on the needs of service users, working across boundaries of care, organisation and role. They will provide **Support**, give **Time** to the service user and thus promote their **Recovery**.'[15] They would not be involved with sectioning or coordinating the **care programme approach**.[16]

Other professional roles

Approved clinician

The functions of the approved clinician (**AC**) include using the s. 5(2) power to detain a patient and examining patients on behalf of a nearest relative with a view to the nearest relative considering discharge of a patient. An approved clinician can act as a responsible clinician for a patient.

Responsible clinician

The **responsible clinician** (**RC**) replaced the role of responsible medical officer. Again, the ambit of professionals who may take on this role is extended. In addition to doctors, others such as nurses and social workers may become responsible clinicians. The RC is the person with overall responsibility for the patient's case, whether detained, subject to guardianship or CTO. Examples of the functions of the RC include: discharging a patient from detention, guardianship or CTO, recalling a patient from leave and varying conditions attached to a CTO. The responsible clinician may change depending on the patient's needs, for example if particular therapies are being used to treat the patient.

The nearest relative

The nearest relative (**NR**) has an important role in terms of admission, care and discharge of patients. A person's nearest relative will often have to be identified by the AMHP and is normally determined simply on the basis of priority on the list of adult relatives contained in s. 26, namely:

- spouse or civil partner (disregarded if separated; cohabitee (including same sex) of six months or more is treated as a spouse or civil partner);
- son/daughter;

- parent;
- sibling;
- grandparent;
- grandchild;
- uncle/aunt;
- nephew/niece;
- any other person with whom the patient resides and has done for five years shall be treated as a relative (s. 26(7)).[17]

Priority is given to anyone on the list who resides with or cares for the patient (s. 26(4)).

Anyone who does not ordinarily reside in the United Kingdom, or anyone under the age of 18 will normally be ignored. Age takes precedence where there is more than one person in a category, e.g. elder sibling. If a child is in care the nearest relative will be the authority named in the care order. The nearest relative can delegate their powers to another person.[18]

The nearest relative is not the same as 'next of kin' and will not always be the person the patient would prefer to act in this capacity. The NR is a 'public authority' under the Human Rights Act 1998 because he is able to exercise functions of a public nature. As such he is bound to comply with the Articles of the ECHR.

Role of the nearest relative

The NR must be consulted before an application for treatment or guardianship is made, and must not object to the application; he does not actually have to consent to the application. If the NR objects to an application for treatment or guardianship, it will not be able to proceed.

The NR can apply directly for a s. 2 or s. 3 order and has a power to require the local Social Services Department to direct an AMHP to consider a case with a view to making an application for admission to hospital. The NR has the right of discharge of the patient. If the NR intends to exercise this right, he must give 72 hours' written notice to the hospital managers. If the RC reports that, in his opinion, the patient is likely to act in a dangerous manner to himself or others, he can bar the discharge. The NR has the right to appoint an independent doctor to visit the patient and view records; this is important in relation to the NR's power to discharge a patient. The NR is entitled to information regarding the patient's detention or CTO and must be given seven days' notice of intended discharge of the patient, by the hospital.

Choice of nearest relative

The European Court of Human Rights considered the nearest relative in *JT* v. *United Kingdom* [2000] 1 FLR 909: a settlement was arrived at in an Art. 8 claim (right to respect for family and private life). The UK authorities agreed to amend the Mental Health Act 1983 so as to permit detainees to make an application to court to have their 'nearest relative' replaced where there was a reasonable objection to having a certain person acting in that capacity. In the instant case, the patient wished to have her mother removed as NR due to their difficult relationship and the fear that her step-father, who allegedly had sexually abused her, would gain knowledge of her whereabouts. Further, in *R (M)* v. *Secretary of State for Health* [2003] EWHC 1094 (Admin), it was held that where the patient reasonably objects to the nearest relative (in that case as there was no relationship of trust), another person should act. Similarly, in *R (E)* v. *Bristol City Council* [2005] EWHC 74 (Admin), the High Court was able to interpret s. 11 MHA compatibly with the convention so that E's sister (the court had said

437

that it would not be in E's interests for her sister to act as NR) did not have to be consulted or informed in relation to applications for E's admission for assessment or treatment on the basis that it was not reasonably practicable. Practicability was not limited to availability and could also encompass whether it was appropriate to consult.

In response to *JT*, the 2007 Act made some changes to the NR scheme. The patient himself can now seek discharge of the NR and a new ground of unsuitability to act is included.

Displacement of nearest relative

There is statutory provision for the nearest relative to be displaced under MHA 1983, s. 29 on the application of the patient, any relative of the patient, any other person with whom the patient is residing (immediately before, if admitted) or an AMHP.

The county court may make an order that the functions of the nearest relative are exercisable by a proper person where the following grounds exist:

(a) the patient has no NR, or it is not reasonably practicable to ascertain whether he has such a relative, or who that relative is;

(b) the NR is incapable of acting as such by reason of mental disorder or other illness;

(c) the NR unreasonably objects to the making of an application for admission for treatment or guardianship in respect of the patient;

(d) the NR has exercised, without due regard to the welfare of the patient or the interests of the public, his power to discharge the patient from hospital or guardianship, or is likely to do so;

(e) the NR is otherwise not a suitable person to act.

Some factors that might lead the AMHP to consider a NR is unsuitable to act are where there is:

- any reason to think that the patient has suffered, or is suspected to have suffered abuse at the hands of the NR (or someone with whom the NR is in a relationship) or is at risk of suffering such abuse;

- any evidence that the patient is afraid of the NR or seriously distressed by the possibility of the NR being involved in their life or their care; and

- a situation where the patient and NR are unknown to each other, there is only a distant relationship between them, or their relationship has broken down irretrievably.

Once an application has been made for displacement of the NR, the NR's power of discharge is immediately suspended. This provision provides, in effect, a 'veto' to the NR's power of discharge, if it is likely to be exercised in a manner the authorities do not agree with. Interim displacement orders are possible (*R* v. *Central London County Court, ex parte London* [1999] 3 All ER 991).

Key Case

In *Lewis* v. *Gibson* [2005] EWCA Civ 587, the Court of Appeal considered the relationship between displacement of nearest relative, guardianship and the inherent jurisdiction. The case merits some attention as it involves a number of related mental health issues.

The case concerned M, a 32-year-old woman with a severe learning disability (as a result of Down's syndrome), who lived with her mother. When her mother's health deteriorated, the council, concerned at the level of care she was receiving, removed M from home having obtained a warrant under s. 135 authorising entry to the house and removal of M to a place of safety. Once at the hospital, an application was made under s. 2 for compulsory admission for assessment. M's mother, who was her nearest relative, sought to discharge her daughter, to which the responsible medical officer (RMO) responded with a s. 25 barring order preventing discharge on the basis that, if M was discharged, she would 'be likely to act in a manner dangerous to himself or others'. The approved social worker applied to displace M's mother as nearest relative; an interim order was made; M was received into the council's guardianship and placed in a care home in the community, where she apparently thrived. The county court, considering the application to displace the nearest relative, was asked to decide whether she unreasonably objected to the making of the guardianship order. The court approved the application and appointed the council as nearest relative.

M's mother argued, first, that her daughter did not fit within the category of mentally disordered person to which guardianship applied, as her mental impairment was not associated with 'abnormally aggressive or seriously irresponsible conduct', and therefore it could not be unreasonable for her to object to guardianship. This was rejected by the court on the basis that it was sufficient that M had a propensity to this conduct even though it was not exhibited at the time of the hearing. Secondly, M's mother argued that the criteria that guardianship is 'necessary in the interests of the welfare of the patient or for the protection of other persons' was not met. She argued that guardianship was not 'necessary' because the council could instead have applied to the High Court to declare whether it was lawful for them to remove M invoking the inherent jurisdiction and relying on the doctrine of necessity. This argument was also rejected. The Court of Appeal found that once the county court was satisfied that M met the criteria for guardianship, there was no gap for the High Court to fill with a declaration. The court did also note that guardianship confers 'extremely limited powers' and that it might be necessary at some point to seek a declaration for matters falling outside the guardian's powers. It seems, therefore, that a best interest declaration could be made alongside guardianship, or instead of guardianship to address matters not covered by guardianship. (High Court declarations are discussed further in Chapter 16.)

Compulsory powers

In certain circumstances it will become necessary for an individual to be detained under a compulsory order in a hospital. The 1999 version of the code of practice stated 'Compulsory admission should only be exercised in the last resort.' Although that specific sentence is omitted from the current code it does note that, 'Before it is decided that admission to hospital is necessary, consideration must be given to whether there are alternative means of providing the care and treatment which the patient requires (para. 4.4 Code of Practice, 2008). Indeed, the emphasis on the least restrictive intervention should mean that compulsory admission is considered as the last resort.

Compulsory powers of detention in hospital are contained in ss. 2–5. Section 2 provides for admission for assessment and s. 3 provides for admission for treatment. Emergency admission for treatment is provided for by s. 4 and under s. 5 it is possible to detain a patient already in hospital.

Table 15.1 Compulsory powers under the Mental Health Act 1983

	Mental health category	Other criteria	Medical support	Duration	Applicant
s. 2	Mental disorder	Warrants detention for assessment in interests of own health or safety, or protection of other persons	2 doctors	28 days	NR or AMHP
s. 3	Mental disorder – nature or degree makes it appropriate to receive medical treatment in hospital. If LD must be associated with abnormally aggressive or seriously irresponsible conduct	Necessary for health or safety of the patient or protection of others. Cannot be treated unless detained and appropriate treatment is available	2 doctors	6 months	NR or AMHP
s. 4	Mental disorder	Urgent necessity	1 doctor	72 hours	NR or AMHP
s. 5	Mental disorder	Urgent necessity	Doctor or nurse	72 hours (doctor) 6 hours (nurse)	Doctor or nurse

Table 15.1 summarises the elements of each section in terms of applicant, duration, medical involvement and criteria. In each case there is no application to court, the operation of the sections outlined being essentially an administrative procedure. The application is made to the managers of the proposed hospital (MHA 1983, s. 11) and carries with it a power to convey the patient to hospital.

Mental health and risk

For each application the relevant mental health definition is stipulated, i.e. mental disorder. This diagnosis is not sufficient in itself. For each case there are further criteria as to the need for detention. For s. 2 the criteria are that he ought to be detained in the interests of his own health or safety, or with a view to the protection of other persons. Other persons could be members of the patient's immediate family or the public. The protection could be required because of the risk of physical harm or the code suggests 'serious persistent psychological harm' (para. 2.9). For applications under s. 3 the criteria are more detailed. The mental disorder must be of a nature or degree which makes it appropriate to receive treatment in hospital, i.e. not in the community or under guardianship. Failure to take medication in the community which leads to deterioration in the patient's mental health could prompt an application under s. 3 or CTO. As with s. 2, there is a reference to detention for his own health or safety or with a view to the protection of other persons. Section 3 carries a stronger imperative, however – it must be 'necessary' under s. 3 rather than 'in the interests of' under s. 2.

Medical support

Applications under ss. 2 or 3 must have the support of two medical recommendations, the authors of which have examined the patient within five days of each other. One of the doctors must be a mental health specialist approved under s. 12, and the other, who should be familiar with the patient, will often be the patient's GP.

Applicant

The applicant for an admission under ss. 2 or 3 may be the AMHP or NR. The code of practice suggests that, as an application by the NR may damage the relationship he has with the patient, and given the training and knowledge of resources of the AMHP, the AMHP is usually the appropriate person to make the application. If the NR does make the application, the hospital managers should notify the local Social Services Department and a social worker will be required to provide a social circumstances report to the hospital (MHA 1983, s. 14).

Section 13(2) requires the AMHP to interview the patient in a suitable manner before making an application for admission under s. 3. It is not unusual for the AMHP to be faced with an uncooperative patient who does not want to participate in any such interview. In *M* v. *South West London and St George's Mental Health NHS Trust* [2008] EWCA Civ 1112, it was found that even fairly brief interaction between the AMHP and the patient may be sufficient to satisfy the AMHP that detention in hospital for treatment is necessary. Equally, a doctor who under s.12(1) is required to have 'personally examined' the patient, may satisfy this requirement by observing conduct even if no actual examination takes place.

Section 2

Detention under s. 2 is appropriate where there is no clear diagnosis of the patient's condition and in-patient assessment is necessary to produce a treatment plan. If the applicant is an AMHP, he should take all reasonable steps to inform the person who appears to be the NR (MHA 1983, s. 11(3)) but the NR's consent is not required.

A person detained under s. 2 may be treated without consent if necessary. It is not possible to renew or extend a s. 2 admission. At the end of the 28-day period, the patient may leave the hospital, remain at the hospital as an informal patient or be detained at the hospital for treatment under s. 3.[19] The duty to provide after-care services under s. 117 does not apply following a s. 2 admission.

Section 3

An admission under s. 3 might be appropriate where a patient is already detained under s. 2 or has been admitted in the past and where a patient has been assessed recently and is known by the clinical team. The patient need not always be detained for the full six-month period and can be discharged earlier by the responsible medical officer (the doctor responsible for the patient's treatment plan). Section 17 provides for leave of absence during the six-month period prior to discharge where a power of recall applies. If the nearest relative unreasonably objects to admission under s. 3, application can be made for the NR to be displaced (see above).

The section may be renewed for a further period of six months, then 12 months (MHA 1983, s. 20). In *R (S)* v. *Mental Health Review Tribunal* [2004] EWHC 2958 (Admin), detention of a patient who was on leave was renewed to ensure that she continued to attend for weekly treatment.

Longer-term compulsory powers may only be exercised if 'appropriate treatment is available' for the patient. This replaces the treatability test which previously applied and required that treatment was 'likely to alleviate or prevent a deterioration in the patient's condition'. Appropriate treatment for a patient must take into account the nature and degree of the disorder and the person's particular circumstances including cultural, ethnic and religious considerations.

Section 4

Section 4 provides for admission for assessment in an emergency on the application of an AMHP or NR. Its use should be limited to emergencies, where there is insufficient time to get a second medical recommendation; it should not be used for administrative convenience or because it is more convenient for the second doctor to examine the patient in hospital. A doctor who knows the patient, and who should confirm that admission is a matter of urgent necessity, should provide the medical recommendation in these circumstances. An emergency situation is evidenced by: immediate and significant risk of mental or physical harm to the patient or to others; danger of serious harm to property; or the need for physical restraint of the patient (para. 5.6). Detention is authorised for up to 72 hours. Once admitted, a patient should be examined by a second doctor as soon as possible to determine whether the patient should be detained under s. 2.

Section 5

Section 5 provides holding powers under which an inpatient, including a patient receiving treatment for a physical condition, and a person subject to a Deprivation of Liberty authorisation, can be detained by a doctor or nurse. The section cannot be used for outpatients. Part IV of the MHA 1983 (treatment without consent) does not apply where the patient is detained under s. 5.

Where a doctor or approved clinician decides that admission under the MHA 1983 is appropriate, a patient may be detained for up to 72 hours, starting from the hospital manager's receipt of the doctor's report (MHA 1983, s. 5(2)). It is good practice for a second doctor to examine the patient as soon as possible to determine whether the patient should be detained under a section. A nurse whose registration with the Nursing and Midwifery Council indicates that his field of practice is mental health nursing or learning disabilities nursing can exercise a similar power under s. 5(4) to prevent an informal patient leaving the hospital, but the duration is limited to six hours (sufficient time for a doctor or AC to attend and use the s. 5(2) power).

Independent mental health advocacy

Independent mental health advocacy services were introduced in England in 2009. 'Qualifying patients' have a right to advocacy. This term includes patients liable to detention, under ss. 2 and 3 as well as patients subject to guardianship and community treatment orders. Informal patients will be eligible if being considered for a s. 57 treatment (see below) or are under 18 and being considered for **ECT** or s. 58A treatment.

Those with responsibility for the patient, e.g. hospital managers or the local authority in respect of guardianship, must ensure that patients are aware that help is available to them from an independent mental health advocate (**IMHA**). The role of the IMHA is potentially broad; to 'be available to help qualifying patients' under s. 130A(1). This will include helping the patient understand his rights under the Act and the rights of others such as the nearest relative, what statutory powers he is subject to including in relation to treatment and how these may be challenged, supporting the patient to participate in decisions about his care and treatment. In order to exercise the role, s. 130B gives the IMHA power to visit the patient in private, interview medical staff and access medical and social services files. An IMHA must have appropriate experience and training, be of integrity and good character and able to act independently.

Human rights and detention

Aspects of the law relating to detention for reasons of mental illness have been considered in a number of cases before the European Court of Human Rights. Article 5 of the ECHR provides the right not to be deprived of liberty except in specified cases, including (Art. 5 (1)(e)) the lawful detention of persons of unsound mind. The leading case on this article is *Winterwerp* v. *The Netherlands* (1979) 2 EHRR 387, which set down the following minimum conditions for lawful detention of a person of unsound mind:

1. detention must be effected in accordance with a procedure prescribed by law;
2. the individual must clearly be of unsound mind on the basis of objective medical expertise;
3. the mental disorder must be of a kind or degree warranting compulsory confinement; and
4. continued confinement must be based on persistence of the mental disorder.

It has been found that *de facto* detention of informal, incapacitated patients may contravene the first requirement that detention must be in accordance with a procedure prescribed by law. This was precisely the issue argued in *R* v. *Bournewood Community and Mental Health NHS Trust, ex parte L* [1999] 1 AC 458 (reported as *HL* v. *United Kingdom* before the ECtHR).

The fourth *Winterwerp* condition was relevant in the case of *Johnson* v. *United Kingdom* (1999) 27 EHRR 296. J was given a conditional discharge from hospital and a plan was drawn up for after care. Four years later he appealed to the Mental Health Review Tribunal, having continued to be detained, as it had not been possible to find a suitable hostel place for him. He was granted an absolute discharge. It was held that the four-year period of detention constituted an unreasonable delay and a breach of Art. 5(1)(e); and he was awarded £10,000 compensation for unlawful detention.

Informal patients in hospital

The discussion of compulsory powers of admission to hospital actually relates to only a relatively small number of patients in hospital at any one time (though numbers are increasing). The majority of patients have not been detained under a section; they are informal patients, sometimes referred to as 'voluntary patients'. Included in this group are patients with dementia who lack proper understanding of their situation, and others who may be compliant in the face of the 'threat' of formal detention.

A person over the age of 16 can become an informal patient and receive treatment in a hospital, and the informal nature of the admission is given explicit encouragement by the MHA 1983, s. 131:

> ## s. 131
>
> Nothing in this Act shall be construed as preventing a patient who requires treatment for mental disorder from being admitted to any hospital or mental nursing home in pursuance of arrangements made in that behalf and without any application, order or direction rendering him to be liable to be detained under this Act, or from remaining in any hospital or mental nursing home in pursuance of such arrangements after he has ceased to be so liable to be detained.
>
> (MHA 1983)

If an informal patient attempts to leave the hospital, and this is not considered to be in their best interests, steps can be taken to convert the status of the patient to a formally detained patient through use of the holding power (MHA 1983, s. 5). The legal status of informal patients was called into question in the case of *R* v. *Bournewood Community and Mental Health NHS Trust, ex parte L* [1998] 3 All ER 289, which reached the House of Lords.

To recount the facts very briefly: L was an autistic man, aged 48, who was unable to agree to or refuse treatment or give a valid consent to admission to mental hospital. He was admitted to hospital after becoming disruptive at the day centre he attended. His carers were anxious for him to return to their care; however, he remained in hospital as an informal patient. It was argued that he was not detained against his will, as he never made any attempt to leave.

The Court of Appeal found that L was detained unlawfully. The implications of the Court of Appeal decision were that a significant number of patients who would not formerly have been compulsorily detained under the Mental Health Act 1983 would need to be and such an increase, it was noted, would have a significant effect on resources in terms of professionals and mental health services, as well as Mental Health Review Tribunals and the Commission.

Second, the Court of Appeal decision left areas of legal uncertainty. It was not clear whether mental nursing homes with patients such as Mr L in their care would have to become registered to receive patients under the 1983 Act, with the ensuing costs and staffing implications; and whether homes currently operating would be obliged to discharge patients. This could include a number of elderly patients who do not have capacity to consent.

Third, on a more positive note, if patients such as Mr L did have to be compulsorily detained, they would benefit from the safeguards contained in the MHA 1983, the current lack of protection being cited as a concern by the Commission. Again, the resource implications of such an extension were noted.

The House of Lords judgment in *Bournewood* focused on the question of whether L was detained and, if so, was the detention lawful; the interpretation of s. 131; and role of the common law doctrine of necessity. The House considered whether this section applied only to patients who have capacity and do consent to their admission ('voluntary patients') or whether a second group, patients who lack capacity to consent but do not object to their admission ('informal patients' such as L), are also covered. Where patients are admitted as informal patients under s. 131(1) but are unable to consent to treatment or care, the House found that the principle of necessity provides the basis for treatment and care. The case of *F v. West Berkshire Health Authority (Mental Health Act Commission intervening)* [1990] 2 AC 1, which sets out the circumstances when necessity would apply, was referred to in support. Under the principle, patients would receive treatment in their best interests.

The House then considered whether L had been unlawfully detained, as the Court of Appeal had decided. Lord Goff found that as detention has to be actual rather than potential, there was no false imprisonment in L's case. Lord Nolan and Lord Steyn found that L was detained and that the argument advanced that he was free to leave the hospital 'stretches credulity to breaking point',[20] but that the detention was justified by the principle of necessity. Ultimately, the difference between the judgments of the House of Lords and the Court of Appeal can be summarised in terms of the extent to which we should rely on the exercise of professional judgment alone to safeguard the interests of informal patients.

The case proceeded to the European Court of Human Rights and is reported as *HL v. United Kingdom* (2004) 40 EHRR 761. The court found the law as described in the House of Lords judgment incompatible with the European Convention on Human Rights, specifically finding breaches of Art. 5(1): 'Everyone has the right to liberty and security of the person. No one shall be deprived of his liberty save in the following cases and in accordance with procedure prescribed by law: … (e) the lawful detention of persons of unsound mind' and Art. 5(4): 'Everyone who is deprived of his liberty by arrest or detention shall be entitled to take proceedings by which the lawfulness of his detention shall be decided speedily by a court and his release ordered if the detention is not lawful.' The first question the court considered was whether L was detained. It found that the fact that L had not attempted to leave the hospital was irrelevant to Art. 5. The key fact in L's case was that the healthcare professionals had complete and effective control over his care and movements and this amounted to a deprivation of liberty. Secondly, the court considered whether the detention was 'in accordance with a procedure prescribed by law' and lawful under Art. 5(1). The court found that L was 'of unsound mind' and that the common law doctrine of necessity includes the minimum condition for lawful detention of persons of unsound mind. It went on to question whether there were sufficient safeguards to ensure the detention was not arbitrary and here the court was not satisfied: there was no formal admission process, nothing stating the exact purpose of admission, no timescales and no equivalent to the nearest relative. Thirdly, the court continued with consideration of Art. 5(4), and questioned whether L was able to challenge the lawfulness of his detention. In the absence of such an avenue, it found a further breach of human rights. In essence, the lack of procedural safeguards of the doctrine of necessity was the incompatibility.

Following the ECHR judgment, the Mental Health Act 2007 introduced the deprivation of liberty safeguards. As the central issue relates to mental capacity, rather than mental health, the deprivation of liberty safeguards (**DOLS**) provisions are inserted into the Mental Capacity Act 2005 by the Mental Health Act 2007. A supplement to the Mental Capacity Code of Practice has also been produced. At the outset it is clear from the code that deprivation of liberty is to be avoided where possible: 'Every effort should be made, in both commissioning and providing care or treatment, to prevent deprivation of liberty. If deprivation of liberty cannot be avoided, it should be for no longer than is necessary' (p. 10). The relevant provisions provide a system of procedural safeguards which were identified as lacking by the European Court. (The DOLS are considered in Chapter 16.)

Guardianship

Guardianship under the Mental Health Act 1983 provides a limited amount of control and support for patients who remain in the community. It is available only for patients over the age of 16. The criteria for an application are:

> ### s. 7
>
> … he is suffering from mental disorder of a nature or degree which warrants reception into guardianship, and it is necessary in the interests of the welfare of the patient or for the protection of others that the patient be received.
>
> (MHA 1983)

Application is made to the Social Services Department (MHA 1983, s. 11) rather than a hospital and must be accepted by the authority. The application may be made by the AMHP (with agreement of the NR) or the nearest relative and requires the written recommendations of two medical practitioners. The guardian may be either a local Social Services Authority or any other person (with agreement of social services and a statement from the guardian indicating his willingness to act).

The code of practice states that the purpose of guardianship is to enable patients to receive care in the community in those situations where it cannot be provided without compulsion. Paragraph 26.4 states: 'Guardianship … provides an authoritative framework for working with a patient, with a minimum of constraint, to achieve as independent a life as possible within the community. Where it is used it should be part of the person's overall care plan.' There is no treatability requirement.

Any application for guardianship should be accompanied by a comprehensive care plan established on the basis of multi-disciplinary discussions, and guardianship should be used in a positive and flexible manner. The plan should include details of local authority support for the guardian, the patient's accommodation, access to day care, education and training facilities, and the patient's willingness to work with the guardian. The code of practice also suggests that the guardian should be willing to advocate for the patient in relation to services (para. 26.22). There is a potential conflict here if the guardian is social services and is advocating on behalf of the patient for services to be provided by social services.

Powers of the guardian

The guardian acquires the following powers under the MHA 1983, s. 8:

(a) to require the patient to live in a place specified by the guardian;

(b) to require the patient to attend at specified places for medical treatment, occupation, education or training;

(c) to require access to the patient to be given at the place where he is living to any registered medical practitioner, AMHP or other specified person.

Guardianship does not provide authority to detain the patient in the specified place, to remove him from it or convey him to it. If the patient is absent without leave from the specified place, he may be returned within 28 days. Guardianship does not authorise treatment to be given without consent. There are no legal sanctions against a patient who refuses to comply with the guardian's instructions. Despite the apparent statutory limitation on the powers of the guardian, a 1997 case suggests that the courts will adopt a more flexible approach. *R* v. *Kent County Council, ex parte Marston* (unreported, 9 July 1997) stated that guardians have a general implied power to act in the interests of the patient, exercisable in a variety of ways provided the behaviour falls short of totalitarian conduct.

Guardianship may be appropriate as a means of providing support to an individual who has suffered abuse or to some people with a learning disability (provided it falls within the definition of mental impairment or severe mental impairment), providing an element of supervision in the community and avoiding hospital detention. A person who has been detained in hospital may be discharged into guardianship by the hospital managers provided the proposed guardian and social services agree (s. 19).

The responsibilities of the guardian include visiting at least every three months, nominating a doctor for the patient and advising social services of any changes of address, of the death of the patient or his discharge from hospital.[21] The duration of guardianship is initially six months, with possible further renewals for six months then 12 months. It may be terminated at any point by the nearest relative, doctor or Social Services Authority (MHA 1983, s. 23).

Short-term powers

In addition to the compulsory powers of detention outlined above, there are a range of short-term powers, which may be utilised, in some cases prior to formal admission, to gain access to a patient or to remove a patient from a problematic situation.

> ### s. 115
>
> An approved social worker ... may at all reasonable times ... enter and inspect any premises (not being a hospital) ... in which a mentally disordered patient is living, if he has reasonable cause to believe that the patient is not under proper care.
>
> (MHA 1983)

There is no power of removal under s. 115; it would be necessary to apply for a warrant under s. 135 if removal is sought.

> ### s. 135
>
> Where a person suffering from a mental disorder has been or is being ill treated or neglected or kept otherwise than under proper control, or being unable to care for himself, is living alone a magistrate may issue a warrant authorising a police officer to enter, if need be by force, premises and remove him to a place of safety.
>
> (MHA 1983)

This power of removal is for a maximum duration of 72 hours. An AMHP can apply to the court under the section following an attempted investigation under s. 115. A place of safety can be a hospital, Part III accommodation, a mental nursing home or (least preferable) a police station.

These powers may have some relevance to adult safeguarding work where there are concerns for a vulnerable adult who is believed to suffer from a mental disorder.

s. 136

Where a police constable finds a person in a public place who appears to be suffering from a mental disorder, he may remove him to a place of safety. The constable must be of the opinion that the person is in need of care and control and that removal is necessary in that person's interest or for the protection of others.

(MHA 1983)

Detention is limited to 72 hours. Any area to which the public has access is included as a public place, e.g. a shopping centre. Police training clearly needs to encompass awareness and recognition of mental disorder. In *R (Sessay)* v. *South Maudsley NHS Foundation Trust* [2011] EWHC 2617 (Admin) the court confirmed that a public hospital, more specifically its Accident and Emergency Department, is classed as a public place. The case also confirmed that where police officers wish to remove persons who appear mentally disordered to a place of safety, they have jurisdiction to do so under ss. 135 and 136 of the Mental Health Act 1983. Section 5 of the Mental Capacity Act 2005 cannot be used for these purpose.

Rights of patients in hospital

As a minimum, patients in psychiatric hospital have the right to a standard of basic care and accommodation. Successive inquiry reports and research suggest the converse is often true.[22] Conditions on wards are poor and patients' rights are given little credence. The rights provided by the European Convention on Human Rights apply to mental hospitals as to any other setting and the introduction of the HRA 1998 may engender greater awareness of rights and aid development of a rights-based culture in mental health.

The framework for dealing with adult abuse (set out in Chapter 17) applies to adults with mental heath problems and, in particular, the right to be protected from abuse is encapsulated in MHA 1983, s. 127. It is an offence for a manager or member of staff of a hospital or nursing home 'to ill-treat or willfully to neglect a patient … receiving treatment for mental disorder … or subject to guardianship'. The new offence within the Mental Capacity Act 2005 may be used in preference as it is of potentially broader application and carries a heavier penalty. As a recent example, however, members of staff at Winterbourne View Hospital[23] were convicted under s. 127 rather than the MCA offence. (Chapter 17 also sets out a range of sexual offences against people with mental disorder under the Sexual Offences Act 2003.)

As a preliminary point, MHA 1983, s. 132 refers to a detained patient's (CTO patient's) right to be informed of their rights by the hospital managers. Information should be provided in writing relating to: treatment; applications to the Mental Health Review Tribunal;

who has power of discharge; the role of the Mental Health Act Commission; and the basis of detention. The patient should also be informed that they will not be automatically discharged or detained at the end of the period of detention. The same information should be provided to the nearest relative. If the section under which the patient is detained changes, the patient should be provided with the information again.

There are a number of important restrictions on the rights of compulsorily detained patients. These restrictions relate to access to the courts, correspondence, voting rights and treatment.

Treatment

Informal patients are required to give consent to treatment just as any other hospital patient would for a physical injury or illness. Application of this principle can become difficult when the patient's mental disorder is such that he cannot give a legally valid consent. Treatment may be given using the authority of the common law doctrine of necessity. The criteria established by *F* v. *West Berkshire Health Authority* [1989] 2 All ER 545 are that the treatment must be given in the patient's best interests, it must be necessary to save life or prevent a deterioration or ensure improvement in the patient's physical or mental health, and accord with practice accepted by a reasonable body of medical opinion. The framework provided by the Mental Capacity Act 2005 now covers this area.

The situation is different for compulsorily detained patients in respect of treatment for mental disorder, which is generally permitted by the MHA 1983 without consent (s. 63). Treatment has been interpreted broadly, with seclusion accepted as an aspect of treatment (*R (Munjaz)* v. *Mersey Care NHS Trust* [2005] UKHL 58). The remit of s. 63 treatment was considered in *R (B)* v. *Ashworth Hospital Authority* [2005] UKHL 20. Section 63 provides:

> The consent of a patient shall not be required for any medical treatment given to him for the mental disorder from which he is suffering, not being treatment falling within sections 57 and 58 above, if the treatment is given by or under the direction of the approved clinician in charge of treatment.

The point considered was whether the section only permitted treatment for the mental disorder for which the patient was originally detained, or whether it extended to treatment for any mental disorder the patient was suffering from during the period of detention. The House of Lords adopted the broader construction, concluding that a detained patient could be treated for any mental disorder he was suffering from, whether or not he was classified as suffering from such on detention.

Part IV of the Act contains procedural safeguards for specific treatments, including psychosurgery: e.g. a lobotomy, surgical implant of hormones to reduce the male sex drive, electroconvulsive therapy (ECT) and courses of medication after three months. Some treatments require the patient's consent and a second medical opinion (MHA 1983, s. 57: psychosurgery and surgical implant of hormones). Before ECT can be administered or drugs continued beyond an initial three-month period, s. 58 requires the patient's consent or a second medical opinion supporting the need for treatment. This was tested in *R (PS)* v. *Responsible Medical Officer* [2003] EWHC 2335 (Admin).

In that case, the patient (PS) had the capacity to make decisions on treatment, did not wish to have the proposed treatment (anti-psychotic medication), argued that his personal choice to refuse treatment should be respected and that to treat him under s. 58 on the basis of a second medical treatment amounted to an infringement of his Art. 3 and Art. 8 rights. The court refused the application for judicial review, and held that administration of the treatment was not an infringement of his rights under Art. 3 and Art. 8. Article 3 was contravened if the proposed treatment reached the minimum level of severity of ill treatment, applied, and the medical necessity for the treatment was not shown. Given the possible benefits to PS and the limited adverse consequences, the administration of the treatment to him did not reach the threshold. His rights under Art. 8 would not be infringed if the proposed treatment was justified under Art. 8(2) as being in the patient's best interests. This was satisfied by the evidence of the responsible medical officer and the doctor and was necessary for the protection of his health and the safety of others.

New safeguards for ECT were introduced by the 2007 Act. Other than in an emergency situation, ECT cannot be given to a patient who has capacity to refuse to consent. For a person who lacks capacity to consent, the treatment can only be given where it does not conflict with any advance directive, decision of a second opinion appointed doctor, or a deputy, or decision of the Court of Protection. (See Chapter 16 for further explanation of capacity, advance directives, the role of deputies and the Court of Protection.)

The safeguards provided by ss. 57 and 58 are disregarded if treatment is needed urgently under s. 62. This will be the case if the treatment is immediately necessary to save life, stop the patient's condition seriously deteriorating, reduce serious suffering, or prevent the patient from behaving violently and being a danger to himself or to others. Complaints about treatment given without consent may be directed to the Care Quality Commission.

The above rules apply to treatment of mental disorder for compulsorily detained patients. Treatment for physical conditions cannot be given to a compulsorily detained patient without their consent, unless the patient lacks capacity to consent and the doctrine of necessity applies. Here it is important to remember that mental disorder and mental capacity are not one and the same. This was clearly illustrated in the case of *Re C (Adult: Refusal of Medical Treatment)* [1994] 1 All ER 819. C was 68 and suffered from paranoid schizophrenia. Against medical advice he refused to have his gangrenous leg amputated. The decision-making process was broken down into three stages: comprehending and retaining information; believing it; and weighing it in the balance to arrive at a choice. Regardless of his mental health problems, C was found to have the capacity to make a decision and refuse the amputation.

Voting rights

Patients who are compulsorily detained by a criminal court have no right to vote. The European Court of Human Rights has ruled that the UK blanket ban on prisoners' voting rights is contrary to the European Convention on Human Rights (*Hirst* v. *the United Kingdom (No. 2)* [2005] ECHR 681, confirmed in *R (Chester)* v. *Secretary of State for Justice* [2013] UKSC 63), but the Government has yet to act to remedy the contravention. Under the Representation of the People Act 2000, all other patients, informal and detained, are entitled to be registered to vote in local and parliamentary elections.[24]

Correspondence

Informal patients may send and receive correspondence without interference. Compulsorily detained patients may receive post, but hospital managers may confiscate any post sent to a person who has asked not to receive any post from the patient. Where a patient is detained in one of the special hospitals, e.g. Broadmoor, his post may be withheld if it is in the interests of safety of the patient or for the protection of others. The patient may be prevented from sending correspondence to a person who has notified the manager or if it is likely to cause distress or danger. Telephone calls of dangerous patients may be monitored: this was considered not a breach of Art. 8 in *R (N)* v. *Ashworth Special Hospital Authority* [2001] EWHC Admin 339.

Visits

Detained patients enjoy the basic right to be visited by friends and relatives and the code of practice recognises that this is an important element of the patient's treatment and rehabilitation (para. 26.1). It is possible to exclude visitors on two grounds:

1. Clinical reasons, i.e. where the visit would be anti-therapeutic and could cause deterioration in the patient's mental health. In some cases the safety of the visitor may be the major concern.
2. Security restrictions, i.e. where the visitor has behaved in a way that is disruptive: e.g. bringing in alcohol or drugs or encouraging the patient to abscond.

Separate policies exist in most hospitals about visits by children and the emphasis will be whether the visit is in the child's best interests.[25] The case of *R (ML)* v. *Secretary of State for the Department of Health* (2000) 4 CCLR 59 unsuccessfully challenged guidance (HSC 1999/160) that restricts visits by children to offenders in special hospitals. Visits will be restricted unless the patient is the parent or relative of the child, had parental responsibility or the child was treated as a member of the patient's household.

Legal proceedings

A compulsorily detained patient cannot take legal action in respect of the exercise of Mental Health Act powers, e.g. by a doctor or approved social worker, without obtaining prior permission from the High Court (MHA 1983, s. 139).

Discharge

As a general principle, a patient should be discharged from hospital as soon as he is found not to be suffering from a mental disorder. Section 23 provides that the responsible clinician, the hospital managers or the nearest relative hold the power of discharge. There are, however, some restrictions on the power held by the nearest relative. The nearest relative must give the hospital 72 hours' notice of intention to discharge the patient. The hospital may prevent this discharge if they do not agree with the nearest relative's proposal and are concerned that if discharged the patient would be a danger to himself or others (MHA 1983, s. 25). This action also prevents the nearest relative making any further attempts to discharge the patient within the next six months. The AMHP can also prevent the nearest relative from acting by making an application to the county court to displace the nearest relative (MHA 1983, s. 29, outlined above).

The informal patient may discharge himself at any point, though detention (probably under MHA 1983, s. 5) can prevent this.

Following discharge, it is possible for a fresh compulsory admission to be made as confirmed by the House of Lords in *R (von Brandenburg (aka Hanley))* v. *East London and the City*

Mental Health NHS Trust [2003] UKHL 58. To avoid a breach of Art. 5 there must be some change in circumstances since the tribunal discharged the patient. This would include the emergence of new information not known to the tribunal.

Mental Health Review Tribunal

The Tribunals, Courts and Enforcement Act 2007 establishes a new system for tribunals (of every nature) comprising a First Tier Tribunal and an Upper Tribunal. Mental health applications will be made to the Health Education and Social Care Chamber of the First Tier. The role of the tribunal is to decide whether at the time of the hearing, the patient should remain subject to the relevant compulsory powers, e.g. s. 3 detention or SCT.

The patient or the nearest relative can also apply to the tribunal for discharge. Hospital staff should ensure the patient is aware of the right to apply for discharge. There are strict time limits within which applications can be submitted (MHA 1983, ss. 66 and 68). The patient can apply for discharge from a s. 2 admission within 14 days (i.e. half way through the period of detention), and for discharge from guardianship or admission for treatment the patient may make an application within the first six months, then once in each renewal period. If, by the end of six months, no application is made, the hospital managers will automatically refer the case to the tribunal. There are also automatic reviews of detention by the tribunal if a long-term patient does not exercise the right to apply to the tribunal. This was introduced because many long-term patients never applied to the tribunal. If a patient detained under s. 3 does not apply to the tribunal within the first six months, the hospital manager must refer his case. If a patient subject to CTO has not been considered by the tribunal for three years or more there is an automatic referral.

The tribunal proceedings are quite formal and a specialist mental health solicitor will normally represent the patient. The panel includes a legal, medical and lay member. A social work report (and other reports such as the registered clinician's) will be submitted to the tribunal. The report should outline the circumstances leading to admission and the current situation. Tribunal rules also require the report writer to consider: the financial circumstances of the patient; the patient's home and family circumstances; the opportunities for employment or occupation and housing which would be available if the patient is discharged; the availability of community support; and medical facilities. The tribunal has no jurisdiction to determine whether the original basis for detention was established. Its role is to consider whether continued detention is justified. The tribunal may also reclassify the type of mental disorder the patient is suffering from. As far as practicable, a medical examination of the patient should take place before the hearing. Hearings are usually held in private, although the tribunal can hold a public hearing if it considers it is in the interests of justice to do so.

The provisions detailing criteria for discharge from hospital detention by the Mental Health Review Tribunal are contained in ss. 72 and 73 of the MHA 1983. The original wording of these sections presented a 'double negative' test and was declared incompatible with the European Convention on Human Rights (Art. 5(4)) in the case of *R (H)* v. *London North and East Region Mental Health Review Tribunal (Secretary of State for Health intervening)* [2001] EWCA Civ 415[26] and a remedial order was made. The burden now rests on the hospital to satisfy the tribunal of the need for continued use of compulsory powers.

R *(AN)* v. *Mental Health Review Tribunal (Northern Region)* [2005] EWCA Civ 1605 has confirmed that the standard of proof in Mental Health Tribunals is the civil standard, balance of probabilities. The patient's application for discharge under s. 73 was rejected by the tribunal. On appeal, Munby J rejected the patient's argument that the criminal standard should apply. He stated that the civil standard applies to the tribunal's consideration of whether the patient is suffering from a mental disorder. The other elements of the detention criteria, nature or degree of the mental disorder and health and safety of the patient and others were matters of evaluation of judgment, not fact, and the standard of proof is therefore not relevant to them.

Article 5(4) of the ECHR provides: 'everyone who is deprived of his liberty ... shall be entitled to take proceedings by which the lawfulness of his detention shall be decided speedily by a court and his release ordered if detention is not lawful'. The opportunity to challenge the lawfulness of detention currently applies only to detained patients (as discussed above in *Bournewood*). Guidance on the application of this Article was provided in the earlier decision, *Megyeri* v. *Federal Republic of Germany* (1993) 15 EHRR 584. According to this case, patients should enjoy the following rights:

- Detained patients are entitled to take court proceedings at 'reasonable intervals'.
- The procedure must have a judicial character and provide guarantees appropriate to the deprivation.
- Patients should have access to a court and the opportunity to be heard in person or when necessary by legal representation.
- Patients cannot be required to take the initiative in obtaining legal representation before having recourse to a court.
- Patients should receive legal representation.

It is necessary to ensure that individual applications are heard as soon as reasonably practicable given the relevant circumstances of the case and within a maximum target of eight weeks.

After-care

> ## s. 117
>
> It is the duty of the [District Health Authority and Social Services Authority] to provide, in co-operation with relevant voluntary agencies, after-care services ... until such time as ... the person concerned is no longer in need of such services.
>
> (MHA 1983)

This provision applies where a person has been the subject of a guardianship or treatment order. It does not apply where a person was detained under s. 2 for assessment or following a period in hospital, however lengthy, without compulsion (voluntary or informal admission). It is a free-standing, independent legal duty jointly imposed on the local and health authority. The duty continues until the health authority and local authority jointly agree that services are no longer needed by way of after-care. As the duty is joint, health authorities can be asked to pay for half of any after-care package. A person in receipt of after-care services will also be entitled to the highest rate of income support. After-care is not defined in the Act, but according to case law it includes social work support in helping the ex-patient with problems of employment, accommodation or family relationships, the provision of domiciliary services and the use of day care and residential facilities (*Clunis* v. *Camden and Islington Health Authority* [1998] 3 All ER 180 at 225). If residential services are provided under s. 117, they should be funded, regardless of the individual's financial status.

The patient is under no obligation to accept after-care and has the legal right to refuse. The status of the s. 117 provision was considered in the case of *R* v. *Manchester City Council, ex parte Stennett; R* v. *Redcar and Cleveland Borough Council, ex parte Armstrong; R* v. *Harrow London Borough Council, ex parte Cobham* [2002] UKHL 34. There were four applications for judicial review based on similar facts. In each case the issue concerned whether each of the respondent Social Services Authorities could charge for residential accommodation provided as after-care services under the Mental Health Act 1983, s. 117. Each of the applicants had been detained in hospital under MHA 1983, s. 3. Upon discharge from hospital they had been provided with residential accommodation by the Social Services Authority. Evidence provided to the court showed that around half of all Social Services Authorities made a charge for residential accommodation provided pursuant to s. 117. It was also submitted that if authorities did not charge, this would impose a cost of over £50 million. The arguments raised were based around differing interpretations of s. 117. It was agreed that residential accommodation was included in the term 'after-care services' and also that s. 117 did not directly confer a power to charge the recipient. The authorities did argue, however, that s. 117 should be seen as a 'gateway' section, imposing a duty on authorities to ensure that after-care services were provided under other legislation. This would include s. 21 of the National Assistance Act 1948, which permits authorities to provide and recover the costs of residential accommodation.

The court concluded that the wording of s. 117 was clear. It did not impose a duty to secure provision of services under other legislation; it was a 'free-standing' duty to provide after-care services. It was therefore not possible to charge for the services by relying on s. 22 of the National Assistance Act 1948. A local government ombudsman decision applied this ruling in *Investigation into Complaint No. 98/B/0341 against Wiltshire CC* (2000) 3 CCLR 60. The local authority were ordered to repay several years' worth of charges made unlawfully for residential accommodation provided under MHA 1983, s. 117. Disputes about which local authority might be responsible for an individual's after care are not uncommon. *R (M)* v. *Hammersmith and Fulham LBC* [2010] EWHC 562 (Admin) rules that the costs of accommodation and after-care should be met by the local authority where the individual was resident or to which they were discharged by the hospital.

Supervised community treatment

Supervised community treatment (SCT) was introduced by the MHA 2007 and replaced the former scheme of supervised discharge (or after-care under supervision). It is the latest attempt to address the 'revolving door' situation where some patients are regularly returning to hospital because they do not maintain their treatment in the community. The intention is to support patients to live in the community following a period of detention while subject to certain conditions and liable to recall if necessary. Supervised discharge will only be available for patients who have been detained for treatment, i.e. under s. 3, not following short-term detention for assessment. As supervised community treatment follows s. 3 detention, the patient will also be entitled to s. 117 support.

A community treatment order (CTO) will be made by the responsible clinician (RC, formerly the RMO) in respect of the patient. An AMHP will have to agree that SCT is appropriate. Section 17A(5) details the criteria for a CTO to be made:

(a) the patient is suffering from mental disorder of a nature or degree which makes it appropriate for him to receive medical treatment;

(b) it is necessary for his health or safety or for the protection of others that he should receive treatment;

(c) subject to his being liable to recall, such treatment can be provided without him being detained in hospital;

(d) it is necessary that the RC should be able to exercise the power to recall the patient to hospital;

(e) appropriate treatment is available for him.

The patient will be subject to conditions relating to their individual circumstances to ensure that the patient receives treatment whilst in the community. All patients must make themselves available for examination by the RC for the purpose of extending the CTO and for examination for the purpose of the consent to treatment provisions. Other discretionary conditions may be set by the RC with the agreement of the AMHP to ensure the patient receives treatment, to prevent risk of harm to the patient or to protect others, e.g. where the patient lives, when and where he will recieve treatment.

A CTO will initially run for six months. It can be extended for a further six months, then yearly. If a patient is recalled to hospital by the RC, there are 72 hours in which to provide treatment and allow the patient to leave, or revoke the order and detain under s. 3, or discharge the CTO.

Leave of absence

A responsible clinician can grant leave of absence, under s. 17, to a patient who is subject to a s. 2, 3 or 4 detention. It can be for a specific period of time or indefinite. The patient remains liable to be detained during the leave of absence and specific conditions can be attached to the leave. It can provide a means to a phased discharge.

Children and young people and mental health

The Mental Health Act 1983 also applies to children and young people, with the exceptions that a guardianship order can be made only from the age of 16 and the after-care provisions do not apply. The criteria for formal detention in hospital are the same for children and adults regardless of age.

If it is considered appropriate for a child to be admitted to hospital, this may be arranged informally provided there is parental consent. A young person of 16 or 17 years of age can give their own consent, as can younger children who are *Gillick* competent. Where a child is an informal patient, after three months the health authority must formally notify the local authority and the local authority must investigate to ensure that the welfare of the child does not require its intervention (CA 1989, s. 85). If neither the child nor the parents consent, as a last resort formal detention under the MHA 1983 may be appropriate. Use of the MHA 1983 provides the same safeguards for children as for adults, including recourse to the MHRT. Where there is a care order in force, the local authority can admit a child to hospital.[27] For children and young people who are not *Gillick* competent, parents can also consent to medical treatment, including treatment for mental disorder.

The law includes a requirement for age appropriate services. Hospital managers must ensure that patients under 18 admitted to hospital for mental disorder must be accommodated in an environment suitable for their age.

In addition to the MHA 1983, provisions of the Children Act 1989 may apply. It is arguable that the CA 1989 does not carry the same stigma as the MHA 1983. If proceedings are commenced in respect of the child, there is the advantage that a children's guardian will be appointed. There is no similar provision for independent representation of the child under the MHA 1983. A child may have mental health difficulties such that he would benefit from psychiatric intervention but does not fall within the MHA 1983 definition of mental disorder. Such a child may be within the definition of a 'child in need' (CA 1989, s. 17), and be eligible for support for the child and his family. Research suggests that there is a strong link between family income and the mental health of children, with children of families in Social Class 5 being three times more likely to have mental health problems than children of families in Social Class 1.[28] It is essential that consideration is given to mental health needs in any child assessment, whether it leads to service input or formal intervention. Services and professionals that may be particularly relevant include the specialist Child and Adolescent Mental Health Service (**CAMHS**), primary child mental health workers, school health services, health visitors and advocacy services. As an alternative to formal detention, it is possible for a child to be accommodated by the local authority with parental consent (CA 1989, s. 20). Particular treatment issues may be dealt with by specific issue orders (s. 8) or in the High Court through the exercise of the inherent jurisdiction where a declaration is sought.

The mental health of a child is clearly an aspect of emotional and behavioural development and it is possible that concerns relating to this aspect of development could lead to formal intervention to seek a care order. It is not unusual for psychologists and psychiatric services to work with children and families, carrying out assessments sometimes leading to the provision of reports to court. Recent research into the implementation of the CA 1989 found, however, that '[a] serious impediment to joint working for children with mental health problems was the absence of therapeutic or mental health services for children and young people'.[29] This is being addressed in part by the Department of Health strategy to improve provision of CAMHS (training and staffing levels), and liaison between CAMHS, primary care and social services.[30]

Criminal proceedings affecting those with mental illness

(Chapter 18 includes discussion of the special position of those with mental health problems who are involved in criminal proceedings.) It is appropriate here to note that in addition to the use of sections under the MHA 1983, an individual may be formally detained via the criminal justice system. A court can make a hospital order or guardianship order at the time of sentence. In addition, a prisoner may be transferred to a psychiatric hospital.

The Mental Health Act 1983 is a complex piece of legislation. Table 15.2 provides an outline of the structure of the Act and summarises the main provisions discussed in this chapter.

Table 15.2 Summary of key provisions of the Mental Health Act 1983

Part I Application of the MHA 1983	s. 1 'mental disorder'
Part II Compulsory admission to hospital and guardianship	s. 2 Assessment s. 3 Admission for treatment s. 4 Emergency admission s. 5 Patient already in hospital ss. 7 and 8 Guardianship s. 13 Duty of AMHP to make applications s. 17 Leave of absence s.17A–G Community treatment orders s. 23 Discharge of patients s. 26 Definition of nearest relative s. 29 Displacement of nearest relative
Part III Patients involved in criminal	s. 37 Power of court to order hospital admission or proceedings or under sentence guardianship s. 41 Restriction orders (see Chapter 18)
Part IV Consent to treatment	s. 57 Treatment requiring consent and a second opinion s. 58 Treatment requiring consent or a second opinion s. 58A ECT s. 62 Urgent treatment
Part V Mental Health Review Tribunals	s. 66 Application to tribunals s. 68 Duty of hospital managers to refer cases to tribunal s. 72 Power to discharge patients
Part VI Removal and return of patients within United Kingdom	
Part VII Management of property and affairs of patients	Repealed by Mental Capacity Act 2005
Part VIII Miscellaneous functions of local authorities and the Secretary of State	s. 114 Appointment of approved mental health professionals s. 115 Power of entry and inspection s. 117 After care s. 121 Mental Health Act Commission
Part IX Offences	s. 127 Ill-treatment of patients
Part X Miscellaneous and supplementary	s. 131 Informal admission of patients s. 132 Duty to give information to detained patients s. 135 Warrant to search for and remove patients s. 136 Mentally disordered persons found in public places

Chapter summary

- Mental health is a complex area of social work practice covered by the Mental Health Act 1983 and a code of practice. All social workers require a basic understanding of the Act but many specific functions are vested in a specialist worker, an approved mental health professional (AMHP).

- The MHA 1983 defines mental disorder and provides a range of short-term and longer-term orders to detain a patient in hospital.

- The majority of people with mental health problems live in the community, possibly with the support of a guardianship order, or a community treatment order, but some will receive care and treatment in hospital either as an informal patient or detained under a section.

- Whilst in hospital there are a number of restrictions on the rights of detained patients and particular provisions relating to compulsory treatment.

- A patient may be discharged at an appropriate time by his nearest relative or at the behest of the hospital or by order of the Mental Health Review Tribunal.

- On discharge, after-care services should be provided to a patient who has been detained long term.

- Mental incapacity is often confused with mental disorder but it is a distinct issue addressed by the Mental Capacity Act 2005 (see Chapter 16).

Exercises

1. George, aged 47, is susceptible to periods of depression and self-harming. He has been admitted to the local psychiatric hospital on a voluntary basis a number of times over the years. He recently lost his job, became depressed, stopped taking his medication and started to drink heavily. He refused to go back into hospital on a voluntary basis and has been detained for five months. His only relative, a sister whom he sees infrequently, has contacted the hospital and insists that George should be allowed home. His living accommodation is very poor and he has very few links in the community. He would also like to be discharged. The hospital are concerned that if discharged he will fail to take his medication and may start to self-harm again.

   Consider any options that would enable George to return safely to the community.

2. Jonathan, aged 33, has a history of manic depression and has received treatment in the past as a compulsorily detained patient. He lives with his mother, who is diagnosed as suffering from schizophrenia and regularly fails to take her medication. Jonathan is found in the town shopping centre, dressed in pyjamas and acting in a bizarre fashion, shouting at passers-by and threatening to throw himself off a balcony. The police are called and take him to the hospital. An approved mental health professional with no previous knowledge of Jonathan is called to the hospital and met by a consultant psychiatrist who instructs the AMHP to do the necessary paperwork, saying that the only way forward for Jonathan is a course of ECT. At the same time, Jonathan's mother appears and insists that if he comes home she will take care of him.

   Consider the steps the AMHP could take.

Websites

Mind – a national charity with over 200 regional offices:
www.mind.org.uk

Mental Health Foundation:
www.mentalhealth.org.uk

Mencap – the organisation which campaigns for equal rights for children and adults with a learning disability:
www.mencap.org.uk

Young Minds – a charity focusing on children's mental health:
www.youngminds.org.uk

Further reading

Texts which provide more in-depth coverage of mental health law include:

Bartlett, P. and Sandland, R. (2014) *Mental Health Law Policy and Practice*. London: Blackstone Press.
Brown, R. *et al.* (2005) *Mental Health Law*. London: Hodder Arnold.
Fennell, P. (2011) *Mental Health: Law and Practice*. Bristol: Jordan Publishing.
Hale, B. (2012) *Mental Health Law*. London: Sweet & Maxwell.
Jones, R. (2013) *Mental Health Act Manual*. London: Sweet & Maxwell. (A detailed reference source.)

Texts with an emphasis on social work practice in mental health:

Barber, P., Brown, R. and Martin, D. (2009) *Mental Health Law in England and Wales: A Guide for Mental Health Professionals*. Exeter: Learning Matters. (This text includes a copy of the 1983 Act, as amended by the 2007 Act.)
Brown, R. (2006) *The Approved Social Worker's Guide to Mental Health Law*. Exeter: Learning Matters.
Golightley, M. (2006) *Social Work and Mental Health* (2nd edn). Exeter: Learning Matters.

Issues within the current law are discussed in:

Hatfield, B. and Antcliff, V. (2001) 'Detention under the Mental Health Act: balancing rights, risks and needs for services' 23(2) *Journal of Social Welfare and Family Law* pp. 135–53.
Herring, J. (2009) 'Losing it? Losing what? The law and dementia' 21(1) *Child and Family, Law Quarterly* p. 3.
Richardson, G. (2002) 'Autonomy, guardianship and mental disorder: one problem, two solutions' 65(5) *Modern Law Review* pp. 702–23.

A number of articles offer a critique of aspects of the reform proposals:

Cavadino, M. (2002) 'New mental health law for old: safety-plus equals human rights minus' 14(2) *Child and Family Law Quarterly* p. 75.
Eldergill, A. (2002) 'Is anyone safe? Civil compulsion under the Draft Mental Health Bill' 8 *Journal of Mental Health Law* p. 331.
Rapaport, J. (2004) 'A matter of principle: the Nearest Relative under the Mental Health Act 1983 and proposals for legislative reform' 26(4) *Journal of Social Welfare and Family Law* p. 377.

Children and young people are considered in:

Darlington, Y., Feeney, J. A. and Rixon, K. (2005) 'Practice challenges at the intersection of child protection and mental health' 10(3) *Child and Family Social Work* p. 239.

Harbour, A. (2008) *Children with Mental Disorder and the Law.* London: Jessica Kingsley Publishers

Kay, H. (1999) *Bright Futures – Promoting Children and Young People's Mental Health.* London: The Mental Health Foundation.

Walker, S. (2003) *Social Work and Child and Adolescent Mental Health.* Dorset: Russell House.

Application of the Human Rights Act 1998 to mental health is the subject of two useful articles:

Hale, B. (2005) 'What can the Human Rights Act 1998 do for my mental health?' 17(3) *Child and Family Law Quarterly* p. 295.

Johns, R. (2004) 'Of unsound mind? Mental health and the European Convention on Human Rights' 16(4) *Practice* p. 247.

Notes

1 Christopher Clunis killed Jonathan Zito shortly after release from detention in a mental hospital. Subsequently, in *Clunis* v. *Camden and Islington Health Authority* [1998] 2 WLR 902, it was held that Clunis had no cause of action against the health authority regarding provision of after-care when he killed shortly after discharge. To provide otherwise would allow him to profit from his own wrong and the case was struck out by the Court of Appeal as against public policy.

2 Secretary of State for Health (1999) 'Reform of the Mental Health Act 1983: Proposals for Consultation' (Cm. 4480). London: The Stationery Office.

3 P. Taylor and J. Gunn (1999) 'Homicides by people with mental illness: myth and reality' 174 *British Journal of Psychiatry* pp. 9–14.

4 Mental Health Bills published in 2002 and 2004 attracted a high level of criticism from practitioners from a wide range of backgrounds and organisations, academics and pressure groups. The Mental Health Alliance was formed as a coalition of charities, such as MIND, user and carer groups and professional bodies, and argued that many of the provisions in these earlier Bills were based on over-reliance on misguided notions of the dangerousness of mental health sufferers. These Bills were abandoned and the final Bill, which became the 2007 Act, was much shorter, though it does still include some of the more controversial measures campaigned against, notably supervised treatment in the community.

5 Department of Health (2011) 'No Health Without Mental Health: A cross government mental health strategy for people of all ages'. London: Department of Health.

6 See D. Browne (1995) 'Sectioning: the black experience' in S. Fernando (ed.) *Mental Health in a Multi-Ethnic Society: A Multi-Disciplinary Handbook.* London: Routledge.

7 'Count me in. Results of a national census of inpatients in mental health hospitals and facilities in England and Wales'. London: Commission for Healthcare Audit and Inspection. The census day was 31 March 2005.

8 '... (2) In this Act – "mental disorder" means mental illness, an arrested or incomplete development of mind, psychopathic disorder and any other disorder or disability of mind; "severe mental impairment" means a state of arrested or incomplete development of mind which includes severe impairment of intelligence and social functioning and is

associated with abnormally aggressive or seriously irresponsible conduct on the part of the person concerned; "mental impairment" means a state of arrested or incomplete development of mind (not amounting to severe mental impairment) which includes significant impairment of intelligence and social functioning and is associated with abnormally aggressive or seriously irresponsible conduct on the part of the person concerned; "psychopathic disorder" means a persistent disorder or disability of mind (whether or not including significant impairment of intelligence) which results in abnormally aggressive or seriously irresponsible conduct on the part of the person concerned. (3) Nothing in subsection (2) above shall be construed as implying that a person may be dealt with under this Act as suffering from mental disorder, by reason only of promiscuity or other immoral conduct, sexual deviancy or dependence on alcohol or drugs.'

[9] P. Fennell (1989) 'The Beverley Lewis case: was the law to blame?' 139 *New Law Journal* pp. 1557–8.

[10] Mental Health (Approved Mental Health Professionals) (Approval) (England) Regulations 2008 (SI 2008/1206), reg. 3.

[11] J. Campbell, G. Wilson, F. Britton, B. Hamilton, P. Hughes and R. Manktelow (2001) 'The management and supervision of approved social workers: aspects of law, policy and practice' 23(2) *Journal of Social Welfare and Family Law* pp. 155–72.

[12] P. Huxley, S. Evans, M. Webber and C. Gately (2005) 'Staff shortages in the mental health workforce: the case of the disappearing approved social worker' 13(6) *Health and Social Care in the Community* p. 504.

[13] See also W. K. Fakhoury and D. Wright (2004) 'A National Survey of Approved Social Workers in the UK: information, communication and training needs' 34(5) *British Journal of Social Work* p. 663.

[14] See DoH (2008) 'Support, Time and Recovery (STR) workers: A Competence Framework, Best Practice Guidance', for a detailed breakdown of the core tasks of the STR role. London: Department of Health.

[15] Department of Health (2003) 'Mental Health Policy Implementaton Guide: Support, Time and Recovery (STR) Workers'. London: Department of Health.

[16] The report of the Workforce Action Team may be obtained from: www.doh.gov.uk/mentalhealth/wat.htm#report.

[17] The five-year residence rule would include carers who have fostered a mentally disordered person under an adult placement scheme.

[18] Mental Health (Hospital, Guardianship and Consent to Treatment) Regulations 1983 (SI 1983/893), reg. 24.

[19] For a discussion of the differences between admission under s. 2 or s. 3, see B. Hatfield and V. Antcliff (2001) 'Detention under the Mental Health Act: balancing rights, risks and needs for services' 23(2) *Journal of Social Welfare and Family Law* pp. 135–53.

[20] See p. 306 of the judgment.

[21] Mental Health (Hospital, Guardianship and Consent to Treatment) Regulations 1983 (SI 1983/893).

[22] N. Stanley and J. Manthorpe (2001) 'Reading mental health inquiries' 1(1) *Journal of Social Work* p. 77.

[23] M. Flynn and V. Citarella (2012) *Winterbourne View Hospital: A Serious Case Review*, Bristol: South Gloucestershire Council on Behalf of South Gloucestershire Safeguarding Adults Board.

[24] Section 5 of the Representation of the People Act 2000 amends the Representation of the People Act 1983, inserting new ss. 3A, 7 and 7A.

[25] See 'Guidance to Local Authority Social Services Departments on Visits by Children to Special Hospitals' (LAC (99) 23); 'Visits by Children to Ashworth, Broadmoor and Rampton

Hospital Authorities Directions' (HSC 1999/160); and 'Mental Health Act 1983 Code of Practice: Guidance on the visiting of psychiatric patients by children' (HSC 1999/222, LAC (99) 32).

26 The first remedial order to be laid before Parliament is to amend ss. 72(1) and 72(3) as declared incompatible with the European Convention: Mental Health Act 1983 (Remedial) Order, laid July 2001.

27 *R* v. *Kirklees Metropolitan Borough Council, ex parte C (A Minor)* [1993] 2 FLR 187.

28 Office of National Statistics (1999) 'Mental Health of Children and Adolescents' (Monograph series (99) 409) cited in Department of Health, Department for Education and Employment, Home Office (2000) 'Framework for the Assessment of Children in Need and their Families'. London: The Stationery Office.

29 Department of Health (2001) *The Children Act Now: Messages from Research.* London: The Stationery Office, p. 106.

30 National Priorities Guidance for Health and Social Services 1999/2002, cited in Secretary of State for Health, Secretary of State for Education and Employment and the Lord Chancellor (2000) 'The Children Act Report 1995–1999' (Cm. 4579). London: The Stationery Office.

Chapter 16

Mental capacity

Learning objectives

To develop an understanding of the following:

- The law on mental capacity as provided by the Mental Capacity Act 2005.
- The meaning of 'capacity'.
- Who can assess capacity.
- The use of High Court declarations and the doctrine of necessity.
- Guiding principles of the Act including 'best interests'.
- Means of delegating decision-making, including the new Lasting Power of Attorney and Advance decisions.
- Deprivation of Liberty Safeguards (DOLS).
- The role of the Court of Protection.
- The roles of independent mental capacity advocate, deputy and Court of Protection visitor.

> ## Talking Point
>
> This article appeared in the *Daily Mail* on 14 December 2007.
>
> A care home boss was facing jail today after he admitted locking three vulnerable residents in his car while he went to a betting shop – for THREE hours. Callous Chris Williams, 43, and his employee Agnes Price, 41, left the three special needs patients in a 'distressed state' and desperate to get out, a court heard. The three men – aged 25, 45 and 56 – are all unable to speak and have varying levels of learning difficulties, including Down's Syndrome and autism. District Judge Mike Layman told the carers they face jail after they were prosecuted under the new Mental Capacity Act 2005 that came into force this year. They each pleaded guilty to three charges of wilful neglect of a person without capacity and will be sentenced at Swindon Crown Court at date to be fixed. The court heard they were seen entering a nearby bookmaker's in Swindon at 1 pm on September 6 after parking their people carrier nearby. Nearly three hours later the police received an anonymous tip-off from a member of the public that three men were shut in a car and distressed. Paula Mulherne, prosecuting, said the caller could see the vehicle's windows were steamed up, and the men inside were shouting, pushing each other and grabbing at the doors. She said: 'A police officer forced entry on arrival and felt a wave of heat from the van…Each of these men is vulnerable in their own right, but the danger of harm to all three of them together is even more concerning'. Police arrived and released the three from the car, where passers-by fetched water for the men and helped calm them down. Officers tracked down Williams and Price, who run Whitman Street Residential Home, where they claim to have 'lost track of time'. Mrs Mulherne added: 'Neither accepted that they had wilfully neglected the men, although Miss Price said it was not professional behaviour'. Williams claimed he thought a window was open and he left music on, but he accepted the patients were locked in through the use of childlocks.
>
> The Mental Capacity Act 2005 introduces a range of measures in relation to adults who lack capacity. One of which is a new offence, discussed below. This tabloid report provides a vivid example of a prosecution under the new offence arising from clearly unacceptable care of three men.

Introduction

The question of mental capacity is especially important when considering whether a person can legally make a particular decision. This is an area of law which originally developed largely through common law principles but is now covered by legislation, the Mental Capacity Act 2005.

There were significant gaps in the old law and the chapter includes a brief discussion of how the courts attempted to fill some of those gaps with declaratory relief. The reasoning of the courts in those decisions will continue to be relevant to courts making decisions under the new Act. Legally and ethically, uncertainty in the law has made this a complex area in which to practise. A further challenge is understanding the relationship between mental incapacity and mental disorder. (Chapter 15 includes extracts from the Mental Health Act Code of Practice, which explore the interface between the two areas.)

The Mental Capacity Act 2005, establishes a much clearer framework for decision-making, provides a universal test of capacity and aims to promote empowerment of vulnerable adults by encouraging first-hand decision-making wherever possible. This chapter provides some background to the previous common law-based framework, then continues to focus on the Mental Capacity Act.

Capacity and decision-making before the Act

The starting point in English law, for adults, has always been a presumption of capacity. In other words, adults are presumed to be autonomous beings able to make their own decisions. This presumption may be rebutted by evidence of incapacity. Whether X has capacity is a legal question, but medical evidence may be helpful to establish the level of capacity, whether it is permanent or transient and whether it is affected by external factors such as drugs or bereavement.

Capacity is not a fixed concept. The capacity required depends on the nature of the decision to be made, e.g. to vote, marry or execute a will. The level of capacity required to manage substantial property and financial affairs may thus be greater than the capacity required to exercise choice over a minor medical procedure. A person may thus have the capacity to make some decisions but not others. *Masterman-Lister* v. *Brutton & Co; Masterman-Lister* v. *Jewell* [2002] EWCA Civ 1889 confirmed that the test of capacity is specific to the issue in question. It follows that no one should be regarded as legally incapable in the total sense. The common law test of capacity is essentially in two parts: the individual must be capable of understanding what is proposed and its implications, and must be able to exercise choice. These principles have largely been incorporated into the new statutory framework.

Difficulties can arise where a person does not have capacity. If X cannot make the decision, who can? Options for delegating decision-making before the Act were limited. The law only recognised substitute decision-making in relation to property and finance matters, with the use of enduring powers of **attorney**, for example, not for welfare or medical issues.

Declarations

In other areas, the High Court (Family Division) jurisdiction to make declarations developed to fill the gap. A declaration states the legal position and will state that a proposed course of action is not unlawful. The use of declarations was first established in medical cases. So, for example, if a surgeon carries out an operation, which has been 'approved' by a declaration, he will not be liable for assault.[1] Someone closely connected, such as a carer or relative, or the local authority may seek a declaration. The Official Solicitor will normally represent the 'patient'. In the case of *Re F (Adult: Court's Jurisdiction)* [2000] 3 WLR 1740, a local authority sought a declaration to protect a young woman from possible abuse (discussed in Chapter 17).

Declarations made by the high court are guided by exercise of the best interests principle. This common law principle has now been incorporated into the statutory framework.

The best interests principle should strive for balance between autonomy and protection but is highly subjective. In another area, where declarations have been utilised to authorise sterilisation of women with learning disabilities, it has been argued from a feminist perspective that the balance has tipped in favour of paternalism.[2] The emphasis throughout a series of sterilisation cases has been on eliminating the risk of pregnancy,[3] yet there are no reported cases of male sterilisation. This was raised in the case of *Re A (Mental Patient: Sterilisation)* [2000] 1 FLR 549. A was a 28-year-old man with Down's syndrome, borderline severe/significant mental impairment. His mother sought a declaration that sterilisation was in his best interests, being concerned that, when she was no longer able to care for him, he might impregnate a woman and be unable to deal with the consequences. The judge adopted a broad definition of best interests, encompassing medical, emotional and other welfare issues. The judge took the view that, for any mentally incapacitated man, neither the birth of a child nor disapproval of his conduct was likely to cause him problems, and on that basis the application was refused. The court did state, however, that if evidence could be presented that, after sterilisation, A would enjoy greater freedom and the opportunity to develop sexual experience, it might reconsider the case.

Another line of cases has addressed the issue of contact with an adult who lacks capacity. *Re D-R (Adult: Contact)* [1999] 1 FLR 1161 considered a claim by a father for access to his adult daughter who had a learning disability. Capacity to marry has also been considered by the High Court. In *Sheffield City Council* v. *E* [2004] EWHC 2808 (Fam), an application was made by a local authority based on their concerns that a young woman of 21 with a learning disability (and described as having a mental age of 13) lacked the capacity to marry. The court agreed that she did not have the capacity to understand the nature of marriage and made a declaration to that effect. The second case, *M* v. *B* [2005] EWHC 1681 (Fam), concerned an arranged marriage proposed by the parents of a 23-year-old woman of Pakistani origin who had a severe learning disability. The court made a declaration stating that she could not give a valid consent to marriage, and also declared that any marriage ceremony would be void and that it would not be in her best interests to leave the jurisdiction. The court noted that the injunction protected her right to private life, which would be jeopardised by her parents' attempts to arrange her marriage.

The cases have illustrated that declaratory relief has extended significantly beyond medical cases, into the area of social and welfare decision-making. (Their continued use in an adult protection context on application by local authorities is discussed further in Chapter 17.) The Court of Protection established by the Mental Capacity Act 2005 has a similar jurisdiction to make single orders addressing the same sort of issues that the High Court has faced. The cases decided by the High Court prior to the MCA continue to be important as a source of reasoning for the new court to draw on.

Litigation friend

A 'litigation friend' can assist a person who lacks mental capacity to instigate legal proceedings.[4] A person may act as a litigation friend as long as he can fairly and competently conduct the proceedings, has no adverse interest, undertakes to pay any costs which may be ordered, and can file a certificate of suitability covering these matters.

The mental capacity of an individual will also be relevant where the court is considering making an order with which that person should comply. In *MJ Harris* v. *HW Harris (Acting by his Guardian ad Litem, the Official Solicitor)* (1999) LTL 22/4/99 (unreported), and *Wookey* v. *Wookey* [1991] 3 All ER 365, issues of domestic violence, enforceability of injunctions and mental health were aired. Both cases concerned elderly couples where there were concerns that the husband might not be able to comply with an injunction because of mental incapacity. In such a case the question was whether the person understood the proceedings and the nature and requirements of the injunction. An injunction ought not to be granted where the person was incapable of understanding what he was doing or that it was wrong, because he would be incapable of complying with it, it would have no deterrent effect and would effectively be unenforceable as he would have a clear defence to an application for committal for contempt of court.

The Mental Capacity Act 2005

Background

The Mental Capacity Act 2005 has its roots in a Law Commission report, 'Mental Incapacity' (1995), which was produced at the culmination of a five-year period of consultation. The opening statement sums up the need for reform: 'The law as it now stands is unsystematic and full of glaring gaps. It does not rest on clear or modern foundations of principle. It has failed to keep up with developments in our understanding of the needs of those with mental disability.' Following a lengthy period of further consultation and publication of draft Bills the Act which applies to England and Wales was introduced. Similar legislation has been enacted in Scotland.[5]

The legislation is divided into three main parts with accompanying schedules. Part I, entitled 'Persons who lack capacity', contains a set of principles to apply throughout the Act, provisions relating to the **lasting power of attorney (LPA)**, general powers of the court and the appointment of deputies; advance decisions to refuse treatment; research; and the independent mental capacity advocate scheme. Part II provides for the new Court of Protection and Public Guardian, with miscellaneous and general provisions contained in Part III. The Act applies to anyone over the age of 16. It will be relevant to people who have difficulty making decisions at any point in their lives, including adults with severe and profound learning disabilities, some people with autism, people with dementia, some people with mental health problems and some survivors of severe head injury. The Act is supported by a detailed code of practice, illustrated throughout with scenarios and case studies, which gives guidance on implementing the law and explains the new provisions. The Act applies to the full range of acts and decisions an individual might face, as described in the code of practice:

> The Act covers decisions made, or actions taken, on behalf of people lacking capacity, whether they relate to day-to-day matters or represent major life-changing events. Actions or decisions may range from choosing what to wear or doing the weekly shopping to carrying out a routine dental check-up, to deciding whether the person should move into residential care or deciding to undertake a major surgical operation. (para. 2.3)

Some decisions will remain outside the scope of the Act, namely those of a highly personal nature and some that are covered by other legislation. The code of practice provides a summary which includes: consenting to marriage or a civil partnership; divorce or dissolution; consenting to have sexual relations; consenting to adoption; discharging parental responsibility for a child in matters not relating to the child's property. Treatment for mental disorder where a person is detained under the Mental Health Act 1983 is governed by that Act (para. 1.9). The code does note, however, that: 'Although the Act does not allow anyone to make a decision about these matters on behalf of someone who lacks capacity to make such a decision for themselves (for example, consenting to have sexual relations), this does not prevent action being taken to protect a vulnerable person from abuse or exploitation' (para. 1.11).

Principles

The principles set out in s. 1 of the Act are an important feature that restate and expand upon some of the common law principles. The principles are:

---

s. 1

- A person must be assumed to have capacity unless it is established that he does not (s. 1(2)).
- A person is not to be treated as unable to make a decision unless all practicable steps to help him to do so have been taken without success (s. 1(3)).
- A person is not to be treated as unable to make a decision merely because he makes an unwise decision (s. 1(4)).
- An act done, or decision made for or on behalf of a person who lacks capacity must be in his best interests (s. 1(5)).
- Before the act is done, or the decision made, regard must be had to whether the purpose for which it is needed can be as effectively achieved in a way that is less restrictive of the person's rights and freedom of action (s. 1(6)).

(MCA 2005)

As these principles are set out with the objective of assisting the range of people affected by the Act, it is important that the Act commences with the presumption in favour of capacity, as the first principle. The code notes:

> It is important to balance people's right to make a decision with their right to safety and protection when they can't make decisions to protect themselves. But the starting assumption must always be that an individual has the capacity, until there is proof that they do not. (para. 2.4)

The burden to displace that presumption falls on the person who questions the individual's capacity. The Act also endorses good practice by requiring steps to be taken to encourage first-hand decision-making. Such steps might include providing information relevant to the decision in a simple format, making sure the person is in an environment in which he is comfortable and there is minimal distraction, or involving an expert or person the individual trusts in helping the person express his views. The Act takes a functional approach to decision-making and does not exclude what might appear to be irrational or eccentric decisions provided the person making the decision has capacity. This 'reflects the fact that everyone has their own values, beliefs, preferences and attitude. A person should not be considered to lack capacity just because other people think their decision is unwise' (para. 2.10). Decisions and actions must be in the person's best interests (discussed further below). Finally, the Act introduces a 'minimum intervention' principle, supporting practices which interfere least with the individual's freedom of action. This principle follows the spirit of Art. 8 of the European Convention on Human Rights (the right to respect for private and family life).

What is capacity?

The test of capacity is contained in s. 2:

---

s. 2

(1) … A person lacks capacity if at the material time he is unable to make a decision for himself in relation to the matter because of an impairment of, or a disturbance in the functioning of, the mind or brain.

(2) It does not matter whether the impairment or disturbance is permanent or temporary.

(MCA 2005)

There are two stages, establishing an impairment or disturbance, and a resulting inability to make the decision. Examples of impairment or disturbance in the functioning of the mind or brain could include a range of conditions such as: dementia; learning disabilities; effects of brain damage; physical or medical conditions that cause confusion, drowsiness or loss of consciousness; concussion following a head injury, and the symptoms of alcohol or drug use. The reference to making 'a decision … in relation to a matter', 'at the material time' clarifies that assessment of capacity is specific not general (*Masterman-Lister* v. *Brutton & Co., Jewell & Home Counties Dairies* [2002] EWCA Civ 1889).

Being 'unable to make a decision', is addressed in s. 3.

---

s. 3

(1) … a person is unable to make a decision for himself if he is unable –

    (a) to understand the information relevant to the decision,
    (b) to retain the information,
    (c) to use or weigh that information as part of the process of making the decision, or
    (d) to communicate the decision …

(MCA 2005)

In most cases the first three criteria will apply. It is not necessary to prove a, b, and c, one element will be sufficient (*RT* v. *LT and A Local Authority* [2010] EWHC Fam 1910). Appropriate assistance from speech and language therapists should mean that few people are unable to communicate a decision. Being unable to communicate a decision may be particularly relevant for people with the very rare condition of 'locked-in syndrome'. 'Relevant information' includes the reasonably forseeable consequences of deciding or failing to make a decision.

An individual will not be considered unable to make a decision until all practical steps have been taken to help him.

The code of practice outlines some of the steps that might be taken to help an individual make a decision:

> 2.7 The kind of support people might need to help them make a decision varies. It depends on personal circumstances, the kind of decision that has to be made and the time available to make the decision. It might include:
>
> - using a different form of communication (for example, non-verbal communication);
> - providing information in a more accessible form (for example, photographs, drawings, or tapes);
> - treating a medical condition which may be affecting the person's capacity; or
> - having a structured programme to improve a person's capacity to make particular decisions (for example, helping a person with learning disabilities to learn new skills).
>
> (MCA Code of Practice)

Issue-specific capacity

The test for capacity is a functional test. This means that capacity has to be assessed for each decision at the time the decision needs to be made. It centres on the person's ability to make a particular decision and the way the decision is arrived at, not the final decision made, nor any test of the individual's capacity in general.

In *Saulle* v. *Nouvet* [2007] EWHC 2902 (QB), the High Court considered whether an individual had capacity to conduct litigation following a serious accident. It limited its enquiry to the particular litigation before it and not generally to all types of litigation.

It was also noted in *Local Authority X* v. *MM (by the Official Solicitor) and KM* [2007] EWHC 2003 (Fam), that an individual can have capacity for some decisions but not others. In this case it was decided it was in the best interests of a young woman to live in supported accommodation and for her relationship with a particular man, Mr K, to be supervised because of her lack of capacity. However, she did have capacity to choose to have sexual relations with Mr K and it was therefore necessary for the local authority to arrange for them to have unsupervised periods of time together.

Assessment of capacity

Consideration of capacity is limited to the particular decision under consideration at the particular time. Assessment of capacity must therefore always be undertaken with a particular decision in mind, not as a general assessment of capacity. The Act also specifies that a lack of capacity cannot be established merely by reference to a person's age or appearance, or a condition of his, or an aspect of his behaviour, which might lead others to make unjustified assumptions about his capacity (s. 2(3)). This rules out stereotyping. The question whether a person lacks capacity must be decided on the civil standard of balance of probabilities, i.e. more likely than not.

Assessment of capacity will often be carried out on a day-to-day basis by people they are in close contact with, such as carers and relatives. Professional involvement may be required for an assessment of capacity in some circumstances, including more complex decisions and the following situations included in the code: where the decision has serious consequences; a person challenges the finding that he lacks capacity; family members, carers and/or professionals disagree about a person's capacity; the person being assessed is expressing different views to different people; somebody has been accused of abusing a vulnerable adult who may lack capacity to make decisions that protect them; and a person repeatedly makes decisions that put them at risk.

In *RT* v. *LT and A Local Authority* [2010] EWHC Fam 1910, the Court of Protection had to decide whether a young woman with mild learning disabilities and mental health problems had capacity to decide where to live and with whom to have contact. The court applied the test in s. 2(1) of the Act. In this case the court found that the woman was 'unable to make a decision' focusing on her inability to use or weigh information, as she had very fixed ideas on certain topics. An expert, Dr K, consultant psychiatrist, provided an opinion to the court, noting the difficulty LT had in using information as part of the decision-making process. The judgment states, 'In his assessment of LT's capacity he noted particular difficulties in LT making balanced judgements, as she was only able to look at a problem from one perspective. The nature of her social disorder ... limited her ability to take in and weigh the relevant information and, in extreme circumstances, communicate it effectively. Thus he concluded, she demonstrated strong dichotomous (black-and-white) thinking: for example, social workers were all bad and only lie; parents were all good and never had any problem' (para 25).

Best interests

All capacity-related decisions must be made in the best interests of the person. All circumstances must be considered in deciding whether something is in a person's 'best interests'. The Act gives further guidance on particular factors to be taken into account in s. 4, set out below. None of the factors carries any more weight or priority than another; the list is not exhaustive but should enable an objective assessment of what is in the person's best interest to be made. The person making the decision must first consider whether the person is likely to have capacity at some time and, if so, when. This recognises that capacity may fluctuate and suggests that non-urgent decisions might be postponed if there is a likelihood of the person regaining capacity. There is also a requirement to permit and encourage the person to participate as fully as possible in any act or decision.

The factors which must be considered include:

- the ascertainable past and present wishes and feelings of the person concerned (including any relevant written statements);
- the beliefs and values that would be likely to influence his decision if he had capacity (including religious beliefs and cultural values);
- other factors the individual would be likely to consider if able to do so (this might include a sense of family obligation);
- the views of others it is considered appropriate to consult including anyone so named, carers and others interested in the person's welfare and any donees of an LPA or deputies appointed under the Act.

In practice, whilst this list should help to structure decision-making, the concept of 'best interests' is likely to remain extremely difficult to apply in many cases. A range of decisions or actions may be considered to be in the best interests of the person who lacks capacity. In such cases the principle that the least restrictive alternative should be followed would apply. It is essential that proper records are kept of all best interests decisions and assessments of capacity. The code advises that:

Any staff involved in the care of a person who lacks capacity should make sure a record is kept of the process of working out the best interests of that person for each relevant decision, setting out: how the decision about the person's best interests was reached; what the reasons for reaching the decision were; who was consulted to help work out best interests, and what particular factors were taken into account. This record should remain on the person's file. For major decisions based on the best interests of a person who lacks capacity, it may also be useful for family and other carers to keep a similar kind of record.

(para. 5.15, MCA Code of Practice)

In deciding where an adult who lacks capacity should live, the best interests test must be applied to the individual, not a blanket application of policy. This was the outcome of *AH* v. *Hertfordshire Partnership NHS Foundation Trust* [2011] EWHC 276. The Council planned to move AH from a rural campus-style residential facility where he had lived for 20 years, to a supported housing project in London, but the Court of Protection decided this was not in his best interests. The first case under the Mental Capacity Act 2005 to reach the Supreme Court gave guidance on best interests: *Aintree University Hospitals NHS Foundation Trust* v. *James* [2013] UKSC 67. The case concerned a life-sustaining medical treatment which a hospital argued would be futile for a man but which his family argued he would want to continue to receive. The Supreme Court confirmed that the test in respect of the wishes and feelings of the person is subjective not objective. In arriving at a best interests' decision some court judgments have usefully adopted a 'balance sheet' approach, comparing the benefits and risks/burdens of a particular proposal (*An NHS Trust* v. *K* [2012] EWHC 2922 (COP)).

Acts in connection with care or treatment

Section 5 provides some legal security for those people, including carers, making day-to-day decisions for a person who lacks capacity. In effect, it deems the person lacking capacity to have given consent to the person acting for him in providing care or treatment, in certain circumstances.[6]

Under the Act, where a person ('D') does an act in connection with the care or treatment of another person ('P'), he will not incur liability so long as he reasonably believes that P lacks capacity in relation to the matter, and that it will be in P's best interests for the act to be done. It is intended to be a positive permission-giving provision. The code of practice provides examples of acts in connection with personal care, including: assistance with washing and dressing; help with eating and drinking; shopping; help with mobility; acts performed in relation to domiciliary services required for the person's care (such as home care or meals on wheels) or in relation to other community care services.

There are limitations to the protection offered by s. 5. It will not authorise restraint unless it is necessary to prevent harm to P and is a proportionate response to the likelihood of P's suffering harm and the seriousness of that harm. The explanatory notes give examples of restraint, including: pulling someone away from the road, putting on a seatbelt or administering sedatives before treatment. Further, s. 5 does not provide a defence to negligence, whether in carrying out a particular act or by failing to act where necessary. In *R (Sessay)* v. *South London & Maudsley NHS Foundation Trust* [2011] EWHC 2617 (Admin) the police purported to remove a woman suffering from a mental disorder from her home to hospital using the authority of s. 5. The specific powers under the Mental Health Act 1983, contained in s. 136 (removal from a public place) and s. 135 (removal with a warrant from domestic premises) should have been used. The police had acted unlawfully.

The general provision in s. 5 is overridden by decisions of a person acting as a deputy or donee of an LPA acting within their powers.

Lasting power of attorney

A new order, the lasting power of attorney (LPA) is created under ss. 9–14.[7] Where an individual has capacity but anticipates possible loss of capacity in the future he may execute a lasting power of attorney, conferring authority to the attorney to make decisions on his behalf. This replaces and extends beyond the previously used enduring power of attorney, and the Enduring Powers of Attorney Act (EPAA) 1985 will be repealed. Any validly registered power under the EPAA will continue to have effect, but will not extend beyond property issues.

The most significant difference between the old **EPA** and new LPA is the extension to 'personal welfare' decisions. The attorney (or attorneys) may be authorised to make decisions about personal welfare, including healthcare, property and affairs where the donor no longer has capacity to make those decisions. As an example of a type of decision a welfare donee could be authorised to take, the code mentions arranging for the donor to access dental or optical treatment and applying for and having access to confidential documents relating to the donor, such as personal files held by social services; where the donor should live and who they should live with; day-to-day care, including diet and dress; and assessments for and provision of community care services (para. 7.21).

The LPA can authorise the attorney to refuse life-sustaining treatment on behalf of the donor (one of the more controversial provisions of the Act, discussed further below in relation to advance directions). An LPA may provide more flexibility in terms of refusal of treatment as the exact treatment and circumstances do not have to be anticipated and stipulated as they do in an advance decision.

This new power reflects the scope of decision-making seen in High Court declarations case law. An LPA can be constructed to deal only with healthcare or property matters or a combination and it can place restrictions on the exercise of powers within those areas. It thus allows a great deal of flexibility for individuals who wish to plan ahead.

Any person over the age of 18 may execute an LPA as long as they have capacity to do so. The LPA can also be revoked by the donor if he has capacity. To be effective, the LPA must be registered with the Public Guardian and comply with certain procedural requirements in Sch. 1. It may be registered as soon as it is executed, contrasting with the current position on EPAs where registration takes place once the person loses capacity, and must be registered to take effect. As an additional safeguard, a 'prescribed person' (most likely to be a doctor) must certify that the donor has not been under any undue pressure which would persuade him to sign, and that he understands the effect of the LPA. The Public Guardian will monitor the operation of LPAs and maintain a register of LPAs. If it is suspected that an attorney is abusing their position, this should be reported to the Office of Public Guardian. If any disputes arise as to the exercise of an LPA, the Court of Protection has jurisdiction to hear the matter and give directions. If the donor lacks capacity to revoke a LPA the Court may do so, as in *Re DP (Revocation of Lasting Power of Attorney)* [2014] EWHC B4 (COP), where the Attorney breached his obligations by failing to keep proper accounts, paying himself an unauthorised salary and making gifts to himself of £38,000. The donor does not lose his power to act as long as he has capacity even if the power has been registered.

Advance decisions

The common law gave some recognition to advance refusals of medical treatment, also known as living wills, advance statements and directives *(Re T (Adult: Refusal of Treatment)* [1992] 4 All ER 649). The MCA 2005 places this on a statutory footing with the introduction of advance decisions (ss. 24–26). It is also possible, as noted above, for healthcare decisions, including advance refusal of treatment, to be delegated under a lasting power of attorney. The greatest autonomy in advance decision-making will be secured by an individual utilising both procedures.

An advance decision to refuse treatment can be made by a person over the age of 18 with capacity. It must clearly specify the circumstances and the treatment which the person wishes to refuse. The treatment may be described in non-medical/lay terms, though this will be subject to interpretation by members of the medical profession. The more precise the terminology used as to both the treatment and the circumstances, the more likely the advance decision is to be followed. As treatments develop with advances in medicine, it is also important to keep the advance decision under review whilst the maker has capacity. The advance decision will also lose validity if the person acts inconsistently with its terms. As the advance decision should be an informed decision by the individual, it must be demonstrated that the maker understood relevant information and the consequences of the decision. To this end, the code of practice recommends ongoing discussions with a healthcare professional. The code also sets out information which it considers useful, to include: details of the person making the advance decision (date of birth, home address and any distinguishing features); details of general practitioner and whether they have a copy of the advance decision; a statement that the decision is intended to have effect if the maker lacks capacity to make treatment decisions; a clear statement of the decision, specifying the treatment to be refused and the circumstances in which the decision will apply or which will trigger a particular course of action; date of document; signature of maker and/or witness (para. 9.19).

Unless the advance decision relates to life-sustaining treatment, it is not required to be in writing; however, evidentially this is likely to be the preferred option.

Deprivation of Liberty Safeguards

The starting point is to remember that the MCA does not permit a person to be deprived of his liberty, though it may be restricted. This is a specific exception to the actions permitted when acting under s. 5. It is unfortunate that there is no clear legal definition of deprivation of liberty in the Act – this will be a matter for professional judgment. The ECtHR noted that: 'The distinction between deprivation and restriction upon liberty is merely one of degree or intensity and not one of nature or substance.' The Deprivation of Liberty Safeguards (DOLS) were introduced in response to the case of *HL* v. *United Kingdom* (2004) 40 EHRR 761. The case had progressed through the UK courts, ultimately reaching the House of Lords as *R* v. *Bournewood Community and Mental Health NHS Trust, ex parte L* [1998] 3 All ER 289. The European Court found that the practice of effectively detaining a person in hospital when he could not consent to that detention and in the absence of the use of Mental Health Act powers of detention, breached Article 5 of the Convention. A further breach occurred as there was no legal procedure by which the detention could be challenged. This absence of authority to detain and to challenge the detention became known as the *'Bournewood gap'*. The DOLS were introduced to fill that gap by introducing a procedure which authorises deprivation of liberty if in an individual's best interests, and provides a mechanism for challenging that deprivation.

The safeguards create two new bodies: the supervisory body, which will be a local authority or PCT; and a managing authority which will be an NHS body responsible for running a hospital or a person registered in respect of a care home. A deprivation of liberty must be authorised: either a standard authorisation or an urgent authorisation. A standard authorisation can be granted by a supervisory body for up to 12 months. It is possible for a managing authority to grant an urgent authorisation for up to seven days if the need for a DOL is urgent and pending a standard authorisation. If a hospital or care home finds that a person who lacks capacity is being, or risks being, deprived of their liberty, they must apply to the supervisory body for authorisation. The supervisory body will conduct a DOLS assessment in six parts:

1. Age assessment – the person is over 18.

2. Mental health assessment – is the person suffering from a mental disorder?

3. Mental capacity assessment – the person lacks capacity to consent to the intervention.

4. Best interest assessment – is it in the person's best interest to be deprived of their liberty to prevent harm to themselves? Is deprivation of liberty a proportionate response?

5. Eligibility assessment – should the person be supported under the Mental Health Act or Deprivation of Liberty Safeguards?

6. No refusals assessment – would the authorisation conflict with any other authority for decision-making?

An authorisation can only be made if the person meets all six requirements. Then the supervisory body can decide on the duration and any conditions of authorisation and appoint a representative for the person. The representative will maintain contact with the person and can ask for a review of the authority if one of the six criteria are no longer met. Appeals against authorisation will be heard by the Court of Protection. The Court of Protection must authorise any deprivation of liberty in respect of a person who does not reside in a care home or hospital setting.

The DOLS have been subject to a high level of critique and the House of Lords Select Committee recommended a comprehensive review and replacement of the safeguards. The Care Quality Commission monitor DOLS and in their report for 2012–13 found that the number of applications for adults over 85 had increased significantly; care homes and hospitals are required to notify CQC of DOLS applications but around two thirds were failing to do so; and, as in previous years, there was a wide variation in application rates between regions.[8]

DOLS have generated a substantial body of case law, much of which concerns the threshold whereby a restriction of liberty becomes a deprivation of liberty, a matter about which there are divergent views.

JE v. *DE and Surrey County Council* [2006] EWHC 3459 (Fam): a 76-year-old man was taken from the care of his wife, because of a risk of harm and neglect, to live in a care home. He consistently expressed the wish to return to his wife but was not permitted to leave the care home. The circumstances amounted to a deprivation of liberty.

In *A Local Authority* v. *A and B* [2010] EWHC 978 (Fam): an adult and a child both suffering from Smith Magenis syndrome lived at home with parents and were locked in their bedrooms at night. This was not considered to be a deprivation of liberty in the context of a happy family life.

In *Hillingdon LBC* v. *Neary* [2011] EWHC 1377 (COP) Steven Neary, a 20-year-old man with autism and learning disability, lived with his father. His father agreed that he should go into temporary residential accommodation for respite following a period of illness. He was retained in the accommodation for his best interests despite the father's opposition and his own expressed wishes to return to his father. The local authority were criticised on a number of levels. The initial detention before a DOLS authorisation was unlawful, the subsequent authorisations were flawed, an independent mental capacity advocate had not been appointed and there was a breach of Article 8, the right to respect for private and family life.

In *Cheshire West and Chester Council* v. *P* [2011] EWCA Civ 1257 the Court of Appeal found no deprivation of liberty in a case concerning a 38-year-old man who lacked capacity to make decisions regarding residence and care, living in supported housing. He needed a high level of care and wore a bodysuit sewn up the front to prevent him removing and ingesting his continence pads. Munby LJ introduced the notion of a 'relevant comparator', i.e. a person with similar needs not an ordinary adult. He also referred to the need to consider objective and subjective reasons for a placement.

The clear authority on DOLS is now the Supreme Court decision below:

Key Case

P (by his litigation friend the Official Solicitor) v. *Cheshire West and Chester Council and another; P and Q (by their litigation friend the Official Solicitor)* v. *Surrey County Council* [2014] UKSC 19.

A conjoined appeal in the Supreme Court has provided much needed clarification on the meaning of deprivation of liberty. The leading judgment was given by Lady Hale and rejected the 'relative normality' interpretation introduced by the Court of Appeal in its Cheshire West judgment. Instead, an objective standard will be applied. The key elements of a deprivation of liberty are that a person is under continuous supervision and not free to leave. The justification for this approach is simply that deprivation of liberty 'must be the same for everyone, whether or not they have physical or mental disabilities', and, further: 'If it would be a deprivation of my liberty to be obliged to live in a particular place, subject to constant monitoring and control, only allowed out with close supervision, and unable to move away without permission even if such an opportunity became available, then it must also be a deprivation of the liberty of a disabled person. The fact that my living arrangements are comfortable, and indeed make my life as enjoyable as it could possibly be, should make no difference. A gilded cage is still a cage' [46].

In assessing whether there is a deprivation the fact that the individual does not appear to object to the placement is not relevant, nor is the purpose of the placement. The judgment also confirms that a deprivation of liberty can occur in a domestic setting (this was the case in relation to P and Q) where the State is responsible for the arrangement.

Since the Supreme Court decision, the numbers of authorisations has increased dramatically and the Department of Health has issued further guidance on the impact of the decisions.

Court of Protection

A new Court of Protection is established under the Act. Sections 15–23 deal with the powers of the court, and the appointment and role of deputies. The court will have jurisdiction to determine disputes relating to capacity, by making declarations and single orders, including whether an individual has or lacks capacity to make a particular decision. The court may make declarations about particular issues, such as contact or residence and declarations as to the lawfulness of any act done or contemplated. As an example, in *City of Westminster* v. *IC (by his friend the Official Solicitor) and KC and NN* [2008] EWCA Civ 198 the court made an order preventing a man with severe learning disabilities from being taken out of the country for a proposed marriage. The court may make a will on behalf of the incapacitated person. The court also has power to revoke an LPA if the attorney has contravened his authority or acted other than in the best interests of the donor. The court can ask for a report from the Public Guardian, a Court of Protection Visitor and a local authority.

The code of practice describes the court's role as being available to 'settle serious and complex decisions'. It notes that 'it may often be more appropriate to explore alternative solutions to solving problems' and refers to advocacy, mediation and use of complaints processes. The scope of the court's jurisdiction and its accessibility as a regional forum would, however, suggest that more cases involving individuals with mental incapacity will be adjudicated on in a judicial setting. This has implications for staff who may be called upon to give evidence or to make applications and the need for training in court skills (see Chapter 4). The exercise of the court's powers is subject to the principles in s. 1 and best interests.

The new court will operate from a central office and registry, but significantly it 'may sit at any place in England and Wales on any day and at any time' (s. 45(3)). In practical terms, this means that there will be regional courts deciding matters under the MCA 2005 in a more accessible way.

Applications to the court may be made as of right by:

- the person who lacks capacity or is alleged to lack capacity;
- the attorney appointed under a lasting power of attorney;
- a deputy;
- a person named in an order of the court, if the application related to the order (e.g. a person who has been named in a contact arrangement with the incapacitated person).

Any other person requires leave of the court (s. 50(3)). That would include new applications by a local authority. In deciding whether to grant leave, the court must consider: the applicant's connection to the person lacking capacity; reasons for the application; the benefit to the person lacking capacity of the proposed order and whether that benefit can be achieved in any other way (para. 8.12).

As a general rule Court of Protection hearings will be held in private, though there is a commitment to greater transparency. The court itself, however, has wide powers to control reporting of its proceedings, attendance of the media at private proceedings and holding hearings in public and this point has been the subject of a series of decisions starting with *A (by his litigation friend, the Official Solicitor)* v. *Independent News & Media Ltd,* [2010] EWCA Civ 343 where it was held that the media had an interest in proceedings concerning a man with severe disabilities who was a concert pianist.

An application was made by members of his family to be appointed as his personal welfare and property and affairs deputies. He lived in a home run by the Royal National Institite for the Blind and that organisation felt it would be preferable to appoint an independent deputy. The media wished to report the outcome of the case. The relevant law is the court of Protection Rules 90–93.

Under Court of Protection Rules, (90) it is a general rule that Court of Protection hearings are to be held in private. It includes a list of people who are entitled to attend a private hearing, including the parties and their legal representatives. An application was made for the media to be allowed to attend the private hearing and to publish information relating to the hearing.

A two-stage test applies: first there must be 'good reason' to make the order, and, second, even if good reason is shown, the court has a discretion to exercise. The case also involves opposing rights under the Human Rights Act 1998 – the individual's right to respect for private life (Article 8) and the media's right to freedom of expression (Article 10).

In this case media representatives were permitted to attend, for three reasons outlined by Hedley, J:

> First, all these issues in principle are already within the public domain and the questions which they raise are readily apparent. Secondly, the court is equipped with powers to preserve privacy whilst addressing the issues in the case. Thirdly, the decision of the court will have major implications for the future welfare of 'A' and it is in the public interest that there should be understanding of the jurisdiction and powers of the court and how they are exercised.

In *G* v. *E and Others* [2010] EWHC 2042 (Fam), the Court of Protection was highly critical of the local authority in a deprivation of liberty case. The authority failed to involve the carer (described as his foster mother) of a young man in their decision to remove him from her care, and prevented any contact between them. The court also commented on the lack of training that had been provided by the council to its employees in preparation for the DOLS scheme. The court decided to name Manchester City Council to hold it accountable for its poor practice.

Practice guidance has been issued on 'Transparency in the Court of Protection' and should ensure an increase in the number of Court of Protection judgments made available for publication, even if suitably anonymised.

Deputies

The court may also appoint a 'deputy' to make welfare and financial decisions for a person who either has not made an LPA and subsequently loses capacity, or could not have made an LPA because of a long-term disability. This system will replace and extend the use of receivership which formerly operated. The court will decide whether a proposed deputy (who must consent to the appointment), is suitable in terms of being reliable, trustworthy and competent. In *R (M)* v. *Birmingham City Council* [2008] EWHC 1863 (Admin), the court confirmed that a council could act as a deputy, but as a deputy is required to consent to appointment, it would not order the council to act. A paid care worker (including care home managers) should not become a deputy because of the potential conflict of interest. Deputies will be supervised by the Public Guardian. Appointment of deputies is subject to the principle that a decision by the court is to be preferred to the appointment of a deputy to make a decision, and the powers conferred on a deputy should be as limited in scope and duration as is reasonably practicable in the circumstances. A deputy does not have power to stop a named person from having contact with the incapacitated person (*Re SK (Vulnerable Adult: Capacity)*) [2008] EWHC 636 (Fam); that would require an order from the court. A deputy is treated as the agent of the adult lacking capacity and is entitled to reasonable expenses. A deputy cannot make a decision on behalf of the incapacitated person if 'he knows or has reasonable grounds for believing that he has capacity in relation to the matter' (s. 20(1)). The scheme for the appointment of deputies was considered in *G* v. *E and others* [2010] and *Re P* [2010] EWHC 1592 and suggested there will often be a preference for a family member to act. An order of preference was sketched out in *Re M, N* v. *O and P* [2013] COPLR 91 beginning with the person's spouse or partner, then other relative with an interest in P's affairs, close friend, professional adviser, local authority representative and panel deputy.

The Court of Protection Visitor

The main role of the Court of Protection Visitor is to provide independent advice to the Court of Protection and Public Guardian. There are two types of visitor: a general visitor and a special visitor, the latter having special knowledge of and experience in cases of impairment of or disturbance in the functioning of the mind or brain. The visitor can visit and interview privately, any person who lacks capacity, attorneys and deputies, and has the right to inspect relevant health and social care records.

The Public Guardian

The role of the Public Guardian, in the Office of the Public Guardian (OPG) provides additional safeguards for arrangements made for adults lacking capacity. This includes maintaining a register of LPAs that comply with the Act, and managing deputies. The Public Guardian will supervise, support and provide guidance for deputies and deal with complaints about attorneys and deputies, sometimes investigating jointly with, for example, social services. He can directly provide reports to the Court of Protection and also directs the work of Court of Protection Visitors.

The independent mental capacity advocate service

The Act includes a scheme for independent advocacy in prescribed circumstances. The object of the independent mental capacity advocate (IMCA) service is that: 'a person to whom a proposed act or decision relates should, so far as practicable, be represented and supported by a person who is independent of any person who will be responsible for the act or decision' (s. 35(4)).

The IMCA service is commissioned by local authorities with social services functions but provided independently.

An independent advocate will be involved: where serious medical treatment is proposed and there is no-one else who could be consulted about the patient's best interests; and where there is a proposal to accommodate a person in a hospital or care home. The role was extended by regulations,[9] enabling (but not requiring) an IMCA to be appointed in adult protection cases. Local authorities (LAs) and the NHS have the power to instruct an IMCA where two criteria are met: protective measures (in accordance with 'No Secrets' guidance) are being put into place; and the person lacks capacity (includes a person who it is alleged has been abused or neglected and a person who is alleged to be the abuser); if satisfied that it would be of particular benefit to the person to do so. Local authorities are expected to have policies in place to guide the discretionary appointment of IMCAs in adult protection cases.

The advocate's role is to represent and support the individual, ascertain his wishes and feelings, obtain relevant information, which may include obtaining a further medical opinion, and consider available courses of action. The independent advocate will be entitled to interview in private the person whom he has been instructed to represent, and may examine and take copies of records relevant to the independent mental capacity advocate's investigation (including records relating to health, social services and residential accommodation).

Criminal offence

Finally, the Act introduces a new criminal offence in s. 44. A person is guilty of an offence if he has the care of a person who lacks capacity or is reasonably believed to lack capacity, or is the donee of a LPA or a deputy, and he 'ill-treats or wilfully neglects the person'. The offence is classified as an 'either way offence' (it may be prosecuted in the magistrates' court or Crown Court), and carries a maximum sentence of five years' imprisonment. The code of practice includes a separate chapter entitled 'What means of protection exist for people who lack capacity to make decisions for themselves?', which addresses abuse and the responsibilities of professionals, agencies responsible for protecting adults, the role of the Office of Public Guardian and the new offence (see further discussion in Chapter 17). The majority of prosecutions under s. 44 appear to relate to incidents in residential settings.

Code of practice

The Act is supported by a code of practice, supplemented by an additional code relating to DOLS. A duty is imposed on various categories of people to have regard to the code when acting in relation to a person lacking capacity. This includes professionals, such as doctors, nurses and social workers; those receiving payment in connection with care of the person, such as a care assistant; the donee of a LPA, a deputy and an IMCA. It notes that failure to comply with the code can be used in evidence before a court or tribunal in any civil or criminal proceedings, if the court or tribunal considers it to be relevant to those proceedings (Introduction, p. 5).

The code is not just intended as a resource for professionals:

> However, the Act applies more generally to *everyone* who looks after, or cares for, some-one who lacks capacity to make particular decisions for themselves. This includes family carers or other carers. Although these carers are not legally required to have regard to the Code of Practice, the guidance given in the Code will help them to understand the Act and apply it. They should follow the guidance in the Code as far as they are aware of it. (Intro-duction, p. 2)

Reflect

The Department for Constitutional Affairs described the Act as follows:

> The Mental Capacity Act 2005 provides a statutory framework to empower and pro-tect vulnerable people who may not be able to make their own decisions. (DCA)

Having read this chapter, do you think the provisions of the Act are likely to fulfil both the objectives of empowering and protecting?

Using the Act

New law often takes some time to become embedded in practice. The Department of Health expressed concern over under-implementation by public bodies with a statement in Circular LAC (DH) (2008) 4 that the necessary 'cultural shift' has hardly begun. Under-implementation is particularly notable in three areas: failure to carry out assessments of capacity; failures to in-struct IMCAs; and best interests assessments. The circular suggests that IMCAs are only being instructed in about 50 per cent of cases falling within ss. 35–41 (decisions regarding long-term accommodation moves and serious medical treatment), and advises that local systems should be reviewed. The circular reminds practitioners that 'assessments of capacity must now be under-taken by everyone' and also that best interests decisions-making is a requirement of the Act and LAs should audit how frequently and comprehensively such decisions are made and recorded.

Chapter summary

- The previous law on mental capacity was largely based on the common law, developed piecemeal and contained a number of gaps or loopholes. A new statutory framework is provided by the Mental Capacity Act 2005, in force since 2007.
- There is a legal presumption in favour of capacity. This means that adults are assumed to be autonomous and able to make their own decisions unless it can be shown (on balance of probabilities) that they lack the capacity to make the decision in question.

- Having capacity means that the individual is capable of understanding what is proposed and its implications, and is able to exercise choice. It varies depending on the nature of the decision to be made, e.g. to marry or to manage complex financial matters.

- The Mental Capacity Act 2005 applies to anyone over the age of 16 in England and Wales. It is supported by a code of practice.

- The Act starts with key principles: a presumption in favour of capacity; all practicable steps should be taken to help individuals to make their own decisions; an unwise decision does evidence lack of capacity; acts and decisions for a person who lacks capacity must be in his best interests; the least restrictive alternative is preferred.

- A person lacks capacity if he is unable to make a decision for himself in relation to the matter because of an impairment of or a disturbance in the functioning of the mind or brain, whether permanent or temporary.

- The Act provides for substitute decision-making in various ways. Section 5 provides freedom from liability for acts in connection with care or treatment for a person lacking capacity and in his best interests, such as day-to-day care matters. A lasting power of attorney (LPA) may be prepared by a person with capacity, to take effect in the future should he lose capacity, and may relate to financial matters but also to health and welfare decisions. In addition, for medical matters, advance decisions to refuse treatment can be made by a person with capacity.

- A Court of Protection has jurisdiction over all aspects of the Act. It can rule on whether a person has capacity for a particular decision, make one-off decisions and declarations, rule on the validity of LPAs and appoint deputies to make decisions for a person who does not have a LPA.

- An independent mental capacity advocate will be appointed for an individual faced with a serious decision about medical treatment or where to live and there is no one else to consult about the proposal, e.g. an attorney, and in some adult protection cases.

- Deprivation of Liberty Safeguards were introduced into the Act as a response to the 'Bournewood' gap'.

Exercise

Josie, aged 25, has a moderate learning disability. At times this causes her speech to be slurred. Following her mother's death, Josie's father emigrated to Australia four years ago with her younger brother, John, now aged 18 and she has lost contact with them. Since then she has lived in supported housing in the community. At times, Josie suffers from depression and she has been known to drink heavily. She does not always get on well with the people she shares her accommodation with, often does not get dressed and her personal hygiene is poor. Her keyworker is becoming concerned that this might not be the best placement to meet Josie's needs. Late on Friday night, one of Josie's housemates finds her in her bedroom clutching an empty bottle of wine in a semi-conscious state with a cut to her face. It appears she may have fallen and hit her head on the bedside table. An ambulance is called and Josie is taken to A & E. The triage nurse assesses that Josie needs stitches to her face and a tetanus injection. Although she has regained consciousness, she appears confused and cannot explain how she got the cut.

She will not answer the nurse, who seeks her consent to the treatment proposed. She becomes tearful and upset.

1. Who should assess whether Josie has capacity to refuse the treatment?
2. When and how should her capacity be assessed?
3. Is it significant that she has been drinking?
4. What is the key practice issue for the person carrying out the assessment?

Josie is left to rest for a while. When she wakes and the nurse tries to talk to her again about treatment for her face she becomes agitated and lashes out at the nurse. The nurse calls for assistance and Josie is restrained by being held down on the bed, then she is injected with a mild sedative to calm her. Whilst drowsy she is washed and changed out of her dirty clothing. Her face is stitched. The hospital contact Josie's keyworker, Phil, who arrives to take her home.

Back at the house, Josie and Phil have a chat about what happened. Josie still can't really remember what happened but says she wants to leave the house. Phil has thought about this and whilst he recognises that Josie is not happy in the house he does not feel she is ready to manage her own flat. He suggests she moves to different all-female residential accommodation. Josie is adamant that she wants her own flat, but also says she would like to share with some other women, and does not appear to understand fully the responsibility of having her own place. Phil leaves Josie a booklet outlining the different types of accommodation available to help her make up her mind.

1. Can Josie be washed and changed without her consent?
2. Is it lawful to restrain Josie?
3. Does Josie have capacity to consent to the accommodation move proposed?
4. Is she entitled to an independent mental capacity advocate (IMCA) to help her at this stage?

Websites

The Official Solicitor has responsibility for representing minors or adults under legal disability, in county court or High Court proceedings in England and Wales, and in the Court of Protection:
www.justice.gov.uk/about/ospt

The Public Guardianship Office is the administrative arm of the Court of Protection:
www.justice.gov.uk/about/opg

Further reading

Specific texts covering the new legislation:

Ashton, DJ, G. (2012) *Mental Capacity: Law and Pratice* Bristol: Jordan Publishing. (A detailed guide to the new law including a copy of the Act.)

Bartlett, P. (2008) *Blackstone's Guide to the Mental Capacity Act 2005*. Oxford: Oxford University Press.

Johns, R. (2014) *Capacity and Autonomy*. Basingstoke: Palgrave Macmillan.

Jones, R. (2012) *Mental Capacity Act Manual* (5th edn). London: Sweet & Maxwell.

The most useful texts, written specifically for people working in mental health, learning disability and old age, and including full text of the Act and some related materials, are:

Barber, P., Brown, R. and Martin, D. (2012) *The Mental Capacity Act 2005: A Guide for Mental Health Professionals* (2nd edn). London: Sage.

Brown, R. and Barker, P. and Martin, D (2009) *The Mental Capacity Act 2005: A Guide for Practice*. London: Sage.

Relevant articles include:

Bartlett, P. and McHale, J. (2002) 'Mental incapacity and mental health: The development of legal reform and the need for joined-up thinking' 25(4) *Journal of Social Welfare and Family Law* p. 313. (This introductory article is the first in an edition of **JSWFL** devoted to discussion of mental health and mental capacity. Written before introduction of the Mental Capacity Act 2005 and the Mental Health Act 2007, all the articles are nevertheless useful for their discussion of the principles involved.)

Dunn, M., Clare, I., Holland, A. and Gunn, M. (2007) 'Constructing and reconstructing "best interests": an interpretative examination of substitute decisionmaking under the Mental Capacity Act 2005' 29(2) *Journal of Social Welfare and Family Law* p. 117.

McDonald, A (2010) 'The impact of the Mental Capacity Act on social workers' decision-making and approaches to the assessment of risk' 40 *British Journal of Social Work* p. 1229.

Redley, M., Clare, L., Luke, L. and Holland, A. J. (2010) 'Introducing the Mental Capacity Advocate (IMCA) Service and the Reform of Adult Safeguarding Procedures' 41 *British Journal of Social Work*, p. 1058.

Notes

[1] See also, for example, in *Airedale NHS Trust* v. *Bland* [1993] 1 All ER 821, a declaration was made that it would be lawful to discontinue life-sustaining treatment for a person in a persistent vegetative state. The law as stated in *Bland* is compatible with ECHR, Art. 2, according to *NHS Trust A* v. *H* [2001] 2 FLR 501.

[2] See K. Keywood (1995) 'Sterilising the women with learning difficulties' in S. Bridgeman and S. Mills (eds) *Law and Body Politics: Regulating the Female Body*. Aldershot: Dartmouth.

[3] See *Re P (A Minor) (Wardship: Sterilisation)* [1989] 1 FLR 182; *Re B (A Minor) (Wardship: Sterilisation)* [1987] 2 All ER 206; *Re W (An Adult: Mental Patient) (Sterilisation)* [1993] 1 FLR 381.

[4] Civil Procedure Rules 1998 (SI 1998/3132), r. 21.

[5] Adults with Incapacity (Scotland) Act 2000.

[6] It was previously referred to as a 'general authority to act reasonably' but the scrutiny process highlighted this as a negative and rather paternalistic term.

[7] The LPA was referred to in the consultation process as a 'continuing power of attorney'.

[8] CQC (2014) 'Deprivation of Liberty Safeguards 2012–13', available at www.cqc.org.uk.

[9] The Mental Capacity Act 2005 (Independent Mental Capacity Advocates) (Extension of Role) Regulations 2006 (SI 2006/2883).

Chapter 17

Adult safeguarding

Learning objectives

To develop an understanding of the following:

- Adult abuse as a recently recognised social problem.
- Definitions, types and the extent of adult abuse.
- The policy framework.
- The impact of the Care Act 2014.
- Social services' responsibility to investigate and take action.
- The use of a range of existing laws to respond to cases.
- Opportunities to prevent abuse.
- Opportunities for the victim to take action.
- Opportunities for formal intervention.
- Safeguarding Adults Boards.

Talking Point

Steven Hoskin was 39 when he was killed by two people who had 'befriended' him. A serious case review was set up by Cornwall Adult Protection Committee to establish the effectiveness of procedures and ways professional worked together in the months preceding his death and to establish whether there are lessons to be learned from the case on which to improve practice. Steven had a learning disability and was described as a 'kind-hearted, generous and understanding young man'. His body was found at the base of a railway viaduct. He had been forced to take paracetamols and alcohol prior to his death, had recently sustained cigarette burns to his body. His neck was bruised and there were footprint marks on his hands and he had the injuries which ultimately caused his death from falling 30 metres off the viaduct.

The evening of his death, he was physically and verbally abused by people he believed to be friends, accused of being a paedophile, tied up and dragged around his flat with a dog collar and lead.

Prior to the events of that evening, Steven had had contact with numerous authorities. He had been in receipt of community care services as a person with 'substantial need', and also had contacts with NHS primary and secondary care services, the ambulance service and the police. Agencies were aware that Darren Stewart (well known to the police and to health services) and Sarah Bullock were spending increasing amounts of time in Steven's bedsit. The report found that 'there were weak and strong "warning signals" that all was not well for Steven'. None of these invoked the 'Adult Protection Procedure' and the report outlines a series of warnings and missed opportunities for intervention.

It concludes that:

> there was no lack of information about Steven and his circumstances and that with better inter-agency working, Steven Hoskin would have been spared the destructive impacts of unrestrained physical, financial and emotional abuse in his own home ... What is striking about the responses of services to Steven's circumstances is that each agency focused on single issues within their own sectional remits and did not make the connections necessary for the protection of vulnerable adults.

Finally, the police commented on the circumstances prior to Steven's murder:

> Steven had lost all control of his own life within his home. He had no say, choice or control over who stayed or visited the flat. He had no voice or influence over what happened within the premises. Darren Stewart recognised the clear vulnerability of Steven Hoskin and had 'moved in' on him ... he recognised the opportunity for accommodation and removed from Steven the little ability he had to make his own choices and decisions.

Cornwall Adult Protection Committee (2007) *The Murder of Steven Hoskin: A Serious Case Review*.

Introduction

Recognition of the existence of adult abuse as a complex social problem, and the need to establish adult protection procedures in response, is of relatively recent origin. Many local authorities through their protection policies now focus on adult protection as a generic category, which encompasses abuse towards specific groups such as older people and people with learning disabilities. Greater consistency between policies around the country should have been achieved under Department of Health guidance, 'No Secrets',[1] which requires local authorities to have policies in place to protect vulnerable adults from abuse. Initially, from the late 1980s and early 1990s responses to abuse were more likely to focus on distinct groups of vulnerable adults, with perhaps the most focus on elder abuse. An early reference had described this phenomenon as 'granny bashing',[2] and was followed by Eastman's graphic account of cases of abuse in 1983.[3] A variety of terms have since been used, including 'elder mistreatment', 'old age abuse', 'inadequate care' and 'miscare'. At the same time, there was growing recognition of the vulnerability to abuse of adults with learning disabilities particularly (it seems) abuse of a sexual nature.[4] The Association of Directors of Social Services have expressed concern that the term 'vulnerable adults' is contentious, adding: 'One reason is that the label can be misunderstood, because it seems to locate the cause of abuse with the victim, rather than placing responsibility with the actions or omissions of others.'[5] In place of 'adult protection', the ADSS prefers the term 'safeguarding adults', and explains: 'This phrase means all work which enables an adult "who is or may be eligible for community care services" to retain independence, wellbeing and choice and to access their human right to live a life that is free from abuse and neglect.' The document sets out standards for good practice and outcomes in adult protection work.

There are issues of similarity to be drawn with the position of adults with learning disabilities and mental health problems and also with the experience of domestic violence, and it is certainly helpful to place any discussion of specific victims of abuse against a context of vulnerable adults. It has also been argued that it is appropriate to address a continuum of 'family violence', ranging from child abuse to elder abuse, as the best way of understanding abuse.[6]

Discussion of rights has been a central tenet of the debate over the relationship between autonomy and protection where adults are subject to abuse. Intervention, in reality, may be paternalistic (framed in terms of best interests and welfare) and may not always reflect the expressed preferences and rights of an individual. As with other areas of law concerning social work, the Human Rights Act 1998 is likely to have an impact. Under the Human Rights Act 1998, there will need to be very precise reasons, taken in a clear decision-making framework, for departing from the principle of autonomous decision-making by all adults.[7] It is clear that the focus under the Act will be on greater access to the courts for effective protection and enforcement of rights as 'the Convention is intended to guarantee not rights that are theoretical or illusory but rights that are practical and effective' (*Artico* v. *Italy* (1980) 3 EHRR 1, para. 33). Abuse is perhaps the most obvious violation of an individual's private and family life; and in *X and Y* v. *Netherlands* (1985) 8 EHRR 235, the court upheld that principle in finding that the sexual abuse of a young woman who was learning disabled violated ECHR, Art. 8.[8]

Adult abuse cases present complex practice and ethical issues for professionals. Central to these is the debate about 'protection versus autonomy'. This is perhaps the crucial defining difference between work with young children and work with adults. For the most part, adults are assumed to be autonomous and entitled to make their own decisions, however eccentric and risky they may appear. In an area where social care professionals are more focused on therapeutic interventions, use of the law may be considered a last resort.[9] Where it is appropriate to have recourse to legal intervention, that action must be informed by values with appropriate emphasis on empowerment and self-determination and seek to achieve an outcome that improves the person's situation. It is also clear that, if legal action is contemplated, appropriate legal advice should be sought especially regarding the extent of evidence required. The need to distinguish this area of practice from childcare has been noted. Nevertheless, there may be useful lessons to be learnt from child protection.[10] This is particularly so at operational level, where practice must develop to produce appropriate responses to abuse in the absence of a clear statutory framework for investigation.

Over recent years a growing commitment from the Government to tackle adult abuse has emerged, issues about vulnerable adults and ageing initially being positioned in the policy against social exclusion. Various legislation will have an impact, including the Mental Capacity Act 2005, alongside a developing policy framework. A review of the 'No Secrets' guidance took place, following a consultation exercise in 2008.[11] Reasons for the review included change in the policy environment since 2000 (including personalisation), weaknesses identified in the implementation of 'No Secrets', and the need to examine the case for legislative change. The most significant legal development for adult social care and with implications for safeguarding is the Care Act 2014. The Act replaces a vast raft of adult social care (as noted in Chapter 14), but whilst providing an anchor for practice in this area, other legislation including the MCA and the criminal law will continue to be of great importance. The 'No Secrets' guidance will also be phased out and replaced by new guidance, but many of the messages of 'No Secrets' will endure within the new framework.

Safeguarding adults practice under the Care Act must comply with the general duty of a local authority to promote an individual's wellbeing as set out in section 1. Within the definition of wellbeing (see Chapter 14), s. 1(2)(c) refers to protection from abuse and neglect. Again, in the principles to apply to functions to promote an individual's wellbeing, s. 1(3)(g) states that local authorities must have regard to the need to protect people from abuse and neglect.

This chapter includes a preliminary section considering the existence and definitions of abuse, and continues to focus on ways of responding to abuse under the headings of preventing abuse, action by the victim and formal responses, the latter incorporating consideration of the role of the criminal law.

Existence and definitions of abuse

There is no clear legal definition of adult abuse. Efforts to arrive at a suitable practice definition illustrate the difficulties inherent in attempting to define an emerging social problem in the absence of comprehensive research, professional consensus or significant grass roots pressure.[12]

Definitions

The first formal definition (which focused on older people) appeared in official practice guidelines in 1993,[13] and focused on abuse within domestic settings, i.e. the family or victim's home, to the exclusion of institutional care settings.[14] The following year, the Department of Health commissioned 'Action on Elder Abuse' to produce a definition which read:

'Elder abuse is a single or repeated act or lack of appropriate action occurring within any relationship where there is an expectation of trust, which causes harm or distress to an older person.' The Action on Elder Abuse definition does not locate abuse within a physical setting but is problematic in other respects. What, for example, is meant by the term 'a relationship of trust'? It would appear to exclude abuse perpetrated by strangers.[15]

'No Secrets' (Department of Health, 2000), offers the following phrase as a basis on which to proceed: 'Abuse is a violation of an individual's human and civil rights by any other person or persons.' This is a much broader statement than earlier definitions of elder abuse, with a different conceptual emphasis which may be linked to the existence of the Human Rights Act 1998. Further elaboration is provided in para. 2.6:

> Abuse may consist of a single act or repeated acts. It may be physical, verbal, or psychological. It may be an act of neglect or an omission to act, or it may occur when a vulnerable person is persuaded into a financial or sexual transaction to which he or she has not consented or cannot consent. Abuse can occur in any relationship and may result in significant harm to, or exploitation of, the person subjected to it.

The Care Act 2014 includes reference to abuse and neglect in s. 42 and at s. 42(3) provides:

---

s. 42(3)

'Abuse' includes financial abuse; and for that purpose 'financial abuse' includes –

(a) having money or other property stolen,
(b) being defrauded,
(c) being put under pressure in relation to money or other property, and
(d) having money or other property misused.

(Care Act 2014)

It is not clear why only financial abuse is defined further in the Act. As 'abuse and neglect' are not so defined, there is the flexibility for broad interpretation under the Act and guidance should add further detail.

Categories of abuse

'No Secrets' goes on to note that beyond that definition there are certain categories of abuse over which some consensus has been reached. The categories are physical, sexual, psychological, financial and neglect, though abusive acts may embrace more than one category. In an area where our knowledge base is rapidly developing, the importance of keeping an open mind to 'new' categories cannot be overstated. In some local authority policies, institutional and professional abuse have separate category status, and chemical abuse is a sub-category of physical abuse. Self-neglect, forced marriage and trafficking may also be addressed through safeguarding adults' policies. 'No Secrets' refers to a separate category of discriminatory abuse including racist, sexist, that based on a person's disability, and other forms of harassment, slurs or similar treatment.[16] Discrimination may be a feature of each of the other categories. Physical abuse or name calling, for example, may be motivated by sexist, racist or ageist views.

Each category includes a variety of types of behaviour. Physical abuse includes hitting, slapping, pushing, unreasonable restraint, hair pulling and forced or over-medication, burning or biting. Sexual abuse has been described as a taboo subject, which is difficult to identify.[17] It may involve physical contact such as touching of genitals or breasts, masturbation or penetration. Equally, activities, which do not involve contact, such as photography, indecent exposure, sexual harassment or forced exposure to pornographic materials, may be considered abusive. Research by Stevenson and Jeary into sexual abuse of elderly people identified cases where abuse occurred in residential care, home care with domiciliary provision and independent living where no formal care was in place. The age of the abused women ranged from 60 to 98 and the abusers were between 16 and 70 years old. The types of cases ranged from sexual harassment through to rape, sexual assault and killing.[18] Psychological abuse includes verbal assaults, threats, humiliation, isolating the elder person, ignoring or being over-protective of the person, racial abuse or intimidation. The most common form of abuse is thought to be financial abuse, which includes theft, use of money or property without consent, forced transfer of assets, misuse of power of attorney or appointeeship and denial of access to funds or property. As one aspect of financial abuse, the Home Office has estimated that as many as 80,000 distraction burglaries and frauds by doorstep fraudsters take place each year targeting vulnerable elderly people. Neglect may be active, being the deliberate failure of a person to provide care; or passive, the unintentional failure to fulfil caring obligations due to inadequate knowledge or understanding. It includes failure to provide medical care, food, clothing, shelter or stimulation and failure to attend to personal hygiene needs of, for example, an adult who is incontinent.

For each category, possible indicators of abuse have been established. Whilst the existence of any of these indicators would not by itself be conclusive proof of abuse, it should arouse suspicion or concern. For example, injuries which are incompatible with history given, or uncared for, untreated pressure sores, bruises in shapes of fingers or belts or other objects, poor skin condition, weight loss and absence of hair are all possible indicators of physical abuse. Certain injuries or medical conditions, e.g. bruising or bedsores, can occur very easily in older people. Where such a condition did not arise out of abusive behaviour, it would nevertheless be a prompt for action to ensure appropriate attention or assessment by a relevant professional, e.g. involvement of district nurse.

Abuse can take place in any context, whether the adult lives alone, with a relative or other person, or in a residential setting. The perpetrator of abuse may be a relative, professional staff, paid care workers, volunteers, other service users, neighbours, friends and associates, people who deliberately exploit vulnerable people, and strangers.[19] The type of intervention (if any) will be dependent on the setting and the relationship of the perpetrator amongst other factors.

Prevalence

Evidence on the extent and prevalence of different types of abuse has been provided from various sources, including a report of calls to the Action on Elder Abuse Helpline.[20]

There have also been specific investigations in particular locations following identification of abuse or even deaths. For example, institutional abuse was found to be 'prevalent in most parts of the learning disability service' in an investigation into Sutton and Merton PCT,[21] and described as 'widespread' in an investigation in Cornwall.[22]

The first published UK study on the prevalence of elder abuse in the community was conducted by Ogg and Bennett (1992).[23] This was carried out using an OPCS survey to interview adults over pensionable age in the general population about physical, verbal and financial abuse. The method used excluded adults in residential settings or adults who were disabled or ill. This is an important limitation, particularly when related to the risk factor, social isolation, and would suggest that the results are an underestimation. The resulting rates found that 1 in 20 older people had suffered verbal or financial abuse and 1 in 50 reported physical abuse. When the same definitions were used to ask adults under 60 if they had abused an older person, the survey produced rates of 1 in 10 for verbal abuse. The Ogg and Bennett study replicated prevalence figures from Pillemer and Finkelhor's 1988 Boston study.[24] It is likely that any measurement of abuse in the future will suggest that the phenomenon is increasing. An increase could be attributable to a number of factors, including demographic changes that have led to a larger population of elderly people, greater awareness and recognition of abuse and more sophisticated and reliable recording of referrals.

Subsequently, a Health Select Committee inquiry into the nature and extent of Elder Abuse 2003/4 made a key recommendation that 'multi-disciplinary research be commissioned by the Department of Health to ascertain the extent of this problem within society'. Arguably a research-based figure would be an effective lever for social policy and political change and be more persuasive than the mass of anecdotal accounts and evidence, for example from the **AEA** helpline.

A national survey was subsequently conducted and found a prevalence figure of 4 per cent, which is based on 'expectations of trust' that the older person may have held about the abuser. This equates to around 350,000 older people being abused each year. In a large proportion of cases, about two-thirds, the abuser was a family member. In a further 9 per cent of cases it was someone employed as domiciliary care staff. Neglect was the highest category of abuse followed by financial, psychological, physical and sexual. More women (5.4 per cent) were abused than men (1.6 per cent). The survey did not cover those with a cognitive inability to participate or those in residential settings.

Statistics published by the Health and Social Care Information Centre (2013) draw on information on safeguarding adults' referrals from councils with social services responsibilities. During the year 1 April 2012 to 31 March 2013 there were 109,000 referrals of which 43 per cent were wholly or partially substantiated, 61 per cent related to women and 62 per cent related to adults aged over 65. There were most allegations of physical abuse (28 per cent), followed by neglect (27 per cent), financial abuse (18 per cent), sexual abuse (5 per cent) and discriminatory abuse (1 per cent). Abuse occurred in the person's own home in 39 per cent of cases and in a residential setting in 36 per cent. The most likely category of perpetrator was social care staff (32 per cent) followed by family members (23 per cent).[25]

Responding to abuse

A duty to investigate

Prior to the Care Act 2014 there was no specific statutory duty to investigate concerns of possible adult abuse in England, although 'No Secrets' clearly envisaged social services as the key agency with responsibility for coordinating procedures for adult protection.

As guidance issued under s. 7 of the Local Authority and Social Services Act 1970, 'No Secrets' should be complied with unless local circumstances indicate exceptional reasons which justify a variation and it is arguable that the Human Rights Act 1998, by imposing a duty on public authorities to comply with the ECHR, may effectively act to 'upgrade' this status. Case law supported this interpretation.

In *Re Z (Local Authority: Duty)* [2005] 3 All ER 280 where a local authority was aware of a woman in their area who wished to be assisted to commit suicide, the court suggested the local authority had a number of duties. These were:

- to investigate the position of the vulnerable adult and consider her true position and intention;
- to consider whether she was legally competent to make and carry out her decision and intention;
- to consider whether any other influence could be operating on her position and intention and to ensure she had all the relevant information and knew all the available options;
- to consider whether to invoke the inherent jurisdiction of the High Court so that the question of competence could be judicially determined;
- if not competent, to provide all such assistance as might be reasonably required to determine and give effect to her best interests;
- if competent, to allow her in any lawful way to give effect to her decision;
- where there were reasonable grounds to suspect that the commission of a criminal offence might be involved, to draw that to the attention of the police;
- in exceptional circumstances to invoke the jurisdiction of the court under s. 222 of the Local Government Act 1972.

The Care Act 2014 clarifies the position with the introduction of a statutory duty to make enquiries, in s. 42:

---

s. 42

(1) This section applies where a local authority has reasonable cause to suspect that an adult in its area (whether or not ordinarily resident there) –

    (a) has needs for care and support (whether or not the authority is meeting any of those needs),

    (b) is experiencing, or is at risk of, abuse or neglect, and

    (c) as a result of those needs is unable to protect himself or herself against the abuse or neglect or the risk of it.

(2) The local authority must make (or cause to be made) whatever enquiries it thinks necessary to enable it to decide whether any action should be taken in the adult's case (whether under this Part or otherwise) and, if so, what and by whom.

(Care Act 2014)

The duty is imposed on the local authority but as subsection (2) provides that enquiries may 'cause to be made', it would be possible for the local authority to work with another agency, e.g. a health professional in leading the actual enquiries. The purpose of making enquiries is to decide whether to take any action, under the Act or otherwise. In many cases this will include an assessment of needs for care and support. It may also trigger a referral to the police. The Act does not include any additional powers to remove the individual or a perpetrator from an abusive situation, unlike the position under Scottish and (to be enacted) Welsh legislation.

If there is to be a safeguarding enquiry and the local authority considers that the individual might have difficulty understanding relevant information, retaining it, using it as part of the process of being involved or communicating wishes and feelings, then an independent advocate must be made available (s. 68 Care Act 2014).

The following stages in an investigation as outlined by 'No Secrets' continue to be relevant:

- reporting to a single referral point;
- recording, with sensitivity to the abused person, the precise factual details of the alleged abuse;
- initial coordination involving representatives of all agencies which might have a role in a subsequent investigation and could constitute the strategy meeting;
- investigation within a jointly agreed framework to determine the facts of the case; and
- decision-making, which may take place at a shared forum such as a case conference.[26]

'No Secrets' envisaged working in partnership with other agencies, including: commissioners and providers of health and social care services; providers of sheltered and supported housing; regulators of services; the police; the voluntary and private sector agencies; other local authority departments, e.g. housing and education; probation; DSS benefit agencies; carer support groups and user groups; advocacy services; community safety partnerships; and agencies offering legal advice.[27]

Since 'No Secrets', the Commission for Social Care Inspection, Association of Directors of Social Services and the Association of Chief Police Officers have produced a joint protocol which outlines the roles of key agencies in multi-agency procedures.[28] The Care Act strengthens this commitment to partnership with a general (s. 6) and specific (s. 7) duty of co-operation (see Chapter 14).

Safeguarding Adults Boards

In addition to the duty to make enquiries, the Care Act 2014 includes a statutory requirement for each local authority to establish a Safeguarding Adults Board (**SAB**) for its area (s. 43). The stated objective of the SAB is to 'help and protect adults' as described in s. 42(1), i.e. with needs for care and support, experiencing or at risk of abuse or neglect and as a result of those needs, unable to protect themselves against the abuse or neglect, or risk of it. Key membership is prescribed, e.g. police and health, and the Board has flexibility to invite others to join. A key function of the SAB will be to arrange for a Safeguarding Adults Review where there is reasonable cause for concern about how professionals worked together to safeguard an adult who has experienced serious abuse or neglect or has died and its is suspected that the death resulted from abuse or neglect (s. 44).

Legal options

As each form of abuse may merit a range of legal responses (or none at all), the law covered in this chapter is arranged in order of levels of intervention rather than according to the specific category of abuse. 'No Secrets' recognises both the various nature of abuse and responses to it: 'Action should be primarily supportive or therapeutic or it might involve the application of sanctions, suspension, regulatory activity or criminal prosecution, disciplinary action or de-registration from a professional body. Remember vulnerable adults who are victims like any other victims have a right to see justice' (para. 6.4).

Separate consideration is given to some of the particular issues, which may arise where the setting for abuse is the residential sector.

The legal framework for dealing with adult abuse remains complex despite the introduction of the Care Act 2014. A number of reasons have been given to explain underuse of the law in relation to adult abuse:

First, some legal procedures, particularly criminal prosecutions, are inappropriate in many cases of elder abuse because the perpetrators of abuse are themselves victims of the situation, for example, carers subject to an excessive degree of stress. Second, legal procedures are often under-utilised because of negative attitudes/lack of experience on the part of professionals such as lawyers and social workers. Third, the notion of abuse is seldom conceptualised in legal terms.[29]

These concerns are compounded by the lack of consensus over definitions and a limited UK research base. It is therefore necessary to be 'imaginative' in the use of existing law and guided by an objective of 'maximum autonomy, minimum intervention'.

Identification of a relevant legal provision will depend on the type of abuse and the desired outcome. Table 17.1 summarises for ease of reference the relevant legal provisions by category of abuse to which they are most likely to be applicable.

Table 17.1 Possible legal remedies by abuse category

Type of abuse	Legal remedies
Physical	Criminal prosecution – Offences Against the Person Act 1861 Domestic Violence, Crime and Victims Act 2004, s. 5 – causing or allowing the death or serious injury of a vulnerable adult Civil action – assault, battery or false imprisonment (restraint) Family Law Act 1996 injunctions – non-molestation and occupation Criminal Injuries Compensation claim Mental Health Act 1983, ss. 115, 135, 127, 117 – after-care Mental Capacity Act 2005 – ill-treatment and neglect Police and Criminal Evidence Act 1984, s. 17 – power to enter to save life and limb Care Standards Act 2000 and Health and Social Care Act 2008 – regulation of care homes and domiciliary provision Safeguarding Vulnerable Groups Act 2006 Care Act 2014 – support
Sexual	Criminal prosecution – Sexual Offences Act 2003. NB specific offences against people with severe learning disabilities Civil action (as above) Family Law Act 1996 injunction for non-molestation Mental Health Act 1983 Care Standards Act 2000 Care support
Psychological	Protection from Harassment Act 1997 Care Standards Act 2000 Anti-discrimination legislation Care support Anti-social behaviour order

Table 17.1 (Continued)

Type of abuse	Legal remedies
Neglect	Mental Health Act 1983, s. 127 Mental Capacity Act 2005 s.44 – ill-treatment and neglect Criminal law – *R v. Stone* [1977] 2 All ER 341
Financial	Lasting power of attorney Court of Protection – use of deputies Criminal prosecution – Theft Act 1968 (*R v. Hinks* [2001] 2 AC 241)
NB	Overarching effect of Human Rights Act 1998

Source: Adapted from L.-A. Cull and J. Roche (eds) (2001) *The Law and Social Work: Contemporary Issues for Practice*. Basingstoke: Palgrave.

Certain legal provisions will be more or less appropriate to particular types of abuse and some will be applicable only to specific categories: e.g. Sexual Offences Act 2003; Theft Act 1968. It is clear, however, that for most cases there will be a range of legal options. The selected option will depend on a number of factors including available evidence and seriousness of case. A major predisposing factor will be the desired outcome in tackling the abuse. Table 17.2 offers a further classification of legal provision by desired outcome or objective. Discussion of the various legal options outlined in Tables 17.1 and 17.2 continues in the following sections, separated into law relating to the prevention of abuse, action which can be taken by the victim, and formal responses. Existing legal options, as outlined in the tables above, are considered in more detail below.

Table 17.2 Adult protection: legal objectives

Objective	Legal provision
Support	Care Act 2014 Domiciliary services Duty to promote wellbeing Mental Health Act 1983, s. 7 (guardianship) Carers support – Care Act 2014 Direct payments Provision of accommodation
Prosecution	Criminal law – statute and common law Investigation by police and Crown Prosecution Service prosecution
Remove perpetrator	Family Law Act 1996 injunction Civil (law of tort) injunction Mental Health Act 1983
Remove subject	Mental Health Act 1983 (provision of accommodation) High Court Declaration, Court of Protection order
Compensation	Civil law Criminal Injuries Compensation Scheme Order of criminal court

Source: Adapted from L.-A. Cull and J. Roche (eds) (2001) *The Law and Social Work. Contemporary Issues for Practice*. Basingstoke: Palgrave.

Preventing abuse

'No Secrets' places great emphasis on the importance of prevention of abuse. 'The agencies' primary aim should be to prevent abuse where possible, but if the preventive strategy fails, agencies should ensure that robust procedures are in place for dealing with incidents of abuse' (para. 1.2). Social services are expected to be the lead agency dealing with a case of abuse and have a duty to provide care and support under the Care Act 2014 where an individual's needs meet the threshold for support. In terms of interventions, except in the most serious cases, provision of an appropriate care package will often be the first step. (Chapter 14 deals with assessment for and provision of care and support in some detail.) In this context it is important to remember that in many situations an individual can legitimately refuse both assessment for and provision of services. In neglect cases such refusal may be one of the central concerns and an initial refusal of support should not be taken at face value. The Care Act introduces a specific exception to this whereby a local authority must carry out a needs assessment in the face of a refusal. The circumstances are where the adult lacks capacity to refuse the assessment and it would be in his best interests. Secondly, if the adult is experiencing, or at risk of, abuse or neglect, the local authority must carry out a needs assessment.

In attempting to provide solutions to abusive situations, it is crucial that workers have confidence in the ability of any services offered to minimise the possibility of an already abused person being subject to further abuse. It was thus of concern that domiciliary or day-care services, often included in care packages, were not subject to any formal regulation prior to introduction of the Care Standards Act 2000.

Support services to carers may help to lessen the risk of abuse to vulnerable adults. (There is no assumption here that carers form a significant body of 'abusers'. Early works on elder abuse suggested that 'carer stress' was a predisposing factor to elder abuse. In fact, research has not found this to be the case.) The Care Act 2014 provides for a separate assessment of the needs of a person providing or proposing to provide care. Services can be provided to enable that person to better fulfil the caring role, e.g. support with shopping. If the subject of a needs assessment or carer assessment is likely to have difficulty understanding relevant information, retaining it, using it as part of the process of being involved or communicationg wishes and feelings, then an independent advocate must be made available.

Screening out unsuitable people

One of the most effective ways of reducing abuse must be to ensure that unsuitable adults do not come into contact with vulnerable adults in a caring role. The Care Standards Act 2000, s. 81 introduced a duty of the Secretary of State to keep a list of individuals who are considered unsuitable to work with vulnerable adults, the Protection of Vulnerable Adults (**POVA**) index.[30] in similar terms to the list established under the Protection of Children Act 1999.

As an example, in *Close* v. *Secretary of State for Health* [2008] EWCST 852, the Care Standards Tribunal found that a care home worker who slept on waking shifts, and verbally abused residents was unsuitable to work with vulnerable adults. In assessing unsuitability, the tribunal noted that it would have regard to (amongst other things): the number of incidents constituting misconduct; gravity of misconduct; degree of recognition by the individual that the conduct was harmful; any extenuating circumstances.

Operational aspects of the POVA list were challenged and have been found incompatible with ECHR Arts. 6(1) and 8; (*R (Wright and others)* v. *Secretary of State for Health and another* [2009] UKHL 3. The whole scheme has been replaced by the Safeguarding Vulnerable Groups Act 2006, as amended by the Protection of Freedoms Act 2012.

Safeguarding Vulnerable Groups Act 2006

The Safeguarding Vulnerable Groups Act 2006 was introduced following the Bichard inquiry and established a new vetting and barring scheme. As before with POVA, any such scheme must be seen as a complement to and not a substitute for effective recruitment strategies. The functions under the Act were invested in a new body, the Independent Safeguarding Authority. There were a number of criticisms of the vetting and barring scheme and operation of the ISA, and the Coalition Government expressed its intention to simplify the scheme. The Protection of Freedoms Act 2012 amended the scheme and integrated the functions of the ISA with the Criminal Records Bureau into a further new organisation, the Disclosure and Barring Service (DBS).

There continue to be two lists, one containing names of people barred from working with children and one in respect of vulnerable adults and it is possible for a person to be included on both lists. It is an offence for anyone on the list(s) to engage or seek to engage in a regulated activity. Organisations must not knowingly engage a barred person. The scheme applies to regulated activities as defined in Schedule 4 of the Safeguarding Vulnerable Groups Act 2007 to include:

- provision of health care to an adult;
- provision of personal care to an adult;
- provision of social work by a social care worker to a client or potential client;
- provision of assistance with general household matters to an adult in need by reason of age, illness or disability;
- assistance in the conduct of an adults affarirs by a LPA, EPA, IMHA, IMCA, independent advocacy services;
- conveying of persons as needed by reason of age, illness or disability;
- other activities as prescribed.

A vulnerable adult under the scheme is one to whom a regulated activity relating to vulnerable adults is provided.

An individual will be added to the barred list where certain criminal offences have been committed, e.g. ill-treatment or wilful neglect and automatically when an offence under ss. 30–41 of the Sexual Offences Act 2003 has been committed; also where a person has engaged in relevant conduct which endangers (or is likely to) a vulnerable adult, including conduct involving sexually explicit images of violence or inappropriate conduct of a sexual nature including a vulnerable adult. Finally an individual's name will be added to the barred list if it appears they may harm, attempt to harm, put at risk of harm, or incite another to harm a vulnerable adult and he has been or may in future be engaged in regulated activity.

Inclusion on the barred list will be for one, five or ten years and appeals may be made to the Upper Tribunal. The DBS can review inclusion if there has been a change of circumstances, error or further information has become available. A criminal record certificate is sent to the individual and may be updated so that it is portable and no longer necessary to apply for a new certificate for new jobs.

One criticism of the scheme is that it does not apply to purely private arrangements. In the context of 'personalisation' this could mean that some vulnerable adults who advertise privately, for example for household support, might employ an individual who is not obliged to register with the scheme. Under the new arrangements there is likely to be a reduction in the number of individuals subject to barring checks.

In addition to POVA, the Care Standards Act created the General Social Care Council to ensure regulation of the social care workforce and promote high standards. Social care workers were required to register with the GSCC. The GSCC was abolished by the Health and Social Care Act 2012 and the professional register is now held by the Health and Care Professions Council (HCPC). The title 'social worker' may only be used by those people who are so registered, an offence is committed otherwise. Where there are concerns about the professional practice of a social worker a fitness to practice hearing may be held. It is possible for the HCPC to remove a person from the register, suspend registration or add conditions to registration.

Preventing financial abuse

In cases of financial abuse[31] it is often difficult to recoup property and, in the longer term, greater emphasis on effective management of financial affairs as a means of preventing abuse may be more effective. If an individual is not able to manage part or all of their financial affairs, which may be due, for example, to a lack of mental capacity or physical difficulty in collecting a pension, there are a variety of ways to delegate that function. The options vary depending on whether the individual has mental capacity to manage their financial affairs. (For a fuller discussion of issues concerning mental capacity, see Chapter 16.)

Agency

Where a person has a mental capacity but needs another person simply to collect their benefits, they may nominate an agent. In the short term, the declaration on the reverse of the benefit order is completed; for the longer term, an agency card from Jobcentre Plus can be completed. There is no monitoring of agency agreements.

Third party mandate

A third party mandate can be used by a person with mental capacity to authorise another person to act on their behalf in bank or building society transactions.

Appointee

If the person is unable to act because of physical or mental incapacity, another person may be appointed to exercise the right to make claims, or receive and spend them for the sole benefit of the individual. This does not have to be a permanent arrangement. Normally, a close relative or friend or someone in regular contact with the adult is appropriate as an appointee. If there is no one else suitable, social services or voluntary bodies may act. Jobcentre Plus should be satisfied that the individual claimant is unable to manage his financial affairs and it should be satisfied as to the suitability of the person who intends to act. If the person is in residential or nursing home accommodation, the proprietor should be appointed only as a last resort, as normally there should be no potential for conflict of interest. Although this provision applies where the individual entitled to benefits lacks capacity to manage the process of claiming etc., the Mental Capacity Act 2005 did not give separate consideration to it.

Power of attorney

A power of attorney is a legal document, which can be used by a person with mental capacity to authorise another person (or persons) to handle his financial affairs. The power may provide general authority or it may be limited to a specific action, e.g. sale of property. The power of attorney remains valid until revoked or the donor loses mental capacity.

Lasting power of attorney

The lasting power of attorney (LPA) is introduced by the Mental Capacity Act 2005 and replaces the old enduring power of attorney.[32]

It is a document which can provide for a person (the attorney) to deal with the financial affairs of an individual (the donor) in the future if that individual loses mental capacity. The LPA can also be used in relation to health and welfare decisions, whereas the EPA was limited to finance and property matters. There are separate forms for personal welfare LPAs and for property affairs LPAs. It is particularly suitable for people who are concerned that they may suffer from some form of dementia or Alzheimer's disease in the future. It must be prepared whilst the donor still has mental capacity. If there is any doubt as to whether the donor has capacity, it is normal practice for the solicitor drawing up the document to obtain medical opinion, having advised the doctor of the test of capacity (*Re K, Re F* [1988] 1 All ER 358). The document must include a certificate completed by an independent third party (e.g. this could be a doctor) to confirm that, in their view, the donor understands the purpose of the LPA, there was no fraud or undue pressure used to persuade the donor to make the LPA and there is no other reason to stop the creation of the LPA.

The Court of Protection, Office of the Public Guardian and deputies

The Court of Protection, established under the Mental Capacity Act 2005, has jurisdiction in relation to adults who lack capacity to make decisions, including decisions relating to property and financial affairs. An application to the court should be made if an individual is unable to manage their financial affairs and has not executed an enduring power of attorney. The court can appoint a deputy to act on the patient's behalf making decisions in the best interests of the person. The deputy may be a relative or friend or a professional (such as a solicitor or accountant) or the local authority. A deputy will be appointed where there is an ongoing need for decision-making. A one-off decision of the court will be preferred if this is sufficient to deal with the issue in question.

The Office of the Public Guardian (OPG)[33] has a role in supervision of attorneys under LPAs and deputies. This supervisory role is conducted in conjunction with other protective measures and other relevant agencies, such as the police and social services, acting within the 'No Secrets' framework. The Public Guardian maintains a register of LPAs and deputies and supervises deputies. The work of the Public Guardian is supported by Court of Protection Visitors, whose role includes visiting people who lack capacity and providing independent advice to the court and to the Public Guardian. If a concern is raised with the Public Guardian in relation to a LPA or deputy or in another respect, concerning an adult lacking capacity, the Public Guardian may carry out investigations itself and/or cooperate with other relevant agencies, most obviously social services, following 'No Secrets', and the police. The code of practice to the MCA provides two examples where a referral might be made to another agency:

> Someone has complained that a welfare attorney is physically abusing a donor – the OPG would refer this case to the relevant local authority adult protection procedures and possibly the police.

> The OPG found that a solicitor appointed as a financial deputy for an elderly woman has defrauded her estate – the OPG would refer this case to the police and the Law Society Consumer Complaints Service. (para. 14.22)

Residential settings

The framework for regulation (which implicitly includes prevention of abuse) of residential care homes and domiciliary care agencies was provided by the Care Standards Act 2000.[34] It is now largely contained in the Health and Social Care Act 2008 and associated regulations. The framework includes a registration requirement and provisions for attaching conditions and cancelling registration. The registration and inspection body, the Care Quality Commission, operates independently of social services and clearly has a role to play where abuse takes place in a setting that is regulated as its stated objective is to promote the health, safety and welfare of people who use health and social care services (s. 3 Health and Social Care Act 2008). Social services will also have direct involvement with care homes in both their care management and commissioning roles.[35] Any concerns of possible abuse, which the home is aware of, should be notified to the registration authority. The Care Quality Commission (Registration) Regulations 2009 stipulate that the registered person for the care home should notify the Commission without delay of: any abuse or allegation of abuse in relation to a service user; any incident reported to the police; any deprivation of liberty request; the death of any service user, including the circumstances of death; anything which is likely to prevent the service providers carrying on regulated activity safely, including shortage of staff, interruption of utility supplies, physical damage to the property and failure of alarms.

If a complaint relating to abuse is received by the inspection unit, adult protection procedures should be clear about the role of the regulatory authority in investigations. Enforcement action (possibly cancellation of registration or prosecution) should be considered if abuse has occurred in a residential setting.[36] It should be recognised that abuse in a residential setting, as in the community, may take many forms. The abuse may relate to poor standards of care or the regime in a home[37] or it may be a single isolated incident, e.g. where a resident is sexually abused during a visit from a relative.

The practice of restraint in some care homes has been identified as an issue of concern.[38] Types of restraint include the use of furniture to prevent a resident moving around freely, bed sides, baffle locks and chemical coshes. Restraint without consent is clearly unlawful unless it can be justified as self-defence or to prevent a crime. The reality of the circumstances of many of the individuals who are subject to restraint means that individual legal challenge is unlikely. It is, however, an important aspect of the way a home is run and should be considered by the regulatory body. Regulation 11 of the Health and Social care Act 2008 (Regulated Activities) Regulations 2010 states that: 'Where any form of control or restraint is used ... the registered person must have suitable arrangements in place to protect service users against the risk of such restraint being unlawful or otherwise excessive.'

The following case provides an example of the need for close regulation of residential accommodation. It reached the Registered Homes Tribunal (whilst the Registered Homes Act 1984 was in force). In *Freeman and Goodwin* v. *Northamptonshire County Council* (2000) Decision 421, 20 December, the decision of the registration authority for cancellation was confirmed. The home in Northamptonshire was registered to accept 16 people with physical disability, or mental handicap and mental disorder. Mrs Goodwin, the Freemans' daughter, was registered manager. Reasons for cancellation included failure to care for a particular resident, Alan (AT), and recognise his care needs. Also there were concerns relating to inability to look after the financial needs of the residents: £19,000 of the residents' money was unaccounted for and some personal money had been used to pay for items for the home. In addition, employment practices, training, induction procedures and staff records were inadequate. Proper records had not been kept, including medication records, and records had been falsified on the instruction of the manager. Mrs Freeman had never played any part in running the home; she should not have been registered and was unfit to continue because of her complete inaction.

Mr Freeman felt it was not necessarily inappropriate for male staff to carry out intimate personal care for female residents. Previous experience of staff was not recorded. One resident, AT, had been kept in conditions of squalor and degradation, he had been deprived of his liberty, his dignity was ignored, his right to property compromised, and he was in pain with a dental abscess and no action had been taken to treat him. One of the inspection officers commented that she had never seen an animal kept in that way. He had effectively been abandoned by Essex County Council 12 years ago and kept in conditions reminiscent of those which led to the closure of many large mental institutions. He spent time sitting on a plastic chair dressed in only a ripped T-shirt, surrounded by urine, in a cold room with no bed linen and a high handle on the door to prevent escape. Of the 15 residents, only four had a care plan.

The human rights implications were noted in the judgment:

> We had in mind that Local Authorities now have a duty under the Human Rights Act 1998 to safeguard the rights of those, like AT, for whom they are responsible. We consider that both Essex and Northampton as public authorities by virtue of section 6 of the Act, behaved in a way which was incompatible with AT's Convention rights. Inspection units and Registered Persons should consider that it may be appropriate to look at how Convention (Human) rights are promoted and protected in Registered Homes when questions of Registration and 'fitness' arise.[39]

In *Freeman* it could be argued that aspects of the regime could amount to inhuman or degrading treatment under ECHR, Art. 3. Application of this article hinges on the definition of the terms used. In *Ireland* v. *United Kingdom* (1978) 2 EHRR 25 five techniques – wall standing, hooding, subjection to noise, and deprivation of sleep, food and drink – were held not to amount to torture but were degrading treatment. 'Torture' was defined as deliberate inhuman treatment causing very serious and cruel suffering; 'inhuman treatment' as intense physical and mental suffering and acute psychiatric disturbances; and 'degrading treatment' as behaviour which aroused in the victim fears of anguish and inferiority capable of humiliating and debasing them and possibly breaking their physical or moral resistance. The case also said that ill-treatment must attain a minimum level of severity. That is a relative issue and will depend on all the circumstances of the case, including duration of treatment, its physical and mental effects, age, sex and state of health of the victim.

The right to enjoyment of private and family life contained in Art. 8 may also have an application in the residential sector. There is potential for it to be relied on in the following examples: moving from independent living in the community to residential accommodation; sharing rooms; communal meals only; no provision for couples to be together; lack of after-care services; covert surveillance; issues involving physical integrity, e.g. tagging; and violations which relate to a person's dignity as an aspect of private life.

The right to respect for a person's home formed part of the argument in *R* v. *North and East Devon Health Authority, ex parte Coughlan* [2000] 3 All ER 850. The health authority intended to close the home in which the applicant lived. Amongst other arguments, it was found that the health authority was in breach of Art. 8 on the basis that Mardon House was the applicant's home and their promise of a home for life for the resident had been broken. The savings the authority would make by closing the home did not outweigh the loss to the applicant of her home.

Action by the victim

It may be effective and empowering for an individual to take private law action to counter abuse. There are clear scenarios where this route would be available legally but may not be at the forefront of professionals' minds as an appropriate intervention. Behaviour, of a physical, psychological or sexual nature, which would ordinarily be classified as domestic violence, might be described as adult abuse where the victim is a vulnerable adult. The conceptual difference and complexities of definition are highlighted in the example of graduated domestic violence. If domestic violence has always been a feature of a couple's relationship, when they each turn 65 years of age does it suddenly become labelled elder/adult abuse? For these purposes the available law does not draw any distinctions based on age. Recourse may be taken to the Family Law Act 1996, the law of contract and the law of tort.

Where an individual lacks capacity to bring legal proceedings, a 'litigation friend' may be appointed to do so on their behalf (Civil Procedure Rules, r. 21) (as in e.g. *R* v. *Bournewood Community and Mental Health NHS Trust, ex parte L* [1998] 3 All ER 289). The implications of this may include the case being heard in a higher court than is routine for the particular application, and also possible involvement of the Official Solicitor.

Family Law Act 1996

The Family Law Act 1996 includes provisions relating to domestic violence. (These were discussed in Chapter 8.) The potential availability of injunctions to prevent abuse in an adult protection context was significantly expanded by this Act. Previously, only where abuse took place between spouses or cohabitees was recourse to injunctions available under a range of domestic violence legislation. The new legislation broadens the range of relationships that are covered.

Orders are available in respect of an 'associated person'. This term is defined in s. 62 and includes spouses, civil partners, cohabitees (including same-sex couples) (and previous spouses, civil partners and cohabitees), people who have had an intimate relationship which is or was of a significant duration (who do not live together), people who have agreed to marry, people living in the same household (but not as lodgers or tenants) and relatives of the person or their spouse or cohabitee. Victims of abuse occurring within a homosexual relationship or at the hands of a grandchild (for example) can now apply speedily for injunctions under the Family Law Act 1996, whereas previously they were limited to an application in the law of tort.

A number of police forces now include adult abuse within the responsibility of domestic violence units. Domestic violence cases are considered at the local MARAC (Multi-Agency Risk Assessment Conference for victims of domestic violence at high risk of serious assault or homicide). It is not currently possible for a third party to make an application for a domestic violence injunction. There is provision for this in **FLA** 1996 s. 60, but the provision has not been implemented. It is arguable that in some cases the victim of domestic violence would prefer a third party to make the application on their behalf and that investing the responsibility in, for example, social services would reinforce the state's responsibility to protect victims of violence. A possible disadvantage might be that if orders are sought by a third party then a police prosecution might be less likely.[40]

Contract

In addition to family law, an individual may also have recourse to the private law of contract and tort. Local authorities can require higher standards in homes they contract with than standards specified under legislation (*R* v. *Cleveland County Council, ex parte Cleveland Care Homes Association* (1993) 17 BMLR 122).

Particularly relevant to financial or property abuse, the law of contract offers protection whereby an individual who enters into a contract under duress or undue influence will not be bound by its terms. For example, if a vulnerable adult is falsely persuaded that it would be advantageous to transfer his house to a younger relative, the remedy in contract will be revocation of the contract or damages. In *Re Craig (Deceased)* [1971] Ch 95, a will which was drawn up under undue influence was set aside. In certain circumstances a presumption of undue influence arises. In *Hammond* v. *Osborn* [2002] EWCA Civ 885, an elderly bachelor transferred over 90 per cent of his assets, amounting to nearly £300,000, to a caregiver. The court was somewhat suspicious that major assets were transferred to a carer of recent acquaintance and found that it was for the carer to rebut the presumption of undue influence by reason of the relationship between them. If the elderly man had taken independent advice, the court would have been more likely to find that he had entered into the transaction of his own free will.

An alternative approach was evident in *R* v. *Hinks* [2001] 2 AC 241. Acquiring property by accepting gifts from a vulnerable and trusting person amounted to 'appropriation' under the Theft Act 1968. The defendant, aged 38 was friendly with Mr Dolphin, a man described to be of limited intelligence, aged 53. In evidence before the House of Lords, a consultant psychiatrist described him as naïve and trusting and having no idea of the values of his assets. Over a six-month period Mr Dolphin visited his building society daily and withdrew the maximum sum of £300, totalling around £60,000, the majority of his savings. The prosecution case was that the defendant had influenced and coerced Mr Dolphin to withdraw the money and she was found guilty of four counts of theft.

Tort

Under the law of tort, civil action may be instigated for assault (reasonable cause to fear direct harm), e.g. pointing a knife at someone; battery (actual direct and intentional application of force), e.g. a punch, unwanted kiss or removal of false teeth without consent; and false imprisonment (infliction of physical restraint not authorised by law), e.g. being tied to a chair or locked inside a room. The use of unauthorised restraint in the residential sector is well documented.[41] Criminal offences of assault, battery and false imprisonment also exist and a separate prosecution may be taken for the behaviour. Negligence may also be relevant (particularly regarding 'professional' care), where a duty of care is established, there is a breach of that duty, by act or omission, and harm is suffered as a consequence. As noted earlier, the previous public immunity enjoyed by local authorities is reduced and negligence claims are now more likely to succeed against local authorities where the elements of negligence are satisfied. The principal remedy is compensatory damages; however, there are examples of the use of injunctions to prevent further abusive acts (*Egan* v. *Egan* [1975] 1 Ch 218; *Patel* v. *Patel* [1988] 2 FLR 179). Vicarious liability may arise in respect of the negligent acts of another: e.g. a care home owner may be vicariously liable for the negligent actions of his staff.

Formal responses

Under the heading of formal responses, legal provisions, which are utilised or commenced by another party in a position of authority, are considered. The options include use of disciplinary proceedings, declaratory relief, the criminal law and the Mental Health Act 1983.

In any case where the abuser comes into contact with the vulnerable adult in the course of their employment (e.g. a nurse, care worker, teacher or social worker), disciplinary action may be taken in respect of that individual. Abuse of a patient or service user would almost certainly amount to a breach of contract of employment and could lead to dismissal. In addition, the relevant professional body may take action in relation to their code of conduct. For example, the UKCC, the professional body for nurses (now the Nursing and Midwifery Council), found that breach of the client–practitioner relationship was the basis of 64 per cent of conduct hearings. More specifically, of those removed from the professional register each year, 10 per cent worked in the learning disability field, 15 per cent in mental health and 30 per cent were employed in the care of older people.[42] Closely linked to this, the Disclosure and Barring Service have been discussed above.

When concerns arise in the workplace, the role of whistleblowing becomes relevant (see discussion in Chapter 4). Whistleblowing in the context of adult protection is in the first instance likely to relate to a particular abuse scenario. It may also have a longer-term effect in preventing further abuse and helping to inform good practice. 'No Secrets' acknowledges whistleblowing, noting '… it is the responsibility of all staff to act on any suspicion or evidence of abuse or neglect (see the Public Interest Disclosure Act 1998) and to pass on their concerns to a responsible person/agency' (para. 6.2). For complaints and concerns about poor practice to be heard, well-publicised and accessible complaints procedures are vital. In the employment context, ECHR, Art. 10 states that everyone has the right to freedom of expression, which should override any gagging clauses designed to prevent whistleblowing and supports the provisions of the Public Interest Disclosure Act 1998.

Declaratory relief

Prior to the introduction of the Mental Capacity Act 2005, a body of case law (in the High Court and above) developed based on declaratory relief to assist in the resolution of disputes about health and welfare issues for adults who lack capacity. Where proceedings are instituted, the Official Solicitor will represent the interests of the person whose capacity is at issue (as his litigation friend). There is no mechanism for the Official Solicitor to instigate proceedings. Cases have reached court on application by local authorities or family members. Declarations are used to determine the lawfulness of a particular position and can provide for injunctions. As interim injunctions are available, there is the potential to use declaratory relief in emergency cases, e.g. if a person is threatening to remove an adult who lacks capacity from their usual place of residence.

Declaratory relief cases originated in the area of medical intervention, and have been used in cases involving sterilisation and withdrawal of life-saving treatment. Their use has extended to the area of welfare decisions and it is this aspect that is most pertinent to adult protection. Decisions have been taken about residence, contact, religion and culture.

In declaratory relief the decision of the court will be based on the best interests principle. (This is discussed in more detail in Chapter 16 relating to mental capacity.) In *Re MB (Caesarean Section)* [1997] 2 FLR 426, Butler-Sloss LJ stated that this includes all relevant information about a person's circumstances and background. A significant case on declaratory relief and adult protection is *Re F (Adult: Court's Jurisdiction)* [2000] 3 WLR 1740. The central issue in the case was whether the court had jurisdiction to grant declarations sought by a local authority as to the place of residence and contact arrangements for a mentally handicapped woman who was unable to care for herself. It was held that, where there was a risk of possible harm in respect of an adult who lacked the capacity to make decisions as to his or her own future, the court had power, under the inherent jurisdiction and in the best interests of that person, to hear the issue involved and to grant the necessary declarations. It was accepted that the woman concerned had the intellectual age of a 5–8-year-old child and she lacked capacity to make decisions as to her future. She did not come within the guardianship provisions of the Mental Health Act 1983, and, as she was aged over 18, the wardship jurisdiction could not be utilised.

The local authority based its application on concern that T was at risk of suffering harm in the family home and sought to determine her residence in a local authority residential home and restrict contact with her mother, Mrs F. She had been placed in local authority accommodation prior to her seventeenth birthday with parental consent, which was since withdrawn. The family circumstances were complex and featured local authority involvement. T was the eldest of eight children; her seven brothers and sisters were in local authority care. The local authority case provided evidence of chronic neglect, a lack of minimum standards of hygiene and cleanliness in the home, a serious lack of adequate parenting, worrying exposure to those engaged in sexual exploitation and possible sexual abuse of the children. Reference was made to the earlier case of *Re S (Hospital Patient: Court's Jurisdiction)* [1996] Fam 1 and the court found that there was a serious justiciable issue in this case, which could be dealt with under the common law doctrine of necessity. In response to argument that the court did not have jurisdiction to act, Butler-Sloss LJ noted:

> There is an obvious gap in the framework of care for mentally incapacitated adults. If the court cannot act and the local authority case is correct, this vulnerable young woman would be left at serious risk with no recourse to protection, other than the future possibility of the criminal law. That is a serious injustice to T, who has rights which she is unable, herself, to protect.[43]

The court was prepared to go beyond the local authority application for T to reside in local authority accommodation and was also prepared to sanction 'the use of such physical restriction as may be needed to keep T there and out of harm's way'.[44]

Such a case, where the individual lacks capacity as defined in the Mental Capacity Act 2005 would now be heard by the Court of Protection, which has powers to make declarations about single issues and appoint deputies to have a continuing decision-making role. (This is discussed in full in Chapter 16.) Nevertheless, the reasoning adopted in these cases is likely to be followed by the Court of Protection if faced with similar issues. This court is also intended to be more accessible than the High Court and less costly.

There may still be some cases that will be heard by the High Court rather than the Court of Protection, if Munby LJ's interpretation of the term 'vulnerable adult' in the case of *Re SA (Vulnerable Adult with Capacity: Marriage)* [2005] EWHC 2942 (Fam) is followed. The case concerned a young woman who needed to be protected from an unsuitable arranged marriage. Evidence suggested that she had capacity to marry and understood the concept of marriage, but would have difficulty understanding a specific marriage contract to a specific individual which would involve moving to Pakistan, where she did not want to live. The local authority wanted her to continue to receive the protection of the court that she had benefited from as a minor under the inherent jurisdiction. Munby J stated:

> ... the inherent jurisdiction can be exercised in relation to a vulnerable adult who, even if not incapacitated ... is, or is reasonably believed to be, either (i) under constraint or (ii) subject to coercion or undue influence or (iii) for some other reason deprived of the capacity to make the relevant decision, or disabled from making a free choice, or incapacitated or disabled from giving a real and genuine consent.

> I would treat as a vulnerable adult someone who, whether or not mentally incapacitated, and whether or not suffering from any mental illness or mental disorder, is or may be unable to take care of himself, or unable to protect himself against significant harm or exploitation, or who is deaf, blind or dumb, or substantially handicapped by illness, injury or congenital deformity. This 'is not and is not intended to be a definition. It is descriptive, not definitive; indicative rather than prescriptive.'

This judgment recognises that there may be adults who do not fall within the scope of the Mental Capacity Act 2005, but nevertheless require some protection. The route in such cases would be to the High Court, rather than the Court of Protection.

A significant recent safeguarding case which applies the 'Munby vulnerable' concept was heard by the Court of Appeal. *DL* v. *A Local Authority* [2012] EWCA Civ 253, confirms that the inherent jurisdiction continues to exist in addition to the Mental Capacity Act 2005, as an important 'safety net', and its existence is compatible with Article 8 of the European Convention. The court responded to a local authority's application for a non-molestation order to prevent aggressive and violent behaviour towards an older couple by their adult son who lived with them, where the couple had taken no steps to protect themselves.

Independent mental capacity advocates and adult protection

In cases where an individual lacks capacity to make a decision about long-term accommodation or serious medical treatment, and has no family or friends, an IMCA must be appointed. (The role of the IMCA was discussed in Chapter 16.) There is also a power for local authorities and the NHS to instruct an IMCA in an adult protection situation, if satisfied that it would be of particular benefit to the person to do so, where two criteria are met:

- Protective measures (in accordance with 'No Secrets' guidance) are being put into place.
- The person lacks capacity (includes a person who it is alleged has been abused or neglected and a person who is alleged to be the abuser). (In adult protection cases there is not a requirement that there is no other person to consult.)

Where the criteria are met the LA/NHS must consider whether to appoint an IMCA. For this consideration local authorities and the NHS are advised to develop a policy statement to be applied when deciding whether there would be a particular benefit. This should achieve consistency within the area, but regional variation is likely. When making a decision about the accommodation review, or about protective measures, the LA/NHS must take into account the IMCA's view or information provided but is not bound to follow it.

Criminal law

In contrast to the United States, there is no specific offence of adult or elder abuse in the United Kingdom. An exception to this statement has been introduced by the Mental Capacity Act 2005 in relation to adults lacking capacity, and is discussed below. Abuse may nevertheless encompass behaviour that constitutes a criminal offence under common law and statute, such as assault, actual or grievous bodily harm, indecent assault, rape and theft. Reservations have been expressed questioning the appropriateness of applying the criminal law to elder abuse cases, particularly where family members are included. Williams argues that use of the word 'abuse' can undermine the impact of the Act, which in other circumstances would clearly be seen as crimes.[45] However, Hugman suggests that, given the complexity and sensitivity of some abuse situations, where it may not be clear who the 'victim' is, criminalising all abusive acts is inappropriate.[46]

Increasingly, inter-agency guidelines will involve the police and provide for some level of joint investigation of elder abuse by the police and social services. Where there is a criminal investigation by the police, this will take priority over all other lines of enquiry. Early involvement of the police can have a number of benefits, including preservation of evidence and avoidance of multiple interviews of the victim.[47] Initially, to start the process it is normally necessary for the victim to make a complaint and be willing to press charges. Ultimately, the decision whether to bring a criminal prosecution rests with the Crown Prosecution Service, who must be satisfied that to prosecute is in the public interest and that there is a good prospect of conviction. Evidential difficulties, including the high standard of proof required, the fact that there will often be no witnesses to abuse and the perceived inability of adults with learning difficulties or older individuals, who may be mentally or physically frail, to give evidence, may influence the decision not to proceed. Encouragingly, the Youth Justice and Criminal Evidence Act 1999[48] introduces provision of **special measures** to assist 'vulnerable witnesses', including use of video-recorded evidence, intermediaries and the presence of a 'supporter' when a vulnerable witness is interviewed. Other practical steps, which can make giving evidence a less stressful experience, include court familiarisation, use of screens and the removal of wigs by judges and barristers.[49] In addition, extension of the role of the appropriate adult to situations where a vulnerable adult is being interviewed as a victim or possible witness, rather than as a suspect, has been suggested.[50] (These provisions are discussed in more depth in Chapter 18.) It is important not to deny the criminal route to vulnerable adults if they are willing to become involved in the criminal process, which serves to position acts of abuse as unacceptable criminal behaviour. 'No Secrets' clearly recognises this position:

> Some instances of abuse will constitute a criminal offence. In this respect vulnerable adults are entitled to the protection of law in the same way as any other member of the public. (para. 2.8)

Sexual abuse

The Sexual Offences Act 2003 (**SOA** 2003) replaces the Sexual Offences Act 1956 and provides specific designated sexual offences. It is a complex piece of legislation, which covers sexual offences generally, including offences against children, adults whose capacity is impaired and familial sexual offences (incest). Under the Act all offences (rape excepted) are gender neutral, unless there is good reason to provide otherwise, so that a female carer who sexually abuses will also be culpable.

The Act includes a statutory definition of consent so that 'free agreement' to sexual relations becomes a prerequisite, and a broad definition of 'sexual activity'. There are particular offences against persons with a mental disorder which can be grouped into three categories – thankfully the old term 'defective' which featured in the previous legislation does not feature in the new law. Sections 30–33 cover offences against people who cannot legally consent to sexual activity because of a mental disorder impeding choice, i.e. because of the mental disorder he is likely to be unable to refuse. A person is unable to refuse if he lacks the capacity to choose whether to agree to engaging in the activity (whether because he lacks sufficient understanding of the nature or reasonably foreseeable consequences of the activity, or for any other reason), or he is unable to communicate such a choice.

Sections 34–37 cover offences against people who may or may not be able to consent to sexual activity but who are vulnerable to inducements, threats or deceptions because of a mental disorder. In such cases the person may appear to have agreed but consent cannot be deemed to have been given freely, because of inducements, threats or deceptions, e.g. telling the person that sex is an expected part of friendship or threatening to hurt family members. The new statutory scheme is not intended to interfere with the right to a sexual life of people who have capacity to consent, as the Guidance to the Act reminds: 'It is important to appreciate that where a person with a mental disorder is able to consent freely to sexual activity, they have the same rights to engage in sexual activity as anyone else.'

Care worker offences (breach of relationship to care) are the third category of offences against people with a mental disorder introduced by the Act. Where a care worker who has face-to-face contact through employment (which includes unpaid work) in a care home, NHS body or independent health setting engages in sexual activity with a person with a mental disorder, an offence is committed. The offences would prohibit relations between patients with a mental disorder and staff; residents and staff; persons receiving care in the community services and the care providers; doctors, therapists and their clients. Finally, a new offence of 'voyeurism' is included. Where a person in a building has a reasonable expectation of privacy and is observed without their consent or knowledge, this would amount to an offence and could be relevant in the residential sector. The existence of these special offences in relation to mental disorder of the victim do not preclude use of other general offences, such as rape, and it will be for the police and CPS to determine the most appropriate offence to charge.

In addition, under the Crime (Sentences) Act 1997, automatic life sentences will be imposed for anyone convicted of a second serious sexual offence.

Crime and disorder

Other developments in the criminal law, which may impact on adult protection, have included certain provisions of the Crime and Disorder Act 1998, such as the introduction of sex offender orders. (The anti-social behaviour order (and reforms under ABCPA 2014) are outlined in the context of youth justice in Chapter 13.) It is an order that may also be relevant to the abuse of vulnerable adults, particularly since stranger abuse has gained formal recognition in 'No Secrets'.[51] Anyone over the age of 10 may be the subject of an application by a council, Housing Action Trust or the police. An order may be made where a person has acted in an anti-social manner and it is necessary to protect persons living in the local government area from further anti-social acts. Anti-social behaviour is that which causes harassment, alarm or distress to people of another household. It is a civil order of not less than two years' duration, intended to deal with criminal or sub-criminal activity, to restrain anti-social behaviour which other individuals cannot be expected to tolerate. The scenario where a gang of youths are bullying and frightening older people or adults with learning disabilities would be an appropriate case for an order. Breach of the order is a criminal offence. Adult protection can be seen as an aspect of community safety, a key focus of the Crime and Disorder Act, and addressed in partnership working between the police and local authorities via crime reduction and community safety strategies.

Harassment

The Protection from Harassment Act 1997 contains a number of harassment offences of possible application in certain adult abuse scenarios, particularly stranger abuse.[52] It is a piece of legislation that has a much broader remit than adult safeguarding and which was not produced with a focus on adult safeguarding. A general awareness of the Act will be useful as part of the law which may apply to a range of service users (and could also be relevant where a professional suffers harassment in the course of employment). The offences included in the Act are: knowingly harassing another person; pursuing a course of conduct amounting to harassment (summary offence); engaging in a course of conduct (at least two occasions) which causes the person to fear violence (either way offence). An offence will be committed if the person knew or ought to have known that his course of conduct would cause the person to fear violence. A course of conduct can include speech. In *R v. Director of Public Prosecutions* [2001] EWHC Admin 17, a 17-year-old youth was convicted for harassing the complainant and her family, all of whom are described in the law report as physically disadvantaged. Evidence was given relating to two incidents: first, where he had a knife and said 'I'm going to slash your ... throat' and, secondly, where he said he would 'blow the ... dog's brains out'. The defendant received a four-month detention and training order.

A restraining order (s. 5) prohibiting any specified action to prevent further harassment can be made by the court in addition to sentence. An example might be a restriction on contacting someone by telephone or letter or approaching within a specified area around a person's home or place of work. It is possible for a restraining order to be imposed without limit. The Court of Appeal provided some guidance on appropriate sentences in harassment cases in *R v. Liddle; R v. Hayes* [1999] 3 All ER 816. The court should consider the level of offence, the seriousness of the conduct, the effect of the conduct on the victim and the victim's family, whether it was necessary to provide protection and whether the defendant expressed remorse and was prepared to undergo treatment or receive help.

Domestic Violence, Crime and Victims Act 2004

The Domestic Violence, Crime and Victims Act 2004 aims to tackle domestic violence and improve victim protection through reform of civil and criminal law. Strengthening of domestic violence legislation is relevant to adult protection but, of particular importance for vulnerable adult protection, the Act introduces a new offence of familial homicide and establishes domestic homicide reviews.

The criminal offence, causing or allowing the death of a child or vulnerable adult (familial homicide), was introduced against a context of cases where a child had died as a result of abuse but it was not possible clearly to identify and therefore prosecute the perpetrator. At the same time, Action on Elder Abuse campaigned for vulnerable adults as well as children to be included in the ambit of the legislation.

The offence is punishable by up to 14 years' imprisonment, which places it at the higher end of the tariff, positioning both adult and child abuse as serious offences, and is likely to be used in the alternative to murder and manslaughter. The parents of 'Baby P' were convicted of this offence. Elements of the offence are that the vulnerable adult dies as a result of an unlawful act of a person who was a member of the same household, and who had frequent contact with him. The death must have either been caused by the defendant, or he was aware of the risk of harm and failed to take reasonable steps to protect the vulnerable adult. What constitutes 'reasonable steps' will depend on the person's circumstances and their relationship to the victim. Death must occur where there is an anticipated risk, for example where there is a history of violence or neglect, and would not include accidents. The offence refers to death resulting from an 'unlawful act'. This term includes commission and omissions and therefore includes neglect. 'Vulnerable adult' in this Act means a person aged 16 or over whose ability to protect himself from violence, abuse or neglect is significantly impaired through physical or mental disability or illness, through old age or otherwise (s. 5(6)). This is a different definition from those contained in 'No Secrets' and in the Care Standards Act 2000.

The Domestic Violence, Crime and Victims (Amendment) Act 2012 amends s. 5 of the Domestic Violence Crime and Victims Act 2004 by adding a new offence of causing or allowing a child or vulnerable adult to suffer serious harm. The new offence of causing or allowing a child or vulnerable adult to suffer serious harm is punishable with up to 10 years imprisonment. 'Serious harm' in this context is equivalent to grievous bodily harm.

Domestic homicide reviews (s. 9) are to take place where a person aged 16 or over dies as a result of violence, abuse or neglect from a person to whom he was related or with whom he was (or had been) in an intimate relationship, or someone of the same household. The multi-agency reviews are to be held with a view to identifying lessons to be learnt from the death. This will place on a statutory footing the 'serious case reviews' that some authorities already hold through their adult protection committees, as illustrated at the start of the chapter in relation to Steven Hoskin.

Mental Capacity Act 2005

The Act introduces a new offence. A person is guilty of an offence if he has the care of a person who lacks capacity or is reasonably believed to lack capacity, or is the donee of a LPA or a deputy, and he ill-treats or wilfully neglects the person. The offence is classified as an 'either way offence' (it may be prosecuted in the magistrates' or Crown Court), and carries a maximum sentence of five years' imprisonment. The code advises that the meaning of wilful neglect varies depending on the circumstances, it usually means that a person has deliberately failed to carry out an act they knew they had a duty to do (para. 14.26).

Criminal Justice Act 2003

This legislation places a duty on the criminal courts to increase sentences for anyone found guilty of an offence which is aggravated by hostility based on the victim's disability or perceived disability. This is sometimes referred to as 'hate crime'.

Compensation

Even if a criminal prosecution does not proceed, the criminal injuries compensation scheme may provide financial compensation. Payments may be made to those who have suffered personal injury directly attributable to a crime of violence (this term includes sexual abuse). (This scheme is discussed in more detail in Chapter 18.)

Mental Health Act 1983

In limited circumstances, the Mental Health Act 1983 may be utilised in respect of the victim or the perpetrator of abuse. An approved mental health practitioner has powers to enter premises in which a mentally disordered patient is living, if there is reasonable cause to believe the patient is not under proper care (s. 115). Further, under s. 135, where a person suffering from a mental disorder is being ill-treated, neglected or kept otherwise than under proper control, or is living alone and unable to care for himself, a magistrate may issue a warrant authorising a police officer to enter premises, by force if necessary, and remove him to a place of safety for up to 72 hours. These short-term powers as part of an investigation may provide for an assessment of a situation causing concern, particularly if access is being denied.

Section 127 makes it an offence for a professional member of staff of a hospital or mental nursing home to ill-treat or wilfully neglect a patient, subject to his guardianship or otherwise in his custody or care (whether by virtue of any legal or moral obligation or otherwise). The phrase in brackets would encompass almost any arrangement for care of a mentally disordered patient. The Director of Public Prosecutions must give consent before a prosecution can proceed and it appears that this section has been little used. The new offence introduced by the Mental Capacity Act 2005 is in similar terms to this offence, but carries the additional requirement to show that the victim lacked capacity. Perpetrators of abuse at Winterbourne View Hospital were convicted under s. 127.

It must be stressed that the definition of mental disorder under the Act will restrict application of these powers to a limited proportion of vulnerable adults.

Chapter summary

- Adult safeguarding is a relatively new area of social work practice. Concerns relating to possible abuse of vulnerable adults – which may include people with learning or physical disabilities, people with mental health problems and older people – are increasingly coming to the attention of social services and must be addressed.

- The Care Act 2014 introduces a statutory duty on local authorities to make enquiries in possible adult abuse situations. It also requires the local authority to establish a Safeguarding Adults Board and hold Safeguarding Adults Reviews in certain circumstances.

- The main types of abuse are physical, sexual, psychological, financial neglect and discriminatory abuse.

- Existing law may be utilised to respond to concerns at three levels: prevention, action by the victim and formal intervention. In each case, respect for the autonomy of the adult is essential and any intervention should present a positive improvement of the situation.

- Prevention may include input of services to a vulnerable adult and support for carers. It can take the form of regulation of sectors of provision, notably residential settings; prohibition of unsuitable adults working with vulnerable adults; and mechanisms to delegate responsibility for an individual's financial and property affairs, particularly important where that person lacks mental capacity.

- The victim of abuse may take action themselves via domestic violence provisions in the Family Law Act 1996, the law of tort and the law of contract. An individual may require support for this and, if lacking mental capacity, a 'litigation friend' may be appointed.

- Formal intervention may be manifest through declaratory relief, criminal prosecution, and use of the Mental Health Act 1983.

- The Domestic Violence, Crime and Victims Act 2004 introduces a new offence of causing or allowing the death of a vulnerable adult, and requires domestic homicide reviews to be held following the death of an adult as a result of violence, abuse or neglect from a relative or someone with whom he was (or had been) in an intimate relationship, or someone of the same household.

Exercises

1. Albert is 82. He lives alone, but has a niece, Diana, who stays with him sporadically. She is an alcohol abuser. Diana collects Albert's pension for him but does not provide any other care. Albert has been physically fit until very recently, when arthritis in his hip has prevented him from walking far. His memory is poor and he is becoming increasingly disorientated. He sometimes gets lost and has mislaid keys and money. He was recently admitted to hospital with burns to his legs from sitting too close to the fire. Albert has unexplained bruising to his chest and upper arms; he spends time talking to a photograph of his daughter, assuming her to be his deceased wife, and has become aggressive towards his son-in-law. His relatives find it difficult to provide support for Albert, and do not approve of his relationship with Diana and their drinking sessions. He refuses to consider domiciliary or residential care.

   Albert often leaves the house unlocked, will let anyone in and has had some possessions stolen. He refuses to throw away rubbish or rotten food, which is piling up at the back of the house. He has a dog, which he can no longer exercise. His capacity for self-care (continence and diet) is decreasing. There is growing concern about his health and conditions in the home.

   What steps should social services take in this scenario?

2. Joe wants to complain about the way his cousin Lucy is being cared for at a residential care home for adults with learning disabilities. Lucy is 19 years old. On his last visit, Lucy told Joe that one of the care assistants is always rough with her and showed him bruising to her wrists. She also said she had been tied to her chair for several hours one day after she refused to eat any lunch. A member of staff told Joe that Lucy has been exhibiting extremely challenging behaviour lately and they have needed to become 'strict' with her, but denied any restraint. Joe explains that he would like to make a complaint and is told that the complaints procedures for the home are under review as they have an inspection looming.

   Joe visits again the following week and finds that Lucy is sharing a room with an 82-year-old woman. There are cot sides on both beds in the room. He notices that the woman appears to be having difficulty focusing and is very sleepy; Lucy told him that earlier that day she fell asleep during her lunch. The manager of the home tells Joe that Lucy is only sharing the room temporarily whilst her room is being decorated. When questioned about the bruises on Lucy's wrists, the manager tells Joe that Lucy is very uncooperative at times and staff occasionally have to hold her by the wrist when walking to and from lunch. She tells Joe that he is welcome to check this with social services but will find that practice is the same in all local homes for adults with learning disabilities.

   How would social services respond if contacted by Joe?

Websites

The Action on Elder Abuse site provides useful resources on elder abuse (the organisation also runs a telephone helpline):
www.elderabuse.org

Practitioner Alliance for Safeguarding Adults:
www.pasauk.org.uk

Counsel and Care merged with Independent Age – provides advice and help for older people, with a particular focus on residential accommodation:
www.independentage.org

Services to people with learning disabilities who have experienced sexual abuse:
www.respond.org.uk

Further reading

The *Journal of Adult Protection* provides up-to-date coverage of adult protection issues incorporating policy, research, practice developments and law.

ADSS (2005) 'Safeguarding Adults: A National Framework of Standards for good practice and outcomes in adult protection work'. London: ADSS. (A guide for best practice drawing on experience since implementation of 'No Secrets'.)

Department of Health (2000) 'No Secrets: Guidance on developing and implementing multi-agency policies and procedures to protect vulnerable adults from abuse'. London: Department of Health. (The key guidance in this area.)

O'Keefe, M. *et al.* (2007) *UK Study of Abuse and Neglect of Older People: Prevalence Survey Report*. London: Department of Health.

Specific texts include:

Brammer, A. (2014) *Safeguarding Adults*. Basingstoke: Palgrave Macmillan.

Mandelstam, M. (2012) (2nd edn) *Safeguarding Vulnerable Adults and the Law*. London: Jessica Kingsley.

Pritchard, J. (ed.) (2009) *Good Practice in the Law and Safeguarding Adults*. London: Jessica Kingsley.

Particular types of abuse and appropriate responses are addressed in:

Action on Elder Abuse (1999) (Working Paper No. 4) 'Bags of money – the financial abuse of older people'. London: Action on Elder Abuse.

Brammer, A. (2014) 'Carers and the Mental Capacity Act 2005: angels permitted, devils prosecuted?' 8 *Criminal Law Review*, p. 589.

Flynn, M. and Citarella V. (2012) *Winterbourne View Hospital: A Serious Case Review*. Bristol: South Gloucestershire Council on Behalf of South Gloucestershire Safeguarding Adults Board.

Jeary, K. (2004) 'Sexual abuse of elderly people: would we rather not know the details?' 6 *Journal of Adult Protection* p. 21.

Perry, J. (2002) *Opening the Gateways? People with Learning Difficulties and Partnership Action against Hate Crime*. London: Values into Action.

Notes

[1] Department of Health (2000) 'No Secrets: Guidance on developing and implementing multi-agency policies and procedures to protect vulnerable adults from abuse'. London: Department of Health (hereafter 'No Secrets').

[2] A. Baker (1975) 'Granny Bashing' 5(8) *Modern Geriatrics* p. 20.

[3] M. Eastman (1984) *Old Age Abuse*. London: Age Concern.

[4] H. Brown, J. Stein and V. Turk (1995) 'The sexual abuse of adults with learning disabilities: report of a second two-year incidence study' 8(1) *Mental Handicap Research* p. 3.

5 ADSS (2005) 'Safeguarding Adults: A National Framework of Standards for good practice and outcomes in adult protection work'. London: ADSS, p. 4.

6 P. Kingston and B. Penhale (1995) *Family Violence and the Caring Professions*. Basingstoke: Macmillan.

7 See further M. Preston-Shoot (2001) 'Evaluating self-determination: an adult protection case study' 3(1) *Journal of Adult Protection* p. 4.

8 See further A. Brammer (2000) 'Human Rights Act 1998: implications for adult protection' 3(1) *Journal of Adult Protection* p. 43.

9 O. Stevenson (1995) 'Abuse of older people: principles of intervention' in Department of Health and Social Services Inspectorate *Abuse of Older People in Domestic Settings: A report on two SSI seminars*. London: HMSO.

10 See O. Stevenson (1996) *Elder Protection in the Community: What Can We Learn from Child Protection?* London: Age Concern Institute of Gerontology, and O. Stevenson (1999) *Elder Protection in Residential Care: What Can We Learn from Child Protection?* London: Age Concern Institute of Gerontology.

11 DH, Home Office and Ministry of Justice (2008) 'Safeguarding Adults: A Consultation on the Review of the "No Secrets" Guidance'. London: The Stationery Office.

12 See discussion in A. Brammer and S. Biggs (1998) 'Defining elder abuse' 20(3) *Journal of Social Welfare and Family Law* p. 285.

13 Department of Health and Social Services Inspectorate (1996) 'No Longer Afraid: the safeguard of older people in domestic settings'. London: HMSO.

14 'Abuse may be described as physical, sexual, psychological or financial. It may be intentional or the result of neglect. It may causes harm to the older person, either temporarily or over a period of time.'

15 For a full discussion of a range of definitions, see A. Brammer and S. Biggs (1998) 'Defining elder abuse' 20(3) *Journal of Social Welfare and Family Law* p. 285.

16 'No Secrets', para. 2.7.

17 Action on Elder Abuse (2000) (Working Paper No. 5) 'The great taboo – sexual abuse of older people'. London: Action on Elder Abuse.

18 K. Jeary (2004) 'Sexual abuse of elderly people: would we rather not know the details?' 6 *Journal of Adult Protection* p. 21.

19 'No Secrets', para. 2.10.

20 Action on Elder Abuse (2004) *Hidden Voices: Older People's Experience of Abuse*. London: Help the Aged.

21 Healthcare Commission (2007) 'Investigation into the Service for People with Learning Disabilities Provided by Sutton and Merton PCT' p. 6.

22 CSCI and Healthcare Commission (2006) 'Joint Investigation into the Service for People with Learning Disabilities at Cornwall Partnership NHS Trust' p. 5.

23 J. Ogg and G. Bennett (1992) 'Elder abuse in Britain' 305 *British Medical Journal* pp. 998–9.

24 K. Pillemer and D. Finkelhor (1988) 'The prevalence of elder abuse: a random sample survey' 28(1) *The Gerontologist* pp. 51–7.

25 See Health and Social Care Information Centre, www.hscic.gov.uk.

26 'No Secrets', para. 6.13.

27 'No Secrets', para. 3.3.

28 CSCI, ADSS, ACPO (2007) 'Safeguarding Adults Protocol and Guidance'.

29 Griffiths *et al.* (1993) in P. Kingston and B. Penhale (1995) *Family Violence and the Caring Professions*. Basingstoke: Palgrave, pp. 198–9.

30 The scheme is administered by the DfES on behalf of the DoH.

31 Financial abuse may also be described as financial or material exploitation, fiduciary, material or economic abuse.

32 Enduring Powers of Attorney Act 1985.

33 The Public Guardianship Office was known as the Public Trust Office until April 2001.

34 In force from 1 April 2002.

35 J. Stein and H. Brown (2001) 'Crossing the divide: the role of inspection units in protecting vulnerable adults' 3(1) *Journal of Adult Protection* pp. 25–34.

36 'No Secrets', para. 6.37.

37 Reports of the First Tier Tribunal Health Education and Social Care Chamber (formerly the Care Standards Tribunal). Reports can be accessed from www.bailii.org. See also analysis in A. Brammer (1994) 'The Registered Homes Act 1984: safeguarding the elderly?' 4 *Journal of Social Welfare and Family Law* p. 423; and A. Brammer (1999) 'A fit person to run a home: registered homes tribunal interpretations of the "fit person" concept in the United Kingdom' 10(1/2) *Journal of Elder Abuse and Neglect* p. 119.

38 See L. Bright (2001) 'Restraint: cause for continuing concern?' 3(2) *Journal of Adult Protection* p. 42; and A. Clarke and L. Bright (2002) *Showing Restraint: Challenging the Use of Restraint in Care Homes.* London: Counsel and Care.

39 Essex was the placing authority and Northamptonshire was the registration authority.

40 For a full discussion of the arguments, see M. Burton (2003) 'Third party applications for protection orders in England and Wales: service provider's views on implementing Section 60 of the Family Law Act 1996' 25(2) *Journal of Social Welfare and Family Law* p. 137.

41 Counsel and Care (1992) *What if They Hurt Themselves.* London: Counsel and Care.

42 R. Bradshaw (2000) 'Preventing abuse of vulnerable adults' 2(1) *Journal of Adult Protection* p. 35. Concerns led to production of new guidance to practitioners: UKCC (1999) 'Practitioner–client relationships and the prevention of abuse'. London: UKCC.

43 [2000] 3 WLR 1740 at p. 1750H.

44 Ibid., p. 1756C.

45 C. Williams (1993) 'Vulnerable victims? Current awareness of the victimisation of people with learning disabilities' 8(2) *Disability, Handicap and Society* p. 161.

46 R. Hugman (1994) 'Social work and case management in the UK: models of professionalism and elderly people' 14 *Ageing and Society* p. 237; and R. Hugman (1995) 'The implications of the term "elder abuse" for problem definition and response in health and social welfare' 24(4) *Journal of Social Policy* p. 493.

47 'No Secrets', para. 6.7.

48 Based on recommendations of a Home Office Report, 'Speaking up for Justice'.

49 See Home Office (2002) 'Achieving Best Evidence in Criminal Proceedings: Guidance for Vulnerable and Intimidated Witnesses including Children'. London: The Stationery Office (a consultation paper).

50 J. Williams (2000) 'The inappropriate adult' 22(1) *Journal of Social Welfare and Family Law* p. 43.

51 'No Secrets', para. 2.10.

52 See N. Addison and T. Lawson-Cruttendon (1998) *Harassment Law and Practice.* London: Blackstone Press.

Chapter 18

Criminal justice

Learning objectives

To develop an understanding of the following:

- The various constituents of the criminal justice system.
- The role of the social worker in the criminal justice system, including the 'appropriate adult'.
- The classification and elements of a criminal offence.
- An overview of the criminal process.
- Police powers as contained in PACE 1984.
- The range of sentences which may be ordered.
- Support for witnesses including 'special measures'.
- The scheme for state compensation for victims provided by the Criminal Injuries Compensation Authority.

> ## Talking Point
>
> The effective operation of the criminal justice system is dependent on a range of professionals being able to work together. An initiative from the Crown Prosecution Service (CPS) provides an example. The CPS website includes a statement from Keir Starmer, Director of Public Prosecutions:
>
> > From June 2009 prosecutors will adopt a 'Community Prosecutor' approach, using creative strategies to help address some of the more negative issues facing our neighbourhoods.
> >
> > In reality there are examples where this has happened already, on an ad hoc basis, but the Community Prosecutor approach takes these achievements to a new dimension.
> >
> > Our role is much broader than preparing case files and prosecuting defendants in court. We are involved in the criminal justice system at an earlier stage, providing pre-charge advice. The Community Prosecutor initiative ensures our staff are aware of the needs and key priorities of the communities for which they are providing pre-charge advice.
>
> The following two examples are provided of CPS working with communities:
>
> > At the Blackbird Estate Thames Valley CPS was recently pivotal in successfully tackling anti-social behaviour. Staff worked closely with the Safer Neighbourhood teams to address a problem where a local woman would regularly cause disturbances on the estate. Through the CPS' involvement the local mental health authority looked into the matter and the woman was re-housed. The disturbances stopped.
> >
> > In Sutton, South London, where the vast majority of overnight remands at court on Mondays were linked to incidents at a local nightclub, CPS prosecutors discussed with the police what evidence they needed to challenge the club's licensing arrangements. With the assistance of the CPS and police the borough council identified the evidence that they needed to revoke the club's licence. This has reduced offending because the club has enhanced security but also knows that its licence is in jeopardy.

Introduction

Criminal justice is a highly politicised and complex area of law. Like youth justice, it has endured enormous policy changes driven by the agenda of whichever political party is in government. Recent years have seen an increasing commitment to get tough on crime, as evidenced by mandatory minimum sentences introduced in the Crime (Sentences) Act 1997. There is no specific Ministry of Criminal Justice; rather, responsibility for criminal justice cuts across three governmental departments: the Ministry of Justice, Home Office, and Office of the Attorney-General (with responsibility for the Director of Public Prosecutions and the Crown Prosecution Service).

The operation of the existing criminal justice system is certainly not without criticism. Some particular areas of reform may be prompted by the introduction of the Human Rights

Act 1998 and its inevitable impact in increasing awareness of the rights of both victims and perpetrators of crime. It is also impossible to ignore the impact of miscarriages of justice and significant reports which have identified major failings in the system; notably, the Macpherson report,[1] which found institutionalised racism within the police.

Recent years have seen significant reforms and development across criminal justice. This has been achieved in large part through implementation of reforms proposed by the Halliday report[2] on sentencing matters and the Auld review of criminal courts.[3] Both the Halliday report and the Auld review were independent reports which must be viewed against the context of the earlier Government report, 'Criminal Justice: The Way Ahead'.[4] Certain of their proposals have been translated into legislation within provisions of the Criminal Justice Act 2003 and the Courts Act 2003.

The Criminal Justice Act 2003 provides for greater involvement of the Crown Prosecution Service in charging decisions, increases magistrates' sentencing powers and introduces a presumption against bail in some circumstances. It allows for judge alone trials in some cases and makes major changes to the sentencing framework. The various kinds of community orders (including community rehabilitation orders and community punishment orders) are replaced by a single community order with a range of attached requirements. A new Criminal Case Management Framework has also been introduced to facilitate active and efficient management of cases from pre-charge to conclusion. The impact of the measures introduced in the Crime and Disorder Act 1998 has also proved to be significant. As well as making new orders available, this Act blurs the line between civil and criminal responsibility: orders such as the anti-social behaviour order (ASBO), introduced as a civil order but with criminal sanctions for breach, will possibly draw more people into the criminal justice system. The Anti-social Behaviour Act 2003 and Anti-social Behaviour, Crime and Policing Act 2014 extends this aspect of law.

Measuring the extent of crime accurately is always problematic. The Crime Survey for England and Wales 2012–13 estimated that there were just over 8 million crimes against adults living in private households. This represented a 10 per cent fall in crimes against the previous year.[5] Fear of crime, however, may be as significant in influencing people's everyday behaviour as actual crime rates, e.g. choosing whether to walk alone after dark. The survey found that perceptions of the level of crime were still high, with 60 per cent of people believing crime in the country had increased in the previous two years. Actual rates of crime have not increased as significantly as fear of crime. The Crime Survey, which is based on interviews and presents information on people's own experiences of crime, is now presented jointly with recorded crime figures, i.e. how many crimes are reported to the police, to present a more accurate picture than could be obtained from either series alone.[6]

The focus in this chapter is on the criminal justice system as it affects adults, i.e. persons of 18 years and over. There are numerous areas of similarity and overlap with the criminal justice system relating to young offenders (considered in Chapter 13). This chapter considers three broad areas: the machinery of the criminal justice system, the process of the criminal justice system and outcomes in the criminal justice system.

Machinery of the criminal justice system

Preventing crime and disorder

The Crime and Disorder Act 1998 (CDA 1998) introduced an important duty on local authorities.

Section 17 provides:

> **s. 17**
>
> (1) Without prejudice to any other obligation imposed upon it, it shall be the duty of each authority … to exercise its functions with due regard to the likely effect of the exercise of those functions on, and the need to do all that it reasonably can to prevent, crime and disorder in its area.
>
> (CDA 1998)

Local authorities, in cooperation with health authorities, probation committees, police and other agencies, are obliged to implement a strategy for tackling and preventing crime and disorder. This is no longer considered the sole responsibility of the police and it is recognised that a wide range of local authority responsibilities and functions may have an impact on local crime rates. Social workers and other professionals employed by local authorities in their various departments will need to be aware of community safety issues. Local authorities are expected to review all services, assessing crime and disorder implications of all aspects of work and develop a coherent plan for implementing the s. 17 duty. The duty is phrased in terms of the local authority doing all it reasonably can to prevent crime and disorder; however, it is unlikely that shortage of resources will be an acceptable reason for not acting. The impact of this section covers a diverse range of actions and responsibilities. For example, leisure departments may be expected to provide additional recreation to reduce boredom that could lead to crime and disorder issues. Housing departments are expected to be particularly vigilant in relation to the anti-social behaviour of nuisance neighbours. Housing Action Trusts are now able to make applications for ASBOs directly. The risk of burglary and vandalism to a range of properties owned by a local authority, such as schools and libraries, may mean a greater emphasis on security measures, including CCTV cameras. Staff such as social workers who enter people's homes and may be at risk of violence could legitimately expect greater training to deal with conflict situations and perhaps the provision of mobile phones or pagers to call for assistance.

Social workers' responsibilities in the criminal justice system

Probation officers carry the vast area of social work within the adult criminal justice system, whilst local authority social workers are likely to have most responsibilities towards juveniles (as discussed in Chapter 13). Nevertheless, it is important that all social workers have an awareness of the elements and process of criminal justice. Service users to whom other responsibilities are owed may come into contact with the criminal justice system as victims, witnesses or offenders and the social worker may be asked about elements of the process. As the probation service is the main professional group working with adults in the criminal justice system, this chapter aims to give only a broad overview of the law. Reference to more in-depth texts is provided in further reading.

Constituents of the criminal justice system

Police

It is the responsibility of the police to investigate crime and arrest and charge suspects. The decision whether to charge a suspect, and with what, used to be the sole responsibility of the police but under recent reforms has been invested in the Crown Prosecution Service. There are approximately 130,000 police officers in England and Wales, divided into 43 police forces, with a significant number of civilians, including traffic wardens, also employed by the service. In addition, the police are supported by special constables (part-time volunteers) and community support officers who have partial police powers and whose role focuses on community safety and deterring anti-social behaviour. In response to the recommendations of the Lawrence inquiry, police forces are taking steps to address diversity issues. The following examples are featured on the Home Office website:

- The Metropolitan Police encourage staff to register their knowledge and/or membership of a community, languages spoken, life skills obtained as a result of ethnic origin, sexual orientation, race, religion and hobbies.

- The Greater Manchester Police have introduced a childcare voucher scheme to help staff balance work and childcare responsibilities.

- South Wales Police use gay officers to break down barriers between police and attendees at Cardiff's gay pride event.[7]

A code of practice on reporting and recording racist incidents was introduced in 2000 and the police are forbidden from membership of the British National Party, Combat 18 and the National Front, by the Police (Amendment) Regulations 2004.[8] Serious complaints against the police, including allegations of racism, are investigated independently by the Independent Police Complaints Commission (IPCC), established in 2004.

Crown Prosecution Service

The Crown Prosecution Service (CPS) was established under the Prosecution of Offences Act 1985 as an independent prosecution service. In essence, it is the Crown Prosecution Service's role to prosecute a person charged with a criminal offence. Within that role, the Crown Prosecution Service will also assess whether sufficient evidence exists on which to charge a suspect, determine the appropriate charge, prepare cases for court and prosecute cases or instruct counsel to prosecute.

A Code for Crown Prosecutors[9] provides guidance on general principles to be applied to ensure fair and consistent decision-making. The seventh edition of the code was introduced in 2013[10] and recognises that the CPS is a public authority within the meaning of the Human Rights Act 1998. The key element of the code is the two-part test for prosecution: first, there must be sufficient evidence to provide a realistic prospect of conviction; and, secondly, that a prosecution is in the public interest. The code lists public interest factors in favour of prosecution. One important factor is where an offence involves racial, sexual or any other form of discrimination or hostility towards a victim based on his membership of a particular section of society. Other factors include the presence of a child at the scene of the crime and the impact of the crime on community confidence. The code is a public document and is currently produced in 14 languages. It is possible to challenge the decision to prosecute or not. In *R (B)* v. *DPP* [2009] EWHC 106 (Admin) the CPS decision to discontinue a prosecution for assault on the basis that the victim who suffered from mental health problems would not be a credible witness, was irrational and a breach of Article 3 ECHR.

In addition to the Crown Prosecution Service, a range of other public bodies may prosecute particular criminal offences. For example, environmental health departments regularly bring prosecutions in respect of food health offences in the restaurant trade, and there is a special body, the Serious Fraud Office, which prosecutes the most complex fraud cases.

Criminal Defence Service

Defence services are provided by salaried defenders and private practitioners, as part of the Criminal Defence Service, for people involved in criminal investigations and proceedings.[11] A defendant will apply to the court for a right to representation when he wishes to be represented at public expense and must satisfy the interests of justice test before the request can be granted. The order is known as a representation order and any solicitor the defendant wishes to act for him must have in place a contract (a franchise) with the Legal Aid Agency. (The role of Citizens' Advice Bureaux, Law Centres and the provision of legal advice and assistance is covered in Chapter 3.)

National Offender Management Service

The National Probation Service and the Prison Service together form the National Offender Management Service (NOMS).

Probation

The probation service is defined as 'a law enforcement agency delivering community punishments, supervising and working with offenders within the terms set by the court or parole board in ways that help offenders to reduce their re-offending and better protect the public'.[12] The aims of the National Probation Service are set out as: protecting the public; reducing reoffending; proper punishment of offenders in the community; ensuring offenders' awareness of the effects of crime on victims of crime and the public; and rehabilitation of offenders.

The probation service carries out most social work functions within the criminal justice system, yet the above definition suggests something of a departure from the social work basis of probation, where the emphasis was traditionally framed in terms of advising, assisting and befriending. Their most important role is supervising offenders in the community (as supervising officers). The service is responsible for implementing community sentences and will provide supervision when the offender is on licence, having been released from prison. Each year the service takes on supervision of around 200,000 offenders. If a pre-sentence report is required, this is prepared by the probation service. Guidance on the contents of pre-sentence reports is contained in 'National Standards for Supervision of Offenders in the Community 2000' (revised in 2002). The service also provides bail information reports and risk and dangerousness assessments for parole and lifer review boards.

Probation officers may specialise in court-based work, prison-based work, or civil work, through care for prisoners and families and work in probation hostels. The probation service has undergone significant changes over recent years and is now part of a new body, the National Offender Management Service, which draws together the work of correctional services.[13] The prison service is also included. The new integrated service has a focus on 'end to end' management of offenders, and targets to reduce reoffending.

The probation service has also had a civil role in providing reports to the court in family proceedings as part of the Court Welfare Service. For these purposes work is allocated to officers of CAFCASS, the body which amalgamated the work of children's guardians, officers of the Official Solicitors Department and the Court Welfare Service (and may include some probation officers).

The Ministry of Justice is introducing major changes which effectively privatise part of the probation service. From 2014 Probation Trusts will be wound up and replaced by Community Rehabilitation Companies (CRCs) who will have responsibility for supervision of medium to low risk offenders. High risk offenders will continue to be monitored by a publicly run service in the form of the new National Probation Service.

Prison service

As at March 2014, there were 85,252 people in custody: this is one of the highest prison population rates in Europe and some prisons are significantly overcrowded. About 15 per cent of prisoners at any one time are on remand. There are 139 prisons in England and Wales, divided into a variety of types, including remand centres, high security prisons, open prisons, dispersal prisons, female prisons and young offender institutions.

The prison service, as part of the National Offender Management Service, is responsible for the operation of the prison system, including prisons run by private companies such as Group 4. There is an Inspectorate of Prisons, which produces regular reports from scheduled and unannounced visits to prisons. Each prison has an Independent Monitoring Board (formerly Board of Visitors), which has a role in deciding offenders' disciplinary offences. Prisoners have different category status ranging from unsentenced prisoners held on remand through to Category A dangerous prisoners.

Courts

The courts which deal with criminal cases are the magistrates' court, Crown Court, Divisional Court, Court of Appeal (Criminal Division) and Supreme Court. (The characteristics of each court are described in Chapter 3.)

The witness service

The witness service, operated by the National Association of Victim Support Schemes, is a confidential and free service provided by a paid coordinator and teams of volunteers, operating from Crown Courts and magistrates' courts. The service can offer support to prosecution witnesses, victims and their family and friends, professionals accompanying victims and defence witnesses. This may include familiarisation visits to court, waiting areas, someone to accompany a witness to court, preparation for the outcomes of cases and practical help, e.g. with expense forms or referral onwards for further help.

Process of the criminal justice system

An offence may be defined by statute, e.g. theft, or it may have its origin in the common law, e.g. murder. Every offence is comprised of two elements, both of which must be proven. The actual commission of the offence, e.g. firing the gun which shoots another person, is known as the *actus reus*. It must be accompanied by the *mens rea*, which is the mental element, the criminal intent – sometimes referred to as the guilty mind. There are different levels of *mens rea*. Intent is required in most cases but there are also a range of offences which may be committed where the person is reckless as to the consequences of his actions. A group of offences exist which are classified as strict liability, where no *mens rea* is required. The commission of the act is sufficient, e.g. speeding, possessing a firearm without a certificate, and selling tobacco to a person apparently under the age of 16.

The standard of proof which must be satisfied in a criminal trial is 'beyond reasonable doubt'. The burden of proof is on the prosecution. Research by Zander (2000), which studied what the standard of proof means to different people, found that whilst there were differences between the understanding of members of the public (who might sit on a jury), magistrates and criminal justice professionals, the difference was not great. However, a higher proportion of the general public than of magistrates said they would need to be 100 per cent sure of guilt before convicting.[14] If the defendant is required to prove an issue – for example, that the knife he carried was for a legitimate purpose – then the lower, civil standard of proof will apply.

Offences are classified as summary, either way or indictable only. Offences which are triable summarily include most road traffic offences, breach of the peace, obstructing a constable, and criminal damage where the value of property is below £5,000. All summary offences are statutorily defined. They are dealt with by the magistrates' court and there is no entitlement to trial by jury. These offences are divided into five levels for the purposes of penalty, ranging from level 1 (a maximum £200 fine) to level 5 (a maximum £5,000 fine and/or six months' custody). For some summary offences it is possible to plead guilty by post and avoid attendance at court. There is generally no time limit within which a prosecution must be brought for an offence; however, as an exception to this principle, a summary prosecution must normally begin within six months of commission of the offence (i.e. the information must be laid). A person cannot be tried for the same offence twice.

Either way offences such as theft, indecent assault and misuse of drugs may be tried at the magistrates' court or the Crown Court. The defendant is asked to indicate his plea and will be dealt with by magistrates if the plea is 'guilty', unless the magistrates' sentencing powers are insufficient. If the plea is 'not guilty', if the magistrates decide that the case should be tried on indictment, the defendant is committed to Crown Court. In addition, the defendant currently has an absolute right to elect trial by jury.

Indictable only offences include the more serious crimes such as murder, rape and manslaughter. The magistrates will send an indictable only offence straight to the Crown Court, having dealt with bail. A vast range of criminal offences exist – too many and varied to discuss here. (Certain specific offences are considered in the context of adult protection in Chapter 17.) It is important to remember that law reform includes the creation of new offences which may reflect particular concerns in society. As an example Section 142 LASPO 2012 introduces a new offence of 'Threatening with an article with a blade or point or offensive weapon in public or on school premises' with minimum sentences of a 4-month detention and training order (**DTO**) for 16- and 17-year-olds and a 6-month custodial sentence for adults.

Arrest

Criminal offences used to be classified as either an arrestable or non-arrestable offences and it was necessary to obtain a warrant for arrest or issue a summons to appear at court for non-arrestable offences. Since 2006 when ss. 110 and 111 of the Serious Organised Crime and Police Act 2005 (amending PACE 1984) the police constable's power of arrest will extend to all offences. Arrests will be subject to the test of necessity based upon the nature and circumstances of the offence and the interests of criminal justice.

Each year the police make around 2 million arrests. When a suspect is identified and arrested he will be taken to a police station (as soon as practicable after arrest)[15] and usually placed in a cell. At that stage the suspect is entitled to free legal advice and to consult his solicitor privately. Even if a person has not been arrested, if being questioned by the police at the station he is entitled to free legal advice. A solicitor may be provided from the duty solicitor scheme or the individual may request another solicitor.

Section 28 of PACE 1984 sets out the elements of a valid arrest. The suspect must be informed of the arrest and of the ground of the arrest and must be cautioned in the following terms: 'You do not have to say anything, but it may harm your defence if you do not mention when questioned something which you later rely on in court. Anything you do say may be given in evidence.'

Since the Criminal Justice and Public Order Act 1994, if the accused remains silent during questioning, at his subsequent trial the court may draw adverse inferences from that silence. A police officer conducting an interview can also give a special warning where the suspect fails or refuses to account for any object or mark on an object or clothing at the time of arrest, or object found at the place of arrest or at the time of arrest, noting that the court can draw an inference if the suspect does not account for the relevant fact.

Time limits for detention

Having been arrested and interviewed by the police, the suspect may be charged with an offence, the police may issue a caution or he may be released with no further action. Once the suspect has been arrested and taken to the police station, specific time limits for his lawful detention apply. Section 37 of PACE 1984 (as amended by the Police (Detention and Bail) Act 2011) provides that a suspect's detention (before charge) is lawful where it is necessary to secure or preserve evidence relating to an offence for which he is under arrest or to obtain that evidence by questioning. There is a requirement for an officer, independent of the investigation, to review the suspect's detention six hours after the suspect arrived at the police station and then every nine hours. In the majority of cases, a suspect should not be detained for longer than 24 hours, at which point, if there is insufficient evidence for a charge, the suspect should be released from police custody.[16] For serious arrestable offences the suspect may be detained for up to 36 hours without charge on the authority of an officer of superintendent rank.[17] Beyond that 36-hour period the police are required to obtain a warrant from the magistrates' court authorising further detention for each subsequent 36 hours up to a maximum period of 96 hours.[18]

In some circumstances an individual will attend the police station on a voluntary basis (i.e. not under arrest) to help police with their inquiries. Such circumstances are covered by PACE 1984, s. 29, which states that the person must be informed immediately if placed under arrest. Until placed under arrest, the person is entitled to leave at any point.

Appropriate adult

An appropriate adult is required where a vulnerable person, being mentally disordered or learning disabled, is being interviewed as a suspect. (The role of the appropriate adult in relation to young offenders was discussed in Chapter 13.) The police have a wide discretion in their interpretation of vulnerability and may also require an appropriate adult where, for example, the individual has speech or hearing difficulties. If the police have any suspicion or are told in good faith that the suspect is a vulnerable adult they should proceed on that basis and request an appropriate adult. Lack of police training on the recognition of mental disorder may lead to the police calling appropriate adults in only the most extreme cases.[19]

The role of the appropriate adult is described in Code C to the Police and Criminal Evidence Act 1984 at para. 11.16:

> he should be informed that he is not expected to act simply as an observer; and also that the purposes of his presence are, first, to advise the person being questioned and to observe whether or not the interview is being conducted properly and fairly, and, secondly, to facilitate communication with the person being interviewed.

An appropriate adult for a person who is mentally disordered or learning disabled may be one of the following:

- a relative, guardian or other person responsible for care or custody;
- someone who has experience of dealing with mentally disordered or mentally handicapped people but is not a police officer or employed by the police; or
- some other responsible adult who is not a police officer or employed by the police.

The custody officer may therefore contact social services and ask the authority to provide an appropriate adult. An approved social worker or social worker on a learning disabilities team could act as an appropriate adult.

If the vulnerable adult is charged or cautioned, the appropriate adult must be present. The adult should not normally be interviewed or asked to provide a written statement unless the appropriate adult is present. The vulnerable adult is entitled to consult privately with the appropriate adult (and legal adviser) at any time. It may be appropriate for the vulnerable adult to consult separately with his legal adviser in the absence of the appropriate adult. One reason for this is that, unlike the solicitor, the appropriate adult is not covered by confidentiality or legal privilege. Appropriate adults may be asked to pass relevant information to the police and both the British Association of Social Workers and the Association of Directors of Social Services support the principle that social workers have a duty to assist in the prevention and detection of crime. In order to do that effectively, some awareness of police powers (as outlined below) is a prerequisite.

The appropriate adult should take a pro-active role and be prepared to challenge the progress of an interview. It would also be good practice to consult the custody record and to keep notes during the interview, noting who is present, what facilities are offered and any remarks which caused concern. If any aspects of detention are challenged (in particular as to the effect on evidence obtained), the appropriate adult may be called upon to provide evidence.

Figure 18.1 reproduces part of the custody record which must be maintained in respect of a detained person.

Police powers

To be an effective appropriate adult, some knowledge of police powers at the police station is essential. There are also some significant police powers, e.g. stop and search, which it is useful to have an understanding of in order to advocate for service users and recognise where individual civil liberties are threatened.

The majority of police powers are contained in the Police and Criminal Evidence Act 1984. This legislation was introduced at a time when serious miscarriages of justice had come to light and the old law, particularly reliance on the Judges' Rules to protect individuals at the police station, was recognised as inadequate. The Act provides a framework of police powers which are supplemented by codes of practice containing detailed guidance for the police and people likely to encounter the police. The codes should be available at the police station to be consulted by the police, detained people, appropriate adults, legal advisers and the general public. There are eight codes, covering the following areas:

Code A: Police powers to stop and search

Code B: Searching premises and seizing property

Code C: Detention, treatment and questioning of suspects

Code D: Identification procedures

PART 3   DETAINED PERSON DETAILS   A209(ii)
(Rev. 4/95)

Custody Record No.   Surname [ ]

Mr/Mrs/Ms/Other

Surname ....

Forename 1 .... Forename 2 ....

Maiden Name .... Nickname ....

DOB [ ][ ][ ][ ][ ][ ]   Age [ ]   Marital Status:

Single	☐	Separated	☐
Married	☐	Divorced	☐
Co-habiting	☐	Widowed	☐

Occupation ....

Place of Birth ....

Skin Colour: Ethnic Appearance:

White ☐   Non White ☐   Unknown ☐   1 White ☐   3 Indian/ ☐
SubContinent

2 Black ☐   4 Other ☐

ADDRESS DETAILS

Address Type (Home, Business etc) ....

Address ....

....

....

Post Code [ ]

Telephone 1 .... Telephone 2 ....

APPROPRIATE ADULT

Mr/Mrs/Ms/Other .... Name ....

Address ....

....

Telephone 1 .... Telephone 2 ....

Relationship to Detainee ....

Figure 18.1   Detained person details
Source: West Mercia Police Authority, reproduced with permission.

PART 4

LEGAL RIGHTS

RIGHTS

Rights Given on Arrival   Yes ☐   No ☐

A NOTICE SETTING OUT MY RIGHTS HAS BEEN READ TO ME AND I HAVE ALSO BEEN PROVIDED WITH A WRITTEN NOTICE SETTING OUT MY ENTITLEMENTS WHILE IN CUSTODY.

Signature .... TIM/DATE ☐☐☐
(Detainee)

Signature .... TIME/DATE ☐☐☐
(Appropriate Adult/Interpreter

LEGAL ADVICE REQUESTED

I want to speak to a solicitor as soon as practicable:

Solicitor's Name: .... Company: ....

Address: ....

.... Tel. No. ....

Signature .... TIME/DATE ☐☐☐   ☐☐☐☐☐
(Detainee)

Signature .... TIME/DATE ☐☐☐   ☐☐☐☐☐
(Appropriate Adult/Interpreter

LEGAL ADVICE DECLINED

I have been informed that I may speak to a solicitor IN PERSON or ON THE TELEPHONE:

Signature .... TIME/DATE ☐☐☐   ☐☐☐☐☐
(Detainee)

Signature .... TIME/DATE ☐☐☐   ☐☐☐☐☐
(Appropriate Adult/Interpreter

I DO NOT WANT TO SPEAK TO A SOLICITOR at this time:

Signature .... TIME/DATE ☐☐☐   ☐☐☐☐☐
(Detainee)

Signature .... TIME/DATE ☐☐☐   ☐☐☐☐☐
(Appropriate Adult/Interpreter

Reasons, if given, for not wanting legal advice: ....

....

NAMED PERSON

YOU HAVE THE RIGHT TO HAVE SOMEONE INFORMED THAT YOU HAVE BEEN ARRESTED. DO YOU WISH TO HAVE SOMEONE TOLD?

| I DO / I DO NOT | want someone informed. I understand that I can change this decision later if I wish. *(Delete)*

Named Person ....

Address: ....

.... Tel. No. ....

Signature .... TIM/DATE ☐☐☐   ☐☐☐☐☐
(Detainee)

Signature .... TIME/DATE ☐☐☐   ☐☐☐☐☐
(Appropriate Adult/Interpreter

DELAY OF RIGHTS

TIME/DATE ☐☐☐   ☐☐☐☐☐

Legal Advice Delayed (S.58)   Yes ☐   No ☐

Intimation(s) Delayed (S.56)   Yes ☐   No ☐

Figure 18.1 Continued

Code E: Tape-recording of police interviews.

Code F: Visual recording with sound of interviews with suspects

Code G: Powers of arrest

Code H: Detention, treatment and questioning of suspects related to terrorism in police custody.

Code C is most likely to be relevant to a social worker acting as an appropriate adult.

The designation of a police officer as custody officer was introduced by Part IV of PACE 1984. Features of the role of the custody officer can be outlined thus:

Characteristics

Sergeant rank or above

Independent of the investigation

Impartial

Role

Keeping a custody record

Determining whether there is sufficient evidence to charge the suspect or release on police bail or detain in police detention.

At the station the appropriate adult and the suspect's solicitor are entitled to access to the custody record. The suspect is entitled to a copy of the custody record on release, a right which also extends to the appropriate adult and solicitor for 12 months after the release. The custody record is an important source of information. It contains personal details about the detainee such as their name, address, occupation, age and also their ethnic appearance. The reason for arrest and details of arrest are recorded and the authority for continued detention, e.g. for preparation of charges, to secure evidence or obtain further evidence by questioning. The time that the appropriate adult was called and actually arrived should be recorded together with details of an interpreter (if used) and solicitor. The suspect will be asked whether they are suffering from any illness or receiving medication and the record should note whether a doctor is called. The detained person will also be asked to sign the form indicating receipt of the notice to detained persons and notice of entitlements and indicating whether legal advice was requested.

Rights at the station

Section 56 of PACE 1984 includes the right to inform someone of an arrest. The suspect should be informed of this right by the custody officer and is entitled on arrival at the station to have one person who is likely to have an interest in his welfare told of his whereabouts. If that person cannot be contacted, at least two further people should be tried.

Section 58 provides the right to legal advice. A suspect is entitled to receive advice in person or by telephone, in private, before questioning by the police. He is also entitled to consult a solicitor privately at any time during questioning and his legal adviser may be present during interviews.

The conditions of detention should be reasonable. Cells should have adequate heat and light and be clean and ventilated. The suspect should be provided with regular meals (taking into account any special dietary requirements) and have access to toilet facilities and outdoor exercise.

A breach of PACE or any elements of the code make a police officer liable to disciplinary action. Breaches may also have an effect on evidence. Any evidence which is improperly obtained may be excluded by the court. Section 76 relates to confessions where, in order to be admissible, it must be shown beyond reasonable doubt that the confession was not obtained by oppression or in circumstances likely to render it unreliable. Section 78 further includes an overall discretion to exclude evidence if its inclusion would make the trial unfair.

Remands

Once a case has been commenced, the court must decide on the issue of remand of the defendant. The court may remand either in custody or on bail. If in custody, the defendant will not normally be remanded for more than eight clear days at a time. Extended periods of up to 28 days are permissible on second and subsequent remands subject to a number of conditions having been met. In some areas prisons now have video links to the court so that it is not necessary for the defendant to attend court for each remand. Any time spent in custody on remand is generally deducted from the eventual sentence to be served. Nevertheless, a significant number of defendants who have been remanded in custody do not actually receive a custodial sentence and there is no compensation available to those who are acquitted of any offence.

The statutory framework for bail is provided by the Bail Act 1976. Section 4 provides a statutory right to unconditional bail in certain circumstances, subject to defined exceptions. These exceptions should be compatible with Art. 5 ECHR. For an imprisonable offence, bail need not be granted if:

1. there are substantial grounds for believing that if released on bail he would:

   (a) fail to surrender to custody, or

   (b) commit an offence, or

   (c) interfere with witnesses or otherwise obstruct the course of justice;

2. he ought to be kept in custody for his own protection;

3. he is already in custody in pursuance of the sentence of the court;

4. there has not yet been time to obtain necessary information so as to take a decision about bail;

5. he has been arrested for having failed to surrender to custody after being released on bail in the current proceedings;

6. the proceedings have been adjourned for inquiries or a report and it would be impracticable to complete them without having the defendant in custody.

The prosecution will make representations to the court if they object to grant of bail for one or more of the above reasons. In addition, the probation service may be asked to supply a bail information report providing verified information for the CPS, e.g. as to the defendant's accommodation and employment, and an assessment of risk of harm to the public.

Bail may be granted conditionally or unconditionally. Conditions can be imposed if they are necessary to secure that the accused surrenders to custody, is available for reports, does not offend, does not interfere with witnesses or obstruct the course of justice. Examples of such conditions include daily reports to police, imposition of a curfew, stipulated residence, perhaps with a relative or in a bail hostel, avoiding certain areas or people and surrender of passport. The court may also request a surety or a security.

If bail is withheld, the court must state the statutory exception(s) which apply and must explain why it feels the exception(s) apply in the particular case. The defendant can apply for the decision to be reviewed by a judge. In *Caballero* v. *United Kingdom* (2000) *The Times,*

29 February, the European Court of Human Rights upheld the concession of the UK Government that automatic denial of bail pending trial was a breach of Art. 5(3) and 5(5) of the European Convention on Human Rights. Section 25 of the Criminal Justice and Public Order Act 1994 stipulated that bail could not be granted to defendants charged with or convicted of homicide or rape after previous convictions of such offences.

First appearance at court

Following charge, the defendant will appear before the magistrates' court. The court will take a plea from the defendant of either guilty or not guilty. If charged with a summary offence, the case may proceed straight to sentencing if the defendant pleads guilty. If there is to be a trial, i.e. where the defendant has pleaded not guilty, the case is likely to be adjourned for preparation of evidence. In either case there may be a further adjournment if reports are required to aid the sentencing decision.

Either way offences may be dealt with by the magistrates unless they decide, after a guilty plea, that their powers of sentence are insufficient, or if it is clearly a serious matter the case may be sent straight to Crown Court for trial. The old committal hearing stage has been abolished.

Indictable only offences are committed to the Crown Court. In the Crown Court a plea and directions hearing will take place in which the indictment is prepared and the defendant is asked to plead.

Trial

A trial in the Crown Court is heard by a judge and jury. Before the trial commences, the jury must be selected and sworn in.

Trials in the magistrates' court and the Crown Court follow standard adversarial procedure as outlined in Figure 18.2.

Each witness must swear an oath or make an affirmation before giving oral evidence to the court. (The terms of the oath and affirmation are set out in Chapter 13.) Notes made contemporaneously (within reason) with the event may be referred to by the witness. The most obvious example of this is the police notebook.

Outcomes in the criminal justice system

Sentences

The sentencing process incorporates a wide range of both expectations and objectives. A number of sentencing theories have been identified including retribution, rehabilitation, deterrence, incapacitation, restitution and denunciation. A combination of aspects from each theory may inform a particular sentencing decision and can also be identified in particular policies.[20] The Criminal Justice Act 2003 specifies the purpose or purposes of sentencing as: punishment; reduction of crime (including reduction by deterrence); reform and rehabilitation; protection of the public and reparation by offenders.

Sentencing decisions should be informed by the facts and seriousness of the offence, including culpability and dangerousness, the circumstances of the offender and be proportionate. There are four levels of culpability: intention to cause harm; recklessness as to whether harm is caused; knowledge of specific risks; and negligence. Within the maximum penalty

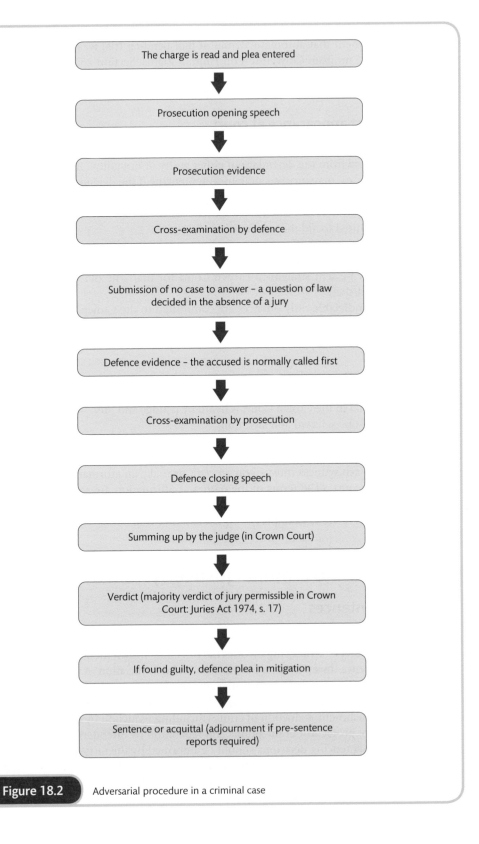

Figure 18.2 Adversarial procedure in a criminal case

stipulated for an offence, the court has a wide discretion to fix an appropriate sentence. It is possible to appeal against sentence and this may lead to change in sentence or in some cases the conviction may be quashed.

Magistrates' courts now have sentencing guidelines produced by the Magistrates' Association to ensure greater consistency between benches. The guidelines' sentencing structure reaffirms the principle of 'just deserts' so that any penalty must reflect the seriousness of the offence and the personal circumstances of the offender. In every case magistrates are required to consider:

- Is discharge or a fine appropriate?
- Is the offence serious enough for a community penalty?
- Is it so serious that only custody will suffice?
- Are sentencing powers sufficient?
- Consider aggravating and mitigating factors, including victim personal statements.

Magistrates start the sentencing procedure by considering the seriousness of the offence before them and will use the guideline starting point contained in the sentencing guidelines. For example, for racially or religiously aggravated common assault, the starting point of 'is it so serious that only custody is appropriate' is a level higher than for common assault, where the guideline is 'is it serious enough for a community penalty'. The court will consider culpability and risk of harm, then all the offence aggravating and mitigating factors, including relevant previous convictions or failure to respond to previous sentences, and determine the extent to which they affect the seriousness of the offence under consideration.

After completing their initial assessment of the seriousness of the offence, the magistrates will form a preliminary view of the appropriate sentence, then consider the offender and any mitigation which has been given on his behalf, such as genuine remorse. If that mitigation is accepted they must reduce the assessment of seriousness, although this may be a minor revision only. If the assessment of seriousness remains at community penalty or higher, then a report from the probation service will be required. Ancillary matters including compensation will be considered. On deciding sentence, discount will be given for a guilty plea, note being taken of the timelines of the plea. In announcing sentence, magistrates will state their reasons. This is done in a structured way and will address: what makes the offence more or less serious than average, including a statement as to culpability (was the offence committed intentionally or recklessly etc.), the harm or risk of harm, aggravating and mitigating factors relating to the offence and the offender. The magistrates will also state the main point of sentence as one or more of: punishment, reduction in crime/deterrence, reform and rehabilitation, protection of the public or reparation.

Sentencing guidelines

The Court of Appeal (Criminal Division) has issued sentencing guidelines from time to time. As an example, in *R v. Billam* (1986) 8 Cr App R (S) 48, Lord Lane set out principles to guide judges on sentencing in rape cases, commencing with a starting point of five years for rape committed by an adult without any aggravating factors, through to a life sentence where the behaviour manifested perverted or psychopathic tendencies. The Sentencing Guideline Council (SGC), an independent body, has responsibility for developing comprehensive sentencing and allocation guidelines. For example, the SGC has issued guidance to courts on the approach to take in giving a reduced sentence depending on the time and circumstances of an admission of guilt.[21] The Council receives advice from the Sentencing Advisory Panel on a particular sentencing topic and uses this to formulate sentencing guidelines on the subject. The court must state reasons if it intends to depart from sentencing guidelines. The Sentencing Advisory Panel was established under CDA 1998, s. 81. It has issued consultation papers on offences involving child pornography, rape, domestic violence, and advice on offensive weapons, racially aggravated offences and minimum terms in murder cases.

Since 1988 it has also been possible for the prosecution to appeal against sentence (for indictable offences) on the ground that the sentence imposed is unduly lenient.[22]

The levels of sentence currently available are discharges, fines, community sentences and custody.

Discharges

The court may order an absolute discharge or a conditional discharge. In both cases the conviction is recorded but no further action to sentence will be taken unless the offender commits a further offence during the period of a conditional discharge. If so, the offender can be re-sentenced for the original offence.

Fines

The most commonly used sentence is the fine, particularly for summary offences in the magistrates' court. The maximum fine is stipulated as a level (1–5) for each offence, and the overall maximum that the magistrates' court can impose is £5,000. There are no financial limits to the fines which can be ordered in the Crown Court. Fines may be recovered directly from income support or attachment of earnings. Prison is the ultimate sanction for non-payment of fines.

Fixed penalties

The Criminal Justice and Police Act 2001 introduced a variety of measures designed to combat crime and disorder including on-the-spot fines. The relevant offences where on-the-spot penalties can be issued are set out in s. 1 and include: wasting police time; being drunk in a highway, other public place or licensed premises; and disorderly behaviour while drunk in a public place. Any uniformed police constable can give a person over the age of 18 a penalty notice. The individual has 21 days to pay the penalty.

Compensation

When an offence which has resulted in a personal injury or damage to property is dealt with, the court must consider whether a compensation order should be made instead of or in addition to another order (Powers of Criminal Courts (Sentencing) Act 2000, s. 130). If a compensation order is made, that takes priority over a fine. The amount of compensation will be determined in the light of medical evidence, the victim's age and sex and other relevant factors. Reasons must be stated if compensation requested is not given.

Community sentences

The Criminal Justice Act 2003 sets out the new structure for community sentences. The previous orders: community rehabilitation order (probation); community punishment order (community service orders); community punishment and rehabilitation order (combination orders); curfew orders; drug treatment and testing orders, no longer exist although elements of these orders are retained under the new structure. A community order may be made for up to three years for offenders aged over 16. The Criminal Justice and Immigration Act 2008 amends the 2003 Act, so that it will only be possible to make a community order if the offence is punishable with imprisonment (the objective is to reduce the use of community sentencing for less serious offences).

A 'community order' may include any one or more of the following requirements:

(a) an unpaid work requirement (s. 199);

(b) an activity requirement (s. 201);

(c) a programme requirement (s. 202);

(d) a prohibited activity requirement (s. 203);

(e) a curfew requirement (s. 204);

(f) an exclusion requirement (s. 205);

(g) a residence requirement (s. 206);

(h) a mental health treatment requirement (s. 207);

(i) a drug rehabilitation requirement (s. 209);

(j) an alcohol treatment requirement (s. 212);

(k) a supervision requirement (s. 213); and

(l) in a case where the offender is aged under 25, an attendance centre requirement (s. 214).

In determining which requirement or combination of requirements are imposed, the guiding principles are proportionality and suitability.

Requirements

Unpaid work – this is similar to the previous community punishment order and the number of hours will be between 40 and 300, to be completed normally within 12 months.

Activity – the offender is required to present at a specified place to participate in specified activities, for a total number of no more than 60 days.

Programme – the offender will participate in an accredited programme recommended to the court by a probation officer or YOT officer as suitable.

Prohibited activity – this requirement prohibits the offender from participating in specified activities and specified days, e.g. avoiding a football ground on match day.

Curfew – the offender must stay at a specified place for between 2 and 12 hours in any 24-hour period, in a similar way to the old curfew. It can last for up to six months and will usually be monitored electronically.

Exclusion – the offender must not enter a specified place or places for a period up to two years, normally monitored by electronic tag.

Residence – after consideration of the home circumstances of the offender, a residence requirement directs the offender to live at a specified place.

Mental health treatment requirement – requires the offender (who must be willing) to undergo treatment by a named medical practitioner or chartered psychologist provided the condition is not so serious as to warrant a hospital or guardianship order.

Drug rehabilitation – the offender will have treatment with a view to reducing or elimination dependency and will provide samples. The treatment and testing period will be for between six months and three years.

Alcohol treatment – the period of treatment cannot be for less than six months and the offender must be willing to comply with treatment as resident or non-resident of an institution.

Supervision – similar to the previous community rehabilitation order, the offender must attend for appointments with the responsible officer with a view to promoting rehabilitation.

Attendance centre – where the offender is under 25, he may be required to attend a centre for between 12 and 36 hours, split into sessions of not more than three hours in a day.

For all community sentences the offender must keep in contact with their supervising officer (probation officer) and advise any change of address. Where an offender does not comply with a community order, the case may be returned to court and the court can revoke the order and impose a sentence which may include a custodial sentence.

Deferred sentences

Deferred sentences were introduced by Powers of Criminal Courts (Sentencing) Act 2000, ss. 1 and 2. These provisions have been modified by the CJA 2003. As well as requiring the consent of the offender, the court is able to impose a wide variety of conditions (including a residence requirement) for the period of deferment. The court can then review the conduct of the defendant before passing sentence.

Suspended sentences

The suspended prison sentence was reformed so that offenders have to complete a range of requirements imposed by the court during the period of suspension. The prison sentence can be suspended for between six months and two years. The court can impose one or more requirements (as set out above for community sentences), and the requirements must be completed within a specified supervision period. The order can provide for periodical review hearings at which the offender must attend.

Pre-sentence reports

Pre-sentence reports are required before a community or custodial sentence can be imposed by the court. The report will be prepared by the probation service. Pre-sentence reports as defined by s. 3 of the Criminal Justice Act 1991 are designed to focus specifically on the offence, provide an analysis of why the crime was committed, the impact on the victim, the offender's attitude to the offence, an assessment of the risk of reoffending, a sentence proposal, and significantly less detail about the offender. The report should be objective, impartial, free from discriminatory language and stereotype, balanced, verified and factually accurate. It should be written following at least one face-to-face interview with the offender and will be based on the use of the **Offender Assessment System** (often referred to as **OASYS**). The court, offender, defence and prosecution will have a copy. The report should be prepared within a maximum period of 15 working days. For many cases in the magistrates' court the report will be required within 5 days and may be delivered orally.

In addition, if a court envisages a specific sentence, e.g. community service order up to 100 hours or probation without additional requirements, a specific sentence report may be requested. This is a briefer report than a full pre-sentence report and is focused on suitability for a particular sentence. It should normally be available to the court on the day it is requested. There is a danger that the desire to speed up the process and avoid delay, and the difficulty of trying to assess someone on the basis of one interview, can lead to situations where the court is not made fully aware of important information regarding the suitability of a person for a community sentence.

Custody

An offender may be ordered to serve a prison sentence in a case where the offence is so serious that only custody is justified; it may be an offence of sex or violence where only a custodial sentence is considered sufficient to protect the public, or it may be imposed where an offender will not consent to a community sentence. The length of sentence for each type of offence is specified in legislation. The time actually served in prison will usually be less than that imposed by the court due to reductions for time spent on remand and the operation of remission. Under the CJA 2003, where a prison sentence of 12 months or more is imposed on an offender who is not classified as 'dangerous', that offender will be entitled to be released from custody after completing half of the sentence. The whole of the second half of the sentence will be subject to licence requirements.

A life sentence is mandatory in cases of murder and may be imposed for other serious indictable offences. The Crime (Sentences) Act 1997 makes a life sentence mandatory for a person who commits a serious offence (attempted murder, manslaughter, attempted rape or rape, intercourse with a girl aged under 13 and armed robbery) having previously been convicted of a serious offence. This is sometimes referred to as the 'two strikes' rule. In addition, the 'three strikes' rule requires that a minimum sentence of three years is imposed for a third residential burglary. A prisoner on a life sentence may apply for release on licence and if released may be recalled to prison at any time. Time spent before release varies but there are few life prisoners who will literally spend the whole of their lives in prison. It is possible to suspend a custodial sentence (of up to two years) if justified by exceptional circumstances.

Vulnerable witnesses

The Youth Justice and Criminal Evidence Act 1999 (YJCEA 1999) introduced measures to tackle problems relating to vulnerable witnesses. Special measures are available to witnesses on the grounds of youth, incapacity, or feelings of distress a witness is likely to suffer in giving evidence. It was recognised in 'Speaking up for Justice'[23] that giving evidence can be particularly stressful for some witnesses and the formality of the process may be intimidating and inhibit their giving best evidence. A vulnerable adult witness is defined as a person suffering from mental disorder or otherwise having a significant impairment of intelligence and social functioning (YJCEA 1999, s. 16(2)(a)), or a physical disability or disorder (YJCEA 1999, s. 16(2)(b)). In addition, a witness may also be eligible for special measures if the court is satisfied that the quality of evidence given by the witness is likely to be diminished by reason of fear or distress in connection with testifying (YJCEA 1999, s. 17). To determine eligibility there is a range of circumstances listed for the court to take into account, including: nature and circumstances of the offence; age of the witness; social and cultural background; ethnic origins; domestic and employment circumstances; religious and political beliefs; and any behaviour towards the witness by the accused or those associated with him, including anyone else likely to be an accused or a witness in the case. The court will make a special measures direction if measures are to be made available to a witness.

The following special measures are provided by the YJCEA 1999:

- screening the witness from the accused (s. 23);
- giving evidence via a live link (s. 24);

- removal of wigs and gowns during testimony (s. 25);
- giving evidence in private (intimidation and sexual cases) (s. 26);
- video recording of evidence in chief (s. 27);
- video recording of cross-examination and re-examination (s. 28);
- examination through an intermediary (s. 29);
- provision of aids to communication (s. 30).

Guidance entitled, 'Achieving Best Evidence in Criminal Proceedings: Guidance on interviewing victims and witnesses and guidance on using special measures' (2011) is in place. All Crown Courts now have video link facilities. And under s. 102 of the Coroners and Justice Act 2009, a supporter can accompany a witness while giving evidence in the live link room. An example of aids to communication are sign and symbol boards, (*R* v. *Watts (James Michael)* [2010] EWCA Crim 1824. An intermediary will be a communication expert, such as a speech or language therapist, and will act as intermediary between the witness and lawyers, judges and juries, will explain to the witness the questions posed and will explain the witness's response to the court, (*R* v. *Cox* [2012] EWCA Crim 549).

In addition, the Ministry of Justice has published, 'The Witness Charter: Standards of care for witnesses in the criminal justice system' (2013) covering the level of service all witnesses (including vulnerable and intimidated witnesses) can expect from all involved in the criminal justice system.

Mentally disordered offenders

There are a number of special provisions and orders affecting those with mental disorder in the criminal justice system. In the Crown Court an accused person may be declared unfit to plead by the jury. The trial may proceed and, if the crime is proven, the court may order detention in a mental hospital, guardianship, or supervision and treatment (Criminal Procedure (Insanity and Unfitness to Plead) Act 1991).

After conviction, the court may remand a defendant to hospital for a report on his mental condition to be prepared, for up to 28 days (consecutive periods not to exceed 12 weeks) where there is reason to suspect that the accused person is suffering from mental disorder and it would be impracticable for a report on his mental condition to be made if he were remanded on bail. The evidence of a registered medical practitioner is required (Mental Health Act 1983, s. 35). The Mental Health Act 1983, s. 36 provides that on the evidence of two medical practitioners the Crown Court can remand the accused person for treatment for a period of 28 days (consecutive periods not to exceed 12 weeks).

Specific orders may be made where mental disorder is apparent at the time of sentence. Under s. 37, a hospital order for six months, which period is renewable, may be made by the Crown Court, where it could have imposed a custodial sentence, on the evidence of two medical practitioners. The criteria are that the defendant is suffering from mental disorder, which makes it appropriate for them to receive treatment (and it is likely to alleviate in the case of psychopathic disorder or mental impairment). The court must be of the opinion, having regard to all the circumstances, including the nature of the offence, character, antecedents, and other available methods of dealing with the offender, that the most suitable method of disposing of the case is by a hospital order.

An interim hospital order may be made under the Mental Health Act 1983, s. 38. A restriction order under s. 41 may be attached to a hospital order. It can be imposed when it appears to the court, having regard to the nature of the offence, character and antecedents of the offender and the risk of their committing further offences if set at large, that it is necessary to impose a restriction order for the protection of the public from serious harm.

A person who is serving a prison sentence may be transferred to a hospital on the direction of the Home Secretary and reports of two registered medical practitioners. In hospital, the offender becomes a patient and is treated in the same way as any other patient compulsorily detained in hospital.

Racism and the criminal justice system

Recent years have seen an increasing awareness of and recognition of racist crimes. Section 95(1)(b) of the Criminal Justice Act 1991 introduced a requirement for the Home Secretary to publish information each year to assist those involved in the administration of criminal justice in fulfilling 'their duty to avoid discriminating against any persons on the ground of race, sex or any other improper ground'. As a result of this provision, ethnic monitoring in police forces was introduced with respect to stop and search, arrest, cautions, homicides and death in police custody. On average, this has shown that ethnic minorities are more than four times as likely to be stopped and searched as white people, and the proportion of black people arrested has been consistently higher than the proportion of white people.

A racial incident is defined by the Association of Chief Police Officers as 'any incident in which it appears to the reporting or investigating officer that the complaint involves an element of racial motivation; or any incident which includes an allegation of racial motivation made by any person' (ACPO, 1985).

A factor in favour of prosecution in the Code for Crown Prosecutors is whether the offence was motivated by any form of discrimination or racial motive. It is also relevant to sentencing decisions. The Crime and Disorder Act 1998 (CDA 1998) introduced racially aggravated offences (Part II of the Act) to deal with racist violence and harassment. Sections 29–32 provide that, where the prosecution is able to prove that the offence was racially aggravated, there is a mandatory requirement to enhance the sentence through additional fines or periods of custody. The prosecution must be able to show either the existence of racial hostility at the time of committing the offence, immediately before or after, or that the offence was motivated wholly or partly by racial hostility (s. 28). Use of racist language during an attack is an obvious example and in such a case the offence becomes a racially aggravated offence. The relevant offences are assaults, criminal damage, public order and harassment. Section 29 also creates three new offences: racially aggravated malicious wounding or racially aggravated grievous bodily harm; racially aggravated actual bodily harm; and racially aggravated common assault. When hearing such a case, the court must state in open court that it is dealing with a racially aggravated offence.

Prior to the introduction of the CDA 1998, it was possible for judges to take account of racial motivation and to increase the final sentence as an aspect of their sentencing discretion (R v. Ribbans (1995) 16 Cr App Rep (S) 698). Given the high profile of the Stephen Lawrence murder and subsequent inquiry, recognition of racial violence is currently high on the agenda. Earlier research suggested that there was significant under-reporting of racial incidents, many of which did not come to the attention of the police.

In determining racial aggravation, motivation and racial hostility are key issues. Prior to the CDA 1998 the offence of incitement to racial hatred existed, in s. 18 of the Public Order Act 1986, as well as the offences of possession of racially inflammatory material and causing harassment, harm and distress. The case of R v. White [2001] EWCA Crim 216 concerned an offence contrary to s. 4 of the Public Order Act 1986, racially aggravated for the purposes of s. 31 of the Crime and Disorder Act 1998. The court found that it was not tied to dictionary definitions in assessing a racial group and race in the case of racially aggravated offences. The defendant admitted calling a London bus conductress from Sierra Leone a 'stupid African bitch'. He asserted that this could not refer to a racial group within s. 28 of the 1998 Act; and there was no offence where the offender and victim were of the same racial group. The court found that African did describe a racial group and it was possible for a person to show hostility to another person of the same racial group. Further, in *R v. Saunders* [2000] 1 Cr App Rep 458, the Court of Appeal held that a person indulging in racial violence must expect a further term of up to two years to be added to their sentence for racial aggravation. This will be the case even if that resulted in a non-custodial sentence becoming custodial.

Sections 28(1) and 29(1)(b) and (2) of the Crime and Disorder Act 1998 provide guidance on the matters to be considered when passing sentence:

1. Nature of hostility demonstrated by language and/or use of a weapon.

2. Whether the location was public or private.

3. Number of demonstrators for and against.

4. Presence or absence of other features such as offensive remarks in a crowded area, such as a synagogue or mosque, or in an otherwise empty room.

5. Discount applied for genuine remorse, guilty plea, previous good conduct.

The Legal Aid Sentencing and Punishment of Offenders Act 2012 adds transgender identity to the personal characteristics which are statutory aggravating factors in sentencing when an offence is motivated by hostility to the victim.

Miscarriages of justice

The Criminal Cases Review Commission (**CCRC**) investigates[24] cases of alleged miscarriage of justice. If the CCRC considers that a miscarriage of justice has occurred it will refer the case to the Court of Appeal. It is then possible for the Court of Appeal to quash a conviction on the basis that it is 'unsafe' (previous wording referred to 'unsafe and unsatisfactory').

Victims

The Code of Practice for Victims of Crime, issued by the Ministry of Justice (2013), sets out the services victims can expect to receive from the criminal justice system including:

- a right to information about their crime, including arrests and court cases, within a specified timeframe;
- a dedicated family liaison police officer to help bereaved relatives;
- clear information from the Criminal Injuries Compensation Authority (CICA) on eligibility for compensation;
- information about Victim Support;
- an enhanced service in cases of vulnerable or intimidated victims;
- the flexibility to opt out of unwanted services.
- a right to make a Victim Personal Statement (VPS) to explain the affect of the crime, and read it aloud or have it read aloud if a defendant is found guilty;

- automatic referral to victims' service by the police;

- a right for businesses who are victims of crime to write an Impact Statement for court explaining how the crime affected them;

- a right to arrange a court familiarisation visit and enter the court through a different entrance from the suspect and sit in a separate waiting area where possible;

- a right to meet the CPS Prosecutor and ask him or her questions about the court process;

- a right to be informed of any appeal against the offender's conviction or sentence;

- a right to opt into the Victim Contact Scheme (VCS) if the offender is sentenced to 12 months or more for a specified violent or sexual offence.

Victims will have the right to appeal if any of the service providers have not met their obligations.

The Attorney-General has set out a Prosecutor's Pledge (2006) describing the level of service that victims can expect to receive from prosecutors. Prosecutors play a key role in protecting victims' interests, in particular when accepting pleas and during sentencing. The pledge is a further step towards the objective of placing victims at the heart of the criminal justice system and is applicable to all prosecuting authorities, including advocates instructed by the prosecuting authorities in the Crown Court. Where there is an identifiable victim the prosecutor will: take into account the impact on the victim or their family when making a charging decision; inform the victim where the charge is withdrawn, discontinued or substantially altered; protect victims from unwarranted or irrelevant attacks on their character; and on conviction apply for the appropriate order for compensation, restitution or future protection of the victim.

Criminal injuries compensation

The scheme for state provision of compensation to victims of criminal injuries is governed by the Criminal Injuries Compensation Act 1995. Claims are made to the Criminal Injuries Compensation Authority. Applications are determined by claims officers and there is an appeal to the Criminal Injuries Compensation Appeals Panel.

A criminal injury is a personal injury (physical or mental) directly attributable to:

(a) a crime of violence;

(b) an offence of trespass on a railway; or

(c) the apprehension of an offender (or suspect), the prevention of an offence (or attempts to do so) or helping a constable.

Ground (b) was included to cover the circumstances where train drivers witness railway suicides or accidents on railway lines. A crime of violence is defined to include: physical attack; any other act or omission which causes physical injury to a person; a threat against a person causing fear of immediate violence in circumstances which would cause a person of reasonable firmness to be in fear; a sexual assault to which a person did not consent; and arson or fire raising.

Claims must be made within two years of the incident that caused the injury. This time limit may be waived where it is reasonable and in the interests of justice to do so, given the particular circumstances of the case. For child victims, applications should be made by an adult with parental responsibility for the child (or, if in care, the local authority). The authority has been sympathetic to delayed applications made while the victim is still a child or on reaching majority in respect of an injury caused whilst a child. A payment will not be made if it is likely that the assailant will benefit or if it would not be in the child's interest. Child abuse cases comprise approximately 10 per cent of all applications and this is an issue which it is appropriate to raise during child protection conferences and reviews. Levels of compensation are fixed under the scheme and there is a minimum threshold of £1,000. If the injuries are likely to receive compensation of less than £1,000, this scheme does not apply. The maximum total amount payable is £500,000. Payments in respect of sexual abuse of children have ranged from £1,000 for minor isolated and non-penetrative indecent acts to £17,500 for repeated non-consensual vaginal and/or anal intercourse over a period exceeding three years.

Application of the scheme to injuries caused by domestic violence is limited. Under the original scheme, applications from incidents of domestic violence were excluded. Under the current scheme, compensation may be paid but only if the perpetrator has been prosecuted (or there are practical, technical or other good reasons for non-prosecution) and, where violence occurred between adults in the family, the perpetrator and the applicant ceased living in the same household before the application was made and are unlikely to live together again. Part of the justification for this rule is to prevent a perpetrator benefiting from an award of compensation.

The incident which caused the injury must normally have been reported to the police. Awards may be refused or reduced if the police were not informed, the applicant did not cooperate with the police or has not cooperated with the authority. It is also possible to refuse or reduce awards based on the authority's interpretation of the applicant's character as shown by his criminal convictions.

Case law has addressed issues of interpretation and procedure under the scheme: *R* v. *Criminal Injuries Compensation Appeals Panel, ex parte August; R* v. *Criminal Injuries Compensation Appeals Panel, ex parte Brown* [2001] 2 All ER 874, where cases which were heard jointly in the Court of Appeal, considered the relevance of consent in determining whether a crime was a 'crime of violence' for the purpose of a claim. In each case sexual offences were committed against the claimants whilst children but with their consent. The court found that the applicant's consent or willing participation was highly relevant to deciding whether he had been a victim of violence. However reprehensible the conduct of the older man involved, a boy aged 13 who was a willing and active participant in an act of buggery with a man aged 53 was not a victim of a crime of violence so as to qualify for compensation.

The Criminal Injuries Compensation Authority is a creature of statute and a public body and, in order to conform to the basic public law requirement of sufficiency, it is obliged to provide proper reasons together with the gist of the supporting evidence for its decision to reduce or refuse claims for compensation. A failure to provide reasons is a form of procedural unfairness (*R* v. *Criminal Injuries Compensation Authority, ex parte Leatherland; R* v. *Criminal Injuries Compensation Board, ex parte Bramall; R* v. *Criminal Injuries Compensation Appeals Panel, ex parte Kay* (2000) *The Times*, 12 October).

Human Rights Act 1998 implications for criminal justice

When the Human Rights Act 1998 was introduced it was anticipated that a number of challenges to prisoners' rights would be voiced. As an example, in *R (P)* v. *Secretary of State for the Home Department; R (Q)* v. *Secretary of State for the Home Department* [2001] EWCA Civ 1151 the human rights implications of prison policy about babies in prison was considered. It was contended that the separation of mother and child once the child reached the age of 18 months was a violation of the right to respect for private and family life contained in

Art. 8. The court held, however, that the Prison Service was entitled to adopt a policy allowing children to remain in prison with their mothers until the age of 18 months but not thereafter. The policy should, however, be applied flexibly, bearing in mind the effect of separation on the mother and child in each case and the alternative placement available for the child.

Chapter summary

- The National Probation Service is responsible for the majority of social work functions towards adults in the criminal justice system. It is important to recognise, however, that other service users will come into contact with the criminal justice system and for that reason it is essential that all social workers have an understanding of this area. In addition, recent legislation has introduced a duty on local authorities to do all they reasonably can to prevent crime and disorder in their area. This will impact on all aspects of social services work and other functions of local authorities.

- Key players in the criminal justice system are the police, the Crown Prosecution Service, the Criminal Defence Service, the National Offender Management Service (combines the National Probation Service and the Prison Service), and the witness service. Each organisation has defined areas of responsibility.

- Offences will comprise both a physical and mental element. The classification of an offence will dictate which court conducts the trial. Criminal offences may be defined by statute or the common law. An offence can be classified as summary, either way or indictable.

- The Police and Criminal Evidence Act 1984 (PACE) is an important piece of legislation which sets out the elements of a valid arrest, time limits for detention in custody, rights in the police station and other police powers. There are eight codes of practice which accompany the Act, including Code C which addresses detention, treatment and questioning of suspects and outlines the role of the appropriate adult in respect to juveniles and vulnerable adults.

- Prior to the trial of a criminal offence the issue of remand must be determined. A suspect may be remanded in custody or on bail. The Bail Act 1976 includes a presumption in favour of bail unless specified circumstances apply.

- The court will proceed to sentence a defendant who has been found guilty. Sentences may be classified into the following groups: discharges, fines, community sentences and custody. A series of requirements can be added to community sentences and imposed during suspended custodial sentences.

- Regardless of the success of a criminal prosecution, a victim may apply for compensation for injuries caused by a crime of violence to the Criminal Injuries Compensation Authority.

- There are a range of special measures available for vulnerable witnesses to enable them to produce their best evidence to the court in a less intimidating environment.

- Specific disposals are available for people suffering from mental disorder who have committed a crime, including hospital orders. It is also possible for a person detained in prison to be transferred to a hospital because of mental disorder.

- Various provisions have been introduced over recent years to address racism in the criminal justice system and to appropriately punish offences that are motivated by racism. The Crime and Disorder Act 1998 introduced a range of racially aggravated offences.

Exercise

The National Front attend a demonstration held in protest against 'loony left racist council policies' which have funded an Asian women's support group in Oldtown. The demonstration soon escalates into violence with others present who object to the National Front demonstration. The police make several arrests including James, aged 31 and white, who was seen attacking a black youth with a wooden post. He was found to be in possession of a large quantity of racially inflammatory material. During the course of his arrest, he was racially abusive and spat in the face of the Asian officer arresting him. He is subsequently charged with several offences to which he intends to plead not guilty. The prosecution intend to oppose bail.

John, a friend of the youth who was attacked, is enraged by the demonstration and makes his way to the squat where James lives, intending to cause minor damage. Seeing racist posters through the window he loses his temper, forces his way in and sets fire to a pile of papers in the house. He was unaware that James' girlfriend and baby were upstairs at the time. They escape with minor injuries. John has a mild learning disability. He is seen running away from the property, is picked up by the police and taken to the station later that evening. The police refuse to call anybody to let them know of John's whereabouts until he tells them 'what he was up to'. They interview him alone, until he confesses to arson. John has never been in trouble with the police before.

Consider what offences James will have been charged with; whether the prosecution may successfully oppose bail; what issues might be dealt with in pre-sentence reports if he is found guilty; any breaches which there may have been to John's rights at the station and the consequences of breach. What is John's potential criminality?

Websites

Liberty:
www.liberty-human-rights.org.uk

The National Association for the Care and Resettlement of Offenders – an independent voluntary organisation working to prevent crime:
www.nacro.org.uk

The Home Office – including information about the police and the national offender management service:
www.homeoffice.gov.uk

The Prison Service:
www.justice.gov.uk/about/hmps

The Crown Prosecution Service, for information and a copy of the Code for Crown Prosecutors:
www.cps.gov.uk

The Independent Police Complaints Commission website has details of how to make a complaint:
www.ipcc.gov.uk

The national Appropriate Adult network:
www.appropriateadult.org.uk

Further reading

Textbooks on criminal justice and guides to legislation include:

Birch, D. and Leng, R. (2000) *Blackstone's Guide to the Youth Justice and Criminal Evidence Act 1999*. London: Blackstone Press.

Gibson, B. (2014) *Criminal Justice: A Beginner's Guide*. Hampshire: Waterside Press Ltd.

Huckelsby, A. and Wahidin, A. (2013) *Criminal Justice* (2nd edn). Oxford: Oxford University Press.

Joyce, P. (2013) *Criminal Justice: An Introduction* (2nd edn). London: Routledge.

Specific aspects of criminal justice are addressed in the following publications:

Bowling, B. and Phillips, C. (2002) *Racism, Crime and Justice*. Harlow: Longman.

Ellison, L. (2001) *The Adversarial Process and the Vulnerable Witness*. Oxford: Oxford University Press.

Gray, N., Laing, J. and Noaks, L. (eds) (2002) *Criminal Justice, Mental Health and the Politics of Risk*. London: Cavendish.

Miers, D. (1997) *State Compensation for Criminal Injuries*. London: Blackstone Press.

White, C. (2002) 'Re-assessing the social worker's role as an appropriate adult' 24(1) *Journal of Social Welfare and Family Law* pp. 55–65. (This article suggests that more guidance and training is required if the role of appropriate adult is to be fulfilled in the spirit in which it was created.)

Winstone, J. and Pakes, F. (eds) (2005) *Community Justice: Issues for Probation and Criminal Justice*. Cullompton: Willan Publishing.

Zander, M. (1995) *PACE Act* (3rd edn). London: Sweet & Maxwell.

Notes

[1] M. Macpherson (1999) 'The Stephen Lawrence Inquiry' (Cm. 4262–1). London: The Stationery Office.

[2] Home Office (2001) 'Making Punishments Work: Review of the Sentencing Framework for England and Wales' (The Halliday report). London: Home Office Communication Directorate.

[3] Sir Robin Auld (2001) 'The Criminal Courts Review Report'. London: The Stationery Office.

[4] Home Office (2001) 'Criminal Justice: The Way Ahead' (Cm. 5074). London: Stationery Office.

[5] Crime Survey for England and Wales 2013.

[6] Findings are published together in statistical bulletins by the Office for National Statistics (ONS).

[7] www.homeoffice.gov.uk.

[8] SI 2004/3216.

[9] The code is issued under s. 10 of the Prosecution of Offences Act 1985.

[10] The introduction to the code includes a useful section describing the role and structure of the CPS.

[11] In matters concerning representation in criminal proceedings, the Access to Justice Act 1999 replaced the Legal Aid Act 1988.

[12] National Probation Service for England and Wales and the Home Office Communication Directorate (2001) 'A New Choreography: An Integrated Strategy for the National Probation Service for England and Wales'. London: Home Office.

[13] For the background to the creation of NOMS, see P. Carter (2003) 'Managing Offenders, Reducing Crime: A review of correctional services in England and Wales'. London: Home Office.

[14] M. Zander (2000) 'The criminal standard of proof – how sure is sure?' 6956 *New Law Journal* p. 1517.

[15] PACE 1984, s. 30.

[16] PACE 1984, s. 41.

[17] PACE 1984, s. 42.

[18] PACE 1984, s. 43.

[19] See full discussion in J. Williams (2000) 'The inappropriate adult' 22(1) *Journal of Social Welfare and Family Law* pp. 43–57.

[20] See M. Davies, H. Croall and J. Tyrer (2005) *Criminal Justice: an Introduction to the Criminal Justice System in England and Wales* (3rd edn) Harlow: Longman, for a detailed explanation of each theory and the types of sentences which most closely reflect each theory.

[21] Sentencing Guidelines Council (2007) 'Reduction in Sentence for a Guilty Plea: Definitive Guidelines'.

[22] Criminal Justice Act 1988, s. 36.

[23] The report which made recommendations on which the Act is based, Home Office (1998).

[24] Criminal Appeal Act 1995, s. 13.

Chapter 19

Welfare and homelessness

Learning objectives

To develop an understanding of the following:

- The obligations of local authorities to provide advice and accommodation.
- The definition of homeless, priority need and intentionally homeless.
- The relationship between s. 20 of the Children Act 1989 and homelessness duties to young people.
- Anti-social behaviour and housing.
- The range of welfare benefits.
- Application of the Human Rights Act 1998.

> ## Talking Point
>
> In *Manchester City Council* v. *Moran* [2008] EWCA Civ 378, the Court of Appeal had to consider the case of a woman who claimed to be unintentionally homeless with a priority need for accommodation. She was staying in a refuge after fleeing domestic violence. The court had to consider whether the refuge was accommodation under homelessness legislation; if so, whether it was reasonable for her to continue to occupy it. She had been expelled from the refuge as a result of her own violent behaviour. The court found that the refuge was accommodation, she had made herself intentionally homeless and was not entitled to rehousing. The court considered the following factors as to whether it was reasonable for her to continue to occupy the accommodation:
>
> - Quality of accommodation, its size, type and whether it was shared.
> - Terms of agreement.
> - Her ability to afford it.
> - Whether the location was appropriate for her and her child and the facilities for her child.
> - How long they had already occupied the accommodation and how long they might expect to continue to occupy.
> - The state of their physical and mental health whilst in occupation.
>
> Specific points relating to the accommodation as a refuge were:
>
> - The nature of the refuge and support it provides.
> - The length of time the refuge might expect her to remain in occupation and the length of time women normally stay.
> - The extent to which the refuge has been full during her stay.
> - Whether her stay has prevented others from benefiting from the refuge accommodation.
> - The extent of her need and ability to accept any support the refuge may offer.
>
> Housing and homelessness legislation can be extremely complex. Decisions of housing authorities as to entitlement to and allocation of limited accommodation often turn on fine points of interpretation. As in the present case the end result can seem harsh to individuals who have no real alternatives for housing. The key elements the court had to consider: the duty to provide accommodation to people vulnerable as a result of violence (amongst other reasons), homelessness, priority need and intentional homelessness, are all explained in this chapter.

Introduction

This chapter focuses on three closely related areas: homelessness, housing and welfare benefits. Each area is characterised by complex regulation and frequent changes in law and policy. This chapter aims to provide an overview of the framework of law and regulation currently applicable. Social services' direct duties in these areas are limited; however, the impact of homelessness, housing and welfare provision on service users is often significant and may interrelate with other duties and powers of social services. These areas mainly fall within the aspect of social work law covering law that service users are likely to experience, though there may not be direct social work responsibilities. Councils have specific responsibilities towards homeless people exercised by the housing department. The principal duties are to provide advice and assistance and suitable accommodation for people who are home-less and in priority need and did not become homeless intentionally. The role of the social worker is identified throughout and these are areas where it is important to be aware of avenues for further information and advice.

Homelessness

The Housing Act 1996 (**HA** 1996) is the key legislation on homelessness, as amended by the Homelessness Act 2002. Responding appropriately to homelessness is important but the 2002 Act also includes an emphasis on strategies for preventing homelessness.

Causes of homelessness are many and varied. Changes to the housing market, including right to buy, demographic changes, unemployment and domestic violence all have their influence. Responses to homelessness have been highly politicised and it is unfortunate that negative perceptions, such as the idea that young women will get pregnant to jump the housing queue, still feature in the popular press. Against this context, and with a limited housing stock, councils and housing associations have to assess each case on its merits.

This section considers relevant definitions, including homeless, priority need and in-tentionally homeless, duties imposed, review of decisions, homelessness strategies and the Homelessness Code of Guidance (2006).[1]

The Government is committed to reducing levels of homelessness. The Department of Communities and Local Government has responsibility for housing and homelessness and has established a Ministerial Working Group on preventing and tackling homelessness. It holds statistics on the number of homeless people and has published research on homeless-ness and the ethnic minority population.[2]

It has also recognised that ethnic minority households are at a disproportionate risk of homelessness and has published two guides: 'Tackling homelessness amongst ethnic minor-ity households – a development guide' and 'The causes of homelessness amongst ethnic minority populations' (**ODPM** 2005).

Specific duties

Councils have two principal duties:

- **Advice and assistance** – Councils have to provide advice and assistance to any person who is homeless or threatened with homelessness who seeks their help.
- **Emergency accommodation** – Beyond advice and assistance councils are also obliged to provide emergency accommodation in some circumstances.

The criteria are that the person is eligible for assistance, homeless and in priority need. Each of these criteria is discussed below.

Eligible

The rules on eligibility provide that most UK citizens are eligible for assistance. Individu-als who have lived abroad, moved to the United Kingdom or come to the United Kingdom seeking asylum are ineligible for assistance (HA 1996, s. 185). The detailed rules on eligibil-ity are quite complex. The Secretary of State is obliged to provide information to a housing authority requesting that information, to determine individual eligibility.

Homeless

A person is homeless if he has no accommodation in the United Kingdom or elsewhere in the world which is available for his occupation.

Potential homelessness is also covered by the Act, as a person is threatened with homelessness if it is likely that he will become homeless within 28 days (s. 175(4)). A person can be homeless even though they have some form of accommodation. For example, a person who is staying with friends or relatives but has been asked to leave, is at risk of violence at home or is about to be evicted, may be classed as homeless. Accommodation will be considered available for the applicant if it is available for him and any person who normally resides with him as a member of his family. If it is not 'reasonable to continue to occupy' (HA 1996, s. 175) accommodation it will be disregarded and the person can be considered homeless. For example, if the accommodation is in really bad condition, having taken into account general housing circumstances in the area (HA 1996, s. 177).

It is not reasonable to continue to occupy accommodation if doing so would result in violence to the applicant or a member of his family. 'Violence' includes threats of violence from another person which are likely to be carried out (s. 177(1A)). Violence is domestic violence where it is from a person who is 'associated' with the victim. The list of associated persons is set out in s. 178 and broadly replicates the list in the Family Law Act 1996 (i.e. married, cohabitants, live in the same household, relatives, parent relation to a child). Clearly there will be cases where social services have involvement with a family as a result of domestic violence concerns and one aspect to be addressed in ensuring protection of children is their housing situation.

It is also not reasonable to continue to occupy if the accommodation is unsuitable because the applicant cannot gain entry to it or it is a moveable structure and there is nowhere to place and reside in it, e.g. a caravan or boat. The cost of a property is also relevant to an assessment of whether it is reasonable to occupy. The housing authority must take into account the resources available to the individual, costs of the accommodation, any maintenance payments and reasonable living expenses.[3]

In *Ali* v. *Birmingham CC*; *Moran* v. *Manchester CC* [2009] UKHL 36, the House of Lords confirmed that it is possible for a person to be 'homeless at home'. In practice this refers to people who have some sort of temporary accommodation but it is unreasonable to expect them to continue living there in the long term. Temporary accommodation of that nature includes a woman's refuge. Two scenarios were addressed in this appeal. In the Birmingham case claims were brought by familes living in overcrowded accommodation, for example a couple who lived with six children in a two-bedroom flat. In the Manchester case a mother and her two children were asked to leave a women's refuge after acting in a threatening way towards refuge staff. As a result Manchester concluded that she was intentionally homeless and the duty to secure accommodation for her in the long term did not apply. (See 'Talking Point' at the start of the chapter.)

The key issue for the House of Lords was the meaning of accommodation 'which it is not reasonable for him to continue to occupy' under s.175(3) Housing Act 1996. The court ruled that there will be some cases where an immediate move from temporary accommodation is necessary because it is not reasonable to continue to occupy, in other cases accommodation may be acceptable in the short term and the authority will have the benefit of some time to locate suitable accommodation for the 'homeless at home' applicant.

Priority need

A person has a priority need if the authority is satisfied that he or she falls into one or more of the following categories:

- A pregnant woman (or person the woman resides with).
- A person with whom dependent children would reside.
- A person who is vulnerable because of a disability, physical or mental health problems, or other special reasons (or a person he would reside with).
- A person who is homeless as a result of an emergency such as fire or flood.
- 16–17-year-olds, provided they are not the responsibility of social services (provided with accommodation under s. 20 of the Children Act 1989).
- 18–20-year-old care leavers.
- A person who is vulnerable having been in custody.
- A person who is vulnerable as a result of service in the armed forces.
- A person who is vulnerable having ceased to occupy accommodation because of violence or threats of violence which are likely to be carried out.

It is usual for the housing authority to require evidence from a midwife or doctor as to pregnancy, but it does not matter what stage of the pregnancy has been reached. From the above it is clear that the status of homelessness and priority need will attach not only to the applicant but also to people it would be reasonable to expect to live with him, i.e. a spouse or cohabitee, dependent children or relatives. In relation to dependent children it is not necessary to have a formal court order (residence, previously custody) before it would be reasonable to expect children to be living with the applicant (*R* v. *Ealing London Borough, ex parte Sidhu* (1983) 2 HLR 45). The phrase 'dependent children' includes children up to the age of 16 and 16–18-year-olds living at home and in education or training. The crucial question will be the degree of permanence and regularity in the arrangement, so occasional ad hoc overnight contact would not be included, but 'joint residence' should be, even though the code notes that 'it will only be in exceptional circumstances that the child will be considered to reside with both parents' (para. 8.10).

Where the applicant may be considered 'vulnerable', the housing authority may liaise with social services and obtain medical opinion to assist with the assessment of vulnerability and suitable housing. A person may also be vulnerable due to old age but there is no automatic age limit. The phrase 'other special reasons' allows others who are not necessarily physically or mentally disabled to be considered as having a priority need.

In *Griffin* v. *Westminster City Council* [2004] EWCA Civ 108, the Court of Appeal confirmed that the assessment of vulnerability is a matter for the council's discretion. A 33-year-old man applied as homeless to the council after leaving his mother's address. He had fallen out with his mother's partner and he had alcohol problems and reactive depression. The council provided temporary accommodation but decided he did not have a priority need. G sought a review of the decision. The review officer confirmed that the test to be applied was drawn from the case of *R* v. *Camden London Borough, ex parte Pereira* (1998) 31 HLR 317: 'whether G when homeless would be less likely to fend for [himself] than an ordinary homeless person so that injury or detriment to [G] would have resulted when a less vulnerable person would be able to cope without harmful effect.' G appealed, arguing that the correct test was contained in the code of practice, which required the authority to evaluate the risk of harm and likelihood of injury or detriment. The Court of Appeal confirmed that the *Pereira* test had been applied correctly and that likelihood of injury did not appear in the statute. The test is whether injury or detriment would occur, not likelihood of it occurring. The statute must prevail over the code of practice.

Where a person is vulnerable because of a disability they have particular housing needs. It is acceptable for the housing authority to offer accommodation on the basis that if it is accepted by the individual it will be suitably adapted. Accommodation provided must be suitable for the applicant and their household but it may be wasteful of a local authority to make extensive adaptations before an offer of accommodation has been accepted. In *Boreh* v. *Ealing London Borough Council* [2008] EWCA Civ 1176 the Court of Appeal explained:

> the suitability of offered accommodation is not to be judged exclusively by reference to the condition of the accommodation at the time of the offer, but that the assessment of its suitability can and should take into account any adaptations or alterations that are, at that time proposed to be made. I would, however, qualify that by saying that I consider that any such proposals would have to be the subject of assurances that the applicant could fairly regard as certain, binding and enforceable.

Where a person is vulnerable having ceased to occupy accommodation because of violence or threats of violence which are likely to be carried out, she has a priority need. This is not limited to domestic violence. The code notes: 'In cases involving violence, the safety of the applicant, and ensuring confidentiality must be of paramount concern. It is not only domestic violence that is relevant but all forms of violence, including racially motivated violence or threats of violence likely to be carried out' (para. 8.26).

Young persons of 16–17 years old who are not the responsibility of social services and provided with accommodation under s. 20 of the Children Act 1989 will be considered to have a priority need. A young person who is provided with accommodation by housing services rather than social services will not be entitled to leaving care services. Previously looked after children, including those provided with s. 20 accommodation as children in need, are entitled to leaving care services. The key distinction is whether the young person requires accommodation under the s. 20 criteria or if he simply needs help with accommodation (e.g. advice on tenancy agreements). If the latter, then the young person would be provided for under homelessness legislation. The same issue arose in *R (M)* v. *Hammersmith and Fulham London Borough Council* [2008] UKHL 14. The case concerned a girl who was excluded from school at 14, became involved with the criminal justice system and was evicted from her mother's home before the age of 17. She approached the housing department and was provided with temporary bed and breakfast accommodation. She was later moved to a hostel for 16–17-year-olds, from which she was evicted, moving then to share a flat with her sister. At no time was a referral made to the children's services department. She was then sentenced to a detention and training order and began proceedings for judicial review whilst detained. Her claim that she had been owed duties under the Children (Leaving Care) Act 2000 was rejected by the local authority.

The House of Lords ruled that

- The housing department should have referred her to children's services. They could not be satisfied that she was in priority need unless they had considered whether she was entitled to accommodation under s. 20.

- Children's services should have conducted an assessment under the 'Framework for the Assessment of Children in Need and their Families', and should have accepted responsibility for her.

- Housing and social services guidance stressed the need to establish and follow joint protocols for assessing the needs of homeless 16- and 17-year-olds. Social services should not avoid their responsibilities by expecting housing to provide accommodation.

- In the immediate term the housing authority should provide accommodation to a 16/17-year-old who appeared to be homeless, but this is pending clarification of children's services responsibilities to the young person.

- In this case the child's circumstances had not been drawn to the attention of children's services at all, she could not therefore be considered to be 'a child who is looked after by the local authority' under s. 22(1) of the Children Act 1989.

The case illustrates the need to take a considered view of a young person's circumstances and not simply focus on housing. Her needs should have been brought to the attention of children's services, who could have provided broader support in the absence of parental guidance and possibly diverted her away from the criminal justice system. It is a further example of the need for a multi-agency approach when facing the needs of young people – in this instance for two departments in the same authority to work together.

Key Case

HL decision in *R (G)* v. *Southwark LBC* [2009] UKHL 26.

Guidance was subsequently issued entitled 'Provision of Accommodation for 16- and 17-year-old young people who may be homeless and/or require accommodation' (Department for Children, Families and Schools and Department for Communities). Key points from the guidance:

- It is important to prevent homelessness by helping young people deal with family conflict.
- Joint protocols between housing and children's services departments are required.
- It may be appropriate to provide accommodation for a homeless 16/17-year-old and his/her partner.
- B & B accommodation is not suitable for homeless 16- and 17-year-olds.
- Housing departments should refer young people to children's services for assessment but may provide interim accommodation.
- Focus should be on whether the young person meets s. 20(1) of the Children Act 1989.
- The young person will only be entitled to the full range of leaving care services after being accommodated for at least 13 weeks.
- If the s. 20 criteria are not met, children's services should consider whether they should provide services under s. 17.
- Housing benefit cannot be claimed by a person accommodated under s. 17.
- A child accommodated under s. 20 should have a placement plan.
- A child who refuses s. 20 accommodation should not be considered intentionally homeless.

Government policy includes a commitment that 16- or 17-year-olds should be placed in bed and breakfast accommodation under the homelessness legislation, and no families except in an emergency and then for no longer than six weeks.

Local housing authorities will have a housing allocations policy which must be fair and reasonable. In *Birmingham City Council* v. *Aweys and others* [2008] EWCA Civ 48, the council's policy was found to be unlawful. It gave higher priority to 'street homeless' than it did to the applicants, all of whom were living in overcrowded accommodation that it was not reasonable to continue to occupy.

Intentional homelessness

Section 191 of the Housing Act 1996 covers intentional homelessness:

> **s. 191**
>
> A person becomes intentionally homeless if he deliberately does or fails to do anything in con-sequence of which he ceases to occupy accommodation which is available for his occupation and which it would have been reasonable for him to continue to occupy.
>
> (HA 1996)

A similarly worded provision applies to those threatened with homelessness (s. 196(1)). The definition can be broken down into four separate elements:

- A deliberate act or failure to act.
- As a consequence accommodation ceases to be occupied.
- The accommodation was available for occupation by the person.
- It was reasonable for him to continue to occupy the accommodation.

An act in good faith by a person who was unaware of a relevant fact will not be treated as deliberate, e.g. leaving accommodation before expiry of the notice period.

A person who leaves accommodation because of actual or threatened domestic violence should not be considered intentionally homeless. In *Bond* v. *Leicester City Council* [2001] EWCA Civ 1544, the court confirmed that under HA 1996, ss. 177 and 191, when deciding whether it was reasonable for the victim to continue to occupy the former home, the authority should only consider whether it was probable that continued occupation would lead to domestic violence, and not whether preventative measures could have been taken by the victim. The variety of circumstances that can lead to homelessness, and about which there is argument as to intentionality, are endless. As examples, failure to pay rent or mortgage payments due to poor financial management is likely to be considered intentional, though if spouse A genuinely believed that spouse B was making payments, spouse A might be considered unintentionally homeless. Becoming homeless as a result of imprisonment is likely to be considered intentional.

In *White* v. *Southwark LBC* [2008] EWCA Civ 792, the Court of Appeal confirmed that a young person may be found to be intentionally homeless where failing to follow reasonable house rules led to her being asked to leave by her parents.

Connection with the area

A person has a local connection with an area if he: is or was normally resident in it as a matter of choice; is employed in the area; has family associations with the area; or there are other special circumstances which result in a local connection with the area. Establishing local connection is the key to which housing authority has the duty to provide accommodation for the applicant.

Duties of the authority

The responsibilities of the housing authority flow from inclusion in the categories outlined above and range from providing advice and information about homelessness to provision of accommodation.

Initially, where the authority is approached by an individual seeking accommodation or assistance, and it has reason to believe the person may be homeless or threatened with homelessness, it must make enquiries under HA 1996, s. 184 as to whether the person is eligible for assistance and, if so, what duties are owed to him. The individual does not have to apply in writing, and it should be possible for an application to be made at any time (24-hour access). Enquiries will include whether the person has a priority need and whether he is intentionally homeless. They should be carried out sensitively by the housing authority. Following enquiries, the applicant must be notified by the authority of its decision. It is possible to provide accommodation pending enquiries (s. 188). The Act does not stipulate a timescale for the conduct of enquiries, though the code suggests a target of completion within 33 days of the application (para. 3.18).

Under the Localism Act 2011, where the local authority is required to provide accommodation, it may meet its homelessness duty with an offer of suitable accommodation in the private rented sector.

Possible decisions and corresponding duties:

Homeless but no priority need

If the applicant is eligible, homeless or threatened with homelessness, intentionally or unintentionally, but not in priority need, the authority has an obligation to assess his housing needs and provide advice and assistance (free of charge). This includes advice as to the likely availability of appropriate accommodation in the area. If the applicant is unintentionally homeless the authority may (but is not obliged to) secure accommodation for him. Much will depend on the resources in the area.

Priority need but intentionally homeless

In this situation the authority must assess the applicant's housing needs and provide advice and assistance. It must also ensure that temporary accommodation is made available for a period it considers will give him a reasonable opportunity to find his own accommodation.

Priority need but threatened with homelessness intentionally

The same advice and assistance duty applies, and once the homelessness occurs the applicant is entitled to a period of temporary accommodation.

Priority need and unintentionally threatened with homelessness

The duty here is to try to ensure the accommodation does not cease to be available for the applicant to enable him to remain in the accommodation. If this is not possible, then accommodation must be provided once the homelessness occurs.

Priority need and unintentionally homeless

The full duty applies here – to ensure that accommodation is available for occupation by the applicant (and any family member who normally resides with him).

The authority has power to make reasonable charges for accommodation it provides. If the applicant refuses an offer of suitable accommodation, the council has discharged its duty and is not bound to provide an alternative. In terms of 'suitability' of accommodation the code advises housing authorities to:

> ... have regard to all the relevant circumstances of the applicant and his or her household. Account will need to be taken of any medical and/or physical needs, and any social considerations relating to the applicant and his or her household that might affect the suitability of accommodation. Any risk of violence or racial harassment must also be taken into account. (para. 12.4)

Bed and breakfast accommodation for more than six weeks will not be classed as suitable accommodation for an applicant with family.

Review of homelessness decisions

Part VII of the Housing Act 1996 provides a scheme for reviewing homelessness decisions.[4] The authority may provide accommodation pending the outcome of a review. A request for review should normally be made within 21 days of notification of the authority's decision. The review should be conducted by a person of 'appropriate seniority ... not involved in the original decision' (HA 1996, s. 203). There is a right of appeal to the county court on a point of law.

In *Runa Begum* v. *Tower Hamlets London Borough Council* [2003] UKHL 5, this was found to be compatible with Art. 6 ECHR. Article 6 was engaged as provision of urgent accommodation to disadvantaged people constituted a determination of civil rights. In terms of independence, the court found that the reviewing officer was not sufficiently impartial or independent, but looked at with the possibility of appeal to the county court, the scheme was compatible. This decision is in a similar vein to *R (on the application of Beeson)* v. *Dorset County Council* [2002] EWCA Civ 1812, where the availability of judicial review was sufficient to make the social services complaints procedure compatible.

Cooperation with social services

Where an applicant with children is considered intentionally homeless (or threatened with homelessness intentionally), the housing authority must request the applicant's consent to refer the case to social services. Local government organisation means that in unitary and metropolitan areas this will be another department in the council, but in county areas the district council will be the housing authority with social services situated within the county council. There is scope under s. 17 of the Children Act 1989 to provide accommodation to children in need and their families; however, as s. 17 provides a general duty, it would also be possible to provide accommodation just for the children.

Section 27 of the Children Act 1989 enables social services to request advice and assistance from the housing department where, for example, social services are concerned with an intentionally homeless family with children. The housing department might respond with advice as to availability of providing rented accommodation but is not bound to provide accommodation itself.

Where a housing authority receives an application for housing from a young person aged 16 or 17, cooperation with social services should enable a joint assessment of housing and other needs to be conducted.

Homelessness strategies

The Homelessness Act 2002 places a duty on housing authorities to publish a homelessness strategy. The strategy should be based on a homelessness review in the area, to include: the level (and likely future level) of homelessness in the area; actions taken to prevent homelessness; ensuring that accommodation is available for homeless people; and providing support for homeless people in the area, together with resources available to the authority and other bodies for such activities. The strategy should be prepared in consultation with social services (who will need to give detail of any activities they provide that are likely to meet the needs of the homeless), and other relevant organisations. The first strategy was to be published soon after the Act came into force and a revised strategy must be published every five years.

Code of Guidance

A Code of Guidance has been issued in support of functions under the Housing Act 1996. The Code (2006) is published by the Office of the Deputy Prime Minister, the section of the Government with responsibility for housing and homelessness issues. Authorities are expressly required to have regard to the code.

What is a home?

The European Court of Human Rights has adopted a broad interpretation of 'home' for the purposes of Art. 8 (right to respect for private and family life).

Buckley v. *United Kingdom* (1996) 23 EHRR 101 decided that: 'the concept of "home" within the meaning of Article 8 is not limited to those which are lawfully occupied or which have been lawfully occupied … Whether or not a particular habitation constitutes a "home" which attracts the protection of Article 8 will depend on the factual circumstances, namely, the existence of sufficient and continuous links.' This position was confirmed in *Harrow London Borough Council* v. *Qazi* [2003] UKHL 43, where it was held that there was no requirement for the occupier to have a legal interest in his home.

The right to respect for private and family life, his home and correspondence, in Art. 8, does not equate to a right to housing however (*Chapman* v. *United Kingdom* (2001) 10 BHRC 48). As with other areas of practice, it is essential that the housing authority (which is a public authority under the Human Rights Act 1998 and obliged to act compatibly with the Convention) makes decisions based on relevant information, follows procedures prescribed by law and makes proportionate decisions.

Anti-social behaviour and housing

Housing law is a complex area and it will almost always be necessary to seek further specialist advice on housing matters. Key legislation includes the Housing Acts of 1985, 1988 and 1996, the latter of which includes the duty of local housing authorities to provide advice and assistance; consider applications for housing under its housing allocation policy; and defines housing associations as registered social landlords. The Landlord and Tenant Act 1985 sets out the scheme for obligation to keep properties in good repair. The Protection from

Eviction Act 1977 provides the scheme for legal eviction and provides protection against illegal eviction. With a focus on those areas most likely to come to the attention of social workers, the chapter continues with consideration of anti-social behaviour and housing.

Where a tenant is affected by anti-social behaviour, there are a number of ways in which this might be tackled:

- All social housing tenancy agreements should include clear clauses which prohibit anti-social behaviour by tenants and their guests, and outline the action that will be taken in response. Breach of the tenancy agreement may provide grounds for eviction. For some time tenancy agreements have included provisions prohibiting racial abuse.

- Under the Anti-social Behaviour Act 2003, all social landlords are obliged to publish their policies and procedures, including their approach to anti-social behaviour.

- Possession orders may be made by the county court under the ground of nuisance.

- When the court is considering possession, it must look at the impact of anti-social behaviour and the likelihood of it continuing.

- The Anti-social Behaviour Act 2003 gives the same powers to registered social landlords as local authorities to apply for injunctions to prevent anti-social behaviour, which causes nuisance or annoyance, including a power to exclude a person from a designated area or from their own home.

- Demotion orders were introduced by the Anti-social Behaviour Act 2003. These orders reduce the status and security of an existing tenancy, where the tenant has behaved anti-socially, and removes their right to buy.

- Possession orders can take some time. The Anti-social Behaviour and Policing Act 2014 introduces an expedited procedure in cases where there is proof from another court of anti-social behaviour or criminality. This gives the landlord an unqualified right of possession, subject only to the court considering proportionality (see case law below).

- In addition to registered social landlords, the police and local authorities retain powers to apply for anti-social behaviour orders in their area.

The Human Rights Act 1998 has an application to housing as to other areas of social work law. Article 8 proportionality has been successfully argued as a defence to possession proceedings. The tenant's personal circumstances may make a possession order disproportionate to the tenant's Article 8 rights (*Manchester City Council* v. *Pinnock* [2010] UKSC 45. In *Southend on Sea Borough Council* v. *Armer* [2014] EWCA Civ 231, possession proceedings were brought because of Mr A's anti-social behaviour. The hearing was 11 months after the behaviour and there was evidence that he had been of good behaviour since. Eviction would be detrimental to his health and affect his 14-year-old daughter and the court found that a possession order was no longer a proportionate response.

Welfare

The Department for Work and Pensions (**DWP**) has overall responsibility for social security benefits, the policy surrounding benefits and their administration. Responsibility for housing benefit and council tax benefit remains with local authorities. Jobcentre Plus is part of the DWP, and administers most pre-retirement benefits. It may do so through old local social security offices and jobcentres or combined centres offering a fully integrated service. Other parts of the DWP include the Pension Service, the Disability and Carers Service, the Child Support Agency and Child Maintenance Service and the Appeals Service. In certain circumstances, social services may make payments to support individuals and families, e.g. covering transport costs to enable parents to have contact with their looked after children.

An outline of the main benefits follows in alphabetical order. It is necessary to have on outline understanding of the main benefits and eligibility for those benefits (and the complexity which can be a feature of claiming), but this is an area where social workers will often need to refer service users for more detailed information and guidance. It is important to remember that, whilst the press often reminds us that some people will fraudulently claim benefits to which they are not entitled, there are in fact thousands of pounds of unclaimed benefits each year. Some people may choose not to claim benefits to which they are entitled, but for many others lack of awareness features and the complexity of the process may be daunting. Jobcentre Plus has benefit advisers and there are other statutory and voluntary organisations that provide information and guidance, such as Citizens' Advice Bureaux and the Disability Alliance, and some local authorities employ welfare rights officers. Even if an individual does not make a claim initially, it should be remembered that some benefits can be backdated. As noted in Chapter 14, individuals often have multiple characteristics and needs and may need to claim a package of different benefits to support their circumstances; for example, a disabled adult may have caring responsibilities for a child and an older adult relative, and be unable to work. For reference, the Child Poverty Action Group publishes an excellent 'Welfare Benefits Handbook' annually, with details of all benefits and their current rate.

Existing benefits can be grouped into various categories. Most benefits are financial payments, made by direct payments into an individual's bank account, in place of the old 'Giro' and order book system. There are also some other benefits that provide subsidised access to goods and services, such as free school meals. Some benefits, such as income support, are income-related or means-tested and others are paid at a flat rate regardless of income. There are contributory and non-contributory benefits. Retirement pensions and jobseekers allowance are contributory benefits, and income support and attendance allowance are examples of non-contributory benefits. A further classification is into taxable and non-taxable benefits, the former including widow's benefits, while maternity allowance is an example of the latter. 'Passport benefits' are payable alongside certain means tested benefits or tax credits, e.g. income support is a passport to free school meals and health benefits such as free prescriptions.

The Welfare Reform Act 2012 introduces major reforms to this area, principally by introduction of Universal Credit. The stated aim of the Coalition Government is to remove disincentives to work and to simplify what has become an overly complex system. Further information about the changes is available from the Department for Work and Pensions, www.dwp.gov.uk.

Attendance allowance

Attendance allowance is a tax-free benefit for people aged 65 or over who are physically or mentally disabled and need help with personal care. Personal care is defined as 'attention in connection with bodily functions', and would include help with washing, eating, communicating needs etc. It may also include people who need supervision of, for example, diet or medical condition, to avoid putting themselves or others in danger e.g. (*Batty* v. *Secretary of State for Work and Pensions* [2005] EWCA Civ 1746).

Carer's allowance

A taxable benefit, payable to carers, 'regularly and substantially engaged in caring', i.e. providing 35 hours per week or more. It applies to carers over the age of 16. The entitlement continues for eight weeks after the death of the person cared for.

Child benefit

Child benefit is payable for all children up to 16 (19 if in education). A higher rate is paid for the first child, then a lower amount for younger children. If the child is 'looked after' for more than eight weeks, the benefit may stop. If the person claiming child benefit or their partner earns more than £50,000, they are expected to opt out of child benefit or if they continue to claim a tax charge is payable.

Council tax benefit and discounts

Council tax benefit is available to people on low incomes on a similar basis to housing benefit. In addition, where a person who is substantially and permanently disabled lives in a bigger property because additional space is required due to the disability, e.g. if extra space is needed for wheelchair use, it may be possible for council tax on the property to be charged at a band lower than the property is worth. To qualify, the property must have a room that has been modified for the disabled person's sole use or an additional bathroom, lavatory or kitchen or extra space to allow a wheelchair to be used inside.

Disabled facilities grant

A means tested grant which may be available for adaptations to a property such as widening doors or installing ramps, stairlifts or a downstairs bathroom.

Disability living allowance

Disability living allowance for adults has been replaced by personal independence payments. New claims may only be made for children under 16 with disabilities including ADHD and other behavioural disorders. It will be necessary to show that the care required by the child is substantially more than that required by a non-disabled child of the same age (Social Security Commissioner Decision CDLA 1797, 2007).

Employment and support allowance

The employment and support allowance was introduced in 2008 replacing incapacity benefit. The new allowance is intended to offer personalised support and financial help where people are not working due to a health condition or disability. Most people claiming employment and support allowance will be expected to take appropriate steps to help prepare for work, supported by a personal adviser. The claimant undergoes a Work Capability Assessment.

Guardian's allowance

A benefit paid to a guardian of an orphan, or where one parent has died and the other is not available (whereabouts unknown, in prison, detained under the Mental Health Act, etc.).

Housing benefit

Housing benefit is paid by the local authority to people who have to pay rent to ensure that, after paying reasonable housing costs, tenants are left with at least equivalent to basic income support levels for day-to-day living expenses. The amount is calculated making allowances for each individual and dependant, including childcare costs, and added premiums, such as lone parent or carer premiums.

In cases where a child spends equal amounts of time living with each parent, any housing benefit entitlement because a separate bedroom is provided for the child, will be paid to the parent who receives child benefit for the child. The Upper Tribunal decided in *TD* v. *Secretary of State for Work and Pensions and London Borough of Richmond-Upon-Thames* [2013] UKUT 0642 (AAC), that this rule did indirectly discriminate against men but could be justified and was not a breach of human rights.

Housing benefit will be reduced if paid in respect of council or social housing and there is a spare room – the so-called 'bedroom tax'. The benefit will be reduced by 14 per cent if there is one spare room, 25 per cent if there are 2 or more spare rooms.

Income support

Income support is an income-related benefit for people between the age of 16 and 60 who are on a low income, or not working, or working on average less than 16 hours a week. Savings of over £16,000 will affect eligibility. If the claimant's partner works, this will also affect the amount of income support awarded. To qualify for income support, most claimants will have to attend jobcentres regularly (exceptions apply to lone parents, people who are sick or disabled or unable to work because they are caring for someone, or registered blind). Income support is made up of a basic personal allowance, allowances for dependent children and may include a family premium, pensioner premium, disability premium, severe disability premium and carer premium. Children under school age and expectant mothers are entitled to free milk and vitamins and children at school will have free school meals.

Income support is one of the benefits which will become an element of Universal Credit.

Jobseeker's allowance

Jobseeker's allowance is a taxable benefit paid to people over 18 who are registered unemployed (or work less than 16 hours a week) and looking for work, up to pensionable age. It will also become an element of Universal Credit.

Personal independence payments

Personal independence payments have replaced disability living allowance to meet the needs of disabled people of working age 16–64. The new assessment will focus on an individual's ability to carry out a range of key activities and the extent to which the individual can live independently. Information will be gathered from the individual, as well as healthcare and other professionals who work with and support them. Most people will also be asked to a face-to-face consultation with an independent assessor as part of the claim process. The benefit comprises a daily living and mobility component paid at standard and enhanced rates. The qualifying period for this payment will be increased from three to six months. This also means that a carer would not be entitled to claim carer's allowance for that six-month period.

Severe disablement allowance

It has not been possible to make a new claim for severe disablement allowance since 2001 – it will usually continue to be paid to those who were receiving this benefit at that time.

Social Fund

Community care grants and crisis loans which were part of the Social Fund have been abolished. The Social Fund now comprises interest-free budgeting loans (which have to be repaid) made to people on income support or jobseeker's allowance for various reasons, including: helping an individual remain in the community or move into the community after a period in residential care; helping an individual who has had an unsettled life settle into the community; and easing exceptional pressures on families.

The Social Fund also includes cold weather payments, winter fuel payments, Sure Start maternity payments and funeral payments.

Universal Credit

The Welfare Reform Act 2012 introduces Universal Credit to provide a single streamlined monthly payment that will combine all means tested benefits and tax credits. It will be capped at £500 per week. The change is being rolled out gradually with the intention that most claimants will have moved to Universal Credit by 2017.

Chapter summary

- The Housing Act 1996 is the key legislation on homelessness, as amended by the Homelessness Act 2002. The legislation gives councils two principal duties: to provide advice and assistance to any person who is homeless or threatened with homelessness who seeks their help; and to provide emergency accommodation in some circumstances.

- The criteria for provision of emergency accommodation are that the person is eligible for assistance, homeless and in priority need.

- Priority need is defined as including: a pregnant woman; a person with dependent children; a person who is vulnerable because of a disability, physical or mental health problems, or other special reasons; a person who is homeless as a result of an emergency, such as fire or flood; 16–17-year-olds, provided they are not the responsibility of social services (provided with accommodation under s. 20 of the Children Act 1989); 18–20-year-old care leavers; a person who is vulnerable having been in custody, as a result of service in the armed forces, or having ceased to occupy accommodation because of violence or threats of violence which are likely to be carried out.

- The council are not obliged to provide accommodation to a person who is considered intentionally homeless. A person becomes intentionally homeless if he deliberately does or fails to do anything in consequence of which he ceases to occupy accommodation which is available for his occupation and which it would have been reasonable for him to continue to occupy.

- Where children are part of a family which is considered intentionally homeless, social services may provide accommodation under s. 17 of the Children Act 1989 as part of their general duty to children in need.

- Where a tenant is affected by anti-social behaviour, it is possible for registered social landlords to obtain an injunction to stop the behaviour and in some circumstances to obtain a possession order evicting the person causing anti-social behaviour. This is in addition to existing responsibilities of the police and councils to tackle anti-social behaviour.

- Many of the people whom social workers will be working with will be entitled to some form of welfare benefits. Benefits may be means tested, contributory or non-contributory; some are taxable and some are passport benefits and are provided alongside an entitlement to another benefit. A summary of some of the key benefits is set out.

● This chapter provides a brief overview of welfare and homelessness, as matters which will affect many service users but where social services do not generally hold key responsibilities. It will often be necessary to obtain detailed advice and further information when faced with cases that touch on these areas.

Websites

The Office of Communities and Local Government, the Government department with responsibility for housing and homelessness, and to access a copy of the Code of Guidance: **www.gov.uk/government/organisations/department-for-communities-and-local-government**

The Department for Work and Pensions resource centre includes leaflets and guides to benefits and services, including downloadable forms:
www.gov.uk/dwp

Further advice and resources can be obtained from the Citizens Advice Bureau:
www.citizensadvice.org.uk

A service for advice workers managed by the London Advice Service Alliance:
www.rightsnet.org.uk/

This advice site was set up by ex-citizens advice service workers. It includes a Quick Benefit guide and is supported by a freephone helpline:
www.welfarerights.net/

The Turn2us benefits calculator can be accessed via
www.entitledto.co.uk

Child Poverty Action Group:
www.cpag.org.uk

Shelter provides useful information and guides on all aspects of housing and homelessness and runs a helpline service:
www.shelter.org.uk

Further reading

Arden, A., Orme, E. and Vanhegan, T. (2012) *Homelessness and Allocations* (9th edn). London: Legal Action Group. (A detailed text including a copy of the Housing Act 1996, as amended by the Homelessness Act 2002 and the Code of Guidance.)

Luba, J. and Davies, L. (2012) *Housing Allocation and Homelessness: Law and Practice* (3rd edn). Bristol: Jordan Publishing. (This text is more practice focused.)

Arden, A., Dymond A. and Hunter, C. (2007) *Manual of Housing Law* (8th edn). London: Sweet & Maxwell. (A detailed resource on housing law.)

Carlton, N., Fear, T. and Means, R. (2004) 'Responding to the harassment and abuse of older people in the private rented sector: legal and social perspectives' 26(2) *Journal of Social Welfare and Family Law* p. 131.

Gervais, M. and Rehman, H. (2005) *Causes of Homelessness amongst the Ethnic Minority Population*. London: ODPM. (A research publication which identifies that ethnic minority households are three times more likely to become homeless than the majority white population, and attributes this to a complex cycle of deprivation.)

Glover-Thomas, N. (2008) 'Joint working: reality or rhetoric in housing the mentally vulnerable' 29(3) *Journal of Social Welfare and Family Law* p. 217.

Rai, S. (2004) 'Accommodating families with children – the final chapter' *Journal of Housing Law* p. 21. (Considers social services responsibilities.)

In relation to welfare see:

Child Poverty Action Group (2014) *Welfare Benefits and Tax Credits Handbook 2014/15.* London: CPAG. (The leading guide and an accessible text written with welfare advisers in mind – updated annually.)

Partington, M. (2012) *Social Security Law in the United Kingdom.* Alphen aan den Rijn: Kluwer Law International

Notes

[1] See also 'Homelessness strategies – a good practice handbook', published for local authority use.

[2] M. Gervais and H. Rehman (2005) *Causes of Homelessness amongst the Ethnic Minority Population.* London: ODPM.

[3] Homelessness (Suitability of Accommodation) Order 1996 (SI 1996/3204).

[4] Allocation of Housing and Homelessness (Review Procedures) Regulations 1999 (SI 1999/71).

Chapter 20

Asylum

Learning objectives

To develop an understanding of the following:

- The legislative framework for asylum seekers.
- Key provisions of the Immigration and Asylum Act 1999 and the background to its development.
- The application and appeals process for asylum seekers.
- The definition of refugee.
- Provision of support for asylum seekers.
- The position of unaccompanied children.
- Remaining responsibilities of social services for asylum seekers.
- Proposals for further reform.

Talking Point

In 2009 the Government issued the 'UK Border Agency Code of Practice for keeping children safe from harm'. It contains a number of objectives to ensure children within the asylum system are safeguarded, stating:

The UK Border Agency will seek to ensure that children

- Are treated in a way that safeguards them, promotes their welfare and promotes their upbringing by their parents.
- Receive full advice, guidance and support about any applications they make or about any contact they have with government agencies.
- Are seen first, foremost and fully as children rather than simply as migrants subject to immigration control, or as adjuncts to a principal applicant.
- Are listened to with respect; and where procedures and services are there to address their needs, a child should be involved as much as possible in applying them to his or her own circumstances.
- Have their experiences taken seriously as well as checked against known records for their country of origin. They should experience a need for confirmation of events, but should not feel that they are up against a culture of disbelief.
- Have their applications dealt with in a timely way that they can understand and that minimises the uncertainty that they may experience.
- Experience contact with the authorities that is characterised by fairness, being listened to, and the absence of conflict. (para 1.7)

Case studies drawn together in a report by the organisation 'Refugee and Migrant Justice' suggest that a real commitment is required to safeguard and protect these vulnerable children within an efficient and fair system for determining asylum claims. The experiences of G and C from their report are illustrative.

G, an 8-year-old boy left his country because his family were threatened by insurgents. Rockets fired by the insurgents had destroyed the boy's family home and school and his father had to move away. The boy was taken to a neighbouring country then smuggled into the UK. On arrival, he had a screening interview without a legal representative. He was asked to complete an application stating his case for asylum, but given no assistance. He was then refused asylum due to his lack of 'credibility'.

C arrived in the UK in 2007 when she was 12 (her age is in dispute and the UKBA are treating her as two years older). Her claim is based on ethnic violence in her country and she had witnessed the murder of her father. She fled to a neighbouring country and was befriended by a man who arranged for her to travel to the UK. He took her to a house and forced her to have sex with him and another man. She escaped and came into contact with social services who accommodated her. She discovered she was pregnant and had a termination. She was interviewed about her claim for asylum but refused. The UKBA did not believe she had been trafficked to the UK despite a letter from the Metropolitan Police confirming they were investigating the matter.

Introduction

The plight of **asylum seekers** is rarely out of the public eye and for many it is an emotive issue. Notable events have drawn further attention to this issue, including reports of deaths of asylum seekers during transit to the United Kingdom. Asylum seekers may flee their country and come to the United Kingdom, whereas others already in the United Kingdom on a temporary basis may apply for asylum if it would be dangerous to return to their country of origin. The number of asylum seekers coming to Britain rose consistently throughout the 1990s. Clearly many asylum seekers are fleeing from conflict. Immigration statistics reveal that asylum applications in 2013 had fallen to 23,507, and there was a decrease in the number of removals. The greatest number of applications were from Pakistan, Iran, Sri Lanka and Syria.

There have been six separate pieces of legislation relating to asylum seekers since 1993.[1] Current law is contained in the Immigration and Asylum Act 1999 (**IAA** 1999), a complex and detailed piece of legislation, based on a Government white paper, entitled 'Fairer, Faster and Firmer – A Modern Approach to Immigration and Asylum'.[2] It has been supplemented by the Nationality, Immigration and Asylum Act 2002 (**NIAA** 2002), which followed publication of a white paper entitled 'Secure Borders, Safe Haven: Integration with Diversity in Modern Britain'.[3] Finally, the Asylum and Immigration (Treatment of Claimants, etc.) Act 2004 (**AIA** 2004) was introduced and a further Immigration, Asylum and Nationality Act 2006. No doubt the legislative activity has in part been an attempt to improve a system which has been characterised by delay and negative media reports concentrating on 'bogus' asylum seekers.

Alongside the IAA 1999, a new body was created to administer the asylum support arrangements: the National Asylum Support Service (**NASS**). New arrangements for support of asylum seekers by the NASS have been in force since April 2000. The UK Border Agency is responsible for the determination of asylum applications. Section 115 of the Immigration and Asylum Act 1999 removed any previous entitlements to social security and housing benefits for new entrants. The law has restricted provision of support to asylum seekers, and allowed more *de facto* detention of asylum seekers whilst waiting for the outcome of tightened procedures for dealing with claims swiftly. It has been argued that over recent years, 'through the progressive hardening of asylum law, the asylum seeker has been subjected to a policy of deterrence, and on occasion of exclusion, either by the introduction of specific restrictive measures targeted at the asylum seeker, or by the categorization of the asylum seeker as *de facto* refugee, economic migrant, bogus refugee, or even quasi-criminal' (Stevens, 2004).[4]

For the purposes of this chapter, a person waiting for a decision on their application for asylum is referred to as an asylum seeker. The term *refugee* applies to a person whose application for asylum has been accepted.

This chapter concentrates on the impact of the three most recent Acts. It continues with an outline of the existing structure for dealing with asylum seekers' claims. The final section has a specific focus on the responsibilities of social services, with particular reference to unaccompanied children and the application of community care law.

Seeking asylum – the current law

It is important to recognise at the outset that discrimination will be a feature of the lives of many asylum seekers and a commitment to anti-discriminatory practice is essential – although it appears to have little support from the law.

Anti-discriminatory practice

Asylum seekers may experience discrimination on a number of levels and it may operate between different groups. At an institutional level, Shah argues, 'the legal system has consistently been favourable to European refugees, whilst it has consistently rejected or been hostile to, the presence of Asian or African groups'.[5] It has been argued that the specific experiences of women refugees are frequently neglected,[6] despite the fact that women and children constitute around 80 per cent of all asylum seekers. Gender persecution is also evident in some asylum seekers' cases, including instances where asylum is sought following extreme domestic violence from which the woman is unprotected in the country of origin, and cases where asylum is sought to escape the risk of female genital mutilation.

Racism towards asylum seekers appears to have increased alongside the dispersal programme. The National Asylum Support Service has a racial harassment investigations team and asylum seekers dispersed away from London may be further disadvantaged because the majority of refugee community organisations, such as the Refugee Council, are based in London and there are fewer legal advisers with appropriate expertise away from the capital. In addition, communities with little experience of refugees may have been influenced by the negative reporting of the media and asylum seekers may suffer both discrimination and social exclusion.

National Asylum Support Service

The **National Asylum Support Service** (NASS) was established by the Home Office[7] and began to function on 3 April 2000. Based in Croydon, it was set up so that a single body would have the responsibility for providing support to asylum seekers whilst waiting for a decision on their asylum status. Before this time, support was provided by the Department of Social Security (DSS) and local authorities, principally through entitlement to welfare and housing benefits. Support provided by the NASS may be accommodation only, financial support only (if the person has somewhere else to stay, e.g. with relatives), or accommodation and financial support. Accommodation will usually be provided outside London at a number of dispersal centres. Support from the NASS is provided to asylum seekers who are destitute or likely to become destitute in 14 days, whilst the outcome of a decision on the asylum claim is awaited.

Refugee status

Asylum will be granted to a person who satisfies the definition of 'refugee'.[8] This is set out in the Geneva Convention Relating to the Status of Refugees 1951[9] as a person who:

> ... owing to a well-founded fear of being persecuted for reasons of race, religion, nationality, membership of a particular social group or political opinion, is outside the country of his nationality and unable or, owing to such fear, is unwilling to avail himself of the protection of that country; or who, not having a nationality and being outside the country of his former habitual residence ... is unable or, owing to such fear, is unwilling to return to it.[10]

If a person is not found to meet this definition of refugee, he will normally be refused asylum. In some circumstances a person who does not fall within the 1951 definition may be granted leave to remain. In April 2003, **exceptional leave to remain** in the United Kingdom was replaced by 'humanitarian protection and discretionary leave'. This recognises that other individuals whose circumstances are not covered by the Convention may still require protection.

Interpretation of 'particular social group' has been an issue for the courts to consider. In *Islam* v. *Secretary of State for the Home Department; R* v. *Immigration Appeals Tribunal, ex parte Shah* [1999] 2 AC 629, the House of Lords reversed the decision of the Court of Appeal and found that Pakistani women sufferers of domestic violence were included. Whilst that might not be a sufficient consideration in other countries, it was noted that: 'in Pakistan women are unprotected by the state: discrimination against women in Pakistan is partly tolerated by the state and partly sanctioned by the state'.[11]

Fear of persecution must relate to current circumstances, as illustrated by *R* v. *Secretary of State for the Home Department, ex parte Adan* [1999] 1 AC 293. The applicant was granted exceptional leave to remain, having fled Somalia in 1988, at which time he had a fear of persecution from the Government. When he applied for his status to be converted to refugee, the House of Lords refused and found that, the Government of Somalia having changed, the applicant had no current fear of persecution. A claim of persecution based on the likelihood of punishment following failure to perform military service due to conscientious objection was not successful for individuals seeking asylum in the case of *Sepet* v. *Secretary of State for the Home Department* [2001] EWCA Civ 681. Interpretation of this key term is likely to continue to be subject to litigation.

An asylum seeker may be recognised as a refugee and granted asylum, not recognised as a refugee but granted humanitarian protection and discretionary leave, or not recognised as a refugee and required to leave the United Kingdom. If recognised as a refugee, the individual is entitled to settle permanently in the United Kingdom (settlement). If the person is granted leave to remain in the United Kingdom, settlement can be applied for after he has lived in the United Kingdom for five years. Once a person is recognised as a refugee or given leave to remain, they become entitled to apply for social security support and their NASS support will end.

Provision of support

Support may be provided for asylum seekers and their dependants who satisfy the criteria in s. 95 of the Immigration and Asylum Act 1999:

s. 95(1)

The Secretary of State may provide, or arrange for the provision of, support for –

(a) asylum seekers, or
(b) dependants of asylum seekers,

who appear to the Secretary of State to be destitute or to be likely to become destitute within such period as may be prescribed.

(IAA 1999)

Support is provided by the NASS; the prescribed period is 14 days. Destitute is further defined. A person is destitute if:

> ### s. 95(3)
>
> **(a)** he does not have adequate accommodation or any means of obtaining it (whether or not his other essential living needs are met); or
> **(b)** he has adequate accommodation or the means of obtaining it, but cannot meet his other essential living needs.
>
> (IAA 1999)

Destitution is a subjective matter and the Secretary of State has a power rather than a duty to support asylum seekers who appear destitute. In providing accommodation, s. 97 directs that the Secretary of State (operating through the NASS) may not have regard to any preference of the asylum seeker or his dependants as to locality. Support can be refused if the person is intentionally destitute. The section below on social services responsibilities outlines the position where a person is not only destitute but has other needs.

Seeking asylum

Economic support may be withdrawn from asylum seekers who do not make their claim for asylum at the first opportunity. It is vital that applications are made swiftly because, under AIA 2004, s. 55, local authorities will only provide support to an asylum seeker who has applied for asylum 'as soon as reasonably practicable' after arriving in the United Kingdom. In reality, this almost always means immediately on arrival, or at least within the first 72 hours. Exceptions apply in cases where the asylum seeker has a dependent child living in the same household or if support is required to avoid a breach of the ECHR.

This provision was challenged, and the House of Lords gave its judgment in a combined appeal, in *R (Limbuela)* v. *Secretary of State for the Home Department* [2005] UKHL 66. Exclusion from NASS support under s. 55 left an asylum seeker sleeping rough in winter with no food or accommodation and no access to washing or toilet facilities. The House of Lords confirmed the decision of the Court of Appeal and stated that in the circumstances it was a breach of Art. 3 ECHR (inhumane and degrading treatment) to deny support to such a person who made a late application for asylum. NASS would have to consider all relevant facts and circumstances, including whether the person was male or female, their age and the length of time they had spent or might spend without support.

Accommodation

Whilst waiting for a decision on their asylum application, an asylum seeker and his dependents may be provided with accommodation by the NASS. The asylum seeker is offered no choice over the accommodation but it should reach a basic minimum standard. In order to ease the burden on London, Kent and the South East, as the areas that accommodated most asylum seekers before the 1999 Act, asylum seekers are now dispersed to cluster areas around the rest of the United Kingdom. The cluster area to which they are dispersed should be appropriate to their language and culture, but the asylum seeker cannot actually choose the area. However, in *R (Blackwood) v. Secretary of State for the Home Department* [2003] EWHC 97 (Admin), it was a breach of Art. 8 to send a woman (and her child) who had been brought up in London and had family there to a cluster area out of London. This was an unusual case, as the woman was seeking asylum having lived and become settled in London for some years. Regulations provide that an asylum seeker must not be absent from his accommodation for more than seven consecutive days and nights without permission or 14 days and nights within any six-month period. The accommodation offered is coordinated by the NASS but may actually be provided by private landlords, housing associations or local authorities. NASS housing inspectors check the standard of accommodation, but it need only be adequate and of a similar standard to temporary accommodation.

The NIAA 2002 introduced 'accommodation centres' which provide services (including food and essentials, healthcare and education) and accommodation to asylum seekers in one place. The maximum period an asylum seeker can be in an accommodation centre is six months (extendable by a further three months) (s. 25). An Accommodation Advisory Group will be appointed (s. 33) and has the power to visit the centre at any time.

Financial support

Support for asylum seekers' essential living needs was originally provided in the form of vouchers, which could be exchanged for necessities at specified shops and outlets. One of the objectives behind introduction of the voucher system and denial of welfare benefits was to act as a deterrent to asylum seekers with unfounded claims. The steady rise in the numbers of asylum seekers coming to this country would suggest that such an objective was not met and indeed challenges the assumption that asylum seekers were motivated to come to the United Kingdom for the cash benefits system. The voucher system was heavily criticised as discriminatory and stigmatising, and various organisations including the Refugee Council successfully campaigned for its abolition. Subsistence payments are now made, at a rate which is equivalent to about 70 per cent of income support rates. Where support is granted, it continues until the exhaustion of the application and appeal process, and for 21 days afterwards.

Appeals

There is one right of appeal against any of a list of immigration decisions (NIAA 2002, s. 82).

The key ground for appeal is contained in s. 84(1)(g) in the following terms: 'Removal of the appellant from the United Kingdom in consequence of the immigration decision would breach the United Kingdom's obligations under the Refugee Convention or would be unlawful under s. 6 of the Human Rights Act 1998 as being incompatible with the appellant's Convention rights.' The time limits for appeals are fairly tight and may not sufficiently accommodate the need to obtain specialist legal advice. Appeals are made to Asylum Support Adjudicators.

The 2002 Act allows for the Home Secretary to require the asylum seeker to return to a safe country he travelled through to arrive in the United Kingdom, and appeal from that country.

Removal of support

Schedule 3 to the NIAA 2002 removed the right to a range of defined services for failed asylum seekers. Services include accommodation, social services and promoting welfare under the Local Government Act 2000. Services to families with dependent children could still be provided until their removal from the United Kingdom. The AIA 2004, s. 9 takes that a stage further, with the insertion of a new paragraph into the schedule. It allows financial support and accommodation to be removed from failed asylum seekers, who have exhausted their appeal rights, if it is considered that they are failing to take reasonable steps to leave the United Kingdom voluntarily or to place themselves in a position in which they are able to leave the United Kingdom voluntarily. This includes support to adults provided as part of a package of support for a child, e.g. accommodation provided to a 'child in need' and her family. Support will be withdrawn within 14 days of the Secretary of State certifying that the family has failed to cooperate. The only way in which a local authority will be able to continue to provide support to a family, and provision of accommodation is the crucial factor, is if the authority consider that to fail to do so would be in breach of the families' rights under Art. 3 ECHR. Following the case of *Limbuela* (removal of support where an application is not made as soon as practicable), it may well be that such a human rights argument would succeed.

There is a limited grant, the hard cases support grant, available to asylum seekers whose application for asylum has been refused, for whom there are no further appeal opportunities and who are unable to leave the country due to physical impediment or exceptional circumstances.

The grant will also be available to an individual who has been granted permission for judicial review of an aspect of his asylum application.

Voluntary sector

The voluntary sector plays an important role in the area of asylum. Voluntary organisations (with funding from the NASS) provide 'One Stop Services' for asylum seekers throughout the United Kingdom. The organisations are: Migrant Helpline; Refugee Action; Refugee Arrivals Project; Refugee Council; Scottish Refugee Council; and Welsh Refugee Council. Other voluntary agencies also provide support for asylum seekers but are not funded by the NASS. Asylum Support Advice Workers, from One Stop Services, can assist with applications for NASS support, explain rights and entitlements to asylum seekers and coordinate emergency accommodation.

Human Rights Act 1998 implications

There are a number of possible violations of the Articles contained in the European Convention on Human Rights in the area of asylum.[12] The Human Rights Act 1998 provides an opportunity to challenge the actions of the NASS, if thought to violate the Convention (by their actions or failure to act), because as a public body the NASS is bound to act in compliance with the Convention.[13] Appeals may be made where an individual alleges a breach of their human rights in connection with their asylum application.

The removal of an asylum seeker to a country where he is likely to face the death sentence could be a violation of Art. 2, the right to life. Article 3 contains an absolute prohibition against inhuman or degrading treatment, punishment or torture. Racial harassment may amount to inhuman and degrading treatment.[14] Again, removal of an asylum seeker to a country where he is likely, for example, to be tortured could be a violation. Article 5 provides the right to liberty and security, other than in specified circumstances in accordance with a legal procedure. The Article also provides for regular reviews of detention and speedy challenges to detention. This Article was relied on in a challenge by four Iraqi Kurdish asylum seekers who were detained for up to ten days in the Oakington Reception Centre whilst they were interviewed and decisions were taken on their claims. The High Court found that detention was lawful under domestic law but did breach Art. 5. The Court of Appeal, however, reversed the decision, allowing the Home Secretary's appeal. The exception in Art. 5(1)(f), 'the lawful arrest or detention of a person to prevent his effecting an unauthorised entry into the country or of a person against whom action is being taken with a view to deportation or extradition', applied and permitted detention whilst the state considered whether to authorise entry. The Court of Appeal decision is reported as *R (Saadi)* v. *Secretary of State for the Home Department* [2002] UKHL 41.

Article 6 provides for fair hearings by an independent tribunal. The independence of Asylum Support Adjudicators may be questioned, as they are appointed and financed by the Home Office. Also, support under IAA 1999, s. 95 has been found to be a civil right under ECHR, Art. 6 in the case of *R (Husain)* v. *Asylum Support Adjudicator* [2001] EWHC Admin 852. It was also noted in this decision that withdrawal of support could amount to inhuman and degrading treatment under Art. 3. Article 8 is a limited article, which provides the right to respect for private and family life. Any interference with this right must be proportionate. It may be argued that the dispersal policy could interfere with Art. 8 if, for example, its effect would be to move an asylum seeker away from a supportive base of friends and family (*Abdi* v. *Secretary of State for the Home Department* [1996] Imm AR 148). Article 14 relates to prevention of discrimination in enjoyment of the rights contained in the Articles. It is arguable that the provision of vouchers rather than cash could breach this Article when an asylum seeker's position is compared with others in receipt of welfare benefits.

Social services responsibilities

The majority of support for asylum seekers is now provided by the NASS. Beyond transitional support for asylum seekers whose application was lodged before the new Act came into force, three important areas, however, remain within the responsibility of local authorities: support for unaccompanied children; support for accompanied children who have needs for support not arising from destitution; and support for adults which is required not as a result of destitution. Some local authorities have specialist social services teams working in this area, e.g. Kensington and Chelsea has an Asylum Team and an Unaccompanied Minors Team.[15]

Unaccompanied children

Social services, rather than the NASS, are responsible for asylum-seeking unaccompanied children. In addition to social services support, on entry to the United Kingdom an adviser from the Panel of Advisers for Unaccompanied Children will provide initial short-term support. As at 31 March 2013, there were 1,860 unaccompanied asylum-seeking children being looked after, 87 per cent were boys and 13 per cent girls.

Unaccompanied (also sometimes referred to as separated) children are perhaps the most vulnerable of all asylum seekers, 'placed as they are at the intersection of two particularly vulnerable populations – refugees and children'.[16] Both groups, it should be added, are particularly vulnerable to discrimination. This disadvantaged position is acknowledged in Art. 22 of the UN Convention on the Rights of the Child 1989, which provides for the right of children seeking asylum or as refugees to 'appropriate protection and humanitarian assistance'. A Refugee Council Panel of Advisers for Unaccompanied Refugee Children (Children's Panel) was established in the United Kingdom in 1994 to provide independent support for children and counselling. Unaccompanied children are the responsibility of social services once they enter the United Kingdom (see below). Children will not be considered 'unaccompanied' by the Home Office if they have travelled with an adult member of their extended family, i.e. they are not 'unaccompanied' simply because they have travelled without their parents or legal guardians. A preferable interpretation is provided by the Separated Children in Europe Programme, which defines separated children as 'children under 18 years of age who are outside their country of origin and separated from both parents or their legal/customary primary caregiver'. The Children's Panel adopts a broader definition of an unaccompanied child than that of the Home Office. The panel looks beyond the presence of an adult to consider the suitability of the adult to look after the child. (See Chapter 2 for a fuller discussion of HRA 1998.)

As a child in need, an unaccompanied asylum-seeking child may be entitled to a range of services provided for in Sch. 2 to the Children Act 1989. Services include advice, guidance and counselling, home helps, assistance with travel to access services and occupational, social, cultural or recreational activities. Many unaccompanied children will be 'looked after' by the local authority and provided with accommodation under s. 20, as in the case of *R (H)* v. *Wandsworth London Borough Council* [2007] EWHC 1082 (Admin). (See Chapter 7 for discussion of responsibilities towards looked after children.) A local authority circular provides that where a child has no parent or guardian in the country there is a presumption that the child will be accommodated under s. 20.[17] The 'Quality Protects' initiative should have a positive impact on outcomes for unaccompanied children in the care of local authorities.[18] The Children (Leaving Care) Act 2000 will also apply, so that support continues after the young person reaches the age of 18 and should ensure that the young person will obtain accommodation in the local authority area rather than being dispersed to another part of the country.

Despite the application of the established framework of the Children Act 1989, the Audit Commission found that unaccompanied children were often receiving lower standards of care than other children in need and only one-third of local authorities produced individual care plans for asylum children in their area. Over one-half of unaccompanied children over the age of 16 were provided with accommodation in hostels and bed and breakfast. A further report produced by the Refugee Council and Save the Children (2001)[19] calls for closer co-ordination between the Department of Health, Home Office and Department for Education and Skills to improve service delivery. This report also identified as a trend the relatively few unaccompanied children who are successful in obtaining refugee status, noting that instead they are more likely to be awarded exceptional leave to remain, usually up to the age of 18, and may be required to leave the United Kingdom at that age. The results of a mapping exercise on numbers of unaccompanied asylum-seeking children in the United Kingdom contained in a report produced by the BAAF and the Refugee Council (2001) are also worthy of note.[20] As with the Save the Children report, particular concerns were expressed about 16- and 17-year-olds, who tend to be treated as having the same needs as adults.

It is established that, for the purposes of support, an unaccompanied child is not classed as an asylum seeker and local authorities are responsible for providing support under s. 17 of the Children Act 1989 to them as 'children in need'. In most cases the local authority will also be bound to provide accommodation under CA 1989, s. 20, it being required due to there being no person with parental responsibility or the child being lost or abandoned. The practical difficulty for local authorities is that in many cases there will be no objective evidence as to the person's age. In *R (B)* v. *Merton London Borough Council* [2003] EWHC 1689 (Admin), the High Court gave guidance to local authorities on how to assess the age of an asylum seeker who may be a child. The factors to be considered include:

- physical appearance and behaviour;
- medical evidence;
- personal history including educational background, ethnic and cultural information;
- documentary evidence, or the lack of.

The court also commented on the need for a fair process. It noted sensible advice contained in 'Practice Guidelines for Age Assessment of Young Unaccompanied Asylum Seekers', being piloted in Hillingdon and Croydon London Boroughs, namely: preference for two age assessment workers; taking account of 'the level of tiredness, trauma, bewilderment and anxiety' of the young person; key focus on ethnicity and culture; adoption of open ended, non-leading questioning; use of interpreters where appropriate; and the young person's understanding of the role of the assessors. If a provisional view is taken that the young person is lying, they must be given the opportunity to address that. The local authority should not simply adopt an earlier assessment, e.g. one undertaken by the Home Office. The local authority must give reasons for its decision, although these need not be long or elaborate. It would be possible for the High Court to interfere with an age assessment if it was one that no reasonable authority could make on the evidence before it.

In *MC* v. *Liverpool City Council* [2010] EWHC 2211, a young person sought judicial review of the Council's decision that he was 18 and not 16 as he claimed. There were many inconsistencies in the young person's account of how he had come to the UK and his experience there and the court ruled that he was 18 months older than he claimed.

The significance of the case is that it confirms for age assessment judicial reviews the court will make its own decision as to age, not just review whether the council's decision was taken lawfully. It also ruled that as it is making its own decision on age, the local authority do not have the burden of proving that the young person is over 18.

In *AS (by his litigation friend the Official Solicitor)* v. *London Borough of Croydon* [2011] EWHC 2091 (Admin), the court provided guidelines on the minimum standards for age assessment:

(1) An appropriate adult should accompany the child and should be present during the interview.

(2) A full and careful explanation should be given to the child of the nature of the assessment and its purpose and of the role of the assessing social worker. A careful check should be made to ensure that there is full understanding between the child and the interpreter and that the interpreter is skilled in both the language and dialect of the child and has experience of interpreting in the kind of situation created by the age assessment process.

(3) The interview should be conducted in a structured, fair, non-adversarial, non-stressful and informal manner and an informal but full note of the questions and answers should be taken by one of those present.

(4) The assessors should pay attention to the level of tiredness, trauma, bewilderment and anxiety of the child and his or her ethnicity, culture and customs should be a key focus throughout the assessment.

(5) The assessors must take a history from the child. All relevant factors should be taken into account including, but not limited to, physical appearance and behaviour. The objective is to undertake a holistic assessment.

(6) Each interview should, if practicable, be conducted by two assessors who should have received appropriate training and experience for conducting age assessment interviews on young and vulnerable children.

(7) The assessors should establish as much rapport as possible with the child (a process known as 'joining'), should ask open-ended non-leading questions using, as appropriate, circular questioning methods. The assessors should be mindful of the child having been 'coached' and that the child may have had to answer questions on relevant topics several times previously thereby unwittingly blurring the possible accuracy of the answers. Giving the child the benefit of the doubt should always be the standard practice.

(8) The assessors should give the child a fair and proper opportunity to answer any potentially adverse findings at a stage when an adverse decision is no more than provisional to so as to enable him or her to provide any appropriate explanation or additional facts which might counter or modify such findings.

(9) The conclusions reached by the assessors should be explained with reasons which, although they may be brief, should explain the basis of the assessment and any significant adverse credibility or factual finding.

(10) The reasons should be internally consistent and should not exhibit any obvious error or inadequate explanation for not accepting any apparently credible and consistent answers of the child.

Accompanied children

Accompanied children are excluded by their status from the support provision of the Children Act 1989, s. 17, except that asylum-seeking children who have a disability will be covered by the Children Act 1989 definition of a 'child in need' (s. 17). (See Chapter 5.) Section 122 of the IAA 1999 states that Social Services Departments may not provide assistance for children in need solely because the child or his family is destitute, so long as the asylum seeker's household (including the child) is entitled to NASS support under IAA 1999, s. 95. Needs not arising from destitution could be supported, e.g. if the child is disabled.

In *R (Ouji)* v. *Secretary of State for the Home Department* [2002] EWHC 1839 (Admin), social services rather than NASS provided support to a 13-year-old asylum seeker in the care of her mother. The girl required additional bedding due to incontinence and suffered from other disabilities.

Education

Local education authorities are under a duty to ensure that children who are asylum seekers or refugees receive appropriate education from the age of 5 up to 16, just as any other child in the country is entitled to. They also have equal entitlement to pre-school facilities including playgroups and nurseries. Asylum-seeking children qualify for free school meals. In practice, some children may not attend school as the cost of school uniform and transport to the school may be prohibitive. An Audit Commission report found that few local authorities collect information about the number of asylum-seeking and refugee children in schools in their area.[21] The Commission recommend that the NASS should advise LEAs of the number of children likely to be placed in the area so that planning enables appropriate support to be provided.

Adult asylum seekers

It should be clear from the above discussion that, since 2000, support for asylum seekers has been the domain of the NASS. The position prior to 2000 was different, with asylum seekers entitled to welfare benefits support and housing benefit. Transitional arrangements have allowed local authorities to continue to provide support for individuals who applied for asylum before the creation of the NASS. There should be few people receiving such support now.

The Immigration and Asylum Act 1999 provides that local authorities are able to provide support in accordance with the arrangements made by the Secretary of State under s. 95 (the section which bases entitlement to support on the destitute test). This enables local authorities to provide support as part of the NASS arrangements, e.g. use of local authority housing stock. In fact, local authorities can be required by s. 100 to cooperate with the Secretary of State in the provision of accommodation under the s. 95 scheme, including providing information about their housing stock. Other local authority functions in relation to asylum seekers (which would have been available before the IAA 1999) have been removed by ss. 116–122. The effect of these provisions is that local authorities will continue to be involved with actual provision of support, but will do so as a NASS resource. In other words, local authorities, in assisting the Secretary of State to carry out his functions, will be secondary not primary providers of support.

Community care

(It may be useful to refer back to Chapter 14 for background discussion of the legal framework of community care.) Under the terms of the 1996 Act, an asylum seeker who failed to make an immediate claim for asylum at the port of entry was ineligible to claim housing assistance, unlike those who made an immediate claim. This position undoubtedly led to some hardship, and the judiciary intervened to bridge this gap in the case of *R* v. *Hammersmith and Fulham London Borough Council, ex parte M* (1998) 30 HLR 10. In this case s. 21 of the National Assistance Act 1948 was applied to the case of asylum seekers who failed to claim at the port of entry. The court found that a destitute asylum seeker (not entitled to welfare benefits) could be in need of care and attention, not otherwise available, under the reference to 'any other circumstances' in s. 21. The court suggested those words could include a lack of food and shelter, and also extended to factors such as inability to speak English, ignorance of the country and the stressful background resulting in the person seeking asylum. A further decision, *R* v. *Secretary of State for Health, ex parte Hammersmith and Fulham London Borough Council* (1998) 31 HLR 475, limited the application of this principle to payments in kind (such as food parcels) and provision of accommodation, rather than cash payments.

The combined effect of these cases was of clear benefit to asylum seekers and overcame the harsh ruling on immediate claims, but led to concern over the burden placed on local authorities. In response, the Immigration and Asylum Act 1999 amended s. 21 of the National Assistance Act 1948. Section 21 provides that a local authority must make arrangements to provide residential accommodation for people over the age of 18 who, by reason of age, illness, disability or any other circumstances, are in need of care and attention, which is not otherwise available to them. The amendment provides:

s. 21

(1A) A person to whom section 115 of the Immigration and Asylum Act 1999 (exclusion from benefits) applies may not be provided with residential accommodation under subsection (1)(a) if his need for care and attention has arisen solely –

(a) because he is destitute; or

(b) because of the physical effects, or anticipated physical effects, of his being destitute.

(NAA 1948, as amended)

Asylum seekers are people to whom s. 115 of the IAA 1999 applies. Asylum seekers applying under the new scheme provided by the IAA 1999 are excluded from benefits provision.

R (Westminster City Council) v. *National Asylum Support Service* [2001] EWCA Civ 512 is now the leading decision on interpretation of this section. Mrs Y-Ahmed, an Iraqi Kurd asylum seeker, was destitute and suffered from a spinal myeloma. The Social Services Department assessed her as needing assistance with mobility and personal care and accommodation with disabled access. The authority argued that as Mrs Ahmed and her 13-year-old daughter were entitled to NASS support, it followed that care and attention was otherwise available to her; meaning she was not entitled to assistance under the National Assistance Act 1948. The NASS argued that she was not destitute because she had the means of obtaining accommodation through her entitlement under the National Assistance Act 1948, and she was therefore not entitled to asylum support. The Court of Appeal decided that the local authority were in fact responsible for meeting Mrs Ahmed's needs. Her need for care and attention did not arise solely because of her destitution or the effects of it. From this interpretation, it followed that s. 21(1A) of the National Assistance Act 1948 (inserted by the IAA 1999) did not exclude her from assistance under the National Assistance Act 1948. Destitute asylum seekers would have their needs met under the NASS, but would also be entitled to community care services if their needs for care and attention exist, even if in funds. This is a significant judgment, which Simon Brown LJ recognises 'raises an interesting and important question concerning the support of a particular category of asylum seeker. The category in question are those who are not merely destitute (that is, without adequate accommodation and/or the means of meeting their other essential living needs) but who in addition have community care needs.'[22]

The House of Lords judgment in this case, reported as *Westminster City Council* v. *National Asylum Support Service* [2002] UKHL 38, confirmed that the council was liable to provide accommodation to the asylum seeker under the responsibilities to provide accommodation imposed by the National Assistance Act 1948, s. 21. Lord Hoffmann stated that the 'infirm destitute' remain the responsibility of social services where they are in need of 'care and attention' under s. 21, as opposed to the 'able bodied destitute for whom NASS has a residual responsibility' under the IAA 1999, s. 95. He suggested further that if the local authority has a duty to provide accommodation under s. 21, NASS has no power to provide support.

In a further case, *R (Mani)* v. *Lambeth London Borough Council* [2003] EWCA Civ 836, the Court of Appeal confirmed that a disabled asylum seeker was entitled to care and attention under s. 21 of the National Assistance Act 1948, to meet needs arising from his disability. Also, in *R (M)* v. *Slough Borough Council* [2006] EWCA Civ 655, the council were obliged to accommodate a destitute asylum seeker who was HIV positive under s. 21.

It can be concluded that, whilst the majority of support is now provided by the NASS, asylum seekers may still be entitled to some support from the local authority and other organisations based on characteristics other than destitution. Community care legislation (as outlined in Chapter 14) therefore does apply to some asylum seekers.

Mental health

The Mental Health Act 1983 applies to asylum seekers as it does to other residents in the United Kingdom. If an asylum seeker is suffering from mental disorder under the Mental Health Act 1983,[23] in certain circumstances he may be admitted compulsorily (sectioned) to mental hospital, or made the subject of a guardianship order.[24] Where a person is detained in hospital under the Mental Health Act 1983, he cannot be removed (for deportation, for example) without the approval of a mental health review tribunal (*X* v. *Secretary of State for the Home Department* [2001] 1 WLR 740). The after-care provisions of the 1983 Act will apply when the person ceases to be detained or subject to guardianship.[25]

National Health Service

Medical treatment provided by the National Health Service is available to asylum seekers (and any dependants) whether they are awaiting a decision, appealing, awaiting deportation, granted refugee status or exceptional leave to remain. This includes the right to register with a GP. Most asylum seekers will also be exempt from prescription charges and related benefits. An interpreter should be provided by the health service where required.[26]

Chapter summary

- The law relating to asylum seekers is now contained principally in the Immigration and Asylum Act 1999, as amended by the Nationality, Immigration and Asylum Act 2002 and Asylum and Immigration (Treatment of Claimants, etc.) Act 2004.

- A person who applies for asylum is known as an asylum seeker. A person whose application for asylum is successful is then classed as a refugee, having satisfied the 1951 Geneva Convention definition of refugee. A person who is not granted refugee status may nevertheless be granted 'exceptional leave to remain' in the country.

- The IAA 1999 introduced a new system for the support of asylum seekers. The system is administered by a new organisation, the National Asylum Support Service (NASS). Previous arrangements for the support of asylum seekers, in the form of welfare benefits and direct local authority support, have ceased to be available to any asylum seekers entering the country since the NASS was established.

- Where an asylum seeker (and his dependants) is found to be 'destitute', the NASS will provide support whilst a decision on the asylum seeker's application is reached. Support may be in the form of accommodation, subsistence for essential living needs or a combination of subsistence and accommodation. Initially, asylum seekers may be accommodated in 'induction centres'. Asylum seekers will be dispersed to accommodation in cluster areas throughout the country, away from London and the South East.

- Unaccompanied children seeking asylum remain the responsibility of Social Services Departments, as children in need. The sections of the Children Act 1989 relating to provision of support will apply, as will the Children (Leaving Care) Act 2000.

- Adult asylum seekers may also be entitled to local authority support under the community care provisions if they have needs which have not arisen solely as a result of their destitution.

- Support may be denied if an application for asylum is not made 'as soon as practicable' upon entering the country.

Exercise

Julianna is 15 and has lived all her life in a village in Kosovo. She witnessed the rape of her mother, her village was burnt down and she does not know what happened to her sister or her parents. She stayed with a family friend, Hugo, in the next village for one month but travelled to England with him and his daughter, Liza, in fear of their safety. Liza is 8 years old and was born physically disabled as a result of spina bifida. On entry to the United Kingdom they have only the clothes they are wearing and the equivalent of about £30. Hugo thinks that his uncle is living in London but cannot get a response from the telephone number he has. They are told initially that Julianna will stay in London and is likely to be accommodated in a hostel, whereas Hugo and Liza will be dispersed to Yorkshire. Julianna is terrified that she will be alone and separated from Hugo and Liza, the only people she knows from home. Hugo wishes to remain in London so that Liza will be able to access the medical support she needs.

Consider the type of support that should be provided to Julianna, Hugo and Liza and which agencies will be involved.

Websites

The Refugee Council provides advice and support to asylum seekers and refugees, campaigns on asylum issues and produces a range of reports and other publications:
www.refugeecouncil.org.uk

The Home Office site has an asylum and immigration section. It publishes statistical bulletins and NASS bulletins:
www.ind.homeoffice.gov.uk

Separated Children in Europe website:
www.scepnetwork.org

Joint Council for the Welfare of Immigrants:
www.jcwi.org.uk

The UK Immigration Advisory Service:
www.iasservices.org.uk

Further reading

Hayes, D. and Humphries, B. (2004) *Social Work, Immigration and Asylum: Debates, Dilemmas and Ethical Issues for Social Work and Social Care Practice.* London: Jessica Kingsley.

A number of publications focus on the special position of asylum-seeking children:

Ayotte, W. and Williamson, L. (2001) *Separated Children in the UK: An Overview of the Current Situation.* London: Save the Children and Refugee Council.

Cobb, N. (2008) 'Better outcomes for unaccompanied or separated children seeking asylum: a case of putting one's money where one's mouth is?' *Child and Family Law Quarterly* p. 183.

Coker, J., Finch, N. and Stanley, A. (2002) *Putting Children First: A Guide for Immigration Practitioners.* London: Legal Action Group.

Coram Children's Legal Centre (2013) *Happy Birthday? Disputing the Age of Children in the Immigration System* Executive Summary. Colchester: University of Essex/Coram Children's Legal Centre.

Fortin, J. (2011) 'Are children's best interests really best?' 74(6) *Modern Law Review*, p. 947.

Kohli, R. (2006) 'The comfort of strangers: social work practice with unaccompanied asylum-seeking children and young people in the UK' 11 *Child and Family Social Work*, p. 1. (Considers social work practice (as criticised in a number of reports) in the complex area of resettlement of unaccompanied minors.)

Kohli, R. (2007) *Social Work with Unaccompanied Asylum-seeking Children*. Basingstoke: Palgrave.

Matthews, A. (2011) 'Landing in Kent: the experience of unaccompanied children arriving in the UK'. London: Office of the Children's Commissioner.

Russell, S. (1999) *Most Vulnerable of All: The Treatment of Unaccompanied Children in the UK*. London: Amnesty International.

Rutter, J. (2003) *Supporting Refugee Children in 21st Century Britain* (2nd edn). Stoke-on-Trent: Trentham Books.

Wright, F. (2012) 'Social work practice with unaccompanied asylum-seeking children facing removal' *British Journal of Social Work* p. 1.

And in relation to vulnerable adults:

Williams, L. (2004) 'Refugees and asylum seekers as a group at risk of adult abuse' 6(4) *Journal of Adult Protection* p. 4. (This paper highlights the vulnerability of refugees to abuse and relates the forms of abuse contained in 'No Secrets' (see Chapter 17) to their situation, with strategies to reduce vulnerability.)

More general guides to asylum are listed below. Note, however, that the most recent changes in legislation and practice may not be included:

Cohen, S. (2001) *Immigration Controls, the Family and the Welfare State*. London: Jessica Kingsley.

Harvey, C. (2000) *Seeking Asylum in the UK: Problems and Prospects*. London: Butterworths.

Newbigging *et al.* (2010): 'Good practice in social care with refugees and asylum seekers', Workforce Development Report 31. London: Social Care Institute for Excellence.

Symes, M. and Jorro, P. (2002) *The Law Relating to Asylum in the UK*. London: Butterworths.

Willman, S., Knafler, S. and Pierce, S. (2001) *Support for Asylum Seekers: A Guide to Legal and Welfare Rights*. London: Legal Action Group.

Notes

1 Asylum and Immigration Appeals Act 1993; Asylum and Immigration Act 1996; Immigration and Asylum Act 1999; Nationality, Immigration and Asylum Act 2002; Asylum and Immigration (Treatment of Claimants, etc.) Act 2004; Immigration, Asylum and Nationality Act 2006.

2 Home Office (1998) 'Fairer, Faster and Firmer – A Modern Approach to Immigration and Asylum' (Cm. 4018). London: The Stationery Office.

3 Home Office (2002) 'Secure Borders, Safe Haven: Integration with Diversity in Modern Britain' (Cm. 5387). London: The Stationery Office.

4 D. Stevens (2004) *UK Asylum Law and Policy: Historical and Contemporary Perspectives*. London: Sweet & Maxwell, p. 164.

[5] P. Shah (2000) *Refugees, Race and the Legal Concept of Asylum in Britain.* London: Cavendish Publishing, p. 1.

[6] C. Harvey (2000) *Seeking Asylum in the UK: Problems and Prospects.* London: Butterworths.

[7] Under the Immigration and Asylum Act 1999.

[8] Interpretation of the definition varies between different countries.

[9] The Convention was initially restricted to European nationals. It was amended by the 1967 Protocol to have worldwide application.

[10] Geneva Convention Relating to the Status of Refugees, Art. 1A(2).

[11] Per Lord Steyn at p. 635.

[12] See Separated Children in Europe website: www.scepnetwork.org.

[13] Human Rights Act 1998, s. 6.

[14] See decision of the Asylum Support Adjudicators 00/12/0135.

[15] See www.rbkc.gov.uk.

[16] J. Bhabha (2001) 'Minors or aliens? Inconsistent state intervention and separated child asylum-seekers' 3(3) *European Journal of Migration and Law* p. 283.

[17] LAC (2003) 13.

[18] Department of Health (1999) *The Government's Objectives for Children's Social Services.* London: Department of Health.

[19] W. Ayotte and L. Williamson (2001) *Separated Children in the UK: An overview of the current situation.* London: Save the Children and Refugee Council.

[20] BAAF and Refugee Council (2001) *Where are the children?* London: Refugee Council.

[21] Audit Commission (2000) 'A New City. Supporting Asylum Seekers and Refugees in London'. London: Audit Commission Publications.

[22] (2001) 4 CCLR 142 at p. 145B.

[23] Section 1 defines mental disorder.

[24] MHA 1983, s. 2 (admission for assessment), s. 3 (admission for treatment) and s. 7 (guardianship).

[25] MHA 1983, s. 117.

[26] See further HC (82) 15 and HSC 1999/018.

Glossary

Throughout the text the reader will notice occasional use of Latin and technical legal terminology. I have attempted to limit this use being a supporter of the movement for plain speaking. There remain some situations, however, where certain terms which might not be part of everyday usage are still used regularly by lawyers or appear in legal documents. In order to be competent in legal settings and in dialogue with lawyers, an understanding of these terms is essential. Other terms and phrases which feature in *Social Work Law* are also included for ease of reference. This glossary attempts to provide clear explanations of terms in the context of social work practice. Terms used are defined consistently with their use in this book, therefore the definitions listed below may not appear as they would in a pure law dictionary.

Adoption agency the body authorised to provide adoption services, either a function of the local authority or a voluntary agency

Affidavit a written sworn statement – now referred to as a 'Statement of Truth'

Affirmation evidence given in court by a person who objects to swearing an oath

Amicus curiae friend of the court

Antecedents previous convictions and other information provided to the criminal court

Appeal complaint to a superior court on the basis of 'injustice' by a lower court, e.g. against conviction

Appellant person making an appeal

Approved mental health professional a social worker with a recognised qualification in mental health, invested with a range of powers and duties under the Mental Health Act 2007

Asylum seeker a person waiting for a decision on their application for asylum

Attorney person appointed to carry out wishes of another

Attorney-General principal law officer, brings prosecutions on behalf of the Crown

Balance of probabilities the civil standard of proof

Barrister a lawyer who typically specialises in court advocacy – also referred to as counsel

Beyond reasonable doubt the criminal standard of proof

Breach violation (usually of a right)

Burden of proof the responsibility to prove a point to the satisfaction of the court, often expressed as, he who alleges must prove

Care management in community care the term encompasses the process of assessment, provision of services and review or reassessment

Care programme approach a term which embraces the provision of services to people with mental health difficulties living in the community

Cause of action the basis of a civil case, the reason for suing

Children and family reporter a social work professional who provides reports to the court in private family proceedings – previously referred to as the court welfare officer

Children's guardian an independent officer who represents a child in court, part of the CAFCASS organisation (formerly known as a guardian *ad litem*)

Children's services authorities those authorities with social services functions, i.e. county, metropolitan and unitary councils

Children's trust an arrangement where services for children and young people in an area are collectively organised into a children's trust with the objective of working together to improve outcomes for children and young people

Codification drawing legislation in an area of law, e.g. criminal or family, into a code

Common law case law, principles of law which can be extracted from decisions of courts of law

Community order a single generic sentencing option including a range of possible requirements, e.g. compulsory work. Replaces the community punishment order and community rehabilitation order

Compellable refers to a witness who may be forced to attend court

Competent being legally able to give evidence

Concurrent system of jurisdiction where the same types of cases can be dealt within different levels of the court system

Consolidation bringing together fragmented pieces of legislation on the same topic into one statute

Contract a legal agreement

Counsel another term for a barrister

Cross-examination evidence given in response to questions from the opponent's advocate, which will challenge evidence already given 'in chief' and may attempt to discredit the witness

De facto in fact, actual

Disclosure providing evidence to the other parties to a case, e.g. exchanging witness statements

Doli incapax the principle that a child of a certain age is incapable of committing an offence

Duty a mandatory obligation to carry out a particular function, something which the authority shall do

Education supervision order an order under s. 36 of the Children Act 1989 which may be made where there are concerns that a young person is not being properly educated

Examination-in-chief presenting oral evidence in court in response to questions from the advocate that calls the witness

Exceptional leave to remain an asylum seeker may be granted exceptional leave to remain and allowed to settle in the UK in circumstances where he is not recognised as a refugee

Ex parte an application made to court without giving notice to the other party, usually referred to as without notice

Fact in issue a point which parties to a case cannot agree upon and requires evidential proof

Family proceedings court the branch of the magistrates' court which dealt with family and child care issues

Green paper a command paper presented to Government containing proposals for consultation

Guardian ad litem term replaced by 'children's guardian' with the introduction of CAFCASS. An independent person who reports to the court as to the best interests of the child

Habeas corpus literally you have the body, a remedy which can challenge legality of detention and order release

Hansard the official record of parliamentary proceedings

In camera a legal hearing which is held in private (press and public excluded)

Independent review mechanism a new review process under which prospective adopters may apply for a review of a decision not to recommend them as suitable to adopt

Indictment the official document in the Crown Court which contains the allegation (against the accused)

Injunction a court order which requires a person to do or refrain from doing a particular thing, e.g. non molestation injunction

In loco parentis in the position of a parent, see s. 5(3) Children Act 1989

Lasting power of attorney introduced by the Mental Capacity Act 2005 to replace the Enduring Power of Attorney, the LPA permits a person with capacity to appoint an attorney(s) to take decisions on their behalf, relating to health, welfare and financial matters, if they subsequently lose capacity

Liability legal responsibility for actions. Liability may be personal or vicarious, for example a residential home owner may be vicariously liable for the actions of staff employed there

Litigant in person a person who conducts a legal case without legal representation

Litigation limit the power to prevent an individual making particular applications

Local government ombudsman the ombudsman who investigates complaints of injustice arising from maladministration by local authorities

Mandamus former name of a High Court order made in judicial review cases which orders action to be taken

National Asylum Support Service the body set up in 2000 to provide support and accommodation to asylum seekers whilst their claim for asylum is being considered

Natural justice more commonly referred to as fairness. The entitlement to the law applying fairly in accordance with its basic principles such as the right to make representations and to know of any allegations made against you, in order to have a fair hearing

Negligence a tort based on three principles: the existence of a duty of care, breach of that duty and damage resulting from the breach

No case to answer a submission made by the defence in a criminal case that the prosecution have failed to establish the existence of a case against the accused

No order principle the principle contained in the Children Act 1989 s. 1(2) that there should be a positive benefit to the child in making a formal court order

Obiter dicta things said by the way in a legal judgment, not binding comments

Offender Assessment System the basis of a Pre-Sentence Report

Parental bindovers parent enters into a recognisance to ensure juvenile is of good behaviour and keeps the peace

Parental responsibility the term which replaces 'parental rights and duties' and is intended to encapsulate the areas in which a parent can exercise responsibility towards their child. Defined in the Children Act 1989, s. 3

Petition an application for divorce

Power a discretion to act, often expressed as something which may be done

Precedent the principle by which decisions of the higher courts bind the lower courts so that case law develops consistently

Prima facie at first sight, on the face of it

Private law the law which operates between individuals, e.g. contract

Pro bono work carried out by solicitors and barristers free of charge

Proportionality the principle applicable to human rights that any intervention or violation of rights should be necessary and proportionate in relation to the matter in question

Public law law in which society has an interest, such as care proceedings, or law concerning constitutional matters

Public Law Outline guidance on the stages of public law care proceedings.

Ratio decidendi the principle of law on which a case is decided

Recorded agreement the formal agreement used to confer parental responsibility

Re-examination the final opportunity for a witness to present evidence to their own advocate's questions. Limited to matters arising out of cross examination

Refugee a person whose application for asylum has been granted

Remedy law deals with a situation by providing a remedy, e.g. compensation

Responsible clinician under the Mental Health Act 1983, the responsible clinician is the person with overall responsibility for a patient's care. The term used before the 2007 reforms was responsible medical officer.

Restricted patient a patient subject to a restriction order made by the Crown Court when a hospital order is made in respect of an offender

Revision of statutes, a process of updating law

Royal Assent a bill becomes an Act when it receives Royal Assent

School attendance order an order issued by the LEA where it is not satisfied that a child is receiving a suitable education either by regular attendance at school or otherwise

Section 8 orders a range of orders provided for in section 8 of the Children Act 1989 which deal with aspects of the exercise of parental responsibility, namely, child arrangements order (incorporating residence and contact arrangements), specific issue and prohibited steps orders

Service technical term for delivery of a legal document

Shared residence arrangements following parental separation a child spends more or less equal time with each parent and residence may be made in favour of both parents

Solicitors members of the legal profession (in addition to barristers). Solicitors provide legal advice and undertake advocacy (mainly in the lower courts)

Special guardians person(s) appointed under a Special Guardianship Order (introduced by the Adoption and Children Act 2002) to have parental responsibility for a child

Special measures measures introduced by the Youth Justice and Criminal Evidence Act 1999 to assist vulnerable witnesses in court, e.g. giving evidence by video link

Standard of proof the level to which a case must be proven. In criminal matters it is beyond reasonable doubt, in civil matters it is on a balance of probabilities

Statement of truth a formal sworn statement of evidence (formerly known as an affidavit)

Statutory instrument secondary legislation in the form of rules and regulations made alongside an Act and often providing additional detail

Sub nom also named. For example the case, *Re H (Minors) (Sexual Abuse: Standard of Proof)* [1996] 2 WLR 8, *sub nom* (or also known as) *Re H and R (Child Sexual Abuse: Standard of Proof)* [1996] 1 FLR 80, HL

Tariff the minimum sentence period that must be served before consideration for early release

Tort the law of civil wrongs, including trespass to the person, negligence, defamation and harassment

Twin track an approach which incorporates concurrent planning for adoption and rehabilitation to birth parents where foster carers are also approved as adopters should attempts at rehabilitation fail

Ultra vires outside the powers given to the body in question, i.e. unlawful action

White paper a command paper presented to Parliament, contains an authoritative statement of Government policy (may follow a green paper)

Witness summons an order which calls a person to attend court as a witness (previously called a *subpoena*)

Youth justice plans an annual plan prepared by the local authority in consultation with other bodies which sets out how youth justice services are to be provided in the area

Youth justice services a range of services to be provided by local authorities and probation stipulated in s. 38(4) Crime and Disorder Act 1998, e.g. provision of appropriate adults, support for juveniles awaiting trial, provision of court reports

Youth offending teams multi-disciplinary teams which coordinate provision of youth justice services

Index

Page numbers in colour relate to entries in the Glossary.